THE **COLLABORATIVE WORK SYSTEMS** SERIES
Building collaborative capacity in the world of work

Other Collaborative Work Systems Series Titles:

Beyond Teams: Building the Collaborative Organization
Michael M. Beyerlein, Sue Freedman, Craig McGee, and Linda Moran

THE **COLLABORATIVE WORK SYSTEMS** SERIES

CENTER FOR THE STUDY OF WORK TEAMS

THE COLLABORATIVE WORK SYSTEMS FIELDBOOK

STRATEGIES, TOOLS, AND TECHNIQUES

Michael M. Beyerlein • Craig McGee

Gerald D. Klein • Jill E. Nemiro

Laurie Broedling

EDITORS

JOSSEY-BASS/PFEIFFER
A Wiley Imprint
www.pfeiffer.com

Copyright © 2003 by John Wiley & Sons, Inc.

Published by Pfeiffer
An Imprint of John Wiley & Sons, Inc.
989 Market Street, San Francisco, CA 94103-1741   www.pfeiffer.com

Library of Congress Cataloging-in-Publication Data

The collaborative work systems fieldbook: strategies, tools, and techniques / edited by Michael M. Beyerlein .. [et al.].
    p. cm.—(Collaborative work systems series)
Includes bibliographical references and index.
  ISBN 0-7879-6375-5 (alk. paper)
  1. Teams in the workplace. 2. Leadership. 3. Management. I. Beyerlein, Michael Martin. II. Series.
  HD66 .C547 2003
  658.4'02—dc21

2002015467

Acquiring Editor: Matthew Davis
Director of Development: Kathleen Dolan Davies
Developmental Editor: Susan Rachmeler
Editor: Rebecca Taff

Senior Production Editor: Dawn Kilgore
Manufacturing Supervisor: Becky Carreño
Interior and Cover Design: Bruce Lundquist
Illustrations: Kelly Emkow

Printed in the United States of America

Printing   10 9 8 7 6 5 4 3 2 1

CONTENTS

            Gayle Porter

Conclusion Reflecting on the Lessons Learned 609

            References 617

            About the Series Editors 635

            About the Book Editors 639

            About the Contributors 643

            Index 655

LIST OF FIGURES, TABLES, AND EXHIBITS

Chapter 21

Chapter 22

Chapter 23

Chapter 24

Chapter 25

IN LAUNCHING THIS SERIES, it is the editors' intention to create an ongoing, dynamic forum for sharing cutting-edge ideas and practices among researchers and those practitioners involved on a day-to-day basis with organizations that depend on collaborative work systems (CWS) for their success.

Proposed publications in the CWS series include books devoted to specific topics, workbooks to guide planning and competency development, fieldbooks that capture lessons learned in organizations experimenting with collaborative work systems, software for facilitating learning, training materials, and assessment instruments. The goal of the series is to produce four new products per year that will build a foundation for a perspective on collaboration as an essential means of achieving high levels of performance in and across organizations. Our vision for the series is to provide a means for leveraging collaborative work practices around the world in for-profit, government, and not-for-profit entities.

Collaborative work systems are those in which conscious efforts have been made to create strategies, policies, and structures as well as to institutionalize values, behaviors, and practices that promote cooperation among different parties in the organization in order to achieve desired business outcomes. While many organizations vocalize support for teamwork and collaboration, collaborative work systems are distinguished by intentional efforts to embed the organization with work processes and cultural mechanisms that enable and reinforce collaboration. New forms of organization continue to emerge with CWS as an essential facet. Team-based organizations and self-managing organizations represent types of collaborative systems. The computer revolution has made possible network, cellular, and spherical forms of organizing, which represent more transorganizational forms of collaboration.

Why the urgency? The challenges organizations face seem to be escalating rapidly. The number of global issues that impact an organization proliferate, including the terrorist threat, continued deforestation of ancient lands by debtor nations, wars, famine, disease, the accelerating splitting of nations' consciousness into the haves and the have-nots around the globe, which fuels hatreds—all aspects of interrelated political, social, economic, environmental challenges that will ultimately reduce quality of life on a worldwide scale if not addressed. These are the systemic, wicked problems that depend on many minds lodged in a common value set committed to improving human welfare in all settings. The business community must work with city, county, and state governments, with nation states, and with transnational organizations, such as the United Nations and the World Bank, to bring enough intellectual and financial capital to bear on the problems to do something about them—demanding collaborative initiatives at all levels.

Individuals working well together—this seems like a relatively simple proposition. Yet barriers abound in organizations that tend to inhibit collaboration at every turn. Social barriers are erected for a variety of reasons, including turf wars and mindsets that lead to hoarding of specialized knowledge rather than sharing. Fear of loss seems to be amplified during economic downturns as operating budgets are trimmed, fueling a multiplicity of negative personal scenarios, including loss of jobs, promotional opportunities, titles, and perks, which in turn can threaten self-esteem and professional identity. Barriers to establishing effective collaborative work systems can also reflect lack of cross-training, cultural norms and reward systems that reinforce individual performance, organizational political realities that reinforce competition for scarce resources among units, and differing technical languages that make communication challenging. However, despite these difficulties, some companies appear to overcome the significant barriers and benefit from the positive consequences of effective collaboration.

People in and around organizations have been experimenting with and learning about designing effective work processes for millennia. Researchers and practitioners have been capturing the lessons learned since the early part of the 20th Century. That process continues as we embark on the 21st Century. There will be much to document as changes in global business practices and new generation technologies enable more effective ways of organizing, operating, competing, innovating, and collaborating. Technical developments during the next quarter century will create unheralded challenges and opportunities in an increasingly interdependent world.

The move from muscle-based work to knowledge-based work has been so profound that some writers have called it the age of the knowledge economy. It demands new levels of collaborative expertise and a shift in focus to intangible forms of capital.

Knowledge grows through the development of organizational routines. Knowledge includes knowing what, but also knowing how and why. Each employee carries a somewhat different library of knowledge and a unique perspective on how to apply it—termed intellectual capital. The network of interaction among knowledge workers creates a rich environment where ideas can grow and blossom in stair-step fashion—termed social capital—and where there is widespread competency around teamwork at all levels of the organization in various forms—termed collaborative capital. This form of capital provides the foundation for leveraging what the other forms contribute, but it demands radically different ways of organizing work and involving employees in its design and practice.

In summary, collaborative work systems provide one of the key competency areas that organizations can focus on for building vitality and excellence, including competitive and collaborative advantage. On a daily basis, people come together to make decisions, solve problems, invent new products and services, build key relationships, and plan futures. The effectiveness of those gatherings and the effectiveness of the systems that emerge from them will depend greatly on the collaborative capacity that has been built in their organizations.

A high level of collaborative capacity will enable more effective work at the local and daily levels and at the global and long-term levels. We can solve our immediate problems more effectively, and we can cooperate more effectively to take on the emerging global issues that threaten us in the 21st Century when we have the skills, values, and processes for effective collaboration. This series of publications is intended as a catalyst in building that collaborative capacity at both local and global levels.

Michael M. Beyerlein, Ph.D.
Susan T. Beyerlein, Ph.D.
Center for the Study of Work Teams
University of North Texas

James Barker, Ph.D.
United States Air Force Academy

ACKNOWLEDGMENTS

THIS FIELDBOOK REPRESENTS a complex project. Nearly five dozen pieces by fifty authors were screened, then three dozen were organized through several rewrites and redesigns of the book to form the final manuscript. Correspondence with authors, editors, and the publisher was frequent. Tact was essential. The editors of the Fieldbook wish to express our deep appreciation to Nancy Gorman for accomplishing the impossible. Her organizational skills kept the project on track and on schedule. She never lost her sense of humor or patience with contributors. There was always such a strong sense of reliability that the editing team could focus on content issues and leave the rest to Nancy. It was a pleasure to work with her on this book.

In addition, we want to thank our editors at Jossey-Bass/Pfeiffer, Susan Rachmeler, Kathleen Dolan Davies, Samya Sattar, and Matthew Davis, for their support and guidance during the publishing process. We especially want to thank Susan Rachmeler for the careful, thoughtful, and extensive suggestions she made on the manuscript. We also express our appreciation for the six reviewers who provided feedback that enabled us to polish structure and clarify wording throughout the book. Bill Lytle contributed his expertise in a consultative fashion. Reviewer and publisher feedback provided many opportunities to hone this work into a useful, accessible tool for readers. We send this group our heartfelt appreciation. Clearly, it takes a team to publish a book!

THIS FIELDBOOK for Collaborative Work Systems (CWS) is intended to improve practice. The purpose is to provide practitioners (change leaders, OD managers, steering team members, design team members, line managers, functional leaders, and so on) a toolkit to assist them in dealing with the struggles and challenges that they face in designing and implementing collaborative work systems, including organizational networks, value chains, partnerships with stakeholders, webs, cross-functional teams, strategic alliances, and team-based organizations.

Teams represent a refined social technology for utilizing collaborative process in the workplace. A great deal has been published on teams in the last ten years. That way of organizing work has spread to all industries, to government, and to nonprofit organizations. However, there have been several gaps in the material published.

First, the approach to teams has typically had a micro focus, that is, individual teams have been the focus of attention in both publishing and practice. That is a necessary but insufficient focus. It must be supplemented with a more macro focus that includes attention to the systems that embed and support the teams, including the culture, the support systems, and the relationships among teams.

Second, the focus on teams has typically been on formal aspects of collaboration and not the informal. A great deal of collaborative practice in organizations is spontaneous, "around the water cooler," community based, and so on, rather than formally structured and explicitly supported.

Third, most of the publications and practices regarding work teams flow from the venerable socio-technical systems (STS) perspective. The STS approach is well-known to some groups of researchers and practitioners and not known to others. We have organized this book to acknowledge other groups' contributions by integrating STS with the Malcolm Baldrige Quality Award criteria; Nadler and Tushman's work on alignment of strategy, work, people, structure, and culture; and our own work on support systems and alignment. The Baldrige criteria have been increasingly used as the basis of business plans because of the thorough coverage of critical success factors (CSFs). The STS approach contributes a balanced focus on social and technical systems that jointly optimizes them. The other perspectives focus on aligning the key facets of the organization to optimize performance. Combining Baldrige and STS in framing the development of collaborative work systems with alignment models provides a richer perspective for organization design. The result enables more thorough coverage of the CSFs in building organizations that can capitalize on the benefits of collaborative work system design.

This fieldbook is designed to be a practical toolkit. It contains ideas, examples, and tools that can be accessed quickly to remind you of what you can't quite recall, to guide your decision making, and to articulate ideas and hunches so you can share more effectively with others involved in the situation.

A fieldbook is designed to be a handy reference. It can be pulled down from the shelf or out of the toolbox at the moment that a problem arises for browsing and reflection. The pieces of the fieldbook provide concepts, tools, and informative examples. Papers were contributed from people employing a variety of approaches to organization change and development, including the Baldrige Award business model, to improve collaborative practices for performance results (www.quality.nist.gov/Business_Criteria.htm).

We hope you find the ideas, tools, and examples in this fieldbook to be of value in solving your collaboration problems. Our goal is to provide you with a toolkit that you can refer to for specific issues and for general design work. Building the capacity to work well together pays off in many ways. The frequent use of the fieldbook will help achieve those payoffs.

The Editors
Michael M. Beyerlein
Craig McGee
Gerald D. Klein
Jill E. Nemiro
Laurie Broedling

Introduction and Framework for the Fieldbook

Michael M. Beyerlein, Craig McGee,
Gerald D. Klein, Jill E. Nemiro, Laurie Broedling

NEW WAYS OF ORGANIZING AND BUILDING HUMAN CAPITAL are emerging and the practices are spreading. One of these is the movement toward use of collaborative work systems (CWS), which includes the creation of team-based organizations. *Collaborative work systems are those in which a conscious effort has been made to create structures and institutionalize values and practices that enable individuals and groups to effectively work together to achieve strategic goals and business results.* Leaders and change leaders are continually seeking ways to make their organizations more effective, adaptive, and relevant. However, leaders have typically not demonstrated a strong understanding of ways to enable collaboration in the design and operation of their organizations. The need to enable is growing—work will continue to be done by people, and those people will have to be able to collaborate and work together as work becomes more complex and knowledge-based.

Although many organizations promote teamwork and collaboration, collaborative work systems are characterized by intentional efforts to create structures, cultures, forums, and practices that reinforce collaboration. One such example is a team-based organization (TBO). *A TBO is an organization in which the team of interdependent contributors is the basic unit of work, and the rest of the organization acts as a system of support processes.* Within a TBO, many forms of teams are utilized, such as temporary and permanent, functional and cross-functional, local and distributed. This wide array of team forms shows that collaborative work is being organized in creative ways to fit the situation.

The Iceberg of Collaborative Practices (see Figure I-1) depicts the formal and informal components of collaboration. There are many opportunities for building collaborative capacity. Nearly all publications on teams focus on the formal, except for that elusive component culture. The effectiveness of the collaborative organization depends on paying attention to both formal and informal CWS opportunities.

Figure I.1. Iceberg of Collaborative Practices

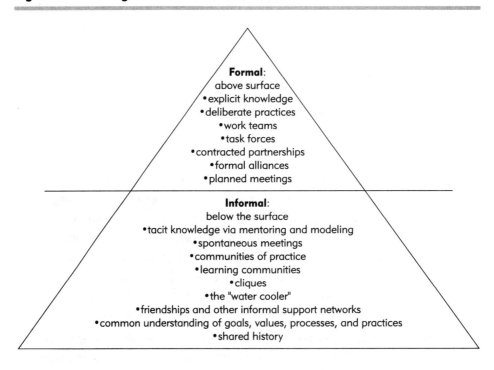

The iceberg structure of Figure I-1 is deliberately chosen to indicate that some aspects of collaborative structure and process are more visible than others and hence seem easier to address. But the less visible components are at least as critical to building collaborative excellence as the visible ones. Collaborative excellence is not a simple goal to achieve, but then neither is sustainable total quality or customer delight. It is obvious that we need to design organizations and their processes so people can work well together and see the value of doing so.

The Need for a Fieldbook

The most common formal collaborative work system is the team. That is where the work gets done—assembly, design, sales, and so forth. As work becomes more complex, individuals and isolated groups cannot do the job well. The synergy of a team is essential to achieving performance goals; the linking of teams with each other into networks is also essential. However, in spite of years of research and practice, at least half of the teams and team initiatives seem to be failures. They fall short of achieving their goals and reaching their full potential. In some cases, the initiatives are abandoned when there is a change of top management. In other cases, businesses fail, downsize, or lose customers, so teams that may have been flourishing are eliminated. Sometimes managers seem to move people in and out of teams by fiat, as if moving people around were more important than giving a team enough time to mature and reach high performance levels. Teams fail for many reasons. Some reasons are located within the teams, such as compatibility of members; other reasons are located outside the teams, such as lack of management support. This book addresses both: systems located outside the teams that have a profound influence on team effectiveness demand even more attention than the teams themselves.

In a study of nine organizations that included 610 interviews, a research team at the Center for the Study of Work Teams (Beyerlein, Hall, Harris, & Beyerlein, 1997) discovered that more than half of the teams and team implementation projects were failing. That is not surprising if one looks at the failure rate of other types of initiatives that promise to transform organizations, such as total quality management (TQM), business process re-engineering (BPR), and enterprise resource planning (ERP). Failure rates for other types of initiatives have been estimated to be as high as 70 percent. Failure rates for mergers have been reported as high as 90 percent. Why do such transformative initiatives fall short of their promise? What should we pay attention to in preventing such failures? The common oversight across these efforts is lack of involvement of the people impacted by the initiatives. Researchers have published powerful evidence to demonstrate that the short-term goal of putting profits first is actually harmful to long-term profitability and that "people centered" organizations are the key to long-term organizational health and prosperity (for example, Appelbaum & Batt, 1994; Beer & Nohria, 2000; Waterman, 1994).

A few writers have written about the failure of work teams (for example, Hitchcock & Willard, 1995; Robbins & Finley, 2000). Those efforts, summarizing experience in a number of organizations, begin to map out the key areas that require early and sustained attention in creating a context for success. In addition, we have identified a number of causes of team failure in our own research (Beyerlein, 1997a, 1997b). Key causes include:

1. Team implementations cannot be adopted from other organizations, they must be adapted, that is, instead of importing an implementation and design process as a whole, it must be tailored to the new site.

2. Teams must be introduced for the sake of performance improvements, not because teams are a fad being used in other noteworthy companies and not just to increase employee satisfaction.

3. Teams will not survive if they are isolated islands of structural change; they must be linked with other teams and receive appropriate resources from support systems.

4. Major change initiatives, including the redesign to a team-based system, must be institutionalized and not depend on a single champion, because when that champion leaves, the efforts built on his/her vision, enthusi-

asm, and expertise will erode back to the prior structure, possibly with backlash in employee attitudes.

5. A key part of institutionalization of the change is obtaining the buy-in of top management; typically, their backgrounds do not enable their appreciation of team structures and processes—they have excelled at working in competitive ways for too long, so lack of top support leads to abandoning the initiative without careful analysis of the long-term costs and benefits involved.

6. Becoming an effective team contributor typically depends on development of significant new competencies, and that requires a great deal of learning—formal training, informal coaching, and so forth; some organizations are unwilling to take the time away from work to provide the learning opportunities, so capability development is stifled.

7. Achieving new peak levels of performance by a team requires time for developing teamwork and the new norms that support it; organizations that rush to achieve peaks become impatient and decide teams were the wrong choice.

8. Leadership requires new meanings and manifestations for teams to work at peak levels; for example, supervisors transitioning into team coaches must make radical changes in style of interaction, and team members must take on leadership responsibilities.

The list above describes a few of the causes of failure of teams and team initiatives. The items on the list represent both factors within the team itself (micro level) and outside of the team (macro level, contextual, environmental). The factors outside the team have not received enough attention in research or in practice and therefore account for more failures than internal factors.

Although a successful transformation to a new organizational design requires changes at all levels—individual, group, department, division, and whole company—we believe that context surrounding the work group or the team is the key piece for sustaining the transition to work teams. That context includes a number of key support systems, including:

- Leadership
- Performance management
- Organization and team design
- Financial and resource allocation
- Learning (formal and informal)
- Physical workspace and tools
- Change and renewal
- Integration

The eight systems are often recognized as processes, but not all are viewed as systems and managed that way. The success of a team-based organization requires that these critical support factors be viewed and managed as systems that are pervasive in the organization. Excellence in each produces competitive advantage; excellence in all leverages resources to a new level of value. Lack of alignment between any of these support systems and the teams they serve will undermine performance.

A study of the relationship between these support systems (Hall, 1998) revealed two critical patterns. First, team design and performance definition contributed the most to team success, which was defined as meeting goals of customer service, resource utilization, growth, and psychological needs like job satisfaction. Second, across the sample of fourteen companies the reward system and the executive management system were the least likely to have been modified to improve alignment with the teams' needs. Alignment of systems in the organization emerges as the foundation of team effectiveness. We have designed the six sections of the Fieldbook following an integrated alignment model to address that issue.

Comparing Alignment Models

Alignment emerges as a key function of management. Managers should focus on both internal and external alignment issues. *External* issues include improving the fit with the customers and markets, with regulations, and with suppliers. *Internal* issues include integration across silos, deployment of information about the mission, vision, and values of the organization, and improving the fit of support systems with groups doing the final work on products and services.

Fred Smith, chairman of Federal Express, says "Alignment is the essence of management" (Labovitz & Rosansky, 1997). Sue Mohrman, an expert on team-based organizations, says "Ninety percent of what caused teams to fail was the context" (Mohrman & Tenkasi, 1997). We agree that both of these ideas are pivotal to the success of teaming processes. However, we think it is extremely difficult to manage entire systems, so we have broken them down into subsystems that are more manageable; we call these subsystems "mechanisms" in order to emphasize the fact that managers can directly impact them and their alignment with the teams' needs. For example, mechanisms for the team design system include direct contact of the team with customers, the team making work-related decisions, and increasing the competencies of the team's members. Mechanisms for the reward system include such facets as pay for achieving or exceeding established goals of the team and of the organization in a timely manner.

Alignment represents managing a complex web of system relationships. Consequently, we define the role of leadership that makes a successful transformation possible as:

1. Developing the resources of the system (including human, social, knowledge, and financial capital);

2. Managing system interfaces;

3. Establishing appropriate infrastructure for sustainable growth and performance;

4. Creating an environment where people care;

5. Building a network of effective relationships; and

6. Recognizing and creating new systems.

Alignment applies across all parts of the organization and across its boundaries with the environment. Whenever boundaries are crossed, collaboration becomes a factor.

The keys to a successful and sustainable transformation to team-based organizing and effective collaborative work systems include a focus on context, the alignment of systems, and a leadership change, but it also includes teams with a balance of accountability, responsibility, authority, and empowerment. It is a challenge to do all of these things well; the option is failure.

The assumption is that an organization is more effective when the various elements are synchronized, which means that each element is chosen and shaped to provide maximum support/reinforcement for the others. An alignment model argues that the elements and parts of an organization should support one another; the elements should not work at cross-purposes. The importance of alignment is widely understood in organizations; however, its effective practice is limited by several factors.

Alignment models focused on teams include those of Sundstrom, DeMuse, and Futrell (1990), Schwarz (1994), and the Center for the Study of Work Teams (Hall, 1998). The models argue that time and attention need to be given to choosing and structuring various organizational elements and that these elements must be synchronized with each other for the organization to be successful.

Nadler and Tushman (1989, 1997) hypothesize that the greater the total degree of congruence or fit between the various components of an organization, the more effective the organization will be. Two components are congruent when "the needs, demands, goals, objectives, and/or structures of one component are consistent with those of another. In other words, congruence is a measure of how well pairs of components fit together" (p. 34). The "components" of concern are described in a couple of different ways. One statement lists them as an organization's "formal structures, personal capabilities, operating environment and work processes." In another paragraph, they describe congruence as "the degree to which the strategy, work, people, structure and culture are smoothly aligned" (p. 34).

Semler (1997) states in his paper "Systematic Agreement: A Theory of Organizational Alignment":

"This theory of alignment looks at the extent to which strategy, structure, and culture create an environment that facilitates the achievement of organizational goals. Well-aligned organizations apply effective leadership and HRD processes to create systematic agreement among strategic goals, tactical behaviors, performance and reward systems, and organizational culture. This agreement helps people to remove barriers to cooperation and performance and thereby increases the performance of individuals, processes, and the organization as a whole." (p. 23)

The alignment model for the Fieldbook incorporated some of these elements and others, specifically:

- The Nadler-Tushman Model—four major elements—from their 1997 book, *Competing by Design.*

- The Baldrige Model—seven major elements. All wording that appears here is taken from the Baldrige website and the Baldrige Criteria for 2000 (Baldrige National Quality Program).

- Craig McGee's Alignment Model—thirteen major elements (including the "culture" item in the center as shown in Chapter 11, "Alignment: The Key to Collaborative Work Systems," and illustrated in Chapter 13, "Creating a Collaborative Work System in an Engineering Department").

- Two alignment models from the Center for the Study of Work Teams, each with many elements: The TBO Model and a "Team Effectiveness Model."(Examples of this can be found in Chapter 1 by Cheryl Harris and Michael Beyerlein, "Critical Success Factors in Team-Based Organizing," and Chapter 17 by Cheryl Harris and Sarah Bodner, "Developing Team-Based Support Systems: Conceptual Overview and Strategic Planning Workshop").

Additional Fieldbook chapters address alignment, as well, including Gerald Klein's "Managing Intergroup and Interdepartmental Conflict to Improve Collaboration" (Chapter 19).

Organization of the Fieldbook

The selected elements from the alignment models were clustered by topic, resulting in six categories that represent the six sections of the Fieldbook. The categories for the six sections of the book are defined as follows:

Part 1. Strategy and Goal Setting. Fitting vision and mission to a collaborative way of designing work; ways in which executive teams formulate, assess, and deploy strategy; bottom-up approaches to strategy formulation; assessing the costs and benefits of CWS as a capital investment; business partner involvement in formulating and assessing strategy.

Part 2. Leadership (Executive, Team, Individual) and Organizational Culture. Unique responsibilities of executives and managers functioning in CWS; norms, beliefs, assumptions, and values that create a culture that either encourages or interferes with collaboration; how leadership is handled at the unit and team level in CSW; collaborative efforts by union and business unit leaders; empowerment as a way of building the leadership system; how learnings are collected and disseminated; changing the organization and aligning organization elements.

Part 3. Structure and Overall Design. Clarification of roles and responsibilities; how authority is distributed and redistributed; the design process; support system alignment; how the work of individuals and teams is integrated; the evolution of organization structure in CWS.

Part 4. Work Processes and Communication Systems. Product and service design, production, delivery, and improvement systems; how work boundaries are delineated; information flow among individuals and departments; managing and improving inter-team relationships; collaborative knowledge generation and sharing; architectural, physical, and technological supports.

Part 5. Human Resource Processes. Collaborative work practices and labor relations; employee selection and staffing; compensation, reward, and recognition policies and practices specific to and encouraging of CWS and other motivation issues; performance management and coaching for both individuals and teams; training programs and career development; the HR responsibilities of work teams.

Part 6. Individual, Interpersonal, and Team Competencies and Skills. For working in collaborative work systems—developing skills in organizing and planning, communicating and giving feedback, creativity and innovation, problem solving, decision making, managing differences and conflict, holding effective meetings, project/work management; needed technical expertise and knowledge.

Enriching the members of the organization builds wealth for the organization; it's a win-win arrangement. Everyone committed to building excellent collaborative work systems already understands that. Where they have room for improvement is by identifying all the pieces of the organization that play a role in collaborative excellence and setting up processes and practices that activate and align the collaboration across those pieces.

Special Features of the Fieldbook

Chapters in the Fieldbook consist of three different types of elements: (1) conceptual pieces, including new frameworks; (2) practical "how to" tools for dealing with collaborative work systems and team-based organizing, and (3) case examples to provide evidence and application of conceptual pieces and/or tools.

The margins are also wide enough for you to add your own notes as you spend more time with the Fieldbook—exploring, reflecting, and experimenting, making it your own. Using Post-it Notes® as bookmarks with labels on them, you can create a set of protruding entryways into the book that will enable you to quickly access key parts. Although this book can be read from beginning to end, it is equally suitable for tracking a topic across chapters by theme, text box, or icon.

In the Search Conference, collaboration is fostered by a self-managing team environment.

The Fieldbook includes several special features to aid the reader in navigating the large amount of material. Margin notes in the left margin, such as the one shown here, contain brief quotes of key material from the text of a chapter to highlight material the reader might want to find quickly or relocate quickly.

These notes also form a high-level outline of the main points of the chapter.

The Fieldbook is the second book in the new Jossey-Bass/Pfeiffer Collaborative Work Systems (CWS) Series. The first book, *Beyond Teams: Building the Collaborative Organization,* was based on ten key principles for building collaborative capability. The content of the Fieldbook is linked to those principles through icons that appear in the left margin, like the one shown to the left of this paragraph.

Table I-1 shows the icons, the principles they represent, and the chapters in the Fieldbook that contain material representing the same principles. The icon system enables a reader of one of the books to easily link to sections describing principles and examples in another book. The same system of icon links will be used in the upcoming workbook and casebook in the CWS Series.

Table I.1. Fieldbook Chapters for Each Collaborative Organization Principle

	Icon	Collaborative Organization Principle	Applicable Chapters																
			1	2	3	4	5	6	7	8	9	10	11	12	13	14	15	16	17
#1		Focus collaboration on business results	■			■		■								■			
#2		Align support systems to promote ownership			■	■				■					■	■			■
#3		Articulate and enforce a "few strict rules"				■										■			
#4		Exploit the rhythm of convergence and divergence												■					
#5		Manage complex tradeoff decisions																	
#6		Create higher standards for discussion, dialogue, and the sharing of information				■			■	■			■					■	
#7		Foster personal accountability		■		■				■									
#8		Align authority, information, and decision making																	
#9		Treat collaboration as a disciplined process													■	■			
#10		Design flexible organizations		■															

■ = Most Relevant Chapters

Icon	Collaborative Organization Principle	Applicable Chapters																
		18	19	20	21	22	23	24	25	26	27	28	29	30	31	32	33	34
#1	Focus collaboration on business results				■			■	■					■				
#2	Align support systems to promote ownership		■				■			■		■		■				■
#3	Articulate and enforce a "few strict rules"																	
#4	Exploit the rhythm of convergence and divergence															■		
#5	Manage complex tradeoff decisions							■										
#6	Create higher standards for discussion, dialogue, and the sharing of information	■		■		■									■			
#7	Foster personal accountability							■			■				■			
#8	Align authority, information, and decision making								■				■					
#9	Treat collaboration as a disciplined process							■	■		■			■		■		■
#10	Design flexible organizations										■							

*This table created by Cheryl L. Harris

The opening chapter of the Fieldbook, "Critical Success Factors in Team-Based Organizing," carries the icon table system another step in linking the principles of the collaborative organization to the principles of team-based organizing, which is a subset of collaborative principles. This represents our attempt to create the print analog of a hypertext system that networks ideas across chapters and volumes.

Conclusion

Think of work teams as a refined social technology for utilizing collaborative process in formal ways. As with new nonsocial technologies, mastery brings competitive advantage. In other words, the competitive landscape is shifting, and those who are quickest to adopt that technology are likely to be the winners. Effective use of team designs for work and creation of a culture that values people is based on a developing social technology. The development of knowledge about informal collaboration has also occurred, but the integration of the two areas has been a weak point.

The development of that social or organizing technology has been going on for some decades. Researchers and practitioners have learned a lot; research, trial-and-error in companies, and careful field experiments have all helped develop an advanced technology of teams. Now a more all-encompassing, advanced technology of collaborative work systems is emerging. Use of that technology can produce competitive advantage, but we will call it "collaborative advantage" here to emphasize how the gains depend on working well together. This enables the optimal development of the intellectual and social capital that provides a sustainable resource for creating the financial capital that a company uses for fuel. This book includes concepts, tools, frameworks, and examples for building a map of ways to build collaborative capital.

Enriching the members of the organization builds wealth for the organization; it's a win-win arrangement. Everyone committed to building excellent collaborative work systems already understands that. Where they have room for improvement is in identifying all the pieces of the organization that play a role in collaborative excellence and setting up processes and practices that activate and align the collaboration across those pieces. The Fieldbook is designed to serve as a resource for such transformative work.

PART 1

STRATEGY AND GOAL SETTING

Craig McGee

THROUGHOUT THE 1970s AND 1980s, more businesses experimented with teams, many with amazing success, including manufacturing sites such as Corning Glass and Saturn and service companies such as Aid Association for Lutherans and Shenandoah Insurance. Then, in the 1990s, businesses moved beyond experimenting with teams to implementing them on a larger scale to achieve their strategic goals. While many organizations struggled with their performances, other American businesses were realizing that their workers

15

were not being used as effectively as they could be. These organizations were team-based, since they used teams to complete their core business (Mohrman, Cohen, & Mohrman, 1995).

As organizations published their success stories, others moved to copy the practices and planned to implement teams, among other strategies. One study (Tudor & Trumble, 1996) reported that one in five companies planned to implement teams in the near future as part of their strategy to meet the new expectations in the marketplace. Another survey (Devine & Clayton, 1999) reported that the number of project teams had exceeded the number of production teams.

Creating a team-based organization is a transformational, strategic decision requiring full leadership commitment and dedication of significant resources. The decision to move to a team-based organization and the broader collaborative work system is a key strategic decision. The decision must be based on the premise that implementing a team-based organization will create competitive advantage.

Too many managers implement teams because "It seems like the right thing to do" and "How can one argue against teamwork?" These managers fail to understand the key strategic decision they are making. They fail to fundamentally shift the distribution of power to workers and managers who are closest to the problems they are trying to solve. Traditional reward systems and information flows remain intact, reinforcing the command and control model. Leaders must drive fundamental changes to the entire organization or the returns are disappointing.

As with the implementation of any strategy, goals must be established and timetables created. Specific actions must occur in a well-planned sequence. One role of leadership is to establish these actions and goals. The goals are not merely financial ones. Goals related specifically to progress toward effectively implementing teams must be established. Such goals may include:

- Number of teams formally chartered;
- Number of teams achieving X level on a team maturity index;
- Cost savings/revenue increases attributed to teams; and
- Numbers of teams operating without direct supervision.

The achievement of these goals results from implementing a series of activities with a conscious strategy in mind. For example, training occurs before chartering of teams; teams demonstrate effectiveness before operating without direct supervision; reward systems are redesigned and implemented at the proper time to encourage teamwork; and so forth. These are just some of the activities that leaders put into a strategic order to create an effective team-based organization.

Creating a team-based organization must be directly linked to the higher-level business strategy. The traditional model of strategic planning includes senior executives and staff assessing the business environment and determining the business strategy. They then communicate this strategy down throughout the organization and expect the lower-level managers and employees to develop operating tactics. Leaders using this model assume that people will naturally understand and accept the business strategy. They trust (or demand) that their employees will develop tactics to support it. This assumption of understanding and blind commitment is often erroneous.

Conversely, high-involvement, team-based organizations adopt different models for linking operational tactics to higher-level business strategy. Team-based organizations directly involve larger numbers of people in the strategic planning process. Methodologies such as search conferences and other large-group events enable people throughout the organization to participate in the strategic planning process. Large numbers of people (hundreds and even thousands) convene for two to three days in order to:

- Assess the business environment;
- Assess the company's competitive performance in that environment and with their customers;
- Examine their culture and values;
- Identify/clarify core strategy; and
- Develop strategic initiatives to meet business objectives.

People support that which they help create. Through their involvement in the strategic planning process, support and commitment is built *during* the planning process, not after it.

This part of the book describes various methods for aligning the involvement strategy of team-based organizations with the higher-level business strategy. The following describe tools and approaches for creating this alignment and actual cases where managers and employees have utilized these tools and approaches. In Chapter 1, Beyerlein and Harris posit ten critical success factors for aligning a high involvement organization with the business objectives. In Chapter 2, Bradshaw, Roberts, and Cheuy describe a method, the Search Conference, that involves a wide range of participants and diffuses the strategy throughout the organization in a collaborative manner. In Chapter 3, Devane illustrates a tool, the Transformation Grid, that can be used to:

- Plan a transformation to a high involvement organization;
- Monitor and adjust the transformation activities; and
- Conduct lesson learned analyses.

In Chapter 4, Dowling describes a team chartering process that ensures that teams are properly aligned with the business objectives. In Chapter 5, Kennedy illustrates a process that ensures that teams generate sufficient returns on the investment put into them. Similarly, in Chapter 6, Levenson describes an alternative approach for calculating the "return on investment" for individual teams.

CHAPTER 1

Critical Success Factors in Team-Based Organizing

A Top Ten List

Michael M. Beyerlein and Cheryl L. Harris

Team-based organizing is a continuous journey.

OVER THE LAST FEW DECADES, work teams have become a popular method for increasing speed, productivity, employee involvement, and collaboration in organizations. This increased use of work teams created the need for organizations to redesign themselves to support those teams. A full redesign effort produces a team-based organization (TBO). However, that term connotes an ending point. The term "team-based *organizing*" represents continuous improvement and continuous reinvention. This chapter identifies the top ten principles of the design and implementation of team-based organizing in the form of critical success factors.

Our definition of team-based organizing applies to an organization that has the following in place:

- Teams as the basic unit of accountability and work
- Teams leading teams
- An organizational design to support teams

Team-based organizing is about organization design.

The team-based organizing approach differs radically from the historically dominant approach that focuses on the individual as the unit of accountability, leadership, and support. Team-based organizing is *NOT* about teams; it is about the organization! Most publications and most examples focus on individual teams. The leap from team to team-based system of work is as large as the leap from individual work to team work. Redesign to a TBO demands redesign of the organization as a whole. The environment the teams work in is critical to their performance level, so redesigning the whole makes effectiveness possible at the lower level.

The goal of team-based organizing is to maximize the ability to cooperate and collaborate appropriately. Collaboration takes time, effort, and investment that working individually does not. Appropriate collaboration occurs when there is:

- Need of diverse expertise;
- Need to build commitment through participation;
- Need to create synergies with the expertise; and
- A supportive environment in place.

Alignment is the process of coordinating system parts and processes.

Collaborative work may not be the best approach when these factors are not present. Working solo is fine when it can achieve performance goals.

Each organization is unique, so there is no roadmap to follow. However, there are principles to guide the journey. Following are ten critical success factors (CSFs) to make appropriate collaboration successful. Please note that these CSFs are not the same as the principles of collaborative organization established in the first book in the Collaborative Work Systems series. However, the CSFs do not contradict the principles of collaborative organization, and do overlap somewhat. We believe that our CSFs warrant discussion in their own right, here in this chapter. A comparison of the CSFs and principles of collaborative organization can be seen in Table 1.1.

Table 1.1. Comparison Between Team-Based Organizing CSFs and Collaborative Organization Principles

Collaborative Organization Principles

Team-Based Organizing Critical Success Factors	Focus collaboration on business results	Align support systems to promote ownership	Articulate and enforce a "few strict rules"	Exploit the rhythm of divergence and convergence	Manage complex tradeoff decisions	Create higher standards for discussion, dialogue, and the sharing of information	Foster personal accountability	Align authority, information, and decision making	Treat collaboration as a disciplined process	Design flexible organizations
Align the organization in multiple ways		■						▦		
The work must be conducive to teams										
Teamwork must fit with and connect to the environment	■									▦
Craft a culture of collaboration and cooperation						▦	▦		■	
Structure the organization with an array of teams										■
Reinforce cooperation and collaboration with organizational systems		■						▦		
Create empowerment and authority at all levels								■		
Foster an atmosphere of entrepreneurship	■									▦
Increase intangible resources of the organization	■					▦				
Design an adaptable organization			▦		▦	▦				■

■ = Most Relevant Principle   ▦ = Relevant Principle

Source: Beyerlein, Freedman, McGee, & Moran (2002).

CSF #1: Align the Organization in Multiple Ways

An organization consists of one system embedded in another, which is embedded in another, and so on, like a nesting dolls toy. Each subsystem is a component of the larger system it resides in and a context for its own components. The most familiar version of this complexity now is that of an ecosystem. And, like an ecosystem, there is interdependence between systems and levels. Alignment is a measure of how well those systems coordinate with each other.

Align Across Systems

Focus on alignment for each decision of the redesign.

Is alignment important? In an automobile traveling down the freeway at 70 miles per hour, a tiny misalignment of the front wheels is noticeable and potentially dangerous. In a company, misalignment also displays "wobbles" and pulls the operation toward the ditch. Alignment is crucial across systems of any organization; effectiveness is directly proportional to it. However, when implementing a major redesign effort such as an initiative to become team-based, alignment has added dimensions for concern. The focus on alignment should be one of the primary principles driving each decision of the redesign. Without such a focus, the following occurs: "These interventions were fragile, and were swamped within months or years by dominant organizational cultures that were static and hierarchical in nature. . . .where changes did result in productivity improvements, it was not long before these innovations gave way to more traditional work systems compatible with the dominant management mindsets" (Cordery, 2000).

Align Change Initiative with Vision

Returning to the auto on the highway again, the driver usually has a destination in mind. Staying on the road is partly a survival issue and partly about goal accomplishment. The vision may articulate that company destination. If the executive effort has been made to share that vision often, well, and widely, it generates an alignment of effort. Any change initiative that contradicts the shared vision will fail. Alignment of the teaming initiative with the vision is essential. An initiative gains acceptance, support, and commitment when alignment is visible.

Align Across Change Initiatives

Typically, companies have multiple change initiatives underway. Initiatives such as enterprise resource planning (ERP), business process reengineering (BPR), total quality management (TQM), lean manufacturing, and others may accompany TBO. The initiatives are typically handled as isolated islands of change, thought, and control and end up competing for resources. An integration of the initiatives through design and oversight, as with a cross-initiative committee, provides the opportunity for alignment.

Align Across Teams

Alignment across teams is crucial for performance leaps. After interviewing managers in major corporations, Steve Jones (1999) concluded that 80 percent of the payoff from using teams occurred between the teams. Improvements in the flow of work occurred because the teams aligned with each other through direct communications.

Align Support Systems and Teams

Most teams fail because of lack of alignment between support systems and teams (Beyerlein & Harris, 2001; Mohrman, Tenkasi, & Mohrman, 2000). Teams are social systems with a hunger for information and resources. When given what they need, the teams can excel. On the other hand, they are typically malnourished, trying to perform without the necessary inputs from support systems and support personnel, including managers, HR, IT, engineering, shipping, and others. However, recognize that achieving alignment between teams and support is likely to require overcoming significant barriers and inertia, including changes in assessment, evaluation, reward systems, and processes.

Align Across Subcultures

There are subgroups and subcultures within an organization. Schein (1996) suggests that the differences in culture between management, engineering, and production are so large that it is as if they were living in different countries. Another major gap is between union and nonunion employees. Alignment across these boundaries can be achieved through participation in the change initiative. Creating a steering team with a vertical slice of the organization as a membership criterion provides the opportunity for input from all the subgroups, so shared understanding can unite them across their current boundaries.

Align with Business Environment

Finally, although teams fail for many reasons, they also fail when the business fails. Alignment of the business strategy with the business environment, including competition and customer needs, is an essential envelope within which to work on the internal alignment issues.

CSF #2: The Work Must Be Conducive to Teams

The work encompasses the task that needs to be completed. Placing work in the center of the change model emphasizes the point that the purpose of organizations is to complete business, whatever that may be. Therefore, the organization must have a business, work-related reason for converting to teams for the transition to be successful.

For team-based organizing to be successful, the organization must have work that is appropriate for teams, that is, interdependent tasks that require more than one person to complete them. However, today, because of the increasingly complex work environment, most work is interdependent, especially over the long term, so teams are appropriate in many situations. For companies involved with team-based organizing, the majority of the work should be team appropriate.

The key is to match the type of work to the appropriate mechanism for carrying out the work.

Contrary to popular myth, however, not all tasks are team tasks, and all organizations would be wise to recognize this and act accordingly. Sometimes work that seems inappropriate for teams actually is; it simply seems to lack interdependence because of the functional structure imposed on it. In this case, work process redesign may uncover interdependent work that is amenable to a team. Or it may be that an individual is most appropriate for the task. The key is to match the type of work to the appropriate mechanism for carrying out the work, whether it is a team or an individual.

Some situations may warrant redesign of the work to become more suitable for a team. Would a team better accomplish the work than would individuals? Are there "hidden" interdependencies that suggest the use of a team? Would value be added by accomplishing the task with a team? Answering these questions will help determine locations where work redesign is appropriate. Work process mapping is one effective tool for identifying these opportunities graphically. (See Jacka & Keller, 2001.)

In team-based organizing companies, the team is responsible for a whole piece of work, so the work is not as segmented. The whole piece of work is usually process or product focused. For example, a team could be responsible for an entire assembly line, rather than the traditional approach in which each individual does his part and throws it to the next person, without regard for the final product.

Work that is conducive to teams creates an opportunity and the need for a team, but not the team itself. Teams represent a complex solution that is too costly when individuals can do the job, but a wise investment when outcomes depend on collaboration.

CSF #3: Teamwork Must Fit with and Connect to the Environment

The environment includes the forces outside the organization, for example, government regulations, communities, competitors, customers, and suppliers.

Today's environment requires more collaborative forms of organization.

Historically, changes in organizational design have followed trends in the environment. A traditional, hierarchical organization was appropriate in the 19th Century and part of the 20th. However, the environment has changed, requiring new, flatter, more collaborative forms of organization. Some of the characteristics of today's environment that are creating a need for team-based organizing include globalization, the fast pace of change, rapidly changing technology, increased complexity, and permeable organizational boundaries.

Because of the fast-changing environment, companies utilizing TBO must create continuous links to that environment. They must have mechanisms to create awareness of the environment and build in ways to change accordingly in order to survive and thrive. Examples abound of organizations that did not survive changes in the environment. Just think of all the organizations that were around at the turn of the 20th Century; how many of them survived to the turn of the 21st? Not many. Strategic planning is partially based on scanning the environment. In traditional organizations, strategy is viewed as the province of top management. In the TBO, all members are responsible for scanning, and teams may contribute to strategic planning (for example, Fogg, 1994).

CSF #4: Craft a Culture of Collaboration and Cooperation

Culture can be defined as a pattern of shared organizational values, basic underlying assumptions, and informal norms that guide the way work is accomplished in an organization. For teams to be most effective, the organization's values, assumptions, and norms must support collaboration and cooperation.

A metaphor for a team-based organizing culture is "teams in the DNA." Organizations that have "teams in the DNA" are so committed to cooperation and collaboration that employees automatically think, "Let's put a team on it" when they see a problem. They immediately understand how to begin a team, how to end one, and the processes in between. Some characteristics of "teams in the DNA" culture include a teams mindset, wherein collaboration is efficient and habitual; respect for expertise instead of position; self-sufficient teams run

their own businesses; continuous improvement, shared responsibility, autonomy, and authority; the ability to make decisions pushed to where the work is
done; all employees engaged and committed; a "not me" but "we" mindset;
and an egalitarian atmosphere of trust and respect.

Strive for a culture that enhances informal, natural learning.

An important, and often overlooked, part of the organization consists of the
informal, natural processes that happen as a part of human nature. Humans
are social beings and naturally create relationships, networks, and communities and share learnings. The successful TBO remembers this and strives for a
culture to enhance, rather than detract from, the informal. These organizations
create the space for connections via time, place, resources, and norms.

Understanding both the existing and the desired organization culture is key
to creating successful change. Without heed to the existing culture, change initiatives may begin in the wrong place, leaving people feeling frustrated and angry
about the gaps and overlaps. Without some emphasis on understanding the
desired culture, initiatives have no hook to the future, no energy, and eventually
flounder. Successful change initiatives must provide the link between the two.

Culture is either difficult or impossible to change directly, depending on
whom you ask. Changing the organizational structure and adjusting systems
represent indirect ways to influence culture.

CSF #5: Structure the Organization with an Array of Teams

Organizational structure includes the ways people are formally organized to carry
out the work. An organization chart is how this is traditionally depicted. However, the formal chart does not necessarily match the reality of the organization.
Charts may be incomplete or out-of-date. They seldom depict types of teams.

Different types of work require different types of teams.

Successful team-based organizing requires using a variety of team types to
support different types of work. Because the environment shifts constantly, the
organization must be able to use different types of teams to meet the needs of
varying situations quickly. Teams can be temporary or permanent, single function or multi-function, inside one organization or across several, and with co-
located or distributed membership. Project and task teams are temporary,
usually with cross-functional membership; they come together for a particular
purpose and disband when that purpose is achieved. Project teams have become
more popular as a method of dealing with the quickly changing environment.
Work teams are typically permanent, long-term teams, with either single-func-

tion or cross-function membership. Management teams are comprised of management members from multiple functions, each usually concerned with particular issues. Virtual teams may never meet face-to-face and instead rely on technology for communication. As the boundaries of organizations become more permeable, more teams have members from more than one organization.

A common belief is that team-based organizing requires permanent work teams, and some believe that this is the only kind of team that can be used. However, we argue that team-based organizing can encompass any type of team and believe that successful efforts require the use of an array of teams.

CSF #6: Reinforce Cooperation and Collaboration with Organizational Systems

Organizational systems form the infrastructure created to support the work and the people doing the work within the organization. Through modifying and creating systems, team-based organizing enables cooperation and collaboration within the organizational context. Because of the need to align with the work and the rapidly changing environment, flexibility in organizational systems is key. As the work processes and structures change, support systems must change to maintain alignment.

For successful team-based organizing, systems must reinforce collaboration and cooperation.

Traditional support systems are set up to reinforce individual work and, often, competition between workers. Team-based organizing requires collaboration and cooperation, so systems must reinforce teamwork. For example, a traditional system typically bases pay solely on individual contributions, which sets up a situation in which individuals are competing for pay. In a team-based situation, if team members are instructed to work together on projects, yet the reward system is based on individual contributions (for example, the person with the highest sales numbers on the team receives a bonus), chances are quite high that the desired teamwork will not occur. Instead, to foster collaboration and cooperation, team-based reward systems need a component to reward team members for accomplishing team goals.

Alignment is required for all support systems, including the following:

Leadership
- Executive leaders
- Direct supervision (active support, boundary management, and interpersonal skills)

- Team leaders
- Team members/shared leadership

Organization and Team Design

- Designating task design/technology, composition, roles, task characteristics, interdependence, boundaries, human resources, and physical environment requirements for each team and set of teams

Performance Management

- Goal setting (goals, priorities, and tasks)
- Performance measurement
- Performance feedback (formal and informal)
- Rewards (individual, team, business unit levels of performance)
- Recognition

Financial and Resource Allocation

- Including the accounting and reporting systems

Learning (Formal and Informal)

- Communication
- Knowledge management
- Training (interpersonal skills training, and business skills training)
- Information (access and sharing, for example, common databases, goals, and priorities)

Physical Workspace and Tools

- Budgets, tools, time, and computers

Change and Renewal

Integration

- Informal integration, formal leadership roles, and policies

The name "support system" has two parts. "Support" comes first—it is the purpose of these systems and the basis of assessing their effectiveness. Ask, "Are they delivering support to those doing the work?" "System" comes next—it represents established processes. But the key point is that the array of support systems should also be viewed as a system. When individual support systems conflict with each other, quality of support drops and team performance drops with it.

For more on team-based support systems, see Chapter 17.

CSF #7: Create Empowerment and Authority at All Levels

Does an eight-cylinder automobile run with greater efficiency, power, and smoothness when all eight spark plugs are firing in synchronization? Yes. Will the car run if one or two plugs fail to fire? Yes, but roughly, with loss of power and waste of fuel. An organization usually has resources that are not being utilized; hence its efficiency and effectiveness are less than optimal. The two most critical under-utilized resources are the hearts and minds of the individual employees and the synergies that emerge from effective collaboration. Empowerment through participation and involvement rectify that problem to a great extent; designing systems with input from all groups completes the equation.

Control of behavior may be exerted from the outside or the inside—telling someone what or how to do something or allowing that person to decide. Because of the hierarchy of decisions (for example, strategic versus tactical), external, high-level decisions will always be required. However, predominantly external decision making results in over-control, micro-management, and alienated workers.

Empowerment represents the shift from external control of work decisions to internal control. It consists of a redistribution of the power to make decisions within the organization—pushing decision making down to the level where the work is done. Both external and internal influences are present all of the time, but the formal shift toward a balance increases involvement and commitment while keeping individual and team decisions in alignment with organizational goals. The two sources of control must be in alignment or they will undermine each other.

Lack of trust and lack of a plan are hurdles to empowerment.

The first hurdle to empowerment is lack of trust. Usually, managers are accused of failing to trust the team members to be accountable when empowered. However, team members may not trust that management is doing something that is win/win; they may suspect hidden motives and agendas. For example, one team of graphic designers grew to the point of being self-managed, but received no extra rewards for the extra responsibility, so they decided to ask to have a manager once again. (For more on this, see Chapter 8.)

The second hurdle to effective empowerment is lack of a plan. Empowerment should proceed in steps that correspond to the developing capabilities of the team. A study of empowerment steps across 117 teams in nine companies by the Center for the Study of Work Teams (Beyerlein, Beyerlein, & Richardson, 1993) showed that the first steps in empowerment were usually team responsibility for problem solving and safety decisions. The last steps were those dealing with disciplining, hiring, and firing of employees. Many other responsibilities were arranged in between these extremes of safety and risk. Even with steps in empowerment, abuse can occur. When given new responsibilities, one team focused on vacation planning and let the more work-related items slide. Alignment to guide priority setting was missing in that plan.

Empowerment releases the energies and imaginations of team members.

Empowerment has the potential to release the energies and imaginations of team members. When handled intelligently, empowerment increases the resources of the organization far more than it costs.

CSF #8: Foster an Atmosphere of Entrepreneurship

Entrepreneurial spirit represents the initiative that some people take to achieve their goals and build their visions. Well-known examples are mentioned in newspapers and magazines on a regular basis. The essence of success is to take risks but do so in an intelligent manner. Calculated risks, experiments that are planned, have tended to work better than risk for risk's sake. Visionaries may often be entrepreneurial, but the great successes are those where the visionary has enlisted the energies of the members of the organization. Successful organizations have an atmosphere of entrepreneurship that surrounds all members.

An effective team provides the best incubator for new ideas. When a member shares a new idea, the team can ask, "How do we do this?" The team can also ask "What if. . .?" "What is. . . ?" and "What should. . . ?" (Pacanowsky, 1995). The idea is protected at conception, receives refining inputs from members with diverse perspectives, and gains momentum before being taken to management. Relationships with customers can benefit in similar ways.

Employees need support through modeling, resources, and systems for entrepreneurship to occur.

Some members of the organization will automatically take risks and develop new ideas, but most will need a sense of permission and support. The naturals will find ways around barriers and use informal mechanisms of information flow. Making formal mechanisms for accessing information, resources, and people user friendly will enable many more members to participate. At the top of the list of support mechanisms is the modeling of entrepreneurial behavior by top management. If conservative, traditional approaches dominate management decision making, that style will cascade down through all layers of the organization and stifle the possibilities at the team level. Removal of barriers to sharing ideas with top management allows them to cascade upward, reversing the trend.

Resources may be necessary for entrepreneurial activity. At 3M, employees may use 15 percent of their time to pursue their own ideas (Coleman, 1999). At Rubbermaid, two-person teams visited homes of consumers to study storage practices and generated three hundred new-product ideas in three days (Stevens, 1999).

CSF #9: Increase Intangible Resources of the Organization

The transformation of work processes and support systems to participative approaches for managing teams requires significant investment of time and money. It is an expensive change. Those who decide to make that change believe that the value gained will exceed the cost. They must be able to answer two questions: (1) How does a team add value? (2) How does a TBO add value?

Each person brings intellectual capital to the workplace.

One of the most common statements explaining change initiative goals has been "faster, better, cheaper." For several decades that statement has summarized the goals of management. Recently, that phrase has changed to include "smarter" and "innovative." Success here depends on building intangible forms of capital—assets that are based on the people of the organization: intellectual, social, collaborative, and organizational. These four types of assets represent a new and emerging focus in designing organizations, supplementing the traditional emphasis on financial and physical capital.

Intellectual capital (IC), also known as knowledge capital, represents what the people in the organization know, including how to find others who know. Each employee brings some IC to the workplace. Social capital (SC) represents the relationships that bind the organization together, including relationships with customers (Nerdrum & Erikson, 2001). IC and SC combined have been referred to as human capital. Collaborative capital (CC) (Beyerlein, Freedman, McGee, & Moran, 2002) represents the organizational, team, and individual processes and competencies for working well together. Organizational capital (OC) represents the strategy, structure, processes, and culture of the organization. Recognizing the value of these four types of assets is the first step toward their systematic development.

Collaboration builds human capital.

Collaboration builds intellectual and social capital. Individuals are assets of the organization—they add value when the situation permits it and encourages it. People in teams add value when collaborative skill enables synergies to emerge and when the hurdles to collaboration have been minimized in the processes and structures of the organization. Then collaboration becomes a source of strategic advantage. The talents and experiences of team members represent valuable assets for the organization. The result of the focus on human capital is a more intelligent organization, one that is more adaptive and more able to acquire, process, and act on information. "The intangible assets are the real drivers of the future business potential" (Sussland, 2001).

CSF #10: Design an Adaptable Organization

Adaptability is critical for survival.

The nature of work, the worker, work organizing, work environments, and collaborative work systems will continue to change, and more of that change will be discontinuous—leaps that will be difficult to anticipate and prepare for.

Adaptability has emerged as a critical capability for companies. Being agile enough to make changes quickly in response to environmental changes enables companies to survive. Change is not new, but the pace is accelerating to new levels. The rate of change is itself changing, so that many areas can be shown by a J-curve of geometric increase. A common example is the amount of memory on a computer chip: It typically doubles every eighteen months. New kinds of chips, such as biochips, may even accelerate that nonlinear pattern. The leap from Six-Sigma quality to nine sigma standards may be another example.

Adaptability requires an awareness of changes and, when possible, an anticipation of changes in the environment. It also requires the capability of making rapid and appropriate internal changes as responses to new environmental opportunities and challenges. This is an intelligence function. Formerly, this kind of intelligence work—gathering information about the environment, assimilating it, and deciding how to respond—was the responsibility of the top management. Increasingly, it became clear that the more members of an organization who paid attention to the environment and brought back observations and ideas, the more effective the adaptation decisions became.

In an organization where all the brains are engaged and sharing of ideas is encouraged, productive communication and interactions abound among all members and across all boundaries. The rich buzz that occurs generates creative and adaptive solutions and identifies new opportunities in a business world characterized by turbulence. "Complexify!" means design your internal environment to match the external environment (Tenkasi, 1997). If the external is complex and dynamic, mirror it with a design that allows similar flow within the organization. Otherwise, the organization is oversimplified and cannot adapt adequately, which leads to extinction.

Self-design is a capability of the most adaptable organizations.

The most adaptable organizations are those capable of informed self-design. The redesign of a major company is an overwhelmingly complex task; so most self-design occurs within smaller business units in a company, such as divisions and plants. The smallest self-designing unit is the work team, which is also the most adaptable level within the organization (Baskin, 2001). The team is closest to the actual work and may be closest to the customer or the supplier. Team consensus decision making may allow for rapid and temporary changes in response to work environment, supplier, or customer issues, whereas a corporate, division, or plant-level response would require formal policy making and take so much time that the need for the change has passed and the appropriateness of the solution evaporated. But the team cannot do the dance of self-design (or mini-self-design of many changes that are quick, temporary, and minor) unless there is sufficient autonomy, and it cannot make appropriate decisions without some skill and information, that is, without some empowerment and development.

Conclusion

To summarize, we suggest ten critical success factors for team-based organizing:

1. Align the organization in multiple ways.
2. The work must be conducive to teams.
3. Teamwork must fit with and connect to the environment.
4. Craft a culture of collaboration and cooperation.
5. Structure the organization with an array of teams.
6. Reinforce cooperation and collaboration with organizational systems.
7. Create empowerment and authority at all levels.
8. Foster an atmosphere of entrepreneurship.
9. Increase the intangible resources of the organization.
10. Design an adaptable organization.

Maintaining a focus on all critical success factors simultaneously is difficult, but necessary, for successful team-based organizing. A tool to help identify where to concentrate your efforts is included as Appendix 1.1. One person cannot do it alone; participation and involvement from members of the entire system are required. Resources are available for those who want them, including the chapters in this Fieldbook. To facilitate your use of the Fieldbook, Table 1.2 provides a cross-reference of CSFs to relevant chapters in the book.

Table 1.2. Applicable Chapters for Each Team-Based Organizing Critical Success Factor

	Applicable Chapters																
Critical Success Factor	2	3	4	5	6	7	8	9	10	11	12	13	14	15	16	17	18
Align the organization in multiple ways		■	■	■	■		■					■	■	■		■	
The work must be conducive to teams																	
Teamwork must fit with and connect to the environment			■							■			■				
Craft a culture of collaboration and cooperation											■			■			
Structure the organization with an array of teams	■																
Reinforce cooperation and collaboration with organizational systems		■	■	■			■					■	■	■		■	
Create empowerment and authority at all levels																	■
Foster an atmosphere of entrepreneurship			■							■			■				
Increase the intangible resources of the organization			■							■			■				
Design an adaptable organization	■																

■ = Most Relevant Chapters

The keys to a successful and sustainable transformation to a team-based organization include a focus on context, the alignment of systems, and a leadership change, but also include teams with a balance of accountability, responsibility, authority, and empowerment. It is a challenge to do all of these things well, but the option is failure.

Acknowledgment

Special thanks to the Center for Creative Leadership for supporting Cheryl Harris during development of some of the conceptual work presented in this chapter.

Critical Success Factors in Team-Based Organizing

Applicable Chapters

19	20	21	22	23	24	25	26	27	28	29	30	31	32	33	34	Critical Success Factor
■				■	■		■	■							■	Align the organization in multiple ways
																The work must be conducive to teams
		■		■	■	■				■		■				Teamwork must fit with and connect to the environment
				■	■	■	■	■	■		■		■		■	Craft a culture of collaboration and cooperation
					■	■		■								Structure the organization with an array of teams
■				■	■										■	Reinforce cooperation and collaboration with organizational systems
																Create empowerment and authority at all levels
		■			■	■					■					Foster an atmosphere of entrepreneurship
				■	■	■					■					Increase the intangible resources of the organization
								■								Design an adaptable organization

Other Recommended Resources

Beyerlein, M.M., & Johnson, D.A. (Eds.). *Advances in interdisciplinary studies of work teams* (Multiple Volume Series). Greenwich, CT: JAI Press.

Lawler, E.E., III, Mohrman, S.A., & Benson, G. (2001). *Organizing for high performance: Employee involvement, TQM, reengineering, and knowledge management in the Fortune 1000 – The CEO Report.* San Francisco: Jossey-Bass.

Lytle, W.O. (1998). *Designing a high-performance organization: A guide to the whole-systems approach.* Clark, NJ: Block-Petrella-Weisbord.

Mohrman, S.A., Cohen, S.G., & Mohrman, A.M., Jr. (1995). *Designing team-based organizations: New forms for knowledge work.* San Francisco: Jossey-Bass.

Mohrman, S.A., & Mohrman, A.M., Jr. (1997). *Designing and leading team-based organizations: A workbook for organizational self-design.* San Francisco: Jossey-Bass.

Mohrman, S.A., & Quam, K. (2000). Consulting to team-based organizations: An organizational design and learning approach. *Consulting Psychology Journal: Practice and Research, (52)*1, 20–35.

Purser, R.E., & Cabana, S. (1998). *The self-managing organization: How leading companies are transforming the work of teams for real impact.* New York: The Free Press.

Sundstrom, E., & associates. (1999). *Supporting work team effectiveness: Best management practices for fostering high performance.* San Francisco: Jossey-Bass.

Appendix 1.1

Team-Based Organizing Critical Success Factor Gap Analysis Tool

Purpose

To facilitate the discussion of critical success factor focus and prioritization among those leading the change effort to team-based organizing. The tool is useful for those considering a transition to TBO, those with a change effort underway, and those wanting to revitalize a transformation effort.

How to Use the Tool

The gap analysis tool can be used in several different ways, including:

- Complete the gap analysis individually and create your own snapshot of the organization.

- Respond to the tool individually, then compile the results of the group to gain an estimate of the group's perception of the situation.

- Create group consensus on each item to cultivate shared understanding and the foundation for planning.

These are all valid uses of the gap analysis tool, each producing different results. Choose the appropriate method according to your needs.

Instructions

1. Answer the questions. Use a circle to indicate where your organization is now. Consider "organization" to be your business unit or department, whatever unit is considering a change or making the effort to transition to TBO.

2. Answer the questions again. This time use a square to indicate where your organization would like to be at your highest level of team-based organizing.

3. Tally subscores for each symbol under each critical success factor.

4. Plot subscores on the graph.

5. Discuss the graph, using the discussion questions.

CSF #1: Align the Organization in Multiple Ways

Conflict and infighting between heads of functions and programs.	1	2	3	4	5	Smooth communication and coordination between heads of functions and programs.
A lot of waste and competition occur because of silos in the organization.	1	2	3	4	5	Resources are effectively leveraged because of integration across boundaries in the organization.
Change initiatives are not aligned and often contradict each other.	1	2	3	4	5	Time is taken to align change initiatives and present them in a unified way.

◯ Subscore CSF #1 = _____   ☐ Subscore CSF #1 = _____

CSF #2: The Work Must Be Conducive to Teams

Individuals do all work or all work is done in teams regardless of type of work.	1	2	3	4	5	A mix of designs (teams and individuals) is used according to the type of work.
The work is segmented with many transitions between different groups or departments during production of the product or process.	1	2	3	4	5	Workers are organized around whole pieces of work, such as whole processes or products.
The work does not require input from multiple types of expertise.	1	2	3	4	5	The work requires input from multiple types of expertise.

◯ Subscore CSF #2 = _____   ☐ Subscore CSF #2 = _____

CSF #3: Teamwork Must Fit with and Connect to the Environment

Employees have little opportunity to receive information about the organization's environment.	1	2	3	4	5	Organization has various mechanisms to create awareness of the outside environment.
Employees are not well connected to customers and suppliers.	1	2	3	4	5	Employees have open lines of communication to customers and suppliers.
Top management is solely responsible for strategic planning, with little to no input from others.	1	2	3	4	5	All members of the organization contribute in some way to strategic planning.

◯ Subscore CSF #3 = _____   ☐ Subscore CSF #3 = _____

CSF #4: Craft a Culture of Collaboration and Cooperation

Employees are uninterested and uninvolved and lack commitment to the organization.	1 2 3 4 5	Employees are engaged, involved, and committed.
Organizational norms inhibit informal learning (for example, no conversations in the hallways).	1 2 3 4 5	The organization supports informal learning by allowing time, place, and resources for informal connections to occur and creating norms to support informal learning.
"Blame culture," that is, time and energy are spent looking for scapegoats; collaboration is forced, not natural.	1 2 3 4 5	"Collaborative culture," that is, time and energy are spent looking for partners; collaboration is efficient and habitual.

○ Subscore CSF #4 = _____   ☐ Subscore CSF #4 = _____

CSF #5: Structure the Organization with an Array of Teams

Regardless of the situation, the organization uses only one type of unit (team, individual).	1 2 3 4 5	Organization uses different types of teams and individuals to meet the needs of varying situations.
Forming a new team takes a long time, so they are not launched to solve problems that arise.	1 2 3 4 5	Teams are formed quickly to solve problems that arise.
Teams are disjointed and often conflict with each other.	1 2 3 4 5	Teams are complementary and integrated and together form a cohesive whole.

○ Subscore CSF #5 = _____   ☐ Subscore CSF #5 = _____

CSF #6: Reinforce Cooperation and Collaboration with Organizational Systems

Systems hinder teamwork, collaboration, and cooperation.	1 2 3 4 5	Systems reinforce teamwork, collaboration, and cooperation.
Individual support systems contradict each other, sending mixed messages to employees.	1 2 3 4 5	Individual support systems align with each other.
Only traditional, formal systems (rewards, performance appraisal) are considered when making changes.	1 2 3 4 5	Formal and informal systems, as well as aspects of systems, are considered when making changes.

○ Subscore CSF #6 = _____   ☐ Subscore CSF #6 = _____

CSF #7: Create Empowerment and Authority at All Levels

Empowerment is haphazard, with no thought-out plan.	1	2	3	4	5	Organization has an empowerment plan for both teams and team managers/leaders.
Teams are told they are empowered, but are not given additional responsibility, authority, or development opportunities, or they are given one but not all three.	1	2	3	4	5	Teams are given more authority and development opportunities to coincide with additional responsibility.
Managers micromanage, withhold information, and do not trust workers to do the job properly.	1	2	3	4	5	Managers empower by sharing power, information, and decision making and by trusting employees to do the job.

○ Subscore CSF #7 = _____   ☐ Subscore CSF #7 = _____

CSF #8: Foster an Atmosphere of Entrepreneurship

Management creates barriers to sharing ideas (especially upward) or does not remove those that exist.	1	2	3	4	5	Management models entrepreneurship and removes barriers to sharing ideas.
Employees are prevented from taking calculated, intelligent risks.	1	2	3	4	5	Employees are encouraged to take calculated, intelligent risks, without fear of being disciplined if they fail.
No resources are provided for entrepreneurial activities.	1	2	3	4	5	Resources (time, money, information) are provided for entrepreneurial activities.

○ Subscore CSF #8 = _____   ☐ Subscore CSF #8 = _____

CSF #9: Increase the Intangible Resources of the Organization

Organization makes little to no effort to develop the intangible capital of the organization.	1	2	3	4	5	Organization actively seeks to develop the intangible capital of the organization (for example, through development of people and teams).
Organization has no recognition of the value of intangible resources.	1	2	3	4	5	Organization measures and accounts for the value of intellectual, social, collaborative, and organizational capital.
Sharing of ideas is hindered, resulting in few new ideas and little creativity.	1	2	3	4	5	All brains are engaged and sharing of ideas is encouraged and supported, resulting in a lot of energy and creativity.

○ Subscore CSF #9 = _____   ☐ Subscore CSF #9 = _____

CSF #10: Design an Adaptable Organization

Organization is slow to move in response to environmental changes and opportunities or does not recognize the need to change.	1 2 3 4 5	Organization is agile and flexible enough to make changes quickly in response to environmental changes and opportunities.
Few new ideas are created, or new ideas are quickly stifled.	1 2 3 4 5	Employees develop creative and adaptive solutions and identify new opportunities, and management listens to these.
Teams must wait for higher-level response that takes so much time that the need for the change has passed.	1 2 3 4 5	Teams create rapid changes in response to work environment, supplier, or customer issues.

⃝ Subscore CSF #10 = _____   ☐ Subscore CSF #10 = _____

Graph of Critical Success Factors Subscores

Directions: Use circles to plot the "where organization is now" scores on the graph below. Connect the circles with a solid line. Then use squares to plot the "where organization would like to be" scores on the graph below. Connect squares with a dotted line.

⃝ Where Organization Is Now   ☐ Where Organization Would Like to Be at Highest Level of Team-Based Organizing

[Graph: y-axis labeled "Subscore" with values 0, 5, 10, 15; x-axis labeled "Critical Success Factors" with categories CSF #1, CSF #2, CSF #3, CSF #4, CSF #5, CSF #6, CSF #7, CSF #8, CSF #9, CSF #10]

Discussion Questions

Gear your discussion to your own situation, particularly to the method of analysis (individual, individual and then group, or group consensus) you have chosen. Some possible discussion questions are listed below.

1. Use the graph to identify the biggest gaps between where you are now and where you want to be. The bigger the gap, the more work needs to be done to get where you want to be.

2. Delve deeper into the biggest gaps by reviewing the scoring of the items within the corresponding subscore. Which item contributes most to the gap?

3. Do you agree with the results? Why or why not?

4. Use these gaps to identify the priority of addressing critical success factors. (Bigger gaps probably indicate a higher priority.)

5. Think of the gaps in terms of sequential order of implementation. Do some of them need to be addressed before others?

6. What can you do to close those gaps? Look at the cross-reference table of critical success factors to relevant chapters in the Fieldbook (see Table 1.2) for follow-up ideas.

CHAPTER 2

The Search Conference

A Participative Planning Method That Builds Widespread Collaboration

Catherine Bradshaw, Joan Roberts, and Sylvia Cheuy

TOO OFTEN, "participative planning" methods flounder in implementation when grand plans receive little or no support from the people on the front lines or in middle levels of the organization. This is because these planning processes paid only lip service to participation by getting input from people and then reverting to control and coordination from an elite group. Plans ultimately feel imposed, and the people who are needed to successfully implement them respond with cynicism, resistance and, at best, low commitment.

In the Search Conference, collaboration is fostered by a self-managing team environment.

Clearly, these efforts don't create contexts for sustained collaboration because things are still done using the traditional system of the control-based, bureaucratic design. This perpetuates a culture of segmented thinking, competition, and abdication of responsibility.

The Search Conference is a tool that goes far beyond these approaches by giving the planners an experience of real collaboration, fostered by a self-managing team environment and by creating and following a strategic plan that diffuses this kind of environment throughout the organization.

The methodology was originally developed by Fred Emery and Eric Trist in 1960 to set strategy in the merger of two aircraft engine makers (which became Bristol-Siddeley, later bought by Rolls-Royce) (Trist & Emery, 1960). Over the last forty years, it has been tested and fine-tuned in diverse contexts around the world. It has been used by major corporations such as Motorola (Cabana & Fiero, 1995), by governments like the Nebraska Mental Health System (Emery & Purser, 1998), and by communities throughout the world to plan strategically and formulate policy in times of rapid change. The authors suggest that it is a vital tool in creating the conditions for successful collaboration for team-based organizations charged with adapting to turbulent environments.

When the process is designed strategically, people throughout the system participate in creating a desirable future for the organization and learn how to work together in a collaborative, self-managing mode. Once people see how it's possible, and feel collaboration in their bones, there's no turning back. The next step is to intentionally restructure the organization into a fully self-managing team environment using methods such as the participative design process described in Chapters 14 and 15. The Search Conference lays critical ground-work for this transformation. Not only does it begin to establish a collaborative environment, but it also builds commitment and responsibility for the strategic plan, and thus ensures that implementation will be smooth and that the change will be sustainable.

In this chapter, we will first outline the theoretical principles that lay the foundation for understanding and applying the Search Conference methodology. We then describe the method itself: we outline the steps that occur during a Search Conference and describe a process for engaging people throughout the organization in the process of strategy development. Finally, we explain the value of the Search Conference in infusing collaboration throughout an organization.

Guiding Principles of the Search Conference

The design of the Search Conference is guided by a number of theoretical principles. Understanding these principles is critical to understanding the methodology.

Organizations must be able to actively adapt to the increasing turbulence of our global environment.

1. Our organizations are currently required to plan in a highly complex and turbulent environment. Emery and Purser (1998, p. 59) describe this turbulence as characterized by a "myriad of unpredictable interactions and enmeshed connections between different facets and groups in society."

Because everything is so enmeshed and interdependent, the smallest actions in one part of the environment can become wildly amplified and lead to unpredictable results.

2. It is therefore critical that organizations be able to actively adapt to their increasingly turbulent world. This means that they must continually scan the broader environment to know what events and trends are happening afar that could have an impact on their system.

   This does not mean passively responding to the turbulence, but rather acting on the environment to improve conditions and ultimately reduce the turbulence. In this way, the organization and its environment evolve together.

3. No designs or plans should be imposed. This means, first, that only people who are part of the system attend the Search Conference because they are the ones who are ultimately responsible for the organization's future, and they will have to implement the action plans that they create during the event. When external stakeholders are in on planning the organization's desirable future, they, in essence, hand their ideas and plans over to the organization's members to implement. Second, this means that a process needs to be developed to diffuse the plans throughout the rest of the organization using the guiding principles outlined in this section, thus ensuring that all organizational members participate collaboratively in creating the desirable future and making it real. A suggested process for doing this is outlined later in this chapter.

4. Complex and unpredictable environments require a more nonlinear approach to planning, one that resembles the process of assembling a jigsaw puzzle: when each piece is put in place, a new picture is created that requires a new set of perspectives and resources to figure out the next step. The search for new possibilities in the current situation is more important than drawing on expert conceptual knowledge. The playing field is leveled, with everyone bringing critical perspectives and resources to the puzzle-learning/puzzle-solving process.

When people hold responsibility for the coordination and outcomes of their work, they fall naturally into an energized, creative work mode.

5. In a democratic structure, the responsibility for coordination and outcomes is located with the people doing the work.

   This puts people naturally into what Bion (1961) calls the *work mode*, which is characterized by high levels of energy, collaboration, and commitment. Bion also explains that when groups feel threatened, emotions intensify, making it easy to fall into one of three *group assumptions*. In *dependency mode,* the group feels reliant on a leader to be able to function. People are in a passive state: they wait to be told what to do; they don't develop creative relationships with their group mates; they aren't interested in learning. In *fight-flight mode,* the group feels it needs to respond to a real or imagined threat from outside the group, which at times is actually a facilitator or "expert" at the front of the room. In *pairing mode,* there is animated discussion between two members of the group which diverts the group's attention toward a new possibility or direction. This can lead a group into work mode, but if the idea continues just as hopeful talk between a few people, the group will remain in pairing.

6. Solomon Asch (1952) specifies four conditions that must be in place for communication to be effective:

- Openness—there are no hidden agendas, things are what they appear to be, all information is shared.

- Shared field—the realization that we all share the same world. We live in a shared context that has objective features that we can all perceive.

- Basic psychological similarity—we all strive for ideals that reflect a basic concern for humanity, for creating beauty, for belonging and for nurturance.

- Trust—this develops as the other three conditions are met. This involves, as Emery points out, the ability to "exercise care about [group members'] own and shared concerns and [to] put away gradually, without risk, the masks of passivity and disassociation" (1999, p. 115). It is therefore critical to working together collaboratively.

7. Successful planning does not sweep conflict under the rug by driving for consensus; it acknowledges conflict and explores it until all sides are understood, then builds on the areas of common ground.

   Called "rationalization of conflict," this process leads to plans that are a thorough integration of the ideas and energies of all participants, plans that feel owned by all.

Description of the Search Conference Method

This section will provide a concise description of the Search Conference Tool, describe some of the key components of a successful Search Conference, and finally, provide an overview of how Search Conferencing can be used specifically to build widespread collaboration across an organization.

The Search Conference combines the best practices of strategic planning, systems thinking, and effective group communication.

The Search Conference uses a format that enables a large group (ideally between twenty and thirty-five people) to develop a set of strategies that they themselves implement. Over two and a half days, these individuals develop long-term strategic visions, achievable goals, and concrete action plans. As a method, the Search Conference combines the best practices associated with strategic planning, systems thinking, and effective group communication to enable participants to rise above self-interest to make decisions for the common good.

It stands out from some of the other large-group processes, such as the Open Space Conference (Owen, 1992), the Future Search Conference (Weisbord, 1992), and ICA's Participatory Strategic Planning process (Spencer, 1989) in that it:

- Rests on a solid theoretical foundation of group dynamics and open systems principles;

- Is carefully designed to put people in a creative working mode and to build a learning and planning community; and

- Combines the environmental scan, system analysis, vision/strategy creation and thorough action planning within the event itself.

The Search Conference is designed to provide a learning environment in which all perceptions are valid, conflicts can be explored and rationalized, and participation is equal and open. People put forward their ideas in large and small groups, using flip-chart paper to record everyone's ideas for all to see. Everything is out in the open and shared in the public domain. Through such an approach, the Search Conference emphasizes the building of mutual trust and people's confidence in their own direct perceptions. This ensures that Asch's (1952) condition of "openness" is honored.

The Search Conference can be used to either set or refine strategic direction for the entire organization.

In an organizational context, the Search Conference can be used to determine or refine strategic direction for the entire organization.

The focus question of a Search Conference can be as simple as "What is the future of the system in three to five years?" but can also be more detailed to

reflect the specific requirements of the system. In general, the design of the Search Conference resembles a funnel because it begins by asking participants to take the widest possible view and gradually narrows the focus to specific goals that the participants are committed to achieving.

In its design, the Search Conference falls into three distinct phases, with each phase taking up approximately one-third of the conference planning time.

The agenda for a Search Conference follows this basic format:

Day 1	Day 2	Day 3
	Phase II: System analysis History Scan: Where have we come from? What has made us? Analysis of the system today: keep, drop, create Determine system's desirable future	Action Plans, cont'd
3:00 Introductions, expectations, dinner	**Phase III: Integration of the system and the environment** Identify constraints and strategies for dealing with them Determine system's achievable future	**Next steps: Post Search Conference** *Diffusion.* The Search Conference grows as it diffuses goals and plans
Phase I: Environmental analysis Scan of changes in the world around us: global and task environment Most desirable and most probable futures	Action Plans Resources needed Responsibilities Timelines	

Phase One: Scanning the External Environment

During the environmental scan, people step outside their immediate concerns to establish a set of shared ideals and perceptions.

Participants always begin with activities designed to help them learn about what is happening in their environment. By taking the widest possible perspective, participants step outside themselves and their immediate concerns to explore a range of possibilities.

This environmental scan helps participants to establish a sense of commonality and honors Asch's (1952) conditions for effective communication by allowing participants to experience the realization that "we all share the same world" and "we all strive for ideals that reflect concern for humanity," which are critical to building trust.

The focus on the broader external environment also reminds participants of the ongoing interrelationship between the system and its environment and the fact that in today's turbulent world it is unwise to assume that the future will look anything like the past. This, in turn, ensures that the plans ultimately developed in the Search Conference will be adaptable and effective. In this way, Search Conference participants have an opportunity to apply "open systems theory." This maintains that for any system to remain viable and healthy over time, it must maintain an open and actively adaptive relationship with its environment (Emery, 1999). When appropriate, a second "task environment" scan is added. This second scan takes a close look at emerging trends in a specific industry or subsystem that is of particular relevance to the system conducting the Search.

Phase Two: Examining Our System

Participants work together to identify the most desirable future for their organization or community.

During this phase, participants explore the unique character of their system and what has shaped it and ultimately reach agreement on the most desirable future for their system. This examination includes reflecting on the past to identify key events and milestones that have shaped what "the system" is today.

The group also analyzes the system's present and specifically identifies what about the current system they must "keep," "drop," or "create" in light of their understanding of the broader environment. During the final activity of this phase, conference participants work together to identify the most desirable future for their system. Out of this emerges a set of strategic goals for making this desirable future a reality.

Phase Three: Action Planning

During this third phase of the conference, the Search community is asked to bring its dreams to earth. During this phase, participants identify the major constraints likely to be encountered during implementation. If necessary, the group may choose to adjust its strategy in light of their constraints. Constraints typically include time, money, resources, and so forth. Once constraints have been identified, participants are asked to devise strategies for overcoming them and then develop action plans that outline who is going to take responsibility for

The last phase of the Search Conference often includes aspects of a participative design workshop so that the organization can create a democratic structure that will ensure success.

each item, by when and how such activities will be monitored and evaluated. Identifying others who need to be involved in the community's emerging plans (people within the organization who were not part of the conference as well as external stakeholders) is another key activity undertaken during this phase.

Often, this third phase of the Search Conference will incorporate aspects of the participative design workshop (see Chapter 15 for more information) to allow participants to design a democratic work structure for themselves that will ensure that they will succeed in carrying out their action plans.

The Importance of Pre-Search Conference Planning

A successful Search Conference requires careful planning and preparation. Typically, a steering team is struck to work in collaboration with the Search Conference manager (typically a consultant who is trained in the methodology) to prepare the organization for the process.

The steering committee is usually comprised of the sponsor or driving force behind the planning process initiative and other members selected to be broadly representative of the system. In a corporate environment, the committee may include various departments as well as labor representation. In a community setting it would involve sectorial representation such as business, education, social services, and equity groups. Some of the tasks that must be addressed include:

- Clearly defining "the system" (and, if appropriate, the "task environment") for purposes of the Search Conference;

- Developing a clear and compelling focus statement for the Search Conference;

- Identifying participants and developing an invitation list. If feasible this should include the entire workforce. Participants generally include the organization's leadership as well as cross-departmental and labor representation. It is advantageous to have as deep a slice of organizational life participate as possible in the planning undertaken at a Search Conference;

- Determining—and supplying—any necessary background information to participants prior to the Search Conference;

- Designing the Search Conference;
- Planning logistics and space for the event itself; and
- Educating participants about the Search Conference design and purpose before the event.

The Role of the Search Conference Manager

The role of the Search Conference manager is different from that of a facilitator because he/she does not act as a helper or guide as it relates to the conference content and does not intervene to manage the group's process.

Rather, the Search Conference manager's role is to create and sustain a healthy, democratic learning environment and process to ensure that participants are able to do the work that they need to do. Specifically, a Search Conference manager's tasks include such things as:

- Monitoring time;
- Providing clear, simple task instructions to participants;
- Integrating group work; and
- Placing boundaries and creating a safe container around conflict using the rationalization of conflict approach, thereby preventing negative group dynamics.

In addition, Search Conference managers play an important role in the pre-Search Conference planning process, working collaboratively with conference sponsors to plan and design a successful event.

Using a Multiple Search Conference Process to Foster Organization-Wide Collaboration

It is possible to use a modified, multi-Search Conference process to engage people at all levels of the organization in working collaboratively to plan for their future. This approach is particularly valuable to those organizations that have already decided to adopt a collaborative team structure but need a clear, shared sense of their strategic direction.

If the organization is small (fewer than fifty people), the entire organization can be involved in a single, traditional Search Conference. With larger organizations, a multi-Search Conference process is effective in diffusing the process of collaboration throughout the system. In this approach, the senior level of management (along with some representatives from lower levels of management) goes through the first two phases of the Search Conference of scanning the external environment and examining the system.

A few strict rules

This Search Conference ends with senior management having defined the organization's desirable future and the strategic goals to achieve that future; no action planning is done at this conference.

Once the broader strategic direction has been set, a series of new Search Conferences is held involving the various functional areas of the organization. In this next level of conferences, the focus is on identifying the most desirable future for each functional area. In the first phase of these Search Conferences, participants conduct both a scan of the world and a scan of their "task environment," that is, the organization. As part of the task environment scan, participants learn about the broader strategic directions developed during the earlier Search Conference. This approach ensures that the desirable futures and action planning of each functional area incorporate the overall strategic goals of the organization into operational goals across each area.

After a series of Search Conferences, an integration conference should take place, involving representatives from all the conferences.

Once Search Conferences have been held for each functional area, an integration conference should be held involving representatives from all the Search Conferences. The purpose of this event is to verify that the action plans will meet the organization's strategic goals and to look for opportunities to combine or assist in the action plans emerging from the various functional areas.

The design of the Search Conference, both the event itself and the process for diffusing it throughout an organization, is powerful in creating a culture of collaboration. It involves employees in the process of creating strategic intent and gives them an experience of working together in a highly collaborative manner.

The Value of Search Conferences in Building Collaborative Work Systems

To sustain a self-managing environment, an organization needs to be clear on what future it is working toward.

Having a clear strategic direction is critical to the success of building collaborative work systems. To be self-managing, an organization needs to know what future it is working and managing itself toward—otherwise the present is generated once again.

The Search Conference is very effective in moving an organization toward truly self-managing work systems. Search Conferences can enhance a team's transition to becoming self–managing by:

- Creating readiness for change;
- Providing a strategic framework;
- Building a sense of ownership;
- Transferring skills; and
- Allowing participants to experience a democratic process.

Creating Readiness for Change

A Search Conference can be used to assess the challenges in the external environment and internal system, thus making explicit the need for change.

Syncrude, a large corporation whose mission is to extract oil from Alberta's tar sands, found that the Search Conference created the internal case for change through its collective learning process. Syncrude's executives convened a number of Search Conferences when they sensed that clear strategic direction by management was needed. In these conferences, functional, departmental, and divisional managers examined the changing business environment, envisioned a more desirable future, critiqued the executives' vision statement and discussed whether it made sense, and made their own plans to help Syncrude begin to change. As a result of this process, many managers in Syncrude's departments and the divisions came to believe that the status quo was unacceptable and that change was needed (Purser & Cabana, 1998).

Providing a Strategic Framework

A Search Conference can be the first step in a total organizational change process and can produce an understanding of shared context and strategic direction by which the subsequent participative design process will be guided. Typical goals coming out of this type of Search include having high morale, a safe and healthy workplace, high productivity and product/service quality, a customer focus, and flexibility to respond to challenges and opportunities (Emery, 1999). The logical next step is to run a series of participative design workshops that allow the organization to thoroughly plan how it will achieve these goals.

The final product of a Search Conference is an integrated vision and action plan with measurable goals and accountabilities that are transferred to other teams to refine, integrate, and eventually implement.

The vision that emerges is derived from the particular character and culture of the organization and concretized with actionable goals, time frames, and champions.

In *Classic Blunders in Team Implementation*, Ellison (1999) explains that one of the greatest mistakes on the road to implementing work teams is the failure to understand the organization's current conditions. A Search Conference is useful not only for an organization to understand the case for change and develop a desired future with goals and strategic direction, but also to assess the system and identify what is working, as well as the roadblocks to change.

Sense of Ownership

A Search Conference can be a first step in promoting a feeling of ownership among the workforce, thus acting as a catalyst for self-management. Successful collaboration requires that employees be invested emotionally in the outcomes of their work.

Jim Heckel, production manager for the Greeley, Colorado, plant of Hewlett-Packard, stated, "We used the Search Conference to develop a plan to build manufacturing flexibility by developing a workplace where employees are supported by management to act as if they are owners. We brought together all of management in manufacturing and a selected cross selection of employees (who would work as self-managing teams) to establish six Year 2000 initiatives for employees acting as owners:

- Rethinking our compensatory/recognition system

- Centering on key core manufacturing competencies

- Getting closer to customer needs

- Exploring information technologies for those which will help us be more productive

- Promoting awareness of diversity issues

- Redesigning and restructuring the workplace."

(Emery & Purser, 1996, pp. 28–29)

Transferring Skills

A Search Conference transfers the skills of active adaptive planning to the participants, including the important skill of continuously scanning the external environment and adapting to trends and opportunities. In effect, scenario planning and strategic thinking skills are developed. Search Conferences can provide a learning opportunity for employees to acquire skills, such as strategy development, that are traditionally held only by senior management. This doesn't mean that senior managers no longer perform this critical function, which is a core responsibility of their jobs, but rather that people throughout the organization are better equipped to contribute their knowledge to the strategy development function. Everyone understands and contributes to the process of continually scanning the environment, analyzing the internal system to see what's working and what isn't, and making changes to adapt to trends in the market and in society.

Everyone understands and contributes to the process of scanning and making changes to adapt to the market.

Once participative teams are created, these skills are shared among team members. Search conferences can be held on an as-needed basis in the various departments of the organization; everyone is thinking strategically, and the various strategies—including the overall vision and strategy for the organization—then relate to each other as an integrated whole.

Experience of a Democratic Process

An important benefit of using Search Conferences when moving toward authentic collaboration is providing the experience of participating in a democratic organization, even if the organization is only temporary at that point. However, the experience of being valued and listened to, and of holding a piece of the puzzle, embodies a new organizational culture and creates the desire to experience it on a continuing basis.

Dan Dotin of Xerox explains the benefits of a Search Conference in creating a shift in his workforce culture:

> "We used the output from the Search Conference action planning teams in our annual planning process to develop the business strategy for the next three years. Our culture has engineered a big shift. We've moved from being highly dependent on top-down planning to acting like entrepreneurs. This is an incredible breakthrough for our employees." (Purser & Cabana, 1998, p. 207)

Conclusion

The Search Conference is a valuable method on the journey toward collaborative work systems. It creates and assesses the system's readiness for change and provides the strategic direction needed for effective goal setting throughout the organization. The collaborative process used throughout the Search Conference builds a sense of ownership, transfers critical skills around strategy development, and gives people an experience of working together in a self-managing environment.

CHAPTER 3

The Transformation Grid

A Framework for TBO Conversions

Tom Devane

Most senior managers recognize that traditional organizations are less responsive to customer needs and market shifts.

OVER THE PAST SEVEN YEARS, there has been a rise in the number of team-based organizations (TBOs).

Most senior managers recognize that traditional organizational forms of multi-leveled hierarchical, functionally organized resources tend to make decisions more slowly and are less responsive to customer needs and market shifts than TBOs.

While the acceptance of TBO *concepts* is gaining widespread acceptance, senior managers have some *practical questions* that need to be answered at the start of a transition to a TBO. Personal experience shows the following questions arise most frequently:

- What high leverage actions will help my organization move to a team-based organization?

- How can we accelerate the transition from a traditional organization to a TBO?

- What can leaders do to facilitate the transition?
- How do we need to manage differently in the new environment?

To address these and other important questions for converting to a TBO, a Transformation Grid is proposed.

The Transformation Grid was developed over twenty-two years of research in over 120 organizations. It has been used to implement Six Sigma and total quality programs, large computer systems, process redesign initiatives, and mergers and acquisitions. Over the past seven years, the Grid has been specifically tailored to address the needs of converting from a traditional organization to a TBO.

In its current form, the Grid domains and starter questions reflect the research and practice of all authors listed in the reference section, in addition to the author's own action research.

This chapter is not about *why* one might want to convert to a TBO. Plenty of other chapters in this book address TBO benefits. This chapter is about *how to do it* in a practical, fast, participative way that focuses attention on critical transformation success factors.

Transformation Grid Basics
What It Is

The Grid is a tool that can be used for:

- Planning a transformation to a TBO;
- Monitoring and adjusting transformation activities; and
- Conducting lessons learned analyses.

The Transformation Grid focuses attention on two aspects of migration to a TBO: time (shown in the top row) and high leverage domains for action (the left-most column). A high leverage domain consists of strategies, tactics, and best practices for converting to a team-based organization. The domains are explained in greater depth later in this chapter.

Organizations have found three variations of the Transformation Grid helpful. Each provides an increasing level of coaching assistance.

The *Basic Grid* (Table 3.1) maps the time to domains and contains blank cells.

Table 3.1. The Basic Grid

	Stage I: Initiation	Stage II: Direction Setting	Stage III: Design	Stage IV: Implementation	Stage V: Operating and Continuous Improvement
Leadership development and key actions					
Participative planning					
Process awareness					
High participation structuring					
Support (HR dept. activity, management, information technology, and so forth)					

The *Typical Profile Grid* (Table 3.2) provides information on the timing of when domains are typically invoked. An "X" denotes a particular domain is invoked during a particular stage. For example, the two Xs in the Participative Planning row show that domain is typically invoked in Stages II and V. All domains are not invoked in all stages. An organization's specific situation determines the timing of invoking a particular domain in a TBO transformation.

Table 3.2. The Typical Profile Grid

	Stage I: Initiation	Stage II: Direction Setting	Stage III: Design	Stage IV: Implementation	Stage V: Operating and Continuous Improvement
Leadership development and key actions	X	X	X	X	X
Participative planning		X			X
Process awareness		X	X		X
High participation structuring			X	X	X
Support		X	X	X	X

The *Starter Grid* (Table 3.3) shows the stage/domain relationships and selected specific actions. This list is intended to be a starter list for productive conversations, not a comprehensive list.

Table 3.3. The Starter Grid

	Stage I: Initiation	Stage II: Direction Setting	Stage III: Design	Stage IV: Implementation	Stage V: Operating and Continuous Improvement
Leadership development and key actions	Ensure business case is made Organize a coalition Model straight talk Develop a clear, succinct, easily communicated message about the burning platform	Obtain education in managing TBOs Coalition models straight talk Seek opportunities for symbolic acts Broaden participation	Use language to help shape new thought (for example, change job descriptions and titles for managers in the old hierarchy) Establish guidelines and boundaries for the redesign	Hold teams collectively accountable Encourage rotating leadership within teams Ask, "How might we be unwittingly reinforcing the past?"	Ensure teams have necessary resources (training, technology, physical facilities) Ensure compensation system rewards teams Reward new thoughts/action
Participative planning		Ensure all critical perspectives represented for planning session Scan the external environment and plan to adapt to and influence it			Develop strategic plans in a participative fashion with multiple perspectives
Process awareness		Conduct process awareness training Map critical process and develop improvement plan	Conduct problem-solving training Teach basic improvement tools (for example, Pareto analysis, cycle time reduction, value-added analysis)		Teach advanced improvement tools (for example, control charts, design of experiment, work cells, pull systems, design for Six Sigma)
High participation structuring			Seek 100 percent participation Have team set own goals and negotiate targets with managers	Adaptively renegotiate goals, targets, boundaries	Workers at all levels restructure the organization as external and internal demands necessitate

Table 3.3. The Starter Grid, Cont'd

	Stage I: Initiation	Stage II: Direction Setting	Stage III: Design	Stage IV: Implementation	Stage V: Operating and Continuous Improvement
High participation structuring *(continued)*			Distinguish between repetitive and non-repetitive work (knowledge work) Satisfy six criteria for productive work in team designs*		
Support	Develop informal feedback system for change proponents and the rest of the organization	Develop communication plan Conduct town hall meetings with information sharing and inquiry	Communicate direction Communicate progress Establish information technology-enabled two-way feedback systems	Provide needed technical training for new teams Publish team metrics and information on intranet Begin restructuring pay	Conduct essential training at workers' request (negotiation, meeting management) Implement pay for skill Investigate gain sharing

*These six criteria are elbow room, variety, learning, mutual support and respect, meaningfulness, and desirable future. For further detail, see Chapter 14.

Underlying Assumptions

All tools have underlying assumptions. The Grid's assumptions are as follows:

- When a group of people with diverse perspectives and a stake in the organizational outcome is assembled, amazing insights result with minimal instruction.
- Feedback systems provide for quick learning and course correction.
- Although most transformation work can be done internally, some external "principle imparting" assistance can be helpful.

Principles for Use

General principles for using the Grid include the following:

- The Transformation Grid is intended to be a foundation tool that organizations can adapt for their own needs. It is not a Procrustean bed* for a TBO transformation. The primary objective of the tool is to encourage senior managers and change agents to think about the truly high leverage actions that contribute to success, and how those might map to stages of a TBO transformation.

- Keep it simple.

- The Grid is not a work plan (though some have found it helpful in developing work plans, the Grid is more of a general framework that ensures the right things will be happening at about the right time).

- No element of the Grid is cast in stone. Users can move Xs, fill in empty cells, and move items between cells.

Experience has shown that people in the organization often come up with as good, or better recommended actions than external strategic planning experts.

- Do not be alarmed by looking at all the blank cells on the Grid when starting. A major benefit of filling it in with a group, instead of having "outside experts" come in, is that the group understands the organization's unique issues and brings a variety of perspectives and experiences to the table.

- Outside help should only be called on if the group is stuck.

- Seek to grow the circle of participation in the TBO transformation when moving from one stage to the next (Figure 3.1). In the figure, the outer boundaries of the circles represent the entire organization and the dark spot in the center of the circle represents the percentage of the entire organization directly involved in the TBO transformation at the beginning of each stage. Strive to encompass the entire organization by the end of Stage III, The Design Phase. Do not focus merely on "inform-people-of-the-change" passive participation. Design meaningful, active participation.

---

*In Greek mythology, Procrustes kept a house by the side of the road and offered lodging and meals to passers-by. To make good his claim to exactly match the size of his guest bed to whoever lay down on it, he would stretch guests if they were too short and chop off their legs if they were too long.

Figure 3.1. Participation Levels

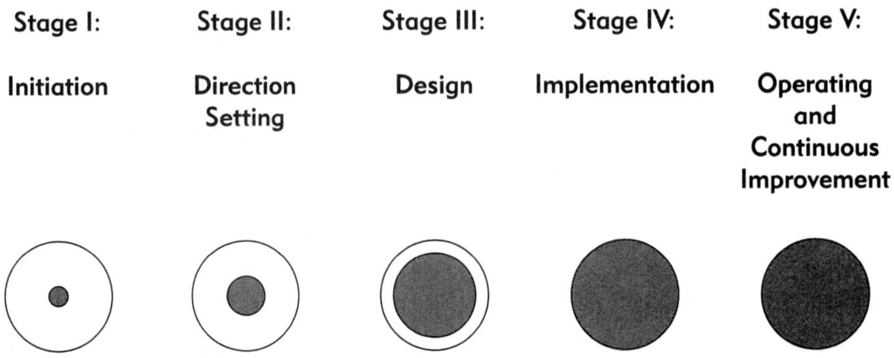

Stage I:	Stage II:	Stage III:	Stage IV:	Stage V:
Initiation	Direction Setting	Design	Implementation	Operating and Continuous Improvement

Rules

The Grid is intended to be a very flexible and adaptive tool. There are only two rules:

1. *Rule #1.* For each domain, place at least two Xs across the Grid. One must be in Stage V, Operating and Continuous Improvement.

2. *Rule #2.* Fill out detailed actions within the Grid with *groups of people* rather than a single individual or two.

Outcomes from Using Grid

The first obvious, visible output of the Grid is the Grid template filled in with activities for a transformation to a TBO. The result will resemble an expanded version of Table 3.3, containing specific action items that senior management and change agents deem necessary for an organization's unique TBO transformation.

The second visible output is an expanded narrative description of Grid action items. Less directly visible, but of equal impact, outcomes are the quality of the transformation effort and ease of operating the resulting TBO. The Grid and conversations about it are beneficial because:

- By ensuring each of the five domains is invoked, an organization ensures the fundamental TBO building blocks for success are present and

- Group conversations about the recommended actions in the Grid help surface different assumptions and bring together different experiences and perspectives resulting in a higher quality plan for the TBO transformation.

High Leverage Domains

The five domains in the Grid represent areas in which a little bit of effort can produce disproportionately significant results. Here are brief descriptions of each.

Leadership Development and Key Actions

Both formal and informal types of leadership authority play a role in a TBO transformation. If formal leaders, that is, those with positional power, are not leading the charge toward a TBO, it will not happen.

Informal leadership is important in a TBO because of the distributed decision making and high demands for personal initiative. In a TBO one goal is to have rotating leadership within teams so that everyone can have an opportunity to lead at some time, based on the knowledge required and the task at hand.

Formal and informal leaders need to constantly develop their personal leadership skills throughout the transformation. Since there are fewer mandates and decision making is distributed, "control" is achieved by providing information, guidelines and visibility of metrics, team-based goal setting and negotiation with management, peer reviews, and center of excellence coaching sessions—not by direct boss-to-subordinate supervision. While senior leaders can still override lower level decisions, this is the exception, not the rule. Formal leaders hold *groups* accountable instead of *individuals*. These leadership elements need to be considered when completing the Grid.

Leaders take actions that others in the organization interpret as either supporting or detracting from new TBO objectives. Therefore, it is important to seriously consider what is done and said as a leader.

Great leaders are constantly on the lookout for opportunities to demonstrate their support for the new ways of thinking and acting. They also need to watch what they say in times of frustration and anxiety since all statements can spread like wildfire—especially statements that make it seem like management is not "walking the talk."

Participative Planning

There are many planning processes in a TBO transformation that provide participation opportunities. Some planning topics include organizational strategy and TBO transformation approach. A well-functioning TBO requires a strategy in place around which to structure teams. If a strategic plan has recently been done, an organization may still wish to conduct a participative planning session that includes wider participation. Although uncommon in a traditional organizational structure, it is not uncommon in a TBO for twenty to sixty people to meet and work productively. An organization's old strategic plan could be used as background for such a session.

Involving others in planning processes is critical, in order to:

- Model behaviors we want to see in the emerging TBO;

- Develop strategic thinking and leadership capabilities for attendees; and

- Demonstrate confidence in people who had previously not been involved in planning processes in which important decisions were made.

Process Awareness

A process can be thought of as a collection of activities and decisions that produce an output for a customer. Processes may be contained within, or may span, departmental or team boundaries.

Whether a process is contained within or spans team boundaries, TBO members need to understand the concept of a process because:

- For exceptional team performance, teams need to know internal or external customer requirements to help negotiate agreements and metrics.

- For teams to improve, they need to understand the activities and decisions that add value to an output for a customer.

- Teams might organize around a process to decrease handoffs among individuals and teams. For example, in a TBO there may be a multi-skilled team composed of engineering, manufacturing, marketing, and purchasing people responsible for developing new products. Having these disciplines in one organizational unit—instead of in traditionally separate departmental silos—minimizes handoffs and reduces opportunities for miscommunication and delays.

It is useful if people understand the concept of processes *before* they begin to restructure the organization into teams.

One of the best ways to teach process awareness is to convene a group session and have members participate in drawing the flow of activities and decisions for one of the organization's processes. The group would first understand the existing process, then design a better one, and then develop plans to migrate to the new process.

A process understanding tends to increase the quality of the new TBO structure because people make conscious design decisions based on customer requirements, reducing handoffs, streamlined workflow, and logical groupings of activities and decisions.

High Participation Structuring

In successful TBOs that this author has worked with, teams are designed to be adaptive organizational units that play a major role in initially *designing* the TBO and then *redesigning* themselves as external and internal conditions change.

Senior managers report that this participation results in a high level of intrinsic motivation and commitment to achieving the organization's goals. For this to happen, of course, teams need to know the principles for designing team-based organizations.

One of the best times to provide this education is in Stage III, Redesign. The Emery method (for more information see Chapter 14), which serves as the foundation for team work that this author has done, recommends that 100 percent of the organization participate in the redesign effort in a series of two- to three-day workshops called participative design workshops (Emery & Emery, 1993).

To many steeped in the management of traditional structure, some key TBO redesign principles may seem counterintuitive:

- Recommendations for redesigning the organizational structure can come from anywhere in the organization—not just top management or the HR department—because everyone is familiar with TBO design principles.

- During the redesign sessions, teams set their own team goals instead of having them handed down from one level above.

- Although teams are considered to be "self-managing," this does not mean they do whatever they want. Controls are designed into the structure at the same time the team-based structure is designed.

- Managers hold *teams* accountable for results, instead of *individuals*.

- The more influence and power a leader gives to teams—accompanied by the appropriate information and rewards—the more power a leader has (Maslow, 1998).

- An effective sequence of a redesign to a TBO is bottom of the organization first, middle next, and top last. In the top workshop, management redesigns the management structure, also integrating the designs from the previous workshops (Emery & Devane, 2000). This sequence permits lower levels to pull down supervisory tasks previously done by higher levels, thus making the teams more self-reliant, motivated, and productive. Higher level teams in the organization can then spend time doing more strategic and customer-related work. (Senior level managers typically spend less than 3 percent of their time on strategy for the corporate future [Hamel & Prahalad, 1994]. In TBOs one objective is to free up senior management time spent firefighting and managing so they can spend more time on strategy.)

Statements like, "Management would never let us do that" and "I can't try that or I'll get my head shot off" disappear from conversations.

In this author's experience, corporate and public sector organizations unanimously agree: having all the people in the organization restructure their work is one of the most effective ways to demonstrate that power is being distributed and that things are really changing.

It is also one of the best ways to create intrinsic motivation and commitment. True change begins when people's experience and perspectives change. No rigorous analysis or clearly written white paper ever changed anyone's mind to do anything new (at least anything major). With high participation restructuring, we seek to change people's experience with workplace interactions and their perspectives on what they are eligible to do.

Support

Even a brilliantly designed organizational structure cannot stand on its own. It also needs the following:

- *Human resources support* (compensation and reward systems);

- *Information technology support* (posting of team data and metrics on intranets, computer support for teams, video teleconferencing, and team Internet access);

- *Management support* (finding teams needed resources); and

- *Facilities support* (rearrangement or remodeling of the physical workplace).

Starter Questions for Each Domain

Following are some questions for each domain to help jump-start filling out the blank cells in the Grid. This is not meant to be a comprehensive list, but rather a "priming of the pump" for additional relevant questions. Keep in mind a key assumption of the Grid: when assembling a group of people with diverse perspectives who have a stake in the organizational outcome, this group can develop some amazing insights and plans.

Leadership Development and Actions

- Who needs to be in our initial coalition group to get the TBO transformation off the ground?

- Are our formal leaders prepared to lead a TBO? If not, what needs to be done and when?

- What is our burning platform for change and how do we communicate it?

- When are good opportunities to model straight talk so people see this as an emerging norm?

- How do we present the notion of a TBO to the organization? Announce it as a directive? Try to sell it? Let everyone analyze it and put it to a vote?

- How can we use storytelling to help get people excited and shift the current cultural mindset?

- How can we hold people collectively accountable as a group—instead of individuals?

Participative Planning

- What types of plans will we need?

- How will we gather global trends, market information, and customer information?

- Should we design our planning sessions from scratch, or use some existing designs? (For some existing designs, see the Collaborative Methods for TBO Transformations section later in this chapter.)

- Are we learning as fast as our environment is changing?

- How can we ensure follow-up after planning sessions?

Process Awareness

- Who needs the initial introduction to the concept of process?
- What is a candidate process to examine first in our organization?
- Should we do process training as a purely educational experience, or should we start immediately with a workshop that targets a process for improvement and then assign resources to work on action plans?
- When is the best time to introduce detailed quantitative quality methods such as control charts and design of experiments?
- Should we handle repeated and non-routine processes differently?

High Participation Structure

- How can we design for collective accountability?
- What market forces do people need to consider as they begin designing their teams?
- How can we ensure that decisions and the control and coordination of work are pushed down to the lowest possible level in the new structure?
- How can we best link the strategic plan and the team goals during redesign?
- If a union exists, when is it best to involve them in restructuring? What should this involvement look like?
- What can we do in the design process to ensure we do not backslide to old ways of thinking and operating when a crisis hits?

Support

- What changes in the current compensation systems are needed?
- What types of training will be necessary? What is the timing?
- How will we fund any large changes in facilities so that teams can be productive as soon as possible?
- What is the process for teams requesting additional resources?

Sample Grid Workshops

The Grid can be used as a tool for planning, monitoring, and adjusting transformation activities or conducting lessons learned analyses. A group should be prepared to take several sessions to fill in all the organization's details in the Grid cells.

Planning Workshops

There are three basic ways to use the Grid as a planning tool, each with increasing levels of coaching assistance:

1. *Planning from Scratch*—For senior managers and change agents who want minimal coaching. Start with blank cells in the Grid and write down activities that need to occur in selected cells.

2. *Planning from the Typical Profile*—For groups who want a bit more guidance than is provided by blank cells. Examine the Xs that appear in a typical Profile Grid (see Table 3.2) and develop appropriate activities for an organization's unique transformation.

3. *Planning from the Starter Grid*—For senior managers and change agents who like some concrete examples of actions in the Grid cells. Use the starter activities as a basis for conversation about which activities are relevant to the organization's unique TBO transformation situation.

Monitoring and Adjusting Transformation Activities

Organizations can use the Grid as a tool to monitor what's happening in the transformation project as it proceeds. If any domains have been missed, corrections can be made before the project proceeds into the next stage.

Example 1. A high-tech electronics firm received feedback during implementation that a group of design engineers felt excluded from the transformation process. At the same time, this company was converting to a TBO, it was implementing a computer aided design (CAD) system. Only two design engineers (of a department of forty-three) were working on the configuration of the CAD system and establishing part numbering standards for the rest of the department. Senior management and a group of change agents initiated a participative planning session for the CAD system implementation that involved ten other engineers in the CAD implementation and standards development.

Example 2. A government agency was three-quarters of the way through its conversion to a TBO when it discovered there was still a fear of making mistakes and this was hindering team innovation. This happened even though senior management had specifically listed the item, "Remove the fear of making mistakes and encourage intelligent risk taking" in Stage I on the Grid. Members of management addressed the issue in the next two town hall meetings. They also provided two awards to individuals who had taken risks—one that succeeded tremendously and one that failed but at the time looked like an innovative approach.

In addition, an organization may find it useful to add actions to a previously empty cell.

Example 3. A pharmaceutical firm believed that its clinical trials process was so troublesome that it invoked the process awareness domain mid-way through the initiation stage, even though it initially was not planned. External benchmarking data revealed the firm's cycle time for that process was twice as long as the industry leader's. The leaders moved cycle time reduction for this process to the top of their TBO transformation guidelines. During the restructuring stage, they combined the four functional departments that participated in the problematic clinical trials process.

Conducting Lessons Learned Analyses Workshops

The Grid can be a powerful tool for figuring out what went well and what to do differently in future transformation efforts.

The Grid can be a powerful tool for figuring out what went well and what an organization may want to do differently in future transformation efforts.

Many organizations have found the basic session format helpful, and there are many variations. These sessions can be conducted at the end of the transformation or throughout. The steps for conducting this workshop follow:

1. Assemble a diverse group of eight to twelve people. Consider all factors for diversity such as functional discipline, age, organizational level within the company, race, gender, length of service with the company, and so forth.

2. Using the organization's completed Grid, ask the group, "Looking at this Grid, what went well?" Record the group's comments on flip charts.

3. Ask, "Looking at this Grid, what might we do differently the next time?" Record these comments on flip charts.

4. Divide people into two to three small groups and ask them to develop action plans to reinforce the positive and correct the negatives for future projects.

5. Combine the results of the small groups and solicit volunteers to do the action items.

6. Plan for a method of reporting progress on implementation and ensuring follow-up on the action items.

Collaborative Methods for TBO Transformations

As mentioned in the Starter Questions section of this chapter, one early decision will be whether or not to develop the collaborative sessions (for example, planning and structuring) from scratch or whether to use pre-existing designs for collaborative sessions. This section contains some collaborative methods that can be used to complete the cells of the Grid for a TBO transformation.

There are many group planning methods available today. Books are available that provide lists and extended descriptions of some of the more widely used ones that can be of assistance in scanning the field (for example, see Bunker & Alban, 1997; Holman & Devane, 1999). In this chapter this author has listed only methods that he has personally worked with and that, in the author's experience, work quite well in combination with each other for a TBO transformation. Other methods may work equally well in combination. Table 3.4 shows the methods that can be used for each domain and some sample uses.

Table 3.4. Group Planning Methods for TBO Transformation*

High Leverage Domain	Method Name	Description and Example of Use
Participative planning	Search Conference	A participative planning process in which people create a well-articulated, desirable, achievable future with action plans for implementing it that include a definite timetable, who will do it, and how to do it. Used for strategic planning, transformation planning, and other plans where people collaboratively plan a future based on common interests.
	Future Search	A participative planning process designed to evolve a common-ground future for an organization or community and develop self-managed plans to move toward it. Used for strategic planning, transformation planning, and other plans in which groups of people collaboratively plan a future based on common interests.

Table 3.4. Group Planning Methods for TBO Transformation*, Cont'd

High Leverage Domain	Method Name	Description and Example of Use
Leadership development and key actions	Search Conference	The same process as described above. It appears in this leadership category because, in addition to its planning benefits, it is helpful in developing formal and informal leaders throughout the organization.
	Future Search	The same process as described above. It appears in this leadership category because, in addition to its planning benefits, it is helpful in developing formal and informal leaders throughout the organization.
	Organization Workshop	A group learning session in which participants experience universal conditions, traps, and dilemmas of organizational life. Participants emerge with concepts, methods, and a common language to improve their interactions in any organization. This workshop is especially useful for training senior and middle managers new to a TBO.
Process awareness	Process Mapping	A participative analysis process in which a group develops diagrams depicting both the current and ideal flows of activities and decisions as they act together to produce an output for a customer.
	Quality Tool Application	A session in which a group of people, trained in quality tools, attack a problem from the perspective of improving the process. (For more information on process improvement tools, see Brassard & Ritter, 1994; Rath & Strong, 2000.)
High participation structuring	Participative Design Workshop	A highly structured and participative process in which people redesign their existing organizational structure to a structure consisting of self-managing teams.
Support	Open Space	A participative session that enables high levels of group interaction and productivity, providing a basis for enhanced organizational functioning over time. This is helpful for teams—and entire organizations—to explore complex issues, disseminate information, create commitment to new directions, and develop action plans for the future.
	Appreciative Inquiry	A participative session designed to enable full-voice appreciative participation that taps the organization's positive change core and inspires collaborative action that serves the whole system. These sessions are useful for creating positive energy and creating culture change.
	Dialogue	A group session designed to build capacity to think together, to surface group assumptions, and to create shared meaning while taking into account the "big picture" perspective. These sessions are useful to explore complex issues, remove organizational barriers, and get out all facts, opinions, and assumptions before taking any group action.

*For all methods except for process mapping and quality tool application, the description and example are adapted from *The Change Handbook: Group Methods for Shaping the Future* by P. Holman and T. Devane (Eds.). San Francisco: Berrett-Koehler, 1999.

Conclusion

The Grid is a framework for thinking about high leverage actions for successful TBO transformations. With minimal external input, groups within an organization can use the Grid for transformation planning and monitoring and for conducting lessons learned analyses.

CHAPTER 4

Chartering Your Team for Peak Performance

Kevin Dowling

CHARTERING IS a formalized process that enables team members to arrive at a shared understanding of team principles and theory and collectively define how they will operate. The result is a working document that is, in essence, the team's statement of identity to the rest of their company (their charter). A charter states who the team is, what they do, who they do it for, and how.

Beyond being the team's identity, however, the charter should also be a set of tools. Ideally, it includes tools the team can use almost daily, such as team norms, process for change integration, team roles and responsibilities, and so forth. As such, it should also be a living document that changes and evolves with the team.

"Chartering" is the process the team undertakes to develop its charter. This would therefore include training of fundamental team theory, principles, and tools for team members to use. This document makes several references to "chartering," and it should be understood that this means not only the process of developing the team charter but also the training process participants under-take to become a team.

Why Have a Charter?

A charter serves as the team's foundation in its efforts to learn teaming princi-ples and put them into practice.

Taking a collection of co-workers through the principles of teaming is one thing, but enabling them to create a charter together, to assemble what will become their identity statement, allows them to immediately put theory into practice by coming together around key learning points. Having teams create a charter creates buy-in, ownership, and responsibility for their learning and development of their performance together.

General Charter Components

A charter reflects basic teaming principles. The transition to a team-based orga-nization is generally stewarded by a steering team. The steering team has the overall responsibility for providing the direction, resources, and leadership for this transition. The steering team, in designing the training material and mod-ules for the introduction of team-based organizations, should structure the learning process so it naturally moves toward a chartering event for teams. Charters work best as a series of "deliverables," that is, a set of end products resulting from completion of training modules. Taking all the deliverables from the introductory teaming phase, then, will create the charter.

Creating a charter should follow the natural flow of training material. (A suggested order for training modules is given below.) Early deliverables in training are designed for immediate creation and application and reflect basic teaming principles. This is a very important consideration, as it will enable the teams to see immediate impact of these tools on their performance and help allay some of the initial concerns, not just among the team members, but among other members of the organization as well (that is, managers, executives, and others). Getting immediate impact from learning about team principles and using the tools creates early success stories to share in the company, which in turn will serve to remove roadblocks later on as teams spread to the rest of the organization. A common first element created in charters is team norms: basic rules of operation that the team agrees to.

While this initial set of norms energizes the team, it is advisable that the team revisit these norms at some later point in the chartering process to create a more comprehensive list incorporating more recent learning experiences.

Later deliverables in the chartering process are more in-depth, incorporating several learning points, and possibly even involving off-line "homework" for the team members. These deliverables must also be open-ended to allow for later revision by the team. For example, to create a better understanding of the team's business flow, team members could be assigned, individually or in subgroups, to create a list of their customers and suppliers, internal and external. In the next training session, these lists can then be shared, and a linkage map listing the team's customers and suppliers can be created.

Suggested Training Flow

Development of the team charter should mirror the team's learning and development during an introductory phase of training modules. As such, the charter should be composed of deliverables resulting from the modules. Following is a suggested flow for introductory material, including deliverables that would comprise the finished charter for the team. The content for this training is based on The Belgard Group's Team Tools training modules (www.belgard.com). It was chosen and utilized by cross-functional steering teams at two different manufacturing companies. While this is the suggested order, any sequence of training that creates a natural flow can work, including breaking up the suggested material into more concentrated modules. It should be noted that, since both companies mentioned above are primarily manufacturing businesses, the material presented may and probably should be modified to match audiences.

Introduction to Teams and Teaming Principles

This module serves as a broad overview of the upcoming training material. Emphasis is on the necessity of teams in the company's future business plan, as well as how the employees will benefit from the new system. It is also most common to introduce teams to Bruce Tuckman's (1965) model of team development here. This model includes *forming* (team members are just getting to know each other and their roles); *storming* (breakdowns between team members); *norming* (members clarify roles and boundaries for working); and *performing* (teams begin truly working together collaboratively). Supplemental information such as testimonials, "before and after" videos, or any material that gives the team members a solid visual of the future are strongly recommended. This will probably be the most theory-intensive module, but participative exercises illustrating these principles helps break up the material (for examples of these exercises, see Module #3, Healthy Team Environment).

A cornerstone of working together as a team is a shared understanding of team members' expectations of behavior from one another, that is, norms. The module therefore ends with a discussion of the importance of team norms and an understanding that the team will be responsible for employing these, not solely their leader or manager.

Norms are the foundation for running a team on a day-to-day basis.

Deliverable for Charter: As this is the first of many training sessions, a set of team norms is developed for an understanding of behavior in future meetings and training. Norms are the foundation for running a team on a day-to-day basis that can be printed and posted in the team's work area.

Sample categories for norms can include meeting/training, workplace behavior, integration of new members, decision making, and communication. Most importantly, there should be some set, agreed-on way to ensure conformity to these norms that the team members are able to use rather than leaving enforcement exclusively to the team's leader/manager.

Coping with Change

This is another theory-intensive module, but it sets the stage for the future training and gives the teams a chance to work through their own concerns about the new system of teams. It builds understanding around the importance of communication and involvement to minimize a sense of random, forced change. This module should be built to allow for group discussion and engagement.

Another part of this module discusses change at the organizational level in a broad sense, and not just the change it is currently undergoing to a team-based environment. Change is becoming a way of life in the global economy, and organizations need to be able to adapt readily to new challenges and ideas. Having a collaborative work environment where front-line employees who know the product best have a say in the company's development is one of the best ways to ensure that company's long-term competitiveness.

Deliverable for Charter: A change communication plan must be developed. The team brainstorms, with its leader's input, major changes that will impact it, what information team members need to know, where to find it, and how soon they will need it.

Also, the team can draw out a more extensive new member integration plan, including such contingencies as new leaders, newly hired employees, and employees who transfer into the team.

Healthy Team Environment

Having seen the necessity for teams in their organization, received a background in team theory, and come to an understanding for the need for change in the company, teams now take a look at their own team environment in this module. The module includes a number of team assessments focusing on the team's own functioning (that is, communication, positive environment of the team, listening skills, and so forth) and also allows for an improvement plan in those areas team members rate themselves low. Other training in the module covers diversity in the workplace and some sort of personality or work style inventory on the teams (for example, Team Work Style Inventory, DISC, or Myers-Briggs Type Indicator). These analyses are fun and memorable experiences for the team members as they get to know themselves and each other a little better and identify reasons for disconnects or potential conflicts between certain members.

A natural offshoot to this diversity training, then, is a segment of learning on dealing with disagreements on the team. Communication skills, listening skills, and giving and receiving feedback can all be covered here.

Finally, this is an activity-intensive module maximizing group involvement. Any sort of activity that illustrates diversity and different personalities at work, as well as team puzzles that members must work together to solve, help to drive home the points in this module and help the team members work together with the principles they have used so far. Good group exercises that illustrate these principles are found in Pam Lindberg and Keith Merron's exercise, "Toxic Waste Dump" (http://web10.eppg.com/training/toolchest/games/0070466076/457.html) or Dutch Driver's "Ring and String Thing" (a.k.a. "Stop on a Dime") (http://home.att.net/~Choragus/library/stoponadime.html).

Deliverable for Charter: This module can have a number of different deliverables linking to the activities suggested above. These include personality or work style assessment of team members; a process for handling disagreements;

and/or a self-assessment of the team's environment and functioning and action plans for improvement in weak areas.

Business Linkage, Stakeholders

Now that the team has come to a greater understanding of team theory and team dynamics, the rest of this introductory phase focuses on giving the team members the business knowledge they will need to operate on a more empowered level. This module covers their company history, products and services it supplies, and how this team contributes to the "big picture." Also included is a discussion of stakeholders—the customers and suppliers for the team and the whole company. The team also gains an understanding of the internal customer, that is, other teams with whom it works closely. The focus of developing these relationships with the customer and supplier should be on how the team can make this stakeholder's job easier. Feedback skills, discussed in the Healthy Team Environment module, are re-discussed here.

Deliverable for Charter: The team develops a linkage map of how it connects to the larger business and a list of major customers and suppliers for the team.

The team also develops a communication plan for its internal customers and suppliers. While the team leader usually handles this communication process at first, this plan should allow for a gradual transfer to other team members so they can eventually serve as the focal point for a certain internal customer or supplier.

Metrics, Goals, and Measures

This module covers the metrics used by the company and the team to assess their performance. Current measures of the team's performance should be available to use during this module. The team also learns the importance of creating goals, what a goal statement is, how to develop action plans to get to these goals, and using company metrics to measure the achievement of these goals.

This module provides the team with a list of its metrics.

Deliverable for Charter: The team will have a list of its metrics and a commensurate set of achievable team goal statements and action plans to achieve them (perhaps using the areas for team improvement plans from the Healthy Team Environment module).

Roles and Responsibilities

The team looks at necessary roles, formal and informal, that are needed for it to function. The list of team roles may include the team scribe, process observer in meetings, devil's advocate, safety focal, focal point for the team customer and suppliers, as well as other company-specific roles. Also, the leader can more fully distribute his or her responsibilities and come up with ways to share these with the team or even to eventually transfer authority.

The explanation of these roles includes a discussion of the responsibilities these roles entail as well as some sort of system for rotation among the team so one member isn't stuck with a role for life.

Deliverable for Charter: The team develops a list of team roles and responsibilities, a rotation system for these roles, and possibly an authority transfer/sharing plan from the leader.

Mission Statement

This capstone module ties the charter and team learning process together as the team writes its mission statement. The team mission statement is the centerpiece of the team's charter. It is necessary to put this learning module toward the end of the team's training process, as it incorporates the learning and understanding from previous modules. The mission statement should identify who the team members are, what they do, how they serve the company, and in what way. Sample mission statements of other teams in the company (including the company's mission statement) can be given as models. The team could also have an exercise in rewriting mission statements to get a feel for them. While this module should be direct in its approach and coverage of materials, it will probably still be lengthy as the team writes its own mission statement. Once finished, this becomes the centerpiece or lead-in for the charter.

Deliverable for Charter: At the end of this module, the team will have its mission statement available for display in its charter and work area.

A Sample Charter

Included below are sample elements of a charter. Comments in parentheses refer to which module or training session the deliverable is from. Some deliverables from the above modules cannot be included as they are too company-specific.

Mission Statement: (Mission Statement) "The human resources organization at [Company X] believes that people are our strength and is committed to proactively providing support and development of its employees to make this a safe, happy, and productive workplace."

Norms: (Introduction to Teams and Teaming Principles)

Meeting Management

- Start on time; end on time.

- Always have an agenda; circulate beforehand if possible.

- Have a deliverable or outcome for the meeting.

- If you are unable to attend a meeting, let the organizer know as far in advance as possible, and it is your responsibility to find out what happened.

Workplace Behavior Norms

- Listen without interrupting.

- Be open and honest.

- Give honest feedback.

Decision Making

- Clearly state the problem or decision to be made.

- Define all solutions and options the group is facing.

- At least half the team must be present in order to make a decision.

- If you are absent from the meeting, you must live with the decisions made.

Communication Plan: (Coping with Change)

- What information do people need to know?

- How should this information be provided?

- Who will provide it?

- Who is impacted by this information?

- When should this information be provided?

Handling Conflict: (Healthy Team Environment)

1. Acknowledge there is a disagreement and describe how it is affecting the team.

2. Get commitment from individuals and/or team to resolve disagreements.

3. Have each party state his or her point of view.

4. Have each party restate the other's point of view.

5. Have each party suggest a solution based on facts, mutual needs, and team goals.

6. Examine solutions.

7. Evaluate process.

What Now?

Once the team has reached the end of the introductory phase, it should have a collection of deliverables that can be put together to form a charter. While the most obvious approach would simply be to put all the deliverables into a book format, allow for creativity from the team, as long as team members cover all the elements of their charter. One team the author worked with turned its charter into a narrative poem set to "Twas the Night Before Christmas," as team members were presenting their charter the day before the company's holiday break!

Some member of the steering team should be present to guide the team through the process.

Once all the modules are completed, the team should sit down with its deliverables and give them a final pass-through for approval and support from all members of the team. Furthermore, the team should decide what its charter will look like and how it will be presented. While reviewing this charter, some member of the steering team should be present to guide the team through the process and point out areas for improvement or clarification in the team charter.

The presentation of the team charter should be done in a ceremonial fashion to all or parts of the steering team, company executives, key customers and suppliers, and anyone else the team wants to invite to see its charter. Team members should participate as much as possible in this presentation, rather than allowing one person or the team leader to cover it all. Part of this ceremony should include a celebration of sorts: a catered meal, a public award ceremony, or something similar.

Once the charter is completed and presented, the team moves on to the next phase of development and empowerment, which involves more advanced theoretical principles building on the basic foundation discussed above. Their charter, while completed, should continue to play an integral role in team members' day-to-day functioning and should change to reflect their development and growth as a team.

Final Tips

The Charter Is a Working Document. Too often teams view their charter as a sacred object that, once completed, cannot be re-evaluated. The charter should be constantly updated and revised.

The team should even allow a periodic (quarterly or so) review of its charter to see what's working and what isn't and to make changes as necessary.

The Charter Is a Tool. In this introductory phase, the team acquires a number of valuable learning tools that it should use on a daily basis, for example, the team norms and the team process for integrating change. Just as teams too often view their charter as a closed document, they also forget about the deliverables they worked on that can help them in their functioning. A suggested solution to this problem is to have deliverables made immediately visible to the team in its daily work environment. Norms should thus be posted in the team's work area and in its meeting rooms. The charter could also be put into a small pocketbook form for team members to carry with them.

Other charter elements, such as the team improvement program, should have concrete goals set around them that the team then reviews regularly in meetings.

Don't Make the Modules Too Lengthy. There are seven suggested modules, which can be combined or broken up as needs dictate. However the training is designed, the actual sessions should be about two to four hours in length, with longer modules taking several sessions. Sessions longer than two to four hours, especially those that are more theory-intensive, tend to lose the team's focus. Resist the temptation to do all-day training events, as experience has shown that these create burnout to the material. Additionally, if the process is done in one fell swoop, the training takes on a certain "bubble effect" in which the team has learned the tools in one long day but doesn't have an opportunity to exercise them back in the "real world." With smaller, broken up doses of training, the team can leave, try to put the tools in practice, and then fine-tune usage in the next team meeting/training.

Don't Make the First Phase Too Lengthy. While there's a lot of material to cover, stretching the first phase of modules out to ten or more meetings may prove too exhaustive for teams, such that they forget where they started by the time they finish. By training two hours a week with seven modules, the process would take seven weeks, a good stretch of time for them to see improvements and feel accomplishment without stretching out the process too far.

Gain a Commitment from the Team, Leader, and Company to Allow Training. If the company is serious about going to a team-based environment, one of the first things it needs to establish is the commitment of time needed to train teams on these principles.

 A schedule for training should be worked out and agreed to by the team, the team leader, steering team, and other stakeholders in that team to allow them to keep to this schedule. Training sporadically, spontaneously, or just whenever the team has time stretches the process out and causes the team to forget earlier modules. If the team does have to get off the training track due to business needs, the first couple of sessions back should be to review what has been covered thus far.

Celebrate Achievements. Regardless of how short the introductory phase may be, it can still be an exhaustive process. If the only sense of achievement and reward the team gets is just in finishing and presenting its charter, the process can prove overwhelming. Create interim milestones scattered throughout the chartering process for the team to reach and celebrate with recognition, such as T-shirts, pizza parties, and so on. Also, the training sessions should allow for group involvement in the form of icebreakers, humor, open discussions, and so forth, so the team can pull back from the intensive training focus to be re-energized during the session.

CHAPTER 5

Return on Teaming Initiative (ROTI)

Measuring Teaming Outcomes to Optimize Their Performance

Frances Kennedy

MANY ORGANIZATIONS INVEST IN team-based systems to respond more quickly to their changing environment and to tap into the expertise of their employees. Making quicker, smarter, more effective decisions enables companies to respond to intense global competition.

Teams require investment in training and other support systems to gain the skills they need and to create and maintain an environment conducive to their success.

Companies are faced with allocating scarce resources strategically within the organization in order to optimize company performance. At some point, companies need to evaluate the decision to invest in teaming in order to determine whether to continue down that path. This issue is a common concern of management: *how to associate gains from team initiatives with company objectives and results.*

Typically, when a company decides to implement teams within the organization, a certain amount of investment cost is expected. Consultants, team training, and materials are common examples of start-up costs. As time passes, new employees require training, the costs of team meetings accumulate, team leaders request pizza and other celebration costs, and a myriad of ancillary costs are incurred. As teams develop and begin to change processes and solve problems, there are benefits and additional costs to the company. These benefits and costs are captured in various ways in the financial records (for example, equipment, supplies). It is common for all these costs and benefits to be buried in various departmental expense statements, making it nearly impossible to discern the financial effect of the decision to establish teams.

Companies need to evaluate the "teaming" decision before investing further in the initiative.

Prior to approving additional funding to develop teaming support systems, a manager would like to know: *Has money previously spent on training, facilities, and other support been worthwhile? Can I see the benefits in my bottom line?*

This chapter reviews obstacles one encounters when attempting to quantify the benefits and costs of teamwork and then presents a measurement system based on estimated cash flow designed to overcome these obstacles.

Obstacles

When faced with valuing teams' performance and contributions to the organization, several common obstacles arise.

How to Measure Team Value. The concept of team value involves "hard" process improvements as well as harder to measure intangible benefits. Examples include better job performance due to ownership and employee involvement, increased communication and synergies among various teams and functions, and the development of intellectual capital.

Separating and quantifying benefits of teaming are *major* obstacles to measurement.

How to Isolate Benefits of Teaming from Other Business Initiatives. Rarely does a company invest in one initiative, wait to see how it works, and then invest in another initiative. Companies implement several initiatives simultaneously, such as just-in-time (JIT), materials resource planning (MRP), and lean manufacturing. With many changes taking place, how can gains resulting from teaming be separated from the benefits of the other changes?

How to Tie this Value to the Bottom Line. Companies have turned to teams as a better, more efficient way of making business decisions. This incremental value, however, is buried in accounting information and throughout various reports: it is difficult to isolate. In addition, team outcome measures are usually quantified using operational metrics, such as scrap rate, number of warranties, or turnaround time. Whereas operational measures provide a clear method to target team goals, they are team specific. A reduction in scrap rate for one team cannot be added to a reduction in turnaround time from another team. There is no common method of measuring different types of teams having different goals.

How to Communicate this Value to Management. Management is continually confronted with allocating competing resources. A team-based organization requires resources to thrive. Its ability to compete with alternative investments requires clear, direct communication of its contributions to the strategy of the company.

How to Gauge Team Progress and Development. All initiatives need to be monitored as they are being developed. Teams are no exception. A measurement system is required to gauge individual team progress. Inadequacies of external support systems can retard individual teams' progress and block achievement of goals.

How to Optimize Team Performance. Sufficient resources and support from the organization are needed for teams to succeed. But what is "sufficient"? A teaming system requires external support in training, information systems, meeting accommodations, and incentives.

As the team system develops and grows, more resources are required and it becomes increasingly important to quantify the incremental value contributed by teams. Developing these resources requires time and money. The underlying issue is knowing where to place resources in order to develop a strong teaming environment.

Measurement Systems

The first hurdle in developing a measurement system is to distinguish areas of responsibilities and decision control. Figure 5.1 illustrates areas controlled by team members and managers.

Figure 5.1. Collaborative Work Systems—Areas of Control

Organizational Environment

Managers make decisions affecting the environment within which
the teams work by providing necessary resources.

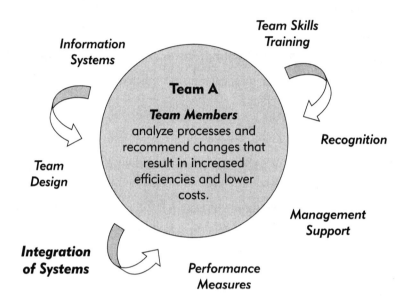

*Team members
control
decisions within
the team
concerning
their goals
and processes.*

Team members come together with the purpose of working toward a common goal. Individually, they have varying levels of experience and knowledge. They need to learn to relate well and manage team tasks such as planning, goal setting, and decision making. Team members utilize all their collective experience, knowledge, and skills in making decisions that lead to accomplishing their goals.

Managers, however, do not sit in team meetings and make decisions for the team. They must remain outside the team and restrict their decision making to that which they do control—support systems. As Figure 5.1 shows, even though managers cannot actively *"make"* teams perform, they can *influence* team performance by ensuring that teams have the support and resources they need to accomplish their goals.

There are two distinct categories of costs associated with team-based organizations that mirror the team members' and team managers' areas of control. The first category is the cost associated with the implementation of process changes and solutions recommended by the team. The second category contains costs associated with maintaining the team system, such as meeting facilities and time, training and performance measures. Each of these cost categories is discussed in the following sections.

The team measurement system consists of six steps tied to both decision responsibilities and cost categories.

The team measurement system is presented in a series of six steps tied to both decision responsibilities and cost categories.

The first four steps take place at the team level and involve the savings and costs associated with team-recommended improvements, focusing on quantifying teaming outcomes. It is critical to note that the team drives all savings and costs. It may weigh various solutions before coming to these recommendations. But the decision to recommend these projects is within the team's control. This is a key element in isolating the benefits of teaming.

Steps 5 and 6 occur at the organizational level and reflect decisions made by managers to invest in teaming. Managers review project solutions and process changes recommended by teams to determine whether to approve implementation. The final result reflects the net benefit of those decisions to the company.

Six Steps to Team Measurement
Team Level

One of the main problems is isolating benefits from teams versus regular operations.

One of the main problems with measuring team performance is the difficulty in isolating benefits from teams versus regular operations.

One way to isolate some of the benefit from teaming is to revert back to the objective of teamworking—to develop new ways to accomplish tasks and to do so more quickly and economically. As teams make decisions to change processes or to recommend project solutions, they are very much aware of the benefits of that change. Benefits normally take the form of increased efficiencies or lower costs. Capturing the annualized net benefit of these changes provides the necessary information to isolate the benefits of teamwork.

Step 1: Identify Specific Changes Initiated by Teams

The first category is the cost associated with the implementation of process changes and solutions. When a team analyzes a process or problem, it will use a variety of tools in developing a solution. The solution is typically based on an analysis of resources expended in a process, and benefits take the form of increased efficiency or reduced resources. A process analysis technique is best illustrated using an example from a team interview with a company we will call *Premium Artists.*

> Example: The "Renaissance Team" is a work team responsible for a delicate painting operation. This process requires using masking tape to manually prepare the precision part for painting with a metallic paint. The team was concerned about the time being spent in this manual process and it recommended a solution that drastically reduced the preparation time. The team recommended using drink cozies to cover the bulk of the area to be taped. Even though a certain amount of hand taping remained, this process change saved twenty labor hours per production run.

It is clear from this example that any benefits accruing from this process change are due to the collaborative efforts of the team members.

Step 2: Associate Dollars with Process Changes and Project Solutions

When teams tackle a problem or a process, they normally utilize various tools in their analysis. Flowcharting, storyboarding, fishbone diagrams, and brainstorming are some examples of activity analysis techniques used by teams. Regardless of the tools used, the process of outlining the tasks performed in an activity for the purpose of making improvements is called activity based management (ABM) (Ansari, Bell, Klammer, & Lawrence, 1999). ABM provides the team with a common understanding of all the tasks and resources included in an activity.

ABM and ABC assist teams in identifying resources consumed in their process.

This process analysis helps teams to identify unnecessary or redundant steps, identifying wasted resources. Activity-based costing (ABC) is a technique that facilitates the assignment of dollars to tasks and activities involved in a process and helps teams quantify, or *dollarize,* resources saved in a process change (Ansari, Bell, Klammer, & Lawrence, 1999).

When the Renaissance Team recommended their solution, they identified and quantified the benefits of using drink cozies (twenty labor hours per production run). They also knew that the unit cost of the cozies was $0.50. By applying this information to production forecast (7,200 units), the team was able to estimate the annualized savings from using drink cozies:

Benefits: Labor savings for 7,200 units	$38,000
Costs: Cozie cost of $0.50 per unit for 7,200 units	$3,600
Net Project Savings	$34,400

As shown, the Renaissance Team estimated the annualized savings from the recommended change to be $34,400. This estimate was based on activity analysis, historical information of the process, and forecast assumptions.

Step 3: Reduce Project Savings to an Effectiveness Factor

PEF measures the net annualized benefit of the recommended change.

The project savings calculated by the Renaissance team show a considerable net benefit to the company. Another way to view the outcome is to divide the annualized savings by the annualized cost. The resulting factor (project effectiveness factor, or PEF) represents a simple return on each dollar of cost.

$$\text{Annualized Benefits}/\text{Annualized Cost} = \text{PEF}$$

$$\$38,000/\$3,600 = 10.6$$

$$\text{PEF} = 10.6$$

The PEF of 10.6 is interpreted to mean that for each $1.00 spent, another $10.60 is saved. The purpose of calculating a return is to provide a measure for evaluating if an investment dollar is spent wisely.

Obviously, a project with zero cost does not calculate to a factor. For this reason, a ceiling of 20.0 was chosen to apply to projects requiring no cost to implement or maintain. Sample tests of this measurement system were used to establish this ceiling (Kennedy, 2002). The PEFs for these sample projects ranged from 3.5 to 17.8. Considering this range, a factor of 20.0 appears to be sufficiently higher than the highest calculated factor.

One of the key discoveries is that many of the teams' recommendations have no implementation cost.

Teams vary with respect to their potential savings due to scope of responsibility and skills. The PEF scales the dollars in a project, allowing projects of various sizes to be compared.

One of the key discoveries in the implementation of this measurement system is that many of the changes and recommendations that teams make have no implementation cost.

Traditional measurement systems require that requests for funding be routed through an approval process and are, therefore, documented. As a result, many of the benefits of teaming are not being documented simply because the teams do not need money!

These projects fall through the cracks because there is no documentation process in place to capture and communicate the changes. Establishing close-out procedures that require teams to summarize changes in process documents the benefits of these previously "lost" projects. Additionally, it allows teams to quantify their efforts and communicate their achievements outside the team.

Step 4: Consolidate Project Savings

Two levels of consolidation are required. The first is at the team level if a team has more than one project recommendation.

TEF measures the consolidated outcome of an individual team.

Let us look again at the Renaissance Team. The team had three process change recommendations during the reporting period, which in this case is one year. By combining the savings and costs from all three projects, a team effectiveness factor (TEF) can be calculated.

Table 5.1 shows three projects with varying savings and costs, including one with no cost involved. The TEF of 8.3 is calculated by dividing the total annualized savings ($364,000) by the total annualized costs ($43,600).

Table 5.1. Calculation of Team Effectiveness Factor

One Team with Multiple Projects

Project	Annualized Savings	Annualized Costs	PEF	TEF
#1	$38,000	$3,600	10.6	
#2	$300,000	$40,000	7.5	
#3	$26,000	0	20.0	
TOTAL	$364,000	$43,600		8.3

The second level of consolidation considers the project savings of all teams in a facility or business unit. Table 5.2 shows the annualized savings for the Renaissance Team as well as four other teams at the same location. The annualized figures are then consolidated to yield an aggregated savings figure.

Table 5.2. Consolidation of Teams' Project Savings

Team	Annualized Savings	Annualized Costs	Net Project Savings	TEF
Renaissance Team (painter team)	$364,000	$43,600	$320,400	8.3
Floor Sweepers' Team (maintenance team)	$55,000	$6,000	$49,000	9.2
Wheelies (forklift team)	$96,000	$26,000	$70,000	3.7
Beanies (accounting team)	$16,000	0	$16,000	20.0
Sculptors (mold maker team)	0	0	0	0.0
TOTAL NET PROJECT SAVINGS	$531,000	$75,600	$455,400	7.0

The total net project savings of $455,400 in Table 5.2 represents the consolidation of outcomes that can be traced to team recommendations at this facility.

Steps 1 through 4 focus on quantifying teaming outcomes. It is critical to note that the team drives all savings and costs. It may weigh various solutions before coming to these recommendations. But the decision to recommend these projects is within the team's control. This is a key element in isolating the benefits of teaming.

Manager Level

The second category of costs accumulates costs of the initial training and ongoing investment in teams.

The second category of costs accumulates costs incurred from the initial training and ongoing investment in the team-based organization.

System costs include the cost of team training, meeting time, celebrations, consultants, team system managers, conferences, materials, refreshments, travel related to team events, information systems, and other systems' development. The previous examples used to illustrate the TEF did not include costs such as the meeting time and facilities incurred by the team during its regular meetings.

It is obvious that these are necessary costs to the team. However, these costs themselves do not relate to the product of the team—a process change. Separating the investments between the project and the system allows decision makers and analysts to consider costs appropriate for different types of decisions.

Step 5: Capture System Costs

Identifying system costs is essential to calculating a return.

Generally, these system support costs are embedded in different cost centers in the accounting system. For example, the costs of meeting time for production teams may be captured in the manufacturing cost center, while the costs of meeting facilities are a small part of a larger overhead allocation. Training and celebration costs may be captured in the human resource department. Because these costs are spread out, accumulating them can be difficult.

Ideally, account codes may be added to the charges that allow these costs to be consolidated from a database as required without changing the original department assignment. In other cases, solid assumptions may be used to estimate the annual costs.

Table 5.3 contains examples and estimates of these costs for Premium Artists.

Table 5.3. Team System Costs

Type of Cost	Cost Estimate
Training (internal)	$35,000
Meeting Time (members and leaders)	$125,000
Celebration Costs	$15,000
Team System Managers	$80,000
Conferences, Dues	$8,000
Materials, Supplies	$3,600
Refreshments	$8,000
Travel	$15,000
TOTAL SYSTEM COSTS	$289,600

The total system costs of $289,600 represent the resources required during a twelve-month period to maintain the teaming environment. These costs are the results of decisions made by managers and are under managers' area of decision control.

Step 6: Calculate Return on Teaming Initiative (ROTI)

ROTI considers system costs as well as project savings.

The final step in the measurement system is to combine the project savings and the system costs in a manner that communicates the financial effect of the teaming initiative on the company—Return on Teaming Initiative (ROTI). (See Table 5.4.)

Table 5.4. ROTI Calculation

Total Net Project Savings (Step #4)	$455,400
Total System Costs (Step #5)	$289,600
Net Teaming Benefit	$165,800
ROTI ($165,800/$455,400)	36.4%

Table 5.5 summarizes the six process steps and their associated outcomes. The benefits of teamworking can be quantified using activity analysis techniques, documenting the resources expended and saved in a process improvement. Worksheets provide a standardized reporting mechanism to enable teams to communicate their projects' benefits. This analysis process also provides a decision tool for the team to assist it in choosing among alternative solutions.

Table 5.5. Team Measurement Process: Steps and Outcomes

Level	Process Step	Outcome
Team	1. Identify process change or problem solution	Isolate improvements originating with team
	2. Associate dollars with improvements	Net annualized savings
	3. Reduce to factor	Project effectiveness factor
	4. Consolidate savings	Team effectiveness factor Net savings (all teams)
Manager	5. Capture system costs	Total investment dollars
	6. Calculate return on investment	ROTI

Overcoming Obstacles

Several obstacles encountered when associating gains from team initiatives with company results were discussed early in this chapter. In the course of discussing the six steps of team measurement, methods to overcome these obstacles were presented. Table 5.6 reiterates the obstacles and summarizes ways to overcome each of them.

Table 5.6. Obstacles and Solutions in Measuring Return on Teaming

Obstacle	Solution
How to measure team value	Use estimates of future cash flow based on assumptions (capital investment techniques)
How can benefits from teaming be isolated from other business initiatives	Track savings and costs associated with recommendations made by teams
How to tie this value to the bottom line	"Dollarize" team outcomes using ABM and ABC techniques
How to communicate this value to management	Return on teaming initiative (ROTI)
How to gauge team progress and development	Team effectiveness factor (TEF)
How to optimize team performance	Use support system costs and ROTI to direct investment in support resources needed by teams

Benefits to Teams and Managers

Measuring return on teaming provides numerous benefits to both team members and team managers. Table 5.7 summarizes these benefits.

Teams primarily benefit from this measurement system because it gives them a means to quantify their outcomes and communicate the results of their efforts to people outside the team. In addition to using the TEF and PEF as a communication tool, team members can also use the PEF to compare alternative solutions in order to optimize the return to the company. Managers can

Table 5.7. Benefits of PEF, TEF, and ROTI

Measure	Team Members	Team Managers
Project Effectiveness Factor (PEF): PEF = Project Savings/ Project Costs (annualized)	Provides a tool to help choose among solution alternatives Quantifies benefits of a specific recommendation Documents net savings for project funding requests Documents all process changes, including those without the need for additional funding	Assists in the review and comparison of potential process improvements
Team Effectiveness Factor (TEF) TEF = Total Project Savings/ Total Project Costs (annualized)	Provides a communication tool by which the team can share its performance Quantifies for the team its contribution to company performance through the "net annualized savings"	Allows for comparisons across teams Provides a common measurement basis that could contribute to a performance measurement system Tracking over time allows managers to discern when teams are stagnating and may need support
Return on Teaming Initiative (ROTI) ROTI = Net Teaming Benefit/ Total Net Project Savings	Provides view of overall teaming contribution to the company	Calculates a return on the entire teaming system, including system costs Makes system costs visible to managers
Net Teaming Benefit = Total Net Project Savings (all teams) minus Total Systems Costs (annualized)		Tracking over time allows for analysis of resource investment and return as the team system matures

benefit by using both the total team project savings and the TEF to compare performance across teams, as well as to identify struggling teams. Managers can also see when a team may be stagnating and in need of additional resources and guidance. By using the ROTI metric, managers can see all the system costs involved in supporting the teams and be aware of what support systems they are and are not developing. Finally, ROTI reflects the percentage of project savings retained by the company after support resources are considered.

CHAPTER 6

ROI and Strategy for Teams and Collaborative Work Systems

Alec R. Levenson

RETURN ON INVESTMENT (ROI) has long been used to evaluate capital spending projects. This chapter explores how to use ROI for teams. The key issues focused on are strategic decision making and performance management.

In order to illustrate the potential and pitfalls of ROI, we consider two different cases. The first is a work team chartered to increase manufacturing efficiency. The second is a management team chartered with acquisition decisions and post-merger integration.

The key aspects of the teams' tasks are shown in Tables 6.1 and 6.2 and include the following:

- *Total time spent on the project.* This is comprised by the "duration start to finish" and time spent working on it "FTE time usage," full-time equivalent days of the team members' time. We need these for the implicit cost of the team members' time.

A team's costs include both out-of-pocket expenses and the implicit costs associated with the team members' and other contributors' time.

The probability of achieving the team's objective is a key component whether forecasting ROI or doing performance management.

- *Resources associated with the team's work.* "Main team resources" and "other resources involved." These include both direct budgetary items and indirect resources used.

- *Outcome metrics.* Some outcomes are readily quantifiable: cycle time, productivity, cost reductions, quality, and customer satisfaction. Others are more difficult: creativity, innovation, and organizational learning.

- *Probability of success.* This is shown as "chance of achieving the outcome." This is the most unusual item for an ROI calculation.

Table 6.1. Examples of the Work Team's Tasks

Task	Duration Start to Finish	FTE Time Usage	Main Team Resources	Other Resources Involved	Outcome Metric	Chance of Achieving Outcome
Troubleshoot assembly defects	7 days	3.5 days per person	Members' time; equipment budget	Functional support (various depts.)	Defect rate back to old level	99 percent (based on prior track record)
Identify maintenance contract vendor	3 months	2 weeks per person	Members' time; support staff time	IT support (new web bidding system)	Uptime improved by 10 percent	50 percent (based on team's internal assessment)
Install new assembly line machinery	3 months	4 weeks per person	Members' and support staff time; equipment; materials	Entire factory idle 7 days until work done	Quicker install; reduced downtime	99 percent for small improvement; 50 percent for large improvement

Table 6.2. Examples of the Management Team's Tasks

Task	Duration Start to Finish	FTE Time Usage	Main Team Resources	Other Resources Involved	Outcome Metric	Chance of Achieving Outcome
Evaluate and recommend acquisition options	6 months	5 weeks per person	Team members' and support staff time	Functional support (various depts.)	Maintain, build market share	0 to 100 percent (depends on alternate scenarios)
Manage integration of acquired company's IT system	3 months	2 weeks per person	Team members' time; new computer system	IT personnel working full-time on project	Bill and pay systems integrated	95 percent (with only minimal bugs in the system)
Design and implement knowledge management system post-merger	3 months	5 weeks per person	Team members' time; new computer system	Cross-functional survey of managers	Best practice sharing	20 to 80 percent (may be hard to measure best practice sharing)

For forward-looking ROI, it is necessary to estimate the time and resources needed. For retrospective ROI, the amounts used can be tallied with precision. Thus forward-looking and retrospective ROI will differ because of the uncertainty involved in estimating the costs ahead of time.

Another difference lies in the probability of achieving the outcome. Forward-looking ROI needs to account for uncertainty to provide an estimate that can be compared to the ROI from other tasks. Retrospective ROI does not require using the uncertainty the team faced. Yet acknowledging that uncertainty can be important when using retrospective ROI for performance management.

Note that the management team's outcome metrics may be harder to assess for forecasting ROI and/or doing performance management:

- It is hard to measure the effectiveness of a knowledge management system.

- It is easy to see whether the company gains or loses market share, but it may be difficult to determine whether an acquisition was the key.

These examples provide the context for our discussion of ROI. As we go through the steps needed for ROI, we often contrast ROI for teams with ROI for capital spending. (For a discussion of ROI for capital spending and investment, see Friedlob & Plewa, 1996; Rachlin & Sweeney, 1996.)

The ROI task itself should not take up an inordinate amount of the team members' time.

Note that it only makes sense to calculate ROI if doing so will not consume a large amount of resources.

One metric to use is the ratio of time needed to calculate ROI over the time needed for the task:

Time to calculate ROI/Time to complete the task

For example, a team might estimate that it will take one month to complete the task and an additional week of the members' time (that is, 25 percent of the time needed) to calculate the ROI from completing the task. This would be an excessive drain on company resources.

While there is no firm rule, a reasonable upper boundary might be 10 percent or one week, whichever is lower. For this task, the 10 percent cap would translate into no more than two days spent figuring out the team's ROI.

Return on Investment for Teams

In the team context, it is not always possible to make a direct link to impacts on the bottom line. Consider a general statement of the ROI formula:

Benefits created by the team/Costs incurred by the team

We start with the task of identifying the relevant benefits and costs first.

Identifying the Benefits

Examples from the work team include reduced defects, improved uptime, and a shorter time to install new assembly line equipment. Secondary benefits from the team's tasks might include improved cross-functional communication, best practice sharing, improved relationships with suppliers, and higher customer satisfaction. These secondary impacts, in particular, may produce benefits that are difficult to trace directly back to the team's work as the source of improvement.

Only benefits attributed to the team's efforts should be included in the team's ROI.

Only those benefits that can be attributed to the team should be considered for inclusion in the ROI calculation. For the work team's maintenance contract, the vendor may offer a volume discount to the company for working with multiple units. If the contract lowers the price to other business units, at least part of the savings should be credited to the team and included in its ROI.

But that benefit should only be credited to the team if its contract contributes "significantly" to the lower price for other business units. Thus, *any benefit that can be only marginally credited to the team's work should not be included.*

What "significantly" means is, of course, subjective. ROI for teams is not widely used, so there are no accepted conventions. This author recommends excluding any benefit contributing less than 5 or 10 percent of the total.

The benefits need to have a true bottom-line impact to be included in the ROI calculation.

A related issue is that *only outcomes that have a true economic benefit should be considered for ROI.* Take the case of the management team's knowledge management system. The vast majority of information sharing through the system might have occurred anyway through informal means. (This might be the case if the system is just a repository of names and anecdotes.) Thus the benefits from the system may not differ much from informal communication.

This brings us to the third key issue: *ROI should be considered relative to the alternative courses of action only.* Best practice sharing across the company may be a key success factor. Thus the management team might claim credit for all best practice sharing that follows implementing the knowledge management system. But if the system does not offer any significant improvement over the best practice sharing that would have happened anyway, the best practice sharing should *not* be included in the team's ROI for the knowledge management system.

Identifying the Costs

Similar issues apply in identifying the costs. *Only those costs that can be materially attributed to the team should be included in the ROI calculation.*

The management team's task of evaluating acquisitions requires the use of the IT system for email, document storage, and so on. The IT department contributes resources to the team via the existing information technology infrastructure and technical support. Yet the team's use of the existing infrastructure represents only a tiny fraction of the load on the system. Thus, for this task, the team's use of IT should not be factored into the cost when calculating ROI.

In contrast, the team's tasks of integrating two companies' IT systems and designing a knowledge management system both require extensive IT support. So for these tasks the IT costs have to be factored in when doing the ROI calculation.

Assigning Monetary Values to the Benefits and Costs

The next task is assigning monetary values to the costs and benefits. Some benefits readily translate into financial terms:

- All of the work team's metrics fall into this category.

- The management team's market share metric also falls into this category.

Some benefits readily translate into monetary terms. Others are much more difficult to quantify.

Other benefits are harder to translate into financial terms:

- Integrating the bill and pay systems across two companies may reduce cost, but the long-run savings from integrating two systems may be counterbalanced in the short run by the costs of transitioning everyone to the new system.

- Integrating the bill and pay systems may lead to increased revenue from those customers who prefer the one-stop shopping that the merged companies offer. If it is the integrated product line that draws the customers in, not the new bill and pay system, then the financial benefits of increased revenue that follow the merger cannot be assigned to the ROI for the bill and pay system.

- What is the value of improved cross-functional communication and collaboration, a key secondary outcome for many teams? The benefits can range widely, from small process improvements that do not measurably impact the bottom line all the way to breakthrough ideas that create entirely new product lines and greatly boost the bottom line.

Organizational Context

Figuring out which intermediate impacts to include in the ROI calculation depends on the company's strategy and philosophy. This idea goes against the spirit of ROI, which is supposed to be objective, but even for capital investment there is significant leeway when calculating ROI.

ROI is subjective. So care needs to be exercised when using it.

Thus, it is impossible to have an entirely objective measure of ROI for capital spending; for teams, this is even more so.

In the absence of a readily available financial metric for evaluating intermediate processes, an alternative for assigning a monetary value to the team's impacts is asking the person with budgetary authority for the team the following question: "How much is the team's outcome worth to the company?" One downside is that this person may not be able to derive a monetary value. But if the team is incapable of producing a realistic monetary value, someone with a better perspective on the company's strategy should be more capable.

If it is too difficult to derive a monetary value for the benefits, the question then is, "How much would the organization be willing to pay to achieve the team's outcomes?" This puts the question in cost terms. The answer is the breakeven point at which the team barely meets its performance objectives.

The Role of Uncertainty

In many cases we want to forecast ROI, but it can be impossible to say for sure whether the team will be successful.

- The work team in our first case cannot guarantee success for large improvements in uptime derived from the new maintenance contract.

- The management team's success with an acquisition depends on factors that are too difficult to forecast.

Construct ROI estimates with differing levels of probability of success.

We need to take account of the uncertainty. Just as in strategic planning, a variety of scenarios that could impact the team's ROI should be considered. This argues for constructing a set of ROI estimates that represent the most likely case, best case, and worst case scenarios, as well as cases in between. (This approach is similar to the real options literature; see Hodder & Riggs, 1985; Luehrman, 1998.)

Consider the work team's maintenance contract. Suppose the annual cost will be $100,000 more than doing the work internally. The team forecasts a worst-case scenario of 1 percent better uptime by contracting out for the services, with an annualized benefit of $75,000, net benefit after costs of negative

$25,000, and negative 25 percent ROI. The most likely outcome they forecast is a 3 percent improvement in uptime, with expected annualized benefits of $110,000 per year; this translates into a positive net benefit of $10,000/year and 10 percent ROI.

The contract also has targets of 10 percent and 20 percent improvements in uptime, with financial incentives for meeting those targets. The incentives amount to an extra cost of $10,000 per year should the vendor meet the 10 percent improvement and $25,000 per year if the vendor meets the 20 percent improvement. But the team also determines that the benefit to the company in each case will be an additional $33,000/year and $52,000/year, respectively.

The ROI figures are summarized in Table 6.3. Note that each scenario has its own ROI. And the overall maintenance contract project has an ROI, too, which is made up of the weighted average of the ROI for each scenario.

Table 6.3. ROI Scenarios for Maintenance Contract

Increase in Uptime	Annual Net Value	ROI	Probability	Probability Weighted Net Monetary Benefit (Annual net value × Probability)	Probability Weighted ROI (ROI × Probability)
1 percent	−$25,000	−25 percent	.05	−$1,250	−1.25 percent
2 percent	$0	0 percent	.15	$0	0 percent
3 percent	$10,000	10 percent	.40	$4,000	4 percent
10 percent	$23,000	20.9 percent	.25	$5,750	5.23 percent
20 percent	$27,000	17.8 percent	.15	$4,050	2.67 percent

Probability weighted net monetary benefit (all scenarios): $12,550
Probability weighted ROI (all scenarios): 10.65 percent

Blank worksheets are provided as tools to assist readers in calculating probability weighted ROIs (see Exhibits 6.1 and 6.2).

Exhibit 6.1. Benefits and Costs for a Scenario

Scenario Name: _____

Type of Benefit	How does it impact the bottom line?	Value of that impact if it happens
Productivity		
Cycle time		
Quality		
Customer service		
Innovation		
Knowledge management		
Creativity		
Team member attitudes		
Other:		
Other:		
Other:		

Total monetary benefit if the scenario occurs: _____

Type of cost	Cost per unit time (week, month)	Total cost over life of the project/team charter
Team members' time: core		
Team members' time: peripheral		
Time of other contributors		
Materials and supplies		
Shared services		
Other:		
Other:		
Other:		

Total monetary cost if the scenario occurs: _____

Exhibit 6.2. Benefits and Costs Across Scenarios

Scenario Name	Annual net value = total monetary benefit less total monetary cost	ROI	Probability that the scenario will occur	Probability Weighted Net Monetary Benefit (Annual net value × Probability)	Probability Weighted ROI (ROI × Probability)
	$ _____	_____ percent		$ _____	_____ percent
	$ _____	_____ percent		$ _____	_____ percent
	$ _____	_____ percent		$ _____	_____ percent
	$ _____	_____ percent		$ _____	_____ percent
	$ _____	_____ percent		$ _____	_____ percent

Probability weighted net monetary benefit (all scenarios): $ _____

Probability weighted ROI (all scenarios): _____ percent

Strategy

Calculating ROI makes sense only when there is uncertainty over the outcome and it is not obvious from prior experience that something is worth doing. Consider the work team's task of troubleshooting assembly defects. Past experience may predict that the vast majority of increases in defects can be solved quickly by a small work team. We do not need ROI to tell us that a small team should be initially assigned to troubleshoot problems. On the other hand, ROI analysis may be helpful in situations where the bottom-line return is obvious to the team members but credibility needs to be built among stakeholders.

ROI can be used to set strategy over whether and how to deploy a team's resources.

ROI can help determine what to do about larger problems. Suppose that some defects cannot be immediately solved by an on-site team. Instituting company-wide policies over spending money on outside vendors versus building an internal team of experts to serve all the company's manufacturing sites is a decision that involves substantial resources with potentially large bottom-line impacts. This case warrants using ROI analysis.

Hurdle Rates

Capital budgeting processes typically specify a hurdle rate that all projects must meet in order to be funded. The hurdle rate is the minimum acceptable ROI, and takes into account the other potential uses of funds. Thus an ROI of 10.65 percent might look reasonable, but only until compared with a company-wide hurdle rate of 15 percent, indicating that the expected return on the maintenance contract is less than the company's goal for invested funds.

Yet there are limits to the usefulness of this kind of analysis. The problem is that ROI is only as good as the assumptions that underlie it. This has long been an issue for capital spending (see Hodder & Riggs, 1985). It is doubly true when evaluating teams, given the subjective nature of ROI.

ROI is a complement to, not substitute for, sound decision making and contextual interpretation of the numbers.

Thus ROI can help increase the objectivity of decision making over strategy and operations, but it is not a substitute for sound judgment and contextual interpretation of the numbers.

Performance Management

How should the team's performance be evaluated in the case of the maintenance contract vendor? It is impossible to evaluate the entire set of scenarios provided by the team because only one of them is realized in the end. However, *the team can be evaluated on the basis of the realized ROI for the scenario that actually happened.* If the contract results in 3 percent improved uptime but with greater costs/lower benefits than the team forecast, the team could be penalized for inaccuracy by withholding any bonus.

It also might be appropriate to give the team a bonus if the vendor meets one of the higher targets. The team should have insights into how to achieve greater uptime through the financial incentives written into the contract. Giving outcome-based rewards to the team members could provide the incentive needed to maximize ROI in addition to creating incentives to increase collaboration.

Note the two different ways to view the gains: ROI (percentage) and net monetary benefit (dollar amount). The annualized net monetary benefit is $4,000 greater for the 20 percent improvement, compared to the 10 percent improvement. Yet the ROI for the 10 percent improvement is *more than* the ROI for the 20 percent improvement in uptime.

Using ROI for performance management can help keep the team members focused on the bottom-line impacts that really matter for the organization.

Thus, incorporating ROI considerations into the team's performance management can help ensure that proper attention is paid to the total return the team's actions provide the company.

A benefit of incorporating ROI into the team's performance management system is the incentive this provides to approach the process. By forecasting ROI for different scenarios, the team should realize before the contract is signed that a $10,000 bonus for 10 percent improvement and $25,000 bonus for 20 percent improvement is not optimal. They could then lower the bonus for the 20 percent improvement, or raise the trigger point for the $25,000 bonus above 20 percent.

Pitfalls

Despite the attraction of ROI for team performance management, it is important to recognize the potential pitfalls as well. Any time subjective valuations are used, they can be biased in favor of a higher ROI number to help the team achieve a higher performance award.

Consider the knowledge management system. The management team might forecast 2 to 25 percent improved cash flow from different new product development revenue streams ten years into the future. Yet if they will be rewarded only for showing at least a 10 percent improvement in cash flow, they might be tempted to downplay the likelihood of the worst outcomes. Doing so, however, could negatively impact the value of the information that the team reports to the CEO. This is a classic performance management problem and not exclusive to teams. The relevant point is that introducing ROI does not alter the subjective nature of performance management. It only provides an additional tool.

Conclusion

This chapter reviewed the complex set of issues involved in considering return on investment for teams. Among the key points addressed:

- *Both out-of-pocket expenses and implicit time costs should be included.* Unless the full cost of team members' and support staff time is factored in, the total costs will be understated.

- *Only benefits with a bottom-line impact should be included.* This means focusing first on productivity, cycle time, quality, customer satisfaction, and so forth. Other benefits that are more difficult to link directly to the bottom line, such as improved innovation, organizational learning, and cross-functional collaboration, should be considered carefully and included if there is a compelling argument for doing so.

- *Only those costs and benefits that are primarily attributable to the team should be included.* In the case of a shared service, the cost of the service should be factored in only if the team uses a significant amount. Similarly, if a benefit would be realized regardless of the team's efforts, its value should not be included in the team's ROI.

- *ROI is subjective, so care needs to be exercised when using it.* While ROI is a metric, it is only as good as the underlying assumptions. Slightly different scenarios can lead to very different ROI numbers.

- *Best-case and worst-case ROI scenarios should be considered.* Because of the likelihood of alternate scenarios, a range of different outcomes should be used to construct a range of ROI estimates.

- *ROI can be used to set strategy over deploying a team's resources.* Acknowledging the range of alternate team ROI scenarios up-front facilitates strategic decision making over how to allocate scarce budget dollars.

- *ROI is a complement to, not substitute for, sound decision making.* The implicit assumptions and underlying uncertainty underscore the reality that ROI typically should play a supporting role only. Without the benefit of understanding the larger organizational strategic context, it is risky to use team ROI calculations as the sole guide to decision making.

- *Using ROI for performance management can help keep the team members focused on bottom-line impacts.* Rewarding team members for maximizing ROI helps align their incentives with those of the organization.

PART 2

LEADERSHIP AND ORGANIZATIONAL CULTURE

Jill E. Nemiro

AS THE VERY NATURE OF THE WORK HAS EVOLVED from routine tasks to more complex and nonroutine work, the nature of the organizations in which this work is accomplished has changed as well. Contemporary organizations have evolved from a traditional, bureaucratic structure to a more team-based system, one in which groups of individuals work collaboratively to solve core business objectives. But the change to a more team-based system is not seamless. Not only have the structure and form of the organization changed, but the leaders and organizational culture that guide the behavior of organizational members have to change as well. How should leadership styles be altered? What new organizational belief system needs to be created and accepted by organizational members in team-based systems? The chapters in this section will provide some answers.

In 1960, Douglas McGregor wrote *The Human Side of Enterprise.* In his book, McGregor objected to the rigid hierarchy of structure and leadership that was found in the bureaucratic organization. His objections were based on the negative assumptions made about people—primarily that employees lacked ambition and would not work unless coerced, controlled, or threatened with punishment (*Theory X*). McGregor argued rather that people enjoy and strive for success in their work and, if committed to business objectives, will exercise self-direction and self-control and will accept and even seek responsibility (*Theory Y*). This same argument is echoed in the first two chapters in this section. In Dennis Romig's chapter (Chapter 7), a new model of leadership is outlined whereby leaders work *side-by-side* with contributors (rather than followers). Michael Beyerlein, in Chapter 8, suggests developing team accountability based on mutual respect, honest and caring feedback, and a sharing of ideas and feelings, rather than fear and reward.

Organizations that are successful in making the transition to a more team-based approach have champions of collaboration at the top levels of the organization. However, not all top management teams are consistent in their support of a team-based approach, and, in fact, not all top management teams even model effective collaborative behavior themselves. In Chapter 9, Mindy Gewirtz and Peter Gumpert track the development and transformation of one such top management team—a combative executive team whose members were resistant to collaboration and teaming. Gewirtz and Gumpert share a set of intervention strategies that was used to transform the executive team to one that could manage on its own in a more collaborative, team-based system.

One cannot talk about leadership without also talking about organizational culture, which has been defined as the shared beliefs, expectations, and core values of the organization. Ed Schein, a key thinker in the area of organizational culture, saw leadership and organizational culture as two sides of the same coin. In 1992, Schein wrote a book called *Organizational Culture and Leadership,* in which he illustrates the importance of leadership in building organizational culture. Schein suggested that organizational culture begins with leaders who impose their own values and assumptions on the members of the organization. And once organizational culture has been established, it tends to be relatively stable and provides a sense of identity for the members within the organization.

But what happens when the identity of that organization drastically changes (as it does when an organization moves from a hierarchical form to a team-based system)? It then becomes necessary for the organizational culture to shift as well. Teams necessitate a fundamentally different set of values and assumptions that will support collaboration and creativity. In Chapter 10, Jill Nemiro outlines the necessary contextual dimensions needed to support creativity for one of the newest forms of teams—the virtual team.

Making the drastic changes in leadership style and organizational culture that are necessary for teams is not an easy path. And not all organizations that have moved to a team-based structure have seen positive results. Why? In Chapter 11, Craig McGee takes a more comprehensive view and suggests that there is a series of organizational and management systems (of which leadership and organizational culture are part) that need to be dramatically changed. If they are not, change initiatives to team-based systems will most likely fail. All the systems need to be re-engineered and aligned to support teaming and collaboration.

CHAPTER 7

Side-by-Side Leaders Promote Breakthrough Results

Dennis Romig

WORK TEAMS AND TEAM-BASED ORGANIZATIONS have achieved significant performance improvements for organizations. The business improvements and benefits are usually significant, particularly when structured team processes are utilized and leaders, as well as team members, are trained in team skills. Documented business improvements of 20 to 40 percent per team across a host of performance improvements have been reported including quality, productivity, profit, cycle time, and customer satisfaction (McLagan & Nel, 1995).

Team systems require a new leadership model.

At its best, a collaborative work system can create team and organizational work cultures where great communication, cooperation, coordination, and creative breakthroughs occur on a daily basis. Cross-functional natural work groups perform their work and share management responsibilities, thus allowing managers the time to be more strategic and forward looking.

The Negative Consequences of Top-Down Leadership

Unfortunately, high performance and a great team culture can become infected and die with bad leadership. One high-technology organization achieved the best results of its peer companies and, in fact, had won industry awards on its performance. The entire organization, composed of interlocking teams, was able to respond rapidly to any major change in customer direction. In part, because of his great leadership, the vice president of the organization was promoted to lead a different division.

I will call the executive who took his place "Fred." Fred thought he needed to make every decision and control every action. Within three months the organization's productivity plummeted to disastrous levels. Fred's response was to become more controlling with frequent eruptions of anger toward his managers. A group of team leaders in Fred's organization came up with a productivity turnaround plan and submitted it to him. Fred let the plan get buried in his in-basket. When Fred was finally fired six months later, the first action his replacement took was to implement the recovery plan the team leaders had developed.

Studies document that 50 percent of leaders are failing.

Unfortunately there are too many "Freds" across all industries and organizations. The "Freds" are part of the 50 percent of the leaders that psychologist Robert Hogan and his colleagues have documented who are failing across all levels of all organizations (Hogan, Gordon, & Hogan, 1994).

Natural systems theory describes important human interactions in terms of reciprocal and mutually influencing behavior patterns. Emotionally close relationships like those between leaders and their followers and managers and their subordinates have been discovered to have observable and predictable patterns. The top-down leadership behaviors of managers like Fred result in corresponding, almost reflexive behaviors that undermine systematic and creative problem solving and goal-directed behavior. (For more information on how to avoid undermining team creative problem solving, see Chapter 10.)

The Side-by-Side Leadership Model

After reviewing three thousand studies of leadership practices from a variety of disciplines, the author developed a systems model of leadership that proved that a third way of leading was clearly superior to either top-down leadership or bottom-up leadership in achieving spectacular business results. This new model is called Side-by-Side Leadership®. Side-by-side leadership is contrasted with the all-too-prevalent top-down leadership in terms of communication, decision making, and teamwork. Research in natural systems documents that when a leader practices one-way communication and authoritarian decision making, subordinates gradually adapt and reciprocate, behaving as non-thinking, order-obeying followers (Kerr & Bowen, 1988; Papero, 1990). Instead, leaders who practice side-by-side leadership use two-way communication and share decision making with others who are qualified and who are impacted by the decisions every day. (For more information on participative leadership, see Chapters 14 and 15.)

The side-by-side systems model of leadership identifies how today's managers and executives are required to practice and model side-by-side leadership in a variety of interactions almost twenty-four hours a day. Leaders have the opportunity to influence performance in five different spheres of leadership: knowledge, personal, interpersonal, team, and organizational (see Figure 7.1).

Figure 7.1. Spheres of Leadership

Reprinted from D.A. Romig, *Side-by-Side Leadership: Achieving Outstanding Results Together*. Austin, TX: Bard Books, 2001.

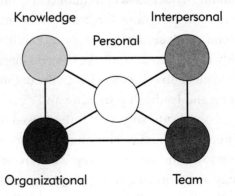

Shading and placement in the figure symbolize both the uniqueness of each sphere and that all spheres relate to the others. Many leadership authors focus on only one or two of the above areas of leadership. The side-by-side systems model addresses all five spheres and the synergy that occurs when all five are present. Research-based practical tools will be presented for each of the five spheres of side-by-side leadership. Leaders can achieve significant performance improvements when they apply side-by-side leadership tools in any one of the spheres.

Vastar Resources, Inc., a subsidiary of Arco Energy Company, had a documented improvement of $5.5 billion in six years during years of low oil and gas prices. The company achieved this 300 percent improvement in shareholder value using side-by-side leadership to involve the hearts and minds of everyone in the organization (Romig, 2001). Side-by-side leadership promotes two-way communication, participative decision making, mutual cooperation, and leaders and contributors working together as thoughtful and creative individuals.

The Five Spheres of Leadership

There is no one single way to lead. Contrast Bill Gates, the founder of Microsoft, with Jack Welch, the eminently successful former CEO of General Electric. What works for one individual will not be as effective for someone else. Different interests and abilities promote strengths in different spheres of leadership. Leaders can be as effective overall, but they have different combinations of skills.

One of Bill Gates' clear competencies is his knowledge of computer programming. In fact, he was a childhood genius in understanding computers and how to write programs for them. In the interpersonal area, he had a network of friends with similar interests and abilities. Jack Welch, on the other hand, quickly moved up the ranks of General Electric with his organizational and personal leadership competencies. In the organizational area, he valued employee training and leadership training and development for all levels of leaders. In the personal leadership area, he espoused honesty, fairness, and directness. He fought against emotional triangles, where one person is critical about another person to a third neutral party. Welch required criticism to be communicated directly and worked out between the parties involved (Lowe, 1998).

Rather than one list of leadership attributes, the five spheres of side-by-side leadership provide a framework for the study and development of leaders. Leaders can succeed with their own unique pattern of abilities and interests.

The size of the circles can be adjusted to depict the actual strength of the leader in that leadership sphere. A successful leader does not have to be strong in every sphere. A leader whose side-by-side team leadership skills are currently the strongest competency would have a model like that in Figure 7.2.

Figure 7.2. Leader with Strong Team Skills

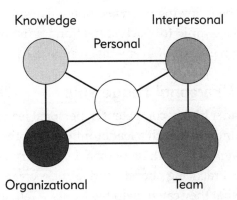

Another leader may have a different assessment. The executive leader, Fred, the top-down leader whose failure was described earlier, had a pattern as indicated in Figure 7.3. His knowledge leadership is his strongest competency, whereas he is weak in everything else, including personal leadership. He was happiest as an engineer solving technical problems, yet he accepted the responsibility to lead a team-based organization. Fred built up frustration and stress

Figure 7.3. Fred's Model

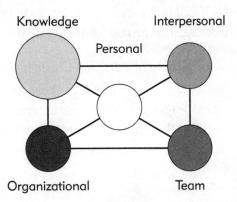

daily because he had to spend all of his time away from the engineering work he enjoyed the most.

The most effective leaders today walk *side-by-side* with their superiors, peers, and individual contributors to get work done. They listen. They respond. They lead two-way—both by listening to others and by sharing their own ideas in an ever-changing internal and external environment. And they frequently do it without organizational power of a formal management position.

The following overview of the five spheres of the model includes a leadership example for each sphere and a list of specific actions you can take to improve yourself in any given sphere.

Personal Leadership

A leader highly competent in personal leadership has strong values, direction, and integrity. Such a leader influences others by example. Leaders who think through and work on personal visionary goals daily inspire those they work with. Practicing honesty and fairness creates the trust by others who will then do what they can to help the leader. "Tell people the truth, because they know the truth anyway," says Jack Welch (Lowe, 1998, p. 35). Natural systems theory proposes that leaders high in personal direction can handle the emotional drain and stress that is associated with the amount of time being spent with others (Kerr & Bowen, 1988; Papero, 1990).

Another factor of personal leadership is maintaining emotional objectivity that can steer the organization in the proper direction compared to changing course with every storm of change and challenge. Two historical examples of great personal leaders are Gandhi and Martin Luther King, Jr.

An integrated self makes it easier for the leader to be naturally side-by-side.

It almost seems ironic, but the people in close relationships with the leader improve the most when the leader works on improving himself or herself. An integrated self makes it easier for the leader to be naturally side-by-side, rather than being overly concerned about always getting his or her way in every interaction.

An Example of Personal Leadership

Frank, a manager of a team-based organization, was high in personal leadership. When the company had to reduce expenses, he went to the teams and told them the situation. Rather than forcing layoffs, the teams volunteered to a reduced workweek for the duration of the crisis. Several individual team members volunteered to leave without pay to go back to school. Later, one of Frank's teams requested and received authority to purchase expensive equipment that ultimately was a waste of money. Everyone was worried what Frank would say and do. When he found out, he calmly asked the group, "What did we learn from this?" (Romig, 2001)

Specific Actions to Improve Your Side-by-Side Personal Leadership

- Identify your personal core values related to work and life;

- Identify and develop one or two personal visionary goals that represent your work and life values;

- Plan your week schedule to always spend at least four hours working toward your visionary goal or doing an activity that supports your highest personal values;

- Identify how to strive toward achieving your personal visionary goals while simultaneously assisting your organization to achieve its most important goals;

- Write down the tasks you do daily or weekly that someone else could do. Work with these people side-by-side to empower them to take over the tasks;

- Identify work tasks where you need more empowerment yourself. Negotiate with your supervisor or manager on how to have greater authority;

- Spend some time alone thinking about your values, visionary goal, and recent achievement; and

- Get enough rest to maintain emotional balance.

Knowledge Leadership

In side-by-side leadership, knowledge leadership involves seeking, developing, extending, sharing, and harnessing all available knowledge. This type of leadership tempers and guides emotional influences.

Knowledge leaders use their expertise to influence the business or purpose of the organization as a whole and in every key area of service or production.

All workers, whether in service or manufacturing, rely on knowledge to do their jobs. Knowledge leaders use their expertise to influence the business or purpose of the organization as a whole and in every key area of service or production (Leonard, 1998). There are three distinct aspects to knowledge leadership: acquiring, sharing, and transforming knowledge. Examples of knowledge leaders include Linus Pauling and Albert Einstein, both of whom worked side-by-side with colleagues and students. The main principle is to create, share, and use proven knowledge side-by-side to rapidly and effectively improve business results.

An Example of Knowledge Leadership

Anthony is an example of a strong side-by-side knowledge leader. He reads books and articles constantly (Romig, 2001). After he reads the information, he analyzes and combines it with other knowledge. Then he naturally thinks of which friends or colleagues would most benefit from the new knowledge, which he then shares. In one situation in which Anthony was coaching a colleague, the first thing he did was to ask the colleague what his learning goals were for the session. He then proceeded to reach the learning goals side-by-side with that colleague.

Specific Actions to Improve Your Side-by-Side Knowledge Leadership

- Identify new proven knowledge that would help you achieve your personal visionary goal and succeed in your current job;

- Contact experts with proven knowledge and share side-by-side with them;

- Before you present new knowledge or skills to others, either in coaching or training, find out what they want to learn and why they want to learn it;

- Before you present new knowledge or skills to others, either in coaching or training, find out what they already know about the topic;

- As you train or coach specific skills, have the team members present knowledge to you and the group where they have expertise;

- Link the training or coaching that you provide to achieving the organization's visionary goals;

- When your team or organization has experienced a success, debrief with the contributors to identify what factors caused it be a success—create organizational learning; and

- Even though you may be an expert in an area of knowledge or work performance, do not act like an expert—practice two-way leadership by being willing to learn from others.

Interpersonal Leadership

Along with the increase in knowledge has been a corresponding rise in the amount of interdependent work in all organizations. Interpersonal leadership is the influence a leader exerts person to person. It also impacts small and large group interactions.

Interpersonal leadership involves listening, speaking, and coaching.

Side-by-side interpersonal leadership emphasizes different ways of listening, speaking, and influencing. Effective interpersonal leadership requires two-way listening, mutual contributing, connecting visionary goals, and diverse networking.

Former U.S. president John F. Kennedy is an excellent example of a great interpersonal leader. He was a great listener, had a huge and diverse network, and could connect to other's values in his speeches and talks.

An Example of Interpersonal Leadership

Another leader, whom I will call Charles, seemed to be friends with everyone in his company, city, state, and industry. He was, of course, not friends with everyone. It just appeared so because Charles took time out to learn people's names and spend time with them. He had a rule to write one card a day to thank someone for a past favor or to recognize the person. In addition, Charles cultivated colleagues who disagreed with his position on key issues in the company and the city. He thought that listening to diverse viewpoints enriched his understanding. He was best friends with both a leading Democrat and a leading Republican politician in his city. Whenever any of his friends or colleagues had a problem, Charles knew to whom he could refer them for the best help. (Pavelek, 2000)

**Specific Actions to Improve Your
Side-by-Side Interpersonal Leadership**

- Lead with great listening;

- Ask people what they think and then listen to their thinking;

- Talk to someone you know who disagrees with you and try and understand his or her point of view;

- Share your personal visionary goal with friends and colleagues. Ask them to share their goals or aspirations with you;

- When you do presentations, think and talk about how the topic overlaps with achieving visionary goals. This will create excitement in your talk; and

- Look for opportunities to help others achieve their goals.

Team Leadership

Side-by-side leadership takes work groups from being "teams" in name only to becoming continuous high-performing teams.

Team leadership is the ability to coordinate and support the efforts of groups of people. In today's complex and interconnected workplace, everyone needs to gain competence in this area. (For information on competencies for teamwork, see Chapter 33.)

Side-by-side leadership takes work groups from being "teams" in name only to becoming continuous high-performing teams. Teams and individuals on a team form interaction fields. Understanding how these interaction fields operate can lead to outstanding improvements in performance. Excellent team leaders lead side-by-side with their team members, the team sponsor, and the managers and supervisors from other interaction fields.

Team leaders are key coordinators, linking individual and team performance and goals to the organization's goals, mission, values, and vision (Romig, 1996). One historical leader who did an exceptional job of building a team of other diverse leaders was U.S. President Dwight Eisenhower; he led British, American, French, and other allies in the successful overthrow of the Nazi occupation of France. He had to mediate conflict with a variety of strong personalities during the most anxious and life-threatening of times.

An Example of Team Leadership

Cathy was the epitome of a great team leader. She was even a team leader before she was formally promoted to that position. As a contributor in a product development organization, she worked across the different boundaries and job descriptions to unify the people working in product development. She promoted the whole team's success rather than focusing on her own accomplishments, which were noteworthy in their own respect. As the team leader, she faithfully ensured that the team met at least once every two weeks and most of the time was able to push for weekly team meetings. She rotated the roles in the team meeting: meeting leader, recorder, and timekeeper. She made sure every team member had equal participation in the team meetings. Cathy also made sure that people had the tools and resources to do their job. Cathy's product development organization received worldwide recognition for the products that were produced with her leadership. (Romig, 2001)

Specific Actions to Improve Your Side-by-Side Team Leadership

- Develop shared team goals that directly support organizational goals;
- Work side-by-side with leaders of other work areas whose success is linked with your team;
- Use a team charter document to gain agreement on team purpose and decision-making authority;
- Involve the whole team in setting team goals and developing actions plans;
- Facilitate team meetings where everyone participates;
- Use structured methods to lead problem solving, decision making, and action planning;
- Develop roles and responsibilities of all team members together; and
- Train all team members in team skills.

Organizational Leadership

Organizational leadership involves understanding organizations as systems that interact in specific ways. (For information on how to align the various systems within an organization, see Chapter 11.) These interactions occur inside and outside the organization. Part of the system aspect of organizational leadership is that it can either pull all other aspects of side-by-side leadership to outstanding success or impose a ceiling and barrier on the performance of other leaders and followers.

Side-by-side organizational leaders facilitate other leaders and followers in achieving visionary goals.

Side-by-side organizational leaders facilitate other leaders and followers in the setting and achievement of the organization's visionary goals (Collins & Porras, 1994). The executives support and build empowered work teams through the organization. Additionally, all organizations move to breakthrough levels of achievement when leaders work side-by-side with the leaders of other organizations to achieve mutual values and goals.

An Example of Organizational Leadership

Bob was a great side-by-side organizational leader because he appreciated the value of every function in his organization, including the so-called "support" functions. Bob also had many contacts outside his organization that he regularly communicated with to find out new and current opportunities and threats to his organization's success. Bob's behavior was consistent with the values and goals of his organization, which were developed side-by-side with a variety of internal and outside leaders. He supported the continuous training and empowerment of teams and individuals.

Specific Actions to Improve Your Side-by-Side Organizational Leadership

- Find out what your customers value most in your organization's products and services;

- Find out what your employees value most in working in your organization;

- Work with a broad selection of other leaders to develop three- to five-year visionary goals for your organization;

- Develop and implement creative strategies for achieving visionary goals; and

- Work side-by-side with the leaders of customer, supplier, government, and partner organizations. Set shared visionary goals for joint ventures.

Continue Your Development as a Side-by-Side Leader

Each of the five spheres of side-by-side leadership was described above, along with some suggested actions you can take to improve in each sphere of leadership. While the suggestions have some proven effectiveness, it would be even better if you developed your own tools for success. To do that, review the side-by-side leadership practices and develop your own action steps.

To improve your overall leadership, first examine the leadership requirements of your current job. Are you in more of a team leadership role with knowledge workers? If you are, the two spheres you should focus on are team leadership and side-by-side knowledge leadership. Notice that I wrote "side-by-side knowledge leadership"; unfortunately, many experts who have considerable knowledge are too authoritarian and top-down. They have the knowledge in their heads, but they do not know how to leverage the knowledge by leading side-by-side and two-way. If you are part of cross-organizational teams or committees, then you may need to increase your ability in organizational leadership.

Breakthrough results occur in organizations where there are different leaders who are strong in different spheres of side-by-side leadership.

The real breakthrough results occur in organizations in which there are different leaders who are strong in different spheres of side-by-side leadership. The best management teams have a variety of leaders, whose combined strengths include all five spheres. Knowledge leadership plus interpersonal leadership equals intellectual capital. (For more information on building intellectual capital, see Chapter 30.) Intellectual capital combined with team leadership and organizational leadership equals a thriving new business. Personal leadership combined with any of the other spheres equals an organization that adds to the community and the lives of every individual the leaders touch.

CHAPTER 8

Team Accountability

A Leadership Responsibility

Michael M. Beyerlein

MANAGERS OFTEN BRING UP THE TOPIC of accountability when discussing work teams. When the topic comes up, it usually focuses on "how to make *others* accountable." That means "how to get others to do what I want" or, at best, "how to get others to act responsibly." Accountability is about *enabling performance.*

Accountability is about enabling performance.

It means "how to *enable* others to act responsibly." Managers should not expect employees to act accountably when they (1) lack the tools and information they need, (2) feel over-controlled, (3) lack the opportunity to learn the necessary behaviors, or (4) have self-interests that conflict with what the managers expect. Managers need to understand that people do the best they can under the circumstances, so if doing better is the goal, circumstances must be improved. That means the managers themselves are accountable for three key prerequisites of employee accountability:

1. Create an environment at work that supports the success of the team and its members;

2. Provide appropriate learning opportunities, so employees have the repertoire of behaviors available to draw on to achieve the goals; and

3. Be accountable to the team. Commitments for support must be kept.

The shift from an individual-focused, command-and-control operation to one based on empowered work teams frightens some managers. The managers in such circumstances believe that the decision making necessary for achieving and maintaining performance at the desired level must remain in their hands to avoid errors and that the people doing the actual work must be carefully watched and motivated. To such managers, the idea of self-management or empowerment means loss of control and decrements in performance. Accountability for these managers means they must protect themselves from errors and failures of the people who report to them.

These controlling managers tend to make the following assumptions:

1. You get what you demand, not what you reward and measure;

2. Workers on the front line are like brainless machines, so management must do their thinking for them; and

3. Performance can be reduced to simple tasks.

Managers with perspectives like this not only resist the transition to team-based organizing but may even work actively to sabotage it. Collaboration seems dangerous to them, because it requires trusting others.

When controlling managers use the term accountability, they typically mean there should be negative consequences for errors, acting "out of line," disagreeing with management, being late or absent, and so forth. They assume that a combination of fear and reward will control behavior. They rely on policies and rules to enforce behaviors they desire. When they use the term "good team members," they mean conformity and obedience, not initiative and innovation. But the style of their interaction with the workers is probably even more important. Dave Hannah (2001) says, "High performance cannot be mandated. It must come from within."

Managers who rely on fear and control anchor one end of a continuum of management perspectives. They believe that what they do and how they do it will get the results they want. At the other end of the continuum is a group of

Enabling managers champion empowerment, collaboration, and teams.

managers who believe in the potential of the people whose work they oversee. Such managers embrace the use of empowered teams and recognize them as the form of organizing that aligns with their own values. These managers champion empowerment, collaboration, and teams.

Such managers use the term accountability to represent the idea that workers on the front line can act as responsible members of the organization when they are given responsibility within a clearly defined task environment and treated with respect and appreciation. High performance can be mutually beneficial; it results from effective coordination and cooperation of all members in the business unit with everyone committing to it and thinking about how to achieve it. These managers rely on mutual respect, with honest and caring feedback; they share feelings, ideas, and opinions and listen hard when others share with them.

Between these two extreme types, a majority of managers fit in the middle of the continuum, where they are somewhat open to new ideas, if the ideas aren't too radical, and believe in the abilities of workers to some extent. They can be swayed by the managers at either pole—toward resisting or toward championing collaborative practices. Figure 8.1 depicts the idea that there are more controlling than enabling managers. Managing the human resources is a core management responsibility (Mabey, Salaman, & Storey, 1988). Accountability is not about control; it is about performance. Consequently, there is a lot of potential for leadership development remaining in organizations.

Figure 8.1. Continuum of Management Approaches to Accountability

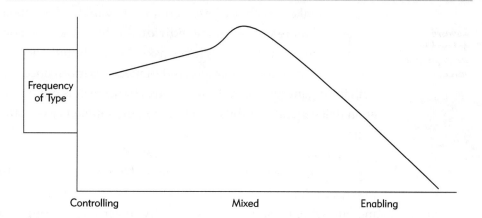

One thing all three types of managers have in common is the desire for workers they are responsible for to receive high marks for performance. Their motivation for getting high marks may vary a little from: (1) commitment to organizational goals, to (2) belief that high performance is good for everyone's morale, to (3) desire for job security and improved odds for promotion. However, the major difference is *how* the motivating energy is created; the how is driven by the manager's assumptions.

Alternate Assumptions

Changing people's basic assumptions can be difficult, but changes in behavior or the systems that reinforce specific behaviors *can* be achieved. Below are some ideas for addressing the assumptions of controlling managers so they will be more willing to create supportive conditions for team accountability.

Rewards and Behavior

Everyone has some understanding of the link between rewards and behavior. However, the term "reward" is often used in a narrow sense as just those objective payoffs that are administered from authorities. Broadening the meaning creates opportunities. Reward has a number of key aspects: (1) originates from either outside the person (extrinsic) or inside the person (intrinsic); (2) is tangible or intangible; (3) provides reinforcement or feedback; and (4) can be a direct consequence of behavior or an indirect consequence or merely coincidental. Whether or not employees can articulate all these points, they do understand them. They choose their behaviors to obtain what is most rewarding for them, and they make that choice based on how they understand their environments.

Reward is defined by what people value.
Reward represents what the individual values. The question of accountability arises here when the employee asks, "Why should I act in an accountable manner?" When the organization is designed so performance generates value for both the organization and the individual, the answer is clear: it is a win/win situation that generates enthusiasm rather than indifference or compliance (Klein & Sorra, 1996).

These aspects of reward are not news. Everyone knows this from subjective experience. These are well-established laws of behavior in both theory and practice. Yet, practice is highly flawed. Examples abound of managers expecting one set of behaviors while actually rewarding the opposite (for example,

Kerr, 1997). If you reward individual contribution, that's what you get, no matter how many times you call it "team work." Expectations for innovation will be frustrated if rewards target proven methods and punish mistakes. People skills will not develop if rewards target technical accomplishments.

A related idea is that "you get what you measure." Measuring means attention is being paid to certain behaviors and consequences of behavior, and assessment is not based on subjective judgments. So a cycle of relationships exists:

> Situation → meaning we make of it → choice we make
> about behaving → behaving → consequences (which
> may include reward) → repeating the behavior to get
> the same outcome or changing the behavior to change
> the consequences → new situation.

The arrows in the cycle link the elements and represent the transition points. The cycle operates continuously at the subjective level in every employee. Management design of the measurement, feedback, and reward systems can generate increased accountability from a reframing of the systems based on the cycle. The design reflects their goals, but is shaped by their assumptions. Some of the limitations of those assumptions can be overcome by taking the cycle into account during the design and implementation process.

Each arrow in this chain of events represents a relationship and an opportunity for impacting behavior. The six arrows are described below:

1. The meaning people make from looking at a situation can be changed by a number of factors, including: what they pay attention to, what they remember about prior situations, what skills they have for making sense of this kind of situation; what information is available; and what people around them are suggesting (including managers who consciously or unconsciously manage meaning-making processes). Meaning drives behavior, and it is personal. But shared meanings are jointly created, so behavior becomes aligned across teams and members. Managers can use a variety of tools for building shared meaning, including mind mapping, five why's, the ladder of inference, and the left-hand column (Senge, Kleiner, Roberts, Ross, & Smith, 1994).

2. The choice people make about what to do, how to act in the circumstances, depends on how they make sense of it. Perhaps people will see

opportunity in the situation, or threat, or perhaps they will see nothing that concerns them or feel helpless and remain indifferent. Choice also depends on their repertoire of responses—what options do they have. For example, "I can't choose to change jobs and become a software engineer, because I don't have the expertise or the credentials for those jobs." Choice is often automatic and reactive rather than reflective and pro-active. It is also often based on emotion rather than data and logic. The latter requires discipline. The best thing a manager can do to influence the sense making is to communicate—to share information readily and openly. Useful tools for doing that include town meetings, Search Conferences, and large group sense making meetings and storytelling (Dixon, 2000). Stories are especially powerful. Managers join organizations like Toastmasters and Story Tellers International to increase their ability to use stories as a tool for communicating about the most important aspects of the organization's culture. (See the chapter on Collaborating in Manufacturing Settings in *Beyond Teams* for more on sense making.)

3. People act; they carry out the behavior they choose. People do this thousands of times a day. The behaviors may be as simple as a head nod at a particular moment to indicate listening to someone or as complex as bargaining with someone in order to build an alliance. Many of those behaviors are habitual, including how people process information in their minds. Habits may be efficient, because they avoid "re-inventing the wheel" each time, but they may also be inappropriate for the situation—thoughtless behavior—and hence ineffective. Managers can contribute to the development of disciplined processes that make analysis, alternative generation, and decision making deliberate. They can also use those processes themselves.

4. Whether people choose to act or not, there will be consequences. The consequences may seem like objective work getting done, but many times the more important consequences consist of interpretations of one's behavior by others. For example, if a manager deliberately chooses not to act in a situation, perhaps with the motive of increasing the confidence of others who must then act, it will be interpreted by others in multiple ways—some meaning will be generated that the others will then base

their behaviors on. Those meanings can be managed to some extent—not completely, but enough to make the effort worthwhile. When a manager provides the rationale for a decision to act or not to act, others can make more productive sense of the behavior and align their reactions more effectively.

5. If people aren't getting the consequences they wanted from their behaviors, they need to change something. The change can occur in the situational factors, the meaning-making process, or the choice of behaviors. An old definition of insanity is "expecting different results while maintaining the same behaviors." The definition has been available for a long time, but the expectation persists. Managers can work with employees to jointly design behavior sets or work processes that add value for the individual as well as for the organization. When employees know this opportunity to co-create exists, they take more initiative to make improvements.

Work with employees to jointly design behavior sets.

6. The situation is always new. Every behavior impacts the cognitive and interpersonal environment people are embedded in, so there is continuous opportunity for change and continuous need to adjust behaviors. That is the nature of a feedback loop. The system continuously changes. Sometimes those changes reach critical points where decisions create major new opportunities. Those opportunities are hard to predict, but the manager who talks with employees and listens to them will have a better chance of pouncing on the opportunity when it comes. Then the new situation is more likely to start an even more productive round of the cycle.

Control behavior by its consequences, negative and positive. This principle has a lot of validity, but the way it is practiced often seems to assume that human beings are as complex as monkeys. Hackman (Hackman & Oldham, 1980) determined some years ago that other major sources of job satisfaction included meaningfulness, responsibility, knowledge of results, autonomy, task and supervisor feedback, significance of the task, wholeness of the task, and skill variety. These are not simple reinforcers like bananas for monkeys. They imply job involvement and complex minds. More recent research makes a strong case for feelings about job success as a major reinforcer (Cote, 1999).

Job success is a major reinforcer.

Enabling the Team

Why address the topic of teams when writing about accountability? Because there is no value in holding teams accountable for tasks they cannot do. If the work requires collective effort, the team or business unit must be held accountable. Although the individual remains accountable to the organization and now becomes accountable to the team, the team is also accountable to the organization. The team should be held accountable when the work requires a team effort. The team should not be held accountable if the work does not require interdependent effort or when the team lacks the skill or the information or the tools necessary for achieving the team's goals; their intent and effort will not suffice. The first level of accountability belongs to the managers; they are accountable for making it possible to get the work done and done well!

Enabling people to do well on the job creates a sense of satisfaction for them. Good performance motivates. For team level accountability, changes must be made in the assessment, feedback, and reward systems. Performance data should be collected from multiple perspectives—customers, peers, and managers (Mohrman, Cohen, & Mohrman, 1995). The differing viewpoints need to be shared and integrated to find the overlap in perceptions that represents the highest priority for change. This process is a form of 360-degree feedback.

Since team performance outcomes impact multiple levels of the organization, assessment should match that complexity. However, when assessment of the team's performance falls short of expectations, the manager must realize that many factors contribute. Perhaps one of the most important and most subtle is that of stress. With increasing pressure for speed, increasing layoffs, and added responsibility to function as an effective team, stress will distract from performance, and most of its causes will be outside the control of the team (Godard, 2001).

There has been a pattern in the evolution of theories of management and leadership away from the focus on the individual toward the focus on context. What are the enabling conditions in that context that remove the hurdles and provide the resources to high performance? This guiding question applies to the work of individuals, as well as teams. In knowledge work, the most elementary variation on this concept is for the manager to "get out of the way." Monitoring one's own behavior and identifying behaviors that impede the team's effort to achieve high performance is a beginning point for enabling.

The next simple level in enabling is sharing information. Teams make many decisions. The quality of the decisions is heavily dependant on the quality of the information they have to work with. Quality decision making depends on clear boundaries of authority, clear goals, effective discussion and decision processes, and good information. Teams that lack any of these resources will make less effective decisions—at any level in the organization.

A more advanced level of enabling involves alignment. Are the resources the team needs available and accessible, that is, are support systems aligned with team needs? If not, the support systems are either irrelevant or they become hurdles to the team. (For more information on support systems, see Chapter 1 on critical success factors.)

Finally, although performance management represents a highly developed tool for controlling worker behavior in traditional organizations, it is too narrow for team-based organizations. It must fit within a culture of commitment with features such as respect and openness, mutual accountability, and enabling systems. Southwest Airlines (Kelleher, 1997) represents a similar culture where there are shared values and goals, shared understanding, and mutual respect.

Enabling Brain Power

People typically get better at what they do frequently, learning from experience. One of the attractive features of managers who work their way up from the bottom is the fact that they will have some experience doing the tasks that line workers perform and of living in that culture. However, they are no longer doing the line work, so their knowledge is not being refreshed. Other managers have no experience at line work at all. Remember, the people doing the work know it best. Although lacking MBA degrees and possibly the ability to articulate some ideas, a team of people working on a machine or process or serving a customer will still have information, knowledge, and ideas that might improve performance and hence the margins. Konosuke Matsushita, founder of Matsushita Electronics, said the Japanese would beat the United States economically because the Japanese use "every ounce of intelligence" from every worker (www.atip.or.jp/ts/wall/). The Investors in People (IiP) organization in the United Kingdom consisting of 42,000 organizations of all sizes relies on the same concept and the idea that "The core of management is the art of mobilizing and putting together the intellectual resources of all employees in the service of the organization" (www.case-jc.demon.co.uk/iip.htm).

Few of us are Einsteins, but then Albert Einstein was only brilliant in one field—he never published a symphony or a best-selling novel or a recipe for a new tortellini in white sauce. We have three tools we can use to build the brain power of our organizations toward Einsteinian levels: (1) lifelong learning, (2) effective collaboration, and (3) multiple perspectives. The organizational environments that are designed to enhance these three tools are smarter; they continuously invent new and better ways of responding to changing markets. (For more information on these tools, see Chapter 33 on team competencies.)

Most organizations are known for doing a lot of things in ways that are not smart—the members know that, even when the customers do not. However, a lot of the dumbness is due to organizations, not to individual members. Treating line workers as incapable of thinking and making decisions dumbs down the organization in several ways. First, it reduces the number of brain cells devoted to examining opportunities for improving the organization. Second, it reduces the involvement of the line workers and hence their motivation. Work becomes "just a job," and there is a tendency to do just what is explicitly required.

The emerging field of intellectual capital (IC) takes a big picture approach to organizational intelligence and identifies ways of showing the business relevance of knowledge and the processes for creating, distributing, and utilizing it (see Bernhut, 2001; Lee, 2000; Stewart, 2001a). To reshape the phrase from finance, "a million here, a million there, and pretty soon you have some real money," consider this variation: "An intelligently functioning team here and another there and pretty soon you have a pretty smart organization." (For more information on intellectual capital, see Chapter 21.)

Performance as an Outcome of Context

Performance has often been defined as something simple, such as the number of widgets that roll off the end of the assembly line or the number of sales made by a salesperson in a quarter. Over-simplification is dangerous. First, it means that only one or two dimensions of performance are being tracked, measured, rewarded, and managed. Second, it makes a short-term perspective more likely. Third, the shift in levels of performance from individual to team to business unit tends to ignore the issue of alignment between and within levels.

Focusing on the micro level of behavior on the job ignores the power of context to influence behavior. Think of job behavior as the figure that stands out and job context as the background in this picture. There is a strong tendency to focus on the figure in any activity. Consider listening to music. The conscious mind tends to pick up the melody and follow it. People tend to whistle or hum the melody when they remember the song. They don't think about the rhythm, harmony, counter-melody, and so forth, that form the context for the melody; hence a lot of the richness is missing. At work, the systems that surround the individual and the team form the context.

Consider the operation of the human body as an analogy. At lunch, a person can pick a salad with low fat dressing, rather than a triple patty hamburger. At the highest levels of decision making, the person has made a choice based on health and longevity; at a lower level there is the need for energy for the day, satisfying the need for hunger, and perhaps social interaction and the taste of the food. At the lowest levels, the body automatically determines which parts of the meal can be utilized and goes through the process of separating those parts from the waste, processing and distributing the protein molecules, the complex carbohydrates, and so on to organs, muscles, nerve cells, and other areas. It is impossible for the diner to monitor the millions of transactions occurring at the cellular level. The data from that level is rolled upward toward the subconscious and conscious decision-making centers, so the next meal is chosen to accommodate cellular needs without noticing the cellular levels. In the organization, individual workers attend to the local; they are close to it, they can focus on it, and they know it well. The manager who attempts to do that over a number of work areas becomes a severe bottleneck to operations. Empowerment and enablement make the organization smarter. Collaboration across levels leverages the local smarts.

Empowerment and enablement make the organization smarter.

The *job description* has been a foundation piece for human resources management for decades. Typical HR practices and processes, the legal system, and even education in technical schools have been organized to use the job description as a tool for decisions about the people in the jobs. But with the shift to a team-based organization, performance must be viewed in broader terms. Accountability in a TBO involves an awareness, a concern, and action related to the bigger picture. Individuals' responsibilities broaden from "the job" to "the role" of team member and organization member. Their accountabilities broaden at the same time.

Performance represents generation of outcomes both short-term and long-term, at individual, team, business unit, and higher levels. It can be assessed by a myriad of measures—hard and soft. Measures at one level may be difficult to adapt to the next level in the organization. For example, counting "widgets" or errors or boxes shipped or other objective information is not an appropriate process for engineers or managers. Counting number of lines of code written in software or number of pages of schematic drawing produced means little without quality information. Counting number of meetings attended or hours in meetings has little value for assessing management productivity. Measurement directs attention and sends the explicit or implicit message "You are accountable for this." Other messages are sent by enabling activities. The messages need to be aligned.

Conclusion

A steel mill in Sweden uses a job description that says, "Responsible person." That's all. That's clearly enough. Acting responsibly in any circumstance that arises at work means making thoughtful, informed, caring responses to problems and opportunities. Who is capable of that? We probably all think that we ourselves are capable. But how do we perceive the others around us?

Three questions: Who is accountable? To whom? About what?

The answers differ depending on the meaning of accountability and the setting. In a TBO, a member of the organization is accountable to himself or herself as well as to teammates and managers and customers. In a customer-centric organization, accountability to a customer usually takes precedence over the others. Of course, there are both internal and external customers.

Accountability to a customer usually takes precedence.

Job description from job analysis is the most common way of defining boundaries of responsibility, but it falls short in two circumstances—knowledge-intensive work and team-based organization. There role descriptions fit better with larger scope of responsibility and more ambiguous boundaries of the task, such as when to leave your work to go help someone else. The role description of "responsible person" for every member of the organization clearly communicates that all are responsible for the success of the whole operation.

Many new initiatives have been launched in organizations in the past decade, including total quality, re-engineering, enterprise requirements planning, teams, empowerment, process management, lean manufacturing, and project management. But the success levels of many of these attempts have fallen short of expectations. One reason for this has been the failure to update the accountability system. The old paradigm for accountability is "based on the conditions of authority, control, and personal responsibility. It focuses on the individual. It divides rather than unites. It encourages blame and competition instead of trust and cooperation, and it reinforces the command and control style of management" (Martin, 2002).

In the frequently quoted definitions of the term "work team" (for example, Katzenbach & Smith, 1993, p. 45; Orsburn, Moran, Musselwhite, & Zenger, 1990, p. 8; Sundstrom, DeMuse & Futrell, 1990, p. 120), responsibility and accountability play key parts. There are other commonalities, but interdependence of members' work is probably the main one. It is the one that justifies a team level of accountability. Teams will fail if they are not held accountable for performance. But the question remains: "When are the conditions right for holding the team accountable?" Management must answer that question first. Because the first answer to the question "Who is accountable" is management.

IST, UC Berkeley's information technology support unit, is a team-based organization that makes clear statements about accountability (Samuel, 1999). Accountability applies to every member of the organization. It means people can be "counted on" to achieve goals that have been agreed to.

Counting on others to provide needed information, become involved in making relevant decisions, give support as needed, and accept support depends on a shared understanding of the goals of the organization. Counting on oneself is also a key to goal achievement that includes changing one's attitudes and behaviors as needed (Samuel, 1999). The following checklist is a self-assessment for accountability based on work at IST (http://ist.berkeley.edu/mission.shtml).

Accountability Self-Assessment

Assess how your behaviors contribute to an organization based on responsibility by checking each of the items that apply below.

Do I . . .

☐ help out or share expertise when needed?

☐ show appreciation for support from others?

☐ practice open and honest communication?

☐ treat each challenge to the team or organization as my own responsibility?

☐ avoid blaming others?

- [ ] believe a solution can be found or created?
- [ ] recognize and praise each example of good performance?
- [ ] confront unacceptable performance in a constructive manner?
- [ ] keep commitments and agreements?
- [ ] accept the responsibility that goes with each assignment and ask for clarification of the responsibility when needed?
- [ ] keep others informed about my ability to meet a deadline, so they can make adjustments when work will be late?
- [ ] think about how coordination and communication can help others in the organization attain their goals?
- [ ] make the effort to understand the priorities of the team and the organization?
- [ ] constructively help surface and resolve conflict?
- [ ] actively commit to the success of projects and services?
- [ ] participate fully in discussions and decisions?
- [ ] examine my own performance and attitudes and make adjustments?
- [ ] express pride in my team and organization?
- [ ] fight the "we versus they" mentality?
- [ ] communicate priorities, schedules, and outcomes clearly to all those affected?
- [ ] make timely decisions?
- [ ] make decisions at the most appropriate level?
- [ ] measure the effectiveness of my results and my team's results and base corrective action on those measurements?

The items in the checklist that you did not check represent opportunities for you to improve the level of accountability the organization is based on. Improvements in accountability ought to translate into improvements in performance.

CHAPTER 9

Sustaining Leadership Teams at the Top
The Promise and the Pitfalls

Mindy L. Gewirtz and Peter Gumpert

CONVENTIONAL WISDOM SUGGESTS that in order to sustain collaborative work in an organization, leaders at the top must champion participation; the belief is that they must create, communicate, and implement both a shared vision of the future and a cooperative operating philosophy. In reality, leaders at the top often have difficulty trusting each other and working together. They may compete instead of collaborate, resist working as a team, and demonstrate ambivalence about teaming in general. This chapter uses a case example to illustrate how teaming in an organization can be sustained despite difficulties and ambivalence at the top. Our premise is that top level teams must also live through the changes we ask organizations to embark on, and that small improvements in the functioning of the top executive group can provide sufficient room for strong teams near the top to sustain teaming in the remainder of the organization. The psychological characteristics of truly intractable top leadership groups are also noted and described, and methods for making necessary improvements in difficult teams at the top are suggested.

**Ideal
collaborative
top leadership
teams are
found in
relatively few
companies—
let us be
generous and
say 20 percent.**

The ideally collaborative top leadership team is found in relatively few companies—let us be generous and say 20 percent. If we depended on ideal teamwork at the top for successful organizational renewal ventures, we would avoid making the attempt in as many as 80 percent of companies. We believe that this view is far too pessimistic. We would prefer to estimate that perhaps 20 percent of companies have top leadership groups whose members are profoundly (not simply due to ignorance or casual opinion) opposed to collaboration and teaming—and are essentially intractable in this respect. This leaves some 60 percent of organizations whose top managers could be characterized as "difficult" or "resistant" to developing collaborative cultures. The purposes of this chapter are

1. To outline ways of working successfully with top leadership teams (that present substantial, but not intractable, resistance to collaboration and teaming) to enhance collaboration at the top, and to reduce their resistance to teamwork in the remainder of the organization;

2. To describe the psychological characteristics of leaders who are likely to make the development of a collaborative culture in their companies exceptionally difficult; and

3. To point out favorable outcomes that can be achieved by persistent work with difficult top leadership groups.

Some Assumptions About Organizational Change

Organizations are living organisms, rather than machines. They do not readily change their fundamental ways of operating. It is abundantly clear to us that they are not easily or durably changed through mechanical or technological means. As Peter Senge has pointed out (Webber, 1999), the successful change manager or external consultant should think of him- or herself as a gardener rather than a mechanic. Perhaps terms like "agronomist" and "ecologist" are also useful.

Many members of organizations are completely convinced, however, that their own organizations and their leaders are, in effect, immutable, and that attempts to change their particular systems are doomed to failure. Often they speak as if the shared social reality of the organization (how we understand and do things around here) was a law of nature rather than an implicit social agreement. We believe that organizations and their members can and do change. The question is not whether change can happen, but what change is needed and how that change can be seeded and helped to take root. (For more information on how to create the strategy for organizational change to team-based organizations, see Chapter 3.)

Relationships between people in an organization are important in many ways, particularly in change efforts. The way people conduct their relationships with each other affects both the people directly involved and others in the organization. Thus, as we all know, the way top leaders behave toward one another affects their subordinates; sometimes these effects are far from subtle. What is less well understood is that it can also work the other way: the ways subordinates act toward one another affects their managers as well as their peers and subordinates. These effects are certainly more subtle, but they are also real and powerful (see Deutsch, 1973 & 1985; see also the meta-analysis from Johnson & Johnson, 1989).

Even though it is easier for people to affect each other negatively rather than positively, positive interpersonal effects are quite common. Other things being equal, for example, if one person is open and truthful with another, the likelihood is greater that the listener will respond in kind. Even external organizational consultants can and do gradually induce change through the ways they behave in the organization.

One metaphor that helps guide the change strategies we use is based on a process known in biology as morphogenesis. In biology, morphogenetic structures or cells are central to the development of organisms. Such cells have the function of directing the differentiation and function of other cells in the organism, permitting the development of essential tissue and organs. Analogously, change can be created by establishing small seed groups in the organization that have the primary function of creating new structures and processes that allow the organization to change and adapt effectively to environmental shifts. These small groups create hope (which energizes change), as well as specific proposals for change. They can eventually stimulate changes in their top leadership groups as well as among their peers and in other parts of the organization.

Occasionally, top leadership groups serve the morphogenetic function we refer to. More often, however, the task falls to others. This chapter deals with the more common situation—in which the top leadership group is, for one reason or another, not fully capable of stimulating and helping to maintain changes that are required.

The Hoped For Ideal of Executive Teaming and Its Intractable Opposite

Some top leaders and top teams are far from ideal and should lead us to proceed with caution and skepticism about beginning a transformation to collaborative work.

Anyone who has tried to do large-scale organizational change hopes to find in a new venture the ideal top executive team—one that will model, champion, and sustain a collaborative system in which people at all levels have the authority to make local decisions on behalf of the organization's goals.

Yet some top leaders and top teams are far from the ideal—indeed, some should lead us to proceed with caution and skepticism about beginning a transformation to broad, sustained collaborative work in the organization. The characteristics of both ideal top teams and exceptionally difficult leaders and teams are outlined in Table 9.1.

Table 9.1. Leadership Team Qualities

Characteristics of Ideal Executive Teams	Characteristics of Exceptionally Difficult Top Leaders and Teams
• The team fosters a jointly created vision of the future and a jointly created roadmap toward that future.	Exceptionally difficult top leaders have three or more of the personal characteristics listed below:
• The team implements consistent communication to everyone about the future, without assuming or expecting that direct reports will tell others in the organization.	• An underlying personal fragility or insecurity, often covered by grandiosity and the appearance of undue certainty about his or her own opinions.
• The team has developed a well-articulated set of operating values—a "philosophy" that makes priorities clear and guides how people will be treated in the organization.	• A tendency to criticize and undervalue organizational subordinates and to treat peers and others with contempt.
• The team communicates a clear set of goals for the current time period.	• A deeply held conviction that only individual "heroes" can accomplish great things, accompanied by a belief that non-heroes should simply do what they are told.
• The team has the ability to resolve internal conflicts productively.	• A consistent inability to trust even when trust is indicated.
• The team maintains a strong and clearly communicated sense of reality about what the organization faces and a reliable respect for the truth.	• A tendency to have a "honeymoon" period with newly hired subordinates, followed by disappointment; new hires "fall out of favor" as easily as they are idealized.
• The team emphasizes joint decision making within the team and a strong and mutually respectful dialectical process that maximizes the quality of their decisions.	• A tendency to hoard information and knowledge. • A demand for personal loyalty among subordinates. • A tendency to use subordinates to achieve political ends. • Overreliance on the use of power (rewards and punishments) to ensure loyalty and compliance.

Table 9.1. Leadership Team Qualities, Cont'd

Characteristics of Ideal Executive Teams	Characteristics of Exceptionally Difficult Top Leaders and Teams
• Team members avoid political maneuvering directed at other executive team members or their subordinates.	• Apparent suspicion that cross-functional collaboration has or can have subversive or disloyal consequences.
• Team members have the capacity to remain calm in the face of adversity and turbulence, and nevertheless recognize openly that others are agitated and distressed by adversity or uncertainty in the environment.	Exceptionally difficult top leadership groups have several (three or more) of the characteristics listed below:
• The team and its members engage in and encourage consistent recognition of the efforts and successes of others, individually and in teams.	• Members systematically withhold information from one another and/or tend to mislead each other about actions or intentions.
• Members show a willingness to delegate action to others without micro-management of methods.	• Members avoid meetings with each other and have great difficulty working in cooperation with each other unless there is a serious crisis.
• The team and its members can be relied on to provide strong, consistent championing of the development of people and teams.	• Members devalue each other in private and talk negatively about other members of top leadership to their own subordinates.
	• "Two against one" coalitions often form in the group.
	• Members feel they must protect themselves or subordinates against one or more other members of the top leadership group.
	• Members have unusual difficulty coming to agreements and frequent difficulty in keeping agreements they do make.
	• Members devalue other members and subordinates.

The systems theory principle of *isomorphism* (the tendency of processes to function similarly across elements in a system; in organizations this may be expressed as the notion that group processes present in one part of the organization tend to be passed up, down, and across to others) leads us to predict that organizations whose top groups have serious interpersonal problems can be expected to have similar difficulties elsewhere, such as the following:

- When people at the top don't trust one another, their direct reports will also have difficulty trusting, especially across functional lines (but also within functions). Mistrust at the top—and the lack of capacity for "benevolent misperception"(assuming the other's motives are non-malicious)—breeds mistrust below.

- Silos created at the top beget silos throughout the organization.

If top executives insist on their own heroism, they will tend to hire and promote "heroes" and encourage them to act as if they were singly responsible for results. Heroes easily become incompetents or villains. Hero status is highly seductive, and hero-designates work very hard to avoid falling from grace, sometimes even if others (and the company) have to suffer in the process.

- "Lone hero" accountability leads people to do whatever they can to protect themselves from the appearance of mistakes and failures. This often leads to blaming others, covering for errors, and making decisions and taking actions that optimize the outcomes of single functions or departments rather than the whole organization. On the other hand, those who are not in special favor tend to avoid responsibility for decisions.

- Both mistrust and sole dependency on the individual accountability method keep information from flowing easily across functional lines and keep people in different functions from using one another fully in the search for optimal decisions and actions that will benefit the whole.

It is less frequently recognized and understood that isomorphism can go both ways: people and teams below the top of the organization can and do have influence on how the top team works. Influence goes upward and sideways as well as downward, particularly if influence attempts are consistent, calmly persistent, and contain consistent actions as well as words. Our own work is grounded in this notion.

Since transformational initiatives can and sometimes do fail because of hostility toward them at the top, it seems sensible at first glance to set the bar for top executive groups pretty high. The reality, however, is that the top leadership groups of many companies show evidence of ambivalence about collaboration and teaming (Katzenbach, 1998).

We can find ways to reduce the skepticism and ambivalence about collaboration and change leadership behaviors to sustain teaming. Instead of writing off these organizations or labeling them as poor risks, can we find ways to reduce the skepticism and ambivalence and change their leadership behaviors enough to sustain teaming? We suggest that despite the difficulties of executive teamwork, and despite difficult individual leaders, top groups can experience enough growth to sustain themselves as a team and can generate sufficient empowerment for the management teams below them to sustain a substantial level of collaborative work throughout the organization.

Case Illustration:
A Difficult, Ambivalent Executive Team

The difficulties of problematic executive teams can appear insurmountable. This was true in the case of one executive committee (three members—CEO, CFO, COO) of a $500M company.* The members of this executive committee had experienced exceptionally serious interpersonal difficulty when we began working with them, and were known to have created much difficulty for the remainder of the organization.

In the context of presenting this case, we will review our methods of facilitating problematic top teams, focusing on the following issues:

- How to recognize the difficulties, unconscious processes, and obstacles to successful teaming at the top—and how the organization can conspire to drive executives apart;

- What can be expected in difficult top teams, and how they can be solidified and maintained;

- How to recognize and understand the limitations of a top team as the champion of a change process;

- How to help top leaders shift from simply "talking or waiting to talk" to creating genuine dialogue that builds trust and effective decision making; and

- How top teams whose members are ambivalent about teaming can nevertheless contribute to the durability of change—and what is needed, at minimum, for them to do so.

Our role in this organization was to help transform the company from a command-and-control system to a collaborative, team-based operation. The initial organizational assessment (conducted through in-depth interviews) indicated serious systemic problems throughout the organization. For example, valuable information was frequently

---

* While based on our client experiences, the information provided in this case illustration is a composite of several of our experiences with top groups. It is not intended to refer to the specifics of a particular group or company.

lost or not shared due to stove-piped, competitive relationships among divisions and departments. Employees experienced operations as poorly planned and executed, which resulted in considerable chaos, quality problems, and late deliveries to customers. Errors were hidden, and finding someone to blame was the most common reaction to falling short.

As part of his determination to transform the company, the CEO became more open to transforming the culture of the organization from a traditional to a more participative and collaborative organization. The proposed culture change, in which we had a part, was intended to support the strategic plan, which required rapid development of increasingly innovative and complex products, without compromising quality and on-time delivery. The CEO renewed his commitment (despite ambivalence from his executive team members) to a multi-level approach to transformation. (For more information on gaining commitment to collaborative, high performing work systems, see Chapter 16.) This approach integrated the creation of cross-functional teams at the senior and middle management levels with team skills development at all levels and individual coaching where required.

Development of the Executive Team

During the year preceding our involvement with the executive team, we worked with a divisional cross-functional steering committee (a cross-functional "seed group") to map and design the strategy and implementation of training and team development for the next eighteen months. In addition to a policy and planning team, a daily operations team was created for each of two divisions. Approximately seven hundred people participated in teamwork training, and twenty-eight teams were developed and sustained during this time. Human resources began to integrate team training into its orientation of new hires.

During the year, we frequently met with the CEO to discuss the change process. He expressed that he was a great proponent of teaming, and he felt he needed to change some of his own style before he could expect other members of the executive group to change. His ambivalence tended to assert itself when financial and marketplace pressures became intense. But the rapidly changing marketplace, coupled with increasing pressure from senior and middle management teams who agitated upward for change, helped persuade the CEO to require the CFO and the COO to join him in facilitated executive team meetings, with an agenda that included both development of teamwork skills and making important day-to-day business decisions.

Thus the top executive group began its own work a full year into the broad transformation process—after several failed attempts to get the group together. Although the CEO supported the transformation process, the COO and the CFO both publicly and privately expressed their disdain for this most recent "flavor of the month," what they called a "make-nice" program. They firmly believed that the future of the company should be in the hands of "a few good men," and that the company needed only to hire those competent senior people.

Managers below the top level put steady pressure on the executive team to change its practices. "Our changing is only a first step," the managers from below argued. "We need the executive group to stop fighting in public and to stop sending us conflicting messages. We need a unified direction if we are to be successful in facing the challenges of the future."

The pressure to "do something" within the executive committee itself began to be more intense as executive committee members found their decisions repeatedly undermined by other executive committee members. The discord had become so great that members had not been able to agree even on a time to meet for six months.

Setting the Stage for the Initial Intervention
The three men—COO, CFO, and CEO—were all politically astute and had worked in the company for a long time. The CEO together with the two other men had successfully brought the company back from the brink of bankruptcy decades earlier. The three men were

consummately skilled survivors of many skirmishes and outright wars within the company.

Each member was used to running his own show without consulting others. We established one ground rule as a prerequisite for proceeding: to create a stable framework of consistent monthly meetings of three uninterrupted hours each. We also suggested that the Executive Committee be renamed the Executive Team.

The psychological impact of creating a special time and a new name signaled an opportunity to change the way members of this group worked together.

When we began working with the executive team, we had already established credibility working with difficult teams elsewhere in the organization. It must be admitted, however, that we were not fully prepared for the pain, secrets, and disappointments that these men had carried with them for two decades. It became easier for us to understand why the three men seldom found "time" to meet. When they did meet, they often had heated conversations. Each member preferred to talk to the others one at a time—or not at all—since reaching consensus was too difficult. Each preferred to "beg forgiveness, rather than ask permission," and to take unilateral action in the organization, earning the anger and resentment of the others. Each person worried that when he went on vacation, one of the others might choose to make a critical decision without consultation. Each man perceived the others as smart, not to be trusted fully, and at times undermining. Yet, they each respected the vision of the CEO, the marketing efforts of the COO, and the ability of the CFO to work magic with the financial community. Indeed, the three individual executives had managed, in the previous decade, to position the organization toward great success.

Creating a special time and new name signaled a change in the way the group worked together.

Early Stage Intervention Strategies Create Safety

We began by meeting with each member of the group individually—and each expressed strong reluctance to meet. Each member told us that the only significant outcome of group meetings would rest on our ability to influence the other members to change their behavior. No one, except perhaps the CEO, had any thoughts about what *he* needed to change. Thus each member shared great frustration about his lack of success in influencing the others. Each expressed a profound distrust of at least one other member, based on unresolved interpersonal incidents that had been festering for years. Each member shared the concern that the organization would be in serious jeopardy if any of the other members ran the company solely from his own perspective. Two members were openly skeptical about whether the meetings could be productive.

Thus we immediately faced skepticism and resistance to change, even to the idea of meeting as a group. According to social psychologist Harold Kelley (1973), the "fundamental attribution error" we all tend to make is to interpret the bulk of human behavior as rooted in the stable personal attributes of the person we happen to be observing. In reality, much of people's behavior is in response to social or environmental forces we as observers don't see directly. What made working in this group particularly difficult was their "pathological certainty" about the correctness of their interpretations of the others' behavior. Each member harbored opinions about the characteristics of the others that made their deep mistrust very difficult to unfreeze. When mistrust is paired with poor and unreliable communication, the use of power and manipulation can become the dominant mode of influence. Members tended to influence each other by determining who could either adopt the most intimidating posture or manipulate information most persuasively in service of an opinion or desired course of action.

Our critical task was to create a containing or holding environment where difficult issues could surface and be discussed.

We felt that our critical task during the first three sessions was to *create a containing or holding environment* (Heifetz, 1994) (see Table 9.2, #1, near the end of the chapter) in which the trio's difficult issues could come to the surface and begin to be discussed and understood differently.

Thus we established norms for the meetings and the authorization to identify and discuss interpersonal or group process issues as they arose. We set firm boundaries that helped members feel safe enough to raise their deeply held conflicts and helped them understand emotional eruptions so they could *identify and manage their "pathological certainty"* (see Table 9.2, #2) when it arose. For the first few encounters, members continued to experience the team meetings as learning how "to make nice"—meaning that they would refrain from shouting to get their ideas across. They still discounted the general concept of teaming, but each could acknowledge the value of having a better relationship with the others. Each member understood how he wanted the others to change and learned quickly that the others wanted him to change as well.

During meetings we helped members reframe their conflicts so their problems could be heard and understood by the others. We also met with members individually between team meetings to give each a safe space to say things they did not yet feel comfortable saying in the group.

We recorded and published confidential, detailed minutes of each meeting *to counter this group's version of organizational amnesia* (see Table 9.2, #3). The minutes became a device that reminded members of what they had discussed and what they had agreed to in the prior meetings. While members were not sure they liked the minutes, they eventually found them useful.

Creating Interpersonal Trust

We began to rebuild mutual trust and respect among members by *creating a structure and process for reframing the most volatile issues* (see Table 9.2, #4) so they could be discussed and resolved. One of the first volatile issues raised about the CEO was the way he defined his "open door" policy regarding employees. The CEO perceived himself as the ultimate advocate of the people. He believed the other two men used command and control as their dominant management style. The other two reminded the CEO that his own change in behavior was of recent vintage and that he often lapsed into the same interpersonal style in his discussions with them. The CEO replied that at least he was willing to try to change, but that the other two were not even willing to acknowledge they needed to change.

The other two members had no problem with the CEO playing the role of ultimate advocate for people. They felt, however, that the CEO used his open door policy as a cover to bring in their subordinates, without the knowledge of the top executive involved. They were convinced that this procedure was disturbing to subordinates and that it was disruptive to internal operations. Both members were distressed that the CEO "went behind their backs to get information." His actions made them feel untrusted by him and untrusting of his motives. The CEO countered that he did not get enough information and worried that the others were shaping the information and not providing the full, accurate perspective that would permit him to be effective. As the dialogue between the men opened up decades-old wounds, they had a difficult time controlling their emotions. The facilitation helped the men *reduce their discomfort by transforming the conflicts of the past into a hope for a different future* (see Table 9.2, #5).

Gradually the men worked out an agreement about the initially presented problem that clarified and resolved this conflict in a way they could all live with. They agreed that employees were always welcome to go to the CEO. Members clarified and agreed about the conditions under which the CEO could meet with their subordinates at his request: he was to inform the others of his intention and be careful to avoid undermining the others' authority. Once this issue was resolved, the next pressing issue emerged: how could each grant the others autonomy regarding decisions that might or might not require the input of the others? This issue, among others, was dealt with in the next stage of the group's development.

Accomplishments of the Early Stage

There were three major accomplishments in the early stage. First, the executives overcame their ambivalence to meeting as it became less painful and agreed to meet on a regular basis for the next several months.

162 The Collaborative Work Systems Fieldbook

Second, the executives were willing to engage in a dialogue regarding some "hot" conflicts in a way that did not lead to explosions, and instead opened the way for productive processing of conflict. Third, senior management subordinates noted to us with great relief that the incidence of difficult encounters in public among the three executives had significantly diminished. Thus, the top executives had begun to move toward a more productive way to air their differences and resolve conflicts.

What We Learned in the Early Stage

We reminded ourselves that consultants have to create safety for themselves as well as for members of the group they are working with. We were able to help the group "hold" (and not act on) long-term resentment about past injuries. We worked with the difficult feelings and members' ambivalence about working with us by creating our own pre- and post-meeting dialogue. We referred to this as our *own detoxification process* (see Table 9.2, #6). We named our fears and our own anger and created useful responses to them. We validated our autonomy and clarified our bottom line. We decided early on that we needed to be truthful and impactful and could live comfortably with the worst-case consequence of being summarily fired.

We experienced a powerful paradox each time we met with the executive team. On the one hand, members hoped that past wrongs would be made right, that they would be less misunderstood, and that they could exert more influence on the others. On the other hand, members shared the conviction that the behaviors of other members would never change. This ambivalence to working with each other, and to teaming in general, extended to working with us. Although it was never fully resolved, it did abate sufficiently for change to occur in the group, which had positive effects on the remainder of the organization.

Ambivalence to teaming is expressed in many ways and is often aimed at the consultants. We knew the resistance was being stirred up when a session began with an overt or covert attack on the entire teaming project or an expressed wish to slow down the project because of the pressure of time or money. We countered this normal, predictable resistance to change by gently shifting members back to working on their own issues. Some of the members poked, prodded, or tried to intimidate us. At times one or another of them attempted to render one of us weak and the other strong to determine whether we could be split and thus made ineffective. We understood and interpreted their probing and prodding of our professional and emotional competence as an expression of their own ambivalence and their need to be certain we were strong enough to withstand the pressure of helping them work through their rage and their disappointments.

We learned that *modeling strong cross-gender teaming* (see Table 9.2, #7), taking turns facilitating and writing minutes, or leading the meeting jointly had a powerful effect on the client group. We modeled collaborative, integrated behavior, interchanging instrumental and care-taking roles, and made it clear that we could not be split.

We learned that our *speaking the truth* (see Table 9.2, #8), no matter how painful, gained the respect of members and challenged them to speak the truth with each other. Members respected that we did not seem afraid of their anger with each other and that we were not concerned about whether their power threatened our long-term work in the company. We learned how to calibrate our internal compasses with each other to make sure we could steer a course for the future without tripping over the many interpersonal minefields we encountered. We learned early on to contain our own expectations for change by identifying realistic goals. The first goal, to have members meet on a regular basis, was achieved. Movement toward the second goal, to provide a safe and containing space for them to air grievances and build trust, was evident.

The Middle Stage of the Work with the Executive Team
Resistance during the middle stage (three to six months) moved from creating structures and boundaries for fundamental safety (scheduling and attending meetings) to *building a track record of success*

for productively resolving conflicts, solving difficult problems, and making difficult decisions (see Table 9.2, #9). (For more information on managing and resolving conflict to improve collaboration, see Chapters 19 and 31.) A severe conflict arose about naming two new vice presidents. The CEO wanted to promote from within, while the other two wanted to bring in people from the outside. The underlying and more explosive issue was succession planning; all three acknowledged this, and nevertheless continued to resist confronting the issue.

We approached the issue gradually, by asking members to clarify the leadership skills required for success in the 21st Century. They could agree on core competence questions, but differed about leadership style. The CEO was committed to promoting people who were collaborative rather than authoritarian. The other two preferred generals who, like themselves, could roll up their sleeves and make things happen by sheer force of will. The problem was that these executive team members had never really developed anyone internally, so no one in the organization was seen as having the requisite experience to take on broader responsibilities. The dilemma of bringing in someone from the outside was that anyone new would require a year or more to get up-to-speed, and time was a critical factor.

We helped members bring to the surface the underlying need for succession planning and leadership development. The team then created a task force charged with developing a process for accelerated leadership development and a solid performance appraisal process for the entire organization. The conflict regarding the two specific vice presidential positions was resolved through a process of dialogue in which the current competence of insiders and their need for development were weighed against the difficulties of bringing someone in from the outside.

The men had considerable difficulty learning the skills involved in *iterative dialogue* (see Table 9.2, #10). They first learned how to check their understandings and underlying assumptions with each other before proceeding with their own argument. They learned how to ask questions in a neutral inquiry tone rather than in attack mode. Their negative assumptions about the others began to diminish in potency, making room for genuine reflection about mistakes and questionable assumptions, and for learning. Slowly they reduced their mistrust, very gradually *building the capacity for interpersonal trust and "benevolent misperception"* (see Table 9.2, #11). The executives finally resolved the promotion issue, for example, by agreeing on the criteria for promoting from within using objective performance measures. Using this strategy, they agreed to promote one of the men from within and to hire the other one from the outside.

What Was Accomplished During the Middle Stage

Team members learned to influence one another through dialogue rather than sheer power and manipulation.

Team members began to learn how to influence one another through *dialogue* as the engine of a dialectical process instead of using sheer power and manipulation. Members learned to articulate what each needed from the others, particularly regarding decision-making autonomy. Members also learned that resolving longstanding conflicts was more important than determining who had been most severely wronged by the others over the years. Some "deep-seated personality" attributions were gradually reframed as systemic conflicts over vision, goals, roles, and the future of the organization.

The earlier issue of the CEO as the ultimate advocate of people was revisited and led the group to clarify what leadership qualities were necessary for a leader who was also the advocate of the people. The others worried that the CEO's new emphasis in this area meant a lessening of his commitment to business needs. The CFO in particular worried that financial concerns would take a back seat to "people" issues. The COO worried that his expansionist vision would be curtailed by the financial conservatism of the CFO. The members clarified their understanding of the issues and came to agreement regarding the emphasis on people as well as business competence.

Members began to use the beginning fifteen minutes of each session to discuss important business issues of the moment. They each took the opportunity to discuss the most important crises of the week. Their team meetings were beginning to have a life and value of their own.

What We Learned During the Middle Stage

We reaffirmed the principle that resistance never stops; it just takes different forms throughout the process of change. We learned that working on business issues and interpersonal issues within each session can be highly effective in creating durable learning. During the first stage, interpersonal conflicts were resolved just enough to free up the team's energy for business issues. In the middle stage, the reverse occurred: business issues sometimes took center stage, but members always came back to their need to understand and resolve interpersonal issues. Successful work on business problems gave them confidence to continue the more difficult work. This looped learning curve seems inherent in the process of changing executive groups with substantial difficulties working together.

Perhaps most important was a discovery that surprised us a bit: that groups such as the one we are describing can actually develop the capacity for dialogue over a few months' time. This capacity is reflected in gradual, observable changes in their behavior.

Sustaining the Team and Terminating the Top-Team Intervention

As the potency of interpersonal conflicts subsided, resistance to change surfaced in members as a kind of "flight into health," in which they tried to end the facilitated meetings by substituting for them a commitment to their own weekly team meetings. In part, they were eager to try to work things out without outside help. The most difficult task, then, belonged to the ending phase: trying to sustain the team's decisions and action plans for the long term.

We did, of course, continue the facilitated meetings for a time. During this stage we were more easily able to *hold up a mirror to members* (see Table 9.2, #12) and worked more openly to show how what they did affected each other and the rest of the organization. They could now accept how their mistrust, lack of communication, and withholding of knowledge had its parallels in the remainder of the organization.

Members now felt more comfortable raising and discussing potentially volatile issues at the beginning of the process, rather than waiting until the conflict became so unbearable that they could only explode at one another. Joint decisions began to be made regarding the criteria and time lines for promoting the inside vice president and hiring a vice president from the outside. Members agreed to expand their team to include a trusted external company advisor. This, they felt, would help modulate the tendency for triangulation among the three original members. The members also agreed to expand the team in the future to include the vice presidents, and in principle agreed to the creation of a cross-functional senior management team that would begin working on the future vision and direction for the company. This structural agreement strengthened the organization's movement toward a team-based organization.

Members decided on a date to end the consultant-facilitated meetings. They immediately began meeting weekly for ninety minutes, and they protected this meeting time for a long period. Members agreed to have *individual coaching* (see Table 9.2, #13) replace the jointly facilitated meetings as a way to solidify individual learning. The CEO had begun to understand that teaming and participative leadership involves far more than effective communication skills—that it requires engaging in dialectic processes and dialogue about ideas to maximize the quality of decisions and to improve performance. Some months later the team created a strategic council empowered to look at the long-range direction of the organization. The strategic council later took on internal organizational issues as well. More broadly, the executive team was less skeptical about the usefulness of teaming in the remainder of the organization, and their changed behavior strengthened other teams in the organization.

What We Learned During the Termination Period

The longer we work in difficult organizational environments, the more we learn about the importance of *honoring, riding, and managing (rather than controlling) resistance* (see Table 9.2, #14). Individual and interpersonal changes in top teams can occur, even when there is little confidence and great ambivalence about them. To the extent that we can work with the ambivalence and resistance in the top team, more support is available for general collaboration within the organization. Thus in contradistinction to conventional theories regarding the absolute necessity of commitment from the top at the beginning of the process, successful organizational strategies can be created in organizations in which resistance is endemic to the system, and there is ambivalence at the top.

We learned once again that having three members in a team creates ideal conditions for triangulation and unproductive coalition formation. Adding a fourth member can help provide a more stable structure for good decision making.

Executives learned that participative leadership is not "icing on the cake" or being polite or "making nice."

We were relieved to find that even these executives could learn through their own experiences that participative leadership is not "icing on the cake" or being polite or "making nice." (For more information on participative leadership, see Chapters 7, 14, and 15.) Only after members live through the process themselves do they begin to grasp certain essential concepts, such as the importance of recognizing the legitimacy of the other's interests; viewing a conflict as a common problem; the importance of "benevolent misperception"; and the importance of honest communication and dialogue. When these and a few other principles are well internalized, a group can move toward being a truly collaborative team.

Intervention Summary

What is the minimum that we must expect from top teams in order to sustain teaming in the remainder of the organization?

1. Although many top teams fall short of the ideal, there is a minimum we should expect. That minimum includes the capacity to work together in a way that does not damage those below them in the organization.

2. There must be at least some positive sentiment in the top executive group about teamwork and collaboration. Teams below can tolerate ambivalence, but not implacable and consistent hostility to teamwork.

3. At least one reasonably strong and consistent champion at the top must be available to help provide initial momentum for the change.

4. Ambivalent top teams must experience enough pain and distress to lead them to take a chance on bringing an outsider into their world to effect change.

What team intervention principles can generate improvement and help top leadership teams sustain themselves during change and turbulence?

1. The establishment *of safety and trust is the* foundation for all progress in top teams and teaming in general. Without a strong interpersonal foundation for safety and trust, issues and conflicts "cycle" back to trust so that people (and the team) cannot proceed toward functioning with greater autonomy or toward further developmental steps.

2. Executives must, from time to time, endure high levels of stress and toxicity as part of their leadership function. Having a safe place to "detox" helps manage negative emotions and releases fresh energy to work productively.

3. Creating a new structure with flexible yet firm boundaries can help establish a safe "holding environment" for even the most troubled group. Creating durable safety, however, requires peeling away at many layers of the onion. Once one difficult issue surfaces and is resolved, members have the courage and energy to reach for the next pressing issue.

4. Every team requires some *level of consistency of meeting structure* and enough interpersonal safety and trust to allow members to bring difficult issues to the team for discussion and resolution.

5. *Resolving interpersonal and organizational issues often are interdependent.* Separating out, containing, and dealing with knotty interpersonal problems can create space for the development of novel approaches to organizational issues.

6. Executives must be motivated *and have the skills to engage in ongoing dialectical conversations* in order to solve problems together. Dialogue in the group becomes a method of normalizing the change and turbulence the group must frequently endure.

All of the principles called out in the case presented are summarized in Table 9.2.

Table 9.2. Intervention Principles

Principle	Description/Comments
1. Creating safety and a holding environment (includes individual meetings between team meetings; absorbing the hostility and toxicity of the relational process)	The term "holding environment" refers to a set of processes that allows people to remain in contact with the experience of distressing internal stimuli (anger, intense anxiety, and so forth) or external circumstances, permitting them to emerge from the difficult experience with an enhanced sense of capability or understanding. The term stems from attempts to understand the interpersonal environment that facilitates childhood and adolescent development.
2. Identifying and reducing "pathological certainty"	We view certainty as a powerful inhibitor of curiosity, further thinking, and creativity. Certainty is particularly "pathological" when the person or group is not conscious of the defensive function it is serving.
3. Countering organizational and member amnesia	The tendency to forget something that has happened or has been agreed to in a group—usually something different from the normal—is a common manifestation of group resistance to change. It is often seen in groups and organizations that are strongly motivated to hold on to familiar patterns of thought and behavior.
4. Reframing/reinterpreting/testing member behavior	Consultant reinterpretations of the actions of a person or group are often helpful in the task of changing the negative assumptions and actions that are usually part of destructive conflict resolution.
5. Reducing distress and creating hope for the future	Both distress and hopelessness interfere with creativity and creative collaboration. Feelings of shame are often accompanied by the wish to be isolated and by other negative feelings. Hope that a solution can be found despite difficulties is required for productive work to be done on serious problems.
6. Creating for consultants safety and a process for consultant "detoxification"	Consultants are frequently affected by the actions taken and the feelings experienced and expressed by the people they work with. In order to understand what is happening and to recover their perspective, consultants can (and should) talk in private about difficult events they have witnessed and the feelings generated by them.
7. Modeling strong teaming	Difficult client groups can attempt in subtle ways to split the consultants working with them. If they succeed in doing so, the consultant intervention is likely to fail; if the team remains strong under pressure, the client group is more likely to feel "held" by the consultants.
8. Giving fearless voice to uncomfortable truths—the role of the barbarian	Difficult issues—including the ones no one in the group will give voice to—must be "put on the table" by the consultants in order to show that the group is not irreparably damaged by their articulation or by discussion of such issues.
9. Building a track record of success: productively resolved conflicts, difficult problems solved, difficult decisions made	Success breeds the confidence needed to tackle the next set of problems.

Table 9.2. Intervention Principles, Cont'd

Principle	Description/Comments
10. Teaching the elements of dialogue	Dialogue is a conversation in which people think together in relationship, requiring that each participant no longer take his or her own position as final. The participants relax their grip on certainty and listen for the possibilities that result simply from working through different perspectives—possibilities that might not otherwise have occurred.
11. Reducing mistrust and (very gradually) building trust and "benevolent misperception"	"Benevolent misperception," a term coined by marital therapists, refers to an interpretation that someone makes of another's ambiguous act or utterance. The act is interpreted in a favorable light, implying good intentions toward the self. Therapists say that benevolent misperception is a key ingredient in good marriages; this is probably true of work partnerships as well.
12. Holding up a mirror to the team and the consequences of its process	Executive groups are often blind to the consequences to others in the organization of the actions they take.
13. Augmenting team building with individual coaching	Frequently individual members of teams lack interpersonal and other leadership skills that cannot be addressed in team meetings. These individuals can sometimes benefit substantially from individual coaching; such a benefit is also reflected in the team's success.
14. Honoring and working with ambivalence and resistance to change	Change and resistance to change inevitably go together. It is far more useful to name and respect the resistance than to try to overwhelm it. Much the same can be said for ambivalence. Often resistance and ambivalence are based on perfectly reasonable concerns that are worth addressing directly.

The Significance of Facilitation Approaches and Challenges Faced by Internal Consultants

With one or two exceptions, the important intervention principles listed in Table 9.2 are not easily translated into "techniques" of facilitation. The shifting interpersonal dynamics involved are complex and delicate and require of the facilitator substantial experience, agility, and sensitivity to intrapersonal dynamics—not unlike what is required of group psychotherapists. We certainly prepared meeting agendas carefully, and did our best through an introduction to set the tone and modest goals for each meeting. We also built and maintained the holding environment in simple ways—by starting and ending on time, holding carefully to our agreements, ground rules, and agendas, and otherwise keeping surprises to a minimum. Beyond that, we listened carefully and empathically and created a flow of events that shifted subtly.

When facilitating difficult top teams, internal consultants should consider how their role in the system might affect their capacity to create safety and trust. Internal consultants may not be perceived as neutral, since they live inside the system, and may report to a member of the top team. Indeed, they may be more vulnerable than external consultants to the implicit or explicit demands top leaders might make. While external consultants can certainly be fired, they are less dependent on a particular client organization.

In preparing to facilitate top teams, internal consultants may find it useful to identify their preconceived assumptions about team members and how their role and position in the organization may affect their work. Setting ground rules for confidentiality within the team sessions and discussing the concerns of team members regarding the facilitation process may help team members feel more comfortable sharing sensitive issues in the presence of the internal consultants. For the consultants themselves, finding an appropriate, confidential way (using either internal or external resources) to process difficult sessions is important; such a resource will help them maintain or recover their perspective.

Concluding Thoughts

Helping top team members to change, as they live through the changes we ask of the organization, can be difficult. The road to enduring change is nearly always full of pitfalls. Senior management groups are seldom completely out of touch with the difficult realities that face their business, however. They can be shaken away from comfortable certainty by judicious intervention, together with persistent demands from the level of management below them. When they do change visibly, even if the process is slow, the change is not lost on their direct reports. The teams near the top are sustained and energized—and this flow helps sustain teaming throughout the organization. Understanding that top leaders have taken the risk of changing their behavior sends a compelling message. It helps others in the organization contain their own ambivalence and provides hope that the organizational ocean liner can finally be turned. Once there is hope, the organization has a fighting chance for durable success.

For the consultant or internal change agent, we have tried to convey three major messages. First, we have argued that the task of changing difficult top leadership groups should not be undertaken as a solo endeavor. Trusted colleagues who can listen empathically and help when necessary should be considered a necessity rather than a luxury for this kind of task. Second, we have suggested that a deep understanding of individual as well as group dynamics may also be essential; we believe that clinical training, and experience with group psychotherapy, can be very useful for consultants who work at this level. Finally, and perhaps most importantly, this task cannot be approached as if there were a technology that can be applied to it.

 It requires consistent, ongoing data collection and interpretation and a consistent willingness to invent solutions as circumstances change. We hope that this perspective on working with resistant and difficult senior management teams can encourage others to take the risk of engaging in this work.

CHAPTER 10

Developing and Assessing a Climate for Creativity in Virtual Teams

Jill E. Nemiro

IN TODAY'S COMPETITIVE BUSINESS ENVIRONMENT, where innovation and "speed to market" are crucial, teaming is essential in order to bring key contributors together to focus on joint work objectives and common problems and to develop innovative solutions. Advances in information technology have enabled the best minds to come together wherever they reside. Today, teaming opportunities exist not only with one's co-workers at the home office, but with people everywhere. Thus, a new type of team is developing, called a *virtual team*. (For more information on virtual teams, see Chapters 22 and 30.) These teams consist of geographically dispersed organizational members who communicate and carry out their activities through information technology (Lipnack & Stamps, 1997; Nemiro, 1998).

Several forces are accelerating this trend toward the accomplishment of work through virtual teams. One key driver for virtual work is increasing globalization. As the marketplace has become more global, organizations must bring members closer to the customer to be responsive to customers' needs. And as competition has grown more fierce, the needed amount of expertise and information has expanded, creating a need to bring diverse talents and expertise to bear on complex projects. Dispersed or virtual teams can leverage the expertise by putting people together on projects without relocating them.

Virtual teams with an eye for creativity are helping businesses meet new market conditions.

Virtual teams with an eye for *creativity* are helping businesses of all kinds meet these new market conditions. Those who manage and are part of virtual teams must be aware of how to enhance creativity in these new work structures. What then can team designers, team leaders, and managers do to help virtual teams realize their creativity? The answer to that question is relatively simple—*create an organizational climate that fosters and supports creativity in virtual teams.* In this chapter, I will describe a theory I have developed to characterize the climate for creativity specifically for virtual teams and will illustrate this theory through the experiences of one particular virtual team. Further, I will introduce a new tool I designed to assess the climate for creativity in virtual teams. Finally, I will offer a set of tips for developing a positive climate for creativity within a virtual team.

A Theory of the Climate for Creativity in Virtual Teams

The theory is based on a two-year investigation in which I primarily examined the work environment necessary for virtual teams to be creative (Nemiro, 1998, 2000a). Selected members from nine different virtual teams (a total of thirty-six individuals) were interviewed about their high and low creativity experiences within their teams. The nine teams varied within respect to the nature of their work. Three teams were organizational consulting firms, two teams were in the field of education, three teams were online service provider teams, and one team was a product design engineering team. From an analysis of the interview data, eleven dimensions that influenced virtual team members' creativity emerged:

1. *Acceptance of ideas and constructive tension.* Ideas and input are encouraged, valued, and accepted by all members of the team without unnecessary criticism; a high degree of honesty exists among team members, leading individuals to feel comfortable not only in sharing their own ideas, but in giving open and honest feedback to one another as well; constructive tension emanating from a mix of differing views and opinions.

2. *Challenge.* A sense of challenge arising from the intriguing and enjoyable nature of a problem or task presented to the group, the urgent needs of a particular situation, or the desire to push for something new and move away from the status quo.

3. *Collaboration.* The ability to pull together and work closely and comfortably together to complete an interdependent task, pursue a mutual interest, or pursue a jointly held intriguing idea.

4. *Dedication/Commitment.* A sense of dedication, intense involvement, and commitment to the work; the ability to work hard on difficult tasks and problems and persevere.

5. *Freedom.* The freedom to decide how to do the work; freedom to do the work at one's own pace; freedom from evaluation, surveillance, or having to meet someone else's constraints.

6. *Goal Clarity.* Clearly defined and developed goals (through constant clarification and feedback); goals shared by all team members.

7. *Information Sharing.* Regular communication; sharing the results of one's efforts; providing needed information; timely updating of information.

8. *Management Encouragement.* Management that is encouraging, enthusiastic, and supportive of new ideas and new ways of doing things.

9. *Personal Bond.* A personal connection among team members; a "family-like" feeling; a sense of connection that goes beyond common goals and commitment to the work to a bond in which team members are also committed to and care for one another.

10. *Sufficient Resources and Time.* Sufficient information, human, and technological resources; sufficient time to creatively think about a project and to experiment and try things in new and different ways.

11. *Trust.* A sense of trust that team members will do their designated tasks within the designated time frame; trust in the accurateness of the information provided by other team members; trust that team members will give honest and constructive feedback on ideas, thoughts, and creative efforts shared electronically; trust in one another's expertise and ability to do the work effectively; and trust that team members will hold ideas shared in confidence if requested.

A theory was then developed to summarize and categorize these eleven dimensions. Three essential components necessary for virtual team creativity were proposed:

- *Connection,* the elements that need to be in place for a team to develop and maintain identity and a sense of community. Connection involves both task (dedication/commitment, goal clarity) and interpersonal (information sharing, personal bond, trust) connections.

- *Raw materials,* the basics on which virtual team members can draw in producing creative work. Once a connection between team members is established, team members need to be supplied with sufficient raw materials, in terms of information, human and technological resources, and time, to accomplish the creative work.

- *Management and team member skills conducive to creativity.* Finally, as creative work is underway, specific types of team member skills necessary for creativity (acceptance of ideas/constructive tension, challenge, collaboration, freedom) and needed management skills conducive to creativity (management encouragement) should be practiced.

Creativity appears to be highest at the intersection of three components: connection, raw materials, and management and team member skills.

Creativity appears to be highest at the intersection of these three components—the area in which the connection is strong, the raw materials supplied are sufficient, and the appropriate management and team member skills conducive to creativity have been developed and are being practiced. The theory is graphically represented in Figure 10.1.

Figure 10.1. A Theory for a Climate for Creativity in Virtual Teams

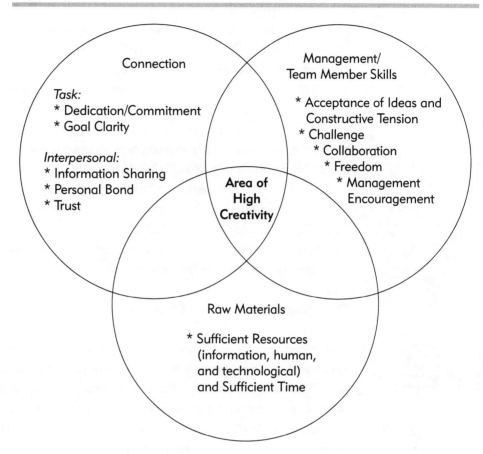

The Case of the ACI Team

I will illustrate each of the three components necessary for a creative climate in virtual work by primarily focusing on the high and low creativity experiences within one particular virtual team, the ACI team.

Description of the ACI Team

The ACI team (name changed to ensure confidentiality) is composed of six individuals who make up an organization development consulting firm specializing in change consulting, primarily in the manufacturing sector. At the time of my investigation, the firm had been in existence (although membership has changed somewhat) for nearly fifteen years. Four of the team members are consultants. The two other team members manage the firm's central office, handling administrative and financial details.

Initially, the team was led by one team leader. However, that leadership structure changed in the mid-1990s, and currently leadership within the team rotates every four months among the four consultant members. The team members fondly call their leader the RIOU, "the rotating intergalactic overlord of the universe."

Three team members reside in North Carolina, two members live in Virginia, and one member lives in Texas. The three members in North Carolina work in the central office for ACI. The three other members work out of offices in their homes. Also, the four consultant team members travel frequently to client sites.

The Climate for Creativity Dimensions
Connection

Dedication/Commitment. In the high creativity stories shared, ACI team members felt a strong sense of commitment and dedication to the work. They worked hard on difficult tasks and problems and persevered. One consultant team member shared her high creativity story.

It involved developing materials within about one week's time frame, but probably should have taken six months to do. There was a very intense focus on a client's expectations, a willingness and assumption that people would and did put an incredible amount of time and energy in that short time period.

In the low creativity stories shared, team members suggested that there was a different degree of commitment to a particular project or goal among the team members. As a result, creativity was hampered and, in fact, the mere existence of the project was jeopardized.

Goal Clarity. The team's goals, and the clarity of those goals, was a prevalent characteristic in the team members' high creativity stories.

Common goals assist in maintaining a sense of connection.

Team members suggested that having common goals assisted them in maintaining a sense of connection. Interestingly, although goals were crucial for success in creative work, some members felt it took more effort in a virtual team to make sure those goals were clear. Constant checking, feedback, and questions were needed to ensure clarification. An ACI team member shared the following:

> "Well, goals need to be more clear and checked more frequently because of the distance, the separation, to keep people on board. Without the personal contact, goals have to be clearer and more frequently reiterated. What we're trying to get out of this, where we're headed, what does it look like when we're done. So that you're not expecting a horse and you get a camel by the time you're finished."

In low creativity stories, team members described situations in which goals were fuzzy or unclear. As a result, misunderstandings and faulty assumptions occurred, and valuable time was wasted. Virtual teams have been created around the need to develop cost-effective, instantaneous responses to customer and market demands. However, the electrifying pace with which business can and does take place electronically sometimes creates the context for confusion when the proper time is not taken to make sure goals are clearly outlined and communicated. Ironically, then, the speed at which the work moves slows the creative process down through unclear goals.

Additionally, creativity suffered due to the indecision that resulted from unclear goals. Consequently, valuable time was wasted, and some projects became unwieldy. An ACI team member recalled the following example:

> "We have had a few little mishaps in my career here. The major one was what we now affectionately refer to as the 'Manual from Hell.' It was a project where three consultants were writing this manual, and they each had a different section that they were supposed to write. And then I was to edit it and put it together and it was going to go to the client. It was actually pretty simple. But it just turned into this massive undertaking. It was like opening Pandora's box. Once they started writing, it was like, 'oh, we've got to talk about this and we've got to go out here and then oh well, let's talk about this.' So, it just grew and grew and grew and grew. And it got to the point where there was no way that it was going to be finished when it was supposed to be."

For some team members, a lack of clarity around the team's goals and roles led to frustration, misunderstandings, and faulty assumptions. Finally, even when goals were communicated clearly in initial face-to-face meetings, as team members dispersed, goals were sometimes forgotten or dropped.

Information Sharing. Information is the fuel that feeds the fire of creativity in virtual teams. Highly creative experiences involved team members who communicated regularly with one another, shared the results of their efforts, offered open and honest feedback, and updated information regularly. (For information on how to create effective communication in virtual teams, see Chapter 22.)

When people meet face-to-face, individuals can be directly asked for information, feedback, or input. In virtual teams, individuals can also be directly asked electronically, but it is easier for individuals to disappear or drop out of the discussion.

It is crucial to create norms for communicating and exchanging information.

To avoid this, the ACI team created norms for communicating and exchanging information. Some of the norms established included the following:

- Members agreed to respond to email at least three to four times weekly, whether working at home or on the road working at client sites.

- A conference call was scheduled every six weeks to review client marketing and business development, to assess ongoing client work, and for a personal check-in.

- Members agreed to respond to all telephone calls within twenty-four hours, whether at home or traveling and working at client sites.

- Face-to-face meetings were scheduled quarterly (referred to by members as "the quarterly gathering of the clan"). These meetings took place in the homes of the team members and lasted for two to three days.

- The central office in North Carolina served as the hub, and all consultants were required to update the hub as to their whereabouts.

Although the ACI team had established norms in place to guide communication exchanges and information sharing, they were not always consistently adhered to. In the low creativity experiences, norms for communication were unclear, ignored, or inconsistent. The ACI team had periods of tremendous information sharing and other periods in which information sharing was limited. One team member related the following:

> "I'd have to say that it's kind of a yin and yang. At some point, there is
> a lot of information sharing, and at other points, you don't know that
> something might be relevant to somebody else. So there is sometimes
> an impact of working in a vacuum where you create something and you
> say, 'Oh, nobody's working on anything like this now.' You don't share
> because you don't want to overload them."

In addition, just as too little information can hamper creativity, so, too, can an overload of information. Team members attempting to deal with the constant flow of information between themselves and their geographically dispersed team members sometimes were overwhelmed with more information than they could effectively comprehend.

Personal Bond. Team members, even though separated by distance and sometimes time, suggested they felt like a family. Developing and maintaining this kind of personal connection is critical for creativity to occur in virtual teams.

A personal connection lessens problematic misunderstandings and faulty assumptions that hamper creativity.

A personal sense of connection can help to lessen the problematic misunderstandings and faulty assumptions that hamper creativity and help to develop the trust, respect, understanding, acceptance, and compassion that team members need to feel comfortable sharing ideas and taking risks across distances. This kind of connection goes beyond common goals and commitment to the work. Team members are also committed to and care for one another. A member of the ACI team described the intense personal bond among the members of the team:

> "This group of six people is up there close to my family in terms of folks
> I feel connected with. And it's not just because we're all in this one life

boat called economic survival, but we have been through each other's personal crises. These people are just supportive. There's just no other way to say that. This is family."

Some of the techniques team members used to help establish a personal bond included the following:

- Scheduling face-to-face get-togethers;
- Electronically sharing humorous stories or incidents;
- Creating playful games to build and maintain team identity;
- Taking the time to show personal interest in one another (by electronically passing along information they thought other team members might be interested in);
- Sharing personal issues and crises with other team members; and
- Functioning as a support network for one another.

Trust. Trust was the most frequently mentioned dimension surrounding the high creativity stories shared. Trust was composed of several elements:

- A sense that individuals would do what they said within the designated time frame;
- Trust in the accurateness of the information provided by other team members;
- Trust that team members would give honest and constructive feedback on ideas, thoughts, and creative efforts shared electronically;
- Trust in one another's expertise and ability to do the work effectively; and
- Trust that other team members would hold ideas shared in confidence if requested.

Team members felt it took a great deal of trust to share ideas and accomplish work electronically. In a virtual environment, without the nonverbal indicators available in face-to-face encounters, trust was viewed as essential not only for the team to be creative, but for the team to even exist.

Although trust was seen as essential in a virtual environment, it was sometimes difficult to establish, and it developed slowly. Trust developed from a sense of accountability, from seeing that others followed through on what they said they would do. A member of the ACI team described how trust developed in her team:

> "I think that in our particular situation, we do have a great degree of trust in all levels. I think it came about by people living up to what's expected of them. I mean, we can be very frank with each other."

Trust was also based on a belief in the expertise of others and on positive, ongoing experiences with one another. The length of time a team has been together also impacts the level of trust.

In low creativity stories shared, the level of trust waned, was lost, or did not exist at all. The most frequently mentioned reason for a decline in the level of trust was low accountability, team members not carrying through on their designated work, or not "pulling their weight." (For information on creating team accountability, see Chapter 8.) Oddly enough, in the ACI team, all of the team members interviewed mentioned the same project in their low creativity stories, the previously mentioned "Manual from Hell." Lack of accountability was a key factor in why the team members felt the experience was low in creativity. One team member shared the following:

> "We were working on a project for a client. It was a new process for us and we were having to, for the first time since I've been here, create something from the ground up. At the beginning, the process was divvied up to different people to do different things. That didn't work well because some of the people didn't do their part by the deadline that they agreed to. So then that caused the process to be pushed out. It caused the envelope to be pushed because we did have a deadline by which we had to have this to the client. So the problem was everyone not getting their piece ready."

Raw Materials
Sufficient Resources and Time. The raw materials for virtual creative work include having sufficient resources and sufficient time to do

that work. The high creativity stories described by the virtual team members were consistently marked by a sufficiency of resources, including information, human, and technological resources. Further, high creativity experiences were characterized by a sufficiency of time.

Networked, virtual team members saw themselves as having an abundance of information and human resources available for creative work. Team members were able to share information with one another by accessing one another's files from their home offices or through shared databases. Electronic links allowed for access to resources outside of the participants' teams and organizations as well. The ability to electronically connect up with geographically dispersed individuals allowed for the inclusion of human resources where they were once limited.

Also crucial in the high creativity stories was having the time to think creatively about a project and the time to experiment and try things in new and different ways. One ACI team member emphasized sufficient time in her high creativity story:

> "I think the first one where it worked so well, we were not under a time crunch, and I had time to really think about things and really be creative and put some graphics in. For me, time makes a big difference. Some people work better under real time restraints. I need time to think about things."

As might be expected, not having enough resources and time hindered creativity. It seems ironic that the same type of team design that offers team members an abundance of resources can also limit resources. However, rather than resources not being available, most of the resource problems in the low creativity stories arose from not being able to *gain access* to available resources. Some of the more frequently mentioned technological difficulties included computer systems failures, broken fax and answering machines, lost email, slow computers, unsophisticated hardware and software, and incompatibility problems between individual team members' computer systems.

Although for some, deadlines and time crunches may provide a sense of challenge that leads to high creativity, it still appears that

**Teams need
sufficient time
to be able
to think
creatively
about a
project.**

teams need sufficient time to be able to think creatively about a project and to try new and different things. Without this time, creativity suffers, as team members scramble to complete projects on time. One ACI team member related the following:

> "It was just such a time crunch. . . As far as I'm concerned, they may have been creative, but there was no creativity for me. It was like, 'I'm going to spell check this, and if it looks like the sentences read okay, then it's going in. And we were handing Matt the binders on his way out the door, and he had twenty minutes to catch a flight. It was just about as stressed as I've ever been without there being a death involved."

Management and Team Member Skills

Acceptance of Ideas and Constructive Tension. In the highly creative situations, team members said they felt their ideas and input were encouraged, valued, and accepted by all the members of their team without unnecessary criticism. In these situations, there was a high degree of honesty, as team members felt comfortable not only in sharing their ideas, but in giving open and honest feedback to one another as well. One of the support staff team members in the ACI team shared the following:

> "What we have to say has value, even though we're not stockholders. It used to be when I first started with this company that the office staff went to tri-annual meetings just to take minutes and did not participate. And now we participate on a very high level at these meetings. And they want to make sure that we know to have input. When this first started happening, we were a little reluctant to speak our opinions. But then we found out that they really did want to know what we thought, and now we tell them."

On the one hand, some team members felt the "virtualness" of their team impacted the degree of acceptance of ideas. For these individuals, ideas and input were more readily offered and accepted electronically. They felt more at ease, comfortable, and less threatened when generating ideas electronically than when doing so face-to-face. However, for others, being virtual had little to do with how accepting of ideas team members were. The key to acceptance was, rather, understanding and appreciating different team members' work styles. An ACI consultant remarked on this issue:

> "I don't think the virtual team part of it has much to do with acceptance of ideas. I think it has more to do with knowledge of, and understanding of, how different people in your team think and how different people in your team work. That is one of the things that I feel really blessed about in our team is the encouragement to experiment, to try things to do within reason."

An atmosphere that encourages acceptance of ideas may also encourage constructive tension.

An atmosphere that encourages acceptance of ideas may also encourage constructive tension, an unusual mix of differing views and opinions (Ekvall, 1983). Constructive tension was mentioned by team members as a positive influence in the highly creative experiences. Creativity arose from the tension, conflict, and differing opinions of team members. Indeed, constructive tension was so valued that there were times when team members actively sought to create it in order to achieve high levels of creativity.

In low creativity stories, it was evident that the dismissal of ideas by management or other team members quickly squashed the motivation to be creative. Stories of low creativity also revealed that not all differences led to constructive tension. In particular, differences in the values held by team members created unconstructive tension, which led to disorganization, confusion, misunderstandings, and, in one case, members leaving the team.

Work that is stimulating, engaging, and fun sparks creativity.

Challenge. Challenge was a major theme in high creativity events shared by team members. A sense of challenge arose from:

- *The intriguing and enjoyable nature of a problem or task presented to the group.* Team members felt creative when challenged by the nature of the work. In particular, work that was stimulating, engaging, and, most of all, fun sparked creativity.

- *The urgent needs of a particular situation.* Members indicated that creativity was high in situations where they felt they were working against the odds. In demanding situations (for example, a tight time deadline), the team felt driven to prove that it could meet the challenge.

- *The desire to push for something new and move away from the status quo.* Team members spoke of the desire to push themselves as a team. Emphasis was placed on creating new ways of doing, rather than relying on old material or previously established templates. For example, one ACI team member commented as follows:

> "We were pushing ourselves into areas that we didn't have any off-the-shelf materials. We've not done that sort of thing before. So we were having to, in a way, make up the response. We had to take our practices and principles and apply them in an arena we hadn't [been in]. And as a matter of fact, this was our first proposal to that client. When they read it, it basically woke them up to a lot of stuff that they hadn't even thought about."

Team members felt their creativity was low when working on tasks they found tedious or lacking in enjoyment or challenge.

Collaboration. The virtual team members described collaboration as characteristic of their highly creative experiences. Collaboration was characterized by team members as the ability to pull together and work closely and comfortably together to complete an interdependent task or to pursue a mutual interest or a jointly held intriguing idea. In high creativity stories, team members shared how they effectively "coordinated things," how the team possessed "an extremely high level of cooperation," and how the situation required them to be "very, very tightly strung together."

Collaborative team members are "tuned in" to each other.

Team members also felt "tuned in" to each other or that they had "just really clicked" with one another. One ACI member shared the following:

> "I think that some of the things we came up with were incredibly good, and energizing, and just came out of our guts and our experience without being a long, rational, you know, planning process. We just kind of sat there and we talked and we talked, and we said, 'Let's try this.' And

one of us would have an insight, and the other would build on it, and lo and behold, by the end of the meal or the third glass of wine we had the design for tomorrow. And we went back in and presented it the next day, and poof, it seemed to work. So it's moments like that where you are with another person; in this case we happened to be face-to-face, and you just play off of each other to create what's the right thing to do for the client at this moment in time. It was kind of like just the recognition that 'here is the problem' and both of us coming up with the same solution at the same time. To me, that's very creative. There's a creativity there or a spark or an intuition. We were really tuned with each other in terms of what our response was, and it just came out."

The key is "not being forced into a 9 to 5 creative box."

Freedom. Three major types of freedom were identified in the high creativity stories:

- *Freedom to work at one's own pace.* In the highly creative stories, team members talked about how they felt free to work at their own pace. Schedules were flexible and adaptable to individual team member's "creative biorhythms" and lifestyles.

  As one ACI team member put it, the key was "not being forced into a 9 to 5 creative box." Flexibility of schedule also alleviated stress and allowed for a better balance between personal and work lives. Freedom with respect to scheduling afforded team members the opportunity of working at times when there were fewer distractions.

- *Freedom to decide how to do one's work.* Team members felt free in highly creative situations to decide how to do their work. A modular approach allowed for work to be parceled out to individual team members. Team members, then, had control over their section of the creative product; they had the freedom to accomplish that section as they saw fit.

- *Freedom from excessive evaluation and surveillance.* In the high creativity stories, a relaxing environment was established where team members felt free from excessive evaluation by management and other team members. Especially in the initial idea generation stage, evaluation has been shown to squash creativity (Osborne, 1963). In addition, working electronically was particularly useful in freeing team members from the negative effects that surveillance can have on creativity. Team members were able to work independently and experiment without the direct presence of others looking on.

In the stories of low creativity, *constraint* or the lack of freedom in deciding what to do or how to do the work was stressed. For these virtual team members, constraint came from inflexible or over-controlling team members and management. An ACI consultant described a low creative experience, in which she worked with an inflexible peripheral team member:

> "I'm working with another consultant right now who has about the flexibility of a . . . the distance between two fly wings. And I don't like it. Oh, it's very difficult. It impacts the trust, it impacts the ability to do the work. It impacts what you're willing or not willing to put on the table. Impacts the creativity. It downright stifles it."

 Management Encouragement. Creativity is fostered when management is encouraging, enthusiastic, and supportive of new ideas and new ways of doing things. The dimension of management encouragement was not specifically addressed by the ACI team (probably because the role of team leader rotates and everyone has the chance to be the team leader). However, members of two of the other virtual teams I interviewed did specifically refer to the encouragement and support they felt from team leaders and management in their highly creative stories. For example, one woman in another organizational consulting team related the following:

> "There is a high level of support for each individual to take initiative, and be, you know, this buzz word now, 'empowered.' But there's truth in that. And so, each individual was empowered to take on an area and develop it, and then we come back, we reassess. We would tweak and fine tune. It became a very creative process, both individually and for the team."

Another member of that same team suggested that management encouragement had actually increased since the team had become virtual.

The ease of electronic communication may increase the frequency with which managers give recognition, praise, and feedback.

The ease of electronic communication helped to increase the frequency with which the firm's managing partners gave recognition, praise, and feedback.

The opposite of management encouragement is an overemphasis on the status quo, on doing things the way they have been done in the past. An emphasis on the status quo was not motivated by a desire to avoid controversial ideas or resist innovation, but rather it was simply more convenient and efficient to do so. The team leader of one of the online service provider teams described how the reliance on old ways of doing, initially set up to automate production of the online publication during her absence, carried over after her return. While production became more efficient, she did not consider it a creative period.

"About things where there's not creativity, I think one thing I've noticed in our team is that when I was gone for two weeks, I did a lot of work to set them up so that they could kind of automate so they wouldn't have to think about things, like how to fill a certain page with promotions. I would say, 'okay, here's a whole list of them and you can just run them.' And it was only for when I was gone, really. But now since I did that, everything is automated. And so it's easier, in a way, to do your work because you don't really have to think about it. But it loses some of the creativity that comes when you sit down and you say, 'okay, we have to have the leads for tomorrow.' And if there's nothing there, then you might come up with something new. Whereas I went ahead and set them all up with a whole bunch of things that they could kind of recycle and made a big spreadsheet for them. And so now we seem to be relying on old material instead of coming up with new stuff."

Context Is Existent

Interestingly, in a working arrangement that some have referred to as "working without context" (O'Hara-Devereaux & Johansen, 1994, p. 150), context for the virtual team members interviewed in this investigation was not nonexistent. The eleven climate dimensions discussed in this section form the "context" in which creativity can be realized in a virtual working arrangement.

A New Tool: The Virtual Team Creative Climate Instrument

Now that we know what makes up a creative climate for virtual teams, how can a specific virtual team begin to understand and develop its own climate for creativity?

The first step must be assessment.

The first step must be assessment. In this section, I will describe a new tool that I have developed to give virtual teams the opportunity to assess their climate for creativity. The tool is called the Virtual Team Creative Climate (VTCC) instrument. While there are other instruments that assess factors supporting or undermining group or team creativity, to date, there are no other instruments (aside from the VTCC) that assess the climate for creativity specifically for virtual teams. In the following sections, the format of the VTCC will be described, the results of preliminary testing of the instrument will be reviewed, and the practical benefits and contributions of the VTCC will be shared.

Instrument Format

Items on the VTCC instrument were written to be descriptive of the work environment and to focus on each of the eleven dimensions in the previously discussed theory. The VTCC instrument has two major parts. Part 1, the Creative Climate Assessment, asks respondents to answer a series of questions about the work environment of their virtual team. Eleven sections (representing the eleven dimensions in the original theory) make up this part of the instrument. Respondents are asked to rate each statement on two different scales: (1) how true or not true the statement is of their *current* team, and (2) how *important* they feel the statement is to their team. A four-point scale is used to assess how accurately each statement describes the current virtual team: (1) never or almost never true; (2) sometimes true; (3) often true; and (4) always or almost always true. A different four-point scale is used to assess how important each statement is to the virtual team: (1) seldom important; (2) somewhat important; (3) important; and (4) very important. Items on the VTCC instrument are both positively and negatively worded to tap into both sides of each of the eleven dimensions.

Part 2 of the VTCC instrument asks specific demographic and background questions about the individual virtual team members and the virtual team as a whole.

Preliminary Testing

Initially, feedback was sought on the VTCC instrument from both practitioners and consultants dealing with virtual teams and academics who have done scholarly work on virtual organizations and teams. Then a preliminary testing of the VTCC instrument was conducted with seventy-seven management students in a major California university. Scale reliability analyses revealed that all but one of the eleven scales in the VTCC were highly reliable. One scale (management encouragement) was moderately reliable. Results from the reliability testing and sample items from each scale are shown in Table 10.1. It is important to note that currently the VTCC instrument is being further tested with existing virtual teams in different business contexts. (If the reader is interested in the full-length VTCC and/or having a team be part of the ongoing testing of this instrument, please contact the author of this chapter.)

Table 10.1. Description of the VTCC Scales

Scale Name	# of Items	Alpha Level*	Sample Items
Connection Scales			
Dedication/commitment	7	.83	Team members are dedicated, intensely involved, and committed to their work.
			Team members are self-driven and committed to the team's goals.
Goal Clarity	15	.82	Goals within the team are clearly defined and developed.
			Team goals are shared by all team members.
			Indecision results from unclear goals.
Information Sharing	20	.83	Team members communicate regularly and consistently with one another.
			Norms for communication are clear to all team members.
Personal Bond	17	.94	Team members are close and feel like a family.
			Team members have compassion for one another.
			Team members take time to show personal interest in one another.
			The team functions as a personal support network for each team member.

Table 10.1. Description of the VTCC Scales, Cont'd

Scale Name	# of Items	Alpha Level*	Sample Items
Trust	18	.79	Team members do their designated tasks within the specified time frames.
			Team members can be frank with one another.
			Team members trust each other's judgment in their particular area(s) of expertise.
			Trust is essential for the team to be creative.

Raw Materials Scale

Scale Name	# of Items	Alpha Level*	Sample Items
Sufficient Resources and Time	14	.73	There are sufficient people to complete the team's work.
			Team members are able to electronically share information with one another, when needed.
			The team has time to experiment and try things in new and different ways.
			Team members are often scrambling to get their work completed on time.

Management/Team Members Skills Scales

Scale Name	# of Items	Alpha Level*	Sample Items
Acceptance of Ideas/ Constructive Tension	13	.74	Team members feel their ideas or input are valued.
			Constructive tension is valued and ways to actively create it are sought.
			Ideas are often solicited and then dismissed by management.
Challenge	12	.74	For the most part, the work of the team is stimulating and engaging.
			Team members have the desire to push themselves as a team.
Collaboration	9	.87	There is a high level of cooperation among team members.
			The work of the team fulfills the mutual interests of its members.
			Everyone on the team benefits from the common result.
Freedom	10	.71	I have freedom to determine my own work pace.
			Over-controlling and inflexible management limits the team's autonomy.
Management Encouragement	9	.57	The team leader creates the opportunity for creativity.
			Management is encouraging and supportive of new ideas and new ways of doing things.

*The alpha level is a statistic called a Cronbach's Alpha, and it is an indicator of how well the items in a particular scale stick together and measure the overall construct of that scale. In other words, this statistic shows how consistently individuals are responding to items that comprise the scale (or construct in a broader sense). In general, scales with alpha levels above .70 are considered reliable scales. Scales with values below .50 have poor reliability.

Benefits and Contributions of the VTCC Instrument

One sure benefit of the VTCC instrument is that it specifically assesses the climate for creativity for virtual teams. Questions are included to assess elements that enhance creativity and those that undermine creativity in virtual teams. An added benefit of the VTCC instrument is the inclusion and realization that not all dimensions are of equal importance to every team. The VTCC instrument allows virtual team members to assess both how they *currently* stand with respect to each of the eleven dimensions and how *important* each of those dimensions is to their team. This yields an individualized assessment of the creative climate for each virtual team, outlining where the team's more pronounced gaps (difference between where the team is currently on a particular dimension and how important that dimension is to the team) lie. Feedback is given on the three major components of the original theory on which the instrument is based—connection, raw materials, and management/team member skills—and on each of the corresponding eleven dimensions. This instrument, then, can be a valuable diagnostic tool for assessing the environment of creativity in a virtual team and for suggesting areas for improvement.

Final Tips and Conclusion

Below are some *final tips* for developing a positive climate for creativity within your virtual team:

> *Take the time to create a connection, both task and interpersonal, among team members.* In virtual teams, connection is not easily attained. Hard work and commitment are required to establish and maintain high levels of dedication, goal clarity, information sharing, personal bond, and trust. One way to start is to set aside funds for team members to get together initially to discuss common goals and shared values and to build trust. Further, once the team is up and running, having periodic face-to-face, social get-togethers or celebrations after completion of particular projects can help encourage and maintain team identity.

In addition, aside from face-to-face meetings, there are other ways in which organizations, managers, and team leaders can encourage connection in virtual teams. Companies or teams can sponsor team games. Or perhaps one team member may function as a team historian, documenting team stories and sending them out electronically to members. For teams that do not meet face-to-face, even low-tech strategies such as sending all team members pictures of one another can be beneficial. (See Nemiro, 2000b, and O'Hara-Devereaux & Johansen, 1994, for further information on creating connection in virtual teams.)

Train virtual team members not only in how to use technology but in appropriate virtual team member skills as well. Virtual team members need to be trained in how to use a range of collaborative software and information technology to enhance the team's work. However, training needs to go beyond how to use the technology to incorporate how to communicate effectively through these kinds of technologies. (For more information on how to communicate effectively while working virtually, see Chapter 22.)

Since many of the traditional nonverbal cues used in communication are lost in electronic interchanges, virtual team members benefit from training in how to use more linguistic precision in their communications (see Townsend, DeMarie, & Hendrickson, 1996). Virtual team members also need training in team management and interpersonal skills such as maintaining esteem, reaching consensus, and conflict resolution. (For more information on managing and resolving conflict, see Chapters 19 and 31.) Further, training and educating the team members in the different working styles of each of the team members is essential. This type of training, if conducted early on in the team's development, will help eliminate misunderstandings that may be disruptive to the creative process. Team members who understand one another's working styles are less likely to attach negative interpretations to incomplete or unclear communications (see O'Hara-Devereaux & Johansen, 1994).

Train team leaders in appropriate virtual team leader skills. Leaders of virtual teams need to be skilled in the ways to help distant members become interpersonally connected. Virtual team leaders also need to take care in the communication of team goals and tasks, making sure their written communications are as clear as possible. (See Fisher & Fisher, 2001, and Wilson, George, & Wellins, 1994, for further information on developing virtual team leadership skills).

 Develop effective communication norms for sharing information among team members. Team leaders must help in establishing an effective communication procedure within the team. O'Hara-Devereaux and Johansen refer to this as creating "a communications drumbeat" (1994, p. 174). Devising a communication routine, whether daily or weekly, is critical to ensure regular and consistent communication and information sharing. (See Chapter 22 and Duarte &

Snyder, 1999, for further information on developing communication norms in virtual teams.)

Particular attention should be paid to matching the message of the communication with the appropriate method. (For more information on linking a particular type of message to a specific communication method, see Chapter 22.) For example, information with emotional context is best communicated face-to-face or via a telephone, while hard data is best transmitted in written form through email. Virtual team members must also be sensitive to the overwhelming amount of information that can be shared electronically and develop ways to deal with and eliminate information overload.

Select individuals who are well suited for virtual team work. Not all individuals "fit" with virtual work, desire to work virtually, or can be creative in this kind of working arrangement. The virtual team members interviewed in this investigation indicated that individuals who need freedom, have a strong sense of autonomy, are self-disciplined and self-motivated, and have a strong drive to complete challenging tasks are those who seem most appropriate for virtual work. Organizations, managers, and human resource professionals will need to incorporate into their selection procedures ways to ascertain what individuals are best suited for virtual work. Finding those individuals who are most appropriate for this new type of work design will be beneficial to employee job satisfaction and productivity and lead to higher levels of creativity as well.

Take the time to assess your virtual team's climate for creativity and, as a result of this assessment, work on areas in need of improvement. Do not just assume that everything is okay. Take the time to empirically assess how your team is doing on the eleven elements necessary for creativity in virtual teams. On what dimensions is your team strong? Strive for even further growth in those areas. On what dimensions does your team need improvement? Address these areas with appropriate action for improvement.

Even in virtual teams, the human side of teams does not go away.

In conclusion, the key point to remember is that even in virtual teams, in which work is accomplished for the most part electronically, the human side of teams does not go away.

As one of the members of the ACI said:

"I don't think that people should get it in their head that because I'm working at a distance with somebody, the human side and the human issues go away. They don't. All of the personality or what people call personality issues, all of the communication issues, all of the need to respect and be conscious of the other person's feelings and where they're coming from, all of that is still there. Whether you're in the same office building and conference room together, or whether you're on the other end of a telephone or a computer terminal, the person doesn't go away in a virtual team. What we have had to do is to work very hard to keep this a very personal relationship. You have to respect the fact that it's another human being who has feelings and emotions, and ups and downs, and assumptions and lenses. That doesn't go away when you are working at a distance. And you have to find ways to manage all of that if your team is going to be successful."

CHAPTER 11

Alignment

The Key to Collaborative Work Systems

Craig McGee

ORGANIZATIONS HAVE BEEN IMPLEMENTING team-based systems and methods over the last thirty years. The expected outcomes have been reduced costs, increased productivity, improved quality, increased customer satisfaction, and so on. And indeed, there are many examples of just these results:

- A greenfield site for Eaton in Kearney, Nebraska, that uses teams and an "empowerment" philosophy is 25 to 30 percent more productive than other comparable plants (Ledford, Wendenhor, & Strahley, 1995).

- Procter & Gamble reports 30 to 40 percent greater productivity at its team-based plants (Hoerr, Polluck, & Whitestone, 1986).

- FedEx reorganized one thousand back office employees into teams, resulting in a 13 percent reduction in service failures (lost packages or incorrect bills) and solved a chronic billing problem that was costing the company $2.1M annually (Dumaine, 1990).

- Tektronix created new product teams of manufacturing, marketing, engineering, and finance employees that cut the time-to-market for new products 50 percent (Fisher, 1993).

Innovative team-based systems can routinely generate 25 to 40 percent improvements.

In fact, innovative, well-designed team-based systems can routinely generate improvements in the range of 25 to 40 percent.

A cross-study comparison of 131 studies reveals that changes in work practices (strongly associated with team-based systems) produces 30 to 40 percent performance improvements (Macy & Hiroaki, 1993).

However, there are more examples of companies that have had disappointing results. Organizations in the 1980s embraced total quality management in the hopes of achieving the same high-performance results as Japanese manufacturing companies. Thousands of managers and executives flocked to Japan, the Mecca of total quality, to learn the total quality methods. But despite their efforts, their organizations failed to replicate the miracles of the Japanese quality machines. American companies have invested millions of dollars and countless hours only to revert to the traditional quality methods or move on to other management methods. The few exceptions, notably Motorola, Kodak, Corning, and Xerox, raise the question, "Why can some companies sustain team-based quality initiatives and others cannot?"

Similarly, self-directed work teams have produced mixed results. Again, organizations like Monsanto, Ford, General Electric, and American Express have implemented self-directed work teams in a number of facilities. Sites like General Foods' Topeka Pet Plant; Saturn; Procter & Gamble's Lima, Ohio, plant; and Westinghouse's Savannah Nuclear Fuels Processing plant are showcases for high-performance, team-based systems. However, these remain pilot sites. Diffusion is incomplete and inconsistent. Even Procter & Gamble, which openly declared their technician system a strategic imperative and a competitive advantage, failed to achieve system-wide diffusion of the technician system.

Team-based organizations require a fundamental reengineering of organizational systems.

So why is it that some organizations can achieve impressive positive results while others fail to obtain these same results or are unable to sustain them over a period of time? The answer to this question is the basic premise of this article: *team-based organizations require a fundamental reengineering of organizational and management systems to support the new dynamics of teams.*

Organizational Systems

Most organizational systems present in today's organizations are the vestige of the longstanding hierarchical, bureaucratic model. The manager or executive in the organization makes decisions. His or her staff develops recommendations and brings them to him or her for approval before implementing them. Work assignments and tasks are made on an individual basis. Merit raises and bonuses are similarly based on individual contribution. Departmental and individual goals often conflict with one another, pitting individuals and groups against one another.

Teams require a radically different environment to flourish than the traditional hierarchical environment. They require a transformed "culture" that supports collaboration and risk taking. They require a leadership style that provides vision and direction setting and empowerment. They require leaders and managers who "coach" without being authoritative. Team-based systems require information systems that provide teams with the right information with which to make decisions. They also require rewards systems that emphasize team accomplishments over individual achievements.

When taken as a whole, leaders must make significant changes to align the organizational and management systems to sustain teams. And while the conventional wisdom that we must change the culture to enable team performance is sound, it fails to provide practical guidance to managers and practitioners. Culture can be broken down into some key elements. They provide action levers to change individual behavior within organizations in order to sustain team performance. The key organizational systems that this article focuses on are

- Norms and values
- Leadership style
- Decision making
- Information systems
- Goals and metrics
- Rewards and recognition
- Selection
- Training

Norms and Values

The norms and values of traditional organizations reflect Emery's design principle #1, a command and control value set (Emery & Emery, 1993). Leaders organize the work and coordinate across functions or business units. They approve decisions and allocate resources. The prevalent norms reflect individual, not team, behavior. Successful team-based systems require a conscious "re-engineering" and institutionalizing of a new value set. This value set includes collaboration, trust, integrity, and open sharing of information and knowledge. These values drive individuals to support one another, to assist peers and colleagues in solving problems and achieving task, and to openly discuss performance, whether it is good or bad.

A few strict rules

The norms emphasize identifying solutions to problems, not finding whom to blame for mistakes. The value set observed by the author in Honda and many other Japanese companies provides a stark contrast to traditional American management styles. In the Japanese companies, when goals and targets are not met, managers and executives analyze their goals and their strategies to understand why "methods" did not work. They practice systems thinking to a greater extent. The above situations are learning opportunities and opportunities to revise their methods. They do not look for individuals to blame. General managers are encouraged to bring forth thoughtful analysis of the situation and the methods used.

Similarly, Jack Welch instituted a new set of norms in GE. During quarterly executive retreats, managers and executives shared ideas about what had worked and what had not. The sustainable team environment includes values of "empowerment" and risk taking. Leaders provide the resources and license to make decisions and implement them. They establish boundaries, and as long as the teams operate within those boundaries, they are empowered. Risk taking is encouraged. Mistakes or miscues are accepted as long as they are learning opportunities. Second-guessing of leaders' desires is eliminated, allowing teams to operate more freely and with more confidence.

A business unit of Sybase provides a vivid example. Started as a classic "garage" software house by a University of Colorado professor and one of his graduate students, it possessed strong values of teamwork, collaboration, and self-initiation. Individuals never received formal team training, nor were there formal team structures. However, the values were so strong that teams formed naturally, accomplished tasks, and re-formed to handle other issues.

Leadership Style

The style of leaders in successful team environments is a second critical factor. The proper leadership style in successful team environments is not laissez-faire. Leaders actively collaborate with the teams in setting direction and monitoring results. They work with teams to set goals and targets that are challenging yet achievable. The key factor that differentiates effective leaders in team environments is that they work *with* their teams to establish these goals, not unilaterally setting them and directing teams to achieve them. Effective leaders in team environments also spend more time establishing and clarifying boundaries for the teams. They establish clear expectations about *what* needs to be done, not *how,* and the parameters within which it can be done.

In successful team environments, accountability is actually greater. The leadership style is one of high accomplishment and results orientation. Leaders continually focus teams on their goals and results.

In successful teams accountability is actually greater.

When goals are not achieved, the team and the coach/leader analyze the situation to understand why goals were not met. They collaboratively assess barriers and devise means to remove those barriers. There are no excuses. Effective team leaders do not let teams under-perform.

Coaching is a critical competency required to sustain teams. Leaders help teams think through problems and solutions in a non-threatening, non-directive fashion. Effective coaches ask questions of teams to help them think about issues or implications that may be overlooked. Effective coaches provide suggestions based on their experience or expertise. They do not force suggestions on the teams, but provide sound rationale, and highlight the benefits and limitations of their suggestions. They focus on the goal of helping the team make an effective decision, rather than on getting their decision accepted.

If additional resources or training are needed, the leader obtains them for the team. The leader's role becomes one of resource provider and barrier remover. Rather than spending time checking work or coordinating activities, the leader focuses on ensuring that the teams have the right resources, skills, and information. "Servant leadership" is the norm.

Decision Making

Teams require new decision-making systems. The structure and purpose of the team generally determines the types of decision-making patterns required. A project team generally has a leader who has stronger decision-making authority and control. A task team may (and probably should) have a more diffused decision-making style, that is, geared more toward making decisions by consensus. A common element, however, is that the decision-making pattern in sustained teams becomes more consultative and participative.

Teams spend considerable effort determining who has authority for specific decisions.

Advanced high performing (a.k.a. self-directed) work unit teams exercise distinctly different decision-making patterns than traditional systems. Rather than concentrating decision making in one individual, that is, the supervisor, team members are provided greater authority for making decisions. This is a conscious choice. Leaders and their teams spend considerable time and effort determining who has authority and responsibility for specific decisions, designating which decisions can be made unilaterally, which decisions require collaboration, and which decisions require group consensus. (For more information on designing decision-making processes, see Chapter 18.)

Decision-making patterns in sustained team environments encourage risk taking.

Decision-making patterns in sustained team environments encourage risk taking. Teams possess a wealth of knowledge and information within their own boundaries. Teams can quickly process this information and make a decision. The norm develops to enable teams to make the "best decision with the information at hand." Leaders need to encourage teams to take calculated risks, especially when all the data is not available.

Information Systems

High-quality decisions require high-quality information. The traditional manager has long been the integrator and gatekeeper of information. However, team-based systems require that the information traditionally retained in the heads and hands of management or staff be distributed to the team members. Given this information, the team can make sound business decisions.

When we empower teams to investigate problems and make decisions, we must provide them with the necessary and critical information. Information, such as production rates, cost estimates, supplier rates, vendor contracts, project costs, and so on are examples of the type of information that is required by teams. The information may be considered confidential or "need to know" by some people.

But teams chartered to solve problems or make decisions do "need to know" this information. Organizations not willing to trust their teams and supply this data are better off with traditional decision-making patterns.

Previously, with limited technology, bureaucratic systems were required to route information effectively. Now, however, newer technology enables broad dissemination of information. Groupware technology enables teams who are not physically co-located to work effectively together. To sustain teams, organizations must invest to design and implement new information systems. Hewlett-Packard provides such technology to its employees (personal communications, 1997). Design engineers spread throughout the world are virtually linked through information technology. Engineers pass their work on to other engineers in other time zones. Design work continues around the clock, with work being passed from Europe to the United States to Asia and back to Europe.

Monsanto provides computer terminals to its production teams to ensure that they have the right information. Whereas traditionally this information flowed to production managers to identify variances and direct corrective actions, the information is now directly accessible by production teams to enable them to assume this role. Production teams track production statistics and take corrective action. Similarly, expert systems are built into reactor operators' control screens. Reactor operators conduct what-if scenarios. They change variables, such as feedstock rate, temperature, pressure, and so forth, and the expert system calculates the financial impact of those adjustments. These expert systems enable teams and individuals to assume decision-making roles that previously resided with a manager or supervisor.

Goals and Metrics

Traditional work systems stress individual performance. Hence, most goals are individually based. These goals often conflict with the goals of other individuals/groups, pitting one group against another. The classic rivalry across shift teams illustrates this point. Members of one shift fail to clean up or do the necessary maintenance in order to maximize their shift's production. Another example comes from a consumer products company with which the author consulted. One group with ownership for inventory management had aggressive inventory reduction goals. However, this strongly conflicted with the manufacturing goal of eliminating out-of-stocks. Also, it was in the plant's interest to schedule long production runs, maximizing plant efficiency, but increasing inventory levels.

Teams focus on aligning their goals with the higher-level business objectives, not merely departmental targets.

Sustaining teams requires different goal-setting systems. These new systems emphasize collaborative goal setting. In fact, the teams tend to establish their own goals (versus having them established in a top-down fashion). The groups focus on aligning their goals with the higher-level business objectives, not merely departmental targets.

The content of the goals tends to be different in successful team environments as well. In addition to traditional operations and finance goals, teams tend to set other goals regarding the effectiveness of team functioning. These include level of skill development or training, stage of group development, and amount of time allocated for team development activities. Specific goals are established to help teams increase their effectiveness.

Successful teams spend more time monitoring goal attainment. They establish their own set of metrics by which to monitor their progress toward goals. Often a specific role exists to collect, analyze, and distribute goal performance data. This is a task performed by leaders in traditional systems. The participative design workshops developed by Fred and Merrelyn Emery (1993) to help teams design themselves feature specific activities for teams to establish their goals and metrics. (For more information on participative design, see Chapters 14 and 15.)

Reward and Recognition Systems

As greater responsibility is shifted to teams, companies must implement different reward systems to sustain teams. Traditional reward systems focus on individual contribution. Group-based incentive systems, such as the Scanlon Plan, Rucker Plan, and Improshare (Graham-Moore & Ross, 1990) have been implemented over the last thirty to forty years. These systems help support team-based environments.

Other reward systems that are more targeted and more directly support team systems have also gained prominence. Teams often require greater flexibility in team member skills. In high-performance work teams, job rotation is the norm. To encourage employees to develop and use skills, pay-for-skills systems have been developed. These systems reward employees for acquiring new skills by increasing the hourly wage for new skill blocks that they learn.

A major manufacturer with which the author worked implemented such a system. Table 11.1 illustrates the pay progression.

Table 11.1. Pay-for-Skills Progression

Skill Block/Job Title	Skills Required	Pay (1998$)
Production Associate	Ability to perform basic operations (material handling, fork truck operations, sanitation, basic production line operations)	$12.60
Production Technician	All of the above, *plus* the ability to run all stations on the production line, start up and shut down the line, and make operating adjustments	$13.60
Production Master	All of the above, *plus* the ability to conduct quality checks and do preventative maintenance; qualified to teach and certify others in these operations	$14.60
Maintenance Technician	All of the above, *plus* the ability to perform advanced maintenance work, that is, troubleshooting, repair, overhaul, process control programming, and so on	$17.00

Employees were slotted into skill blocks and earned the associated pay rate no matter what job they performed. For example, if a maintenance technician operated a fork truck one day, filling in for an employee attending training, the maintenance technician would receive the normal maintenance pay of $17.00 per hour.

Not only did this provide for staffing flexibility, but it also encouraged employees to rotate jobs to share both the more routine work and the more interesting work. The pay systems were consciously designed to encourage employees to develop new skills, thereby creating greater flexibility in the production teams.

Similarly, gainsharing compensation systems have been developed to reinforce team behavior. Whereas Scanlon, Rucker, and the other earlier plans focus on division/company-wide performance (Graham-Moore & Ross, 1990), the more recent gainsharing plans focus more narrowly on specific team performance. The scope of the plan is not so narrow as to pit teams against one another, but instead is designed to create synergies within a logical organizational unit. Examples of logical operational units include a product business team (sales, development, R&D, and manufacturing), a plant, or a service center.

Effective gainsharing plans focus on performance metrics over which teams have direct control. The metrics include sales volume (units or dollars), cost (scrap, overall production costs, overall business costs, unit cost, etc.), attendance, safety, and quality. Specific performance targets are established for each. A gainsharing design team typically establishes these targets for the entire site/business unit. If the teams exceed the target, producing a financial gain for the company, they share in that gain by some prescribed formula. The percentage tends to be substantial, as much as an equal split of the gain between the company and the teams.

An example of one such plan follows. One manufacturing plant established six criteria for team gainsharing:

- Volume

- Units held for inspection (HFI)

- Number of customer defect reports (CDRs)

- Scrap

- Safety

- Attendance

Targets were established for each criterion. A team of production employees worked with the plant manager to establish the performance targets and adjusted them annually. If the teams exceeded the targets for the criteria, percentage points were accrued. The percentage points reflect the percentage of their base salary that they would earn. Specific ranges for exceeding the targets were set and percentage points associated with each range (see Table 11.2). Each quarter, the bonuses were calculated and paid to teams. Bonuses averaged $5,000 to $6,000 annually on base wages of $30,000.

Table 11.2. Sample Gainsharing Plan

Factor	Weighting	Maximum Bonus Payout %	Thresholds
Volume (avg. M units/day)	40	4%	5925 = 0 points—Acceptable 6000 = 2 points—Good 6075 = 4 points—Excellent
Hold for Inspection (HFI) %	20	2%	6.0% = 0 points—Acceptable 4.5% = 2 points—Good 3.0% = 4 points—Excellent
Scrap	20	2%	5.1% = 0 points 5.0% = ½ point—Acceptable 4.5% = 1 point—Good 4.0% = 2 points—Excellent
Absenteeism Rate	10	1%	Over 1.0% = 0 points—Acceptable .75% = 1 point—Good .50% = 2 points—Excellent
Safety	10	1%	Over 3 lost worker days = 0 points—Acceptable 3 lost worker days or less = ½ point—Good No lost days = 1 point—Excellent
	100%	10%	
Customer Defect Reports			Not to exceed .7. If this is exceeded ALL payments are cancelled for that quarter. If the rate is .3 or less, a bonus of 1 point will be awarded for this excellent quality. This point will be added to the total of those earned in the above categories for payment calculation.

Since quality was so important, if the threshold performance level for this criterion was not met, no bonuses were paid. Instead, the money earned in the other criteria was accrued in a reserve fund. The reserve fund was used for paying bonuses that normally would have been earned, but for special reasons (plant shutdown for installing new equipment, major "act of God" events, and so on) the teams were prohibited from earning the bonuses.

Selection

Traditional organizations frequently select employees on the basis of technical skills. Successful team environments require the steady influx of people with the capability and skills to work in teams; thus some organizations place heavier weight on interpersonal skills and problem-solving skills. They believe it is easier to teach the technical skills versus the interpersonal skills.

The selection systems for team-based environments balance technical skills with interpersonal skills as selection criteria. The skills required to work successfully in team environments include the following:

- Flexibility
- Conflict management
- Giving and receiving feedback
- Problem analysis
- Decision making
- Initiation
- Facilitation
- Persuasion
- Oral communications

Another key competency is analysis and critical thinking, being able to analyze data and develop sound conclusions. While this competency may be built into the selection process for managers, supervisors, and "leaders," it is often lacking for team members. Traditional selection systems typically fail to increase the weight placed on this criterion.

The above skills are pretty well recognized as skills or competencies required for working in teams. One competency that is not as well recognized is the ability to deal with ambiguity.

Selection systems for team-based environments balance technical skills with interpersonal skills as selection criteria.

In traditional environments, tasks are structured and provided by a supervisor/manager. In team environments, there often is less direction. Teams must first identify what the problem is (traditionally a function of management), then solve it. The parameters of the problem may or may not be clear. They must define the parameters and relevant attributes.

Successfully staffing team-based organizations requires additional selection tools.

The means to select for these new qualities differ in team-based environments. In traditional environments, a heavy reliance is placed on the interview for making selection decisions. Successfully staffing team-based organizations requires additional selection tools.

These tools rely on, to a greater extent, exercises that simulate the work environment. They use role plays and group exercises extensively to assess an individual's interpersonal skills. Assessment-center type processes are used, even for rank-and-file applicants. Assessment centers are series of activities (role plays, problem-solving exercises, group activities, and so on) designed to simulate the work environment. By placing job candidates in situations that mirror the actual work, better employment decisions result.

An example of such a selection system is one the author co-created for the startup of a major brewery. Fifty thousand applications were received for five hundred jobs. The company utilized the State Employment Commission to solicit the applications and conduct the initial screening. Based on criteria provided by the company, the Commission conducted preliminary application screening and eliminated 72 percent of the initial applicants. The state then used the General Aptitude Test Battery (GATB), a well-established, validated battery of tests to further qualify applicants. The company wanted people with fundamental cognitive abilities and physical abilities that the GATB assessed. The Commission then provided the company with a small percentage, relative to the initial applicant pool, of applicants for more extensive screening. Essentially, the state screened out 97 percent of the initial applicants at basically no cost to the company. And, as an additional benefit, the company eliminated 97% of the EEO/AA liability.

The company then interviewed those applicants the state referred. Teams of interviewers from the company used a structured, behavioral events interview format to assess applicants. Behavioral events interviews focus on what the applicants have actually done in the past in specific situations. They are based on the premise that the best predictor of future behavior is past behavior.

For specialty areas such as the lab and maintenance, applicants passing the interview phase were given a technical assessment. Situations that mirrored the actual work tasks were provided to candidates. Qualified assessors evaluated the applicants' ability to perform such tasks.

The final hurdle for all candidates was a twenty-five-hour "training course." The course provided basic skill development in math, problem solving, safety, and group dynamics. Trained observers attended the course and evaluated candidates. This provided greater contact with the applicants and the opportunity to observe applicants in a variety of situations. Specific team-related exercises were designed that not only helped the candidates develop skills, but also provided observers with a chance to assess how well candidates worked in team situations.

It took a total of six weeks to complete the process and involved five distinct hurdles. The company estimated that each employment decision represented an investment of $1.25 million dollars in wages and benefits alone over the course of an average employee's tenure. Given this investment, the company wanted to minimize selection mistakes.

Training

Teams are the "Ferraris" of organizations design.

Ed Lawler has called teams the "Ferraris" of organization design (Dumaine, 1994). They are high performance, well engineered, and deliver results that far exceed other organizational forms. However, along with high performance comes high maintenance. Teams require maintenance in the form of ongoing training and development. The time required to train effective teams can be two to four times that of traditional work groups. Training includes skill development in problem solving, group dynamics, interpersonal skills, and so on.

Similarly, to help teams reach sound business decisions, teams must become more business literate. Basic financial concepts and business management tools help teams reach sound business decisions. Again, these are the types of things we tend to teach managers and supervisors, but as we shift decision making to teams, business literacy becomes more important for all members of the organization. Republic Steel provides monthly modules in business economics. Employees learn how to decipher balance sheets and income statements to better understand data about the steel industry (*American Workplace*, 1995).

Related to training are the ongoing development activities. Routine team meetings that focus on assessment of team functioning and correct actions are required to keep teams highly tuned. Traditional managers frequently (daily/weekly) conduct operational reviews to track how well the production systems are functioning; sustaining teams requires similar frequent reviews of the *organizational* system. Similarly, teams need to critique their decision-making processes, provide feedback to team members, and organize their work. This type of ongoing team building is required to keep the "racer's edge."

Summary

Organizations have been strongly attracted to the benefits of teams. Numerous examples exist of high performing teams that have produced dramatic benefits. While appearing on the surface to be a simple exercise, the implementation of teams is actually more complex than most assume. The under-performance of teams generally stems from failing to re-architect the organization's culture and systems to support teams. Sustaining teams requires radical transformation of organizational systems from a bureaucratic, hierarchical model to a more participative model. The systems described in this article (decision making, leadership style, norms and values, reward, selection, information systems, goals and metrics, and training) must be redesigned to support the new team-based organization.

PART 3

STRUCTURE AND OVERALL DESIGN

Gerald D. Klein

THE INTRODUCTION TO THIS BOOK and previous chapters have suggested how the structure of an organization is an important influence in collaboration. What unites the remarkably diverse chapters in this section is their common and primary interest in structural elements rather than other aspects of organizations, such as leadership and culture, organizational goals and strategy, and work processes, although in truth, these aspects are also discussed. In fact, the focus of two of the chapters here (14 and 15) is primarily on one structural element, the locus of decision-making authority.

So that a reader is better able to discern what in each of the chapters is relevant to organization structure, it is useful to start with a definition and description. The different elements or components of structure are identified next, and we will indicate how each is handled in organizations that are collaborative work systems. Concluding this introduction are overviews of the section chapters. The relevance of each to organization structure will be highlighted.

There are a number of formal definitions of organization structure, most very similar. Robert Miles, for example, defines an organization structure as those aspects or elements that either delineate its parts or that function to bring the parts together (Miles, 1980). Arthur Bedeian and Raymond Zammuto define structure as consisting of the segmenting or departmentalization of activities and the connections (between the segments thus created) established within and between departments (Bedeian & Zammuto, 1991).

With these definitions, it is possible to identify four elements of organizations that are properly part of structure. The four are an organization's hierarchy of authority or chain of command; the departmentalization or clustering of employees; role definitions throughout the organization; and an organization's integration mechanisms.

Organization authority is the right to command and expend resources. The hierarchy of authority (chain of command) indicates the individuals in the organization who possess authority and reveals the various levels of the organization. Individuals at higher levels theoretically "command" and are able to overrule those at lower levels. As one ascends the hierarchy, one encounters individuals who oversee and direct the work of larger numbers of employees and groups. Traditionally, and in many organizations today, information flows up in the organization and decisions and information flow downward. The traditional view holds that it is the responsibility of the executive and managerial group to make organization decisions.

Long ago, it was realized by Rensis Likert that there were many sound reasons to challenge this arrangement. To increase employee satisfaction and motivation and improve the quality of decision making in the organization, he favored, and field data he collected supported, the idea that *influence as well as information should flow upward as well as laterally* (cross-unit, cross-department). Likert proposed a linking-pin organization design in which each manager was a superior in his or her organization unit and simultaneously a subordinate (along with his or her peers) in the unit at the next higher organizational level. Managers at all levels were encouraged to manage in a group-centered, participatory manner. Accordingly, at higher organizational levels managers were encouraged to permit decisions to be influenced by managers at lower levels—managers bearing important information from and representing the perspective of those they supervised. Individuals throughout the organization were also encouraged to be more open to lateral influence (Likert, 1961, 1967).

Following Likert, other prominent researchers, including Fred Emery and Eric Trist, were to recommend the greater participation of employees at all levels in organization decision making, including major decisions concerning organization change (Emery & Thorsrud, 1976; Emery & Trist, 1978). Because of the increasing rate of change and the need for rapid organization response, the authority to make decisions must today reside at lower organizational levels and reside in more employees. Tom Peters and others have for some time argued that it is vital to have lateral communication and problem solving among, and permit decision making by, those at lower organization levels (Peters, 1988, 1992). Those at lower levels are guided by the vision, goals, and strategy articulated by those at the top. Jeffrey Pfeffer has assembled impressive data indicating that companies can achieve a competitive advantage when they use and treat people well. Pfeffer identifies sixteen practices by these companies, including top-down information sharing, the decentralization of decision making, and the extensive use of different kinds of empowered teams (Pfeffer, 1994, 1998).

The traditional bases for clustering employees are well-known. We can group or cluster employees primarily by their functions or occupational specialties, such as accounting, human resources, and engineering, and can cluster them further by their specialties *within* a function, for example, recruitment and selection within human resources. Alternatively, we can cluster employees into units and divisions, each responsible for particular (one or more) products, services, regions, customers, or projects. Although employees are grouped or clustered in these traditional designs, these groups or clusters are seldom "teams." With these designs every employee is primarily responsible to a single supervisor or superior.

In collaborative work systems, it is common to find employees formally grouped or clustered into teams, and the number of teams can be great.

Departments and groups within departments are conceptualized and organized as teams, and teams are collectively responsible for the work. Each team member may have particular tasks for which he or she is responsible, or rotate between tasks. Nevertheless, team members are expected to help the team solve problems and reach sound decisions and pitch in to help the team meet its goals.

Collaborative work systems are characterized by various kinds of teams. Work teams are responsible for some part of the basic work of the organization. The responsibilities of a management team at the top often include organization goal setting, value identification, and external relations. Staff teams in such areas as human resources, information technology, and engineering, ideally, assist and support the work teams. Standing and ad hoc cross-functional teams may develop new products or integrate the activities of teams. Continuous improvement teams look for ways to improve and strengthen the organization.

Two other components of an organization's structure are role definitions across the organization and the mechanisms used to achieve integration between individuals and units. In the past, organizational roles were defined so that mainly those in supervisory positions had coordinating responsibilities. In a collaborative work system one would expect to find that many roles and roles at *all* levels would have a collaborative component, that is, a requirement for interaction with others for the purpose of securing or transmitting information, mutual planning, and performing other coordinative acts. Most employees in collaborative work systems will enjoy contact with others both within and external to their organization units. That contact may be lateral or vertical, that is, involving individuals at other levels. Other changes in organization roles as collaboration increases were discussed above, for example, the extra responsibilities of an individual when he or she becomes part of a team.

Integration mechanisms function to bring the parts of an organization together for the purpose of unified action. There are a number of different mechanisms or devices that exist, and an organization can employ a few or many of them. In a collaborative work system, one would expect to find many of these mechanisms employed. The major mechanisms of integration include (1) the organization's hierarchy of authority; (2) job descriptions, which will specify an individual's regular work contributions to others in the organization; (3) informal contact and interaction; (4) organization goals and strategies; (5) formal plans and schedules; (6) organization policies, procedures, and rules; (7) computerized data bases that many can access; (8) integrating roles and in some cases integrating departments; (9) cross-functional teams and ad hoc or permanent committees; and (10) email and shareware or group software that permits several parties at one time to respond to a common document.

In Chapter 12, William O. Lytle compares four strategies for rapidly changing organizations: the modified design team approach; the cascading, macro design approach; the sequenced, multiple-conference approach; and the hybrid approach. Widely employed in organizations today, these strategies typically permit many employees and, in smaller organizations, all employees to participate and exert influence in the crucial task of changing the organization. When these methods are used, it is intended that the open, cooperative, and egalitarian relationships that develop between groups and levels during the change process continue in the new organization. Each method typically requires the temporary amendment of organization structure—new groups and teams are created to oversee, plan, and implement the change. This chapter contains an assessment instrument to help an organization decide which of the four strategies is most appropriate.

Craig McGee in Chapter 13 describes an effort to change an engineering department in a South American mine to improve turnaround time on projects, reduce costs, and improve customer satisfaction. Departing from past practice in this department, the entire department designed, attended, and shaped the outcomes of three large-group conferences. The focuses of the three conferences were the department's environment and vision, work processes, and key support systems, such as compensation and performance management. Many of the significant outcomes achieved were structure-related: greater collaboration between and integration of the work of the department's work units; the establishment of project teams as the primary structure for the department; the clarification of roles on these teams; and the redesign of support system roles to support the project team structure.

Both Chapter 14 by Catherine Bradshaw, Joan Roberts, and Sylvia Cheuy and Chapter 15 by Donald W. de Guerre focus on a particular approach to organization change, the participative design process. Bradshaw, Roberts, and Cheuy sketch its history and foundations and discuss conditions that are necessary for success. Its major purpose is to create a permanent democratic organization structure. Obviously, for most organizations this involves a significant shift in the distribution of organization authority, but the authors describe the benefits. Another goal is a workplace that reflects sociotechnical ideals, that is, a workplace that is both good for people yet also productive and effective. In addition to the decentralization of authority, movement in this direction invariably involves the redesign of jobs and work (usually expanded roles and responsibilities), the creation of better integration devices, and may involve the clustering of employees into teams—important structural changes. In their chapter, Bradshaw, Roberts, and Cheuy compare "bureaucratic" and democratic organizations and offer criteria that can be used to judge the adequacy of an organization from a people point of view.

The participative design workshop is mentioned as part of the participative design process in Chapter 14 and is the primary focus of Donald de Guerre's Chapter 15. The workshop is described as usually a one- or two-day intervention. In a larger organization a longer workshop or several workshops are held. De Guerre describes the workshop in its two basic forms, one for redesigning a traditional, bureaucratic structure and the other for creating a new organization. Examples of each application are offered. For the former, implementation requires that organization leaders agree in advance to change the "design principle" of the organization, that is, to move toward democratic practices. While workshop activities are ostensibly focused on designing a new organization, they are also intended to stimulate excitement and build the commitment of the participants and to create egalitarian and mutually respectful relationships between individuals, groups, and organization levels that will carry over to and continue in the new organization. Examples of participative design workshops tailored to different settings are provided.

In Chapter 16, Gina Hinrichs and Kevin Ricke report on an effort at a brownfield plant of John Deere to apply high performance work systems thinking and methods in a continuous improvement program. Targeted for intervention were a selection of manufacturing departments. The departments were not equally successful in identifying and completing continuous improvement projects and Hinrichs and Ricke suggest the reasons for these differences in their chapter. The variation in department performance is attributed, in part, to structural elements, including the ability of department members to assume the new responsibilities connected with continuous improvement and successfully handle as well their other responsibilities—the issue of role overload; the ability of departments and department members to carry out new role requirements, such as accessing department, plant, and company data; and good or poor integration of the department subgroup receiving special training in high performance work systems with the rest of the department.

Finally, in Chapter 17 Cheryl Harris and Sarah Bodner emphasize the need to align organization support systems so they assist the work of teams. This is especially important when teams constitute the organization's structure. Support systems include those that are familiar to the reader—reward and compensation, information, and performance management—and those that may not be so obvious, such as leadership and renewal, and integration. The authors describe in very useful detail a support systems strategic planning workshop. Its implementation is likely to lead eventually to one or more kinds of structural change: the decentralization of authority within support systems, usually occurring when support personnel become responsible for serving one or more teams; change in the roles and responsibilities of support system personnel; the creation of new temporary and permanent groups within individual support systems, or which combine support system and team personnel; and new integration mechanisms.

CHAPTER 12

Accelerating Organization Design

Choosing the Right Approach

William O. Lytle

WITH THE DEMANDS AND OPPORTUNITIES in today's business world shifting so abruptly, organization leaders are seeking ways to rapidly reconfigure strategies, work processes, structure, and culture. They are well aware that the fast expansion of internal capabilities can give their organization a true competitive advantage in the marketplace. The search for faster and more effective ways of organizing and functioning has become imperative. One critical need is for a design process in which the rapid reconfiguration of key organization elements enables the achievement of exceptional business and human results.

This chapter describes four approaches to accelerated organization design and identifies eight key factors that influence the use of each approach. Also included is a set of assessment questions that will help a group of senior leaders choose the accelerated design approach that is right for their organization and its design effort.

Organization Design

Organization design, as used in this chapter, denotes a deliberately planned process that concurrently reconfigures key elements of an organization's work processes, structure, people, and culture. A successful design must satisfy the disparate requirements of the business environment, work processes, and human systems.

The outcome of accelerated organization design is the reduction of the aggregate time for planning, design, and implementation with no sacrifice of quality.

The process of organization change occurs in five phases, with the first four of limited duration and the fifth of indeterminate length. These five phases are *exploration, planning and preparation, analysis and design, implementation,* and *renewal* (Lytle, 1998). The outcome of accelerated organization design is the reduction of the aggregate time for planning, design, and implementation with no sacrifice of quality.

Four Options for Accelerating the Design Process

Four accelerated design approaches are used by organizations today: the modified design team approach; the cascading, macro design approach; the sequenced, multiple-conference approach; and the hybrid approach. A description of each of these approaches follows along with a brief example; the author of this chapter was one of two external consultants who worked with the organizations described. For a more detailed explanation of these four approaches see Lytle (2002). The subsequent section presents eight key factors and associated assessment questions that will help an organization's leaders choose the best approach for their organization.

Modified Design Team Approach

To appreciate the "modified" design team approach, it is first necessary to understand the "traditional" design team method. This will help clarify what is being modified and why.

Traditional Approach: In the traditional design team approach, two temporary groups, a steering committee and a design team, play key roles in the design effort. The steering committee is a group of senior managers and, when present, union leaders, who address key planning issues, commission the design effort, provide necessary resources, develop support among stakeholders, approve proposals, and oversee the change process from start to finish

(Kotter, 1996; Lytle, 1993). The design team, typically six to ten people representing a cross section of the organization, meets for four to six months to analyze the current organization, create the blueprint of the new organization, and develop a plan for the implementation of the proposed features. While this "traditional approach" has produced excellent results in the past, over the years it has evolved into the "modified approach."

Modified Approach: In the modified design team approach, a variety of activities are used to accelerate the change process and build support for the new design.

> *Examples:* The steering committee in one company saved its design team time by prescribing the use of certain proven organization features, such as self-managing work teams. A design team in another company commissioned several employee task groups to help it work out the details of specific changes, for example, new training needs and facility modifications.

Cascading, Macro Design Approach

In the cascading, macro design approach, the steering committee is responsible for the normal planning activities, but it also assumes the task of producing a design that determines the broad features of the entire organization. This "macro design" establishes the higher-level structure and systems that may include, for example, new unit boundaries, team structure, information systems, human resources systems, and the like. This macro design is then "cascaded" or handed down to individual work units, each responsible for deciding how the prescribed features will be implemented in its respective area (the micro design).

> *Example:* In the Milwaukee, Wisconsin, brewery of the Miller Brewing Company, a steering committee of senior managers and union leaders met four days a week and completed a macro design and implementation plan in two months. Within four months, the unit micro designs were completed and implementation was well underway throughout the plant.

Sequenced, Multiple-Conference Approach

In the sequenced, multiple-conference approach, the majority of the visioning activity, data analysis, organization design, and broad implementation planning is done in a series of linked conferences attended by large groups of employees (50 to 150) who make up a cross section of all units and levels in the organization. The conferences occur within a compressed period of time (Axelrod, 2000; Dannemiller, James, & Tolchinsky, 2000; Emery, 1993; Weisbord, 1992). Key external stakeholders, such as customers, are also invited to attend and contribute.

Typically, each carefully structured conference lasts from two to three days, and conferences are held every three or four weeks. This spacing permits participants to absorb the results of a conference and prepare for the next. Each conference focuses on one of the design steps and builds on the work of the ones before it. During a conference, participants spend time working both in small groups and in the total community. The macro design for a large organization can be developed in four conferences over a four- to five-month period.

> *Example:* The Consumer Credit Division of First Union used four conferences to create a new macro design for its organization. The original functional organization was reconfigured into four regional groups. Members of each new regional group then met separately for a two-and-one-half-day conference, during which they developed the micro design and the detailed implementation plan for their unit.

(Chapter 2 of this fieldbook provides an overview of Search Conferences, a very similar approach for changing an organization. A number of chapters in this section also discuss methods of organization change. See especially Chapters 13, 15, and 17.)

Hybrid Approach

The hybrid approach to organization design is not a single prescribed method but rather is a combination of elements borrowed from the other three approaches. For example, an organization design effort might entail the use of a design team, multiple task groups, and several conferences to create a macro design and unit micro designs. This hybrid approach accelerates the design process through the mixing and matching of components.

Example: In the Winslow, Maine, mill of the former Scott Paper Company, a joint union-management steering committee commissioned nine parallel design teams to create team-based work systems in various production and support units. Then two back-to-back conferences of two days each were held to first integrate the nine separate unit designs and then develop the implementation plan for the site.

Process Outcomes of Accelerated Approaches

These four accelerated design approaches have the capacity to speed up the organization design process. Each approach produces one or more of the following process outcomes to varying degrees:

- Increases the number of people who support the need for rapid change;
- Enlarges the scope of the design effort;
- Focuses the design work on the most essential tasks;
- Expands the number of high-quality design ideas;
- Tests design options against the requirements of multiple stakeholders;
- Develops broad support for the implementation of the new design through the direct participation of employees;
- Shifts the culture in a direction supportive of the new design; and
- Uses the resources of people, time, and funds prudently.

Choosing the Right Approach

Once senior leaders understand the alternative approaches for accelerating organization design, they must carefully assess their current situation and choose the approach that is right for their design effort. In conducting this analysis it is important that leaders understand how the following eight factors influence the choice of a design method.

1. Need for rapid change;
2. Scope of the design effort;
3. Key relationships;
4. Employee involvement;

5. Management control;

6. Resources;

7. Past experience with organization design; and

8. Leadership readiness.

In the following section, "Assessment of the Organization," each factor is explained and questions are provided that help leaders assess their organization and select the most appropriate design approach. An experienced internal or external consultant may be used to facilitate this assessment process.

The following five steps describe how the material in the next section should be used. It should take each senior leader an hour or less to answer all the questions and interpret the results. Discussion of this material by a group of leaders may take several hours.

1. Every senior leader is given a copy of this material.

2. Working alone, each leader reads the explanation of one factor and then answers its assessment questions.

3. The leader then considers the implications of his or her answers and, in the space titled "Conclusion," indicates the design approach that seems most appropriate.

4. When a leader completes all eight sections, he or she reviews the conclusions reached in each section and decides which design approach, on the whole, is most appropriate for the organization. The leader may assign different weights to each of the eight factors. This final decision is written in the space titled, "Summing Up."

5. The senior leaders meet to compare their answers, discuss design alternatives, and make a final choice for their organization.

Assessment of the Organization
1. Need for Rapid Change

The need for a rapid shift in an organization's capabilities may be driven by both external and internal demands and opportunities. For example, customers, without warning, may specify new product requirements that must be met, or the implementation of new technology may unexpectedly call for a new form of organization for those responsible for its operation and maintenance. However, for such changes to occur, key stakeholders in the organization must agree on both the general nature of the change needed and the necessity for its fast design and implementation.

Key individuals and groups must be in substantial agreement at the start about the need for rapid change.

For the cascading, macro design and the sequenced, multiple-conference approaches to be effective, key individuals and groups must be in substantial agreement at the start about the need for rapid change. If any of these parties have reservations about the nature of the change or its pace and if these issues cannot be easily resolved, then the modified design team approach may be most appropriate. This method gives people more time to work through their concerns as the design process slowly unfolds.

Assessment Questions

1a. To what extent do key stakeholders agree on the general nature of the changes needed in the organization?

1	2	3	4	5	6	7
Limited			Moderate			Great

1b. To what extent do these stakeholders also agree that the organization must change as rapidly as possible?

1	2	3	4	5	6	7
Limited			Moderate			Great

1c. If disagreement about the nature or pace of change arises among these stakeholders, how easily can it be resolved?

1	2	3	4	5	6	7
Not at all easily			Fairly easily			Quite easily

Given your answers to the questions in this section, which approach seems to be most appropriate for your organization design effort? Why?

_____

_____

_____

_____

2. Scope of the Design Effort

The scope of a design effort is the number of individuals, groups, units, levels, locations, work processes, and the like to be involved in the change. It may be very broad and inclusive, extending even to external groups such as customers or suppliers, or it may be relatively narrow with a focus on more limited parts of the organization. If particular units in the organization are interdependent to a substantial degree, that is, where a significant change in one necessitates changes in the others, then all should be included in the design scope. The various groups that will be directly affected by the changes should be represented in the design effort, as well. The scope of the effort will also be influenced by the resources available and the degree of stress the organization can manage.

When the scope of the design effort is very broad, the cascading, macro design and sequenced, multiple-conference approaches are particularly appropriate. They handle this broad scope by creating a macro design for the whole organization, which is then followed by detailed micro designs developed by employees within each new unit. If the scope is relatively narrow, any of the approaches may be used. The modified design team approach is especially useful if the design process requires in-depth organization analysis.

Assessment Questions

2a. How interdependent are the various units in the organization, that is, where change in one requires changes in the others?

1	2	3	4	5	6	7
Not at all			Moderately			Highly

2b. How many people in the organization are likely to be directly affected by the kinds of changes being considered?

1	2	3	4	5	6	7
Only a few			About half			Almost everyone

2c. How broad will the scope of the change effort be? (Consider what will be included: individuals, groups, units, levels, locations, facilities, products/services, work processes, technologies, external groups.)

1	2	3	4	5	6	7
Narrow			Moderate			Broad

2d. How much in-depth analysis of the business environment, work processes, and human systems will the design process require?

1	2	3	4	5	6	7
Little			Moderate			Considerable

Given your answers to the questions in this section, which approach seems to be most appropriate for your organization design effort? Why?

_____

_____

_____

_____

3. Key Relationships

Constructive working relationships provide the very foundation for all of the accelerated design approaches.

Mutual respect, open communications, and teamwork are necessary characteristics of any successful organization. Constructive working relationships provide the very foundation for all of the accelerated design approaches. If individuals or groups are greatly concerned with protecting their turf, then the implementation of new designs that cut across organization boundaries may be resisted. In unionized settings, it is very helpful if management and the union have had some successful cooperative experiences before undertaking the design process. In general, if relationships among key groups are badly strained, senior leaders must concentrate on improving relationships *before* initiating a design effort.

The sequenced, multiple-conference approach, with its very public give and take, depends on especially positive relationships among the many individuals and groups involved. When relationships contain elements of mistrust, then the modified design team or cascading, macro design approaches may be more suitable. These two methods provide time for groups to improve their relationships and work through issues as the change process proceeds.

Assessment Questions

3a. To what extent are key working relationships in the organization characterized by mutual respect, open communications, and teamwork?

1	2	3	4	5	6	7
Limited			Moderate			Great

3b. To what degree are people or groups in the organization concerned with protecting their turf?

1	2	3	4	5	6	7
Limited			Moderate			High

3c. (If applicable) To what extent is the union-management relationship constructive and based on successful cooperative experiences?

1	2	3	4	5	6	7
Limited			Moderate			Great

Given your answers to the questions in this section, which approach seems to be most appropriate for your organization design effort? Why?

_____
_____
_____
_____
_____
_____
_____
_____

The more people who participate in and take responsibility for creating a new organization, the better the design.

4. Employee Involvement

As a general rule, the more people who participate in and take responsibility for creating a new organization, the better the design, the greater the commitment to its success, and the faster its implementation. The involvement of large numbers of employees in the design process depends to a great extent on both the organization's past experience and the readiness of the people to participate. If participation in the past has been rewarding for both the organization and the employees, then all parties are likely to support its use in the change effort.

The success of the sequenced, multiple-conference approach depends on the contributions of large numbers of employees during the macro design, micro design, and implementation phases of change. The cascading, macro design method involves all employees during the micro design and implementation phase, while the modified design team approach may use more limited participation for gathering information and testing ideas.

If the sequenced, multiple-conference approach is to be used in a unionized organization, the union leadership must feel comfortable having individual members express their opinions publicly. Traditionally, union officers speak for the membership as a whole, and this capacity to speak as one body has been an important source of a union's strength. Some union leaders may not wish to have disagreements among members aired publicly. They also may be concerned that bargaining issues such as pay levels will be discussed in an inappropriate setting.

Assessment Questions

4a. In the past, how much success has the organization had with employee involvement, where, for example, employees at all levels were involved in identifying and resolving important issues?

1	2	3	4	5	6	7
Little			Moderate			Great

4b. To what extent does the senior leadership want employees to be directly involved in the design process?

1	2	3	4	5	6	7
Limited			Moderate			Great

4c. To what extent will employees want to participate actively in the change effort?

1	2	3	4	5	6	7
Limited			Moderate			Great

4d. (If applicable) How comfortable will union leaders be having their members participate in a public design process where disagreements between members may be openly expressed?

1	2	3	4	5	6	7
Not at all			Somewhat			Very

Given your answers to the questions in this section, which approach seems to be most appropriate for your organization design effort? Why?

_____
_____
_____
_____
_____
_____
_____
_____

5. Management Control

Senior leaders must decide on the degree of control they want to exercise over the design process, the issues it addresses, and the outcomes. The current culture of the organization and their perception of the risks involved will influence their decisions. If management has traditionally valued predictability and control, top-down decision making, and avoidance of risk, then it may want to maintain close control over each step of the design effort.

The cascading, macro design approach provides senior leaders with the most control of the design process and its outcomes. The sequenced, multiple-conference approach provides the least direct control of the process and outcomes, while the modified design team approach lies somewhere between the other two.

Assessment Questions

5a. To what extent does the senior leadership value predictability and control, top-down decision making, and avoidance of risk?

1	2	3	4	5	6	7
Limited			Moderate			Great

5b. How much risk is inherent in the kinds of organization changes being considered?

1	2	3	4	5	6	7
Limited			Moderate			Great

5c. How much direct control do the senior leaders want to exercise over the design process, the issues that will be addressed, and the outcomes?

1	2	3	4	5	6	7
Little			Moderate			Total

Given your answers to the questions in this section, which approach seems to be most appropriate for your organization design effort? Why?

_____

_____

_____

_____

_____

_____

6. Resources

The leaders of a change effort must understand clearly the resources that will be required by the accelerated design approach they choose and have a plan for acquiring them. If sufficient time, people, and budget are not available, the scope of the design effort may need to be reduced and perhaps a different approach selected. Leaders must also anticipate events that could reduce future resources and have a plan in place to respond to such potential problems.

The design effort must be assigned a high enough priority to compete for resources with other organization projects, programs, and activities. Those efforts in which senior leaders directly participate stand the best chance of obtaining and maintaining resources.

The different accelerated design approaches require different kinds of human resources for different lengths of time. For example, the modified design team approach requires a relatively small cross section of people, the design team, who work full or part time for several months, augmented in some cases by small task groups. In addition, a senior-level steering committee meets from time to time to manage the overall change effort. The cascading, macro design approach calls for the full participation of a group of senior leaders over a period of a month or two and then the participation of all employees in the micro design and implementation stage. The sequenced, multiple-conference approach requires a large cross section of people working for several short periods of time. All employees are then involved in developing and implementing the micro designs.

Assessment Questions

6a. Given the current demands for resources, how likely is it that the organization will be able to provide time, people, and budget sufficient to support the scope of the change effort?

1	2	3	4	5	6	7
Not at all			Somewhat			Very

6b. How possible is it that unpredictable events could undermine the priority assigned the change effort and reduce the resources available?

1	2	3	4	5	6	7
Not at all			Somewhat			Very

6c. To what extent will the senior leaders directly participate in the design process?

1	2	3	4	5	6	7
Limited			Moderate			Great

Given your answers to the questions in this section, which approach seems to be most appropriate for your organization design effort? Why?

_____

_____

_____

_____

_____

_____

_____

_____

7. Past Experience with Organization Design

An organization that has enjoyed success with organization design in the past will have gained a great deal of knowledge about change and is in a better position to undertake another design effort. In addition, if the organization has had success with large-scale change of any kind, for example, the installation of new technology, it will have learned a great deal about project management and the change process.

The modified design team approach requires the least amount of past experience with organization design. However, an organization that has had success with this approach may have gained enough confidence to move on to the use of one of the high-involvement methods—the cascading, macro design or the sequenced, multiple-conference approach. Those organizations that have experience with large-scale change may be prepared to manage design efforts with a very broad scope. Such efforts commonly use either the cascading, macro design or the sequenced, multiple-conference approaches, which create a macro design for the whole organization.

Assessment Questions

7a. How much positive experience has the organization had using the traditional or modified design team approach to design?

1	2	3	4	5	6	7
None			Moderate			Considerable

7b. How much success has the organization had in the past with large-scale change of any kind, for example, the implementation of new technology?

1	2	3	4	5	6	7
Little			Moderate			Great

7c. How much confidence does the organization have in its ability to use a high-involvement design approach?

1	2	3	4	5	6	7
Little			Moderate			Considerable

Given your answers to the questions in this section, which approach seems to be most appropriate for your organization design effort? Why?

_____

_____

_____

_____

_____

_____

8. Leadership Readiness

It is important that leaders fully understand and are prepared to carry out their role in the method they choose.

Because the different design approaches make different demands on the senior leaders of the organization, is important that they fully understand and are prepared to carry out their role in the method they choose. In the modified design team approach, the leaders serve on a steering committee that secures resources and provides an important oversight function during the design effort. With the cascading, macro design and the sequenced, multiple-conference approaches, the leaders are personally involved in analysis and design activities for significant periods of time. The sequenced, multiple-conference approach challenges senior leaders the most because here they will feel direct pressure from multiple sources, have limited personal control over events, and experience uncertainty about design outcomes; in addition, their personal style will be fully visible in very public settings. To some extent, then, the personal comfort of the leaders with particular approaches will influence the one they choose.

As the senior leaders discuss this "leadership readiness" issue, they may well change their assessment of some of the other factors. For example, if they become more confident of their ability to assume the responsibilities required by the high-involvement approaches, they may also come to believe that the scope of the design effort can be enlarged, more employees can be directly involved, and additional resources can be made available.

Assessment Questions

8a. How ready are the senior leaders to devote large amounts of their time to the change effort?

1	2	3	4	5	6	7
Not at all			Somewhat			Very

8b. How willing are the senior leaders to be directly involved in organization analysis and design activities?

1	2	3	4	5	6	7
Not at all			Somewhat			Very

8c. During the design effort, how prepared will the senior leaders be to deal with pressure from many sources, limited personal control over events, uncertainty about design outcomes, and a high level of public exposure?

1	2	3	4	5	6	7
Not at all			Somewhat			Well

Given your answers to the questions in this section, which approach seems to be most appropriate for your organization design effort? Why?

_____

_____

_____

_____

_____

_____

Summing Up

As you look back over your answers to the questions in all eight sections, which approach do you now believe is the most appropriate for your design effort?

Why? What must be done to ensure the success of this method? Which other approach might be a good backup to hold in reserve?

_____
_____
_____
_____
_____
_____
_____

Making a Wise Choice

Each accelerated design approach has the potential to nudge an organization's culture in a particular direction.

In determining the right design approach to use, decision makers need to consider other factors in addition to the ones above. Each accelerated design approach has the potential to nudge an organization's culture in a particular direction. The modified design team approach affirms the value of developing a thorough understanding of the current organization, including its human dimension. The cascading, macro design approach supports the value of building a partnership among senior leaders. The sequenced, multiple-conference approach reinforces the value of a high level of employee involvement and information sharing. Thus, even if the answers to the questions suggest the use of one particular approach, leaders may elect to use another method that embodies more of the qualities of the preferred culture. If there is not too large a gap between the current and the preferred cultures, then the alternative approach can succeed in producing both a sound design and a modest shift in the culture.

Note that as an organization moves from the modified design team to the sequenced, multiple-conference approach, the number of employees directly involved in the design process increases significantly. Generally, when people help design a new organization they become committed to its rapid implementation. Faster implementation is a major reason why these approaches are able to accelerate the change process.

Finally, remember that the questions and explanatory material presented here are just tools to help clarify the design options and facilitate informed discussion. What really counts is the leadership group's careful assessment of the organization and its considered judgment about the right design approach to use.

CHAPTER 13

Creating a Collaborative Work System in an Engineering Department

Craig McGee

THIS ARTICLE PROVIDES A CASE STUDY of an engineering department for a South American mine owned by a large international natural resources company. The mine implemented high-performance work teams approximately five years ago. The engineering department, being a support group, was not included in the initial implementation. The engineering department provided basic engineering and construction management services for projects for the mine. They developed the engineering design for capital projects, worked with the operating departments to ensure that the design met their requirements, developed cost estimates, oversaw actual construction of the project and so on. Over several years, the department had developed a reputation for being more expensive, slower, and harder to work with than external engineering contractors.

The leadership of the mine was committed to improving the effectiveness of the department. In the words used in this book, they wanted to create a collaborative work system. They hired the author as a consultant to develop and

**Expected
outcomes:**
• **Reduced
  costs**
• **Reduced
  cycle time**
• **Improved
  customer
  satisfaction**

facilitate a design process for the engineering department. The expected outcomes for the redesign process were

- Reduced time to complete engineering/construction projects;
- Reduced costs for completing those projects; and
- Improved customer satisfaction.

The process used for achieving these outcomes, while custom designed for the engineering department, can be adapted for a variety of other settings.

The engineering department consisted of approximately forty people organized into three major sections: project control, design, and construction. The employees in the department possessed primarily technical skills. They possessed both four-year university degrees and technical school certifications. The employees were a combination of payroll employees (on the corporate payroll) and contract employees (outside contractors with six- to eighteen-month contracts that could be, and were, routinely renewed to fulfill project demands).

The project started with an initial visit by the consultant. During that visit, he met individually with each of the section chiefs and a sample of the employees. Using a semi-structured interview format, he queried about the following:

- Strengths and weaknesses of the department;
- Customer perceptions; and
- Interest/willingness to change to a more team-based environment.

The focus was on breaking down functional barriers between the different sections and integration into more dynamic, flexible project-oriented teams.

Based on those interviews, the consultant drafted options for a design process to create a more collaborative work system. The consultant provided three design options to the department's leadership team, ranging from a traditional design team (that is, a diagonal slice task team of four to eight people who do the design themselves) to a large group, whole system approach. During the presentation of these options, the leadership team selected the whole system, large group approach. They desired to involve the whole department and wanted to use the whole system approach to develop greater commitment to the resulting design. Furthermore, they provided sound suggestions and modifications to best utilize the time of the people involved.

The key point was that the leadership team co-developed the process with the consultant. This process alone began the shift toward aligning the systems to support collaboration. Rather than the leaders alone, or a design team alone, making design decisions for the group, this decision to involve the whole department symbolized the shift to a more participative, collaborative work environment. The consultant and the leadership team began modeling behaviors that they wanted to instill in the department. (For more information on the transition to participative approaches, see Chapters 3 and 12.)

The process consisted of three large group events in which the whole department was invited. (See Figure 13.1.) In the first work session (*Create Vision*), participants clarified values and examined the business context in which they worked. During this work session, participants identified key leadership characteristics and the leaders made commitments to develop that leadership capability. In a second department-wide work session (*Define Team Structure*), they evaluated the basic work process and created a collaborative project development process. The process emphasized greater collaboration among different groups within the engineering department and with the clients. Participants defined roles and responsibilities and the decision-making process. In a third work session (*Systems Alignment*), the department analyzed key organizational systems (compensation, performance management, and so forth) and identified how to better align them to support collaboration. Each of those large group events is described in detail below.

To support the redesign effort, a curriculum of team skill training, team leadership training, and upper management leadership training was developed. This curriculum ran concurrently with the design sessions and provided team members and leaders the "right" skills to work more collaboratively.

Figure 13.1. Engineering Department Design Process

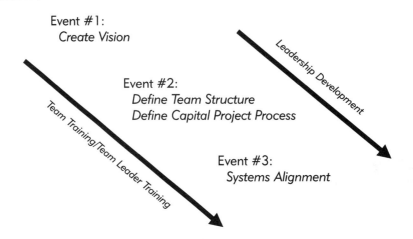

 ## Large Group Event #1: Create Vision

There existed a vision for the mine overall. This vision provided the framework for the mine's transition to a team-based organization. However, this was developed several years previously and the process had not included broad representation of the engineering group. Also, the initial interviews with the engineering personnel identified some misalignment between leadership behaviors and a collaborative work environment. A planning team (primarily the engineering leadership team) and the consultant designed the first work session to create a vision specific to the engineering group and align their (the engineer group's) leadership behaviors with the vision. They also designed the first work session to achieve a collective understanding of the business requirements for the group. They established the following objectives for a two-day work session:

- Better understand *customers' perspectives and requirements*;
- Better understand *business conditions* that the engineering group can support;
- Establish a *common vision* for the engineering group's future; and
- Build a *strong sense of teamwork* among the engineering staff.

The following agenda was developed for the work session:

- Introduction: an appreciative inquiry activity (see below) to understand team members better and establish the proper communications tone;
- Understand the customers' perspective;
- Understand the leader's perspective;
- Understand the employees' perspective;
- Tell our stories . . . understand the history of the department;
- Keep, discard, create . . . define the elements for the vision;
- Draft vision statements;
- Integrate the different vision statements;
- Agree on one vision statement;
- Identify drivers and barriers to achieving the vision; and
- Action plan to remove barriers.

The work session began with an Appreciative Inquiry exercise. Participants selected a partner and shared some of the best experiences they remembered in the engineering group. The exercise focused on shifting the mental frame to a positive, forward focused mindset. It also created a different communications pattern, one based on hope and dreaming, versus a focus on the past with all the negative baggage associated with it. Participants remarked that this work session was probably the first time they had all come together and provided an opportunity to get to know everyone else in the department.

The next activity focused on understanding the business context. The business context was defined from three different perspectives: that of internal customers and clients, senior leadership of the mine, and employees within the engineering department. These three perspectives collectively defined the business context. To help the team understand the customers' perspective, a panel of customers shared their perceptions of the engineering group. Customers provided some candid impressions of what it was like to work with the engineering group. They provided examples of both positive situations as well as difficulties they experienced working with engineering.

RESPONSIBILITIES

Next, the director of engineering shared his view of what the engineering department needed to do to support the mine's business objectives. The key messages he conveyed were:

- The need to work collaboratively with the customers;

- Involving other groups within the engineering group early on . . . breaking down inter-departmental barriers;

- The notion of the project team leader who has full responsibility of a project from inception to completion; and

- Representing the financial interests of the mine . . . working with the customer to minimize costs while providing the required functionality. Customers often requested elaborate, expensive projects that did not support the financial goals of the mine overall.

Last, the group examined the employees' perspective. This was done through an exercise called "Glads, Sads, and Mads." Small groups of employees identified elements of the engineering group they were *glad about,* those they were *sad about,* and those they were downright *mad about.* The author facilitated a discussion that identified those elements the group wanted to carry forward into the future and those elements they wanted to change.

In addition to the business context, the history of a work group influences its vision. To understand the influence of history, participants next explored their history. First, each participant shared a couple of stories about the department. They recounted stories that were significant to them individually and/or to the department. From these stories, they identified elements of the department that they wanted to *keep, discard,* or *create.* These elements provided the basis for a vision statement and, more importantly, developed shared alignment around what team members wanted to create.

Next, in small groups of six to eight, they drafted vision statements. The consultant provided samples of vision statements from other companies as well as the vision statement for the corporation overall and the mine site. Participants used these statements as models, but the consultant encouraged them to draft a statement that best expressed their personal vision.

The groups created four different vision statements. This activity finished day one of the work session. Two representatives from each group volunteered to stay after and integrate the four draft statements into one. Over the next two hours, this working group pulled different elements from the statements and created one common one.

The next morning, the subgroup presented this vision statement to the rest of the department. The rest of the department willingly accepted this vision statement. The final vision statement read:

> "We are a leading team in the development of projects and services in engineering and support areas, with focus on quality, efficiency, safety, and environmental protection."

The bulk of day two focused on identifying how to operationalize the vision. Many groups participate in vision exercises that produce nice statements that hang on walls but that result in little visible change. The planning team designed this work session to generate concrete actions to help the group achieve the vision.

Participants identified "drivers and barriers" to achieving the vision. Some of the barriers they identified were:

- Lack of technical knowledge;
- Poor interpersonal skills;
- Lack of a project control system; and
- Departmental focus.

They next identified actions they could take to remove the barriers. Initially, they generated a large "laundry list" of actions needed. They recognized that this list was too large and that focusing on a smaller set of the vital few increases the likelihood of these actions occurring. Using a multi-voting process, the participants identified seven key actions to take to institutionalize the vision:

- Create a training and development system;
- Deliver a training course to develop interpersonal skills;
- Create a system to ensure client satisfaction;
- Develop strategies to develop better teams and improve employee morale;
- Create department awareness of what goes on in other areas (job rotation, rotation of managers, education);
- Implement a system that recognizes results; and
- Develop a system to optimize the use of department's resources.

The session concluded with a summary of the actions and a preview of the next session. (For more information about agendas and activities for related visioning work sessions, see Chapter 2.)

Large Group Event #2: Define Capital Process and Team Structure

Over the next two months, the leadership team proceeded with the actions that were identified at the previous large group event as necessary to move the department toward its vision. It also planned the next work session with the consultant. They designed the next work session to focus on the process by which they managed projects and the team design to support that process. They established the following objectives for the next session:

- Develop a project delivery process;
- Agree on the appropriate team structures for engineering;
- Create better understanding of the interdependency among different teams and specific roles; and
- Determine levels of empowerment for different roles.

The author/consultant continued to work with the leadership team to develop the agenda for the work session and to provide support in the actions identified in the visioning work session. The leadership team developed the following agenda for this work session:

- Review progress on implementing the vision;
- Define the values to support the vision;
- Assess the current project delivery process;
- Develop a new project delivery process;
- Review the project team structure;
- Develop project team roles;
- Define levels of empowerment for the project team roles;
- Define how to select project team leaders;
- Review project team chartering; and
- Define metrics for success project teams.

Demonstrating progress on implementing the vision was critical.

During the planning process, the planning team and consultant discussed the need to demonstrate progress on implementing the vision. To that end, they developed a module to review progress on implementing the vision.

During the gap between the two work sessions, the leadership team had taken actions to support the implementation of the vision. Some of these actions were visible to the rest of the department, others were not. The planning team wanted to clearly communicate to the rest of the department the number of actions that had been implemented to support the vision.

During the planning process, the planning team also determined that the engineering group needed to create a set of values to support its vision.

During the work session, small groups identified key values to support the vision. Each small group presented its set of values to the entire group. These values were aggregated into one collective list and the entire large group then identified the eleven values they believed were most important. The values included:

- Teamwork,

- Integrity,

- Customer satisfaction, and

- Involvement.

To ensure alignment among everyone, the group identified practices and behaviors for each value.

To ensure alignment among everyone in the department, the group developed a working definition for each value and identified practices and behaviors that illustrated each value.

At this point in the work session the focus shifted from vision and values to process. The work session facilitator broke the entire department down into four groups of six to eight participants each. Each group constructed a flow chart reflecting its perception of how the current capital planning process worked. The capital planning process was the engineering group's core work process that drove all its activities. They also identified what was working in the current process and where breakdowns, disconnects, or delays occurred. Each group shared its flow chart with the rest of the group. The group discovered that the engineering group had no consistent process. Furthermore, the process did not support customers' expectations around involvement in the process, clear communications, or timely project delivery.

Participants, again in four small groups, now began drafting a new process. The four small groups produced four different processes. At this point, two activities were conducted simultaneously, one activity to consolidate the four draft processes into one, and the second activity to define the key roles that had emerged in all four draft processes. To complete the first activity, the process integration, two representatives from each of the original four groups formed a new group that then integrated the four processes into one.

To complete the second activity, defining roles in the process, the rest of the participants defined key roles required in the process and the responsibilities for each role. An underlying premise for this activity was that some sort of project team structure would best support the new process. The consultant provided participants with an overview of what a project team was and what roles could be included in a project team structure. Prior to the work session, the planning team and consultant had drafted a set of proposed project team roles and responsibilities; they did this to provide the group members with a concrete example that they could react to. The participants agreed that the project team structure presented by the planning team and the consultant was appropriate. They then identified the key roles/representatives to include on a project team:

- Project team leader
- Project control
- Design
- Construction

These were consistent with what the planning team had developed, but were modified somewhat by the work groups.

For each role/representative, the group also identified specific responsibilities and tasks for which that person was responsible. This became the basis for the project team structure that the group agreed to. The model project team included all of the key functions required to execute a project.

The model project team included all of the key functions required to execute a project.

By having them all included as core team members, they could plan timing and resources early on in the project. This enabled greater collaboration and resolution of problems.

After a period of time, the large group reconvened. At this time, the process team reviewed the integrated process. They presented key features critical to creating greater collaboration with the customer and within the engineering group. These key elements included:

- Clear agreement with the customer on the scope of the project;
- Early involvement with the customer regarding design decisions;
- Providing the customer with design options and the customer accepting responsibility for the design choice; and
- Initiating a project kickoff meeting that would include all project team members, relevant support groups, and the customer.

Similarly, the remaining participants presented the project team structure they had agreed to, along with the explanation of the roles and responsibilities in the project team structure.

The next activity in the work session focused on levels of empowerment and how to involve different parties in different decisions. The group recognized that much of collaboration was based on how decisions were made and how they involved people in those decisions. Participants reviewed the process developed by the subteam and identified what decisions needed to be made or where key activities occurred. For each of those decisions/activities, they identified key parties to include and how to include them. The consultant provided an empowerment model to guide this effort. For each decision/activity, the group identified:

- Which parties needed to be *consulted* with;
- Which parties needed to be *informed* about the decision or activity;
- Which party (or parties) needed to *approve* the decision;
- Which party was *responsible* for driving the decision or activity; and
- Who *did not need to be involved* in the decision/activity.

 This activity established the patterns of collaboration among the different stakeholders. (For more information on defining communications and decision-making processes, see Chapter 18.)

The remainder of the work session focused on how to implement the project team structure and associated project delivery process. Participants discussed subjects such as:

- How do we select project team members (including the project team leader)?
- How do we charter a project team?

- What training is needed to develop specialized skills in project team members?

- What metrics should be used to gauge the effectiveness of project teams?

The work session concluded with a summary of action items and a preview of the next work session.

Large Group Event #3: Systems Alignment

Aligning the organizational systems is a critical element in creating effective collaborative work systems.

Aligning the organizational systems is a critical element in creating effective collaborative work systems. Organizational systems can reinforce behaviors incongruent with collaboration. The consultant worked with the planning team to identify the key organizational systems that impacted the proposed process and team design. The planning team and consultant developed a work session to examine the organization systems and identify ways to better align those systems with the redesigned process and project team structure. The objectives of the third work session were as follows:

- Understand the impact of organizational systems on work processes;

- Assess current organizational systems;

- Align organizational systems to support team structures; and

- Agree on an implementation plan for moving forward with the vision and the team structure.

Rather than focus on all organizational systems, the planning team and consultant prioritized the systems and agreed to focus on five:

- Compensation and rewards,

- Performance management,

- Metrics,

- Leadership, and

- Project control.

The planning team and consultant designed a three-day work session to examine these organizational systems and develop redesign recommendations. Given the facts that the engineering group did not own many of these systems and that corporate policies governed a significant portion of these systems, the framing of the exercises in the work sessions was more sensitive. The objective of the exercises was to develop recommendations and suggestions for changes that the engineering leadership could pursue with the proper staff personnel. The planning group was careful not to create expectations that could not be met.

The first system the group tackled was compensation. The planning team scheduled a conference call with the manager of compensation. He planned originally to attend in person, but was called away to another site, so he participated via a conference call with the group. He explained many of the compensation components, such as job grading, job evaluation, merit increases, and so on. Other representatives explained the recognition programs. There existed some misunderstanding about how the programs were designed and what approvals the engineering leaders needed to utilize them. The session helped answer some questions (for example, "As a project team leader, can I give a team member a gift certificate for a job well done?") about the programs and how they could support the new processes and team structure.

The group next focused on the performance management system. The consultant presented some material on performance management and a draft performance management process. Performance management is fairly complex, so the planning team and consultant felt that the group needed something concrete to react to. The consultant encouraged the group to "add to, delete from, and modify" that draft as necessary. Elements of the performance management process included:

- Formal annual reviews;
- Interim reviews throughout the year to gauge progress;
- Personal objectives linked with organizational goals and key result areas;
- Project related objectives for each team on which an individual participated; and
- Ongoing coaching.

The group also determined that a significant part of the development efforts should be focused on developing skills and abilities necessary to lead and work in projects. They identified specific actions to select, assess, and develop project leaders.

The group then turned its attention to the metrics system. The group had already developed a set of draft metrics for the project teams in the previous work session. However, there remained a "functional, administrative" team to which people reported administratively and that served as a home base for people not assigned to projects. The group focused on creating metrics for these administrative teams. The metrics they identified included:

- Development of technical competencies;
- Storage and processing of information;
- Development of teamwork and a collaborative environment; and
- Systems/process development; continuous improvement.

(For more information on metrics, see Chapter 26.)

The fourth system the group examined was the leadership system. The planning team and the consultant developed a draft set of competencies for project team leaders and functional leaders. The consultant presented these to the group and the group added to, deleted from, and modified this set of competencies. Similarly, the group examined how leaders were selected and developed. They created a process for selecting and developing both functional leaders and project team leaders. This process included assessment centers for selection and development, creation of a pool of potential team leaders, ongoing assessment and development of team leaders, and certification of project leaders that enabled them to assume larger, more complex projects. (For more information on team leadership, see Chapter 7.)

The last system the group examined was the project control system. Representatives from the project control group provided details about what information systems and templates were available for managing a project. The larger group provided suggestions for additional tools that would support the project team concept.

The work session concluded with a discussion of an implementation plan. Key actions for moving forward were summarized and reviewed with the group. The planning team and consultant had identified a series of training activities to support the transition to the project team structure. They reviewed this training curriculum with the entire group and provided a draft schedule. (For more information on the whole subject of system alignment, see Chapter 11.)

Summary

This engineering group identified a basic need to change its work structure and process to better suit its customers' needs. Furthermore, team members recognized the importance of aligning the organizational systems to support the new processes and structure. A series of large group events in which the entire department participated provided a vehicle for not only redesigning the systems, structures, and processes, but also for building commitment and support for those systems, structures, and processes. The process engaged everyone in the department directly, eliminating the need to "sell" the proposed changes. Changes were not proposed; they were developed and agreed to in real time.

This project provided some interesting learnings that may be instructive to others embarking on similar work:

- *Good work can be done in large groups.*

- *However, large group work sessions must be carefully designed and facilitated.* There were times during the work sessions when more thoughtful design could have improved the work session.

- *Support systems can be difficult to change.* They often span the entire organization, and owners of those support systems can be reluctant to make the changes needed to support the new work structures.

- *Working in another language (even with good translation services) can be difficult.* Some terms and phrases that American consultants and practitioners commonly use do not always have an equivalent in a foreign language.

- *Models for work group design in manufacturing settings often do not apply in knowledge work settings.* There were significant differences in the team design in the engineering group versus the operations groups. Some people at the site were uncomfortable with the lack of consistency. Significant effort at times was required to ensure support for these differences.

In spite of some of the "challenges" presented, the engineering group members are now actively engaged in implementing the redesigned systems, structures, and processes they created.

CHAPTER 14

Real Collaboration Requires Power Sharing
The Participative Design Approach

Catherine Bradshaw,
Joan Roberts, and Sylvia Cheuy

O VER THE LAST TWO DECADES, "self-directed work teams" have been of great interest to organizations. Many leaders and managers have jumped on the bandwagon, flattening the organization by removing supervisors and mid-level managers, forming work teams that cut across traditional departments, and cutting teams loose to manage their own work, all in the name of creating collaborative work systems that are flexible, productive, and innovative. Unfortunately, all too often these efforts fall short of expectations. Teams flounder with unclear goals. Newly appointed "team leaders/coaches" evolve into traditional supervisors, fostering employee resentment and cynicism. Productivity and quality can plummet.

In this chapter we suggest that sustainable and system-wide collaboration is possible. Indeed, collaboration can be introduced and sustained over a short period in any organization, but how can collaboration occur throughout an entire organization on an ongoing basis?

**Real and
sustained
collaboration
requires a
democratic
workplace.**Real and sustained collaboration requires a democratic workplace in which people participate directly in making decisions that impact their work and performance. This is achieved only through a fundamental shift in the power and control relationships of an organization that results from realigning the organization's structure and design principle.

The participative design process described in this chapter provides such realignment and goes beyond most redesign efforts by:

- Making a conscious shift in the power dynamics of the organization, thereby redefining the nature and quality of working relationships, and

- Engaging the entire system, both employees and managers, in the process of redesigning the whole organization.

Such an approach creates a workplace that is more rewarding for employees and also makes sound business sense. Employees are committed to the success of the organization, are more highly skilled, and are able to contribute those skills; consequently, productivity goes up, costs go down, and quality is improved.

In this chapter we will present:

- The assumptions and theoretical framework underlying participative design;

- The design principles that are at the core of any organizational structure;

- The conditions that must be met to ensure a successful shift to collaborative work systems through participative design; and finally,

- The value and benefits of (that is, the business case for) making this shift.

The Participative Design Approach

The participative design process is a way of engaging the entire organization in determining how the system should be designed. The core technology of this process is the participative design workshop (PDW). During the PDW, people learn the basic principles of organizational design (which are described in Chapter 15). *They then intentionally design or redesign their organization to best create the conditions that will allow people to produce high-quality work, which ultimately leads to a democratic organization structure.* In such an organization, people are directly involved in deciding on the issues that impact them. They continuously gain knowledge and skills, see a desirable career path for themselves, and get support and respect from their colleagues.

The participative design workshop utilizes the following basic format:

- *Analyze the current structure*: participants learn about the bureaucratic design principle; assess their work on six criteria; identify the skills that are needed to do the work; and locate their work section.

- *Redesign the structure*: participants learn about the democratic design principle; draw the current workflow and structure; and redraw the structure to better meet conditions for workplace productivity.

- *Plan for implementation of the new design*: participants draft a comprehensive set of measurable goals for their section; develop training goals based on needs identified through the skills held analysis—this includes designing career paths for individuals; determine other requirements for implementing the design, for example, changes in the technology, in the hardware layout, in mechanisms for coordination; and show how the new design will meet the six criteria for productive work.

Each participative design process needs to be tailored to the context and needs of the particular organization. However, there are a number of principles that guide the design of any participative design process. The following principles are implicit in the participative design framework and essential for establishing collaborative work systems:

- People are purposeful and ideal-seeking (Ackoff & Emery, 1972), that is to say, people welcome opportunities to live meaningful lives and they actively strive for their ideals.

The most effective organizational designs come from the people doing the work.

- The most effective organizational designs come from the people doing the work; everyone who will be impacted should have hands-on participation in developing the new organizational design.

- The organizational structure has a strong impact on how people work together—their culture and their social interactions.

- When responsibility for control, coordination, and outcomes is in the hands of the people doing the work, a climate of collaboration and creativity is established.

- People should be paid according to their skills and should be rewarded for social and business skills, for example, decision making, strategy development, conflict resolution, or problem solving, as well as technical skills.

From Bureaucracy to Democracy: A Shift in Design Principle

For more than forty years, Fred and Merrelyn Emery and their colleagues have done groundbreaking research that has highlighted the role that organizational design plays in creating productive and humane workplaces. They've discovered, through studies beginning in the English coal mines of the early 1950s (Trist & Bamforth, 1951), that organizations are designed along one of two basic design principles: the *Bureaucratic Design Principle,* often referred to as Design Principle 1 (DP1), or the *Democratic Design Principle,* often referred to as Design Principle 2 (DP2). In addition, there is a third mode that organizations often fall into when there is an absence of any clear structure or design principle; we call this *laissez-faire.* Each of these organizational forms drives people to adopt particular ways of thinking and behaving.

Bureaucratic Design Principle

In Design Principle 1, people are segmented into narrow job functions and are treated as replaceable parts (flexibility is built into the system through redundancy of parts), and the responsibility for control and coordination lies at least one level above where the work is performed (with the supervisor or manager).

We've all had experiences with these kinds of workplaces:

- People are more concerned about pleasing their bosses than about supporting co-workers in meeting goals;

- People feel competitive with co-workers;

- Information only moves up and down the hierarchy and not across work teams;

- People must go through elaborate chains of command to take action on the smallest detail;

- People are focused on their small piece of the work rather than on the broader goals of the organization; and

- People follow orders and therefore don't feel responsible for the outcomes of their actions.

Design Principle 1 can also be understood as a "dominant hierarchy" in which levels of the hierarchy are defined by the control that they have over the levels below them.

Democratic Design Principle

In Design Principle 2, each person performs multiple functions using multiple skills, including social, business, and technical skills (flexibility is built into the system through redundancy of skills). The individual is therefore more valuable to the organization and is not easily replaced. The responsibility for control and coordination is in the hands of the people doing the work.

This structure creates a self-managing team environment in which people share responsibility for meeting the measurable goals that they've jointly agreed to as a team, goals that link directly to the broader targets of the organization. To meet their goals, teams set their schedules, determine their work processes, and monitor the contribution of their members. They have the skills in the group—planning, analysis, technical, and social—to be able to handle the work. It is in the individual's interest to help colleagues out because they are mutually responsible for the same goals: critical information is shared across the organization and skills are applied where needed to get the work done.

Design Principle 2 can be thought of as a "non-dominant hierarchy" (Emery, 1993, p. 38), one in which teams at different levels of the organization are responsible for functions critical to supporting the whole enterprise but not for controlling and coordinating the work of those at lower levels.

A few strict rules

This kind of structure ensures that people are getting certain human needs met, thus generating a creative, productive working environment. The following six criteria for productive work have been identified through field research in Europe, Scandinavia, Australia, India, and North America (Emery & Thorsrud, 1969). In a DP2 organization these requirements are maximized. The first three refer to the content of work. The optimal amount varies for each person—that is, you can have too much or too little of them. The second three refer to the climate of the workplace; people can never have too much of them.

1. *Adequate Elbow Room.* People need to be able to make decisions about how they do their work, but also have enough direction and structure so that they know what to do.

2. *Opportunities for Continuous Learning.* People are able to get feedback that is specific and timely and set goals for themselves that are reasonable challenges.

3. *Sufficient Variety.* Each person has the amount of task variety that is right for her/him, enough to prevent boredom, but not so much that it prevents settling into a satisfying rhythm of work.

4. *Mutual Support and Respect.* Conditions are conducive to people providing support and respect to their co-workers.

5. *Meaningfulness.* People have a sense that their work contributes to the social good and are able to see how their part of the work leads to a final use or purpose.

6. *A Desirable Future.* People have a career path that allows for personal growth and the acquisition of new skills and knowledge.

While meeting workers' psychological needs is ethical in itself, the bottom-line results are equally important. When these human conditions are met, people work more productively and feel committed to the broader goals of the organization. Clearly, getting maximum effort and quality from employees translates into real financial gain for the business.

Laissez-Faire

In a laissez-faire organization, a design principle is effectively absent and people operate without any parameters or direction to guide their work. There is a general feeling of "do your own thing," without any thought for or knowledge of the needs of the broader system. Unfortunately, this system is often confused with a democratic design because people are thrown into "self-directed teams" with no sense of direction or knowledge of the broader context to guide their work. People in a laissez-faire organization will frequently revert to DP1 behavior as a way to regain some control over the situation. Examples of this include the "team leader" who is a supervisor in disguise or the manager who flies in to fix a team's problem by telling its members how they need to do the work. This leaves people feeling confused and then resentful of being treated differently from the professed style of the organization. Early experiments conducted by Lewin, Lippitt, and White (1939) showed that laissez-faire systems create the same negative energy and emotions that one finds in the autocratic environments of Design Principle 1.

Necessary Conditions to Support a Successful Participative Design Process

In this section, we present an overview of the conditions that should be established to ensure a successful participative design process. *Not surprisingly, considerable information, education, and planning are necessary.* Critical success factors to be addressed prior to conducting a participative design workshop include the following:

- Building awareness and commitment at all levels of the organization;
- Preparing the various levels of management for their changed role in a DP2 structure;
- Designing the sequence and makeup of the various participative design workshops;
- Developing a legal agreement that details the guiding principles for redesign;
- Establishing partnerships with staff unions; and
- Ensuring that explicit organizational goals and strategies exist that work teams can use to set clear and measurable goals.

Building Awareness and Commitment Throughout the Organization

Once the leadership has made the decision to transform its organizational structure to DP2, education is needed to build awareness and commitment at all levels of the organization. Front line staff, middle managers, executive leaders, and even board members and shareholders all need to understand the bottom-line results that the new system will realize. When presenting this information, leaders need to highlight the opportunities that such a shift in structure provides. For example, today's rapidly changing and unpredictable business climate makes adaptability a necessary survival skill for all organizations. *The DP2 organization is able to quickly adapt to changes in the environment by infusing design skills throughout the organization, building skill flexibility into the system, and continually tapping into the intellectual and scanning capacity of all employees.* Many employees are also attracted to the increased opportunity to diversify their skills and assume more responsibility for their work.

While it is important for people at all levels of the organization to be well-informed about the organization's intended shift to a democratic design, it is particularly important that senior management receive the education necessary to support this transformation. It is well-known that a major cause for failure of organizational change initiatives is lack of endorsement by senior managers. *It is therefore critical that senior managers have a deep understanding and appreciation for why a shift to a DP2 structure is in the long-term, best interest of the organization as a whole.*

Preparing Management for Its Changed Role

The DP2 structure changes the very nature of management. In traditional organizations, a manager's role is largely to set goals, issue orders, set schedules, and manage performance. *However, in a democratic organization, the role of management is to encourage teams to set their own goals and coordinate their own work.* This does not mean allowing people to do whatever they want, but rather providing the leadership and "goal focus" necessary to promote and support team self-management. Table 14.1 describes management roles at different levels in a democratic or DP2 organization.

Table 14.1. Management Roles in a DP2 Organization

Management Position	Role and Responsibilities in Democratic (DP2) Organization
Overall Management at All Levels	Hierarchy of functions—teams establish relationships of mutual dependency and cooperation with other functional areas.
President	Interface with the outside world.
	Respond if functional managers feel organization's strategic plan needs updating. Intervene in situations where certain functional managers can/will not cooperate.
Senior/Executive Management	As a team, assume responsibility for day-to-day operations.
	Establish and negotiate with the president the coordination goals and targets that relate to the president's goals.
	Actively adopt and practice the new way of working.
Senior Management with Specialist Expertise	In situations where multi-skilling is not possible because work is highly specialized (for example, finance, human resources), each specialist continues to control his or her own work.
	Take group responsibility for the coordination of the team's work and for meeting the social goals of the team as a whole.
Plant/Business Unit Management	Maintain a two-way flow on policy, strategy, goals, performance problems, needs, and capabilities.
	Continually assess whether plant/unit goals are being accomplished, processes are effective, behavior is consistent with new structure, capabilities are being developed and maintained.
	Focus on team processes and responsibilities and use participative approaches to regularly review the way work is organized.
Plant Middle Management and Line Management	Focus on operational team processes and responsibilities
	Work together with teams, as equals, but from different functional perspective.
	Assist teams in becoming more proficient in self-management.
	See and communicate the "big picture" beyond any one function.
	Regularly monitor team performance based on agreed-on goals.
	Intervene when teams move outside their mandate.
	Temporarily transfer to other parts of the organization to assist with troubleshooting in other functional areas.
	Provide teams with timely, relevant information.
	Connect teams with management.
	Facilitate ongoing work redesign as part of a continuous improvement process.

Source: The Nuts and Bolts of PD: A State of the Art Process for Creating and Sustaining Adaptive Organizations. Melbourne, Australia: The Amerin Consulting Group.

Managers need to be reassured that they will be involved in the redesign of the organization, since they are often left out of such processes. Often managers are concerned that the organization will fall apart if they aren't "in control" of things as they were in the traditional, bureaucratic structure and, from a place of fear, they can be masterful at pulling political maneuvers that sabotage the move into DP2. They need to be reassured that they will perform functions in the new structure that are critical to the success of the organization and that the DP2 structure will include a new system of accountabilities and controls.

This shift in the manager's role can be very difficult for some because it requires the "unlearning" of many traditional management approaches. For this reason, senior managers need support in learning how to manage differently and in adapting to the personal change this new organizational structure requires. Having managers who model a willingness to learn and apply new ways of doing things is a powerful motivator for the structural change overall.

There is no supervisory role within a DP2 organization since control and coordination of work becomes the responsibility of the teams.

There is no supervisory role within a DP2 organization since control and coordination of work becomes the responsibility of the teams doing the work. In an organization's transition from a DP1 organization to a DP2 organization, ex-supervisors can assume valuable, new roles. Some examples of this include:

- Becoming part of a special projects, resource, or support team;
- Joining an operational team; or
- Scanning the external environment, including clients and suppliers, thereby enhancing the organization's capacity to anticipate and adapt to change.

An excellent way to identify important tasks or special projects that can be undertaken by ex-supervisors is to create a list of all the important tasks and/or projects that have not been getting done in the organization because of time constraints. Use this list to develop specific goals for special work teams of ex-supervisors.

Sequencing and Composition of the Participative Design Workshops

The design, sequencing, and workshop composition of any participative design process need to be carefully planned (again, see Chapter 15 for more details on the PDW). Overall, the objective of such a process should be to move the entire organization into a democratic or DP2 structure. Design decisions deal with who should be designing what sections with whom and when. It may make sense to have whole sections in the same workshop or to have only a deep slice team designing a section and then taking their draft design to the broader group in a town hall kind of format for a final decision by the whole group. In situations where only certain areas of the organization are open to redesign, it is critical that the boundaries between the redesigned area and the broader organization be carefully managed. "Pilot-testing" of a democratic structure does not work, not only because it is impossible to have two competing organizational structures operating at one time, but also because in such tests the required shift in power relations is never clearly made within the organization.

Developing a Legal Agreement of Guiding Principles for Redesign

There are three essential guiding principles at the core of participative design, and these principles must be in place as a legal agreement between staff, management, and the union, if one exists, before embarking on the redesign:

1. An acknowledgement of the organization's intent to shift from a bureaucratic structure to a democratic structure, where responsibility for control and coordination of work shifts to those doing the work;

2. A commitment from the highest level of the organization that no involuntary layoffs will occur as a result in this shift of organizational structure; and

3. A commitment from the highest levels of the organization that there will be no reductions in pay as a result of a change in individual roles or in the organization's overall structure.

Since a fundamental belief of this approach is that no organizational designs be imposed, it is essential that workers at all levels of the organization be engaged fully in developing the redesigned structure. The guiding principles listed above emphasize the intent of the PD workshops and provide people with the necessary assurances that free them up to be creative and fully engaged in the task at hand.

In addition to these three guiding principles, additional principles that clearly describe the features that are and are not open for change in the redesign process must be clearly articulated at the outset. These typically include such things as strategic goals and personnel policies.

Establishing Partnerships with Unions

Unionized organizations need to ensure that their union reps become thoroughly educated and informed about participative design and its intent. *It is critical that the unions be involved in the redesign as current collective agreements may identify issues that cannot be changed during the redesign process.* It is also important to negotiate an agreement with the union for its overall support of the participative design process. Ultimately, a formal, legal agreement outlining the guiding principles for redesign needs to be endorsed by management, union, and employees.

Ensuring Explicit Organizational Goals and Strategies Exist

Explicit organizational goals and strategies are necessary to ensure effective redesign workshops. The search conference (see Chapter 2) is an excellent way to establish such organizational goals if none formally exist or if they need to be updated. These organizational goals guide each team in developing a comprehensive set of clear and measurable goals for itself during the PD workshop. Examples of such goals might be "Reduce waste by X amount" or "Shorten product design time by X amount." Each team's goals are later negotiated with management and should include both task goals (such as quantity and quality of production) and human components (such as skill development, performance management, and team coordination) in keeping with the overall organizational strategic plan.

Benefits of the Participative Design Process

There is a solid business case for organizations to adopt a democratic structure.

In this section, we demonstrate that there is a solid business case for organizations adopting a democratic structure.

The benefits to organizations can include the following:

- A happy and healthy workforce with reduced employee turnover and absenteeism;

- Attainment of organizational performance goals;

- A workforce able to adapt to changing environmental conditions; and

- Extraordinary productivity gains.

As mentioned earlier, a DP2 organization responds to the human need for productive work. People are involved in decision making, continuously gain new knowledge and skills, see a desirable career path for themselves, and gain support and respect from their colleagues. This leads to a healthy and more satisfied workforce. The employee benefits, but so does the organization: absenteeism and turnover are reduced, productivity goes up, and quality is improved.

A recent Health Canada study, *Best Advice on Stress Risk Management in the Workp*lace (Shain, 2000), presents three models of stress in the workplace.

All three models agree that certain workplace conditions are key to the production of stress and that these conditions are largely a result of how the work is organized. Shain states that "fairness at work," that is , the level of control and reward, is missing in unhealthy workplaces. When work is felt to be unfair, people feel depressed, angry, demoralized, and anxious; when it is felt to be fair, they feel satisfied, calm, and enthused. The "six criteria" outlined earlier in this chapter ensure that the conditions to create "fairness at work" are embedded into the participative design process.

Once a PD process is underway, an organization's goals are often quickly implemented and attained. DP2 organizations are decisive. Goal focus is very high as employees accrue the benefits that result in the successful implementation of organizational and team goals, including pay for skills, opportunities to increase and diversify their knowledge and skill base, and often some form of financial gainsharing. Since everyone is involved in deciding what their workplace design is, and they have control over their work process, they are highly motivated to contribute their wisdom and productivity to the work team. In addition, they are able to hold their peers accountable for high quality input to the work process, resulting in a work team poised to take advantage of the opportunities and challenges that present themselves on a day-to-day basis.

In *People in Charge,* Rehm (1999) describes how Southcorp, an Australian wine company, embarked on a PD process. In this example of meeting performance goals, the Karadoc Winery:

- Reduced inventories from three to four weeks to ten days for wine casks and from two months to four or five weeks for bottled wine;

- Dramatically improved safety performance from 1,500 hours of lost time to fewer than eighty hours; and

- Improved productivity across the board by 7 percent.

Another major benefit of a PD process is that the organization becomes more adaptable to continuous change in turbulent environments by tapping into the wisdom of all employees. The PD workshop results in a design that ensures flexibility, continuous learning, and the full utilization of employees' skills and knowledge. By releasing management control over work processes, sharing information on the demands of the marketplace, and providing a democratic structure for employee participation, a PD process allows employees to understand and be an integral part of meeting the organization's challenges.

Productivity gains can be extraordinary. Financial performance is dramatically improved when the intellectual capital of all employees is fully engaged. It is clear from the literature that the greatest potential to significantly improve the financial performance of a firm comes from integrated design strategies that deal directly with power and control levers within an organization (Macy & Izumi, 1993).

Barry Macy and Hiroaki Izumi's (1993) seminal work, *Organizational Change, Design, and Work Innovation,* examined 131 North American organization change and work innovation studies. The study identified the design features and action levers of change projects and assessed them in light of the desired effects and resulting impact. Fifty percent of the action levers were correlated with financial improvement for the client organization. Specifically, they found that the following action levers were most influential in improving financial performance:

- A holistic change strategy;
- Structural changes to the authority and accountability grid (flattening the hierarchy);
- The use of self-directed work teams;
- An open flow of information throughout the organization and formalized employee involvement in decision-making functions;
- Multi-skilling;
- Common job classifications; and
- Job enrichment and job enlargement.

A PD process incorporates all the levers identified by Macy and Izumi.

Syncrude, in Alberta, Canada, is the world's largest oil sands crude oil production facility. After attempting a number of organizational design efforts, including three weeks of human relations training for its employees, Syncrude heard about the successful implementation of participative design in an Exxon plant in Rotterdam. Dr. Donald de Guerre was hired to implement a participative design process.

Productivity improvements as a result of Syncrude's redesign were astounding, with an overall productivity improvement of over 75 percent (Purser & Cabana, 1998, p. 297). Table 14.2 details this performance improvement.

Table 14.2. Syncrude's Productivity Improvements

Measure	1989 (before PD)	1995 (after PD)		1997	
Production (Mbbls)	54	74	+37%	76	+40%
Revenue ($M)	$1174	$1764	+50%	$2107	+79%
Operating Costs (as spent $/bbl)	$17.17	$13.69	−20%	$13.78	−20%
Workforce	4,704	3,672	−22%	3,513	−26%
Productivity (Mbbls/person)	11,500	20,200	+76%	21,550	+84%

By 1998, Syncrude was operating with 50 percent fewer middle managers and administrative staff (Purser & Cabana, 1998, p. 295).

We believe that the improved financial performance and productivity of the cases cited presents a strong case for authentic collaboration and real power sharing. Although the magnitude of the shift in organizational power and the role of management may seem daunting, the benefits are clearly compelling.

Conclusion

To develop a collaborative, team-based organization, leaders need to be willing to design a structure that allows employees to control and coordinate their own work, support one another, continuously learn and apply new skills, and feel connected and committed to the broader goals of the organization. Efforts that create collaborative teams without changing the underlying power structure, or that aim to change the structure using autocratic means, are unable to sustain system-wide collaboration over the long run. Participative design uses a participative, democratic process to move an organization's structure into a democratic design. It recognizes the importance of improving conditions for employees and how this leads to solid business results.

The proven benefits of the PD process are that:

- It is fast and economical; there is no need for a lengthy and expensive redesign process that depends on expert consultants or design teams that consume company resources;

- It builds workforce commitment in implementing and sustaining the new plan;

- It creates a workplace that is flexible and highly adaptive to environmental change; people are able to quickly redesign their workplace whenever they need to; and

- It increases quality and productivity and reduces costs over time.

Additional Resources

Aughton, P. (1996, March). Participative design within a strategic context. *Journal for Quality and Participation.*

Cabana, S. (1995, November/December). Can people restructure their own work? *Target,* 11(6).

Cabana, S., & Fiero, J.D. (1995, July/August). Motorola: Strategic planning and the search conference. *Journal for Quality and Participation.*

Ellison, S. (1999). Classic blunders in team implementation: Lessons learned from the 90s [On-line]. Available: www.workteams.unt.edu/orderfrm.htm [last accessed August 29, 2001]

Rehm, R. (1995). *Participative design.* Unpublished paper.

CHAPTER 15

The Participative Design Workshop and Its Variations

Donald W. de Guerre

THE PARTICIPATIVE DESIGN WORKSHOP (PDW) and its tools are conceptually grounded in a socio-ecological open systems theory (OST) developed by Fred and Merrelyn Emery (1976).

The PDW is a concept-based approach for developing and maintaining collaborative work systems.

The PDW is a concept-based approach for developing and maintaining collaborative work systems found in team-based organizations (TBOs). In this chapter we will briefly review this theory and how it applies to organizations, briefly review the development of the PDW, and then describe how is can be used to create and sustain TBOs. Several variations of the basic PDW, including its use to design a new organization, will also be discussed. (Chapter 14 provides additional background information on the PDW, including extended discussion of organization design principles mentioned below. For alternative approaches to organization redesign that lead to rapid transformation see Chapter 12.)

OST defines three inter-relations that are necessary and sufficient to characterize any human system, such as an organization. For an organization, these include:

1. Relationships within the organization, for example, horizontally between departments and vertically between levels;

2. Relationships between organizations who are stakeholders in an organization, such as government units, financial and educational institutions; and

3. The many two-way relationships between the organization and its external stakeholders. All organizations must learn from their environments, must meet the demands of stakeholders, seek to survive, and seize opportunities to grow. Organizations may also make plans and take action to compete in their markets.

Conceptual Background

There are four historical landmarks in the development of OST and the PDW that are helpful to review in order to understand the conceptual basis of this tool:

1. Lewin, Lippitt, and White (1939) identified three social environments in which people live and work: the totalitarian, democratic, and laissez-faire. Laissez-faire social environments, which are characterized by an absence of structure, are not democratic. Rather, they generate a negative affect and low energy similar to what people experience in totalitarian environments. This is important because TBOs should not be laissez-faire. Teams do best when they have goals and measures, methods to record progress, opportunity to analyze performance, and are encouraged to improve performance.

> **The PDW is a tool for people to create organizations that are well-run and productive and good for people.**

2. Building on Lewin's work, Emery (1959) described organizations as sociotechnical systems. The PDW is a tool for people to create organizations that are well-run and productive and good for people, as well.

3. As people are the core of any human system, including collaborative work systems, it is beneficial to have some view of what people are like. Ackoff and Emery (1972) provide one such view and describe people as: ideal seeking; in possession of *will*; able to produce different outcomes when placed in the same or different environments; and able to achieve the same outcome in different ways. This view suggests that flexibility is key in leading, organizing, and managing people.

Another important point: human beings live in groups and do not work well isolated from others. Even highly independent, high-need achievers find ways to work well in team-based organizations; they find specialized, individual tasks that they can perform best for their team. So team-based organizations are generally more healthy environments for purposeful people.

4. Sociotechnical systems analysis and design was tested in Norway in the 1960s (Emery & Thorsrud, 1976). It was empirically demonstrated that self-managed team-based organizations were clearly more effective for both people and productivity. However, sociotechnical systems analysis and design (STS) at that time required the extensive involvement of consultants and it was not always well-received by workers. Though STS helped consultants and perhaps a few managers learn about the work performed in a particular work area, the people who did the work already knew it well enough to redesign it. So Emery (1967) developed a more inclusive approach for creating sociotechnical systems, *participative design*. In participative design, employees are directly involved in the design of their own workplace, they learn OST, and experience what it is like to be in a democratic organization. At first called the developing human resources (DHR) workshops, it was not until 1974 that Emery was able to develop an elegant and simple one-day workshop, including only what was necessary for organization analysis and design. It is now called the participative design workshop (PDW), and it has been implemented around the world. Many variations of the workshop have been tried.

A few strict rules

The Participative Design Workshop

The PDW is a workshop with the single purpose of producing a democratic organization structure. In the PDW participants are provided with six criteria for a work organization that often they design back into their organization. The six criteria, which are presented in Chapter 14, as well, are

The PDW is a workshop with the single purpose of producing a democratic organization structure.

1. *Adequate Elbow Room.* People need to be able to make decisions about how they do their work, but also have enough direction and structure so that they know what to do.

2. *Opportunities for Continuous Learning.* People are able to get feedback that is specific and timely and set goals for themselves that are reasonable challenges.

3. *Sufficient Variety.* Each person has the amount of task variety that is right for her or him, enough to prevent boredom, but not so much that it prevents settling into a satisfying rhythm of work.

4. *Mutual Support and Respect.* Conditions are conducive to people providing support and respect to their co-workers.

5. *Meaningfulness.* People have a sense that their work contributes to the social good and are able to see how their part of the work leads to a final use or purpose.

6. *A Desirable Future.* People have a career path that allows for personal growth and the acquisition of new skills and knowledge.

The PDW comes in two basic forms. One is for redesigning existing bureaucratic organizations and the other is for designing new organizations. In large organizations, a series of PDWs is used. The total system participative redesign process includes the redesign of production or service delivery systems, management systems, and support systems and the necessary realignment of company policies and practices. Prior to implementing the PDW in a bureaucratic organization, management must agree that the "design principle" on which the new organization will be based will be changed from a bureaucratic to a democratic one. (For more information on design principles, see Chapter 14.)

The PDW used to create a new organization is called a Greenfield PDW. In using this approach there is less analysis since, of course, there is no existing organization to analyze. Each of the two basic forms of the PDW will be discussed in more detail later.

In order for employees to accept responsibility for self-management, it is important that they be involved in designing their section or area of the organization. In a one-day PDW, participants analyze their existing work organization, propose a new design, and prepare an implementation plan for that design. A benefit of this process is that all participants learn a great deal about the work that others do.

In a two-day PDW it becomes possible to get the whole system in the room. Participants are able to see how the parts of the organization fit together.

In a two-day PDW it becomes possible to get the whole system in the room. Participants are able to see how the parts of the organization fit together and to work together to design a new organization. While the basic design of the workshop is the same as a one-day one, the two-day version permits the use of mirror groups. A mirror group is a joint design team composed of two natural work groups from different areas, for example, a production team and a maintenance team. On the first day, they would redesign the production area with maintenance acting as the mirror group, contributing ideas and critiquing the new design. On the second day, the maintenance area would be redesigned and production would be the mirror group. If the pair of teams work well and it is appropriate the two teams may wind up creating a new design for one integrated unit. The use of mirror groups in a PDW is useful in working with large organizations having many departments or areas.

Each PDW is designed specifically for a particular organization. The next section outlines the basic PDW. It is followed by a description of variations of the basic design.

The Basic PDW Design

The following is an outline of the basic design of the PDW when it is used for *redesign*:

Phase 1. Analysis

- Natural work groups analyze their organization in terms of the six criteria listed earlier.
- The groups complete a matrix of skills available.
- The groups present analyses of the existing organization.

Phase 2. Change

- The groups draw up their current workflow.
- The groups draw up their current organizational structure and redesign it.
- The groups present their reports and discuss the new designs proposed.

Phase 3. Practicalities

- The groups identify a comprehensive set of measurable goals for all aspects of their work;

- They identify training requirements (from the skills matrix) for the new self-managing, team-based organization design;

- Identify other requirements, such as mechanisms for coordination between teams and changes in technology;

- Find career paths through the organization based on the skills required at different steps; and

- Show how the redesign improves scores on the six criteria.

In brief, the first phase is an analysis of what currently exists. In Phase 2, workshop participants develop a proposal for a new organization design. Phase 3 covers practical matters that are important in implementation.

In Phase 1, the PDW manager, a specialist trained in the design, implementation, and evaluation of PDWs, presents the six criteria and describes a bureaucratic organization structure and its consequences (see Chapter 14). Natural work groups then evaluate their organization using the six criteria and prepare an inventory of group member skills.

In Phase 2, the PDW manager describes the democratic organization structure and its consequences and variations appropriate for specialists and multiskilled, self-managing teams. Groups briefly draw up the workflow in their organization area. These products are shared so that all participants can see what occurs in each section of the organization. Groups then analyze the formal structures of their sections and redesign these structures. When each has the best possible democratic structure, the groups undertake Phase 3.

In Phase 3, groups draft the goals for work of their section, identifying the training and other requirements necessary in order for the new structure to work in practice. The groups also develop a draft identifying new career paths based on the new design. These drafts are later discussed with others, including one or more experts in designing career paths. The final system design, often unique in some way because of the organization's members and its strategic goals, will be some variation of one of the models shown in Figure 15.1.

Figure 15.1. Variations in Democratic Organization Systems

Source: Adapted from Emery, 1993, p. 108.

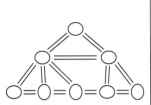 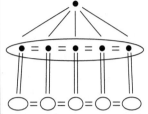 

Large self-managed organization with non-specialized people at strategic level requires three levels in the hierarchy. Work is controlled and coordinated at the level at which work is done. A non-dominant hierarchy of funtions.	Small to medium organization with specialized people at strategic level. Also known as "Democratic Modified," where responsibility for control is still one level above where work is done, but responsibility for coordination is in the self-managing team.	Small "knowledge work" organization that has only one level in the hierarchy. Whole organization is the decision-making body. It is composed of temporary, overlapping project teams that change as the work changes.

PDW Variations

The basic rule is that there must be no imposition of a design.

Flexibility is possible with the PDW. The basic rule is that there must be no imposition of a design. Thus, if an organization or section is too large to involve all employees, even in a series of PDWs, then a town-hall-type meeting is planned for all employees. In brief, at the town-hall meeting, the six criteria are shared, the organization is assessed against them, and a final design is developed, the final design usually taking the best of the ideas developed in earlier PDWs.

Apart from the above rule, PDWs can be designed in different ways. A workshop can be created for a single area or section. A workshop can be held for one or more deep slice teams, which are teams composed of members from every level of the hierarchy in an area but not including any member's immediate supervisor. In a workshop, multiple teams can be assigned to redesign one or more areas. These choices depend on the nature of each individual workplace.

An Extended PDW Process Example

An information technology (IT) department with several different sections including help desk, software, hardware, and architecture was not able to participate in a one-day PDW. Instead, a PDW was planned that required two-hour weekly meetings held over a six-week period. Members from each section redesigned their own areas and, with management approval, implemented their new designs beginning the seventh week. Department members then participated in a second PDW process over another six weeks. In this one, the sections worked on a design for the whole department. At the end of six weeks the department reached these conclusions: software decisions could be left to user departments, although architecture and related hardware decisions would be made by IT; better linkage between the department and its customers could reduce user problems and complaints; and work assignments to IT specialists could be better matched to specialist interests. As a consequence of the PDWs in this department, a process was began that eventually engaged senior management and all end-user departments in discussion about the role of IT in the company. Eventually, significant new investments were made, a new open information system was designed, and the IT organization design created in the PDWs was put into place.

The Greenfield PDW and an Application

The goal of this version of the PDW is to create a design for a new organization, including project teams and or communities of practice. Because there is no existing organization to analyze, the following occurs:

- The six criteria are not scored. Instead, they are evaluated as a possible set of guidelines for the design of the new organization.

- To undertake the design of the new organization participants must have enough technical knowledge. Sometimes a briefing is required that involves specialists such as engineers. This may lead the PDW to become an iterative process as engineers attending an initial PDW may then modify the technical specifications, requiring a second PDW. The second one ensures that the new design is compatible with the new technical specifications.

A Greenfield Example

In a large mining company opening a new mine, two PDWs were held. The first was held at the funding request stage and the second held once the project was approved. The first PDW helped the engineers understand how operators would experience the new technology. This workshop helped them make wise technical choices. It also permitted management to better estimate total project and operating costs. The PDW also generated a lot of interest in the organization.

In the second PDW, held a year after the first, final design decisions were made. Eventually, this breakthrough design performed beyond everyone's expectations.

Unique PDW Designs

Unique workshop designs use OST and its tools creatively. They are unique rather than modified PDWs because the design process is vastly different. Unique designs may take from two hours to three days or more, depending on the characteristics of the organization and the nature of the assignment.

One approach involves creating a design that combines the methodology of the Search Conference (SC) with a PDW. In a Greenfield design, it may be useful to do the first part of an SC, an environmental scan and analysis, before a PDW. This permits participants to obtain an understanding of the demands (threats) and opportunities that will be present for the organization they will be designing. It may also be useful to use another part of the SC and have participants sketch out a desirable future organization, as this would identify the performance requirements that they would have to design for. (For further information on Search Conferences see Chapter 2.)

The Management PDW

The creation of a democratic organization often requires that all work, including knowledge work, be organized on a team basis. This transition is often most difficult for managers. In bureaucratic organizations, managers are expected to own and manage their own territory and they are often naturally resistant to teaming. What can assist managers in making this transition is for them to identify what its work or tasks *as a team* will be in a self-managing team-based organization. It is important that they do this in advance of the organization's redesign. Managers must identify how they will add value because in a democratic organization with self-managed teams a number of their responsibilities will be assumed by the teams. In a PDW for managers, preparing an affinity diagram that captures all their current tasks could be used to clarify their new role.

Every Organization Needs to Design Its Own PDW Process

In very large organizations where it seems logical to keep three levels in the hierarchy—senior and middle management and an operating level—one or more senior management teams may participate in redesigning their roles while mirrored with "middle teams," in a two-day mirroring process similar to the one described earlier. "Middle teams" include specialists such as human resources, accounting, engineering, and the like, as well as middle managers. Similarly, middle management teams may participate in redesigning their roles mirrored with senior management teams, operating teams, and specialist teams. Designing a series of two-day PDWs, mixing and matching groups like this will create an aligned and integrated and "tight" management system.

Through a series of creatively organized PDWs, design teams in large organizations can have an ongoing conversation about the design of the whole organization. This may include the elimination of entire departments or the merging of departments, such as maintenance with operations. It is useful to start with two or three PDWs on the shop floor, then perhaps one or two middle management and staff PDWs, and then another shop floor PDW. A senior management PDW followed by a town-hall meeting in which all participants present their designs can quickly create a new organization structure.

A key rule is that there will be no imposition of a design. At a town-hall meeting each person has one vote. With a series of PDWs of the kind described above, the results of a PDW can be fed into the next one and the resulting conversation can create significant new designs. The rule of thumb is to stay as close as possible to the normal PDW design, but modify it as it makes sense.

Readiness

Organizations may not be ready for the PDW because they are not prepared to commit to the implementation of the resulting redesign.

In some cases, organizations may not be ready for the PDW because they are not prepared to commit to the implementation of the resulting redesign. In these instances a one-day PDW can be done for the purpose of educating and informing. In the PDW a fictional organization could be the focus of the redesign work by participants or the actual organization redesigned but only as an exercise.

Conclusion

This chapter has presented an outline of a conceptual framework, described a specific tool, the participation design workshop, and several variations of that tool that have been applied to help create collaborative, democratic work systems. Over time, the application of this framework and its tools has created healthy and productive organizations, where the structure of the organization is such that, by virtue of coming to work, purposeful people continuously learn on the job and continuously improve their organization.

CHAPTER 16

Gaining Commitment to High Performance Work Systems

John Deere Case Study

Gina Hinrichs and Kevin Ricke

ORGANIZATIONS ARE FACING increased complexity and global competition, which requires an increase in performance and responsiveness to changing conditions. Organizations need to increase their capability to respond effectively to change as the pace of change continues to accelerate. Performance increases and ability to respond to change can be enhanced with the creation of high performance work systems (HPWS) that utilize self-managed teams as a critical component. Involving employees at all levels is a basic tenet for continued success.

For more than thirty years, there has been interest and experimentation of organizations to move toward HPWS. Research has verified that increases in productivity, quality, and job satisfaction are achievable. Despite successes, few organizations have implemented this powerful organizational design.

John Deere Case Study

An approach to deploying and gaining commitment to HPWS was created from a case study that explored the theoretical and practical problems of implementing HPWS at John Deere Harvester Works (JDHW). Through a longitudinal study, insights and methods to enhance deployment and overcome barriers of progress toward HPWS were identified (Hinrichs, 2001). The study dealt with progress toward HPWS at a seventy-year-old manufacturing operation. The study examined enactment of HPWS across five departments utilizing a HPWS intervention referred to as AIM & IMPACT (discussed later). The departments were tracked for eighteen months for performance differences.

The departments studied and intervention dates were as follows:

- Subassembly and Weld—Dept 450, Summer 1999
- Main Assembly—Dept 950, Winter 1999
- Primary—Dept 150, Winter 1999
- Assembly—Dept 550, Spring 2000
- Primary—Dept 100, Summer 2000

AIM & IMPACT was not the first attempt at John Deere to increase employee involvement. Many efforts over decades were introduced by external consultants and perceived as "programs of the month." However, they did provide learning and foundation that supported a shift to HPWS. These were programs such as employee involvement (EI), "Working Together," and team building though outdoor activities.

AIM & IMPACT

The HPWS intervention was based on AIM & IMPACT, a methodology for process management (AIM) and improvement (IMPACT) (see Figure 16.1).

AIM is a process that Aligns business processes, Initiates projects through a charter to improve processes, and Manages the processes. AIM sessions are conducted with unit management. The sessions involve understanding cus-

Figure 16.1. AIM & IMPACT Process

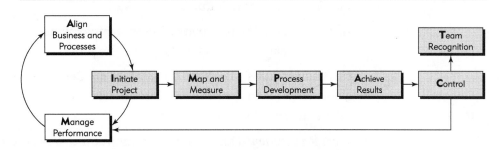

tomer needs, business needs, and process capabilities. The process capability gaps are determined and projects Initiated to close the gaps.

IMPACT is a process for continuous improvement of business processes.

- *Initiate the Project:* A charter is created by management to provide clarity to guide the team. It establishes commitment for both management and the team. The team questions and revises the charter as they see it. The seven areas of the charter follow:

    1. Business Case—why are we doing this project?

    2. Situation Statement and Goal Statement—Where are we now? Where do we want to be?

    3. Mission and Vision—What does the future look like?

    4. Project Scope—What is the process definition? What are the resources, constraints?

    5. Schedule and deliverables including logistics.

    6. Assignments and Roles—What are the expectations? Who does what?

    7. Implementation Perspective—How does this impact the organization?

- *Map and Measure:* The current process is mapped, metrics established and baseline data collected. Team members understand the process and identify problem areas and gaps.

- *Process Development:* Solutions for an improved process are proposed, input from stakeholders gathered, and an appropriate solution identified.

The team identifies changes to the organization, information systems, metrics, values, and culture.

- *Achieve Results:* The improved process is implemented, standardized, and altered as learning occurs in the pilot. The process is documented.

- *Control:* Methods to control the process are designed and incremental improvements to the process continue. This step addresses a feedback loop and corrective action plans.

- *Team Recognition:* This is done throughout the project to recognize the team and stakeholders who have adopted the new process. It is an opportunity to discover lessons learned and share best practices.

At John Deere Harvester Works, AIM & IMPACT was facilitated by internal consultants from the process improvement department collaborating with the wage team facilitators. The wage team facilitators were wage employees on nontraditional assignments to facilitate team building.

The design of the HPWS intervention also included the following:

- Ongoing meetings with management and union representatives for aligned communication;

- Appreciative Inquiry (Cooperrider & Whitney, 1999) to uncover when the group was at its best (see below);

- Team building to improve group dynamics;

- Understanding of customer and business needs to shift employees to more strategic thinking;

- Documenting department processes and workflow (for example, welding, assembly);

- Initiating projects with business case justification, implementation plans, and persons responsible;

- Tracking four key metrics (safety, quality, delivery, and performance); and

- Tracking attitude changes utilizing interactive surveys and interviews.

Appreciative Inquiry

The Appreciative Inquiry begins with a definition of terms, interviews, and a consolidation of themes for use in the process design.

Appreciative Inquiry (AI) operates from the following assumptions:

- In every organization, group, or individual something works and can be valued;
- What we focus on becomes the reality we create;
- The language we use creates our reality;
- The act of asking a question begins the change; and
- People have more confidence to journey to the future when they carry forward the best parts of the past.

Interview. Participants are instructed to take notes for the consolidation step:

- Think of a time in your entire experience when you felt best about coming to work, when you felt your group performed best. What were the circumstances during that time that made it great?
- Describe an incident when you or someone you know went the extra mile to improve quality, cost competitiveness, or a new product introduction. What made that possible?
- What do you value most about your work, your group, and our organization?
- What are the three most important hopes that you have for our organization for the future?

Consolidation. From individual notes, the team creates common themes of the stories:

- From the themes, create statements about how we want our future to be based on the best of the past.

Outcomes

Utilizing the intervention and follow-up, JDHW experienced success with a few of the teams. Primary departments 150 and 100 were successful based on organizational outcomes and adoption of more empowering social agreements. Dept 450 had moderate improvement that has not been translated to improved organizational outcomes. Dept 950 was just beginning to improve. Dept 550 made no progress during the study. Organizational outcomes of productivity performance (CIPP Output—standard hours /Input—actual hours) follow (see Figure 16.2).

Figure 16.2. Departmental Performance

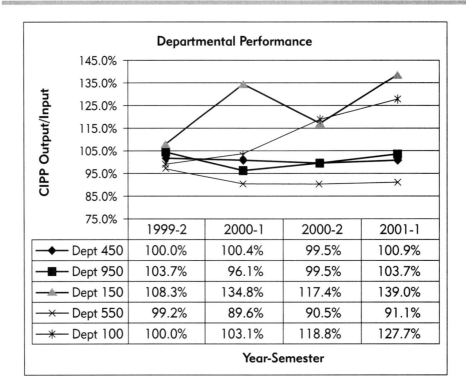

	1999-2	2000-1	2000-2	2001-1
◆— Dept 450	100.0%	100.4%	99.5%	100.9%
■— Dept 950	103.7%	96.1%	99.5%	103.7%
▲— Dept 150	108.3%	134.8%	117.4%	139.0%
✕— Dept 550	99.2%	89.6%	90.5%	91.1%
✳— Dept 100	100.0%	103.1%	118.8%	127.7%

The analysis of the case studies is provided at two levels. The first level is a first-order analysis on what occurred due to organizational systems, structures, and relationships. A second-order analysis is provided on sense making and the dynamics of social agreements within a group. The social agreement of the group was uncovered as a key variable in the enactment of HPWS.

First-Order Analysis—Organizational Systems, Structures, and Relationships

The first-order analysis provides a holistic approach using current approaches for transformational change. The first-order analysis focuses on foundational elements of systems, structures, and relationships (see Figure 16.3), including the following:

- Union support/contract
- Metrics

- Payment system

- Information systems

- Training

- Business understanding

- Management support

- Group dynamics

- Supervisory behavior

- Trust

Figure 16.3. First-Order Analysis

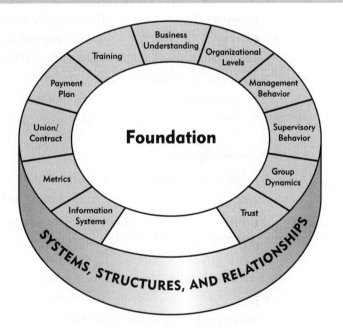

Union Support/Contract

The union did not visibly support HPWS effort for the first four departmental interventions, but it did not present a barrier. The union committeemen adopted a "wait and see" stance. By the fifth intervention, the union became supportive. Because the union represents most of the employees, its opinion and action carry considerable weight. Thus, it was important to communicate with union leadership so, at least, they did not oppose change.

An implication for practical application is creating a relationship with this stakeholder group, encouraging their participation, and ensuring they do not become a barrier. Enactment does not require the union be completely on board at the beginning.

Metrics

The main metric for manufacturing was to meet schedule. Focus on this metric encouraged a short-term view, rather than the long-term view supported by HPWS. However, the schedule metric was not a barrier to those departments that were not directly connected to the main line. The main line was where the schedule metric was measured. Having distance from the main line meant less attention on the driving metric. Distant departments were able to make improvements that could impact the schedule metric. Since the main line department (Dept 950) had no distance, it had an additional challenge in its enactment of HPWS.

An implication for practical application is to create a goal and metric that measures progress of HPWS. At minimum, understand the impact of the organization's driving metric on progress toward HPWS and design distance or a buffer so the driving metric does not prevent process improvement experimentation.

Payment System

The payment system is a critical organizational design subsystem that had a major impact on the progress toward HPWS. In general, gainsharing compensation systems complement organizational development efforts such as HPWS (Doherty, Nord, & McAdams, 1989). The gainsharing plan (Continuous Improvement Payment Plan—CIPP) at John Deere did support productivity increases with a bonus, but was also a barrier to employees working on continuous improvement (CI) projects. Employees who took time to work on CI projects impacted the productivity measure by increasing the input hours (denominator) without immediately increasing output (numerator). This lowered individual and group performance and impacted short-term pay. In theory, CIPP supported HPWS, but in practice, it created a challenging barrier.

An implication for practical application is to ensure that any payment plan supports and benefits employees' contribution to the HPWS process.

Information System

Data availability is important to a successful HPWS, thus information systems play a crucial role. Access to both internal and external data provide improved decision making. At JDHW, information technology was emphasized. Even though employees had access, many did not know how to access the data. Information access is a foundation for first-level business understanding and to the second-level sensemaking resources.

An implication for practical application is to provide access to both internal and external data for better decision making through information systems and training.

Training

This study supports the observation that supervisors' training in a new role as coach, facilitator, and integrator is a major issue in the success of HPWS (Lawler, 1992). None of the departments at JDHW benefited from supervisors with skills needed to manage group dynamics. Some supervisors had more experience and a stronger belief in self-managed teams than others, but none had a competency in dealing with group dynamics. In several cases, wage team facilitators provided on-the-job training for supervisors in group dynamics. Many supervisors learned group dynamics skills but lacked experience or a depth of knowledge in group dynamics.

An implication for practical application is to provide training in the value of HPWS, facilitation, and group dynamics for supervision.

Business Understanding

Employees need to gain a holistic view of their business. Understanding the whole system in which one works was an important cognitive shift for the John Deere groups. This understanding increased employees' ability to communicate with management because of the introduction of new language and concepts like return on investment (ROI), business case, and project management. To facilitate understanding, employees must have data about their business.

An implication for practical application is to provide training, experience, and access to information systems for a critical mass of employees to understand the holistic business system in which they operate.

Management Support

Multiple organizational levels add complexity for each level with which the employees must deal. The management levels should be aligned so that one level does not become a barrier to what the other levels are attempting to accomplish. When there are two levels of management supporting enactment of HPWS, there is a greater likelihood of success (Stewart & Manz, 1997). At JDHW, successful groups benefited from alignment of supervision and middle management.

When middle management was visibly supportive, groups showed progress. Middle management that moved quickly from an active democratic style to a passive democratic style (Steward & Manz, 1990) provided the most encouragement for progress to HPWS (see Figure 16.4).

Figure 16.4. Stewart and Manz' Leadership Behavior Impact Model

Source: Stewart & Manz, 1990.

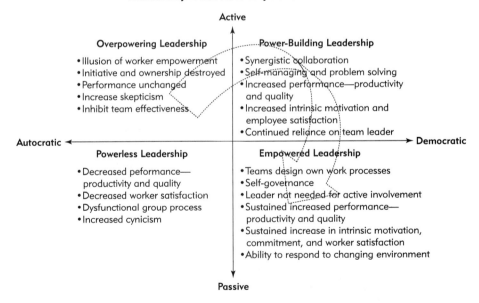

Leadership Behaviors Impact on Team

Active

Overpowering Leadership
- Illusion of worker empowerment
- Initiative and ownership destroyed
- Performance unchanged
- Increase skepticism
- Inhibit team effectiveness

Power-Building Leadership
- Synergistic collaboration
- Self-managing and problem solving
- Increased performance—productivity and quality
- Increased intrinsic motivation and employee satisfaction
- Continued reliance on team leader

Autocratic ← → Democratic

Powerless Leadership
- Decreased peformance— productivity and quality
- Decreased worker satisfaction
- Dysfunctional group process
- Increased cynicism

Empowered Leadership
- Teams design own work processes
- Self-governance
- Leader not needed for active involvement
- Sustained increased performance— productivity and quality
- Sustained increase in intrinsic motivation, commitment, and worker satisfaction
- Ability to respond to changing environment

Passive

An implication for practical application is to help management understand the implications of their behavior and coach towards a passive democratic style.

Members of top management were interested in results rather than specific details for achieving results so they became involved if breakthrough results were achieved or a project caused a major disruption.

An implication for practical application is to gain alignment of organizational levels. The optimum situation is for top management to lead the effort. Strong committed leadership can shorten transformation to HPWS. However, HPWS can progress without top management leadership.

Group Dynamics

Group dynamics—how individuals within groups act toward and respond to one another and the group as a whole—are an important aspect of organizational relationships. At JDHW, each group was as unique as the individuals who comprised the group. Group dynamics presented different challenges for each group. Large groups had a more difficult time arriving at group consensus, sensemaking, and creating social agreements. Cohesion, which usually benefits groups, became a barrier to Dept 550 unlearning previous social agreements that were no longer effective.

An implication for practical application is skilled facilitators are needed to guide group dynamics to enhance sensemaking and creating social agreements. Optimally, a supervisor should be trained to handle this role, but in the absence of supervisory competency, a skilled facilitator/coach is needed.

Supervisory Behavior

Supervisory behavior has been covered in Management Support and Group Dynamics sections. Supervisors need to have a passive democratic style and be competent facilitators and coaches to enact HPWS. Supervisors who lack these skills could be the greatest barrier to enactment.

An implication for practical application is supervisors must understand and be committed to HPWS. They must receive training for their new role and be supported by the organization.

Trust

Trust was a barrier to enactment of HPWS at JDHW. Because of a historic lack of trust between management and employees and the large number of long-term employees, employees were less willing to risk new behaviors required in HPWS. The groups only trusted to the management level that they felt showed support. Trust was established quickly when middle management was supportive. It was destroyed just as quickly if top management did not follow through on commitments or communicate.

An implication for practical application is that maintenance of trust requires communication and keeping commitments.

First-Order Analysis—Conclusion

It can be seen that a holistic approach to gaining commitment to HPWS requires a comprehensive effort. The study of five manufacturing departments showed the foundation did not require that all aspects be optimal. The progress of HPWS was supported by many, but not all subsystems. In many cases, it was more important that subsystems "did no harm" rather than strongly support enactment. Progress toward HPWS has been evolutionary and piecemeal, which made progress difficult but possible. Even without optimal organizational structure design and approach, progress towards HPWS occurred at JDHW due to the dynamics of sensemaking and social agreements.

Second Order of Analysis— Sensemaking and Social Agreements

It became necessary to move to another level of analysis when the first order of analysis was insufficient to explain the differential success rates of the departments studied. The departments had the same environment and foundation, yet progressed differently towards HPWS. Dept 550 provided a clue to the unexpected results since Dept 550 had the most optimal organizational systems, structures, and relationships of the five departments, yet was the least successful. What became evident was high performing groups were more successful in sensemaking and creating social agreements.

A social agreement is created through social construction based on shared language, relational understanding, shared meaning, sensemaking, and enactment. There can be no agreement if language, understanding, and meaning of the situation are not shared within the group. Each individual shares the group's construction of what is "real" and "good" (Gergen, 1999, p. 122). This means that there is implicit understanding built through shared history and experience.

The social agreement is created when a group has made sense of its situation. Group members have gained consensus about how things are perceived and what they mean. Through action, the group can test the appropriateness of its sensemaking (Weick, 1979).

Over time, environmental changes may render social agreements inappropriate for the current situation. Then, the group will need to make sense of the new situation. This may require unlearning previous social agreements and recreating more effective social agreement.

Karl Weick's approach using the seven properties of sensemaking (SIR COPE) is employed for a second-order analysis of the departments (see Figure 16.5).

Figure 16.5. Second-Order Analysis

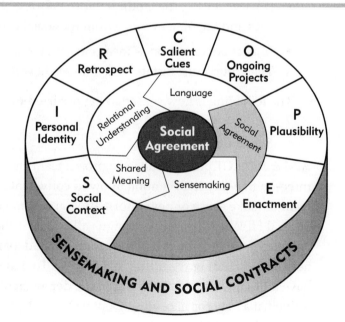

Weick's seven properties of sensemaking follow:

- (S)ocial Context is influenced by actual or imagined presence of others. Meanings come from social support and conversation. To change meanings changes the social context.

- Personal (I)dentity is the employee's own perception of his or her role in the group.

- (R)etrospect is influenced by how the group interprets what has occurred. Access to information is needed to have effective retrospection.

- Salient (C)ues is the group's taking cues and expanding them into explanations. Hunches are expanded to self-fulfilling prophecies. The group searches for confirming evidence. Contradictory or unstable cues cause the group to question its stories and a paradigm shift may occur.

- (O)ngoing Events Employees group events to keep pace with the ongoing nature of events. Boundaries allow sensemaking when employees are thrown in the middle of things and forced to act without knowing everything.

- (P)lausibility is the credible sense (stories) the group makes of salient cues and ongoing events within the social context.

- (E)nactment is action as means to gain more sense of what is happening. The group must test its system to see how it reacts (Weick, 1999, p. 43).

The following is how sensemaking occurred for the JDHW departments.

Social Context

AIM & IMPACT process utilized a project team chosen by the department. The three- to five-day intervention allowed conversations needed for the project team to make sense of new information and come to individual discoveries. Several HPWS intervention designs allowed for the project team to conduct daily updates with the rest of the group so the department was able to reach a new understanding regarding its business. Two unsuccessful groups did not have a design to involve the rest of the department, so only the project team arrived at a new social context. Dept 950 and Dept 550 did not achieve critical mass in the shift of employees to change its social context.

This study emphasized the importance of conversation to sensemaking and creation of social agreements. It follows that the more effective the conversations the more effective sensemaking and social agreements. This further emphasizes the need for competency of managing conversations.

An implication for practical application is to make available competent facilitators/coaches and provide supervisor training in their role as facilitator/coaches.

Personal Identity

In most groups, employees had a sense of their role in the group before the intervention. These identities tended to be passive victims or clever saboteurs. In successful groups, AIM & IMPACT disrupted employees' roles as it challenged self-imposed boundaries. When employees became active in developing their business, they adopted more empowered roles.

For Dept 950 and Dept 550, there was no disruption of roles because there was no conversation or project work to create new roles. Employees did not risk changing roles or challenging the current system. In these departments, the "toxics" (deeply negative employees who dominate employee meetings) or informal leaders worked to maintain current role relationships. Eventually, Dept 950 stopped listening to "toxics" and began to allow more empowering roles. This is when progress began.

This study uncovered that there is personal risk involved in adoption of new roles. Reducing risk of adopting a new role is facilitated by exposure to alternative roles and encouragement of co-workers. There also needs to be enough stability in an employee's role to consider adopting a new role.

An implication for practical application is to understand and minimize risks involved in facilitating employees adopting new roles.

Retrospect

The groups had systems to access data that allowed increased understanding of its business. More successful groups had employees who learned how to access and interpret data. When some data was restricted, groups were less successful. Dept 450 management restricted access to data regarding in-sourcing of work. Dept 950 and 550 self-imposed a restriction of data due to lack of interest outside of the department or due to informal leaders maintaining power through control of information.

Data is key for retrospection. Employees need data from their local area and data on how they fit into the whole organization. If data is nonexistent or limited only to the local area, employees may not get complete understanding for effective sensemaking. Incorrect assumptions lead to poor sensemaking, ineffective social agreements, and bad decisions.

An implication for practical application is creating information systems and providing employees with training and tools to access data they need to run their business.

Salient Cues

Salient cues provided reinforcement or disruption to current social agreements. Dept 150 and Dept 100 had cues from successful project implementation that its emerging social agreements were appropriate. Both departments had moved from a social agreement of "us versus them" (wage employee versus company) to "we can make money." Dept 950 and Dept 550 had cues that provided feedback that its social agreements were inappropriate to current reality. Dept 950's social agreement to "get rid of Alex (current general supervisor)" began to be reevaluated. Dept 550 defended its old social agreement, "save union jobs." Dept 550 had a social agreement that addressed loyalty among group members and the union movement so it met employees' hierarchy of needs: money, membership, and meaning. Its social agreement was so strong that it was resistant to salient cues. Because of this resistance, the group was not receptive to feedback on whether cues, its actions, and its social agreement fit current reality.

Salient cues are needed to provide the feedback loop to sensemaking. If sensemaking and social agreements are effective, salient cues will be consistent and support the social agreement. Groups cannot afford to be insulated from cues.

An implication for practical application is ongoing exposure and heightened awareness to salient cues. Effective facilitation aids groups in gaining competency in interpreting cues.

Ongoing Events

Binding the day-to-day flow of experience into meaningful groupings with boundaries is needed to make sense and to test social agreements (for example, before intervention, after intervention). Dept 450, Dept 150, and Dept 100 employees operated differently following AIM & IMPACT. They shifted their actions and interpretations to a democratic participative way of operating.

HPWS was seen as having pragmatic relevance when the departments were able to enact it through daily tasks. Dept 950 and Dept 550 did not have CI projects to provide feedback for their actions and interpretations.

Resiliency is required to overcome interruptions (excessive boundaries) to CI projects if the interruption negatively impacts progress toward HPWS. Dept 450 and Dept 950 did not have the resiliency to overcome interruptions they faced. In both cases, there were business reasons for the interruptions but lack of communication and mistrust of management derailed progress. Dept 150 had resiliency to interruptions due to their access to information and participation in project management. When project schedules were changed, they were part of rescheduling so they accepted changes.

Ongoing experience does not have boundaries, but for sensemaking to occur, boundaries need to be applied. Interruptions represent excessive imposed boundaries. If there are too many interruptions, resiliency and a stable sense of what is happening is lost.

An implication for practical application is the need to help a group create logical markers and minimize interruptions.

Plausibility

Plausibility utilizes the other sensemaking resources to allow the group to create a story to answer the question, "What's going on here?" Since plausibility is so powerful in the process of sensemaking and creation of social agreements, plausible accounts must be shared that support the shift to positive change. Most departments had a forum to exchange plausible accounts. Only Dept 550 did not provide a forum due to control by informal leaders and lack of departmental meeting attendance by employees. Effective facilitation would have allowed introduction of salient cues and given more employees a voice. Facilitation could have helped in Dept 950, where "toxics" dominated creation of plausible accounts. This domination led to disempowering social agreements. Facilitation could have managed competing stories that occurred in Dept 450. Exchange of plausible accounts should be strengthened to support group interpretations that lead to empowering social agreement.

An implication for practical application is the need for facilitation competency so groups improve sensemaking resources to create empowering social agreements. Facilitators should help the group deal with ambiguity and provide some sense of stability while the group creates a story to answer the question, "What's going on here?"

Enactment

Action is necessary to provide information about the system and to verify the usefulness of social agreements. Action is also needed to prove to the group that the effort is worth the risk of investing the group's energy and trust. Without action, momentum and emerging social agreements are lost. Only in those groups where action orientation was sustained was there a creation of empowering social agreement. Dept 950 and Dept 550 were derailed so there was no action in the form of implementing CI projects. Neither of the departments was allowed time to work on projects. Dept 450, Dept 150, and Dept 100 experienced immediate action after AIM & IMPACT and began to progress. Only Dept 150 and Dept 100 had sustained action. Dept 150 and Dept 100, the most successful cases, were able to create new social agreements and see that their social agreements were appropriate for protecting the interests of members.

Both union and management have critical roles to play in trusting the process by supporting action, thus reducing risk to the group. Union and management need to support action even when they are not sure of the ultimate outcome.

An implication for practical application is the need to work with union and management to support action even if it appears messy and iterative.

Conclusion

The unique journeys of five departments towards HPWS made it evident that there are many variables to consider. Despite having shared the same industry, geographical location, organizational structures, top management, and the intervention; the five departments took different paths. It was learned that transformation cannot be adequately explained by studying single interventions, at one level, over a short period of time.

Progress toward HPWS did not occur only as a result of integrated organizational systems, structures, and relationships, though these were the foundation to transformational change. The enactment occurred as a result of effective sensemaking, which created empowering social agreements. Two groups were more capable of sensemaking and creating effective social agreements. As a result, they were significantly more successful in improving performance and quality.

In a perfect world, organizational systems, structures, and relationships would be aligned in support of transformational change needed by the organization. In the real world, as long as there is some support for the change and organizational systems, structures, and relationships do not become barriers, effective sensemaking and creating empowered social agreements could move the transformation forward. With empowered social agreements that drive behavior and enactment, organizational structures and relationships could be improved to support the transformational change. Conversely, a weak sensemaking system could produce, at best, no progress toward transformation and, at worst, destruction of the organization.

The model for enactment of HPWS depicts the dynamics of first level organizational systems, structures, and relationship to the second level sensemaking and social agreement (see Figure 16.6).

Figure 16.6. Enactment of HPWS Model

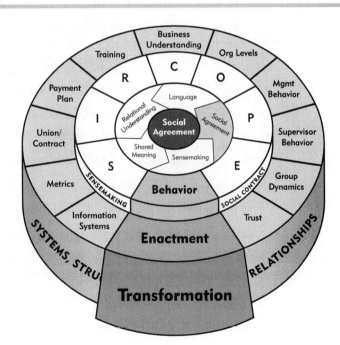

The practical implications suggested in this study that lead to actions that should be taken by management and OD practitioners to progress toward HPWS are summarized as follows:

- Engage the union so that it does not become a barrier. Work for their support through proven success.
- Provide a HPWS progress metric or design distance if the organization's driving metric does not directly support the enactment of HPWS.
- Design the payment plan so that it supports and benefits employees' contributions.
- Gain alignment of organizational levels and work towards leadership by top management, but do not wait for management's leadership to begin enactment.
- Provide training in facilitation, group dynamics, and the value of HPWS for supervision. While supervision is increasing their skills, provide skilled facilitators to handle group dynamics and become a resource to support effective sensemaking.
- Provide training and experience for employees to gain a holistic view of their business.
- Provide information systems that allow employees access to internal and external data to understand and run their business.
- Coach management and supervision on the implications of their support behavior and move to a passive democratic management style.
- Provide open communications for trust and value trust as social capital.
- Coach management to support the risks for adopting new roles and taking action to test the system.

The overall implication of this study is that sensemaking and creation of empowered social agreements can compensate for unsupportive organizational systems, structures, and relationships in progress toward HPWS. An organization does not have to wait for perfect conditions to start implementing, since improving sensemaking resources can help create those conditions.

CHAPTER 17

Developing Team-Based Support Systems

Conceptual Overview and Strategic Planning Workshop

Cheryl L. Harris and Sarah L. Bodner

USING TEAMS TO ACCOMPLISH COMPLEX, difficult tasks faster and cheaper has become a mainstream management strategy. Despite its popularity, reports of team failure far outweigh those of team success. Almost everyone you ask can tell you about a "bad" team experience, but few can speak of a "great" one.

Why do so many teams fail? One reason is failure to change the context of the team, which includes all the elements outside of the team that impact it. Typically, when a team has a problem, the response is to look within the team for the solution. This often involves process interventions such as conflict management. However, if the true problem is in the team's context, the appropriate place for an intervention is at the context level.

The context of the team can be defined in terms of support systems. Support systems are the infrastructure created to support the work and the people doing the work in the organization. Reward systems and training and development systems are examples. Supervisory techniques and organizational leadership, although often not thought of as support systems per se, are other examples. Every organization has support systems; but in organizations using teams it is important that these systems support collaboration and cooperation. The emphasis of this chapter is on helping organizations to design team-based support systems. The first section of the chapter presents a conceptual overview and examples of team-based support systems. The second section describes a workshop that can be used to develop support systems appropriate for a team-based organization. (The importance of changing units and other elements of the organization to support teams is the focus of other chapters in the Fieldbook. See especially Chapters 3, 11, and 13.)

Conceptual Overview

The following are important to keep in mind when working with team-based support systems:

Forming teams is not enough—changing the team context is crucial to team success. When teams are formed without regard to the context in which they operate, they tend to become isolated and cut off from the rest of the organization. The isolated team becomes akin to a disease in the body; the larger organization acts as an immune system doing whatever it can to expel the disease. This phenomenon acts to ensure that collaborative systems fail, especially when they are introduced as an isolated practice.

Creating a successful context for teams requires intentional effort. Creating an environment where teams can thrive does not happen by chance. Teams and the larger organization must give some careful thought to what is needed to support teams. Time must be set aside to intentionally review and modify the context to support teams.

Support systems must be flexible to deal with various team types, as well as individual and team work. Different types of tasks require different kinds of teams (for example, management, project, work, parallel, cross-functional, and integration teams). Despite the common myth that teams are a panacea for all problems, some tasks may require an individual instead of a team. Support systems need to be flexible in order to accommodate these various team types and individual work. Support systems should create an umbrella so the organization can remain a cohesive whole, yet be flexible enough to meet the needs of various teams and individuals. Systems that are too rigid limit teams, forcing them to find a way to work around the obstacles that the system presents. Systems should be enablers of, not barriers to, team success!

Support systems must be flexible to deal with needs of the external environment. Much attention has been paid to the escalating rate of change and complexity in the increasingly global world environment. Organizations and organization units, including support systems, must be able to react quickly to and even anticipate change in the environment. Because change occurs so often, it is important that support systems be able to adjust to meet new requirements. Systems should exist that help the organization stay attuned to the external environment. Ideally, the organization has one or more systems that permit it to be informed of important changes involving customers, suppliers, competitors, and regulatory agencies.

Structure influences, but does not create, teaming. Unfortunately, the famous movie quote, "If you build it, they will come" does not always apply in the case of team-based support systems. The presence of team-based support systems does not automatically result in good processes (Mohrman, Cohen, & Mohrman, 1995). The potential problems of team-based support systems are the same as in traditional organizations. Some of these problems can include over-formalization, rigidity, and emphasis on rules over common sense.

What Is a Team-Based Support System?

Considering changing the internal environment of an entire organization is overwhelming. Our concern here is with one part of that environment—the part that supports the work and the people who do it. Stated formally, a support system is "part of the organizational infrastructure that facilitates carrying out the processes necessary to do the work; to manage, control, coordinate, and improve it; and to manage the people who are doing it" (Mohrman, Cohen, & Mohrman, 1995, p. 302). Every organization has support systems.

Traditional versus team-based support systems. In general, support systems in traditional organizations are structured to support climates emphasizing individual performance and competition. In organizations attempting to maximize collaboration, support systems must be modified and created to facilitate team performance and cooperation. For example, in a traditional system pay is based on individual contributions, which creates a situation in which individuals are competing for pay. Using this system in a team-based organization will hinder the teamwork desired. Here, in order to foster collaboration and cooperation, team members should receive rewards when team goals are accomplished.

Support system mechanisms. Because support systems are so big, they are difficult to conceptualize. It is helpful to discuss support systems in terms of mechanisms, which are subparts of support systems that can be managed. By changing mechanisms, you ultimately change the system. For example, a mechanism in the performance appraisal system is "group members give each other regular, informal feedback."

What Are Some Types of Support Systems?

Some support systems, such as reward and compensation, come readily to mind. Others, such as leadership and renewal, are just as prevalent in organizations, but are not always considered "systems." However, this chapter defines "support system" as anything in the organizational context that supports or hinders the people doing the work.

Recent work (Hall, 1998) examined nine support systems and the mechanisms within each support system that were most important for team success. Table 17.1 lists for each of the nine a definition and the top five of fifteen mechanisms, in order of importance as indicated by the results of this study. The nine support systems are

- Executive management
- Direct supervision
- Defining performance
- Training
- Performance appraisal
- Reward
- Information
- Group design
- Integration

Table 17.1. Team-Based Support Systems Overview

Support System	Team-Based Definition	Top Five Mechanisms in Order of Importance
Executive Management	Develop the organizational context that makes team work possible Determine and communicate organizational goals and priorities Develop support systems Model team-based norms	1. Managers and executives expect work groups to succeed 2. Managers and executives help provide work groups the resources they need to perform work 3. Managers and executives are dedicated to meeting customer needs 4. Managers and executives are open to multiple perspectives (such as different points of view) 5. Managers and executives make sure that different areas of the company work well together
Direct Supervision	Develop skill sets (for example, design skills, leadership skills, and coaching skills) Clarify roles between supervisors and teams Facilitate inputs and outputs from the team into the organization and vice versa Develop the internal processes of teams	1. Direct supervisors expect groups to succeed 2. Direct supervisors are dedicated to meeting customer needs 3. Direct supervisors provide groups the resources they need 4. Direct supervisors support group learning 5. Direct supervisors involve the work group in decision making
Defining Performance	Align performance of business units and teams with organizational goals Align goals vertically and horizontally Utilize systematic goal-setting procedures Ensure team member participation in goal setting	1. Work group's priorities are clear 2. Individual group members have clear priorities 3. Group goals are aligned with company goals 4. The work group has goals that require high levels of performance 5. The work group's goals are aligned with business-unit goals
Training	Develop the performance abilities of teams Build skills (interpersonal, learning, leadership, decision making, facilitation, consensus building, task performance) Ensure effective training experiences	1. Work groups can easily get training to help us develop new technical skills 2. Work groups can easily get on-the-job training 3. Training opportunities are of high quality 4. Training is available and timely 5. Training is an ongoing part of the job
Performance Appraisal	Identify growth areas and develop abilities of the performer Include multi-level assessments Use well-defined metrics and procedures Appraise frequently and informally Use reliable rating scales	1. Group members give each other regular, informal feedback 2. Work groups use performance measurements that are easy to understand 3. Work groups use measurements to improve performance 4. Direct supervisors use performance measurements that are easy to understand 5. Group members feel good about the measurements in use

Table 17.1. Team-Based Support Systems Overview, Cont'd

Support System	Team-Based Definition	Top Five Mechanisms in Order of Importance
Reward	Reinforce desirable goals and priorities Reinforce desired group behaviors Align with organizational strategies, structures, and culture Account for eligibility, participation, and measurements Structure to meet organizational needs	1. The pay system is fair 2. Pay for individual group members is based on actual performance 3. The recognition program is fair 4. As more responsibilities are taken on, work groups get rewarded (or recognized) in a timely manner 5. After achieving goals, work groups are paid (or are recognized) in a timely manner
Information	Provide informational resources and tools to facilitate team task performance Give teams the information necessary to make decisions and correct errors Use information tools that integrate work between teams and team members Facilitate appropriate task strategy selection	1. Work groups can easily collect, organize, and store information needed to perform their jobs 2. Individual group members can easily share learnings (such as new knowledge) with other group members 3. Individuals in a group try to learn from other group members 4. Work groups can easily get information from their direct supervisors 5. Work groups can easily get information about their customers
Group Design	Integrate organizational support systems to facilitate the performance of tasks Ensure appropriate team tasks Select appropriate team members and team size Clarify leadership structures and roles Design and clarify boundary functions Design appropriate individual jobs	1. Individuals are skilled at doing their work 2. Members of a group take responsibility for work 3. Work groups have the skills they need to perform work well 4. Group members have good people skills 5. Work groups make many work-related decisions
Integration	Link performing units horizontally and vertically Prioritize decision making and trade-offs to protect integration Standardize work processes and work content Contract between support services and teams Develop integrative leadership roles	1. Groups conduct information-sharing meetings 2. Work groups can easily work with other groups or work areas 3. Groups routinely coordinate work with other work groups 4. Work groups have meetings with customers to share information 5. Performance review systems are consistent across the company

Source: Adapted from Hall, 1998.

Other important support systems include the following:

- Organization design
- Team design
- Business environment awareness
- Financial
- Communication and information
- Knowledge management

- Leadership
- Between-teams integration
- Resource allocation
- Physical workspace
- Renewal
- Selection

Strategic Planning Workshop

The team-based support systems strategic planning workshop is a comprehensive learning and planning experience for groups leading the implementation of teams in their organization. The workshop focuses on educating participants about support systems for effective teams and creating plans for implementing team-based support systems in their own organization.

Key Tenets

Participation and involvement. The goal of creating team-based support systems is to enhance collaboration and cooperation. It makes sense to match the planning mechanism to the desired result; therefore, participation and involvement in the planning and implementation of team-based support systems is crucial. Workshop leaders should seek and encourage participation and involvement whenever possible and set up an environment conducive to this.

"Working" workshop. A workshop generally is not intended to be a series of lectures. Here, as in others, participants are expected to do real work, creating plans for their organization.

Flexibility to meet needs of participant group. Each group will be different. The workshop leaders need to be aware of this and be willing to adjust the workshop plan.

Collect information from the larger system between sessions. Multiple sessions over several weeks are preferred so participants can acquire additional information between sessions. Those attending the workshops should be encouraged to collect information and dialogue with those not attending. Experience suggests that successful change will not occur if workshop participants rely solely on their own personal knowledge.

Workshop Logistics

Outputs of the workshop. The many outputs of the workshop are not theoretical; they are actual working documents:

- Team-based support systems strategic plan;
- Preliminary action steps and deadlines;
- Preliminary plans for support systems committee composition;
- Shared understanding of where the organization is going with its teams efforts, including what changes to the support systems are needed; and
- Increased commitment to the plan because of participation in its creation.

Workshop participants. The participants should include a cross section of the affected area of the organization, that is, representation from multiple functions and levels. Key decision-makers with the power to implement changes and key implementers of those changes should also participate.

Time requirement. The workshop consists of approximately ten hours of interactive educational and work sessions that are, ideally, spread over four weeks. There should be enough time between sessions to provide participants with the opportunity to collect information from others. The length of time of a workshop session or meeting can be modified to meet the needs of the organization. However, giving participants enough time to thoroughly discuss plans is needed to ensure success.

Recommended workshop environment. Ideally, this workshop is conducted off-site to avoid distractions. A comfortable room with appropriate audiovisual equipment, tables appropriate for small group work, and a flip chart with markers for every four or so participants is recommended.

Workshop pre-work. Prior to the workshop, the organization should have an empowerment plan for teams that summarizes how the teams' and the team coaches' roles will change as the team matures (see Exhibit 17.1). Also, participants should receive information to help them develop a common understanding of the organization's teams effort and its support systems. The following are recommended as supplemental pre-reading:

- Chapter 10: Developing Organizational Support Systems (Mohrman, Cohen, & Mohrman, 1995).
- Chapter 11: Supporting Work Team Effectiveness: Best Practices (Sundstrom, 1999).

Exhibit 17.1. Sample Empowerment Plan

Notes:
- An empowerment plan may also indicate the transitioning role of the direct supervisor. This may help to clearly depict the transfer of responsibilities from supervisor to team as well as the new responsibilities taken on by the supervisor.
- Some items are filled in below. They are meant purely as examples; each organization should take the time and effort to create its own empowerment plan.
- Phase names are examples.

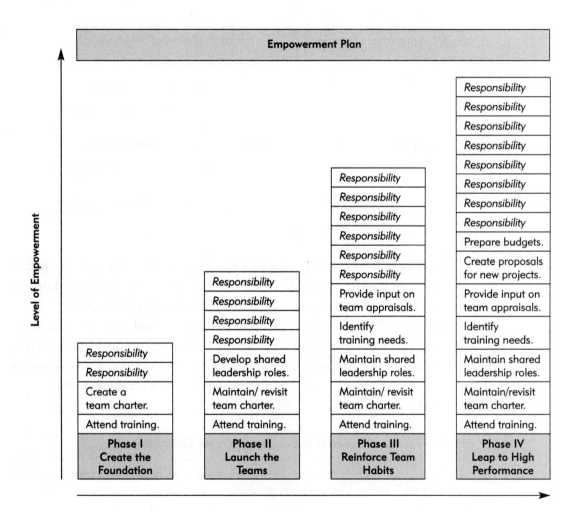

Workshop Overview

The three phases of the workshop are educating, planning, and implementing. The approximate time and content of each phase is shown in Table 17.2.

Table 17.2. Workshop Overview

Phase (Time Required)	Content
Educating (4 Hours)	Workshop Introduction
	What Is a Support System?
	Why Are Support Systems Important?
	What Are Some Types of Support Systems?
Planning (4 Hours)	Determining Support System Categories
	Support Systems Strategic Planning Tool
Implementing (2 Hours)	Implementing Support Systems

Educating. The goals of this phase are to begin exploring the concepts concerning team-based support systems and to start creating a shared understanding of how the concepts apply to the participants' organization.

Material for the educating phase pieces can be pulled from the conceptual overview that begins this chapter. An activity to promote discussion of types of support systems is described in Exhibit 17.2. The support systems descriptions in Table 17.1 or a similar resource will be needed for this activity.

Exhibit 17.2. Understanding Support Systems Exercise

Purpose: To allow participants to further explore types of team-based support systems and to begin creating a shared understanding.

Time requirement: Approximately forty-five minutes for each round

Supplies: Flip chart and markers for each subgroup

Exhibit 17.2. Understanding Support Systems Exercise, Cont'd

Process:

1. Divide group into subgroups of three to four people.

2. Assign each group one of the nine support systems. You likely will need to repeat this exercise several times to cover all of the support systems.

   - Executive management

   - Direct supervision

   - Defining performance

   - Training

   - Performance appraisal

   - Reward

   - Information

   - Group design

   - Integration

3. Ask each group to answer the following questions about its assigned support system. Ask groups to write their answers on a flip chart and to be prepared to share their answers with the rest of the group. It is useful at this point to share Table 17.1 with the groups so that they have a place to begin their conversations. Allow at least twenty-five minutes for the groups to work on this.

   - What is it?

   - Why is it important?

   - What values do you want?

   - What practices could you utilize?

4. Bring the groups back together and debrief. Encourage discussion among groups during this time and check whether they have any questions or additions to make.

Planning. The goal of this phase is to create the first draft of the support systems plan using the strategic planning tool (see Exhibit 17.3).

To tailor the process, the organization should prepare a list of support systems that will serve to organize future discussions and work. For example, one organization listed four areas: communication and information systems; training and education; reward and performance management; and leadership, group design, and renewal. Some questions for participants to consider when creating support system categories are

- Which support systems naturally go together?
- How many categories do you want to organize around?
- What is a manageable number of committees to manage when working on support systems design?
- How much development work can one committee realistically handle?

When support system categories have been determined, the support systems strategic planning tool can be introduced (see Exhibit 17.3). This tool should correspond with the existing empowerment plan. The tool permits viewing all support systems at once, thereby better ensuring alignment of the support systems with each other and with the empowerment plan. Looking at the tool document raises potential sequencing conflicts as well. Some things simply have to be done before others.

The selected support systems categories go in the left column of the tool. An empowerment plan's phases are arrayed from left to right. Within each box, representing a category and phase, the group will plan key action items and target dates. The goal is to match support system development with the empowerment of teams.

The objective of the workshop is to create a first draft of the support systems strategic planning tool. After the workshop, the tool becomes an invaluable planning and discussion document that can be used for years as the roadmap for support systems implementation.

Exhibit 17.4 describes an exercise to begin the planning process. As the participants begin to work in subgroups, it is important to have the groups learn from each other. One benefit is that common best practices can be identified and used. From time to time, the workshop leader should intentionally bring up the idea of common subgroup guidelines.

Exhibit 17.3. Support Systems Strategic Planning Tool

Notes:

- Number of phases and primary phase focus are determined by the organization's empowerment plan for teams. If the organization does not have an empowerment plan for teams, it would be wise to at least discuss with the group the number and types of phases of empowerment they would like to have to begin creating shared understanding of the foundation of the teaming effort.
- Number and subjects of support systems categories is determined by the organization.
- It is helpful to include dates for each action item to instill accountability.
- The sample support systems (performance and direct supervision) provided below are oversimplified and very general. They should not be seen as a concrete process to follow in the development of support systems.
- Primary phase focus areas also are shown as examples only.
- This is a living document; it should be reviewed and updated frequently.

	Phase I	Phase II	Phase III	Phase IV
Primary Phase Focus	Create the Foundation	Launch the Teams	Reinforce Team Habits	Leap to High Performance
Performance	Develop informal feedback methods	Research team appraisal systems	Develop appraisal system for teams	Implement new appraisal system
	Develop informal reward system	Review current appraisal system	Determine integration needs	Refine system as needed
	Discuss performance needs with team	Discuss ideal appraisal system	Develop implementation plan	
Direct Supervision	Determine supervisor's role	Provide leadership training	Develop appraisal system for supervisor	Review role of supervisor
	Select appropriate supervisors	Develop informal feedback methods	Implement appraisal system	Continue development
	Provide initial training in teaming	Address fears and concerns		
	Provide resource information	Create developmental plans		
Support System Category #3	Action Item	Action Item	Action Item	Action Item
	Action Item	Action Item	Action Item	Action Item
	Action Item		Action Item	
Support System Category #4	Action Item	Action Item	Action Item	Action Item
	Action Item	Action Item	Action Item	Action Item
		Action Item	Action Item	
Support System Category #5	Action Item	Action Item	Action Item	Action Item
	Action Item	Action Item	Action Item	Action Item
		Action Item		Action Item

Exhibit 17.4. Planning Support System Exercise

Purpose: To begin planning the team-based support systems transition process

Time requirement: 4 hours during workshop, lots outside of workshop

Supplies:

- Flipchart and markers for each subgroup

- Copies of support systems strategic planning tool

- Computer and projector, or overhead projector and transparencies may be useful

- Other materials as deemed necessary by the subgroups

Process:

1. Divide the group into subgroups, according to the categories of support systems they chose to organize around. Ask the group to consider appropriate selection to groups—is there someone with particular expertise who needs to be in a particular group?

2. Subgroups brainstorm specific tasks that must occur within the support system category in order to align with the team development specified by the empowerment plan. Remind the groups that they will likely need to gather information from outside sources in order to make a good plan.

3. Subgroups can move the tasks they brainstormed into the planning tool, placing them in the phase of empowerment in which they must be developed to support the teams.

4. Subgroups come back together to meet as a whole to debrief their progress. Some alignment will occur here, as subgroups ask each other questions and make decisions about things such as:

   - Under which subgroup does this task fall?

   - Which phase should contain this task?

   - Where do we have redundancies? Who should take responsibility?

   - Where do we need to integrate to pass off a piece of work from one group to the next? How can we do that?

   This is an iterative process; alignment changes should continue to occur throughout planning and implementation. Remind the group that there is no "right" answer, but they need to come to a common agreement of the way they will do it.

5. The group as a whole puts a tentative timeline on the empowerment plan, so everyone has a basic understanding of when the tasks of each phase need to be accomplished.

6. Subgroups go back to work to develop some firmer dates for tasks to be due.

7. The group as a whole meets to continue sharing and alignment of plans.

Implementing. The goal of the final phase of the workshop is to think through and identify what needs to be done to begin implementation of the planned support systems changes.

As a group, workshop participants should create guidelines for committee membership. Who should belong? How many people should be on each committee? Should the committees be leaderless or should there be a chairperson for each? Will committees be allowed to call on additional help in the form of external consultants and others with support systems expertise?

After reaching consensus on some guidelines for membership, participants should identify the key individuals to serve on each committee. It is important to remind them to involve relevant individuals from all parts of the organization, not just those who are in the room. A plan is then created for inviting individuals to join the committees.

To maintain alignment, integration must occur among the groups comprising each committee and across all committees. The last activity in the workshop is to create mechanisms for post-workshop integration. Some possible methods of integration are

- Key individuals of different committees meet regularly to maintain alignment;
- Committees present at regular coordination meetings;
- Ongoing information sharing by telephone, email, hall conversations; and
- If committee areas are highly overlapping, some members could belong to two or more groups.

Some questions important for participants to ask are

- Which key support systems members will meet regularly to maintain alignment?
- How often will they meet?
- When and how will coordination meetings involving all support systems committees occur?
- What are the other ways in which integration will occur?

Workshop conclusion. By the time the workshop is over, the participants have done quite a bit of work! Remind them of all they have done, and congratulate them on their efforts. Before the closing celebration, find out when they will meet again in committees and as a whole to continue to refine and implement the plan. Following up with them on a regular basis will help maintain the momentum of the workshop.

Conclusion

Modifying systems to support teams is crucial to team success.

Modifying systems to support teams is crucial to team success. Support systems are huge; it will take lots of effort to change them. One person or even a small group of people cannot do it alone; they will need the help of others in the organization. It will take time and effort, but the results of a successful teaming effort will be worth it.

PART 4

WORK PROCESSES AND COMMUNICATION SYSTEMS

Craig McGee

EFFECTIVE TEAM-BASED ORGANIZATIONS fundamentally change their work processes and information flows. Employees and managers change fragmented work systems where individuals perform narrow, fragmented jobs to jobs where they perform a complete piece of work and can better manage their individual work processes. Effective team-based organizations consciously examine their work flows and redesign them to minimize errors, rework, and delays.

A critical component for accomplishing work tasks effectively is the information systems. The first aspect of the information system to be redesigned is the basic flow of task-related information. This is more than the traditional definition of the hardware and software that typically define information technology. It focuses more on the information individuals require to perform their work effectively. It includes quality information to provide them feedback about their work performance, customer requirements to ensure they produce the right product, shipping information to allow them to schedule their work properly, and so forth. High performing, team-based organizations spend considerable time, energy, and money to ensure that the right people have this information. The "right" people are typically those directly producing the product or providing the service, not their managers or supervisors. With this information they can adequately monitor their performance and make the proper business decisions. Technology remains part of the solution, but low-tech approaches, such as designing effective meetings, defining who needs to talk to whom, and what critical pieces of data to share are equally important.

This section focuses on how team-based organizations create more effective work and social interaction processes. In some cases these interactions are face-to-face, but increasingly are becoming virtual (separated by space, time, or geography). And these interactions involve many different perspectives. Effective team-based organizations consciously design and implement processes to bring diverse viewpoints together and synthesize those perspectives to create knowledge for the benefit of the organization. The contributions were specifically selected to illustrate both the analytical and intuitive elements required for creating these processes. The contributions also illustrate that work flows and social interactions have become increasingly broader and more complex. In addition to exchanging information between departments, team-based organizations are turning their focus to designing knowledge creating systems with other companies and across geographic/cultural boundaries.

In Chapter 18, Craig McGee provides a simple tool for intentionally designing the information flows and decision-making processes for a high-performing team. In Chapter 19, Gerald Klein provides a summary of the key elements that create conflict between teams and disrupt the communication flow. He also provides strategies for preventing and alleviating the counterproductive aspects of that conflict. In Chapter 20, Kevin David and John Lloyd provide tools and approaches for improving communications among dispersed teams. In Chapter 21, David O'Donnell and Gayle Porter discuss communities of practices, illustrating how greater intellectual capital can be developed through the effective use of communities of practice. In Chapter 22, Jill Nemiro expands on the theme of dispersed teams and addresses the specific issues that affect the communications patterns of virtual teams.

CHAPTER 18

The CAIRO Tool

A Tool for Defining Communication Patterns and Information Flow

Craig McGee

ADVANCED HIGH-PERFORMING (a.k.a. self-directed) work unit teams exercise distinctly different decision-making patterns than traditional systems. Rather than concentrating decision making in one individual, that is, the supervisor, team members are provided greater authority for making decisions. This is a conscious choice. Leaders and their teams spend considerable time and effort determining who has authority and responsibility for specific decisions, designating which decisions can be made unilaterally, which decisions require collaboration, and which decisions require group consensus.

This paper describes a tool for helping teams clarify the nature of their decision making and the information flow to support that decision making called the CAIRO tool. CAIRO is an acronym (see Figure 18.1) that defines the involvement different people have in different activities or decisions.

There are five designations that indicate what kind of involvement different parties have in making a specified decision. A pentagon is used to visually represent the different designations. The elements of CAIRO are defined as follows.

Figure 18.1. CAIRO Model

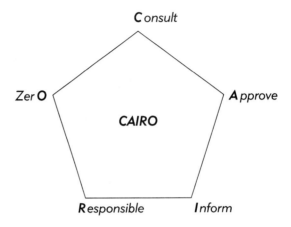

Consult

Parties with a *consult* designation should be actively consulted during the decision-making process. Their input should be sought. They typically have unique expertise or experience that should be weighed heavily when making the decision. They may also be greatly impacted by the decision and need an opportunity to discuss what the impact of the decision on their operation will be. Attempts should be made to reach consensus among those parties with a consult designation.

Approve

The person(s) with an *approve* designation must formally approve the decision. While he or she may be involved earlier in the decision-making process, the recommended decision must be brought to him or her for formal approval. If multiple parties have this designation, a numerical suffix indicates the flow of decision making. A1 approves the decision first, then it is passed to A2 for the next approval, and so on.

Inform

Parties with an *inform* designation should be informed about the decision once it has been made. Parties with an inform designation typically need to understand what the final decision was, as they may process paperwork or materials that support the decision. Alternatively, they may need to understand what decision was made in order to track trends.

Responsible

Parties with a *responsible* designation are responsible for raising an issue, driving the decision, and collecting all relevant data. They are the ones chartered with "making it happen" even though they may not have full decision-making power or authority. They are the ones who initiate meetings and discussions, consult with all affected parties, bring different parties together, and formulate recommendations and present them to those who must approve the decision.

zerO

These people have no involvement in the decision. The decision does not involve them or affect their work. The tool represents an adaptation of Beckhard and Harris' responsibility charting (Beckhard & Harris, 1977, pp. 77–80). The key difference is the addition of the zero designation. Too often, one or more parties get too involved in decisions. The zero designation clearly indicates those parties who do not have a role in the decision-making process and should not try to be involved.

Using the Tool

To use this tool, follow these steps:

1. Identify all the key decisions or activities that must occur during the target work process. List these on the left hand side of the CAIRO matrix (see Exhibit 18.1).
2. Identify the different parties (individuals or groups) who may need to be involved in the activity or decision. List these at the top of the matrix.
3. For each activity or decision, identify how each party needs to be involved.
4. If a decision needs multiple approvals, use numbers to indicate the approval chain. Use A1 for the first level of approval, A2 for the next level of approval, and so on.

Accomplishing these first four steps is best done in a facilitated work session with the team and the critical stakeholders. An experienced, independent facilitator can lead the team through a constructive discussion of the decision-making process and ensure that the right stakeholders are involved in designing the decision-making processes.

5. Validate with parties who were not present or involved with the initial development of the matrix.

Exhibit 18.1. Sample CAIRO Matrix

Target Area: Product Management

Involved Parties

Activities/Decisions	PST Team	Product Manager	Design and Engineering	Sales	Sales Administration	International	Finance	Forecasting	Purchasing
Manage gross margins (by product and overall portfolio)	A/R*	R	C	R		R	C		C
Develop overall marketing strategy	A	R	C	C		C	C		
Develop product line strategy—establish goals for products and markets (including international)	A/R	R		R		R			
Pricing deviations		I		A	I		I		
Price protection strategy		A		C	R		I		C
New product ideas (features, fabrics, size, and so on)	A	R	R	R		R			
Initial design and costing	I	R	C	C		C			I
Determine need for market research	A	R							
Design and conduct market research		R	C	C		C			
Develop retail price point	A	R	C	C		C			
Develop sample	A	C/A**	R						
Obtain sample		I	R						C
Interface with factories regarding design changes and schedules (prior to product concept approval)		I	R						C
Develop packaging design		A/R	C	C		C			C
Develop business case (includes contribution analysis)	A	R		C		C			
Establish launch dates	A	R	C	C		C		I	C
Develop critical path		R	C	I		I			C
Develop manifests (preliminary and final)		A	R						C
Develop Bill of Materials									R

Exhibit 18.1. Sample CAIRO Matrix, Cont'd

Target Area: Product Management

Involved Parties

Activities/Decisions	PST Team	Product Manager	Design and Engineering	Sales	Sales Administration	International	Finance	Forecasting	Purchasing
Develop drawings and performance specifications		C	R						C
Develop final cost estimates (product, packaging, and labor)		C	R						C
Final product approval (product approval meeting)	A	R	C	C		C			
Project manage entire process (cradle to grave)—establish project management tools/forms; convene/facilitate milestone meeting		R	C						
Maintain project milestone chart		R	C	I		I		I	C
Maintain critical path charts		R	C	I		I		I	C
Manage pilot/production test runs		I	C						R
Manage component and package delivery schedules		I							R
Develop packaging literature		A/R							C
Develop sales/marketing collateral		A/R		C					

Finalize package design
  master carton
  structure
  graphics
		A
		A/C
		A/R
				C
				C
				C
						C
						C
						C
									R
									R

Develop bundled product sets and retail price points	A	R	C	C	C	C	C		C
Develop introduction strategy		R	C	C		C		C	C
Establish initial inventory level		A/R		C	C	C		C	C
Establish monthly inventory levels		C		C	C	C		A/R	C
Special promotions/projects (within financial parameters)		A/R	C	C	C	C		C	C

Exhibit 18.1. Sample CAIRO Matrix, Cont'd

Target Area: Product Management

Involved Parties

Activities/Decisions	PST Team	Product Manager	Design and Engineering	Sales	Sales Administration	International	Finance	Forecasting	Purchasing
Identify slow moving products	I	I		R	R	I		I	C
Develop corrective actions for slow moving products	C	R		C		C		C	C
Develop marketing programs	A/C	R		C		C		C	C
Maintain competitive information databases and files		R		C		C			
Obtain competitor samples		R							
Assign model numbers		R							

Notes:
C = Consult
A = Approve
I = Inform
R = Responsible
Blank cells indicate zero involvement.
*In some cases the same party will have the responsibility for initiating action (R) and also the approval authority (A). This is indicated on the chart with an A/R designation.
**In some cases, the same party should be consulted (C) and also has approval authority (A).

Summary

The primary purpose of the CAIRO tool is to clarify roles in the decision-making process and ensure that the proper communications occur. The tool has been used in many different situations. These include:

- Clarifying the roles and decision-making processes when implementing a product management concept in a consumer products company (shown in Exhibit 18.1).

- Clarifying project managers' roles versus developers' and marketing in a new product development process for a software development company.

- Identifying roles and responsibilities in a new plant startup for a major brewery.

- Clarifying the responsibilities of a team leader when implementing self-directed work teams in a plastics plant.

Its value lies in ensuring that the right people have the right information and the proper level of involvement when making decisions.

CHAPTER 19

Managing Intergroup and Interdepartmental Conflict to Improve Collaboration

Gerald D. Klein

IT IS DIFFICULT TO IMAGINE a group or department in a modern, complex organization that does not regularly interact with, contribute to, or rely on the work of other groups or departments. Specialization and the division of work characterize complex organizations by necessity. Groups and units have responsibility for certain organization activities, yet interdepartmental work and relations are vital and contribute significantly to an organization's success.

While relations between groups and departments may be harmonious in a few organizations, personal experience and reports from business and university colleagues and graduate students suggest that in most organizations, the quality of intergroup and interdepartmental relations could be improved.

That groups and departments experience conflict is almost inevitable, as each has some purposes and goals that are unique to the group or department and are not shared. Tension and conflict also occur because units typically compete for resources, influence, and prestige and hire employees who differ in perspectives, interests, background, and training. Conflict between groups and

> In most organizations the quality of intergroup and inter- departmental relations could be improved.

between departments also arises because of changes in the organization's environment. Shifts in such factors as market conditions, material costs, and customer and regulatory requirements can alter the priorities and plans of groups and departments, which, in turn, will often have consequences for other units in the organization.

Conflict and Inter-Unit Relations

In this chapter we are concerned with conflict between the groups and departments of an organization and with what can be done to reduce and prevent conflict and improve collaboration. To simplify the presentation that follows, the term "unit" is used to refer to either a group or department and the phrase "inter-unit conflict" is used to mean conflict between groups or departments.

Inter-unit conflict can range from mild to severe and will be expressed behaviorally. At one end of a continuum, inter-unit conflict consists of mild tension, stress, and distrust within one or both units that work with one another. At the other end of the continuum are units that communicate minimally, far less than they should, or not at all because of past and/or present grievances. At this end of the continuum, too, are units engaged in heated, strident, and virulent debate and opposition.

Conflict of any type reduces cooperation, coordination, and information flows between units; can hurt customer relations; and is a distraction, causing time and attention to be taken away from important work. Some level of conflict is desirable in organizations and beneficial because it can identify problems and lead to needed change. In fact, some organizations may have too little conflict (Miles, 1980). However, in many organizations conflict occurs that is not productive or functional, interfering with collaboration beneficial to the organization.

Antecedents to Inter-Unit Conflict

There are at least fifteen antecedents or sources of conflict between units.

A purpose of this chapter is to pinpoint the sources of inter-unit conflict in organizations. There are at least fifteen antecedents or sources of conflict between units that are described in the following section. These include:

- The need to share or compete for resources;
- Work overload;

- Obstacles to communication;
- Jurisdictional ambiguities; and
- Dependence on other units.

In addition, proposed for each source or group of sources are actions that can be taken by an organization's leaders, managers, and members to either reduce the likelihood of conflict or permit better "management" of conflict. The following discussion is a product of the author's experiences and draws primarily on these sources: Litterer (1966); Miles (1980); and Walton and Dutton (1969).

Two important points should be kept in mind. First, in any inter-unit relationship, more than one of the antecedents to conflict may be present. Improving inter-unit relationships in this circumstance requires the implementation of countermeasures of the kind indicated for those multiple antecedents. Thoughtful analysis using the framework provided by this chapter can reveal the antecedents present in a particular relationship. Secondly, collaboration between organization units is less likely to occur or be successful if the antecedents to conflict are ignored and the action steps below are not implemented. The reader is encouraged to mark or note actions steps below that are important to undertake in his or her organization.

Antecedent 1. Units Having to Share or Compete for Scarce Resources

Resources in organizations are limited and units may be required to share or compete for resources such as: physical space, including access to certain spaces (for example, conference and interview rooms); equipment; personnel; operating and capital funds; and centralized services.

Actions to Minimize Conflict That Occurs Because Units Have to Share Common Resources or Compete for Scarce Resources

- Separate the units by giving each what it needs, or arrive at an equitable solution for sharing resources.
- Attempt to balance allocations to different units. For example, it is common to find that the opportunity to hire new personnel passes sequentially from one department to another.

- Give priority to new projects that will generate benefits for two or more units.

- Place projects that are proposed by units on a long-range funding plan, especially those projects that are not approved for the current year. This will result in less conflict than approving some and rejecting others. Fewer units will see themselves as "losers" in the funding process (Pondy, 1964).

- Develop investment "categories" for the organization that preempt debate and conflict over what evaluation criteria should be used in assessing different investment opportunities. For example, each year invest in a *range* of desirable projects in such areas as government compliance, cost reduction, replacement, and employee satisfaction and retention (Pondy, 1964).

- Choose investment projects that are well related to the organization's strategy (a form of superordinate goal—a goal whose achievement benefits all units) (Sherif & Sherif, 1953); relate allocation decisions to the overall strategy.

Antecedent 2. Units That Must Rely On One Another in Performing Their Respective Tasks

Here, units are mutually dependent—Unit A relies on Unit B, and vice versa—and literally need each other to carry out their responsibilities. In a manufacturing organization, for example, a production department needs information from sales on a regular basis for scheduling purposes. Similarly, sales requires information from production regarding product availability. A similar relationship exists between purchasing and sales in a wholesale distributorship. In these circumstances, there is a high incentive for inter-unit collaboration and coordination, but also the potential for conflict (Walton & Dutton, 1969). Thus the relationship of units that enjoy mutual task dependence needs to be monitored carefully by unit members and leaders.

Actions to Minimize Conflict Occurring Because Units Are Mutually Dependent

- Encourage broad and frequent communication between units, including notification about workflow interruptions as early as possible.

- Develop and "institutionalize" procedures to be followed when inter-unit differences arise.

- Identify "integrators" or trouble-shooters for mutually dependent units, individuals who are able to work skillfully with other units, or train all to have the requisite skills (see Antecedent 15).

- Introduce buffer stocks, working ahead and the stockpiling of outputs to reduce the dependence of one unit on the performance of another unit.

- Combine mutually dependent groups in one unit. This helps eliminate organizational boundaries that promote conflict.

- Permit units to become self-contained, that is, eliminate the mutual dependency.

- As a superior, work with the different units to achieve clarity about how they are to work with one another and monitor the relationship. Clarify timing and quality requirements for deliverables.

Antecedent 3. One Unit Relies More on a Second Unit than the Second Unit Relies upon the First

The dependence here is one-way, that is, Unit A relies on Unit B but Unit B does not rely on Unit A. Under these circumstances, conflict between the units may arise because Unit B may lack an incentive to cooperate and meet the needs of Unit A. Line and staff relations in organizations are one example of unequal dependence.

Line and staff relations in organizations are one example of unequal dependence.

Staff often depend on line personnel to implement new programs and processes they propose, yet line may lack a sufficient incentive to cooperate. Staff members are also required to understand the problems of line groups and get along with them but there are not reciprocal requirements on line personnel (Walton & Dutton, 1969). The high reliance of operating groups on information technology and maintenance departments are two other examples of non-symmetrical, non-reciprocal dependence. Those in information technology and maintenance do not, in turn, depend on the units they support.

Other "unbalanced" situations in organizations that are likely to prompt conflict between units include the following four.

Antecedent 4. The Unequal Influence of Units in Organization Decision Making

Antecedent 5. The One-Way Flow of Requests or Demands from One Unit to Another

For example, various service groups or departments, such as purchasing agents, programmers, financial analysts, data entry and word processing personnel, are often on the receiving end of requests from other units.

Antecedent 6. One Group Reporting on the Activities of Another Group, That Is, Various Auditing Activities in Organizations

Antecedent 7. A Lower Status Group Influencing, Directing, or Setting Standards for the Work of a Higher Status Group

One example would be an environmental quality group in an organization attempting to influence the processes and procedures of scientists in research and development.

Actions to Take in the Above Circumstances

- Since the one-way dependence of a department, a one-way (unbalanced) pattern of initiation, and other unbalanced and status situations promote conflict:

    - Balance the workflow, creating mutual task dependence and symmetrical relations wherever possible. For example, indicate to personnel in information technology how highly satisfied internal customers lead to improved organization performance from which they are likely to benefit. Alternatively, form teams consisting of specialists from different departments and hold teams responsible for accomplishing particular projects.

    - When making a decision, consult with all units that will be affected by the decision. Hold additional discussions when a decision is not likely to match the preferences of units.

    - Permit staff from units always at the receiving end of requests to occasionally impose, when reasonable and within limits, certain requirements or constraints on the requests of other groups. Purchasing agents and information technology and secretarial staff often do this in organizations.

- Provide service groups with occasional tokens of appreciation.

- Establish auditing practices that minimize the likelihood of resistance and conflict, and select auditors with strong interpersonal skills. Resistance and conflict are reduced when auditors are flexible in scheduling the audit; convey that they are there, in part, to help improve the practices of a unit rather than to "catch" and report mistakes; and report their findings to the unit at the audit's conclusion.

- Place an inspection/auditing unit organizationally in a high status group.

- Permit units to air or raise grievances and provide units with considered responses to them.

Antecedent 8. Work Overload Experienced by One or More Units

The unit experiencing the overload can be one or both units that mutually rely on one another, or the unit on which other units are dependent.

Under overload conditions, units may be unable to comply in a timely and/or satisfactory manner with the expectations of other units.

Under overload conditions, units may be unable to comply in a timely and/or satisfactory manner with the expectations of other units for assistance, information, compliance, and other coordinative acts. Conflict is likely to arise as a consequence.

Actions to Minimize Conflict Caused by Task Overload Conditions

- Permit an overloaded unit to acquire additional and temporary resources to deal with the overload.

- Adjust deadlines, loosen schedules, or adjust the deliverables where and if possible so as to reduce the overload.

- Enable units to have the ability to duplicate the work of another unit, thus reducing requests to a unit that is temporarily operating under overload conditions.

Antecedent 9. Units That Are Focused on Meeting the Goals or Expectations Established by Top Management and Striving to Obtain the Rewards Available if Expectations Are Met

An organization's leadership, by the expectations and rewards it establishes for units, can either increase or decrease the potential for inter-unit conflict. Cooperation and collaboration among units may be reduced when each is held accountable for achieving goals that are not shared by other units. For example, we find in many organizations that a production department, concerned with meeting production schedules and keeping the per unit cost of production low, often lacks incentive to work with sales to meet the special production and scheduling needs of a large customer. Similarly, marketing department staffers may have great difficulty involving sales personnel in discussions concerning new products because the primary concern of sales personnel is meeting immediate sales quotas and generating commissions. Research and development staff, who are expected to add new products to a company's pipeline, may lack sufficient incentive to work with manufacturing staff to resolve production problems.

Actions to Minimize Conflict That Occurs Because Units Strive to Meet Different Performance Expectations and Secure Rewards

- Recognize collaborative, cooperative acts by units or activities/accomplishments that benefit many units or the entire organization.

- Call attention to the need for inter-unit cooperation and the importance of this to overall department and/or organization success.

- Develop measures that reveal the extent of inter-unit cooperation.

- Make unit contributions to inter-unit tasks the focus of unit performance review and unit rewards; create reward systems that elicit greater harmony and cooperation between groups.

  For example, (1) hold the production department accountable for cooperating with sales in being responsive to requests from large customers for product modifications and certain delivery dates; (2) hold production and quality control groups equally responsible for reducing customer returns; (3) reward production, sales, and research and development based on the number of new products brought to the production stage; or (4) hold line and staff jointly responsible for making process improvements during the year. In each of these examples two or three units are responsible for accomplishing a common objective.

Create reward systems that elicit greater harmony and cooperation between groups.

Antecedent 10. Units Not Sufficiently Understanding or Appreciating the Work Done by Other Units

The members of each unit, by virtue of their specialized training and primary focus on certain organization issues, may come to value their contribution to the organization too much and value the contribution and work done by other units too little. In the absence of information about other units, negative stereotyping may also occur, for example: "those myopic engineers" or "the bean counters in accounting." These negative stereotypes of other units, of course, increase the potential for conflict. Additionally, when a unit knows relatively little about another unit's work and its work cycles, it is possible for it to make requests and hold expectations that are unreasonable. Actions that can be taken to remedy these problems are grouped with those for Antecedent 11.

Antecedent 11. Various Obstacles to Inter-Unit Communication

These include (1) distance between units that regularly or on occasion work together, including situations in which interacting units are on different floors, in different buildings, or in different towns, states and countries; (2) synchronization difficulties, that is, units attempting to communicate across shifts or different time zones; (3) semantic misunderstandings and differences—including jargon used by the members of a unit not fully understood by the members of other units; (4) the uneven distribution of information in an organization, for example, a unit may receive and act on information having a bearing on its work, plans, and priorities. However, this information may not have been received or read by units affected by these changes.

Actions to Minimize Conflict Caused by Communication Obstacles and an Under-Appreciation of the Work Done by Other Units

- Place the workplaces/workspaces of interacting units in close physical proximity, to permit frequent interaction of the units.

Create the possibility architecturally of informal, unplanned inter-unit contact.

- Create, through architecture, the opportunity for informal, unplanned inter-unit contact. Especially helpful in this regard are central spaces individuals must pass through on their way to other places. Examples of central spaces are organization reception areas and atriums (Steele, 1979). A lot of unplanned contact also occurs in company cafeterias.

- Establish areas that are suitable for inter-unit meetings.

- Establish a pattern of regular meetings between units, where inter-unit problems can be raised and ironed out before they get serious.

- Establish the means whereby the members of different units who work at different time periods can nevertheless communicate with one another (email, voice mail, mailboxes, overlapping shifts, message boards, and lists of home phone numbers).

- Provide intensive training in communication and listening. (For more information on communication and listening skills see Chapter 31.)

- Allow participation in inter-unit projects (for example, cross-functional teams), inter-unit problem-solving teams, and periodic presentations by one unit to other units. These permit units to learn of the work being done in other units and to learn about demands typically placed on these units. Units are therefore less likely to unintentionally make unreasonable demands or requests of other groups.

- Don't assume that all groups have received or read reports, memoranda, and other items that potentially affect inter-unit relations.

- Establish training programs for new hires that involve the lateral movement of employees through different units.

- Include articles in company newsletters that describe the work done by different units.

- Begin "brown-bag" lunch meetings in which a unit describes the work that it does.

Antecedent 12. The Presence of Various Ambiguities in the Organization

These include (1) jurisdictional ambiguities, where each of two units may believe that the resolution of a problem is the other unit's responsibility. Conversely, two or more field offices may believe they have a legitimate claim on the business of a particular client, or a field office and headquarters may vie for the same client; (2) difficulty in assigning credit or blame between two or more units, that is, accountability ambiguities, increases the likelihood of conflict, as does (3) uncertainty over the best means to accomplish goals, and (4) an absence of communication about an organization's long-term goals. A lack of communication and clarity here lessens the likelihood that units will work together in the same direction.

Actions to Minimize Conflict That Occurs Because of Ambiguities

- Define unit jurisdictions and specify a process to be used in the future if jurisdictional differences arise.

- Create the means so that credit and blame can be more easily assigned to different units. For example, create action plans in which the responsibilities of individual units are clear.

- Have units critique their own proposed solutions to problems and identify commendable points in the proposed solutions of other units.

- Formulate and communicate organization goals.

Antecedent 13. Perceived Inequities in the Distribution of Organizational Rewards

The potential for inter-unit conflict is increased when a unit believes that its contributions are undervalued.

The potential for inter-unit conflict is increased when a unit believes that its contributions are undervalued, underappreciated, and inadequately rewarded, especially in relation to the rewards received by those in other units. For example, customer service departments that work hard to serve and retain customers may be resentful of the rewards lavished on those involved in sales.

Action to Minimize Conflict in this Situation *(see also Antecedent 4)*

- Permit units to air or raise their grievances and provide units with considered responses to them.

Antecedent 14. Members Unhappy with Their Roles, the Status of Their Unit, and the Opportunities for Recognition and Advancement

Unit members here have career and other aspirations that are unfulfilled, and this can lead to conflict with other units. In early research, purchasing agents and others in staff roles were identified as experiencing dissatisfaction of this kind (Dalton, 1959; Strauss, 1962).

Actions to Minimize Conflict That Occurs Because of Role Dissatisfaction

- Conduct a thorough interviewing and screening process for new employees that includes realistic job previews. A realistic job preview involves providing a candidate with honest, undistorted information about the job and organization. The positive and negative aspects of the job are presented and an effort is made to convey a balanced, realistic picture of the opportunity (Greenhaus, Callanan, & Godshalk, 2000).

- Provide professional career counseling and planning for employees.

- Implement organization policies and career development practices that permit people to move out of areas where they are not happy. For example, establish a job posting system, in which a firm gives preference to its internal workforce in filling vacancies; or encourage and permit lateral, including cross-functional, transfers.

- Design broader roles that allow people to better use their skills and abilities.

Antecedent 15. The Personal Qualities and Skills of Unit Leaders and Members

Certain personality attributes such as high authoritarianism, high dogmatism, and low tolerance for ambiguity are antithetical to inter-unit relations that are cordial, congenial, trusting, and characterized by mutual respect (Walton & Dutton, 1969). Conflict between units is also likely when unit leaders and members lack skills to address and work through interpersonal and inter-unit differences or diversity issues, have poor listening skills, or are technically incompetent or inept.

Actions to Minimize Conflict That Occurs Because of Personal Skills and Traits

- Provide training that encourages the early surfacing and quick resolution of conflicts and that discourages "issue aggregation." Provide people with the skills to address and work through differences and conflict.

- Establish the ability to work collaboratively and cooperatively with others, including other groups, as an important criterion in rewarding and promoting people.

- Be selective in recruitment, that is, select new hires who have qualities likely to make them successful in working with others.

Remove unskillful and abrasive personalities as unit leaders and representatives.

- Remove unskillful and abrasive personalities as unit leaders and representatives.

- In extreme cases as a manager, restrict inter-unit contact and negotiation so as to involve only certain designated individuals, each of whom possesses the required experience, skills, and qualities.

- Arrange to be present when inter-unit interaction occurs so you can minimize the damage caused by an abrasive unit leader or member.

- Provide alternative channels for resolving disputes, for example, ombudsmen or review panels.

- As personal dissimilarities between unit leaders or representatives can increase the potential for conflict, establish a culture that does not tolerate discrimination, and provide effective diversity training.

Conclusion

In this chapter, we have identified the major sources of conflict between groups and departments in organizations and the actions that can be taken to prevent, reduce, or better "manage" conflict. We will conclude this chapter with three major points.

First, the list of fifteen antecedents reveals that only some of the conflict in organizations arises because of the qualities and absence of skill of particular leaders and members. It has been suggested that much more conflict occurs because of the features of the organization, that is, the context within which groups and departments operate (Walton & Dutton, 1969). To improve collaboration between organization units, this context must be a primary focus of attention.

All **levels of an organization have a role to play in reducing conflict and improving collaboration.**

Second, the lists of actions suggest that *all* levels of an organization have a role to play in reducing conflict and improving collaboration.

Certainly, some of the actions suggested to prevent and reduce conflict require the direct intervention of an organization's leaders. For example, an organization's leadership allocates organization resources (Antecedent 1); conveys expectations for department performance and allocates rewards (Antecedent 9); often has a strong influence in the physical arrangement of organization units (Antecedent 11); formulates and communicates organization goals (Antecedent 12); crafts staffing policies and practices (Antecedent 14); and determines the broad criteria used for rewarding and promoting people (Antecedent 15).

At one level lower in the organization, the department manager level, there are many actions they can implement. They can, for example, attempt to balance resource allocations to the different groups they supervise (Antecedent 1); encourage frequent communication between units, and monitor inter-unit relations (Antecedent 2); provide service units with occasional tokens of appreciation (Antecedent 7); permit overloaded units to acquire additional and temporary resources and to negotiate adjusted deadlines for these units (Antecedent 8); recognize cooperative acts by units and call attention to the need for inter-unit cooperation (Antecedent 9); and resolve jurisdictional ambiguities (Antecedent 12).

Continuing down the organizational hierarchy, individuals can prevent and reduce conflict, as well. For example, employees can function as integrators/ trouble-shooters for their units (Antecedent 2); express appreciation for cooperative acts by other units (Antecedent 9); use clear, jargon-free language when communicating with members of other units, and suggest regular meetings between units where problems can be ironed-out (Antecedent 11).

Without detailing them specifically here, there are many action steps in the above lists in such areas as recruitment, training and development, and performance review that require the full involvement, energy, and contributions of human resources. It is clear that everyone in an organization can take steps to mitigate conflict.

Finally, the reader is encouraged to expand on the ideas presented here and to implement actions that increase the frequency and improve the quality of collaboration in his or her organization. In developing the lists of remedial actions that follow the antecedents, there was no attempt to make these lists exhaustive. Quite likely there are other countermeasures that can be taken in relation to each antecedent. The reader is encouraged to draw on his or her experience to supplement these lists.

CHAPTER 20

Learning and Communicating About Collaboration in Dispersed Teams

Kenneth David and John R. Lloyd

IN THIS CHAPTER WE FOCUS ON TOOLS for organizational learning and organizational teaching about effective practices for dispersed team projects. The chapter begins by situating the study (business impacts of dispersed teaming) and by defining needed terms.

The following section sets out challenges for dispersed teaming by reviewing (1) power issues, (2) cultural issues, and (3) multimedia communications issues that must be addressed by the dispersed team.

Second, we set out a series of tools that meet these challenges by (1) making individual experience accessible to the dispersed team member (organizational learning) and (2) turning individual experience into accounts that are communicable to others in the team or elsewhere in the organization (organizational teaching).

The concluding section of this chapter connects these tools with types of knowledge (fugitive knowledge, accessible knowledge, communicable knowledge, and transmitted knowledge) that are produced in accord with processes of organizational learning and organizational teaching.

Introduction
Business Impacts of Dispersed Teams

Coordination of dispersed team activities is a growing strategic necessity. Effective (or ineffective) communications practices strongly affect the coordination of dispersed team activities.

A large manufacturing company (with many operating divisions) has multiple fabricating sites within each division. The monitor division (twelve sites worldwide) co-designs components to provide to one another. Dispersed teams experience communications difficulties when they try to co-design components. The results are serious: the cost of defective goods due to misfits of components at $200 to $300 million per year. More effective teamwork could eliminate most of this loss.

A truck manufacturer in northern Europe has competitive advantage because it co-designs repairs for trucks, no matter where the truck has broken down. Global positioning locates both the truck and then the closest repair shop. A central repair advisor helps the local shop diagnose and then repair the truck. This is effective dispersed teamwork that provides a strategic advantage.

Definitions

As just indicated, due to strategic needs of multi-site organizations and alliances among separate enterprises, organizations increasingly depend on dispersed team projects—in which interaction and collaboration take place among geographically distributed teams (sometimes called "virtual" teams or "distributed" teams).

A *co-located* team is a set of persons who work in a face-to-face situation. A *virtual* team is a collection of individuals located at diverse locations who work together via electronic communications. We focus on the *dispersed team* composed of two or more *subteams* in different geographic locations; local subteams work together via face-to-face communications; dispersed subteams work with each other via electronic communications.

We define the entire distributed team as the *dispersed* team. Within the dispersed team is a *proximate subteam* located close to the team's client and one or more *distant subteams* located farther away. (See Figure 20.1.)

Figure 20.1. Dispersed Team and Subteams

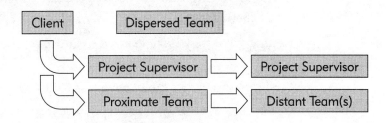

Effective Teaming

Effective teaming coordinates *interdependent activity* within the dispersed team.

We define *effective dispersed teaming* as the coordination of interdependent project activity within the geographically dispersed team. We suggest that the benefit of collaboration comes from harnessing complementary competencies or knowledge of these local teams. Then the additional costs and efforts of working at a distance are worth the trouble.

Our approach to effective dispersed teaming can be briefly stated: dispersed teams have the opportunity to be *learning* as well as *teaching* organizations.

Dispersed teams have the opportunity to mutually construct their practices and policies.

They can mutually construct their practices and policies. Norms (or at least informal routines) must be developed for working together and then communicated around the dispersed team.

Management literature introduced the notion of *learning organization* over twelve years ago (Senge, 1990). Learning from project experience is already a recognized task. During inter-organizational interaction, organizations learn from other organizations. Learning from others is a dynamic process that often involves active adaptations to the knowledge held by other organizations (Levitt & March, 1988). Experience, particularly non-technical knowledge about effective work practices, is not retained very long by project team members unless they record it. Why take the trouble to learn from project experience unless you make the complementary effort to communicate what has been learned to those who need to use it? Therefore this chapter stresses the complementary notion of *teaching organization*.

Business needs for coordination of dispersed activities is a growing necessity in collaborative teaming. Team-based organizations, especially when the organizations engage in cross-border teaming, become more effective when they become proficient at:

- Learning about effective project work practices: gathering pertinent, timely knowledge about effective teaming (instead of relying on intuitive experience);

- Putting what they have learned in a form that others can understand; and

- Communicating what they have learned to others so that it can be organizationally useful.

When all three tasks are organized, it is fair to say that both organizational learning issues and organizational teaching issues are operative in an organization.

Power, Culture, and Multimedia Communications Issues in Dispersed Teams

Because most studies of group team work concentrate on "co-located" teams (see Sundstrom, 1999, for an extensive literature review), the current challenge is to learn how to improve collaboration in dispersed teams (Duarte & Snyder, 1999; Kostner, 1994; Lipnack & Stamps, 1997). Members of dispersed teams are more likely to be working in different cultural contexts, less likely to have worked together before, and less likely to have opportunities for face-to-face interaction (Jarvenpaa & Leidner, 1998). Such teams require different methods to create and maintain relationships to coordinate and manage interdependent work. In particular, team members face *power, cultural,* and *communications* issues.

Power Issues

Is there perceived inequity or perceived fairness in the relationship among dispersed subteams?

Neutralizing perceived power problems is necessary to foster and sustain group cohesion, motivation, and morale. Team members may be confronted with various power issues: various subteams *may perceive* that they have unequal access to the client, control of information, control of material resources, or distribution of credit for project accomplishments.

As the report in Exhibit 20.1 illustrates, when team members perceive such inequities in the relationship, the project partnership will likely suffer in terms of interdependent activity. A common response in dispersed teams is not to rebel overtly, but to act covertly and disrupt (subvert) the activity. This response occurred in a dispersed team design project between a U.S. based subteam and a Singapore based subteam.

Exhibit 20.1. Transcultural Incident Report 1

Business Situation

An engineering team from the United States collaborated with a team from Singapore on a distant engineering research project. The U.S. project supervisor told the team to propose and to check out four options for the item to be designed. The U.S. team followed orders but thought that only options #1 and #2 were worth the effort.

Cultural and Power Issues

The U.S. team started working with the Singapore team; they initiated the work assignment: they *told* the Singapore that the U.S. team would check out options #1 and #2, while the Singapore team would check out options #3 and #4. In email messages, the Singapore team apparently agreed to this division of work.

Boundary-Spanning Action

No further action was taken after exchange of email messages. Teams worked independently.

Outcome

Three weeks later, the two teams communicated results. To the surprise of the U.S. team, the Singapore team had also checked out options #1 and #2.

After inconclusive discussion, during which the U.S. team began to get irritated with the Singapore team, the latter reluctantly and diplomatically explained their action: "We knew that options #3 and #4 were worthless. Since you suggested them, we thought you would lose face if we checked them out and made it perfectly clear that they were not feasible options. So we decided to turn our effort to the two more feasible options."

Lessons Learned

Further discussion clarified that the Singaporeans were actually sending another message: do not simply order people around and expect them to comply.

Dispersed teams may agree to a unilateral order of command. Norms (or at least, informal routines) must be developed for decision making. If there is no agreement, then you are buying trouble.

Imposition of a work plan by one design team on a partner distant design team may incite surprising action and, sometimes, covert subversion of the plan.

Alternatively, team members can act so as to neutralize these power issues and promote relative equity (fairness) in the relationship, as the following example illustrates.

A tri-national Whirlpool Emerging Technology project team initially encountered and overcame the "gatekeeper" issue stemming from unequal access of the three local teams to the client. The U.S. team was the *proximate* team, the team geographically closest to the client. The other two teams (Dutch and Chinese) were located farther away.

The Dutch and Chinese teams both thought that the United States had been explicitly briefed by the client at the beginning of the project and was withholding information (like a "gatekeeper"). In fact, no one was highly briefed because the client wanted to "empower" the tri-national team to think creatively.

The "gatekeeper" image was not resolved at a distance. The three teams scheduled two face-to-face meetings (U.S. and Dutch and U.S. and Chinese) to build teamwork and share information. In the course of these meetings, the "gatekeeper" image that was negatively affecting the project was dispelled (see Figure 20.2).

Figure 20.2. Perceived "Gatekeeping" in a Dispersed Team

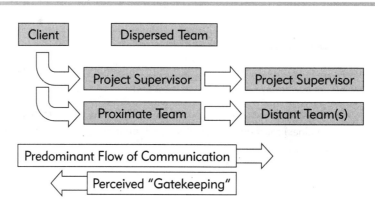

Cultural Issues

Do we understand each other?

Bridging cultural differences is necessary to foster coordinated activity. Culture is defined as shared understandings. Humans acquire shared understandings only when they are similarly socialized in cultural classifications, cultural codes for conduct, and cultural priorities for action (David & Lloyd, 2001; David & Terpstra, 1991).

Cultural classifications. Culture classifies phenomena into discontinuous units. People learn and then perceive what is around them with these classifications. Children classify bushes and trees together until they learn to classify them as different. Companies also classify reality. Some companies never classify difficult situations as "dilemmas" or "crises" but always refer to "challenges," "issues," or "opportunities."

Cultural codes. What are proper codes for behavior? People learn not only to classify items but also how to behave toward them. Consultants in a particular company learn various "codes" including time codes: they look down on clients who rush to leave the office at 5 p.m. Some companies are known as very formal when working with external clients but push formality backstage in the office.

Cultural priorities. What are priorities among codes for conduct? Priorities are necessary because different social situations call for different actions. For example, an engineer flew out of town at short notice to repair a major client's equipment. Because the work took a week, she found it necessary to buy some clothes. When the accounting department rejected her claim for these expenses, the CEO publicly overruled them, thus demonstrating that the firm's code for customer service was more important than its policy (company codes) for travel expenses.

Cultural issues are present in dispersed teams because, by definition, a dispersed team is culturally disparate. Cultural disparity means that team members do *not* initially share cultural classifications, codes, or priorities. Said again, dispersed team members do not initially share *work practices.*

Dispersed team members do not initially share *work practices.*

In order to become an effective team, team members must take the time and effort to develop mutually acceptable norms for interaction.

In the example described in Exhibit 20.2, a Dutch-U.S. dispersed team displays good teaming skills by learning from a cultural miscue. They learned how to develop shared understandings needed to work together at a distance.

Exhibit 20.2. Transcultural Incident Report 2

Practical Situation

The Microchannel heat-exchanger engineering design team was composed of Dutch plus U.S. team members. The dispersed team met in a cordial and professional videoconference and began defining the project specifications. They assigned tasks to be done before the next videoconference.

Cultural and Power and Contextual Issues

This first conference took place on a Monday. The dispersed team agreed that it was most convenient to meet every Thursday. As the conference was ending, a U.S. team member suggested they schedule a meeting "for next Thursday." The Dutch team member agreed: "Fine. We will meet *next* Thursday."

Three days later, the U.S. team tried to make a video connection but got no answer. A telephone call confirmed that no one was present at the Dutch end.

Boundary-Spanning Action

The U.S. team was irritated but sent a mildly worded email asking why the Dutch had not kept their appointment. The Dutch, in turn, sent back an email, asking why the U.S. team expected them to show up when the meeting had been firmly agreed for one week later.

After two more emails, both sides understood that the American English denotation of "this" and "next" differs from the Dutch denotation. When Dutch say "this Thursday" [deze Donderdag], the word "this" means a day in the current week; when Dutch say "next Thursday" [volgende Donderdag], the word "next" means a day that occurs in the following week. The dispersed team further learned that American date notation (month/day/year) differs from Dutch date notation (day/month/year). They learned that Americans use the twelve-hour clock while Dutch use a twenty-four-hour clock.

Outcome

The dispersed team decided on a time-scheduling protocol for scheduling events. Dates would be designated with an alphanumeric sequence such as 18 Oct 1999. Time would be in twenty-four-hour notation with time zone attached.

Lessons Learned

This usage is a cultural difference that is a common source of misunderstanding between Dutch and English speakers.

Working through this cultural misunderstanding led to a very constructive attitude of checking on arrangements and developing shared understandings for the project work. The dispersed team learned how to deal with cultural disparities that could affect project performance.

Power and Cultural Issues Must Be Analyzed Together

Power issues (perceived fairness *versus* perceived inequity among dispersed subteams) directly affect cultural issues (developing greater understanding *versus* fostering misunderstanding). Y.R. Isar, a keynote speaker at the 1996 International Congress of the Society for Intercultural Education, Training, and Research, stated the objectives of the society as "building bridges for intercultural communication, shaping shared understandings, . . . working for human rights, and promoting equity" (Isar, 1996). We suggest that the opposite processes also occur. In situations of perceived inequity, people are moved to create cultural distance and create misunderstanding among organizations. For example, after a "merger of equals" between two Dutch banks, ABN and AMRO, each *informatica* department tried to take power. For a while, each was unwilling to share professional knowledge but rather fostered misunderstandings in order to avoid giving away knowledge that might lose the battle. This power struggle was only "resolved" when one department effectively took over the other department. It was a takeover—not a merger of equals.

Another case illustrates the intertwining of cultural and power issues: BDDP, a French advertising firm, attempted to acquire BMP, a British advertising firm. Both parties addressed contrary messages to a set of stakeholders. As part of its takeover attempt, BDDP attempted to construct a perception of cultural togetherness and of organizational complementarity vis-à-vis BMP. As part of its takeover defense, BMP attempted to construct a perception of cultural distance and of organizational disarray vis-à-vis BDDP.

This case demonstrates that cultural distance is not a fixed factor but a constructed event, that is, a perception that participants can emphasize or deemphasize, depending on their vested power interests. In studying dispersed teams, we always study cultural and power issues together. Depending on the power situation, team members can either work to *bridge* cultural misunderstandings or work to *create* further cultural misunderstandings (David, 1996).

Multimedia Communications Issues

Have we established conventions for using media?

Dispersed team members must choose from a variety of advanced telecommunications media and decide which media are appropriate for different phases of a design project (Duarte & Snyder, 1999). Dispersed team members face both time zone and cultural challenges. When working together across time zones, synchronous ("real time") interactions are reduced. Asynchronous modes of communication such as email increase.

 Problems of information distribution and interpretation occur (Cramton, 1999). Team managers must decide which modes of communication can and should be supplied, which types of computer-based coordination and support are needed, and which project and information management approaches enable groups to work effectively.

In addition, dispersed team members must recognize that media use is shaped by power and by cultural issues. Power impact is illustrated in the following example:

> A general manager of a Chinese branch of a European multinational received a central server, a set of computers, local area networks, and company-wide intranet connection. Headquarters was surprised that the system was not being deployed. A vice president visited the branch and reported that the central server was sitting in the general manager's office, not in the information systems department. The general manager found it wrong for his subordinates to have better equipment than he had.

Further, media use is partially shaped by culture. Conventions for how a telecommunication medium is used are totally determined by the technology; conventions are shaped by the national culture, professional culture, and organizational culture of the users (for more information, see David & Terpstra, 1991).

The following case illustrates that media conventions are shaped by different organizational cultures. Americans from different companies miscommunicate due to different media conventions.

> Two Americans from different companies are located in the same city in the United States. They tried to arrange a business lunch.

The two companies are preparing for the annual renewal of a major contract.

"Why didn't you show up for lunch yesterday?" said a manager from one company.

"You didn't invite me," replied the manager from a second company.

"I certainly did. I emailed you three times to confirm the appointment."

"Forget it. At my company, you have to *telephone* if you want to make a meal appointment."

A major contract was coming up for renewal and no more mistakes could be tolerated. The two managers reviewed norms for communications and telecommunications within the contract negotiating team. This simple cultural misunderstanding led to a very constructive attitude of checking on arrangements and developing shared understandings for the project work.

Transcultural communication, therefore, can occur even within the same city. A cross-border relationship involves people from different national cultures. They can have rather different ideas on what it means to use a particular medium.

In the Whirlpool Emerging Technology project involving U.S., Dutch, and Chinese teams, the subteams wanted to use different media during project launch because they had contrasting cultural ideas about how one should launch a project. The project objectives were not initially strongly defined by the client, who wanted to "empower" the dispersed team to think innovatively.

How did the various teams respond? The U.S. and the Dutch teams were task-oriented during the project launch: they worked hard to define the project; they predominantly communicated by email to express their ideas. The Chinese, by contrast, responded to "under-definition of objectives" by making a strong effort to establish harmonious social relationships with their counterparts until the time that project became better defined. They preferred to use telephone or Net meeting for this purpose.

In all cross-border projects, use of various telecommunication media involves understanding and responding to different cultural priorities. Two subteams prioritized task orientation (defining the project) while the other subteam prioritized social orientation (seeking harmonious relationships).

In dispersed teams, then, everyone is a multimedia communicator. Multimedia skills are especially important in dispersed project team management. Dispersed teams have the opportunity to negotiate how each medium should be used in order to foster effective communication.

Summary: Challenges of Dispersed Teaming Projects

The previous sections have discussed a series of challenges that dispersed teams must deal with if they are to implement strategic objectives:

- *Power Issues:* Is there perceived inequity or perceived fairness in the relationship among dispersed subteams?
- *Cultural Issues:* Do we understand each other?
- *Multimedia Communications Issues:* Have we established conventions for using media?

Meeting the Challenges: Implications for Collaborative Teaming Practice

What are the implications for collaborative teaming practice? The point is to enhance communication and coordinate activity within the dispersed team in order to improve project performance.

Collaborative team members require additional communications and teamwork competencies in addition to technical competencies.

Our position is that collaborative team members require not only the usual technical competencies; they also require additional communications and teamwork competencies for developing and communicating project knowledge.

Dispersed team members have the opportunity to construct and negotiate "practices" and "policies" for their dispersed team. That is, they can develop norms for working together—designing ways to overcome cultural and power issues and to overcome multimedia communications issues.

Successfully performing these activities requires two sets of skills:

- Transcultural communications skills are skills that attempt to neutralize (and sometimes overcome) cultural and power issues in the dispersed team.

- Multimedia communications skills are skills for helping dispersed team members to understand and respond to the diverse cultural conventions that team members expect when they use particular telecommunications media and skills to negotiate how media should be used in order to foster effective communication.

Summing up the situation in one phrase, we need a framework and a toolkit for developing and communicating project knowledge.

Activity Framework and Project Reporting Tools for Learning and Teaching Project Knowledge

A contribution to a book on collaborative work practices should not only specify *what* to do, developing transcultural and multimedia communications skills, but should indicate *how* to do it. In this next section, we propose a framework whose purpose is to diagnose and correct *cultural* and *power issues* that impact on the coordination of *project activity by the dispersed team*. We also propose an additional set of project reporting tools for learning and teaching project knowledge: field notes, transcultural incident reports, project case studies, contract case studies, and project archives. The Culture, Power, and Project Activity framework helps summarize lessons from each of these project reports.

The Culture, Power, and Project Activity Framework and Its Application to Dispersed Teaming

This framework is one of a set of organizational teaching tools that can be used by dispersed teams as an addition to standard project management techniques. We note that teams who have been informed of the framework shown in Table 20.1 tend to avoid dysfunctional practices or to recognize problems before they get out of hand.

Table 20.1. Power, Culture, and Collaborative Team Activity Framework

	Do we understand each other?	
Do we have power problems?	No. We do not share cultural understandings.	Yes. We do share cultural understandings.
No. We do not have power problems.	*Disorganized Activity* Ambiguous definition of project objectives. Erratic peer consultation. No agreed method for decision making.	*Coordinated Activity* Clear definition of project objectives. Peer consultation about issues. Negotiated and agreed-on method for decision making. Coordinated division of work.
Yes. We do have power problems.	*Turmoil* Conflicting project objectives. Purposive misinformation or miscommunication among team members. Overt rebellion against coordinated action.	*Adverse Activity* Competing project objectives. Compliance with resentment. Staff defection. Covert subversion of activities.

This framework can and has been applied to collaborative teaming in the following ways:

- Serve as a dispersed team "report card" to quickly chart the progression of team activities during the course of a project;

- Call attention to (in)effective activity and thus lead to problem identification;

- Focus effort for correcting problems; and

- Provide a summary statement about the project for archival purposes.

To illustrate the use of this framework, we revisit the U.S.-Singapore project reported earlier in the chapter.

- There was no problem in the project launch phase when the project was initially defined. The subteams moved from an ambiguous to a clear definition of the project objectives: they moved from *disorganized activity* toward *coordinated activity*.

- Later, a problem arose when the dispersed team divided design work between the two subteams. The U.S. team divided work between the two teams without peer consultation. They bluntly told the Singapore team what to do. The Singapore team indeed understood what the U.S. team wanted but rejected the unilateral orders issued by the U.S. team. They refused to work on design options they found worthless. Their response was to *covertly subvert the activity (adverse activity)*.

- At the end of the project, the U.S. team recognized they had unintentionally caused a power issue. The two sides then agreed on a particular design option; as a result, they achieved reasonably *coordinated activity*.

Project Reporting Tools for Learning and Teaching Project Knowledge

This section proposes additional tools for learning and then communicating knowledge about effective collaborative work practices for dispersed teams:

- *Field Notes:* Field notes are taken while or shortly after dispersed teams have interacted. They preserve detailed information on cultural and power issues that may affect the project outcome.

- *Transcultural Incident Reports:* Transcultural incident reports use a specific format to report on particular events that occur during a project. The report highlights effective practices for dealing with cultural and power issues that affect the coordination of project activities.

- *Project Case Studies:* A case study is an overall project account. A case study records basic project information and then pulls together the set of pertinent incident reports in order to draw lessons about effective practices.

- *Contrasting Case Studies:* These are a pair of case studies. Organizational communication is enhanced by pairing two cases that illustrate effective and ineffective work practice on the same topic.

- *Archive Materials:* Archives consist of a growing collection of observations on completed projects. Archives contain all of the tools listed above: field notes, communications practices, transcultural incident reports, and case studies of previous dispersed engineering projects. Archives preserve knowledge and transmit lessons around the organization.

These tools are a nesting structure: the first tool is a building block for the next tool, the second for the third, and so on. Taken together, they are a toolkit that spans the gap between learning and teaching processes within the organization, as represented in Figure 20.3.

Figure 20.3. Project Reporting Tools

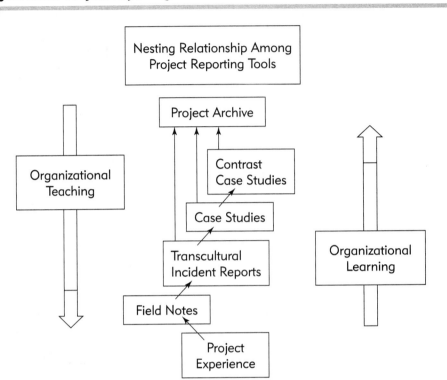

We shall now present a set of tools for imparting effective communications practices for collaborative teamwork. The order of presentation follows the scheme presented in Figure 20.3: from organizational *learning* tools to organizational *teaching* tools.

Field Notes

Field notes are the first step in developing knowledge on effective project practices. Field notes are written during or just after team members participate in a particular project encounter (such as a videoconference among dispersed team members).

The objective of field notes is to make project experience accessible for future use. They preserve detailed information on cultural and power issues that may affect the project outcome.

What you observe is fugitive knowledge until you write it down.

Field notes should be recorded quickly: what you record quickly is more accurate than what you try to record later. What you observe is *fugitive knowledge* until you write it down.

Recording what you observe makes it knowledge that is *accessible* to yourself— it is the first step in creating project knowledge that will be useful elsewhere in the organization or when working with another organization.

Debriefing soon after a meeting with another participant observer can be useful. Joint debriefing adds depth and perspective. Everyone has selective perceptions. Debriefing with another observer enlists the various perceptions and yields a more complete account. Exhibit 20.3 provides an excerpt from a field note.

Exhibit 20.3. Field Note: Wind-Driven Generator Project

Dispersed team composition: Engineers from Michigan State University (United States) and Technical University of Delft (Netherlands)

Establishing communication between the distant team and the sponsors: The U.S. side was concerned about the lack of information the U.S. had received from the Dutch. The Dutch have direct contact with the client; they learn more about what the sponsors want. Some may consider this gatekeeping, but we don't think it is. The Dutch are not purposefully withholding information. They just do not know they should be telling the information to the U.S. They assume the U.S. knows what the client is saying. This is an unfounded assumption. The U.S. has, however, notified the Dutch that they need to be updated. Perhaps the U.S. could try to contact the client directly. No one told them not to do this. The meeting ended with the two teams creating a schedule for next week and brainstorming a list of assumptions about the project and a list of criteria for a good design.

The field note was reported by a transcultural observer attached to the particular dispersed project team. *Transcultural observers* are social science students trained in observation and recording techniques. To produce this field note, the transcultural observer made notes during the videoconference. Observations were followed by a discussion between the engineers and the transcultural observers. This was one of a series of field notes recorded during the project.

The field note reported in the exhibit preserved for the transcultural observer some basic observations about social and task-oriented behavior within the internationally dispersed team. By discussing and writing them down, these observations became knowledge that was accessible to the project team members.

Transcultural Incident Report (TIR)

Transcultural incident reports are *more formal, formatted accounts* of incidents that affect project conduct and performance and deserve further attention. The report highlights effective practices for dealing with cultural and power issues that affect the coordination of project activities. Transcultural incident reports, then, are the second step in developing communicable knowledge on effective project practices.

After initial observations are recorded in field notes, project participants or transcultural observers may produce further notes on communications practices. These are short, anecdotal accounts of project events such as project launch, project definition, options generation, evaluation, design choice, or design presentation. Or they may recognize that some events require further attention because they potentially affect the performance of the engineering design team. This recognition is the signal to produce a transcultural incident report.

Format for Transcultural Incident Reports. Both project observers and project participants can and have contributed transcultural incident reports. This co-production of knowledge is facilitated if everyone shares a common format that includes the following elements:

- Practical situation—What were we doing when the incident happened?
- Cultural and power issues—What was the incident that challenged us?

- Boundary spanning action taken—What did we do about the issues?
- Outcome—What happened? How did the incident end?
- Lessons learned—What did we learn from the incident?

Examples of transcultural incident reports appeared earlier in this chapter (see Exhibits 20.1 and 20.2).

A transcultural incident report should be done when the events are likely to affect the coordination of activities within the dispersed team. For example, we have various reports on the project definition phase: What are the goals and objectives of the project? Sometimes the client gives too little information to the project team to help define the project and sometimes too much. In either case, geographically dispersed, culturally disparate teams must develop norms for making a decision and then they must make a decision about project definition.

Transcultural incident reports are the most widely used of the archival materials. They address specific problem areas that occur during dispersed projects and given discrete lessons on effective practices. They can be written by project participants who have just had several hours of briefing and are provided with the report format and with examples of incidents previously written. They can be written and read relatively quickly. They do, however, lack the overview and context of case studies.

Case Study

A case study records information on the context of a dispersed design project: who, what, where, when, and why activity occurred. A case study then focuses on how the work was done, that is, the particular issues that affected the coordination of activities among the various subteams comprising the entire dispersed team.

Transcultural incident reports are the usual building blocks for the case study: each TIR corresponds to an issue potentially affecting project activity. The outline in Exhibit 20.4 gives an idea of the breadth of topics addressed in the full case study.

Exhibit 20.4. Outline for Case Study

Cultural, Power, and Communications Issues Reported in the Case Study on a Wind-Driven Generator Project (a U.S./Dutch Engineering Design Project)

I. Project Design Issues
   Project Definition
   • Perceived lack of direction
   • Team expectations
   • Decision matrix used to define project
   Specification Alterations
   • Mid-project alteration of specifications
   • Adopting assumptions concerning related subsystems in order to achieve clarity and closure concerning the current design task

II. Media Issues: Conventions and Use of Media
   • Selection of multimedia communication devices
   • Server difficulties
   • Software compatibility
   • Media choices
   • Technical difficulties

III. Team Communication
   • Meeting profiles
   • Agenda setting
   • Administrative availability
   • Primary communicator

IV. Teaming Organization
   • Roles
   • Attitudes

Case studies of dispersed projects are the main deliverable of transcultural observers and can become a secondary deliverable of project participants. Engineering project teams produce and then deliver to their client both the commissioned engineering design report and a modest case study on lessons for dispersed teaming.

Contrast Case Studies

The presentation technique of contrast cases is borrowed from an old anthropological presentation method called controlled comparison. The ethnographer first presents ethnographic cases that can be defined as equivalent in certain salient features. The ethnographer next presents a pattern of divergence between the two cases that leads to a highly credible and instructive analysis.

Contrasting case studies can be a very powerful tool in dispersed team management. It is used most commonly when there are two projects that have similar geographic and cultural composition within the dispersed team but in which the pattern of interrelations between the local teams differs significantly. This is a good presentation method to point out the consequences of one strategy versus another. Different actions have different consequences. The cases can be short, but the points related to the diverse actions and practices must be clearly evident.

Contrast cases have several strengths:

- Whereas a single case presentation shows a single perspective on an issue (action and consequences), a contrast case presentation shows variations on a theme (contrasting actions and contrasting consequences).

- Variations on a theme are pedagogically more effective because human meaning is, at heart, a question of contrasts: we cannot understand "day" without understanding "night."

Therefore, contrast cases deliver knowledge on cultural and power issues very effectively to persons who have not been exposed to social analysis and reporting. They can be presented in short summary form to diverse audiences, as shown in Exhibit 20.5.

Exhibit 20.5. Contrast Case Study

Two Engineering Design Projects

This report contrasts two specific cases of corporate-sponsored, mechanical engineering design projects. The Microchannel project and the Evaporator Plate project were both thermodynamic projects concerned with optimizing heat transfer device design.

Similarities

This is a controlled comparison:

- The two separate projects ran concurrently.
- Two U.S. mechanical engineering teams worked together with counterpart engineering teams from the Netherlands.
- The teams learned advanced telecommunication media skills and were briefed in transcultural communication skills in order to carry out the dispersed-team design process.

Exhibit 20.5. Contrast Case Study, Cont'd

A further similarity between the two dispersed projects was a disparity in professional engineering culture between the Dutch and U.S. participants. In both U.S. local teams, the engineers wanted to launch the project by getting into the laboratory and building a first prototype device. U.S. professional culture prioritizes an experimental approach to the engineering design process. By contrast, in both Dutch local teams, the engineers wanted to launch the project by doing library research on previous solutions to the design at hand. The Dutch professional culture prioritizes an analytic approach to the engineering design process.

Differences

- Socially bonding versus socially aversive behavior

One contrast between the Microchannel and Evaporator Plate teams was a contrasting tendency to social bonding versus socially aversive behavior.

The Microchannel team made sure that every international videoconference included some time for social interaction as well as task interaction. One project member referred to the sequence of social/task–social/time as "the sandwich." This interaction was quite symmetrical between the Dutch and the U.S. engineers in this regard.

In the Evaporator Plate project, by contrast, interaction between Dutch and U.S. team members was not very social. The Dutch tried to get to know their U.S. project partners but were met with a "let's get to work" attitude that was rather aversive. The Dutch settled for a polite but more formal relationship for the remainder of the project.

- Learning and using each other's competencies.

A second contrast was the degree to which the two teams effectively learned and used each other's competencies. In both project teams, the Dutch engineers were more analytically oriented, while the U.S. engineers were more hands-on, design-object oriented. The Dutch wanted to use analytical processes to define the limits of feasible design. The U.S. engineers wanted to use experimental techniques in the laboratory, that is, building prototypes.

In the Microchannel project, the Dutch indeed reduced the total work done by defining a range of options before the U.S. team took to the laboratory.

In the Evaporator Plate team, the Dutch proposed the same procedure, but this offer was ignored by the U.S. team. They spent far more time in the laboratory than the Microchannel U.S. team did.

- Greater quality design/lesser quality design

When the projects were submitted by the Microchannel and Evaporator teams, the client judgments varied considerably.

Clients of the Microchannel team rated the quality of design to be innovative, thoroughly researched, and effective in design.

Clients of the Evaporator Plate team, on the other hand, were disappointed by the lack of creativity and understanding of the underlying thermodynamic processes involved, processes needed to design an effective device.

The differences in project launch drove the dispersed team apart, and the two local teams proceeded down two different paths. When the project came to completion, the U.S. team recognized that they could have benefited from the knowledge gained by knowing what others had done relative to the project solution. Their solution was deficient. The Dutch team acknowledged that they should have started on prototype building sooner so that they could have had a satisfactory completion to the project. Two different pathways through the project, two different outcomes, and neither half of the "team" was satisfied that they had done their best.

Project Archive

Project archives provide the basis of corporate knowledge when dispersed teams are involved in projects. Without archives, the knowledge gained is dispersed as fast as the team members are. Project archives are *critical* for sustained proficiency in effective dispersed team projects. Important points to remember are

- Project archiving must overcome barriers. Contributors must be incited to contribute and the audience must know that accessing the archive will pay off for them in real terms.

- Contributors to an archive are partially motivated by the perception that they are imparting lessons to a specific audience. They give lessons to real people who are undergoing similar project difficulties because they are facing cultural and power issues for which they have not been professionally educated.

- The audience to an archive can be motivated when accessing the archive becomes a normal phase of project management. It is often useful to begin a project with a project briefing. Archival materials serve as a strong basis for briefings and help to alert project team members about issues that tend to occur during dispersed projects.

- Archives should not be thought of as a recipe for success, but should be seen as an enabling mechanism that allows recognition of otherwise unfamiliar terrain and thus allows some degree of anticipation.

- Project archives store the organization's collective knowledge concerning projects. Knowledge development starts with data collection. It continues with presentation of the data to develop information that can be used to create knowledge. Project archives are the basis for corporate project wisdom, especially when the barriers of time, distance, culture, language and such work against effective collaborative teaming.

Some companies have already implemented elements of the program of learning and teaching project knowledge. As illustrated in the following account of Maersk, a company can beneficially use tools similar to what we are about to represent:

> To ensure quick, responsive service to customers while meeting company objectives, Maersk invests heavily in a *two-year training program* of corporate cultural as well as technical training. During

this program, future country managers are systematically exposed to *incident reports* of managers abroad who had to respond to different cultures, different bureaucracies, and different logistics systems. This program equips future managers with transcultural communication skills as well as the technical skills of shipping.

As a result of using this *archived knowledge,* Maersk employees act confidently under pressure, even when faced with tricky situations and no time to confer with the Danish headquarters or with colleagues located in distant locations. The Maersk world-wide shipping line from Denmark has an outstanding record of customer service in its multiple country offices.

Project Reporting Tools and Types of Knowledge

Our toolkit is a set of project reporting products. The tools include both *learning* tools and *teaching* tools for imparting effective communications practices for collaborative teamwork: field notes, transcultural incident reports, case studies, and contrasting case studies. These reports may all be stored in an archive.

These reporting tools are supported by the power, culture, and collaborative team activity framework, another teaching tool. This framework serves as a dispersed team "report card" to chart the progression of team activities during a project. It highlights problem areas reported in the various teaching tools and helps focus effort for correcting problems while the project is still underway. It provides a summary statement about the project for archival purposes. The objective of these tools is *communicable knowledge.*

It is not enough to have knowledge; you must also share it within the organization or, as necessary, with strategic partners with whom one is working. The act of sharing or *transmitting* of knowledge must overcome problems of resistance to reporting to archives and resistance to accessing an archive. Overcoming resistance relates to other organizational arrangements such as the evaluation and reward systems. Companies employ a variety of systems to incite contributions to knowledge archives: rewards that direct people's attention and effort toward providing others with this sort of knowledge for collaboration and direct people to access the archive as part of the project launch.

Figure 20.4 represents the relationships among the various tools, the kind of knowledge produced, and the organizational communication processes (learning and teaching) involved.

Figure 20.4. Summary of Project Reporting Tools, Types of Knowledge, and Organizational Communication Processes for Learning and Teaching

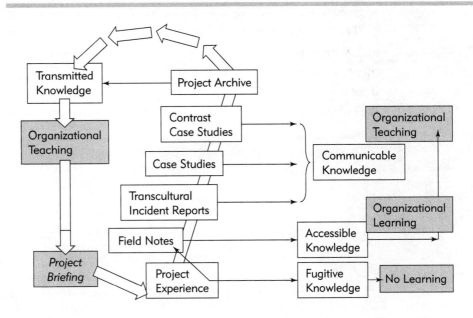

Key to Figure 20.4	
Transmitted Knowledge	Knowledge that has been made available to others in the organization. Lessons from previous projects that are shared in an archive. Processes such as evaluation incentives to the organization's members are typically necessary to incite transmitting (sending and receiving) such knowledge.
Communicable Knowledge	Knowledge about effective communication practices, incident reports, or cases that is understandable to those who did not directly experience it.
Accessible Knowledge	Knowledge that the project participant or observer can recall about project events.
Fugitive Knowledge	Knowledge that has not been recorded and tends to be forgotten or just perceived as not pertinent because it has become part of "normal" experience.

Final Remarks

A dispersed collaborative team design project has two deliverables: first, the practical deliverable that is defined as the project objective, and second, lessons for effective dispersed teaming. This chapter has provided a set of tools that are useful in learning and then teaching lessons about effective dispersed teaming. These tools complement rather than replace standard project management tools such as critical path analysis. These learning and presentation tools have been successfully taught to engineers working in dispersed teams as well as to transcultural observers who have learned these tools and assist engineers. Both engineers and observers have produced lessons for future project teams.

The success of archival endeavor (recording lessons, submitting lessons, archiving lessons, accessing lessons) depends on other organizational arrangements such as the processes for evaluating and rewarding behavior. Only then does learning and sharing project knowledge become routine, that is, part of the culture of collaborative dispersed teaming project management.

CHAPTER 21

Making Space for Communities of Practice

Creating Intellectual Capital Through Communicative Action

David O'Donnell and Gayle Porter

A PARABLE. A nomadic merchant spent long days selling his wares traveling throughout the Land of Biz. At night, he would stop for rest. While he attended to his inventory and assembled the accounting records, his tent staff of four people would create a warming fire. The merchant received great comfort and rejuvenation from this fire that burned throughout the long cold nights. He was able to rest well and awaken each morning with renewed strength and enthusiasm.

During a time when the Biz economy was struggling, as economies tend to do from time to time, a proclamation arrived from the Grand Emir, Ruler of Biz, requiring that all tent communities be reduced to only three people. This created a problem for the merchant, mainly due to a quirk of tradition that restricted members of tent communities in the Land of Biz to being able to carry only one item. By tradition, one person carried the portable stove, one the flint, one the kindling, and one the longer burning fuel (usually wood, occasionally coal) that provided warmth throughout the long cold desert nights.

For several nights, the merchant experimented with creating warmth using only three elements, in order to accommodate the new "lean" operating philosophy proclaimed by the Grand Emir. But without the flint, the kindling and wood sat cold and inert within the stove all night. Without the kindling, sparks from the flint gave a hint of fire but could not directly ignite the longer burning fuel. Without the wood or coal, the kindling showed initial promise but very soon exhausted itself—and the nights remained very, very cold. Finally, without the stove, they were able to create a warming fire using flint, kindling, and wood. The person who had heretofore taken charge of the stove was given some small recompense by the merchant and, sadly, sent back to his own village. All went well for a brief time. However, having no proper structural containment, the fire soon spread out of control, destroying the merchant's tent and his entire inventory!

Moral: Staff reductions, without a well-thought-out plan for the continued performance of essential functions, can be hazardous to survival in the Land of Biz!

Business Reality

Are we so different from the merchant and tent community in this parable? Are we not also subject to strong external forces that push our organizations to reduce costs and introduce more intensive forms of working? Organizations now have to cover essential functions with fewer people. Somehow we are expected to keep generating the warmth of continuous profit—and without burning down the tent in the process. It is generally acknowledged that good people are the prime source of sustainable competitive advantage in an increasingly knowledge-intensive and turbulent business world (Pfeffer, 1998; Sveiby, 1997). Yet organizations continue to struggle with how to retain key people and best utilize their expertise, innovativeness, and strategic agility.

In an effort to increase "collective knowing," companies have experimented with work teams and a variety of knowledge management initiatives. Some succeed; many do not. Discussions, both recently and historically (Brown & Duguid, 1991; Wenger & Snyder, 2000), have incorporated the idea of communities of practice (CoPs). CoPs are groups formed around a shared interest in which discussions build on the motivations of the members. From a traditional industrial era perspective, CoPs are often less structured than other means of creating and sharing knowledge. CoPs may span levels, functional distinctions, and even organizations. Although there is a future point at which the more developed ideas can be considered for business applications, the structure of ongoing members' exchange is interest-based rather than a path toward pre-established goal attainment. Typically, a "topic champion" organizes meetings (time, place, notification, and so on) and keeps things moving, but CoPs are not directly managed through the traditional organizational hierarchy. This "spaghetti-like" sidestepping of hierarchical control and a lack of specified outcomes from the group often makes managers from business environments based on performance metrics, deliverables, and the more familiar evidence of doing "real" work uncomfortable.

After all, wouldn't we all like to sit and chat for a while about a shared interest in some new idea? Add to that the unusual inclusion of people who do not have obvious expertise in the topics under discussion. Might we not question the depth of their true interest and their ability to contribute in any meaningful way? For all our talk about valuing fresh perspectives and diverse viewpoints, managers find it difficult to allow the conditions to exist in which broader and less structured discussions can occur.

Creation of intellectual capital doesn't always look like traditional work but may be the source of sustainable advantage.

There is also an increasing realization that the creation of intellectual capital, facilitated through various communities of practice, may be *the* competitive advantage that others cannot easily imitate; there seems to be no equivalent substitute. While the concept is relatively simple, it is far from easy to implement.

Sustainable advantage comes from achieving those things that others cannot easily replicate.

Intellectual Capital Through Communicative Action

Intellectual capital is a dynamic process of collective knowing.

Intellectual capital creation can be defined as a dynamic process of "collective knowing" that is capable of being leveraged into economic or social value (O'Donnell, O'Regan, & Coates, 2000).

As all organizations are forced by external pressures to shift their attention further up the value chain, the intellectual capital created by people is becoming as important as financial capital. To consider communities of practice as a source of unique intellectual capital requires, however, that we must step outside the self-imposed constraints of current business practice. What we have learned to accept as the traditional nature of doing business may be imposing unnecessary restrictions in a changing economic climate. Definitions of efficiency that rely on strictly measured input against highly specified outcome goals are similar to proclamations from the Grand Emir of Biz. They often obscure opportunities that may be essential to our long-term well-being.

Communicative action is the exchange among people in which they establish shared understanding about a situation and agree to some coordinated action (Habermas, 1984, 1987). This is an evolutionary process. People must have the opportunity for these exchanges, with boundaries only to ensure that they maintain a quality process. The communicative action perspective is one in which the focus is on the quality and depth of conversational interaction, rather than on the members as individuals.

Who makes a particular contribution is not as important as the fact that all have an opportunity to do so and that various contributions are allowed to build toward the concerted action of the group. All interaction has the effect of increasing shared understandings, without which focused action is simply not possible.

While goal-oriented activity is valuable, true growth requires that there also be activity that evolves without rigidly determined end goals. Traditional management advice is to always have clear-cut goals as well as a plan for meeting those goals. It is true that this process will focus energy in the directions specified. However, effort may cease when the goals are achieved. Managers sometimes try to enhance this process by setting "stretch" goals that reap higher rewards. Further increases in productivity are then encouraged by raising the goals each year. Communicative action suggests that true growth is more evolutionary than simply raising the bar to demand more and more of the same. Without giving up the guiding structure of goals with specific targeted outcomes, much can be accomplished by also allowing space and time for less structured ideas to grow into possible business applications. Communities of practice are one means to allow for communicative action and the growth that this makes possible.

Four structures must be present for the organization to generate intellectual capital.

There are four knowledge-relevant structures in the communicative world of any organization: (1) the overall culture; (2) communities of practice; (3) people; and (4) language (Habermas, 1984, 1987).

For organizations to adapt, grow, and generate intellectual capital, each structure must be present and each must exhibit levels of development, socialization, more extensive social integration, and cultural reproduction. Table 21.1

provides a matrix of these structures and processes, which may be used as a blueprint to aid practice.

In summary, these elements of structure and process emphasize communicative collaboration, particularly when achieved in ways that allow the freedom for evolutionary growth in addition to the more usual goal-oriented activity. To support the existence of more free-flowing collaboration, management must give attention to creating and sustaining these four separate structures in the organization.

Table 21.1. A Matrix for Creation of Intellectual Capital

Processes Needed to Sustain the Organization	People	Culture	Communities of Practice	Language
Cultural Reproduction	Behavior patterns and specified learning goals	Enactment of shared assumptions and values	Growth opportunities, compatible with or to shift culture	Organized expression of shared identity
Social Integration	Social memberships	Obligations of agreed-on social contracts	Legitimately ordered interpersonal relations	Channels and modes of communication
Socialization	Personal identities and the ability to interpret others'	Negotiated roles and norms for behavior	Progressive integration of individual interests and motivation	Instruction as formal training plus informal discourse
Self-Development	Openness to continued learning and growth	Balancing history and tradition with the need for adaptability in dynamic environments	Encouraging growth in understanding and idea generation	Evolving uniqueness in message content and mode of transmission

Here are some examples of how the matrix reasoning flows.

People

Self-development of the individual requires achieving openness to continuous learning, challenge, and growth. This openness contributes to an understanding of personal identity and the ability to interpret information about others (*socialization*). This identity and interpretative ability allows for social memberships to form (*social integration*), which then influence ongoing behavior patterns and learning goals (*cultural reproduction*). Consider the parallel to hiring new employees, who undergo an orientation process to help them understand who they are in the total organization and how they will be expected to interact with others. They become part of a specific work group and, additionally, may have membership on task teams or other committee assignments. Their behavior and future goals evolve from these identities and social memberships that are initially learned through open and reciprocal dialog.

Organizational Culture

At the level of organizational culture, considering the balance of the organization's history against current conditions and its resulting needs for adaptation is the large-scale equivalent to an individual's openness to self-development. It is the culture's *self-development.* Within this culture people negotiate norms of behavior (*socialization*). Individuals and groups gradually agree on boundaries for pursuing personal preferences as well as having some consideration for each other's needs. These norms eventually become part of a social contract that guides behavior without the need for continual renegotiation (*social integration*).

Culture, people, language, and communities of practice must all develop as mutually supportive structures in the organization.

At some point, the assumptions and values represented in this social contract become so embedded as to be understood at a subconscious or tacit level and shape the ongoing life of the organization (*cultural reproduction*). Any manager who has attempted to implement a culture change can testify to the difficulty of first raising these issues into conscious thought and then proposing that the old ideas might no longer be valid.

Communities of Practice

The third structure, communities of practice, is central. A CoP self-develops as people grow an understanding of their shared interests and begin to generate ideas about its meaning. The socialization process is a gradual integration of individual interests and motivations into a shared focus. As this develops in the organization, CoPs take on a certain orderliness in how people gather and interact, gaining legitimacy without becoming over-institutionalized. Providing the CoP is compatible with the existing culture of the organization (*or* is being nurtured as one that can stimulate needed cultural adaptations), it is capable of providing growth opportunities that otherwise would probably not exist. Not growth in size, necessarily, but growth in ideas—expanded and malleable approaches to products, customers, internal work processes, inter-company relations, and many other organizational factors.

Language

Language develops in ways that are unique to the business world, to the industrial sector, to the organization, and to the functional specialty of a person's work and unique life history. Eventually, language and means of communication become incorporated into a shared identity. We have featured language here as one of four indispensable knowledge structures, progressing through the four processes as shown. Additionally, language can also be viewed as a connecting thread throughout the organization. When emphasizing communicative action, the language structure will either facilitate critical processes across the other structures or, when not developing appropriately in its own right, hamper the entire network of processes within the matrix.

Putting the Elements Together

Linking back to our introductory parable, this matrix reminds us of the four elements carried by the merchant's tent staff. The organization's culture is the stove, which offers containment. On the one hand, if it does not allow enough space, over-containment will stifle the fire. On the other hand, lack of any supporting structure can allow flames to become destructive rather than a constructively focused source of warmth and efficiency (read as: revenue-generating ideas!). The people represent kindling through their ideas, without which there is no beginning to the creation of a warming fire. Language is the flint that sparks the kindling into an initial flame, transitioning a loose collection of individuals into the potential for continuous fire. Finally, communities of practice serve as the longer-term fuel—the opportunity for rejuvenation and renewal, growth, and adaptation to changing circumstances.

Elimination of or damage to any one of these structures dashes any hope of sustainable advantage. Some structures are there, but efforts may be misdirected. Every organization has a culture, but rarely does it strongly support communicative action. Individuals are bound by the traditional expectation that all working time must be goal-driven, time-driven, and perhaps rules-driven in order to be considered productive. Language of course exists, but it may be directive and restrictive, rather than connective and collaborative, by not allowing for open discussions that can include sincerity, social rightness, or areas of accomplishment beyond immediate profit motives.

Regarding the people, organizations struggle to recruit and retain the best talent, while at the same time cutting back on the total workforce. The impact on surviving members is usually a level of anxiety that interferes with open sharing of information and know-how. The preceding examples all suggest an existing structure that can be better utilized. The one piece most likely to be missing, rather than simply under-utilized, is the forum for growth than can exist through communities of practice.

Applying the theory of communicative action creates something of a paradox for organizational leaders, and paradox is typically difficult to manage until it is fully accepted and embraced as a worthwhile truism. To pursue the goal of sustainable competitive advantage, managers must be willing to relax their strong bias toward goal-oriented activity for some portion of daily operations. It is not enough to simply tolerate a few meetings.

Leaders must manage in a way that aligns the people, culture, and language structures.

Leaders must demonstrate commitment to the freedom of communicative action and manage in a way that aligns the people, culture, and language structures needed to support CoPs. In the following section, we briefly provide an example of such leadership.

Oticon: Case Study in CoP Leadership

In this section we draw on Morgan-Gould's (1994) award-winning case study of Oticon and Oticon's website to illustrate our discussion. Oticon, a Danish hearing-aid organization, was founded in 1904 by Hans Demant, whose wife had a severe hearing loss. Its humanistic philosophy originates from this time. In 1988, Oticon introduced a number of new products, and in 1991 a new and very flexible organization structure was established to strengthen this knowledge-intensive organization. During the ten-year (1988 to 1998) presidency of Lars Kolind, this company achieved a truly remarkable transformation, as shown in Table 21.2.

Table 21.2. Performance at Oticon

Oticon was listed on the Copenhagen Stock Exchange in 1995. Selected results shown below are impressive, especially when viewed in terms of *pre* and *post* the 1991 turn-around.

	1988	1989	1990	1991	1992	1993	1994	1995	1996	1997	1998
Return on Equity %	−3.9	13.0	6.7	−0.2	5.8	37.1	37.9	25.7	24.3	30.6	35.7
Revenue in mill. DKK (kronar)	433	450	456	477	539	661	750	940	1087	1413	1613
Gross profit in mill. DKK (kronar)	197	213	195	214	258	322	411	512	591	765	893
R & D in mill. DKK (kronar)	12	14	16	30	40	43	49	78	99	118	146
Employees (avg. #)	1064	1087	1049	1086	1069	1073	1192	1485	1443	1760	1925

One product developed during that time was the world's first 100 percent digital hearing instrument at ear level (what most people think of as a hearing aid). Commenting on Digifocus, Kolind notes that he initially focused on tight cost control but eventually:

Our company functioned not because of our organization, but in spite of it.

We realized that our company functioned not because of our organization, but in spite of it. This had to change, and I saw no other solution except to discontinue the concept of a formal organization. So, we threw it all away, and we introduced something new, which has been named the spaghetti organization (Morgan-Gould, 1994). . . . We abolished job titles and introduced flexible work teams (www.oticon.com).

Kolind envisioned that the various functional units would have to work together in a fully integrated manner in crafting innovative customer-driven products and services. This, he believed, could not be achieved by normal structural or procedural change. The company accomplished this by making people work together, which required breaking out of traditional thinking patterns. One breakthrough from their new creativity was the reduction of the product development cycle by 50 percent.

Instead of the industry norm of a couple of years to produce a new product, they began doing it in less than twelve months. Kolind believed that the newer approach—being flexible, having multi-jobs, using know-how intelligently, and being open and transparent—was a sustainable advantage. The difficulty of changing from a traditional hierarchical, departmental, slow-moving organization was not something competitors would be able to implement easily.

Two structural, yet deeply psychological, innovations were central to this turnaround. One was the construction of a new, open plan head office. In this configuration, there are no walls. All employees have identical desks with only a work station and a mobile phone/charger on the desk. Each employee has a portable trolley for "essentials," which allows employees to move desks and link up with various project teams in minutes. All employees can access common office applications and all their own files on the servers, independently of which work station they use. Further, tea or coffee on desks is prohibited. Coffee bars on both floors exist to stimulate interaction, ideas, face-to-face communication, and "dialog and action." This dialog and action contributes to an environment in which CoPs, the exemplar of communicative action, will thrive.

A second major innovation was initiation of a new IT system, which led to the almost total elimination of paper.

This paperless system remains today. As paper enters the Oticon head office, it is scanned into an integrated database and then 95 per cent of it is immediately shredded (legal and contractual documents still require hard copy). The shredded paper cascades down a highly visible transparent chute through the two floors. Kolind insists that:

> There is absolutely no way that works better than having transparency and fostering dialog. Maybe I make it sound like a religion with me, but I am a very strong believer in the value of transparency. This is a company designed for dialog. We have shifted from formal communication to dialog and action. In order to have this kind of flexible workplace, you had to get rid of the paper." (Morgan-Gould, 1994, p. 5)

In Oticon, *language* is the carrier of knowledge, which plays a key role in intellectual capital creation, innovation, and renewal. Learning is constantly stimulated among and across various project teams. They focus on dialog, communication, knowledge absorption, and value-adding action. Intellectual capital creation is possible through their consistent attention to these activities. All job descriptions and formal job titles were discarded. Kolind abandoned the practice of fitting the person to the job, in favor of enabling people to apply skills to different and emerging positions.

They chose to focus on people rather than continually diagnosing business processes.

Rather than continually diagnosing business processes, they chose to focus on *people*. In a knowledge intensive industry, this represents a rational business strategy—one that encourages innovation and deployment of value adding new knowledge.

Top management at Oticon clearly recognize that the pace of technological change makes it critical to both develop and maintain knowledge and competencies within its diverse *CoPs* in order to remain competitive. Its *culture*, which facilitates risk taking, optimizes utilization of the diverse skills available. The nature of management within this culture has changed considerably. Managers note that the task is different from when they used power to push things through. Now things are negotiated, but their ability to react to both new problems and new opportunities is faster than it was before.

The key question remains: Is there a relationship between Oticon's emphasis on dialog, action, self-managing teams, and CoPs and its financial and operational results? Although we cannot prove direct cause and effect, the striking metrics in Table 21.2 suggest linkages between the company's change in operating philosophy and its positive financial outcomes. During Kolind's term, investment in R&D increased by a factor of thirteen; sales revenue and gross profit increased by a factor of four; and the return on equity figures would bring a smile to the face of any investor. In an era where downsizing is often proposed as a panacea for all business ills, it is worth observing that employment has doubled in the period. In his ten-year presidency, Lars Kolind proved to be an outstanding pioneer in the area of humanistic business strategy. These financial results could be coincidence, but it seems much more likely that they are not.

Lessons for Merchants
(and Managers) in the Land of Biz

Our friend the merchant was unable to *manage* a solution to his having to function with only three out of four essentials, and he lost everything. Many organizations today are similarly chasing cost cutting without an appreciation of better options that might exist. In contrast, the Oticon case illustrates a success story, showing how all four structures may be integrated in practice to achieve competitive advantage. Through their efforts, they have realized:

- *Value that is non-substitutable,* because their people are knowledgeable AND learning oriented, and willingly became multi-skilled;

- *Rarity,* because their people exchange layers of knowledge on R&D, marketing, technology, and customers; and

- *Advantage not easily imitated,* because the employees view work as conversation and action, a belief facilitated through encouragement of communities of practice as seen in both the physical layout and in the elimination of paper exchanges.

Did the merchant too readily accept the limitations of the existing goals, job descriptions, and processes that had become tradition? Was there an alternative to cutting staff? Could the stove carrier have returned to get the fuel while the flint and kindling were being used, rotating assignments so that the two-trip job was shared with the others? Should the merchant have gotten up off his pillows to put the stove in place for his people and then stepped aside to let them get on with doing their jobs? It would not be prudent for us to declare a single right answer to this dilemma, judging as we are from a great distance of time, space, and culture.

However, we can be so bold as to add one observation. There is no evidence that the merchant made any attempt to employ his greatest potential asset—the ideas of the people closest to the task. What innovations might have been possible? His management task would have had to shift to a focus on creating the setting for free discussion from a variety of perspectives. He might have had to shiver and shake through some initial loss of productivity while his people learned to use this unusual freedom in a focused way. And he might have needed a new level of open-mindedness in order to entertain suggestions from outside his own area of expertise and authority. Yet, could anything have been worse than his assumption that the only path was to muddle through as best he could with only three out of four of the essential elements? Think about it before you burn down your own tent!

Our framework of culture, communities of practice, people, and language provides an outline of four essential structures necessary for the creation of intellectual capital, *the* source of sustainable competitive advantage. The description in each cell of the matrix offers checkpoints, which will facilitate open-minded observation or inquiry about people's perceptions of critical processes across all four structures. Monitoring the status of these structures and processes will supply an ongoing picture of the situation. From any specific current position, the next higher process description supplies a signpost for desired movement. Should differences arise across organizational levels, departments, or work groups, this information will also suggest possible actions needed to bring everyone into the same experience.

This matrix can be used to create an awareness of what happens in the organization or as a blueprint for action steps in generating more communicative action. The most unfamiliar, and most contrary to traditional management, is the idea of communities of practice. Yet, making space for this knowledge structure is the one option that offers opportunities for growth.

CHAPTER 22

How to Effectively Communicate Virtually

Lessons from Case Studies of Virtual Teams

Jill E. Nemiro

THE NATURE OF WORK in contemporary organizations has changed and will continue to change. Contemporary work has been classified on a continuum from routine to non-routine activities (Mohrman, Cohen, & Mohrman, 1995). Routine work is conceptualized as work that is programmed, involves repeated patterns, is static, and can be easily understood. Non-routine work, on the other hand, is emergent in nature, varied and unique, interdependent, dynamic, complex, and uncertain. Today, routine work is becoming automated, and much of the work that remains is *knowledge-based and non-routine*.

The complexity of non-routine work has led to an increase in work being performed by teams of knowledge workers, rather than by individuals. Teams offer a way for organizations to bring together key individuals to work jointly on problems and develop innovative solutions. Further, advances in information technology have enabled these key individuals to work together on teams regardless of where they live. Team members need not be in neighboring offices, but rather can be located anywhere throughout the globe. Thus, a new type of team has emerged, called a *virtual team*. (For more information on virtual teams, see Chapters 10 and 30.) These teams are "characterized by members that are geographically separated from one another, who communicate mostly through electronic means, and whose boundaries may be stretched by the inclusion of core and peripheral members, members from multiple departments, and smaller teams subsumed by larger teams" (Nemiro, 1998, p. 111).

In collaborative, non-routine work accomplished in teams, whether virtual or not, *communication is key*. If there is faulty or no communication, collaboration is hampered. Duarte and Snyder (1999) share: "When every team member has a piece of the puzzle, robust communication pulls the pieces together and plays a key part in solving problems. Communication is paramount in an adaptive world and is essential to collaboration" (p. 209).

Communication is the vehicle for creating synergy, for keeping a team together and moving it forward. However, one of the key challenges facing virtual teams is how to effectively communicate with one another across the miles. Communication problems may be magnified by different time zones, differences in technology proficiency among team members, and cultural differences between team members. Virtual teams potentially face a much greater strain on communication as team members attempt to interact, share meaning, and reach consensus in the absence of rich face-to-face interaction (Kayworth & Leidner, 2000).

Why is it difficult to communicate and exchange information virtually? One answer might be the rate or speed at which communication flows. The rapid speed with which one can send off messages electronically may cause individuals to not take adequate time to clearly encode and process thoughts and messages. In addition, a second answer might stem from the ease with which one can communicate electronically, which can ultimately lead to a potential overload of information for those on the receiving end. As virtual team members attempt to deal with information overload, they may block out potentially important communication exchanges. A third answer might emerge from the fact that much communication between virtual team members is asynchronous (not at the same time). Feedback and confirmation, then, may be delayed, leading to potentially disruptive misunderstanding and miscommunication and to time not well spent (Cramton & Orvis, 2001).

A key answer to why communication poses a challenge for virtual teams lies in the difficulty of transmitting messages through methods limited in information richness.

Finally, a key answer to why communication poses such a challenge for virtual teams lies in the difficulty of transmitting complete messages through the electronic communication methods often used by virtual teams, methods which are limited in *information richness*. The concept of information richness was developed to explain information processing behavior in organizations (Daft & Lengel, 1984). Richness was defined as "the potential information-carrying capacity of data" (p. 196). Daft and Lengel suggested that communication channels differed in their ability to handle multiple cues simultaneously, facilitate rapid feedback, and be personal. Face-to-face communication was seen as the richest channel because it has the potential to transmit the maximum amount of information. Multiple cues (words, posture, facial expression, gestures, and intonations) and immediate feedback (both verbal and nonverbal) can be shared. In addition, face-to-face encounters create the personal touch of being there. But for virtual teams, where face-to-face interaction is not frequent, and in some cases, non-existent, the inherent limited richness in communication exchanges can lead to misunderstandings and miscommunications among team members.

Thus, there is a *real need for virtual team members to learn how to be active and effective communicators.* Indeed, their very survival depends on the ability to exchange critical information despite the challenges of time and place. In fact, virtual teams may need to over-communicate and to have more structured communication patterns and norms in place than their co-located counterparts.

The purpose of this chapter is to describe how nine successful virtual teams communicated. What methods of communication did these teams use to exchange information, and for what purposes did they use these methods? What norms were in place to guide their communication behavior? In addition, four major areas that emerged from the descriptions of the nine teams' communication behavior will be discussed: (1) the degree of structure, or lack of structure, used in each team's communication behavior; (2) the appropriate matching of communication methods to specific purposes of messages; (3) how the nature of the team's work may have influenced the choice of communication methods used; and (4) the evolution of communication methods used in these teams. Finally, the lessons learned from each of the nine teams' communication behavior will be shared.

Description of the Teams

Selected members from nine virtual teams (a total of thirty-six individuals) were interviewed individually over the telephone. In the interviews, team members were asked to discuss a variety of topics related to their virtual team's functioning and communication behavior. Team members also completed a survey, providing information on various aspects of the virtual team—size, duration, mission, specific tasks, frequency with which team members used various methods of communication, and specific types of information technology used by the team.

The nine teams varied with respect to the nature of their work. (*The names of the teams, individual team members, and other company specific information have been disguised to ensure confidentiality.*) Three teams were organizational consulting firms: Alpha Consultants Incorporated (ACI), specializing in assisting clients with organizational change; Vital Training Group (VTG), specializing in personal productivity and time management training and helping clients streamline their workflow; and Jacobs/Taylor, who assisted clients in technological diffusion.

Two teams were in the field of education. The Job Search Consortium (JSC) team was composed of a group of career development professionals from universities with small, but high quality, MBA programs that had come together to put on an annual recruiting event for their students. The Electronic Learning Consortium (ELC) team was composed of four developers responsible for developing and maintaining a text-based, educational virtual community for primary, secondary, and university students.

Three teams were online service providers. Two of these teams resided in the same organization, Worldwide Software Development, a large software development company. The WN-Current Events team was responsible for producing an online publication that featured a calendar of events and directory of content of what was happening on the online service network. The WN-Religion Forum team managed an online chat on religion. The third online service provider team resided in OfficeTech, a large, multinational organization that manufactures business machines and computers. The major work of the OfficeTech team was to develop and sustain a company virtual community to foster knowledge sharing among globally dispersed workers in the corporation.

The final team was made up of product design engineers, all of whom worked for AutoMax, a large auto manufacturing company. The engineers were responsible for designing the electronic side of the car—designing circuit boards for radios, clusters, odometers, anti-lock brakes, and electric windows.

Members of the nine teams were mostly located within the United States, but were widely dispersed across the country. The size of the teams varied from three to twelve individuals. Team tenure (defined as the time from when the team was initially formed to the time of the interviews) also varied, ranging from one team who had been in existence for only six months to one team who had been in existence for fifteen years.

Methods and Norms of Communication for the Nine Teams

"Communicating is key. That's what we're all about."

—ELC team member

"Communication is the most important thing when you have a virtual team, making sure that everybody knows what everybody else is doing, and what you're supposed to be doing."

—WN-Current Events team member

As the above quotes of individual team members emphasize, communication was considered to be *key to the success of their virtual teams.* So how did these virtual team members communicate with one another? Data from both the surveys and interviews was used to describe what communication methods the teams used, how frequently they used these methods, and what norms, if any, guided their communication behavior.

In the survey, team members were asked to rate how frequently their team used each of twelve different communication methods: face-to-face, telephone, fax, mail, voice mail, email, computer conferencing, shared databases, remote screen sharing, videoconferencing, teleconferencing, and bulletin board services/listservs. There were several overall trends in the methods used by these nine virtual teams to communicate:

- For seven out of the nine teams, email was the most frequent method of communication;

- Overall, the most frequently used communication methods were email, phone, shared databases, and voice mail;

- Overall, the least frequently used communication methods were face-to-face exchanges, mail, and videoconferencing; and

- The extent of face-to-face (FTF) communication within the teams varied, with two teams meeting FTF a few times weekly, one team meeting FTF a few times a month, four teams meeting FTF a few times a year, and two teams who had never met one another FTF.

In the interviews, team members were asked to discuss in more detail the communication behavior of their virtual teams. The results from the survey ratings and the interviews have been summarized in Table 22.1. Both the frequency of methods used by each of the nine teams and the communication norms developed and agreed on by team members to guide their communication behavior are described. Representative quotes from team members are also included for illustration.

Table 22.1. Communication Methods and Norms

Teams	Frequency of Communication Methods Used	Communication Norms Agreed On by Members
The Organizational Consultant Teams		
Alpha Consultants Incorporated (ACI)— a team of six who assist clients with organizational change.	Email and phone used several times weekly. Voice mail and fax used nearly several times per week. Mail, shared databases, teleconferencing used monthly. FTF interaction limited to a few times per year. Additional FTF contact occurred as needed on client sites and for product development. None of the twelve communication methods received a rating over "a few times a week," indicating that team members were not in daily contact with	Members agreed to respond to email at least three or four times per week. Consultants on the road traveled with computers to be able to respond. Members agreed to return phone calls within twenty-four hours, even when traveling and working out of client sites: "This is an expected norm, if one of my partners calls me, for whatever reason, I am expected to, as soon as possible, get back to them. And if I have a problem and call, generally within 24 hours, more often within a few hours, I'm going to get a return call."

Table 22.1. Communication Methods and Norms, Cont'd

Teams	Frequency of Communication Methods Used	Communication Norms Agreed On by Members
The Organizational Consultant Teams		
	one another (except for the team leader and support staff).	Email exchanges were used to convey: (1) client developments; (2) requests for advice; and (3) schedule and calendar changes.
		Phone calls were used for checking in with one another.
		A scheduled conference call was held every four to six weeks for discussing client marketing, assessment of ongoing clients, and personal check-in.
		Unscheduled conference calls were used for emergencies.
		Formally scheduled FTF meetings occurred four times a year and lasted two or three days (called the "quarterly gathering of the clan"). These meetings were held in members' homes to solidify connection between team members.
		Corporate office team members served as the "central hub" and all consultants were required to update the hub as to their whereabouts.
Jacobs/Taylor (J/T)— a team of eight who assist clients with technological diffusion and implementation.	Telephone was used once and sometimes more than once a day.	Senior members of the team agreed to have daily phone contact: "We talk to each other, all four of the senior members, every day including weekends. I know every night at 5:30 p.m. Pacific time, my partner is going to call me from wherever he is, or I will call him."
	Email and voice mail were used daily.	
	Fax was used a few times weekly.	
	Shared databases and mail were used a few times per month.	Sensitive personnel issues were dealt with FTF; other personnel issues were dealt with over the phone.
	Formally scheduled FTF "company celebrations as a family" occurred twice a year.	
	Other FTF interaction occurred as needed, on the average of once a month.	Email was used for routine correspondence and status checking.
	Teleconferencing, bulletin board services, videoconferencing, remote screen sharing, and computer conferencing were rarely used.	

Table 22.1. Communication Methods and Norms, Cont'd

Teams	Frequency of Communication Methods Used	Communication Norms Agreed On by Members
The Organizational Consultant Teams		
Vital Training Group (VTG)—a team of six who specialize in personal productivity, time management training, and helping clients streamline workflow.	Shared database (Lotus Notes) were used frequently, several times a day. Email was used heavily, ranging from five to forty email exchanges daily. Telephone was used on average several times a week. Voice mail, bulletin board services, teleconferencing, and fax were used monthly. Methods used rarely or not at all were mail, FTF, remote screen sharing, computer conferencing, and videoconferencing.	Team members were required to replicate (post relevant information into the shared database) daily. The majority of team meetings were asynchronous, accomplished through Lotus Notes: "We don't need to get together to have a meeting. Lotus Notes holds the meeting and we participate as we feel like it, as we log in and log out. It's pretty amazing. "
The Education Teams		
Electronic Learning Consortium (ELC)— a team of four responsible for developing and maintaining an educational virtual community.	Only team (out of the nine) to use computer conferencing frequently, several times a day. Bulletin boards, shared databases also used daily. Remote screen sharing used once a month. All other methods rarely or never used, including phone and FTF.	There were no formal rules to guide communication exchanges: "Well, there are no rules, actual written rules as to how we communicate. I would call it an unwritten set of rules . . . anything that is unusual, you communicate." All members were expected to be online daily. No formal FTF meetings were scheduled. In fact, only two of the four team members had met FTF. Telephone was used for emergencies only (for example, computer system went down; personal crisis experienced by team member).
Job Search Consortium (JSC)—a team of twelve MBA career development professionals that put on an annual job recruiting event for students.	Email was used most frequently, at least a few times weekly. Telephone, fax, and voice mail were used a few times per month. FTF meetings occurred twice yearly, to assess the previous year's efforts and set future goals. Additional FTF interaction sometimes occurred between subgroups of the team. One teleconference was held during the year. Mail and shared databases were used, but rarely. Remote screen sharing, computer conferencing, bulletin board services, and videoconferencing were rarely or never used.	In electronic communication, distribution lists were used so that all communication went out to all team members. There were no established guidelines for how often members were to check and respond to email. Rather, it happened naturally, as team members were constantly connected to email in their work.

Table 22.1. Communication Methods and Norms, Cont'd

Teams	Frequency of Communication Methods Used	Communication Norms Agreed On by Members
The On-Line Service Provider Teams		
OfficeTech—a team of three that develops and sustains a company virtual community.	Email contact several times a day. Daily telephone calls. Monthly planned teleconference calls. FTF contact occurred three times during the year.	Communication occurred on an as-needed basis. There were no formal rules or norms in place to guide communication exchanges. This may have been because of the team's small size (three members).
WorldWide Network—Current Events (WN-CE)—a team of five who produce an online publication.	Email was the most frequent method used. Informal phone contact, voice mail, and scheduled teleconferences were used at least a few times per week. Shared databases were used weekly. FTF meetings occurred several times per week for team members who were in close proximity. In these meetings, geographically dispersed members attended through tele-conferencing. Bulletin board services were used monthly. Computer conferencing, remote screen sharing, mail, fax, and videoconferencing were rarely or never used.	Even though email contact occurred daily, there were no formal rules or norms in place to guide email exchanges; rather they occurred as needed. Email was used when it was crucial to document something in writing. Shared databases or networked tools were used in building the online publication. Telephone contact was used to touch base and check on things. Formal FTF meetings were used to review information, make decisions, and assign work.
Worldwide Network—Religion Forum (WN-R)—a team of four that manages an online forum on religion.	Most communication was through email: "Email is probably about 98 percent of how we communicate." Telephone was rarely used. Although team members were required to monitor bulletin board services and host chats in their work, they did not use these methods to any extent to communicate among themselves. Computer conferencing and remote screen sharing were used rarely (only two members used remote screen sharing). Mail, fax, teleconferencing, and video-conferencing were never used. Members of this team had never met FTF.	Communication among members was described as a random exchange, occurring as needed. There were no regularly scheduled formal meetings (FTF or electronic) among members. Telephone was used for emergencies only. At the time of the investigation, members did acknowledge the need for more structure in their communication behavior: "What we need is not this random exchange, a sort of moment-by-moment exchange of notes. We will write each other literally fifty times a day. We need a system."

Table 22.1. Communication Methods and Norms, Cont'd

Teams	Frequency of Communication Methods Used	Communication Norms Agreed On by Members
The Product Design Engineering Team		
AutoMax—a team of five engineers who design electronics in cars.	Used a variety of methods to communicate with one another. Most frequently used methods (a few times per week) were email, phone, FTF (only for the subset of members who were in close proximity), and voice mail. Shared databases, remote screen sharing, teleconferencing, computer conferencing, and bulletin board services were used a few times per month. Videoconferencing was used, but sparingly. Fax and mail were rarely used.	Weekly meetings were held through tele-conferencing and remote screen sharing to review product design: "Instead of shipping a paper down to the plant, and then having them [other team members] mark it up and send it back, we can actually look at the circuit board on the computer, and they can say, 'We would like to know what would happen if we moved this part over here.' And they can move the part right in front of my eyes, or I can move it for them."

Reflections on Virtual Team Communication Behavior

As I reflected back on the descriptions of each team's communication behavior, four areas of discussion emerged: (1) the degree of structure, or lack of structure, used in each team's communication behavior; (2) the appropriate matching of communication methods to specific purposes of messages; (3) how the nature of the team's work may have influenced the choice of communication methods used; and (4) the evolution of communication methods used in these teams.

Structured Versus Unstructured Communication

Common sense may suggest that when individuals are geographically dispersed, it takes a lot of structure to create communication exchanges between these individuals. Unstructured, spontaneous "water cooler" type discussions are not easily accomplished in virtual teams (O'Hara-Devereaux & Johansen, 1994). The teams in this investigation had varying degrees of structure to their communication behavior. Some teams had a high level of structure, while for others communication was merely a random exchange of information. Some teams established rules to create structure in their communication behavior. For example, VTG required members to replicate daily; Jacobs/Taylor required senior members to call in daily; and ACI required consultants to return calls within twenty-four hours. Structured exchanges also occurred through formally scheduled face-to-face meetings and conference calls. For example, ACI, Jacobs/Taylor, the Job Search Consortium, and VTG teams had face-to-face meetings scheduled a few times a year. The WN-Current Events team had bi-weekly face-to-face morning meetings. The AutoMax team had weekly review meetings through conference calling and remote screen sharing. The ACI team had monthly conference calls, and the Job Search Consortium team had a yearly conference call.

Day to day, most communication was unstructured.

On a day-to-day basis, however, the majority of communication between team members was unstructured, occurring as needed. Further, two of the teams (OfficeTech and WN-Religion Forum) lacked much of any structure in their communication behavior. Even in looking at the team with the most amount of structure in their communication behavior, ACI (with nine conference calls and three face-to-face meetings), the majority of that team's contact came through unstructured exchanges in email and over the phone.

One may wonder how teams who work across physical distance and different time zones can survive when the majority of their communication behavior is unstructured. The answer may lie in the type of individual who seems most appropriate to work in these teams. The interviews of the nine teams in this investigation revealed that team members believed that, to work effectively in virtual teams, individuals must be self-disciplined, self-motivated, and self-directed.

However, even if virtual teams are composed of self-directed individuals, I suggest that communication behavior still needs to contain a balance of structured and unstructured communication. In the teams studied, for the most part, structured exchanges were used for reviewing and assessing work and the business and for keeping personal bonds alive; unstructured exchanges were used for exchanging information, asking for advice, and keeping one another informed. It is interesting to note that in the two teams (OfficeTech and WN-Religion Forum) that lacked structure in their communication behavior, the team leaders and members felt the need and were planning on implementing structure into their communication exchanges. The OfficeTech team was planning on implementing a morning meeting conference call, and the WN-Religion Forum team was anticipating beginning chat room staff meetings.

Communication Method Appropriateness

Different communication methods were used for different purposes. In this section, some of the more salient connections between selected communication methods and purposes of messages are discussed. (In reviewing the teams' salient method-message connections, it is assumed that each team chose what it felt was an appropriate method for a particular communication exchange.)

Email was used for a variety of purposes.

Email. Six teams (ELC, Jacobs/Taylor, OfficeTech, VTG, WN-Current Events, and WN-Religion Forum) reported using email on a daily basis. The other three teams (ACI, AutoMax, and the Job Search Consortium) reported using email a few times a week. Clearly, email was used for a large portion of each team's communication behavior. Email was used for a variety of purposes:

- To exchange information;
- To update members on schedule and calendar changes, client status, and other developments;
- To make and answer requests;
- To give and get advice;
- To develop policy and set rules;
- To keep in touch and have personal conversations;
- To quickly send a message to the entire team; and
- To document what was being said.

Telephone/Teleconferencing. Some teams used the telephone infrequently (ELC and WN-Religion Forum). In those teams, phone calls were used to interact only when there was an emergency, such as a computer system failure or a personal crisis. Other teams (ACI, Jacobs/Taylor, OfficeTech, and WN-Current Events) used the telephone more frequently. In these teams, phone calls were used to touch base and catch up, to establish personal contact, or to ask questions. One team also used phone calls for business management (the leader of the ACI team called the support office daily). At least four teams (ACI, AutoMax, the Job Search Consortium, and WN-Current Events) used teleconferencing to review and assess current and previous work. One team (the Job Search Consortium team) used teleconferencing as a motivational technique.

Shared databases. Shared databases were used in several teams to organize, manage, and archive information. The most frequent user of shared databases was the VTG team, who used Lotus Notes® for pretty much everything.

The majority of teams had face-to-face contact, even if only a few times a year.

Face-to-Face. The majority of teams had face-to-face contact, even if only a few times a year. Face-to-face meetings were used:

- To discuss the overall direction of the business;
- To assess and review previous and current projects;
- To prepare members for work assignments by establishing agendas, assigning roles and tasks, and setting goals;
- To make creative decisions on current work assignments;
- To deal with sensitive personnel issues; and
- To establish and solidify human bonds.

The Nature of the Task and Its Influence on Communication Methods Used

The nature of a team's work may influence the types of communication methods used and how frequently or infrequently those methods are used. Consultants, who travel frequently to work with clients on-site, need to have portable methods of communication. A team member from Jacobs/Taylor explains:

> "Part of the challenge is that you have to be ready to be 100 percent self-sufficient if anything goes wrong. You can't assume that all you need to do is walk down the hall the other way to find a Xerox machine, or that somebody will be there in the morning to sign for the FedEx. You have to do much more contingency planning and be ready to take on whatever needs to be done if a communication link fails or a logistical problem arises. We've gone so far. We've got briefcases that are packed for that. Also I wear a fishing vest because it's got all the pockets. I can have everything stuffed in it, my cell phone in one pocket and so on. I don't have to think about it. I just put it on and I go. You get on the plane and you're ready to go."

The most frequently used methods in the three organizational consulting teams were easily accessible or portable—email and shared databases (via a laptop computer), telephone, and voice mail. More sophisticated, and less portable methods, such as videoconferencing, were not frequently used by consultants.

The nature of the team's work also influenced the methods used by the education teams. The major tasks for the Job Search Consortium team were to organize and handle the logistics of an annual career recruiting event. To accomplish these tasks, email, phone, and fax were most frequently used. However, the ELC team was responsible for designing and maintaining a text-based educational, virtual community. To that end, members needed to use more sophisticated electronic methods, such as computer conferencing, bulletin board services, shared databases, and email.

Online service providers most frequently communicated through email. Two of the three teams also used the telephone, shared databases, and teleconferencing regularly. I must admit I was surprised that these teams, who were in the business of providing online service, did not more frequently use some of the more sophisticated methods of communication—computer conferencing, videoconferencing, and remote screen sharing. Lipnack and Stamps (1997) also found the same phenomenon in one of the teams they studied (from Sun Microsystems). The co-leader of that team said that because of the small size of the team (fifteen), a highly structured project management system (in this case, videoconferencing) would have slowed things down. Each of the online service provider teams in this investigation was even smaller (OfficeTech had three team members; WN-Current Events had five team members; and WN-Religion Forum had four team members).

The nature of the work of design engineers is non-routine knowledge work, specifically product design. To accomplish this work, engineers used mostly email, telephone, and voice mail. The mission of this team was to develop products with input from all stakeholders in order to achieve first-pass success. The more sophisticated methods of communication—remote screen sharing and videoconferencing—were essential in allowing team members to accomplish this mission by bringing globally dispersed stakeholders into the design cycle sooner.

The Evolution of Communication Methods Used

The nature of communication behavior is apt to change as virtual teams use more sophisticated methods of communication.

The nature of communication behavior, and team effectiveness in general, is apt to change as more sophisticated methods of communication become more prevalent in virtual teams. It is interesting to note the infrequent use in these teams of methods that once were considered standard—mail, fax, and face-to-face. The most frequently used methods were email, phone, shared databases, and voice mail. Although the communication methods used in these teams have evolved from more standard methods, the teams have still not incorporated frequent use of more sophisticated methods such as computer conferencing (used frequently only by the ELC team), remote screen sharing (used somewhat frequently only by the AutoMax and ELC teams), and videoconferencing (used rarely and only by the AutoMax and ELC teams).

In some of the more longlasting teams, members have begun to notice the effects of the evolution of communication methods used in their team. For example, the Job Search Consortium team, whose members initially communicated primarily through phone, fax, and face-to-face meetings, has evolved to where the majority of communication now occurs through email. With this change, notes one JSC team member, "We've discovered that what we used to need to meet for, we can communicate a little better on now." Another team member from the JSC team shared that she felt this change to more frequent use of email allowed the team to make decisions more collaboratively.

As teams evolve into more frequent use of communication methods that allow for real-time, synchronous communication and the inclusion of both visual and audio components (for example, computer-, video-, and teleconferencing), perhaps much of the misunderstanding and miscommunication that result when communicating through more limited channels of communication may be lessened.

Lessons Learned

This section outlines some of the key learnings from the nine cases on how to effectively communicate when working with team members who are separated from one another by distance, time, or both. These lessons provide valuable recommendations for those embarking on designing communication plans for their virtual teams.

- *Early on, establish agreed-on norms for regular communication.* These norms can and should be tailored to the individual needs of a particular team. The important point is that whatever the established norms are, team members need to commit to them and follow through. So if the team has a norm that all members will call one another back within 24 hours, all team members need to follow through with the appropriate action.

- *Establish guidelines for appropriate matching of the message and the medium used to communicate that message.* It is crucial that all team members discuss and agree on what purposes and in what situations specific communication methods are appropriate and not appropriate.

- While two of the nine teams had never met face-to-face (FTF), the majority of team members had and agreed that *formally scheduling FTF meetings of team members at least two to three times yearly is necessary* for review of the business and work and for revitalizing human bonds.

- *Recognize that members of the team are individuals and each may have different needs for "warm human contact."* Agreed-on norms are important, but it is also important to understand the communication needs of the individuals within the team as well. For example, although the members of the VTG team had little FTF and phone contact, the team leader recognized the individual need of one of the team members for FTF contact and scheduled this contact as needed.

- *Do appropriate preparation work and circulate to all members before information exchange meetings.* This was evident in the ACI team, where the staff members sent out to all consultant team members relevant reports for review prior to scheduled conference calls and FTF meetings.

- *Have a plan for how you will handle communication within subgroups of the team.* For example, the JSC team simply agreed that all communication (even if intended for a subgroup of the team) was to be forwarded to the entire team. The ACI team, on the other hand, allowed for the opportunity for subgroups of consultants to meet FTF when together at a client site.

- While much communication between virtual team members may appear random and occur as needed, *there needs to be a balance of structured and unstructured communication.* And as the size of the virtual team increases, so may the need for more structure in the communication behavior between members.

- *The use of multiple methods of communication is crucial.* The AutoMax team effectively used a variety of methods to accomplish a complex task (product design) virtually.

- Build into the repertoire of methods used to communicate, if possible, *more frequent use of methods that allow for real-time, synchronous communication* to lessen misunderstanding and miscommunication that often occur in virtual teams.

- *Create a personalized communication plan for the team.* Communication is a key challenge for virtual teams. However, virtual teams can rise above this challenge by developing individualized communication plans for their specific teams. A team's communication plan should include a description of the expected frequency of use of particular methods, the appropriate situations in which certain communication methods are to be used, and the developed and agreed on norms for guiding communication behavior. Devising a communication plan is critical to ensure regular and consistent communication and information sharing in the virtual workplace. (For information on defining and analyzing communication patterns, see Chapters 18 and 20.)

- *Last, realize that communication is key.* Without information exchange and communication, there is no team. A team member from the ACI team shares: "There are a lot of balls in the air with a virtual team. In order for a virtual team to work effectively, you can't just be out there spinning in your own universe. You've got to communicate and let people know what is in your universe, or it really is not a team."

PART 5

Laurie Broedling

THE BASIC BUILDING BLOCK OF TEAMS is people. Therefore, there is no substitute for the basics to support people: their selection, motivation, recognition, competencies, and leadership.

One of the most fundamental human resource processes is that of employee selection. Not everyone is qualified or predisposed to work well in a team setting. While there are a variety of employee selection tools available, Chapter 23 in this section describes a particularly powerful one and describes a case in which it was used by a team.

407

We all know that recognition of accomplishment is a major motivator of human behavior. Therefore, recognition of successful team-based accomplishments is another critical process. While recognition programs can be developed in-house, Chapter 24 describes an existing external recognition program that can be used by any organization, either by simply using the criteria or by competing in the award program.

While it is laudable to empower teams to take responsibility and improve work processes, this move will be self-defeating if the members are not equipped with analytic tools to do so. Therefore, they also need knowledge in systematic approaches to problem solving and process improvement. Both Chapters 24 and 25 include frameworks for teams and their members to use in this regard.

As organizations move toward becoming team-based, one of the main changes is the expectation that people will explicitly demonstrate collaborative behaviors toward one another. The reason teams can be more productive than single individuals or traditional groups lies in the extent to which they know how to truly collaborate. The adage, "two heads are better than one" is only true if the two heads can work together successfully. Chapter 26 describes specific ways in which people can be trained to collaborate, as well as ways to measure the extent of collaboration.

The move toward team-based organizations has profound implications for how people are treated and what is expected of them. These expectations need to be communicated by leaders, who must function differently in team-based organizations than they would in traditional organizations. Chapter 27 details how team members need to be coached and supported, rather than managed and controlled. Moreover, team-based organizations often involve not only teams but also self-directed teams. These particular types of teams require even more changes to the traditional leadership and management styles.

In addition to changes in style, leaders in TBOs must make other changes, so management training and development becomes especially important. Chapter 28 describes a specific technological tool that can be used to help deliver training and development to managers on an ongoing basis.

The point of covering a variety of human resource processes in this section is that they all need to be addressed with a systems mentality in order for an organization to successfully transition to a team-based organization. If people are encouraged to act consistently with a team philosophy, they must be encouraged on all dimensions, not just some. They will quickly see the inconsistency of being told to improve a work process as a team but be disparately rewarded for doing so as individuals, or being compensated as a team but not being allowed to select new team members. Examples of these inconsistencies abound in today's organizations. Hopefully, the sum total of tools, not only in this section but throughout the book, give practitioners a full spectrum toolbox to make sure that such inconsistencies are eliminated.

CHAPTER 23

Team Member Selection

"Tell Us About a Time When . . ."

Carole Townsley and Susan Larkin

HIRING NEW EMPLOYEES is an important function in any organization. Traditionally, employee selection has been the responsibility of line managers and HR departments. But in team-based organizations, where the success of new employees depends on how well they can work with their team, we believe that a new team-based method of selection outperforms traditional hiring techniques.

This chapter presents a team-based behavioral interviewing method of employee selection that is based on the principle that a candidate's past performance is the best predictor of future performance. Considering the high cost of employee turnover (Whitely, 2000), organizations recognize the need to become more strategic regarding their personnel selection process. And as work teams mature and begin to make more of their own decisions, it seems only natural that the responsibility for hiring a new team member would shift from the manager to the teams themselves. (See Chapter 14 for a description of why collaboration requires power sharing.)

Traditional Hiring Methods

Traditional hiring methods, or "resume-based" interviews, are popular for several reasons: most interviewers are familiar with and comfortable using this method, it requires little preparation because questions can be made up as you go, and it lets interviewers rely on "gut feelings" (Bell, 2001). There are drawbacks to the traditional approach, however. Interviewers who rely on gut instincts or intuition may be responding to a personal bias rather than a real indication of skill or ability on the candidate's part (Bell, 2001). Additionally, traditional interview questions typically don't provide a direct link to actual job performance.

If challenged in court, an employer must be able to demonstrate a job-related necessity for asking every interview question; some traditional interviews may not be legally defensible (Cascio, 1998). Finally, because of the unstructured nature of the questions, interviewers using traditional interview questions may find themselves focusing on one major aspect of the job and overlooking other important job elements (Larkin, Theismann, & Stephenson, 2000).

Benefits of Behavior-Based Interviewing

Behavior-based interviews are designed to overcome some of the drawbacks of traditional interviews. Behavior-based interviews are *structured,* meaning that the interviewers know ahead of time what questions they will ask and what to do with the information once they get it. This helps provide a more consistent sample of behavior across applicants and improves the accuracy of the ratings (Cascio, 1998). Structured interviews have a higher success rate than others (Leibler & Parkman, 1999) and a structured hiring method that focuses on what an employee has done is a better indicator of future job performance and offers numerous benefits to the organization.

New hires can more quickly align with organizational strategies and goals, their orientation time decreases, and their level of satisfaction increases as they experience better job fit (Larkin, Theismann, & Stephenson, 2000). Selection methods that assess the competencies that predict job performance have much higher validity than unstructured interviews that permit the interviewer to ask anything he or she chooses (Cascio, 1998; Klinvex, O'Connell, & Klinvex, 1999).

A structured hiring method that focuses on what an employee has done is a better indicator of future job performance.

But there are disadvantages to this method that are worth mentioning. For one thing, behavior-based interviewing penalizes for lack of experience and may give a slight advantage to the more experienced candidate. Secondly, using this method requires more preparation time and more time to conduct the interviews (Bell, 2001).

Team-Based Behavior Interviewing Method

The following team-based behavior interviewing method combines the best of both traditional and behavior-based interviewing and does it in a team setting. As in traditional hiring methods, you can still probe for information, check references, and administer pre-screening assessments, but you gain the added benefits of using the more valid, quantifiable, and legally defensible approach that comes with behavior-based interviewing (Bell, 2001).

The following are the steps and key actions involved in the team hiring process:

1. Confirm authority to hire.

2. Form a hiring subteam.

3. Learn behavioral interview methods.

4. Define job dimensions.

   - Identify job tasks
   - Validate task list
   - Identify task categories
   - Determine human qualities
   - Identify methods for obtaining proficiencies and qualities
   - Determine job dimensions

5. Determine critical job dimensions.

6. Define preferred behaviors.

7. Prepare behavioral interview questions.

8. Determine scoring method and produce scoring matrix.

9. Produce data collection worksheets.

10. Prepare for interviews.

11. Conduct interviews.

12. Conduct candidate selection session.

13. Extend offer and set reporting date.

Step 1: Confirm Authority to Hire

Team hiring begins with a shift in authority from the traditional manager to the team members. The team must be *empowered* to select new team members based on the interview data it collects. "Second interviews" by someone other than a hiring team member are discouraged because the team will collect all the necessary data required to make the hiring decision.

Empowerment is a term that has been used by many organizations in many different ways; thus we would like to explain our definition of "empowerment."

$$\text{Empowerment} = \quad \text{Authority} +$$
$$\text{Responsibility} +$$
$$\text{Capability} +$$
$$\text{Capacity}$$

Empowerment, from our point of view, is the act of shifting authority and responsibility for work; in this case the "work" is the responsibility for hiring new team members. Deployed successfully, transitions in empowerment will improve business performance, stimulate personal and group development, and improve customer satisfaction. Casual attempts in empowerment lead to confusion, fear, frustration, distrust, and failure (Pavelek, 1998).

Empowerment is not delegation, abdication, or a directive. Instead, empowerment should begin with an invitation or offer to be explored and negotiated by the person offering the empowerment and by the team members who are receiving the offer. Empowerment is the result of calculated, deliberate, specific transitions in authority and responsibility (Pavelek, 1998):

> The five members of the Human Performance Team in Sabre's Performance Technology and Training Department were winding down

their meeting. After an hour of discussion, the team arrived at the general consensus that in order to round out the team's competencies, it needed to hire a new team member. Critical skill sets were missing from the team and there was more work than team members could handle. George, the team's leader and manager, empowered his team to take on this challenge and, in fact, believed that the job of hiring a new team member rightly belonged to them. From this point on, he would act as a resource as needed, but the responsibility and the process of hiring a new team member resided with the existing team members.

Because the team had attended his two-day workshop on behavioral interviewing, no further training was needed; however, the team did need to decide which three members would form the hiring subteam. Team members understood that hiring a new team member would require extra work, but they also believed that the time invested would pay off in the long run.

Step 2: Form a Hiring Subteam

Once the team has accepted the authority and responsibility for hiring additional team members, members need to decide who will participate on the hiring subteam. A subteam of three can provide the necessary variance in perspective but still be small enough to reach consensus quickly.

The members of the hiring subteam do not necessarily need prior hiring experience but they do need:

- Experience performing the job for which they are hiring;
- Thorough understanding of the performance requirements associated with it;
- Participation based on their personal desire and time available; and
- Redistribution of work projects as necessary to help accommodate participation.

Because one of the Human Performance Team members had just begun a new project that would require 100 percent of her time, the three remaining members agreed to become the hiring subteam. The first thing they needed to do was to define the job the new team member would be performing. Realizing that this would require some time, they scheduled a half-day session for later in the week where they would define key job dimensions and identify behaviors for each dimension.

Step 3: Learn Behavioral Interview Methods

The hiring subteam members can learn and practice behavioral interview methods by:

- Reading articles and books and attending workshops;
- Creating job dimensions together; and
- Asking other team members to participate in a mock interview.

Because most behavioral interviewing methods are used by individuals rather than teams, slight adaptations may be needed to apply to a team-based organization. For example, for decision-making purposes, team members must become proficient in reaching consensus, and most behavioral interviewing methods do not include this kind of information (Cascio, 1998; Leibler & Parkman, 1999; Werther & Davis, 1996).

Step 4: Define Job Dimensions

A job dimension should articulate behaviors that lead to desired performance. Dimensions may be defined during a facilitated session or collaborative team dialogue. The following actions will help hiring teams define the dimensions for a job:

- *Identify job tasks*: The task list should answer the question, "What is the employee required to 'do' when performing the job?"
- *Validate task list*: Distribute the task list to job performers and managers, and request their feedback.
- *Identify task categories*: Group similar tasks together with the goal of creating task categories. Table 23.1 represents possible task categories for additional skills needed on the Human Performance Team.

Table 23.1. Task Categories for the Position

Task Category	Tasks
Basic Math Skills (evaluated through prescreening assessment)	Calculate return on investment variables Perform cost/benefit analyses
Managing Performance Improvement Projects	Plan, monitor, and implement performance improvement projects Gather customer requirements Contract with the client to determine project plan, project scope, deliverables, and timeframe
Communication Skills	Communicate with personnel at various levels within the organization Collaborate with team members and client contacts regarding projects Provide feedback to both clients and team members
Problem Solving	Assist clients in solving problems Help clients improve their business performance Facilitate both scientific and spontaneous problem-solving methods Facilitate innovation and continuous improvement
Basic Technical Skills	Create presentations using presentation software Create participant and moderator materials to be used in the classroom Track projects using software Secure and monitor business travel itineraries using internal software applications

- *Determine human qualities*: Human qualities are personal characteristics or attributes that enable individuals to interact successfully in their work environment (Leibler & Parkman, 1999). Table 23.2 represents a list of human qualities for the human performance consultant position.

Table 23.2. Human Qualities for Position

Human Quality	Rationale
Manage stressful situations	Essential when dealing with condensed project timelines and when managing a heavy project load
Cooperation	Important when collaborating with other team members, as well as when meeting customer requirements
Integrity	Paramount in building trust with both clients and team members

- *Identify method for obtaining proficiencies and qualities*: Review the task categories and human qualities and identify which are essential to the job. For those essential tasks and qualities, divide them into three types: those which are best measured by testing (test), those which are best obtained by on-the-job development (develop on the job), and which are best measured during the interview (selection). (See Table 23.3.)

Table 23.3. Methods for Obtaining Proficiencies and Qualities

Task Category	Decision
Basic math skills	Test
Managing performance improvement projects	Selection
Communication skills	Selection
Problem solving	Selection
Basic technical skills	Develop on the job
Human Quality	
Manage stressful situations	Selection
Cooperation	Selection
Integrity	Selection

- *Determine job dimensions*: After analyzing the task categories, job task list, and human qualities list, create job dimensions that will be used for employee selection. In order to keep the length of the interviews within a reasonable timeframe, consider limiting the number of dimensions to ten or fewer. Each dimension adds approximately ten minutes to an interview, so allow about one hour for every five to six job dimensions. Table 23.4 shows the dimensions identified for the new Human Performance Team member.

Table 23.4. Job Dimensions for Position

Task Category	Job Dimension
Manage performance improvement projects	Manage performance improvement projects Navigating change
Communication skills	Communicate with the organization at all levels Collaborative networking
Problem solving	Problem solving
Manage stressful situations	Handle stressful situations with calm and helpful demeanor
Cooperation	Work easily with others toward a common purpose
Integrity	Display personal honesty and sound judgment

On the morning of the half-day session, one of the members facilitated, although she also provided her input throughout the day. Standing at the chart easel with a marker in hand, she began the session by asking: "What are the key dimensions of the job we will be asking our new team member to perform?" Using brainstorming techniques, the team systematically generated ideas one by one. After everyone had a chance to add their ideas, the facilitator helped the team reduce the list by eliminating duplications and by grouping related tasks. Their final list included six job dimensions.

Step 5: Determine Critical Job Dimensions

Review the dimensions and determine which are *most* critical for performance. Consider the following criteria:

- The dimension is fundamental to success in other dimensions of the job.
- Impact on the team will be significant if the person cannot perform the dimension.
- Complexity of the learning curve is high.

Step 6: Define Preferred Behaviors

Preferred behaviors describe successful job performance and should answer the question: "What does this dimension 'look like'?" These behaviors may include knowledge of a specific method or product (such as "demonstrates an understanding of market and industry trends and the potential impact on the business"), a skill (such as "capable in the use of Microsoft PowerPoint"), or human quality (such as "gains the respect of others and easily develops rapport").

> Now that the key job dimensions were understood, it was time to go through each one and identify the preferred behaviors. The facilitator used an example from a time when she had participated on a team that hired a new project manager. One of the job dimensions for that job was "planning and task coordination," and the preferred behaviors had included the following items:
>
> | | |
> |---|---|
> | Establishes a systematic course of action for self or others to assure accomplishment of specific objectives. | Determines priorities and allocates time and resources effectively. |
> | Controls expenses within acceptable limits. | Delegates and empowers others. |
> | Follows through on set milestones. | Allows for and contributes needed resources. |
> | Removes obstacles. | |
>
> One by one, the members worked through the job dimensions and agreed on preferred behaviors for each. Afterward, they discussed how they would go about validating their list with the others on their team.

Step 7: Prepare Behavioral Interview Questions

The behavioral interviewing method involves providing candidates with a situational prompt and asking task, action, and result questions for each dimension. The situational prompt requires the candidate to recall a specific time when he or she completed a task or displayed a skill or quality.

The situational prompt requires the candidate to recall a specific time when he or she completed a task or displayed a skill or quality.

Task, action, and result questions gather more detail regarding the candidate's performance. Listed below are two examples of situational prompts:

- *"Give me an example of a time when you* were required to use persuasion to successfully convince someone to see things your way."

- *"Recall a specific occasion when you* conformed to a policy with which you did not agree."

The *task* question, "What was your role and what were your responsibilities?" helps interviewers understand more about the candidate's past experience.

The *action* question, "What was your approach?" or "How did you go about it?" allows interviewers to capture the candidate's approach, method, or application of knowledge.

And the *result* question, "What was the outcome?" provides interviewers with specific results of the approach taken by the candidate.

Step 8: Determine Scoring Method and Produce Scoring Matrix

Dimensions may be scored using either objective (yes/no) or subjective (high, medium, low) criteria. These decisions will depend on the nature of the dimension.

Candidate responses to the interview questions will be checked against the preferred behaviors for the dimension. A "yes/no" score is appropriate for dimensions that are not subject to individual interpretation. If subjective criteria are used, team members must come to agreement on the meaning of a high, medium, or low score and assign a quantitative value to each. The following scale is one option:

- High (3) = Master: depth, breadth, complexity of experience, can teach others

- Medium (2) = Novice: can do with coaching

- Low (1) = No experience or cannot do at all

Team members can use the scoring template in Exhibit 23.1 to record individual scores and tabulate results.

Exhibit 23.1. Scoring Template

Job Dimension	Candidates			
	C1	C2	C3	C4
1. Manage performance improvement projects.				
2. Communicate with the organization at all levels.				
3. Handle stressful situations with calm and helpful demeanor.				

Step 9: Produce Data Collection Worksheets

Data collection worksheets are to be provided to each hiring team member. Exhibit 23.2 presents an example of the worksheet for the Human Performance Consultant dimension "Handles stressful situation with calm and helpful demeanor." For every interview, the interviewers will have one data collection worksheet for each dimension. These worksheets are to be filled out during the interviews, although it is not uncommon for hiring teams to take five or ten minutes after each interview to work individually to complete their worksheets.

After the interview process is complete, the data collection worksheets should be archived in the event that a non-selected candidate pursues legal action.

Exhibit 23.2. Data Collection Worksheet

Worksheet (to be completed during each interview).

Candidate: _____   Interview Date: _____

Dimension 8: Handles stressful situation with calm and helpful demeanor.

Objective: ☐ Yes (2)   ☐ No (1)
or
Subjective: ☐ High (3)   ☐ Medium (2)   ☐ Low (1)

Preferred Behaviors *(Defined by the team prior to the interview):*

☐ Allows customer to vent   ☐ Rephrases issues to check understanding
☐ Listens to perceived problems   ☐ Follows through on commitments

Situation Prompt: "Recall a specific time when you dealt with a stressful situation."

Task Question: "What was your specific role/responsibility?"

Action Question: "What was your method/approach?"

Result Question: "What was the outcome or result?"

Other comments:

Step 10: Prepare for the Interviews

The degree of involvement of the human resource (HR) department will vary depending on the size and structure of your organization. HR may recruit candidates at colleges or job fairs, collect resumes, pre-screen candidates, and administer pre-tests. We recommend working closely with your HR department throughout the hiring process.

Behavioral interviewing usually requires more time than traditional interviews and, in general, you might allow ten to fifteen minutes per job dimension. Each interviewer will need a data collection sheet for each job dimension.

Typically, candidates prepare for a job interview by rehearsing answers to traditional interview questions. A simple orientation just prior to the interview conducted by someone who is not a member of the hiring team can help the candidate understand how this interview will differ. Exhibit 23.3 provides a sample agenda.

Exhibit 23.3. Candidate Pre-Briefing Agenda

1. Welcome and thank the candidate for his or her interest in the job.
2. Introduce the behavioral interview process that will be used to conduct the interview:
   - Three-member panel
   - Each will ask questions and record responses
   - Informal and relaxed environment
3. Read each job dimension and explain that each dimension will be used for questioning during the interview (*without* revealing preferred behaviors.)
4. Define the interview process, stating:
   - "As prompted, you will be asked to recall a specific workplace memory of a time when you experienced the job dimension."
   - "In doing so, take your time and be specific. Respond using first-person, singular responses, using 'I,' not 'we.'"
   - "If a job dimension is introduced to you that you have not experienced in the workplace, but you have experienced elsewhere, feel free to communicate the experience."
   - "After recalling your past experience, we will ask questions about your role and responsibilities, methods and results. Please take your time and be specific."
   - "You are encouraged to ask questions as necessary."
5. Ask the candidate what questions he or she has prior to meeting the hiring team.

Step 11: Conduct the Interviews

Creating a relaxed atmosphere and establishing rapport early on will help put the candidate at ease. In general, it is a good idea to provide water or something to drink, and, at the onset, let the candidate know that questions will be rotated among the team members and notes will be taken throughout the interview.

As the candidate answers the questions, each team member should be recording responses and noting preferred behaviors revealed in the candidate's answers. Many times, after completing the first couple of job dimension questions, the candidate will anticipate the rhythm of the interview process and begin answering task, method, and result questions prior to being asked. Interviewers should:

- Allow silence when a candidate has problems responding to a situational prompt;
- Encourage the candidate to take time when responding;
- Remind the candidate that a non-business example is okay;
- Refocus the candidate on a specific dimension when necessary;
- Score candidates for each job dimension *following* the interview, using a template like the one in Exhibit 23.1; and
- Refrain from discussing their thoughts and feelings about a specific candidate until all candidates have completed the interview process.

The team posted the job opening with the HR department and asked that HR personnel conduct the initial pre-screening of applicants and forward appropriate applications to the hiring team. The hiring team scheduled the first interview for a Monday morning from 9:00 to 12:00.

When the candidate arrived at 9:00 a.m. sharp, a team member who was not part of the hiring subteam greeted her and led her to her office. After the candidate was given an overview of the interview process, she was shown into the conference room, where the interviewers were waiting. After greetings and introductions, the candidate was shown to a chair at the conference table. Trying to control her nervousness, she sat down, opened the bottle of water that had been provided, and the interview began.

"Think about a time when you. . . ."; "Tell me how you went about. . ."; "When you did it that way, what was the outcome?" One by one the hiring team members took turns asking questions. After one dimension had been thoroughly covered, another team member took the next dimension and began the process again. As the candidate answered each question, hiring team members took notes on their data collection sheets and listened carefully for evidence of their previously agreed-on preferred behaviors.

Once the final question had been asked, one of the interviewers smiled at the candidate and said, "Okay, now it's your turn. What questions do you have for us?" Taking a deep breath and sitting back in her chair, she looked at the three of them and said, "Well, what I'd like to know from each of you is this: What do you like most about working here and what do you like least about working here?" She listened to their responses and began to feel more at ease.

After the candidate left, the interviewers took a few minutes to finish their notes and review their individual score sheets. Knowing they would wait until the last candidate had been interviewed before discussing their scores, each finished writing and left the conference room.

Step 12: Conduct Candidate Selection Session

Once all candidates have been interviewed, the hiring subteam follows these steps to make the hiring decision:

- Conduct a dialogue to discuss data gathered for each candidate;
- Review each dimension; and
- Transfer individual scores onto a scoring matrix. (See Exhibit 23.4 for a completed sample.)

Exhibit 23.4. Sample Completed Scoring Matrix

Job Dimension	Candidates				Hiring Team Scores
	C1	C2	C3	C4	
1. Manage performance improvement projects.	3	1	1	2	Team Member 1 (name)
	2	2	2	2	Team Member 2 (name)
	3	2	3	2	Team Member 3 (name)
2. Communicate with the organization at all levels.	3	2	2	2	Team Member 1 (name)
	2	3	3	2	Team Member 2 (name)
	3	2	2	1	Team Member 3 (name)
3. Handles stressful situation with calm and helpful demeanor.	2	1	3	2	Team Member 1 (name)
	2	2	3	2	Team Member 2 (name)
	3	1	2	2	Team Member 3 (name)
Total Scores	23	16	21	17	

Note. Score values are high (1), medium (2), and low (3).

It is not necessary for team members to reach complete consensus when scoring *individual* dimensions, but significant differences in scoring should be discussed in greater detail. (In this example, a two-point difference was considered significant, that is, a score of 1 versus 3.)

Members should discuss the logic behind their scoring decisions until *understanding* is reached. When two or more candidates share similar *total* scores, the team may narrow its focus and consider certain dimensions that have previously been identified as absolutely critical to success.

Admittedly, there is no foolproof method of selecting high-performing team members, but for the hiring subteam, reaching consensus on the *final* hiring decision is crucial. If consensus cannot be reached, the team may decide to seek additional candidates and continue interviewing.

> After the last candidate had been interviewed, the subteam scheduled another half-day session to discuss the scoring and arrive at a hiring decision. Referring to their data collection sheets, they took turns discussing each candidate. Being careful not to compare one candidate to another, but to instead score them according to the preferred behaviors, the team talked through their scores and recorded them on the scoring matrix.
>
> On those dimensions where team members had a difference of 2 points, they discussed the candidates' responses and tried to bring their scores closer together. At the end of the session, the final scores were tabulated. One candidate clearly stood out by demonstrating more of the preferred behaviors than the others demonstrated.

Step 13: Extend Offer and Set Reporting Date

Depending on the HR hiring practices within the organization, the hiring offer may be extended to the selected candidate by one of the hiring subteam members, team lead, or an HR representative. In any case, the employee must be notified, salary negotiated, and an employment start date arranged.

> After the subteam advised George of their decision, he notified the HR department so they could begin the appropriate personnel processes and make the initial offer to the candidate. Within a matter of days, George was on the phone welcoming the new team member.

Conclusion

Selecting the right members for your team is not an easy task, especially since there are so many variables that impact an organization's ability to attract and retain high-performing employees. While there may not be one right way to select new employees, this team-based behavioral interviewing method offers significant benefits over traditional interview practices and places the authority and responsibility of hiring new team members with the people they will be working most closely with—their teammates.

George met Carole for the first time when she arrived for her first day at work. As they walked to his office, George stopped a few times to introduce her to others in the department. After they'd had a chance to get acquainted, Carole was shown to her new office where Susan, one of her new teammates, was waiting to help her get settled. They sat together and reviewed the orientation handbook that Susan had prepared, which included a schedule for Carole to meet with various members of the department over the next three days.

Later that day, Carole received developmental feedback from the hiring subteam based on the results of her interview. She appreciated the fact that her new team members offered her feedback in a way that made her feel valued and excited about developing new skills that would help her contribute to the team.

As Carole headed for the parking lot at the end of the day, she walked by George's office and stuck her head in to say goodbye. He looked up, smiled, and said, "I'm sure glad to have you on the team. Have a great weekend, partner."

CHAPTER 24

The Team Excellence Award Program

Recognizing Successful Team Problem Solving and Process Improvement

Laurie Broedling

ONE OF THE LEAST DEVELOPED AREAS within the field of team-based organizing is that of rewards and recognition, yet it is extremely important. Many team-related initiatives stall or fail because the organizational reward system continues to reinforce individual behavior rather than teamwork. This is a prime example where organizational support systems frequently are misaligned with the new intent of fostering collaboration. On average there is a dearth of formal programs to recognize team achievements.

Fortunately, one formal award program, the National Team Excellence Award Program, does exist to recognize and celebrate outstanding accomplishment on the part of teams who employ a systematic approach to problem solving and process improvement. It is a vehicle that any organization can use to reward and recognize teamwork, either internally or by participating in the external evaluation and competition. Several states also have an affiliated award program, such as the California Team Excellence Award (CTEA) program. At both the national and state levels, this program can be used to advantage by anyone who is interested in encouraging teams to apply a valid methodology and in rewarding them for doing so. The Team Excellence Award Program bears the same relationship to fostering team-based organizations nationwide as the Malcolm Baldrige Award program has to fostering overall organizational excellence and improvement nationwide. Both programs lay out clear criteria, are based on sound organizational theory, and have well-trained evaluators. (See Chapter 7 for more information on the criticality of aligning organizational support systems with teams.)

Participation in the award program offers several benefits including the following:

- *Methodological framework*—The award criteria represent a valid approach to problem solving and process improvement.

- *Educational and developmental opportunities*—When team members learn about the criteria, they acquire important skills in systematic problem solving and process improvement. These skills are generalizable to any setting.

- *Enhanced employee motivation and commitment*—The criteria set a high standard. Attempting to meet them fosters a shared goal and framework, which in turn enhances pride in workmanship and team spirit.

- *Celebration*—Moving a step beyond intrinsic motivation, the program offers an opportunity to give formal recognition to team accomplishments and celebrate together.

- *Bottom-line improvements*—Winning teams have made significant contributions to the functioning and profitability of their organizations. For example, the top team in the 2001 national competition had a 32.5 percent increase in productivity.

Similar to the Baldrige Award, the program's criteria can be used to advantage, even by organizations and teams who choose not to participate in a formal competition.

Program Scope

This program has wide-ranging applicability. It is targeted to teams when they are engaged in structured improvement activities of two types:

1. *Problem solving,* in which there is a definite cause-effect relationship.

2. *Process improvement,* in which the team is either improving an existing product, process, or service or developing a new one.

Because there is a pervasive need for systematic problem solving and process improvement, all types of organizations can benefit from using this approach. It is appropriate for teams in both the private and public sectors. It is equally applicable to product-based organizations and service-based organizations. Past participants have come from a wide variety of sectors, such as health care, financial services, manufacturing, and public service agencies. This program is also applicable to any type of team, whether it is an intact work team or a project team formed for a finite period of time. The team can be comprised of members from any organizational level. The program is applicable whether the team is co-located or operating virtually.

Evaluation Criteria

At the heart of this program are the evaluation criteria. They are used to determine the degree to which the team has employed a credible, systematic approach to successful problem solving and process improvement. The criteria represent a framework for teams that is based on sound theoretical underpinnings. Generically they follow the logic of the plan-do-check-act (PDCA) cycle developed by Walter Shewhart and popularized by W. Edwards Deming (1982).

The criteria emphasize identification of root causes and also the testing of various proposed causes and solutions before institutionalizing the recommendations.

Employing this disciplined approach greatly enhances the chance that a team will be successful in solving a problem or improving a process. Unfortunately, even the most motivated team cannot be successful in this regard if they lack the analytic skills to ferret out root causes, if they do not identify and involve stakeholders, or if they do not employ appropriate measures. Too many teams chase superficial symptoms or are ill-equipped to use credible data in order to justify their proposed changes.

The evaluation criteria used for the 2001–2002 National Team Excellence Award are presented in Exhibit 24.1. Also included is the number of points assigned to each criterion. The evaluation criteria used for the 2001–2002 California Team Excellence Award are presented in Exhibit 24.2. Both sets of criteria are organized around the same principles. The state award criteria are made simpler to assist entry-level teams in understanding what is expected. A summary of what both sets of criteria cover resides in the answers to the questions: What? Who? How?

What?

- What project was selected and why?
- What are the potential versus actual root causes?
- What was the potential versus actual solution?
- What were the results achieved and were they related to the original organizational goal?
- What were the anticipated versus actual results?
- What impact did the project have on the organization in terms of sustainable change?

Who?

- Who are the team members?
- Who are the stakeholders?

How?

- How was the project selected?
- How were the team members chosen and what is their involvement?
- How did the team involve the stakeholders and how were the stakeholders affected?
- How did the team identify potential root causes, narrow them down, and validate the final root cause?
- How was the final solution implemented?
- How was the impact measured?

Overall, the criteria emphasize the methodology itself more than the outcome. The criteria are meant to guide teams in correctly diagnosing the causes(s) and correctly selecting the solution(s). They are not meant to recognize teams that simply achieved large-scale results without going through proper analysis. Impressive outcomes in and of themselves will not result in a high overall point score unless they were derived from systematic application of appropriate analytic tools. A higher score will accrue to a team that has adhered to a systematic methodology, even if they do not achieve a large-scale outcome. There are several reasons for the relative emphasis on methodology:

- It recognizes that improvements, no matter what the magnitude, are not sustainable if they are derived from solutions that do not address root cause, even though they may appear superficially appealing.

- It levels the playing field. It does not favor teams that simply picked "low-hanging fruit" problems or processes.

- It emphasizes the need for teams to select projects that are clearly tied to organizational priorities and goals.

- It recognizes that others in the organization who are involved in implementing and institutionalizing the solutions, such as management and other stakeholders, will be expecting thorough justification.

- If the team presents a solution based on insufficient or poorly analyzed data to a sophisticated audience who asks tough questions, they will not get very far. The world of teams is littered with an inordinate number of proposed solutions and improvements that have failed to gain organizational support for precisely this reason. Needless to say, this leads to discouragement and disillusionment, not success and enthusiasm.

Another aspect to be noted about the criteria is that they are not overly prescriptive. While they specify an overall methodological framework, they do not specify which individual tools should be used. Therefore, teams have discretion to choose the data collection tools and analytic approaches they feel are most appropriate.

Teams have discretion to choose the data collection tools and analytic approaches they feel are most appropriate.

In this regard, the conceptual approach is similar to that of the Baldrige Award criteria. The Baldrige criteria specify a general framework for organizational excellence and improvement but do not specify the detailed ways by which an organization should achieve those criteria.

Award Program Structure

The national level program is administered by the Association for Quality and Participation (AQP), a subsidiary of the American Society for Quality (ASQ). This AQP award program has been in existence since 1985. A total of 660 teams have competed during the program's history. Its purpose is to provide recognition and rewards to teams as well as to enable benchmarking and assessment. The award is administered on an annual cycle culminating in a live competition and award ceremony during AQP's national conference. Teams that apply submit a video presentation on their project that is no more than twenty-five minutes in length. The submission should cover a project completed in the current business year and should track the project from origin through implementation and outcomes. Applicants must also submit a hard copy of the slides that they use during their presentation. In this preliminary round of competition, trained judges evaluate the presentation according to the criteria and assign a total point score. They also develop written feedback that is provided to the teams along with the point score. A maximum of the twenty-seven highest scoring teams are selected as finalists, with the provision that a finalist must have scored a minimum of seventy points.

The finalists are invited to give a live presentation at the national conference and be judged again at that time. While the judging is based on the live presentation, all team presentations are videotaped. This provides a record of each team's final product. A video containing presentations of all three top winning teams is made available for purchase to enable others to benchmark outstanding team performance. At the conference, all finalists are presented with a finalist award, recognizing their achievement in getting to that stage. The top three scoring teams are awarded gold, silver, and bronze medals. A major celebration is held honoring the winners and recognizing all the finalists. The judges are also recognized and honored at this time. This event is a very motivational experience for the teams and the conference attendees, with a lot of team spirit being demonstrated. There is also extensive publicity afforded the finalists, and especially the winners. Along these lines, the winners and their accomplishments are posted on the AQP website throughout the following year. Moreover, the opportunity for the team members to travel to the conference and give a live presentation is in itself an honor. For those team members who are unaccustomed to participating in professional association conferences, this is a particularly motivating and memorable experience.

An additional feature to the recognition process is the People's Choice Awards. The conference participants who attend the live presentations are encouraged to vote for the teams in various categories, such as best team spirit, best visual aids, best team-vendor relationship, and best costumes. The People's Choice Awards are distributed at a separate celebratory event the day before the major award event. The winning teams are frequently benchmarked by other teams and organizations throughout the following year, thereby receiving continuous recognition.

State-Level Award

California is one of several states that have affiliated award programs. The CTEA is administered by the California Council for Excellence (CCE), the organization that also administers the state's Baldrige-type award. The state-level program provides teams more opportunities for recognition and celebration, given that the competition at the national level is much stiffer. The California Team Excellence Award (CTEA) has been in existence since 1998. It was originally started by San Diego State University (SDSU) as the first team award in the region. In 1999 CCE assumed overall management of the CTEA program with sponsorship from SDSU. While it is its own self-contained program, it also serves as a feeder to the national program.

Teams that apply for the CTEA submit a video of their presentation that is no more than twenty-five minutes in length. A panel of four or five trained judges reviews the presentation and assigns point scores according to the criteria. The judges also generate a feedback report for the team that describes both strengths and opportunities for improvement.

Team members find both the formal recognition and the opportunity to share their work to be very motivating.

The awards in this program are based on point scores. All teams that score above a pre-determined point level receive a gold medal; the same is true for silver and bronze medals. All others receive an honorable mention. All teams are formally recognized at a celebratory event during the CCE annual conference. Moreover, the top team is invited to give its presentation and answer questions in a conference session.

The top California winners are eligible to go forward in the competition process. The very top winner is guaranteed a slot at the AQP national competition as long as they meet or exceed a minimum score pre-determined by AQP. Any other CTEA team can resubmit a video to AQP's preliminary national competition. Based on their new scores, they may also receive a berth at the national competition.

Winning Teams

Recent winning teams and their accomplishments are as follows:

AQP Winners

Gold medal 2001–2002. Merrill Lynch Production Technologies Mail Efficiency Partnering Team. This Six Sigma process improvement team included the five major suppliers. It was tasked with improving equipment efficiencies, including increasing throughput, reducing rework, and driving down cost. The team achieved an annual savings of $1,088,000, while simultaneously strengthening supplier partnerships.

Gold medal 2000–2001. Blue Cross Blue Shield of Florida State Account Operations Claims Quality and Productivity Improvement Team. Their goal was to exceed the claims processing standards established with that state. Their improvements resulted in a 32.5 percent increase in productivity and a 19 percent decrease in cost per claim. This team also won the Florida State team excellence award.

Silver medal 2001–2002. Hermetic Perfectors from Emerson. This problem-solving team addressed the problem of six hours of daily rework and repairs that had been a longstanding problem with a certain product. Through use of problem-solving tools, the rework was completely eliminated, for a labor savings of $13,204.

Silver medal 2000–2001. Lucent Technologies Grease Masters Team. Their goal was to improve factory test yield for an electronic circuit assembly process by increasing first test yield from 62 percent to at least 85 percent. Their improvement resulted in a first test yield of 92 percent and a savings of $2M.

CTEA Winners

Gold medal 2001–2002. Grundfos Pumps Reduce the Juice Team. This problem-solving team was tasked to find ways to reduce energy consumption in one of the company's manufacturing facilities. A careful analysis of energy usage patterns enabled the team to identify several major improvement opportunities. These changes resulted in a 28 percent reduction in energy usage in the first year.

Gold medal 2000–2001. Emermex-Liebert Royal Team. Their goal was to improve the accounts payable process so that their suppliers would be paid within thirty days. Their improvements resulted in a significant reduction in overdue invoices and a 16 percent increase in monetary discounts.

Gold medal 1999–2000. Hoag Memorial Hospital Pneumonia Treatment Team. Their goal was to improve clinical outcomes while reducing cost and length of stay. Their improvements resulted in a reduction of almost one day in average length of stay, reduction of $2,000 in cost per patient, while keeping mortality rates and re-admissions low.

To elaborate on one of the winning teams, the Emermex-Liebert Royal Team was from a company that manufactures uninterruptible power supply products. The company determined that it had a problem with delayed payments to suppliers, which resulted in suspended, deferred, and/or delayed credit, which in turn resulted in production stoppages and delayed product deliveries. The company assembled an associates action team to improve the accounts payable process. The team employed a six-step methodology used by the company to continuously improve processes:

1. Select/identify the project;

2. Analyze the process;

3. Evaluate alternatives/solutions;

4. Test solutions;

5. Implementation and standardization; and

6. Communication.

Within each of these steps a variety of appropriate analytical tools were employed, such as flow charts, run charts, check sheets, brainstorming, decision matrices, surveys. The team set up a test plan to verify the results of their potential solutions before institutionalizing them. They engaged their stakeholders every step of the way. They also demonstrated commitment and involvement of all team members. They did a superior job of presenting their project in an articulate manner and took obvious pride in the professionalism they demonstrated. Their enthusiasm was not only obvious, but it was infectious. Most importantly, they achieved demonstrable productivity improvements that were directly related to organizational goals. (Chapter 5 on return on investment of teams emphasizes the importance of calculating teams' contributions to the bottom line.)

Benefits

There are a wide variety of benefits to this program. The primary goal is to provide formal recognition to teams that engage in systematic problem solving and process improvement. As such, it fills an important niche in the field of teaming and collaborative work systems. It provides a way to motivate and celebrate with teams using external recognition. One of the less obvious motivational components is the fact that any team can compete and derive benefit, not simply the top winning teams.

Any team can compete and derive benefit, not simply the top winning teams.

In the CTEA program, for example, every team that applies receives some form of recognition, no matter what their total score. Second, at the California state level any team that scores at a certain level is eligible for the "prize" at that level. In other words, they are competing against the criteria, not against each other. Moreover, everyone is treated as a winner simply for trying. This approach encourages teams to become involved, even if they are relatively inexperienced in systematic problem solving and process improvement. Participation is not reserved to expert teams. It fits within the philosophical approach of continual improvement, which is that the starting level of performance does not matter. What matters is that the team continues to improve its performance. The program is meant to be encouraging to all teams, not to be exclusionary or elitist. A conundrum exists in any awards program, which is how to recognize excellence while encouraging everyone else. The program deals with this conundrum by recognizing participation and developing pride in all teams while giving special recognition to teams that make respectable, permanent improvements by using the most systematic approaches.

Organizations can use this program to great advantage. It offers many other potential benefits aside from the formal external award and recognition component. Its core is a sound methodological framework. Use of the framework will improve any organization's performance. Teaching team members this framework provides them with a valuable skill set. These skills are not only useful for the particular problem or process selected but also for working on future improvements. Moreover, there is a continuum of skills associated with this approach. Team members can learn how to use progressively more sophisticated analytic tools to be applied within the improvement framework.

The program can improve the communication necessary to turn a team's recommendations into reality. Since a team rarely controls all the resources or procedures that will be affected, the approval by some set of management and other stakeholders is almost always required for the recommendations to be implemented. One of the most potent motivators for teams is to see their recommendations adopted. Conversely, one of the demotivators is to have their hard work left on the table. Yet this is a too frequent fact of organizational life and a big detractor in the advancement of teaming. It is one of the most frequent junctures at which team-based improvement projects break down. It is rarely a result of organizational intent, but rather a result of the lack of a formal approach to ensure that the requisite dialogue takes place. Often there is no routine protocol to make this happen; instead the approach is ad hoc.

Moreover, videotaping a team's final presentation both increases the professionalism of the product and improves the communication among the team, management, and other stakeholders. It provides a discipline to what the team is doing and how they describe it. It also provides the team an opportunity to review its own work before giving a live presentation to management. Also, a videotape can easily be provided to a broader constituency of stakeholders, especially ones who are not geographically co-located with the team.

Last, management can take the opportunity to celebrate team accomplishments internally, irrespective of whether the teams participate in an external competition. This provides organizations with a well-developed and professionally credible basis on which to provide recognition and celebration.

Conclusion

The goal of collaborative work systems in general, and use of teaming in particular, is to enhance organizational effectiveness. Many organizational teaming efforts do not have their reward systems adequately aligned to support a team-based organizational approach. Therefore, more ways to reward and motivate teams to use systematic improvement methods must be introduced. Their long-term effectiveness and survival depend on it. The Team Excellence Award Program and use of its criteria are ways to provide formal and informal recognition as well as enhance the likelihood that team contributions will be accepted and institutionalized.

Also, on a national level, it would be beneficial if more states would sponsor state-level team excellence award competitions. Having this program expand nationwide at the grassroots level would make it possible for even beginning level teams to participate, no matter where they are located. Given the major challenge in shifting from traditional to team-based organizations, the more venues for reinforcement that are available, the better.

For the most current information on AQP's National Team Excellence Award Program, go to www.aqp.org/awards/teamaward.htm.

For the most current information on the California Team Excellence Award Program, go to www.calexcellence.org/cce/awards/index2.htm.

Exhibit 24.1. AQP Team Excellence Award Criteria for 2001–2002

1. Project Selection and Purpose

   9 factors × 3 points = 27 points possible

   1a. Explain the methods used to choose the project. (Provide specific examples of techniques and data used.)
   - Reasons why the project was selected.
   - Types of data and quality tools used to select the project, and why.
   - Involvement of potential stakeholders in project selection.

   1b. Explain how the project supports the organization's goals.
   - Listing of affected organizational goals/performance measures.
   - Types of impact the project will have on each goal area.
   - Degree of impact the project will have on each goal area.

   1c. Identify the potential stakeholders (those impacted by the project) and how they may be impacted by the project.
   - Affected internal and external (if applicable) stakeholders.
   - Types of potential impact on stakeholders.
   - Degree of potential impact on stakeholders.

2. Current Situation Analysis

   6 factors × 4.5 points = 27 points possible

   2a. Explain how the team used a formal process to identify the improvement opportunity or the potential root causes(s).
   - Methods and tools used to identify improvement opportunities or possible root causes.
   - Analysis of data to identify possible improvement opportunities or root causes.
   - Example of other actions taken to identify improvement opportunities or possible root causes.

   2b. Describe how the team analyzed information to identify the final improvement opportunity or root cause. (Include any appropriate validation.)
   - Methods and tools used to identify the final improvement opportunity or root cause.
   - Analysis of data to verify that the best improvement opportunity or primary root cause was selected.
   - Demonstration of how validation was ensured.

Exhibit 24.1. AQP Team Excellence Award Criteria for 2001–2002, Cont'd

3. Action Plan Development

   9 factors × 3 points = 27 points possible

   3a. Explain the methods used to identify the improvement actions or potential solutions.
   - Methods and tools used to develop improvement actions or possible solutions.
   - Analysis of data to develop possible improvement actions or possible solutions.
   - Demonstration of how validation was ensured via methods, tools, etc.

   3b. Explain how the final improvement(s) or solution was determined.
   - Criteria used to select the final improvement action or solution.
   - Use of methods, tools, and data to select the improvement action or solution.
   - Involvement of stakeholders in the selection of the improvement or solution.

   3c. Explain the justification/benefits of the improvement(s) or solution.
   - Types of tangible and intangible benefits that are expected to be realized.
   - Use of data to justify the project.
   - Comparison of budgeted-to-actual costs, or use of other justification methods.

4. Project Buy-In, Implementation, Progress, and Results

   9 factors × 3 points = 27 points possible

   4a. Explain how buy-in/agreement was achieved for implementation.
   - Types of internal and external (if applicable) stakeholder involvement.
   - How various types of resistance were addressed.
   - Proof/validation that buy-in existed.

   4b. Explain the methods that were developed/installed to ensure the results.
   - Use of stakeholder feedback in implementation.
   - Procedure or system changes that were made.
   - Creation and installation of a system for measuring results.

   4c. Describe the results achieved.
   - Types of tangible and intangible results that were realized.
   - Linkage of project impact on organizational performance and goals.
   - How results were shared with stakeholders.

     The team will also be evaluated on:

     3 factors × 3 points = 9 points possible
   - The clarity and organization of the presentation.
   - The effective use of presentation aids (charts, graphs, etc.)
   - The demonstration of involvement by all team members throughout the project.

Exhibit 24.2. California Team Excellence Award Criteria for 2001–2002

1. Project Selection and Purpose

   12 points possible

   1.1 How & Why Was the Project Selected?

0 points	No evidence provided as to why the project was selected.
1 point	Anecdotal evidence of problems led project selection.
2 points	Analysis concluded that the organization will substantially benefit if the purpose of the project is accomplished.
3 points	Project selection is part of a systematic process of evaluation and analysis. Beginning stages of data-driven decision making and an understanding of organizational "as is" condition.
4 points	Fully integrated data system, including systematic use of quality tools, drives project selection. Project impact on organization is measurable and substantial relative to alternative projects.

   1.2 How Were Members Chosen?

0 points	Ad hoc assembly of interested employees formed the team.
1 point	Team chosen based on workload availability and impacted work areas.
2 points	Internal stakeholders were considered in team composition.
3 points	Internal *and* external stakeholders (or up/downstream processes) were considered in team composition.
4 points	Team chosen through a defined standard organizational process that assures representation of all internal/external stakeholders, and needed skills, aptitudes, knowledge, and styles.

   1.3 How Was the Project/Team's Objective Aligned to the Organization's Goals?

0 points	Team had an informal goal/objective.
1 point	Team developed a formal goal/objective.
2 points	Team subjectively quantified its formal goal/objective with some evidence of organizational alignment.
3 points	Team quantified its formal goal/objective. Their approach included use of appropriate quality tools. Beginning stage of understanding "as is" condition of impacted processes. Goal/objective aligned to organizational priorities.
4 points	Team quantified its formal goal/objective. Quantitative "as is" assessment of impacted processes undertaken or reviewed. Goal/objective aligned to organizational priorities and quantitatively expressed.

2. Root Cause Analysis

   12 points possible

   2.1 How Did You Identify Your Potential Root Causes?

0 points	No potential root causes identified. Team essentially went from problem identification to solution.
1 point	Potential root causes or existing conditions identified by assumptions, brainstorming lists, nominal group technique, fishbone diagrams, and/or intuitive tools.

Exhibit 24.2. California Team Excellence Award Criteria for 2001–2002, Cont'd

2 points	Data analysis integrated into the identification of potential root causes. Baseline measures established.
3 points	An advanced statistical tool or technique was used to identify potential root causes.
4 points	Multiple statistical tools and techniques were used to establish potential root causes.

2.2 How Did You Narrow Down to the Potential Final Root Cause(s)?

0 points	Team did not employ a process to narrow potential root causes to the final potential root cause(s). Team essentially went from problem or potential root cause identification to solution.
1 point	Team narrowed list to final potential root cause(s) through assumptions and intuitive knowledge.
2 points	Team narrowed list to final potential root cause(s) through the use of basic quality tools and limited data analysis.
3 points	Team reviewed to determine if all necessary data were considered when narrowing down to the potential final root cause(s). May have conducted a one-time data-collection process to support decision.
4 points	Team utilized a systematic and data-driven process in narrowing down to the potential final root cause(s).

2.3 How Did You Validate the Final Root Cause(s)?

0 points	Once the potential final root cause(s) was identified, team went straight to solution development without considering validating its findings.
1 point	Team attempted to validate the potential final root cause(s) through anecdotal and/or qualitative methods.
2 points	The team sought to validate the potential final root cause(s) using simple data analysis tools.
3 points	Team conducted systematic statistical validation studies of potential final root cause(s).
4 points	Team utilized multiple tools, data points, statistical methods, and techniques to validate the potential final root cause(s).

3. Solution Development

12 points possible

3.1 How Did You Identify Your Potential Solutions?

0 points	Team relied on personal experience, intuitive knowledge, and assumptions without association to identify potential root causes (2.1).
1 point	Team identified a number of potential solutions related to the potential root causes identified (2.1).
2 points	Team relied on final potential root cause(s) process (2.2) in identifying potential solutions. Solution selection tied to the final potential root cause(s) through basic quality selection tools.
3 points	Team utilized a formalized selection process. May have identified additional information and/or data to collect as part of this process.
4 points	Team relied on validation process (2.3) in identifying potential solutions. Statistical data and root cause analysis data were integrated to identify potential solutions.

Exhibit 24.2. California Team Excellence Award Criteria for 2001–2002, Cont'd

3.2 How Did You Narrow to the Potential Final Solution(s)?

0 points   Team essentially chose solution(s) based on personal experience, intuition, knowledge, and assumptions.

1 point   Team narrowed its choices based on non-data-driven techniques such as voting.

2 points   In addition to using basic quality tools to prioritize solution(s), the team relied on data to justify their selection.

3 points   Limited one-time trial/evaluation developed and conducted. Results led to the selection of a potential final solution(s) relative to alternative solutions.

4 points   Formal trial/evaluation developed and conducted. Multiple data points utilized. Multiple potential final solutions integrated into trial/evaluation efforts. Trial/evaluation results critical to selection of a potential final solution(s).

3.3 How Did You Validate the Final Solution(s)?

0 points   Final solution(s) did not undergo a validation process.

1 point   Team sought to support the final selection(s) through qualitative methods.

2 points   Team sought to support the final selection(s) through basic quantitative analysis and tracking. Team conducted tests to prove that solution(s) worked as expected.

3 points   Team sought to support the final selection(s) through statistical review/evaluation.

4 points   Team developed and implemented a validation process including the use of statistical tools and techniques to verify impact of final solution(s) selected upon the original goal/objective. Correlation statistically valid.

4. Implementation and Impact

  12 points possible

  4.1 How Was Your Solution(s) Implemented?

0 points   Implementation of project undertaken with no formal plan or process for evaluating impact.

1 point   Implementation of project undertaken by team with some consideration given to downstream impact and/or organizational effect.

2 points   Implementation of project undertaken by team. Efforts communicated and involvement sought of management, customers, and stakeholders as applicable.

3 points   Plan developed for implementation. A system to measure and track results was put into place prior to implementation.

4 points   Detailed plan developed for implementation. Contingencies and training identified. Standardization of processes formalized.

  4.2 What Results Did You Achieve?

0 points   Results showed little to no improvement over time.

1 point   Final results were positive, but didn't relate to the original goal/objective or were significantly lower than anticipated.

2 points   Final results directly related to original goal/objective. Results matched expectations.

Exhibit 24.2. California Team Excellence Award Criteria for 2001–2002, Cont'd

3 points   Final results directly related to original goal/objective, and were achieved in a more timely and cost-effective manner than anticipated.

4 points   Final results exceeded original goal/objective. Ancillary results/benefits of project identified. Improvements sustainable and permanent.

4.3 What Impact Did Your Project Have on the Organization?

0 points   Impact to organization has not been identified.

1 point   Project impact has minimal effect on the organization's overall goals/objectives.

2 points   Project had one-time impact on the organization.

3 points   Project resulted in the establishment of new standards, policies, procedures, or processes and has been documented. Project may be replicated elsewhere within the organization.

4 points   Project has resulted in a major change that impacts the organization's goals/objectives.

5. Presentation

12 points possible

5.1 How Well Did You Tell Your Story?

0 points   Presentation focused on one or two elements at the expense of a full telling of activities.

1 point   Presentation told a logical story from selection to results.

2 points   Presentation told a complete story with efforts made to enhance the audience's ability to understand all of the steps the team took.

3 points   Presentation told a robust story that was dynamic, exciting, and entertaining to the audience.

5.2 What Lessons Did You Learn?

2 points   The team provided limited insight into lessons learned and what the audience could learn from the team as a result.

3 points   The team identified potential lessons learned at the project/organizational level.

4 points   The team tied lessons learned to personal/professional growth.

5 points   The team conveyed how and why their activities created learning opportunities for the audience. Examples were provided that resonated with the audience on a personal and organizational level.

6 points   The team demonstrated evidence of personal and organizational transformation based on lessons learned by the team on this project.

5.3 Visual Presentation

0 points   Charts, graphs, and other aids supported the presentation.

1 point   Charts, graphs, and other aids enhanced the presentation.

2 points   The overall visual and aesthetic effect helped make the presentation interesting and entertaining.

3 points   The overall visual and aesthetic effect created a dynamic and exciting element to the full presentation.

CHAPTER 25

A Problem-Solving Training Program for Groups of Service Engineers

A Case Study

Ad Kleingeld and Harrie van Tuijl

SEVERAL YEARS AGO, a performance measurement and feedback system was developed in the field service districts of a supplier of photocopying equipment in The Netherlands. After implementation of the system, significant performance improvement was observed in the area of cost performance, while quality performance remained stable. This result led to the hypothesis that providing service engineers with performance feedback alone is not enough to improve performance in those areas lacking knowledge of cause-effect relationships (for example, quality), compared to areas where such information is more readily available (for example, cost).

Based on the assumption that cause-effect information is necessary in order to select or develop adequate task strategies, a training program was set up to help group leaders to gain a better understanding of the causes of performance variation among and within their teams. The training program closely followed the three phases of a problem-solving process: (1) defining the problem; (2) establishing problem causes; and (3) finding solutions to the problem. In Phase 1, statistical tools were introduced to assist in interpreting performance feedback in terms of the presence or absence of "problems" (defined as significant departures from an intended performance level or target). In Phase 2, a tool was developed participatively to categorize potential problem causes, with the help of team leaders and engineers. In Phase 3, the tool was used as an instrument in the search for causes of particular problems. These problems were defined both at the level of team performance and at the level of individual engineer performance. Details of the training program are presented and examples of the tools are shown.

Preliminary experiences with the program indicate that the tools were successfully applied to detect performance problems, establish causes, and implement solutions, both at the individual and the group level. A cooperative environment where individuals and groups actively share information is considered a precondition for effective use of these tools.

Background

The program described in this chapter was developed as part of a long-running project in eleven service districts of a company selling and servicing photocopiers in The Netherlands. Each district was headed by a district service manager and was made up of approximately twenty service engineers and two or three district technical specialists (very experienced engineers). The service department management wanted to optimize both quality and cost of service by providing the service engineers with valid feedback on their performance. A performance management approach was adopted in all service districts (Kleingeld, 1994) based on the Productivity Measurement and Enhancement System (ProMES) (Pritchard, 1990, 1995). The system provided service engineers with individual performance feedback on several performance indicators, all of which could be grouped into two main service engineer responsibilities, quality and costs. See Table 25.1 for a summary of the indicators and their relative importance.

Table 25.1. Performance Indicators

Responsibility Area (Product)	Measure (Indicator)	Description	Weight of the Indicator
Quality	Mean copies between calls	The average number of photocopies the client's machine has produced between two consecutive service calls	70

Table 25.1. Performance Indicators, Cont'd

Responsibility Area (Product)	Measure (Indicator)	Description	Weight of the Indicator
	Mean days between calls	The average number of days between two consecutive service calls on the same machine	30
	Percentage repeat calls	The percentage of calls that occur within five working days from the previous call on the same machine	65
Cost	Labor time per call	Average time spent per service call on maintenance and repair activities (minutes)	50
	Parts cost per call	Average amount spent on spare parts used per service call (monetary value)	55

Providing performance feedback to individual engineers caused a significant increase in overall performance (Kleingeld, 1994). This performance increase was mainly attributable to improvement on cost indicators, whereas performance on quality indicators remained stable. An assumption was made that cost performance can be improved by sticking to prescribed routines in servicing photocopiers, whereas quality improvement requires a problem-solving approach in order to find out the exact causes of performance variation. In order to improve quality problem-solving processes by service engineers, additional information was provided about their individual performance on the quality indicators (for example, which clients had called for a repeat visit, which types of complaints occurred most frequently, and so on). A performance increase on quality indicators was observed in the period following the provision of this information (Van Tuijl, Kleingeld, Schmidt, Kleinbeck, Pritchard & Algera, 1997).

Since the start of the project, a period of almost ten years using the ProMES system to measure and feed back performance information had elapsed, and performance increases had leveled off. Nevertheless, the assumption was that there was still room for improvement, given the existence of extensive performance variation both among and within service districts.

In other words, service engineers could learn from one another how to develop and apply effective and efficient task strategies, exchange relevant information, and experiment with alternative strategies.

A project was set up in order to teach service engineers a systematic problem-solving approach that could help discover optimal task strategies.

The premise was that performance variations within and among groups are opportunities for performance improvement.

In other words, the hypothesis was that further performance improvement would be possible only if the causes of performance variation could be found and removed, and if those causes were directly or indirectly controllable by service engineers.

The Problem-Solving Training Program

With the aim of furthering service engineers' insight into the causes of the underlying variation within their ProMES performance scores, a training program was set up for the districts' technical specialists, highly experienced service engineers with special responsibility for particular types of photocopiers. The machine malfunctions that appear to be irreparable by regular service engineers are assigned to these specialists. They also head technical meetings in their districts, in which they disseminate information on their types of photocopiers to other engineers and in which they provide technical support to individual engineers (for example, coaching of inexperienced engineers). In the last few years, the function of these specialists had expanded from merely being highly experienced service engineers to being responsible for the technical performance of the photocopiers and engineers within their segment of photocopiers (several similar types). The idea was that these district technical specialists would be able, given proper training, to act as problem-solving coaches for the service engineers.

The problem-solving model used was based on ideas developed by Kepner and Tregoe (1981) and consisted of three consecutive phases, also found in other prevailing problem-solving models (see, for example, Lipshitz & Bar-Ilan, 1996). The phases are (1) definition of the problem; (2) determination of the problem cause(s); and (3) selection of the problem solution. Following this problem-solving model, the training program design consisted of three phases, each providing the indicated tools, which are described further in the following sections.

Phase 1   Do we have a problem? If so, how should the problem be defined? (tools 1A, 1B, and 1C: locating significant performance differences)

Phase 2   Which potentially relevant problem causes can we think of? (tool 2: comprehensive set of potential problem causes)

Phase 3   Which particular cause could be responsible for this particular problem? (tools 3A and 3B: interactive search exercises)

Phase 1: Tools for Problem Definition

In this context, a problem was said to occur when an observed score on a performance indicator significantly deviated from a target value on that performance indicator, and the performance of the best-performing district/engineer was regarded as the target. Thus, the occurrence of statistically significant differences among the performance of districts (or among the performance of engineers within a district) was considered a "problem." This definition, although different from known approaches that focus on results remaining within specifications, was considered appropriate within this context, where the aim was to learn from performance differences.

In order to be able to detect significant performance differences among districts and among service engineers within the same district, three tools were developed. The aim of Phase 1 of the training was to teach the district technical specialists how to use these tools. All trainees took part in a general one-day introduction to problem solving, emphasizing the importance of a good problem definition as the basis for successfully analyzing and solving problems (Kepner & Tregoe, 1981). They also received a short introduction into descriptive and inferential statistics (in layman's terms to be able to interpret the graphical information in the three tools).

Although the ProMES system could provide feedback summed across types of photocopiers, all three tools (developed by the authors) provided information at the level of distinct photocopier models. This detail information about the individual and group performance had not been included in the feedback previously available and was considered to be the most useful for the trainees.

Tool 1A presents graphical information for one type of copier on the results obtained on the five performance indicators in the ProMES system plus an aggregate overall effectiveness score for the eleven districts (A through K) and the country as a whole (see Figure 25.1). The graphs should be interpreted as follows: if two intervals do not overlap, one should assume that the difference between the two means is significant. In other words, there is a low probability that the difference occurred by chance. If the intervals "touch," this probability is 5 to 10 percent. For example, the "overall performance" graph shows that only one district (D) has an overall score that differs significantly from the national score. Also, the scores in districts B, H, and K are significantly higher than the scores obtained by districts C, D, F, and G. For this particular type of photocopiers, the District D technical specialist should be interested in taking a closer look at his group's performance.

Figure 25.1. Perforance Data for All Districts over a Period of Six Months

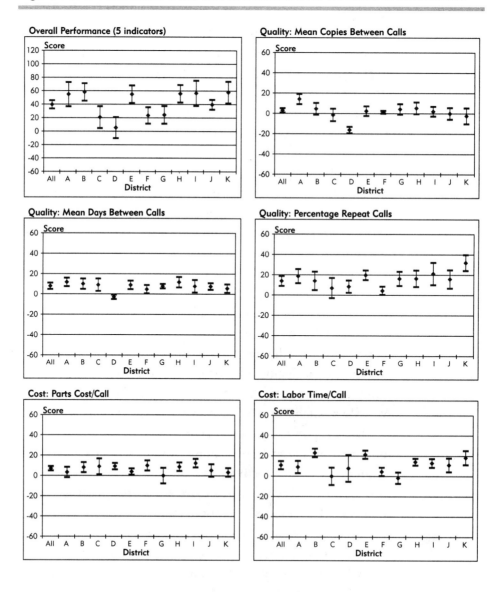

Figure 25.2 presents an example of the output from tool 1B for District D (excerpt). Whereas tool 1A provides mean scores and intervals irrespective of the actual sequence of the monthly scores, tool 1B enables a comparison of a district's monthly effectiveness scores over time to other districts or to the average of all districts. Figure 25.2 shows that the difference between the overall score of District D and the national score appears to increase. The sudden decrease in district D on the indicator "labor time/call" (only shown in tool 1A as a comparatively large interval) especially seems grounds for further analysis.

Figure 25.2. Performance Trends of District D Compared to All Districts

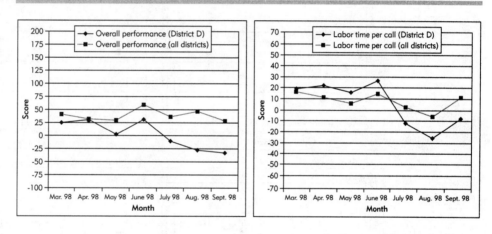

Whereas tools 1A and 1B can be used to identify differences among the performance of districts, tool 1C identifies significant differences within a district. Figure 25.3 shows tool 1C for District D. The engineers ID numbers 97 through 499 are in descending order of number of years with the company. Number 204 is the district technical specialist, while number 499 joined the company three months ago. In this example, attention is drawn to the results of the two least experienced engineers, which explain the sudden decrease of the "labor time/call" indicator seen in tool 1B. Also the difference among the more experienced engineers (204, 324, and 347 versus 97, 119, and 380) is of interest.

Figure 25.3. Performance Data for District D over a Period of Six Months

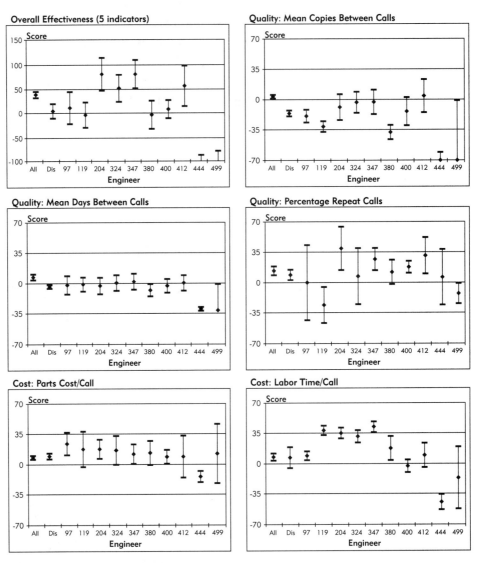

Note: All = all districts, Dis = District D

Phase 2: A Tool for the Discovery of Problem Causes

On the basis of Phase 1, in which the district technical specialists learned how to use tools 1A, 1B, and 1C, the trainees were able to identify performance differences worth further investigation. The purpose of Phase 2 was to define a set of potential problem causes underlying the performance differences. So in this second phase, a general search for potentially relevant problem causes was undertaken with the purpose of developing a search tool to be used later on in Phase 3 when the technical specialists would be looking for the causes of specific problems as detected by tools 1A, 1B, or 1C.

The knowledge and experience of specialists and engineers was used in generating a comprehensive list of possible causes of performance variation.

In Phase 2, six groups of district technical specialists and one group of service engineers went through a brainstorming session in which they had to develop all possible causes of performance variation on each of the five performance indicators. Fishbone diagrams were used as a framework for generating causes.

The result was a list of over four hundred possible problem causes. These causes were first categorized by the researchers by clustering related causes and by removing duplication. Next, the district technical specialists and a group of representatives from the service engineers refined the categorization proposed by the researchers. The final list of fifty potential problem causes consisted of nine main categories (number of items in parentheses). A representative example is given for each.

1. Work procedures: keeping up with procedures, customizing procedures (7), such as "adhering to repair and maintenance procedure."

2. The service engineer (7), such as "knowledge."

3. Group (vs. individual) performance focus (3), such as "cooperation."

4. The client's photocopier operator (7), such as "operator's knowledge of and commitment to photocopier."

5. The photocopier (6), such as "right machine at the right place."

6. Materials (4), such as "availability of spare parts."

7. Circumstances (4), such as "time pressure."

8. Environment (7), such as "support and instructions from technical specialists."

9. Measurement and control system (ProMES, appraisal and reward) (5), including "weighting factors/priorities, competition."

Through a questionnaire, the Phase 2 participants indicated (1) whether each cause could in actual practice affect performance differences (yes-no); (2) how strong the effect of each cause would be on the quality and cost indicators (very strong, strong, weak); and (3) which individuals or groups are the main factor of influence on each cause.

On the basis of the results, four checklists of causes were composed (quality—district differences; cost—district differences; quality—individual differences; and cost—individual differences), comprising tool 2. The fifty causes were ranked according to perceived impact. The impact score was calculated by multiplying the average ratings on the first question—likely cause, value between 0 and 1—and the second question—strength of the effect, value between 0 and 2. For each cause, the influential individuals or groups (constituencies) were shown. As an example, Figure 25.4 shows the fifteen causes ranked highest for district differences on "quality."

Figure 25.4. Top Fifteen Possible Causes of Differences Among Districts

Rank	Factor	Description	Category	Impact	engineer	group	district technical specialist	district service manager	central technical support	planning, call reception	service management	human resources	marketing and sales	logistics	client	supplier	university	nobody	other
1	2.1	Knowledge of the engineer	service engineer	1.32	+++	+	++	+	+++	+	+								
2	2.2	Experience of the engineer	service engineer	1.17	+++	++	+++	++	+	++									
3	1.2	Following the repair and maintenance procedure	work procedures	1.10	+++	++	+++	+	++										
4	3.1	Interpretation and sensible application of procedures	group focus	1.00	+++	++	+++	++	++	+									
5	1.3	Repair and maintenance; exceeding the requirements	work procedures	0.93	+++	++	+++	+	+										
6	3.2	Cooperation	group focus	0.87	+++	++	+++	++	+										
7	2.7	Motivation of the engineer	service engineer	0.85	+++	+	+	+++	++		++	+			+				
8	8.5	District technical specialist: support and instructions	environment	0.82	++	+	+++	+++	++	+	+								
9	3.3	Long vs. short term effectiveness focus	group focus	0.72	+++	++	+++	++	+										
10	4.1	Expectations of the client/key operator	key operator	0.70	++	+	+	+		+	+		+++		+++				
11	5.3	Photocopier state	machine	0.65	+++	++	++	+	+		+		+		+				
12	8.6	District service manager: support and instructions	environment	0.59	++	+	++	+++		+	++								
13	1.4	Customizing repair and maintenance	work procedures	0.59	+++	++	+++	+	+				+		++				
14	1.1	Arrival procedure	work procedures	0.57	+++	++	+++	+		+									
15	9.2	Weighing factors, priorities in the ProMES system	meas't/control system	0.55	++	++	++	+++	++		++						++		

Constituency

Note: the higher the number of +, the higher the perceived influence

Phase 3: Using the Tools in Interactive Search Meetings

The purpose of the third phase was to let groups of technical specialists (all responsible in their own district for the same type(s) of photocopiers) define actual performance problems by means of tools 1A, 1B, and 1C and find the most probable cause(s) of those problems by means of the list of causes developed in Phase 2.

A summary of the group meetings, which comprise tool 3, is given in Table 25.2.

Table 25.2. Interactive Search Meetings (Tools 3A and 3B)

Tool 3A: Meeting on Group-Level Problems	Tool 3B: Meeting on Individual-Level Problems
Training group composition	Presentation of problem by focus specialist (tools 1C, 2)
6–8 specialists	
variation: high and low scores on quality and cost	Round-robin discussion by colleagues (specialists of other districts)
Presentation by specialists of hypothesized causes of high and low scores for each indicator separately (tools 1A, 1B, 2)	Formulation of advice by pairs of specialists
	Reaction of focus specialist
Discussion of potentially effective actions	Experimentation period (put advice into practice)
Experimentation period	Evaluation
Evaluation	

The groups were composed such that each group had a member with significantly higher scores in his district on one or more of the performance indicators compared with the other group members. Preferably, the mixture of scores in a group would be such that there would be no clearly superior or inferior performers; every technical specialist would do well on some performance indicators and less well on other ones. The intent was to create a learning environment for all group members so that everyone could both learn from others and be able to teach others how to improve.

Before the training sessions, each participant had to fulfill two homework assignments. The first assignment involved using two different tools to identify causes. First the participant was to locate high/low scores his district had realized on a particular performance indicator on a certain model. (These high/low scores could be made visible by tools 1A and 1B.) The participant then was to search for causes of these high/low scores by means of tool 2, the list of problem causes. Most trainees got both a high and a low score to investigate. This was possible because sometimes a high score on one performance indicator was accompanied by a low score on another indicator and also because most district technical specialists were responsible for more than one photocopier model. At the training session, they had to present the results of their search processes.

The second assignment was to scrutinize the performance of his district's service engineers by means of tool 1C and to detect significant performance differences among engineers on a particular photocopier model. Next they were to search for potential causes of those differences using the list (tool 2). At the training session, they had to present the results of their search process, on the basis of which their colleagues asked questions and made recommendations. The following is an example of an interactive search meeting on a group level problem.

In one of the sessions, it became apparent that two districts achieved significantly higher overall effectiveness scores on a particular type of photocopier. Both specialists attributed this to the same primary cause: "Going beyond the minimal maintenance requirements." They pointed out that the standard preventative maintenance procedure was not sufficient to take care of specific weaknesses of this photocopier model. By consistently checking all the critical features, malfunctions would be prevented and a higher long-term quality would be achieved. In fact, the overall score consisted of a very high score on the quality indicators combined with just below average scores on the cost indicators, strongly suggesting that gains on the quality indicators more than offset the additional investment of parts and labor. One specialist also mentioned the cause "long-term versus short-term focus." The other specialist stressed the importance of creating a team that enjoys tackling these technical issues ("cooperation" and "motivation"). Together with his engineers, he had compiled a checklist for use on this type of copier.

One of the specialists whose group had achieved significantly lower effectiveness scores attributed them to a single large customer, whose key operators had insufficient "knowledge of and commitment to the photocopier," notwithstanding attempts to remedy this condition. Tool 1C showed that engineers in his district who did not service this customer had higher effectiveness scores than those that did, albeit mostly lower than the scores obtained in the two high-scoring districts. Other specialists' explanations for their districts' lower scores included the causes "key operator's knowledge of and commitment to the photocopier" and "machine design failures." The latter cause reflected a passive attitude rather than the proactive attitude chosen by the high-scoring districts. Eventually it was decided to use the checklists in four districts (instead of one) and to use the tools to evaluate whether these checklists should be used nationwide.

Thus the interactive search meetings led to a more widespread adoption of procedures developed by high-performing groups.

This type of approach fits very nicely into the problem-solving and process improvement criteria cited in Chapter 24.

Preliminary Results

Most specialists were able to analyze performance differences using the tools for problem definition and determination of causes. In several instances, specific and controllable causes were detected, often referring to differences in work strategies (for example, helping and instructing the customer's key operator, weighing the pros and cons of replacing a spare part versus repairing or cleaning it, conducting thorough preventative checks, and so on). Specialists were generally pleased with the insight the tools provided them into the technical performance of their group and its members. The tools helped focus attention on those types of copiers where problems had been signaled or where future problems were developing. In several districts, specialists used the tools together with their group of engineers as a basis for optimizing group strategies. The tools, especially tool 1C, were considered useful for determining coaching needs of individual technicians.

In most cases where specialists had to explain their high district scores, they attributed it to teamwork.

In most cases where specialists had to explain their high district scores, they attributed it to teamwork. The authors drew the conclusion that those district technical specialists were good at coaching their service engineers.

As a result of the training program and the use of the tools, three issues came to the fore that deserve mentioning: controllability of causes, preferred strategies of engineers, and reward distribution and cooperation within and among districts.

Often the causes for performance differences were not under the direct control of all specialists or engineers. We have seen, for example, that uncontrollable customers' characteristics have a significant impact on the performance effectiveness. When we consider the way the work is structured, we observe that service engineers are information-dependent on their colleagues, on their own technical specialist, and on support groups. (See Chapter 20.) Also, service engineers directly influence one another's performance. Every service engineer can in principle be assigned to service any photocopier of a particular type in his district; therefore his point of departure always is the previous service quality level. Therefore, the data could imply differences where none really exist (or fail to show differences that do exist). In order to take into account the interdependencies between engineers, system boundaries could be redefined from the individual to the group. The focus should be the performance of the group, and individual service engineers should be made primarily responsible for contributing to overall group performance instead of individual performance.

With respect to the second issue, there appeared to be roughly two types of service engineers: *"costs strategists"* and *"quality strategists."* Typical for the first group was a short-term time perspective. By working quickly and neglecting preventative maintenance, they realized good scores on costs indicators, without endangering quality in the short-term. Typical of the second category was a long-term perspective. By using adequate labor hours and spare parts, this group invested in long-term quality. Although this group knew that doing so might decrease their ProMES scores, at least in the short term, they "felt responsible toward the client" and "went for quality." It became evident that district level performance was influenced by the mix of costs strategists and quality strategists present.

In the case of a well-balanced mix, two important objectives came closer to realization. One objective was a fast response to clients who call for repair. Realization of this objective became more difficult in periods with a high workload, and even more difficult when the majority of service engineers belonged to the quality strategists category. The second objective was long-term effectiveness. Realization of this objective was easier in periods with a lower workload, when ample time was available to work on quality. Of course, this objective was difficult to realize when the majority of service engineers in the district belonged to the category of costs strategists. Solutions to this problem include regrouping engineers to obtain a better mix of cost and quality strategists or, preferably, making a conscious decision to change the strategies depending on circumstances.

However, this presupposes that engineers are willing and able to be flexible in their strategies.

The need for exchange of performance-related information created by the problem-solving program made obvious the rather high task interdependence, both within a district and among specialists across different districts. When the tools were first put into practice, the researchers noticed some reluctance on the part of engineers and specialists to exchange information. An important reason appeared to be hidden in the company's appraisal and reward system, which was based on relative ratings of employee performance within a district.

This approach apparently stimulated competition between service engineers instead of cooperation. This is the third issue that surfaced as a result of the training program. When group members consider themselves negatively goal-interdependent and reward-interdependent, cooperation will be less likely (Van Vijfeijken, Kleingeld, Van Tuijl, & Algera, 2001; Wageman & Baker, 1997). Yet, cooperation is required to stimulate the sharing of insights about cause-effect relationships. The more the engineers and specialists perceive themselves as cooperatively interdependent, the more their problem-solving activities will be in line with the intended problem-solving model.

When the company became aware of the inconsistency that competition was rewarded where cooperation was required, it agreed to implement a more appropriate appraisal and reward system.

Conclusion

This problem-solving training program was developed as an answer to the problem that feedback alone, even if accepted and accompanied by accepted goals, is not enough to improve performance improvement where there is inadequate knowledge on cause-effect relationships. Groups of service specialists and engineers were provided with tools to successively define problems, find causes in line with the problem definition, and arrive at solutions consistent with the most probable cause(s) found.

Preliminary experiences indicate that this approach has been successful. It, however, presupposes the availability of a performance measurement system for detecting valid and controllable performance differences among groups and individuals. In this specific context, having a reward system that promotes cooperation and an increased exchange of information appeared to be a necessary precondition for turning these groups of engineers into high-performing teams.

CHAPTER 26

Creating and Measuring Ways to Win Together

Theodore A. Wohlfarth
and Michael J. Stevens

THE IMPORTANCE OF TEAMS is conventional wisdom in business today, but many managers struggle to build teams that collaborate effectively. Why is this the case? The answer to this question is, in many ways, the premise of this Fieldbook. At the heart of the answer is a systemic issue: teamwork requires fundamental changes to traditional organizational and management systems. This chapter describes how teams can become more effective if people understand how to practice and measure both collaboration and competition. The goal is to give people a new way to experience and measure collaboration between teams, the EnTeam approach. This approach consists of two elements:

1. Creating learning opportunities for teams to collaborate with each other; and

2. Measuring the teams' performance in collaboration.

Both elements are addressed, first in the simple realm of sports, where the rules are static, the goals are predefined, and scorekeeping is unambiguous, and second in business, where the rules are not static, goals are diverse, and scorekeeping is often nebulous. Comparison between sports and business is useful because both must be restructured from win-lose contests into win-win events before collaboration between teams is practicable.

The chapter is organized into the following sections:

- Why measuring collaboration is important;
- How collaboration in sports and games can be structured and measured;
- How collaboration in business can be structured and measured; and
- How this process for measuring collaboration can help work teams to be more collaborative and successful.

In order to create a context for the EnTeam approach, it is first useful, however, to consider the general issue of how people's mental models affect their ability to change.

Mental Models and Change

Companies must overcome some deep-rooted assumptions if they want to succeed with collaborative work teams. One of the assumptions is thinking that the only way to measure success is on a win-lose, or competitive, basis. Teams need a scoreboard that measures collaboration.

American society has a very strong cultural bias in favor of spontaneously and intuitively perceiving relationships as win-lose contests, and in many respects this very thinking contributes to our economic and even democratic successes as a people. Win-lose contests such as elections and sales contests give the competitors an objective way to measure their successful performance. Measurement is an essential step for improving performance. This has always been true with win-lose competition. However, the thesis of this chapter is that business teams can improve their success as collaborators by measuring their performance in win-win situations. If managers want to improve collaboration, they need to develop ways to measure it.

If managers want to improve collaboration, they need to develop ways to measure it.

Part of the explanation for management's intuitive bias in favor of measuring performance in win-lose contests is the mindset that grows from experience with organized games and sports. Most people grow up watching or playing on sports teams. Although traditional sports can teach many useful lessons about teams and teamwork, the sports metaphor is hazardous to business teams because it perpetuates the zero-sum mental model that is inherent in win-lose contests. But our premise in this chapter is that companies that want to foster a culture in which collaborative work teams can thrive need to counter the idea that work relationships should be seen as zero-sum games.

One step toward building a collaborative culture is to introduce games and sports that measure success in terms of win-win strategies rather than win-lose. For example, traditional games like baseball or poker do not give players any insights into the possibility that one can win by helping outsiders to succeed. Imagine what would happen if a player left his dugout during a Little League baseball game, walked over to the other dugout, and gave the other team ideas for how they could improve their score. This would be an absurdity in the eyes of baseball players. This form of collaboration would be "treason" and might even lead to dismissal from the team.

The same would be true with poker: only a fool would trust the opponent by openly showing his or her hand. However, our argument is that such behaviors are foolish only when viewed through the lens of win-lose competition. The rules to these traditional games are human inventions. We are free to change them.

By changing the rules, collaboration among teams and individuals can be measured as accurately as traditional win-lose competition is measured.

Why Measure Collaboration?

"What you can measure you can manage" is an essential tenet of management thinking. Without measurement, the development of a coherent improvement strategy is problematic. Measurement is at the heart of most continuous improvement efforts, such as total quality management (TQM). Unless individuals and teams can measure whether or not they are improving, they have no basis for gauging their progress. For example, a baseball coach can fine-tune a team by tracking specific measurements of performance, such as batting averages and fielding percentages. Typically, the coach uses these measurements to find ways to improve the team, and the goal is that one team wins more games. However, quantification can be just as useful for improving collaborative performance, with the goal being that all teams improve performance.

The following illustration demonstrates how the way performance is measured directly affects the kind of performance people give. A printing company running three shifts kept separate production records for each shift. Managers evaluated the shift workers based on each shift's separate production performance. As one would predict, the result was that competition between the shifts was intense. Employees devoted significant time and energy to making sure that their own shift always had better production numbers than the next. Some of this competition was good. For example, it helped workers focus on output and efficiency. But some of the effort was counterproductive, such as when workers would run machines to the very end of their shift and leave the next shift to do the needed maintenance and cleanup. Supervisors tried to control the problem through various work rules and regulations, but these strategies proved ineffective due to the complicated nature of the work runs and variations in production run length.

After considering ways to measure collaboration among these three shifts, the managers began to measure results that reflected the ability to work together. For example, the managers stopped measuring the production of each shift separately and began to measure the total production of the three shifts together. The result was eliminating the temptation to manipulate the work to make one's own shift look good.

Just as competitive skills and strategies must be developed, measured, and coached to improve performance, so must collaborative skills and strategies. In fact, because of its novelty for many employees and managers, *collaboration often requires even more coaching and nurturing than does competition.* For many of us, the most familiar measures of competitive contests are the numbers shown on the scoreboard at sporting events. Yet there is nothing inherent about competition that makes it more easily measured than collaboration.

There is nothing inherent about competition that makes it more easily measured than collaboration.

Both are equally abstract concepts—quantification of one is no more difficult than the other. However, few of us grow up learning how to measure collaboration. This logic was the motivation behind the development of the EnTeam system for rethinking the rules and scoring strategies for a wide variety of games and sports. EnTeam games grew out of experiences coaching children's sports, recognizing that children could benefit from keeping score on a win-win basis, as well as a win-lose basis.

This logic also extends to business. If managers want employees to understand how to operate on a win-win basis, they need to give them experience using new rules and a scorecard that measures win-win performance. Why limit the mental models when it is easy and practical to measure success both on a win-lose and a win-win basis? Organizations have used a wide variety of EnTeam games such as volleyball, baseball, bowling, pool, poker, checkers, and tennis to build more collaborative cultures. By using the collaborative EnTeam rules and scoring tools as they play the games in an experiential training format, new concepts of teamwork, interpersonal communication, and collaboration unfold for participants. This occurs because the scores in EnTeam games measure the ability of two sides to bring out the best in each other. EnTeam games can score collaboration just as effectively as traditional scoring systems can measure competition.

How to Measure Collaboration
Measuring Collaboration in Games and Sports

Since most people learn to measure competition through watching or participating in games and sports, it is useful to introduce the process for measuring collaboration by modifying these traditional activities. EnTeam games are modified versions of sports and games that would be familiar to most employees. When people see that they can score collaboration as accurately as they can score competition, they begin to see new possibilities for measuring collaboration and teamwork on the job.

In traditional games, the score measures the performance of one side in outperforming the other. When the game is over, one side is the winner and the other side is the loser. However, it is fairly simple to change a win-lose game, like poker, into a win-win game that measures collaboration. Traditional poker is a win-lose game replete with behaviors that are destructive to cooperation: bluffing, withholding information, deceiving other players, and concealing the truth. Poker is also highly individualistic because it pits each person against everyone else. It is the classic zero-sum game: the amount of money won is equal to the amount of money lost.

The process of redesigning poker from a win-lose game into a win-win game starts with changing the objective. In traditional poker, each player's objective is to win the pot (the money paid by all the players for the right to participate in the game) either by getting the best hand or by inducing players with better hands to drop out of the game. EnTeam poker, however, discards the traditional poker objective of redistributing the pot of money among the players and redefines the objective as increasing the total amount of money in the pot. The EnTeam rules challenge the players to work together as a team in competition against the statistical probabilities of poker. A team wins by beating a pair of aces, which is the most probable winning hand in five-card stud with eight players (Wohlfarth, 2001). The players are thus in league with each other against the statistical odds of poker. A team can win if it can best what Hoyle denotes "the most probable winning hand" (Morehead, 1959). The successful player in traditional poker has a combination of luck, an understanding of the laws of probability, and a talent for mind games—reading other people and deceiving them. However, the successful player in EnTeam poker is the one who has the ability to work with the other players (against the odds of poker itself), rather than against the other players. In EnTeam poker, players will all win the pot (or all lose the pot) together. Thus, the objectives, the rules, and the scoring strategy of poker are redesigned to measure the ability of players to work together as a team.

Measuring competitive performance is also familiar to anyone who has played on a sports team. For example, a volleyball team measures its success by scoring the number of times it hits the ball so that the other side cannot return it. At the end of the game, the numbers on the scoreboard measure which team outperformed the other. But in EnTeam volleyball (Wohlfarth, 2001) teams score points by hitting the ball so the other side *can* return it. The rules and scoring for EnTeam volleyball are set up such that both sides race against the clock to hit the ball over the net as many times as possible in three minutes with everyone participating. In other words, each person on the receiving side of the net must hit the ball before it can cross the net and score a point. To further emphasize the collaborative nature of the game, the players from each team are on *both* sides of the net (that is, half of the members of the two teams are on either side of the net). Therefore the players understand very clearly before the game even starts that the teams are in a new relationship.

EnTeam volleyball is different from traditional volleyball (as invented in 1895 by William Morgan) in a number of other ways, as well. For example, three or more teams participate in a match, and a match consists of each team playing one game with each of the other teams. The teams also have the option of using two balls simultaneously, and the coaches from both teams plan strategy together. At the end of the match, the teams all have individual scores, collective scores, and an overall match score. The scores thus reflect the performance of the teams individually and collectively, and depend on:

- The skill of the players on the teams;
- Their ability to collaborate with each of the other teams in the match; and
- Chance—the random bounce of the ball.

The thrill of the contest is focused on who is best at working with the other side, rather than who is best at outperforming or dominating the competition. The hero is the one who is the best collaborator. In EnTeam games, the score measures the skill, cooperativeness, and luck of both sides working in collaboration.

Measuring Collaboration in Business

Business and sporting games have many useful parallels. Sometimes business is a simple win-lose game like traditional sports, but more often businesses involve complex webs of both win-win and win-lose relationships. One useful way to sort out the complexities of business is economic game theory. Game theory can help companies identify when they are in win-lose contests and when they are in win-win relationships. Game theory can also help companies change some win-lose contests into win-win relationships. Game theory gives a disciplined approach to thinking about the way decisions are made in interdependent situations. In their lucid exposition of game theory for business, Brandenburger and Nalebuff (1996) introduce the concept of "co-opetition," which is their term for the dynamic interplay of competition and cooperation that exists in most business relationships.

For example, if you are buying a car, the dealer seeks a high price and you seek a low price. It is a competitive contest. The dealer "wins" and you "lose" to the degree that the final price you pay is extremely high, and vice versa. However, the potentially complex nature of this business relationship can be reflected in such questions as: What are the chances you will buy a second car from that dealer? What will you tell others about that dealer? Are you the motor pool buyer for a large corporation? In the long run, unless the buyer and seller both walk away from the deal with a "win," then both have "lost" in important ways. Brandenburger and Nalebuff suggest that competition and cooperation are present in every transaction.

Businesses can thus be more successful if they understand how to keep a proper balance between competition and cooperation. Businesses can thus be more successful if they understand how to keep a proper balance between competition and cooperation, and one very useful step for finding this balance is to measure *both* competition *and* cooperation.

Our experience with measuring collaboration is that it can be successful even in some very challenging business situations. However, introducing such measurement is not a silver bullet. The qualities of open-mindedness and the willingness to participate are requisite. When the company is ready to learn, the results can be significant.

By way of illustration, Illinois Power used collaborative EnTeam games to transform a zero-sum culture at a power plant where hostility between management and labor was seriously damaging productivity. First, the managers and supervisors learned how to set up and measure cooperation in EnTeam games. They learned to transform win-lose games like Ping-Pong and poker into win-win opportunities by playing EnTeam versions of those games. New ways of approaching previously intractable relationship problems began to come to mind. The manager in charge of operations said it was like "taking down a brick wall one brick at a time" as gradually the relationships began to change. However, playing the EnTeam games was only the beginning. A key to maintaining the newly emerging relationships was to figure out ways of measuring those behaviors and results that reflected collaboration on the job.

For instance, one of the specific troubles that plagued the plant was the habit of finding fault with the person who caused a problem, rather than finding a solution to its underlying root cause. People spent time pointing fingers at each other, rather than exploring together how the processes could be improved. Time and energy were thus wasted, and productivity was undermined.

The situation improved when a group of managers and union members worked together to form process-improvement teams. They followed the same model used to change games from win-lose to win-win, namely:

- Establish an environment in which both sides can win;
- Define a goal that can be achieved collaboratively;
- Create new rules that make clear how people are to interact; and
- Set up new measures of cooperative performance.

One measure used by Illinois Power was the number of ideas for improving work that were initiated by each of the four shifts. Another measure was the number of initiatives that made the transition from concept into action. A third was the specific benefits generated by the initiatives (such as time saving, reducing cost, and increasing production). By keeping score of their ability to collaborate, people continued to focus on ways they could win together. According to the union steward for the plant, one noticeable result was that the work environment improved significantly.

 In another example, one of the teams created a cost saving in excess of $200,000, while yet another resolved an environmental issue that could have led to a costly penalty from the Environmental Protection Agency.

Steps for introducing people to the process for converting win-lose contests into win-win relationships include the following:

1. Identify an actual low-risk collaboration challenge where two sides must work with each other to perform successfully;

2. Relate the actual collaboration work challenge the team members face on the job to one of the EnTeam games (for example, people in risk management, such as insurance, could use EnTeam poker);

3. Play the EnTeam game and measure the performance of the two sides collaborating together;

4. Debrief the exercise by discussing ways to improve the skills needed to compete against the actual problem on the job—not against people;

5. Play again to see how much the teams can improve their scores together; compare scores between the first challenge and the second;

6. Identify the strategies used in the game and then explore how they might be applied to the process of building teamwork for the organization; and

7. Put the strategies into practice on the job and continue to measure progress for a period of time long enough to get meaningful results.

By applying these steps to an actual low-risk work challenge, participants can develop strategies to apply the process of measuring collaboration to their own work and eventually to higher risk situations. Then it is a relatively straightforward matter for them to develop their own plan of action for building teamwork. (For an example of directly applying a win-win to a particular set of activities, namely meetings, see Klein's chapter in Part 6 on new meeting behaviors.)

Participants in EnTeam games accrue the following benefits:

1. Discovering how to move the power of competition away from *competition against people* and toward *competition against problems* (the skills needed to excel in collaboration are fundamentally different from the skills needed to make someone else lose);

2. Learning new ways to transform win-lose situations into win-win relationships (starting with familiar win-lose sports such as baseball, volleyball, and tennis or games like poker, pool, or chess, participants play the games with EnTeam rules and scoring methods);

3. Experiencing a paradigm shift to a new mental model that defines "winning" as the process of helping others perform their best (with EnTeam games, the better you can get the other team to perform, the more points you can score); and

4. Seeing ways to apply the process to building collaboration with people from diverse groups and backgrounds (the EnTeam games create a metaphor that people can naturally and easily extend into other areas of work and life).

Although there are many enlightening parallels between businesses and sporting teams, there is one difference worth noting, which is that businesses can typically transition to collaboration with much greater ease than sports teams. This is so because businesses often find it in their long-term best interest to establish win-win relationships with others. For instance, a printing machine vendor and a printing company might be viewed in some ways as competitors on different teams. That is, the win-lose business model would suggest that the vendor "wins" in this relationship if it sells a basic machine with few features at a higher price, whereas the printing company can "win" only if it buys the most elaborately featured machine at the lowest price. However, these two businesses are also in a collaborative relationship, because if the vendor fails to deliver the needed equipment on time, then the printing company cannot fill its orders and suffers. In a similar fashion, if the printing company fails to provide a stable source of business income over time for the vendor through its purchases, then the vendor suffers. Thus, one can see how these two businesses have a complex relationship that allows for *both* adversarial *and* collaborative relationships. If the vendor and the printing company can determine a way to keep score of how well they work together, they could improve their collective chances of success.

Measuring Collaboration Among Teams

Building teamwork between teams adds another level of complexity.

While building teamwork among the members of just one team is challenging work, building teamwork between teams adds another level of complexity.

For example, if the engineering and design groups are working together efficiently and productively as an operations team, we cannot necessarily assume that they will work with the marketing and sales teams in an equally effective manner. However, the EnTeam approach for measuring collaboration can also be applied to the relationships between teams. The following illustration provides a good example of this.

> Collaboration between the managers and unionized employees was dramatically improved at the James River Corporation's Hazelwood, Missouri, plant by using EnTeam's experiential games. The games were only one part of a comprehensive, integrated six-month training and development intervention that also included debriefing discussions focused on different aspects of team building, as well as the creation of consensus-based action planning strategies for improving communications and collaboration among employees. To start, the twenty-eight managers and supervisors set a goal in June 1996 to improve teamwork among all workers. This program included a series of two-hour workshops held bi-weekly. Each workshop included an EnTeam game, combined with a discussion focused on a relevant aspect of team building. In the process, the management team created an action plan for improving its communications and cooperation with the union members, who then prioritized the top three objectives for the manager into the following statement:
>
> "During the upcoming months, the managers and supervisors will have:
>
> 1. Treated employees the way they want to be treated;
>
> 2. Found solutions, not fault; and
>
> 3. Communicated clearly and honestly."
>
> Each month during the EnTeam program, and again six months later, the union members graded the managers and supervisors as a team. On a four-point scale, the employees scored their agreement with statements about the behavior of managers and supervisors. The result was a significant improvement in each of these three priorities during the EnTeam program. And, more importantly, the union members gave the team of managers and supervisors high scores six months after the program was over. Net revenue at the plant went from $10 million in the red the year before the program to $4 million in the black following it. The managers and

supervisors continue to use the action plan that they developed during the EnTeam program.

See Chapter 11 for a description of the importance of rewarding team performance rather than just individual performance.

Figure 26.1 shows the progress the union employees saw in their managers and supervisors. The dark bars show the percentage of workers who agree that their managers were communicating clearly and honestly.

Figure 26.1. Progress on Honest Communication

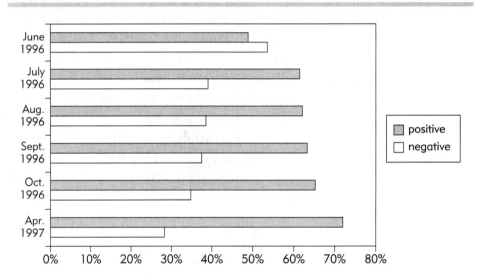

The percentage of the union members who reported that managers and supervisors were "communicating clearly and honestly" increased from 47 percent at the beginning of the EnTeam Program to 72 percent following the program, while disagreement with the statement went from 53 percent to 28 percent. The plant manager during this period reported that the EnTeam program "helped improve communication skills among the management, supervisors, and hourly ranks, which was key to the turnaround that has kept the facility open."

Conclusion

This chapter explored ways in which an individual's mental models can unobtrusively predispose him or her for competition rather than collaboration. This can be a significant roadblock, keeping teamwork and collaboration from emerging. EnTeam's unique and innovative approach to playing and scoring traditional games can be used as a practical method for getting people to become receptive to new modes of thinking about teamwork and collaboration. The success of this approach is based on the assumption that the way things are measured can very powerfully predispose or constrain the way people perceive their options. The natural predisposition to see everything in terms of a competitive contest can be countered by introducing methods to measure cooperation. People have an instinctive desire to improve what they do, and measuring cooperative performance gives them a method for gauging their rate of improvement. Just as traditional games provide an objective score for measuring competition, EnTeam games provide an objective score for measuring cooperation. One of the underlying premises that makes the EnTeam approach work is that it can be an intuitively appealing and non-threatening method for people to start exploring these new possibilities in a powerful new learning environment.

CHAPTER 27

Keeping Teams Afloat

Critical Coaching Competencies in Today's Team-Based Organizations

Sarah L. Bodner and Lori Bradley

MOST ORGANIZATIONS MAKING THE TRANSITION TO TEAMS have put forth effort to educate and prepare employees to become effective team members. Often, however, insufficient effort is given to the training and preparation of managers and team coaches. This approach is inconsistent with research showing that the transition to teams is most difficult for managers and team coaches.

Considering the level of difficulty and the crucial role managers and coaches play in the success of teams, their development should be considered a priority. This need should be taken into account in the initial planning and development stages of moving to a team-based structure; and the need should continue to be met, through various support functions, as the organization moves through the stages of a teaming initiative. An extensive survey of teaming and leadership research was performed in order to identify the most critical competencies needed to succeed as a team coach.

**Those
competencies
and their
subsequent
skill sets were
found to fall
into three
groupings—
knowledge,
tools, and
actions.**

Those competencies and their subsequent skill sets were found to fall into three groupings—knowledge, tools, and actions. The *knowledge* grouping comprises the *theory component* of coaching competencies, which is the "why" part of the coaching equation. It includes knowledge of organizational culture and environment, of teams and organizational design, and of transitional leadership. The *tools* grouping is the *skills component* of coaching competencies, serving as the "how" in the coaching equation. Skills that fall under the tools grouping include coaching skills, the skill to develop teams and individuals, understanding of team dynamics, and communication skills. The *actions* grouping is the *application component* of coaching competencies, providing answers to the questions of "when" to do "what." Here knowledge and tools combine with the wisdom of knowing when to apply the competencies of effective coaching. Each of the three broad groupings and their respective competencies is shown in Table 27.1 and will be discussed further in the following sections.

Table 27.1. Coaching Competencies and Subsequent Skill Sets

Knowledge	Tools	Actions
Organizational Culture and Environment	Coaching Skills	Team Processes
Team and Organizational Design	Individual Team Member Development	Performance Guidance
Transition Leadership	Team Development	
	Team Dynamics	
	Communication	

It is important to note that while categorizing the coaching competencies, the authors have purposefully refrained from assigning a sequence. The order of importance varies largely from organization to organization and from team to team. A competency that may be the most critical for one particular coach may be the least important for another. Competency importance depends largely on the type of team, the stage of team implementation, and the stage of team development.

Knowledge

An understanding of the theory of teams and organizations serves as a knowledge base for a team coach. This knowledge creates the foundation that guides the coach in the use of various coaching tools and actions. Knowledge competencies include organizational culture and environment, team and organizational design, and knowledge of transitional leadership.

Organizational culture and environment is the knowledge of the context of the organization—the organizational norms, behaviors, and expectations. The coach must understand how the culture and environment affect the team, when he or she should act as a buffer between the team and the organization, and what cultural habits need to be changed.

A coach also needs to have an understanding of organizational change so that he or she can effectively guide the team through the challenges that come with change. Chances of success increase when the coach knows how the change will impact the team, what ripple effects the team and organization will have to deal with, and what changes the organization should make to support the team. Knowledge of organizational change also helps the coach handle fear components, which can be dramatic during times of organizational change or transition.

Knowledge of organizational change also helps the coach handle fear components, which can be dramatic.

Organizational learning is a powerful tool when the coach knows how to utilize it to meet the needs of the team. The coach needs to know what methods exist for knowledge acquisition and sharing, what collaborative processes exist, and how the team can use them. By understanding the existing organizational learning structure, the coach can then determine whether or not the team is utilizing this structure and if the current structure meets the needs of the team(s).

Team and organizational design is the knowledge of the structures, procedures, and functions to which organizations and teams adhere. More importantly, it is the knowledge of the logic behind them, the business reasons for them, and their effect on the team. Knowledge in this area involves focusing on the future of the organization. Understanding the vision of the organization is particularly important because it provides clarification and inspiration and lets the team and the coach know where the organization is heading. It also ensures that the team's efforts are in alignment with the organization's goals.

A vision is essential, but the coach also needs to be aware of current realities. This includes the knowledge of existing policies and infrastructures and how they affect the team. The coach also needs to know how to influence organizational policies and infrastructures, since the team must function within them.

In order for a coach to help the team be effective, he or she needs to have knowledge of the partnerships and collaborative arrangements that are needed and those that already exist. The coach should know how to create, utilize, and maintain partnerships and collaboration.

It is important that the coach also ensure that there is a connection between the team and its customers, that the connection is supported through customer advocacy, and that the team stays focused on the purpose of the organization.

Transition leadership is the knowledge and ability to guide teams during times of change. Organizational transition can be confusing, so the coach needs to have a clear vision of the desired outcome of the change and the ability to communicate that vision to the team. Learning and development is crucial to transition leadership. It is important for the coach to obtain new knowledge and learn new skills that will help the team and coach in the new design. The coach also must provide the team with learning and developmental opportunities to assist in successfully weathering the transition. Change can be traumatic, but when the team feels it is involved in the change rather than having it imposed, there is more support and more involvement in the change. The coach can help this occur by developing ownership within a team. The coach needs to possess the ability to adapt quickly and to be cognitively flexible in order to assist the team through transitional times.

Former managers, who often become team coaches, must be willing to relinquish control to the team.

The transition to teams often involves a perceived loss of power by the manager. Knowledge of manager roles and the ability to communicate those roles is critical, whether or not the team coach is the manager.

Former managers, who often become team coaches, must be willing to relinquish control to the team. The team coach must know and be able to communicate what the new role of the manager and team coach will be.

Coaches need to be able to change their roles, to be able to function in different roles, and to communicate the purpose behind their functions. Team members' roles may also be changed or created during a transition. The coach must identify what roles need to be changed or added and then support the team members through their transition into these new roles.

An important element of transition leadership is trust. For this reason, one of the most crucial coaching competencies is the knowledge of how to develop trust. Insecurities frequently arise during transition periods, and the coach needs to have trust of and in the team. He or she must also encourage trust within the team.

Tools

Another dimension of coaching effectiveness is the mastery of various coaching "tools." These tools go beyond simply understanding the principles or theory of coaching. The tools build on the knowledge competencies and concern the abilities required to be a team coach. These include general coaching skills, the ability to develop individuals and teams, an understanding of team dynamics, and communication skills.

Coaching skills are the actual tools and techniques that a coach uses to assist the team in becoming effective. One such skill is modeling, which is one of the primary ways in which people learn. The coach is very influential in modeling both good and bad behaviors, so it is essential that the coach display the type of behavior that supports effective teams.

It is essential that the coach display the type of behavior that supports effective teams.

Taking a facilitative approach, as opposed to a dictatorial approach, is important. A facilitator assists groups in solving problems and making decisions. A facilitator's goal is to build competencies in the group, rather than creating dependence. It is important that a facilitator stay focused on process rather than content. In cases where the team coach has expert knowledge, exhibiting facilitative behavior can represent a challenge.

The primary responsibility of a team coach is to lead, not manage. This distinction often gets lost for coaches, as the majority of coaches in today's organizations come from a managerial background. Managerial skills are helpful, but leadership contributes most to a team's success. An important aspect of leadership is boundary management. An effective boundary manager serves as a buffer or gatekeeper to help guard and protect the team from external obstacles and influences. This skill also requires that the coach act as a team advocate and serve as a communication link for the team with management and other teams.

Although it may be unpopular in a business environment to speak of nurturing, the reality is that the team needs space to develop and to be helped along in a trusting environment. A coach also needs to motivate, foster team growth and spirit, and create a space within which the team can grow, improve, and learn from its mistakes.

Finally, a coach needs to have the skill of mediation. It is inevitable that a team will require help solving problems or resolving conflict. The coach needs to have the skills to help their team through those times. (See Chapter 31 for more information regarding the dynamics of conflict resolution.)

Individual team member development means taking a developmental interest in each team member so that each can grow and contribute to the effectiveness of the team. The coach must understand what the team needs, who possesses what competencies, and who has the potential to develop certain competencies. The coach uses that knowledge to help team members develop. Developing technical or behavioral skills is not enough. A coach needs to have an understanding of human behavior and an understanding of the reasons behind individuals' behaviors. This will help the coach understand team members and will help team members understand each other.

A coach also needs to be able to apply the principles and practices of adult learning in order to educate team members effectively. There can be a great deal of rigidity behind adult behaviors and beliefs. In order to help team members change, a coach needs to be able to utilize adult change processes to help overcome that rigidity.

Team development is the understanding and guiding of the growth processes and cycles that the team goes through to become effective. Essentially, the team can be thought of as the coach's customer, where the deliverable is guidance in the team's growth process. Team growth occurs in cycles. A coach must understand what to expect from a team at certain points in its development.

A coach must understand what to expect from a team at certain points in its development.

Based on this knowledge, the coach can determine where to "meet" the team. This also helps in setting expectations for the team.

Regardless of team growth cycles or team design, empowerment will come into play in some form. The coach needs to have a clear understanding of what empowerment is, how it works, when and how to utilize it, and the level of empowerment for which the team is ready.

Much of the research and literature on teams concerns team building. This is an important skill for the coach to have, as it helps the team to develop as a cohesive unit and helps ensure success. In addition to helping team members understand one another and get along, the coach needs to help team members develop teaming skills. A team also has to know where it's going and how it will get there. A coach can ensure this through chartering and visioning. Finally, team coaches need to be able to teach the team to deal with the inevitability of change.

Team dynamics applies the concepts of group dynamics to the team. Team emotions play a large part in team dynamics. The coach must understand that teams have emotions as a collective unit, be able to read this emotional climate, and be able to adjust, adapt, and address those emotions. Should team emotions be ignored by the coach, it can severely hurt team effectiveness.

A team is a unit comprised of different individuals. Individual differences can be a tremendous asset to a team when correctly utilized. Those same differences can also cause turmoil. A coach needs to be aware of individual differences and must be able to make the individual differences benefit the team. Individual differences can be harnessed to benefit the team; however, they may also lead to interpersonal conflicts. When this occurs, the coach must be able to use conflict resolution skills to help team members and protect the team.

Regardless of the best retention efforts, team membership does not remain stable over a lengthy period of time. The manner in which a team and its coach select and incorporate new team members can make a large difference in the impact that new membership has on team effectiveness. The coach needs to know how to select and incorporate new members so that the experience is a positive and beneficial one for all involved.

Perhaps one of the most important tools that a coach may possess is the ability to develop team leadership. Whether or not a team is fully empowered, the team needs to be self-led to some extent. The coach can help this by developing leadership within the team.

Whether or not a team is fully empowered, the team needs to be self-led to some extent.

Communication includes both conveying and receiving information and is one of the most important tools of the team coach. The coach must act as both an effective communicator and as an advocate for effective communication within and between teams and outside entities. The team relies on the coach to make sure that it has the information that it needs in order to perform well. The coach has to recognize the value of the information that he or she has or can obtain and must not manipulate others from that position. The coach must understand and disseminate information relevant to business analysis, since a team is a business unit making business decisions. The coach also needs to be willing and able to help the team members to find those same information resources on their own and to avoid reliance on the coach for all information.

A coach must possess and be able to develop communication skills in others. This includes developing and guiding dialogue. The coach can model and encourage effective dialogue between team members. The coach can also help the team to develop strong listening and speaking skills. Helping people to "be heard" and to express themselves contributes greatly to team decision making. In addition to hearing and understanding one another, team members need to be able to give one another feedback so that they can continue to grow. A coach can help a team to understand effective ways of doing this, and in turn help to foster trust in the team. However, no amount of positive communication will prevent occasional conflicts. A coach must be able to deal with and help others deal with conflict. Conflict can be a productive component of teams when dealt with in a positive and affirming manner.

Actions

Coaching knowledge and tools are critical, but without the ability to apply the knowledge and tools, the coach will not be successful. This section discusses the action competencies of team processes and performance guidance.

Team processes involve understanding and helping teams to utilize the tools and methods that they have to assist them in their work. This includes problem solving, decision making, and effective meeting guidelines. A coach must understand how the team's work is performed so that he or she can guide the team in improving its process.

Part of improving work processes is problem solving. The coach should know various problem-solving techniques and must be able to guide a team through them. This often involves an education component in basic and/or advanced problem-solving techniques. The coach should also model problem-solving techniques in his or her work with the team. The coach plays a large role in helping the team to develop the ability to make and review decisions as it takes on an increasingly larger decision-making role. Teaming requires many meetings and, if those meetings are not effective, the process will bog down. The coach must make sure that meetings are being conducted as effectively and productively as possible. This may require training to support the team in its meeting process.

Performance guidance is often thought of as a control function. For this reason we refer to this skill as "performance guidance" rather than "performance

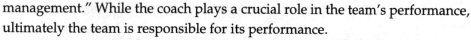

management." While the coach plays a crucial role in the team's performance, ultimately the team is responsible for its performance.

In this capacity, the coach acts to ensure that the team is performing effectively and that the job gets done. In order to do this, the coach must focus on both individual and team performance. Individual performance refers to what each individual team member is expected to do in order to support team effectiveness.

The coach must evaluate an individual's performance and assist the individual in performance improvement.

The coach must also focus on team performance. This is often done by using metrics, set either by the coach, by the team, or by some combination. Metrics help the team to know what it needs to work on and what it needs to maintain. There is a common adage that "what gets measured gets done." While this is true, the coach should also keep in mind that not everything that is measured and/or done contributes to team effectiveness. Metrics should be chosen wisely and used sparingly so as to provide clear focus. While tracking and evaluating team performance is valuable, it is little more than an exercise if effort is not made toward continuous improvement. The team and coach need to know where they are and where they want to go in order to push them beyond the status quo.

Continuous improvement is an attitude and is not developed overnight; it is a challenge for both the team and coach. Organizations are constantly changing and so are the expectations of the team, both internally and externally. The coach needs to know and share the new expectations, so that he or she can help the team adjust.

In an ideal world there would be no need for disciplinary action. However, sometimes it is required in order to achieve team effectiveness. While disciplinary action holds a negative connotation, it does not necessarily have to be so. It is important for the coach to know how to use discipline to help the team and the individuals know how their behavior affects the team and to help instill accountability within the team. While discipline may be required, it should be balanced with rewards and recognition. Rewards help the team to know when they have done well and when they should celebrate. Celebration keeps morale high, promotes further improvements, and enhances the coach's rapport with the team.

While the coach plays a crucial role in the team's performance, ultimately the team is responsible for its performance.

RESPONSIBILITIES

The Development of the Coach

Having reviewed the coaching competencies above, a question arises: Who is responsible for the development of the team coach? Ultimately the individual is responsible for his or her own development. However, the individual looks first and foremost to the developmental resources that are provided by the organization. The organization and the individual need to take joint responsibility for the development of the team coach.

Organizations should consider coach development to be a priority, given that team success is so dependent on the quality of the coaching. This need should be taken into account in the early stages of moving to a team-based structure; and it should continue to be met as the organization moves through the stages of a teaming initiative.

Some of the support functions that the organization can provide the coach are simple and require little time or effort. Others are more complex and require a substantial commitment.

One support function is simply the careful selection of coaches. It is unfair to both the team and the coach to place an individual in the role of coach when he or she does not have the desire or the basic ability to serve as a coach.

It is unfair to place an individual in the role of coach when he or she does not have the desire or the basic ability to serve as a coach.

Careful selection of coaches can ensure that people selected have at least the basic requirements to become successful team coaches. Once selected, team coaches need to have a clear definition of the coach's role and a clear explanation of the organization's expectations. This helps ensure that both the team and the coach start off with a common understanding of who and what the coach is and what is expected.

From the beginning there should be skill development for the coach. This initial skill development should be followed with a co-created developmental plan. The organization should make efforts to assist the coach in following and succeeding in the developmental plan, including information about the resources available. (See Chapter 34 regarding relevant employee development issues.) In addition, there should be a mechanism for evaluation and feedback for the coach. This serves to focus the coach's efforts and assist in his or her development.

While all of the above organizational support is imperative to coach success, it is often a support network that provides the most valuable learning and support. This support network may be a forum of team coaches from across the organization who meet occasionally to share problems, ideas, and experiences or it could be an occasional meeting of team coaches from different organizations to share experiences and best practices. Regardless of the form that it takes, it is very valuable to provide the coach with contact to other people in similar roles.

Coaches are critical to the success of a team, and with so many factors affecting the success of a team coach, it is important that organizations provide effective support for their coaches. It is often difficult for an organization to assess whether or not it is supporting its team coaches.

The following list of diagnostic questions is intended to help organizational leaders in determining the level of support available. This list can serve as a springboard for discussions between team coaches and those who are responsible for their development and support. It can also be used as a planning tool when implementing new teams and orienting new coaches or as a report card when assessing whether or not the current system is providing sufficient support for coaches. If given thorough thought and discussion, this list should help organizational leaders avoid common mistakes. The questions are grouped into the *knowledge, tools,* and *actions* categories that have been used throughout this chapter to assist in easy reference back to those sections of the chapter concerning those topics.

> **It is often difficult for an organization to assess whether or not it is supporting its team coaches.**

Diagnostic Questions

Knowledge

- Do coaches go through a selection process?
- Is there agreement among the organization, the teams, and the coaches as to what the role of the coach is?
- Does a process exist to help coaches understand the organizational culture?
- Do resources exist to help the coach understand the concept of organizational change?
- Have the coaches received information as to the design, policies, and procedures of the organization and how teams fit into that?
- Does the organization value coaches as critical resources?

- Do the coaches feel supported?
- Are coaches recognized and rewarded for superior performance?
- Are coaches utilized to their full extent?

Tools

- What forms of training are the coaches required to complete?
- What developmental opportunities exist for the coaches?
- Has the coach received leadership training?
- Has the coach received facilitation training?
- Is the coach held responsible for developing team members?
- Does the coach have information regarding adult learning and change?
- Has the coach received training as to the changing nature of developing teams?
- Is the coach evaluated on his or her ability to develop team cohesiveness?
- Has the coach received training on group dynamics?
- Has the coach received training in communication, giving and receiving feedback, and conflict resolution?
- Is the coach supplied with needed information resources?
- Has the coach been given training regarding problem solving, decision making, and meetings?
- Is there a system in place for the sharing of knowledge between coaches?

Actions

- Does the coach have a clear understanding of the difference between being a manager and being a coach?
- Is the coach allowed to play his or her role as boundary manager?
- Does the coach understand the team's work processes?
- Does the coach have the resources to instill accountability within the team?
- Does the coach understand and have access to performance management tools such as metrics, evaluations, rewards, and recognition?

- Is the coach able to take appropriate disciplinary action when required?
- Is the coach encouraged to practice self-care such as time management, stress management, and so forth?

Conclusion

One of the main conclusions that came out of this survey of literature was that being a team coach is a much more complex and demanding role than it appears on the surface. For this reason, it is all the more important that people not go blindly into this territory and that they not be sent unprepared into this role by their organizations. If organizations utilize teams and do not invest in the selection, training, and support of their coaches, they are missing a crucial link in the team success chain. This chapter is not intended to be used to train a team coach, but rather the purpose was to highlight the many competencies needed by a coach and to assist in designing or evaluating a training program for the team coach.

As has been discussed, it is strongly recommended that organizations invest time and effort into building an educational program for their coaches and an organizational system that supports the coaches. Investing in the coach in this way is an investment in the team as a whole and could prove the critical factor that "keeps the team afloat."

CHAPTER 28

A Web-Based Electronic Performance Support System for Managers

Garry McDaniel and Bijan Masumian

Brad was tense as he left the morning department meeting. Brad was worried about the increased production goals for each work team. As a work-team shift manager, Brad understood that the demand for more product meant increased sales for the company. As he sat down in front of his PC, Brad wondered how to share this information with team members so they would see the importance of the work request and not become too resistant. Six weeks ago, he was just one member of a work team, and now he was in charge. He reflected that it was one thing to carry out orders, and quite another to be the one who had to communicate orders and motivate others to carry them out.

Brad was scheduled to attend a team leadership workshop in another month or so, but this work request had to be accomplished now! As he sat at his desk, he noticed an icon on his PC screen that linked to the company intranet site designed to provide managers and supervisors with information, training, tools, and links to solve real-time problems. "That's it!" he thought as he double clicked on the icon. In seconds he had chosen a path that led him to an online training program on "Leading a Team." Over the next fifteen minutes, Brad reviewed the suggestions and tips provided on fostering commitment to team goals. He then printed out a handy checklist to review with team members to help facilitate a discussion on how they could collectively accomplish the new work request. "Maybe this won't be so bad after all," he thought, as he walked out to the production floor.

Management has never been easy. This is particularly true in today's fast-paced, high-tech world, where time-to-market and constant product and service improvement are not just expected, but critical for survival. For collaborative work systems to work most efficiently, structure and support must be put in place to enable employees and managers to work together effectively in order to drive business success. Managers are key players in the effective and efficient implementation of collaborative work systems within any organization. This chapter describes a nationally recognized electronic performance support system that provides managers with the information, tools, and training they need to excel in their jobs. It also provides a case example of how a cross-functional team at a major high-technology company designed and developed this tool.

Management Training: What's the Problem?

The management of an organization is formally tasked with the primary responsibility for the tactical and strategic operations and results. Management generally involves working collaboratively with others to coordinate and align work, expectations, and goals so that the business succeeds. Given the importance of this role, it should follow that ensuring that new managers are appropriately trained and supported to excel in their jobs would be a high priority. However, research conducted by the Corporate Leadership Council suggests that organizations are not addressing the need for good management. In a study titled *The Compelling Offer: A Quantitative Analysis of Career Preferences and Decisions of High Value Employees,* the Corporate Leadership Council (1999) found that poor management continues to be the top reason employees leave a company.

This may be due in part to the approach organizations take to prepare managers to perform their new roles after being hired or promoted into a position for the first time. We find that organizations approach management development from one of three frames of reference.

Some organizations take a "sink or swim" approach to preparing new managers, in which little support or assistance is provided to ensure an individual is properly trained to perform the new role. Adherents of this approach believe that you can get the results you want if you just "throw them in the deep end and see if they swim."

In other organizations, new managers are provided a standard training session after assuming the job, and that is all they ever get. This is the "just teach them the absolute basics" approach. Followers of this method seem to think that once you've learned to dog paddle, that's all you will ever need.

A third approach involves identifying individuals with management potential, ensuring they are appropriately prepared before promotion, and providing them with ongoing training once they assume their new roles. Organizations that follow this method assume good managers need to receive proper development and coaching to serve as leaders in a collaborative work environment.

Managers need to receive proper development and coaching to serve as leaders in a collaborative work environment.

Organizations that approach management development from this perspective recognize that if the goal is to compete with world-class swimmers, constant coaching and ongoing training are needed.

Like many of the organizations following this latter approach, Advanced Micro Devices (AMD) recognizes that new managers need to learn fundamental supervisory knowledge and skills to allow them to excel in their role. However, research (Brown, Hitchcock, & Willard, 1994; Robinson & Robinson, 1989) has suggested two areas that are problematic for new managers, not just at AMD, but at other organizations as well. First, despite the best of intentions, there is often a gap between the time new managers are placed in their roles and when they actually begin to attend basic management training programs. For example, in today's lean environment, it is not uncommon for new managers to spend the first six to twelve months just trying to learn their jobs and stay ahead of their workloads. The longer one puts off needed training, the more difficult it is to go back and pick it up later. Second, interviews conducted by human resources staff with experienced managers within AMD also highlighted that some situations involving employee problems, budgets, or planning occur so infrequently that managers forget the correct procedures for addressing those issues. Or more commonly, procedures had changed over time and the new approach was unknown to the manager.

Both of these problems impact the manager's job. Employees expect managers to be competent in their role. When managers cannot deal with common employee problems, employee morale, trust, and commitment diminish. When managers do not know how to perform basic tasks such as budgeting, performance management, and communicating vision, mission, and values, employees lose focus and the cost of getting work done increases.

Managers.Compass: Online, Real-Time Support for Managers

One method of addressing these two gaps is to provide a customized curriculum focused on different levels of management. However, the problem still remains that some issues occur so infrequently that managers forget how to respond appropriately. Despite their best intentions, most managers found that it is extremely difficult to stay ahead of the flood of information and demands on their time due to workload and yet remember all they need to about basic management skills. In many organizations, many with the title of "manager" are finding that their true role is primarily that of an individual contributor with the responsibility of managing being extra duty if time allows or a crisis occurs.

If we agree that the purpose of training is to provide individuals with the information and skills they need to accomplish their jobs, and that the role of "full-time manager" is becoming increasingly scarce in today's fast-paced world, then new methods of helping managers do their job are needed (Ruttenbur, Spickler, & Lurie, 2000). To address the reality of the manager's role and learning needs within Advanced Micro Devices, a cross-functional team of professionals was drawn from a variety of disciplines including learning and development, human resources, organization development, finance, library sciences, information technology, public relations, and marketing. This team was formed to conceive and design a structure for institutionalizing manager work requirements and practices. The resulting intranet site, called *Managers.Compass,* was created to meet the growing developmental and performance support needs of over eight hundred managers within the United States. The purpose of this structure was to bring the right information to the right people at the right time so they could be as productive as possible.

Background

To fully understand the needs of AMD's managers, a subgroup of the design team reviewed information gathered from several corporate-wide surveys and focus groups that pointed to a number of skill gaps in the repertoire of new and incumbent AMD managers. As the team reviewed the skill gaps, it became evident that the shortcomings could be addressed via the following remedies:

- Set clear roles, responsibilities, and expectations for managers;
- Create a comprehensive matrix of managerial competencies;
- Enable managers to assess their current skills and define a learning plan for addressing their deficiencies;
- Provide managers with world-class training and support tools to help them implement their learning plans; and
- Create a system of accountability for performance improvement.

One-Stop Shopping for Development and Support

After considering several alternatives, the team decided that a website would provide the optimal solution for this problem. An online website would allow managers to address their developmental and performance support needs in a real-time, seamless, integrated environment.

An online website would allow managers to address their developmental and performance support needs in a real-time, seamless, integrated environment.

The team decided to use the metaphor of a compass in the title of this site (Managers.Compass) to highlight providing *direction* to the development and support needs of AMD managers. Managers.Compass was built around the AMD leadership model, which contains four areas of managerial and leadership responsibility along with specific competencies expected of the ideal AMD manager. The four areas of leadership responsibility are

1. Sets direction;
2. Creates a positive and supportive environment;
3. Gets results; and
4. Builds for the future.

The home page of the site (Figure 28.1) features a prominent display of the four quadrants of AMD's leadership model at the center.

Figure 28.1. Managers.Compass Home Page

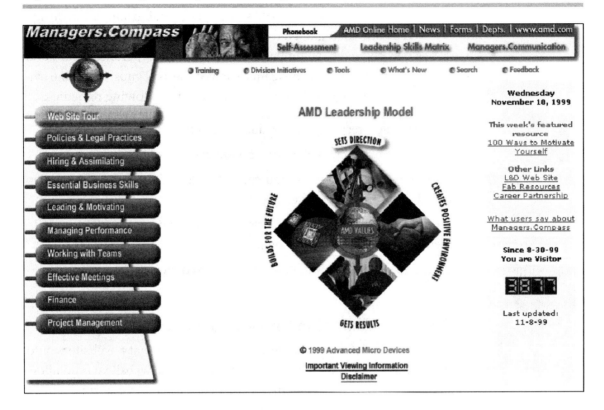

Clicking on any of the four quadrants of the leadership model allows a manager to see a specific list of competencies constituting that responsibility (Figure 28.2). For instance, clicking on "Creates Positive Environment" allows the manager to see the nine competencies that describe this broad responsibility. One of these is "helps build and maintain effective teams."

Figure 28.2. Skill Sets as a Quadrant

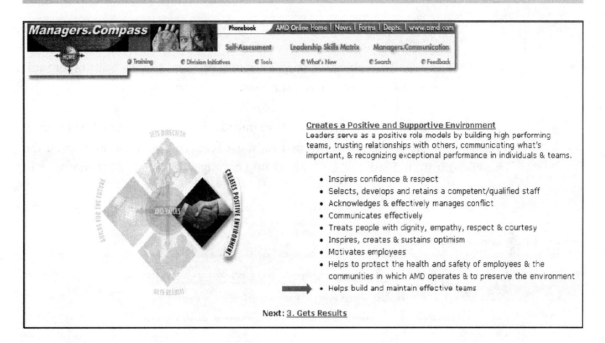

Creates a Positive and Supportive Environment
Leaders serve as a positive role models by building high performing teams, trusting relationships with others, communicating what's important, & recognizing exceptional performance in individuals & teams.

- Inspires confidence & respect
- Selects, develops and retains a competent/qualified staff
- Acknowledges & effectively manages conflict
- Communicates effectively
- Treats people with dignity, empathy, respect & courtesy
- Inspires, creates & sustains optimism
- Motivates employees
- Helps to protect the health and safety of employees & the communities in which AMD operates & to preserve the environment
- Helps build and maintain effective teams

Next: 3. Gets Results

If desired, managers can then click on any single competency. If the manager clicks on "Helps build and maintain effective teams," he or she is taken a level deeper. This level (see Figure 28.3), called the Leadership Matrix, allows the manager to see specific *behaviors* and *actions* associated with each skill in the above list, as well as specific online training, tools, and resources that can help the manager acquire each skill.

Among the tools and resources to be found in the Leadership Matrix are the following:

- Short, just-in-time tutorials that are seamlessly integrated into Managers.Compass;

- Links to websites, online job aids, forms, and worksheets to help master specific competencies; and

- Links to specific classroom training available in the Texas or California sites. Employees can view course information and, if needed, immediately send a web-based registration request to AMD's training organization, all without leaving the Managers.Compass site.

For example, if a manager wants to improve or simply review team leadership skills, he or she can select the Leading a Team option illustrated under the skill column in Figure 28.3. Clicking on Leading a Team takes the manager to

Figure 28.3. Leadership Matrix

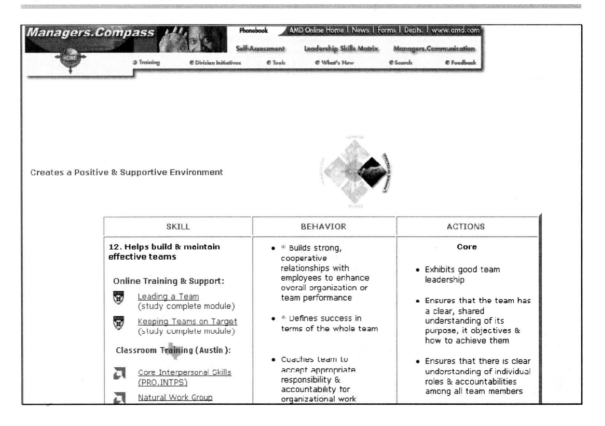

a short online tutorial by Harvard Business Publications (Figure 28.4). This tutorial provides a complete, focused development program on how to form a team and foster collaborative teamwork. (For a detailed discussion of a leadership approach to fostering teamwork, see Chapter 7.) In addition to core team leadership skills, managers can also view:

Figure 28.4. Harvard ManageMentor Tutorial

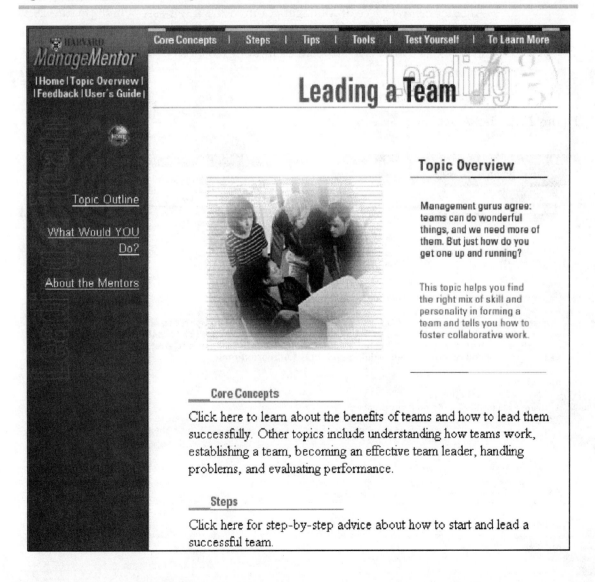

- Steps for starting a team;

- Tips for selecting team members and enhancing team performance;

- Checklists for assessing, monitoring, and/or developing team interactions and operations;

- A self-survey to assess their own personal baseline knowledge of leading a team; and

- A list of recommended articles, books, and other media on the subject of leading a team.

Another central piece of Managers.Compass is a self-assessment (Figure 28.5) that enables managers to rate themselves on each of twenty-four competencies in the skills matrix and compare their ratings to those of their peers in the growing database.

Figure 28.5. Self-Assessment Screen

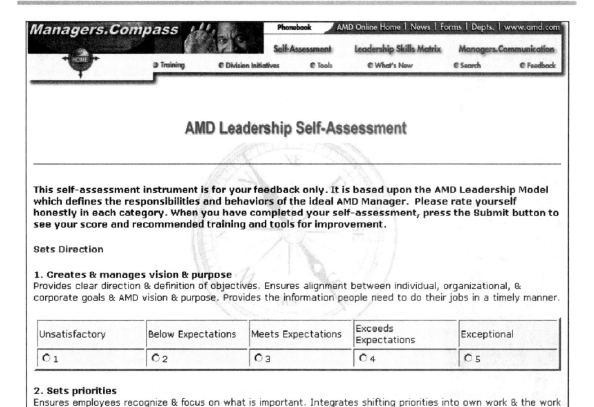

After completing the online self-assessment, managers can view a screen that displays a summary of their strengths and areas in need of improvement. This page also shows how the manager's personal self-assessment rating for each competency compares to the average rating of all AMD managers who have completed the self-assessment. (Managers can only view their own ratings and the cumulative ratings for all managers, not the individual ratings of other managers.) Finally, the feedback page also includes a shopping cart feature that enables managers to identify specific skill sets on which to focus. Managers can define their own individualized short-term and long-term development plans and modify their choices at any time.

Managers can define their own individualized short-term and long-term development plans and modify their choices at any time.

The skills sets are also dynamically linked to the Leadership Skills Matrix that includes links to support tools and resources displayed in Figure 28.3. The seamless integration of the Leadership Skills Matrix, self-assessment, development planning, and online learning opportunities for improving skills provides a complete, closed-loop, professional development system for identification of skill deficiencies and acquisition of those skills. (For a full description of required team competencies, see Chapter 33.)

A final feature of Managers.Compass is a performance support component that is designed to address the daily needs of the AMD manager. The design team surveyed a sample group of managers drawn from various functional areas and asked them to identify the most common problems encountered in their role. Managers identified problems or issues that fell into the nine major categories listed below and on the left-hand side of Figure 28.1:

- Policies and legal practices;
- Hiring and assimilating;
- Essential business skills;
- Leading and motivating;
- Managing performance;
- Working with teams;
- Effective meetings;
- Finance; and
- Project management.

Clicking on any one of these categories takes the manager to a list of classroom or online training, specific books, articles, or other media; tips and checklists; and links to public websites that offer information, advice, or skill-building opportunity on that topic.

Usability and Pilot Assessment

The design team conducted pilot tests prior to implementation to assess the functionality of the site. Nine managers from several functional backgrounds were individually brought to a controlled environment that included two video cameras: one focused on the PC screen to follow the paths managers chose as they navigated through the site, the other focused on their faces to register their reactions to different screens and features. Managers were asked to "think out loud" as they explored Managers.Compass and accomplished eight specific tasks. These tasks included completion of the self-assessment, defining individualized learning plans, reviewing online tutorials, and finding specific forms and other resources on the site to accomplish the tasks. This usability study revealed numerous opportunities for improving the structure and design of the site, including adjustments in the location, alignment, and association of several buttons on the home page.

In addition to the usability study, a pilot was conducted with forty-one randomly selected managers from both the California and Texas sites. The participants were asked to accomplish the same list of tasks as had the managers in the usability study from their own desktops. They were also asked to complete an online evaluation of Managers.Compass and rate the accessibility and usability of each of the main features of the site.

Outcomes

Managers.Compass was launched at AMD's Austin and Sunnyvale sites on the last day of August 1999, and it quickly became a frequently used manager tool at AMD. As a testament to its usability, within a month, Managers.Compass had received close to two thousand hits. To date, the site has received over 21,000 hits by managers accessing information, taking the self-assessment, and reviewing online skill development workshops or topical tools and checklists. Many managers use the site with such frequency that they have installed a shortcut on their desktops that launches Managers.Compass as their opening home page.

The team is now working to provide Managers.Compass to AMD's international sites. AMD's newest manufacturing facility located in Germany and sites in Malaysia, Singapore, China, and Thailand have indicated strong interest in adapting this resource to the cultural needs of their employees. The design team plans to conduct detailed user pattern analysis, generate site traffic reports, and hold follow-up focus groups in a continuous attempt to evaluate the functionality and usefulness of the tool and improve the Managers.Compass site accordingly.

Conclusion

Understanding how to work effectively with one's team members, employees, and peers is vital for managers in today's collaborative work environment. Further, it is important that managers do the right thing the first time to avoid wasting time, energy, and organizational resources. Feedback from AMD's management has clearly communicated that Managers.Compass has achieved the desired outcomes of providing managers at AMD with targeted information, tools, and training to ensure that they can perform their roles in a manner that enhances team performance, development, and motivation.

PART 6

INDIVIDUAL, INTERPERSONAL, AND TEAM COMPETENCIES AND SKILLS

Gerald D. Klein

THE CHAPTERS IN THIS SECTION discuss team member skills and team practices that contribute to team effectiveness. While the chapters here share this general focus, each provides a distinct and different view on this issue.

There is little question that certain team member skills and team practices are important to achieving successful team outcomes. Certain competencies, skills, and behaviors are required for teams to succeed, such as competencies and skills in communicating, listening, managing differences and resolving conflict, and planning and organizing work. However, there is significant division of opinion on how the necessary competencies and behaviors are best acquired by an organization. This is, of course, an important issue for organizations that are in the process of implementing, or are contemplating the implementation of, an organization design that makes extensive use of teams.

Richard Walton (1972, 1977), J. Richard Hackman (1977), Edward E. Lawler III (1992), and others who are experienced in attempts to create greater collaborative activity within and across organization units and between levels, hold that organization-level factors and support at the top are vital in order to achieve and sustain these outcomes. When those at the top fail to support a workplace innovation such as increasing collaborative activity, it is very unlikely that the behavior of employees will change. Specifically, an organization's culture must support collaboration within and between units if collaborative behavior is to be demonstrated.

Another approach for obtaining the requisite competencies for collaboration and collaborative behavior is exercising great care in selecting employees and managers. There is a long history of carefully selecting and employing particular individuals to achieve certain organization outcomes, including greater collaborative behavior. At the pioneering and then new General Foods plant in Topeka, Kansas, Richard Walton (1972, 1977) and his associates carefully selected team leaders, plant managers, and other employees who would work well within and support a plant based on interacting self-directed teams. Prominent work design expert J. Richard Hackman emphasizes the importance of careful employee selection in creating teams to handle work (Hackman, 1977). One report of a successful Lucent facility emphasizing self-direction and self-management by employees and self-managed teams indicates a preference for hiring "attitude over aptitude" (Pettinger, 1997, B1).

Finally, at Corning, Inc., Johnson & Johnson, and other leading companies, job applicants are hired and employees are retained and promoted—all selection activities—based, in part, on their predisposition, willingness, and ability to work collaboratively with other individuals and departments (Johnson & Johnson, n.d.; Klein, 1992).

A third approach for developing certain characteristics, competencies, and skills that are desired in employees is through training. The research on training constitutes an extensive body of knowledge and suggests different approaches in training design. Faced with sorting through and working with these findings, a trainer is not to be envied! David Kolb (1984, 1985) and others, for example, indicate the importance of individual learning styles in training outcomes.

Building on the pioneering work of Locke, other researchers have discovered that the conscious establishment of specific goals by learners, in combination with high trainer expectations, has a positive and significant impact on training outcomes. An entirely different approach to training that has been demonstrated to be effective is behavior modeling. Here, learners are exposed to a specific set of behaviors thought to be effective when used to handle a particular and recurring situation—problem solving with employees, conducting performance appraisals, disciplining, and terminations. The behaviors are portrayed several times, preferably by different models, and learners have numerous opportunities to practice these behaviors and to receive feedback and be coached on their performance (Fox, 1988; Kraut, 1976).

Illustrating yet another approach to training is research suggesting that better training outcomes are achieved when learners are deliberately exposed to various obstacles and challenges in training that require investigative and exploratory behavior (Nordstom, Wendland, & Williams, 1998).

Summarizing this discussion, it is clear that there is probably not a single best approach for obtaining the skills, competencies, and behaviors that are important in collaboration. It is probably prudent for an organization that wishes to create or increase collaborative activity to remain open to using various means to accomplish this end.

The chapters in this section address various ways to impart necessary behaviors and skills.

In Chapter 29, Kelly Rupp presents an assessment instrument and discussion tool that can help newly formed teams quickly begin work on their goals. The instrument is designed for completion by individuals prior to discussion, but can be discussed and completed by a team. The UATTRA model (Up And To The Right Arrow) that guides assessment and discussion requires that a team begin with its customers and become clear on what the customer expects from the team. By answering questions on the "Self and Others" part of the assessment, team members become clear concerning such issues as the willingness of team members to be on the team; the experience, abilities, and resources of team members; and the norms that should govern the team.

Through work on the "Objectives Versus Time" portion of the instrument, team members clarify the goals of the team, establish an action plan for its work, and evaluate the plan in terms of time and resources. The final part of the assessment addresses team member motivation. Here, each team member is encouraged to identify what rewards or outcomes for team service would be valued. The rewards available to members are also discussed.

Deborah Hurst and Scott Follows in Chapter 30 describe a two-phase, six-week distance training module on team dynamics provided to members of a professional organization. The goal is for participants to learn about teams and to develop team skills by taking part, first, in a team simulation using CD-ROM technology and then discussing this experience with others who have also completed the simulation. This discussion is carried out online at scheduled and unscheduled times. At scheduled times, a group facilitator is involved. The chapter reports the reactions of both learners and facilitators to this experience and their learning. Hurst and Follows identify the challenges involved in this approach to training and describe its promise and potential benefits.

Jimmy Nelson explores the important organizational issue of interpersonal conflict in Chapter 31. Nelson describes five common methods of handling conflict, which he illustrates with examples, and indicates the consequences of each. Integrative solutions to conflict, win-win solutions, are best and typically better than compromise and competition, two of the other approaches. While integrative solutions are sometimes difficult to fashion, it is important to seek these. Also addressed by this chapter are specific interpersonal skills and techniques that are useful when a person is involved in a conflict. These skills really are relevant to any interpersonal encounter and include listening, observing, and questioning. A list of ten behaviors for a person involved in conflict provides an effective summary for the chapter.

Chapter 32 by Gerald Klein is concerned with the problem-solving meetings that are central to collaboration in organizations. Klein identifies a series of meeting problems and indicates that meetings can be made more satisfying and productive. Key here is new behavior by meeting leaders and members, behavior that most would be capable of demonstrating. It is argued that just a few of the new behaviors can improve meeting climate, member satisfaction, and meeting results. The chapter concludes with other tips for having successful meetings and refers readers to additional resources.

Drawing on his knowledge of teams and team training, Michael Beyerlein in Chapter 33 identifies various categories of learning required of team members that he labels tool sets. Although important to team effectiveness, these are areas that formal training usually ignores in favor of others. Beyerlein suggests that increased proficiency in each or at least some of these areas would be reflected in improved team performance. In the chapter all of the tool sets are described and the implications for team training are indicated.

Gayle Porter in Chapter 34 suggests that much training at work, including training to develop interpersonal and team skills—training that is common when an organization shifts to a team-based design—is often ineffective. This is so because participants have not adequately resolved issues of personal identity and commitment. Commitment to an occupation and organization may be prerequisites to real learning and the application of learning, as the new knowledge is viewed by a person as helping him or her do a better job in a profession and organization that he or she really cares about. Porter discusses the consequences for organizations of not helping individuals establish a place for themselves in the world and of encouraging a great or an exclusive focus on the job and the organization. In sum, Porter believes that when efforts to improve collaboration and collaborative skills do not seem to be succeeding, individual employee development may be needed. The chapter contains a number of specific recommendations for organizations and managers.

CHAPTER 29

UATTRA Performance Assessment for Fast Formed Teams

Kelly Rupp

K NOWLEDGE WORKERS IN BUSINESS TODAY routinely collaborate in work groups in order to get things done. We are expected to "team up." But how, exactly, are we to do this? We are asked to work with people we hardly know, accomplish things that may never have been done before, and do it all within an absurdly short timeline. To build effective teams that successfully address today's rapid-fire and ever-changing business challenges, a new model of self-directed team guidance is proposed. The UATTRA model (Up And To The Right Arrow) focuses first on the customer. That customer is always someone real, someone human, who will benefit from the team's deliverables. The model proceeds to frame the customer within three dimensions from which to build and execute the tasks of the team. These three dimensions are interrelated and lead us to look inward and outward in our daily work activities: sense of self and others, balancing objectives versus time, and motivation. By mapping these dimensions to lessons in basic communication, problem solving, and relationships that we universally learned during our childhood and adolescence, we can realize greater effectiveness in teams, sooner, with increased satisfaction.

Why UATTRA?

Surviving Y2K was a picnic. Surviving the ups and downs of the stock market roller-coaster is emotionally trying, but bearable. And surviving the sudden shocks of energy scarcity may ultimately lead us to more responsible and sustainable consumption. But will we survive each other—joined in teams in our workplaces—trying to get along together while we collaborate at breakneck speed to whip our business indicators "up and to the right"? This is the direction that portrays success over time in conventional illustrations of financial growth or well-being (see Figure 29.1). The UATTRA is adopted herein as a symbol of success and preferred direction for our teams' growth.

Figure 29.1. Up and to the Right Arrow

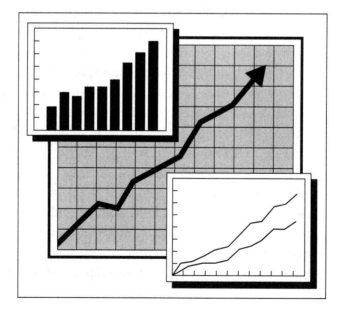

Today's business environment requires us to "fast form and fast norm" into teams, with people we may hardly know, in ambiguous and often pioneering situations. There is little if any time for our teams to step away from our demanding and already shortened deliverable schedules to "school" ourselves in the relationship-centered skills training of negotiation, assertiveness, conflict resolution, or social styles understanding. Nor will we always have the benefit of great leaders who will provide us with clear direction and remove the inevitable roadblocks that threaten our team's success.

The challenge is daunting. Just how will we "fast form" into an efficient work team that produces both business results and satisfying work experiences for team members?

The UATTRA Assessment

To build and exercise effective teams for today's rapid-fire business challenges, we must consider new models for self-directed teams (Kline, 1999; Urdan & Weggen, 2000). One such model is UATTRA, a new assessment tool for newly formed teams of knowledge workers "thrown together" for first-time collaboration.

UATTRA is a new assessment tool for newly formed teams of knowledge workers "thrown together" for first-time collaboration.

The UATTRA assessment, a copy of which is provided in Exhibit 29.1, approaches our work team interactions with the same openness, innocence, and even selfishness for our own well-being that once guided us as youth when we joined in team play with our friends. This assessment methodology is rooted in deeply ingrained behaviors that provide fundamental orientation to personal and team success. Its foundation is the assumption that, at the end of the day, people don't change that much and that attempts to provide "just-in-time" skills training in collaboration and team play will fail (Buckingham & Coffman, 1999). Of chief concern is that skills hastily learned are not retained. Unless intensely reinforced and repeatedly exercised, skills training disappears from our behavioral repertoire at the very moment we need these skills—when faced with real-life business tensions that test our ability to work effectively with others. Moreover, even if skills training is available, all team members are unlikely to have common training experiences, as they are increasingly likely to come together from widely differing educational and cultural backgrounds. (For additional perspectives on convening new teams and team development, see Chapters 4, 9, and other chapters in this section.)

UATTRA assessment begins with an understanding of our team's customers.

UATTRA assessment begins with an understanding of our team's customers and welcoming their virtual presence at the worktable. We then proceed to consciously examine our team's effectiveness along each of the following three dimensions: *self and others, objectives versus time,* and *motivation* (see Table 29.1).

Table 29.1. The Three Dimensions of UATTRA

Dimension	Behavior
Self and Others	Balancing our own interests, needs, and capabilities with those of other team members
Objectives Versus Time	Understanding exactly what the group is expected to deliver or produce, in what timeframe
Motivation	Ensuring that each team member is motivated to contribute based on intrinsic (personal and private) drivers as well as external expectations for reward or outcome.

The team's customer personas and the three dimensions of effectiveness provide a framework that helps improve team interactions. In the UATTRA assessment, an "up and to the right arrow," the framework becomes a kind of "jungle gym" for team members to hang onto while working toward their objectives. The assessment is practical and easily applied by team participants and leaders throughout early stages of team development. Individually and as a team, members assess, chart, and discuss their positions along each dimension.

The UATTRA scoring template is presented in Figure 29.2; a sample "scored" assessment is shown in Figure 29.3, illustrating an individual's personal assessment of her team's positions on all three dimensions and her understanding of the team's two customers.

Figure 29.2. UATTRA Scoring Template

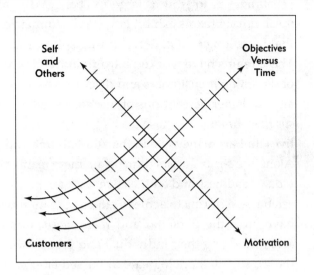

Figure 29.3. Sample UATTRA Score

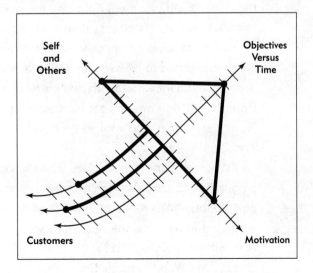

The "up and to the right arrow" orientation of the scoring template visually encourages us to grow as large and balanced an arrow as possible, which is the ideal. Strong teams exhibit large and symmetric "up and to the right arrows" that have long tail(s), representing solid understanding of their customers. These teams have worked hard to understand their clients. They may have observed their customers and discussed as a team customer objectives, needs, and customer perceptions of the team's deliverables. Along the *objectives versus time* dimension, these teams have contracted among themselves on objectives that are achievable in the allotted time and satisfy the teams' customers. Along the *self and others* dimension, these teams have acknowledged their individual readiness and enthusiasm for team participation and clarified roles and established norms to achieve effective team interaction. Finally, strong teams have built the personal and team *motivation* to work together, partly by acknowledging their individual and group "wins." The three dimensions and the scoring methodology are discussed later in this chapter.

Let's take a peek at a real-life team environment and see how these dynamics play out.

Planning the Sales Kickoff

Kari enters the conference room somewhat flustered: "This is the room for kickoff planning, right? Hi, everybody, I'm Kari. Give me a minute to set up this laptop; then we'll begin."

Kari takes a mental snapshot of the assembled group. Eight people are supposed to be here; six are in their seats, not counting Kari. Todd, from finance. Elizabeth and Larry, both from marketing. Tina, from the outside agency contracted to host the creative content. Nancy, an admin who's taken on travel coordination responsibility. And Ed, the web guy.

"Who's missing?" asks Kari, while stooping under the table to plug in the AC cord. Various responses overlap from the assembled participants: "Was Ken coming?" "And where's Steve?" "Isn't there supposed to be someone here from sales?" "Yeah, where *is* sales? After all, we're doing this for them, right?"

Ed, "Mr. Web," already looks uncomfortable sitting among the others. He's doodling with his palm unit, saying nothing, and avoiding eye contact with others. "So, what kind of day is he having?" Kari asks herself while plugging in her laptop's mouse.

Across from Ed sits Tina, who's engaged in an animated and bubbly, if one-sided, conversation with two others, Elizabeth and Larry. Kari muses, "Sure, she's got the contract for this gig; I can imagine she's feeling pretty comfortable."

Elizabeth and Larry force smiles and offer polite responses to Tina's banter. "Half-engaged," Kari judges to herself while waiting for her laptop to power up. She knows that Larry and Elizabeth have come to this meeting from a group staff conference where it was announced that their parent corporation's latest acquisition would bring aboard another marketing group and a new director of marketing. Kari privately sympathizes, "A new boss with something new to prove. Oh boy."

Todd sits attentively and passes the cable to the projector to Kari. "Thanks," Kari mumbles while making the connection. "Don't know Todd very well," muses Kari. "Been onboard how long? A month maybe?" She squints at the folders displayed on the laptop's desktop and clicks through to the PowerPoint® presentation that will guide this afternoon's meeting.

Nancy interrupts her search for the presentation. "Kari? Do I need my employee lists that shows who's traveling to the kickoff?" Kari looks up. "Uh, I don't think so, not for today," she assures. But privately to herself, "Just great. Here's an ambitious admin who wants to be something more but has never done travel logistics before. Geez, I don't know what's needed either. . . . This is like the blind leading the blind."

Kari hits the control keys to trigger a slideshow of her PowerPoint presentation. With the setup complete, Kari takes a deep breath and addresses the group. "Okay, 'team,' welcome. We've got about two months to plan the sales meeting. This is the group that will make it happen!"

And they're off and running. The word "team" is first used to describe the collection of individuals in the room. The task and timeline are more or less defined. Roles and responsibilities are perhaps less clear. The abilities of the team's participants are mixed and largely unknown by team members.

Will a strong corporate script or playbook of meeting norms facilitate a successful outcome of this planning effort? Maybe, but what about the team members who haven't read the playbook? Like the new guy, Todd, or the outside partner, Tina? Would every team participant understand the rules in the same way? And would they commit to them?

This group has a big task ahead. Many people will ultimately be affected. A lot of money and time will be spent to train and motivate the salesforce. This group has to come together and function collaboratively in a short time. It has no time to invest in extensive skills training designed to forge harmonious relationships or help the group solve problems or resolve conflicts. Discipline alone will not be sufficient; nor will an authoritarian leader with a prepared list of action assignments to dole out to team members. Commitment from all members will be needed to find creative solutions to problems not yet envisioned by the group.

Frank team member discussion is required for effective use of the UATTRA tool.

An important prerequisite for success is open communication. Frank team member discussion is required for effective use of the UATTRA tool. The single factor in achieving effective work team results are team members who are aware of their feelings and are willing to talk about these and team experiences.

What to do next?

The Prime Need: Acknowledge Our Team's Customers

First, identify the team's *customer*. All work teams have at least one customer. The team was formed to do some*thing* for some*one.* Customers may be "big C" customers (the buyers of your company's goods and services) as well as "little c" customers (individuals or groups internal to your business who rely on your team's deliverables to complete their work better or faster). Perhaps the team members themselves are also customers in some way. For example, a group of employees working collaboratively to learn new skill sets or an executive team creating a strategic plan both count themselves as customers of their team efforts. Most likely your teams have both "big C" and "little c" customers.

As a workgroup, discover your customers. Name them. Understand their needs and the intentions that drive their behaviors. These behavioral intentions form the basis of a "persona" for each customer. A *customer persona* is a fictional characterization of the model customer for your team's outputs. Personas are different from "target user" demographics, which may include an ideal age range, income range, job title, or education level. Personas go further, to include the specific needs of the profiled individual as they relate to your team's outputs. Moreover, personas represent individuals, each with a unique name, gender, age, educational and job background, and specific cultural and social characteristics. Personas are specific people, not an abstract list of customer "wants" or "needs" (Cooper, 1999).

The persona of the customer provides conscious focus for the team. Delivering on your commitment to the customer—as defined in your team's objectives or outputs—is the core reason for the team's existence. A strong customer persona will therefore help arbitrate disputes and resolve conflicts in your team's journey to results (Fisher, 2000).

> The first slide of Kari's PowerPoint presentation appears on the screen. The slide is simply a digital photo of a business setting where a young man appears to be leading a discussion or is perhaps explaining something to his audience.

"Hey, isn't that Dean Kato in the picture?" interjects Larry. "He sells for us in Dallas, right?"

"You got it," announces a newcomer to the meeting after a hurried glance at the screen while finding a seat. Ken, the regional sales director, slides around the table to an empty chair. "Sorry I'm late; we were on the phone with a customer."

Kari clicks to the next slide. Another photo appears showing a woman with a telephone headset. She seems to be speaking into the phone and may be focusing her attention on an image on her monitor. "Anyone recognize her? "Kari asks. "This is Joan Bell, from applications." Ken, Nancy, and Elizabeth confirm that they each do, while Kari again advances the slideshow on her laptop. This photo shows two executives seated next to each other at a conference table. "The guy on the left is Ed Koss, our manager of UK operations," volunteers Ken. "He just came on last year."

"These are *our* customers for this sales kickoff," emphasizes Kari as she clicks to the next slide. "And this is their customer." This photo shows casually dressed engineers at a CAD station. "This is Chris and his team, engineers with Monmouth Engineering. Dean (our company salesman), Joan (our corporate app's engineer), and Ed (our UK sales manager). These are *our* customers. And Chris, here in this picture, is *their* customer." Kari pauses for emphasis: "He is our customers' customer."

Used effectively, the various customers that Kari highlights—salesperson, applications engineer, sales manager, and end-user—and their personas become virtual members of the work team and a conscious part of their psyche. These customer personas become vital contributors who show up in spirit at team discussions:

Customer personas become vital contributors who show up in spirit at team discussions.

- "What would *Dean* think of this message?"

- "Would *Joan* be able to use this?"

- "Is this value proposition sufficient for *Dean* to justify the sale to *Chris*?"

- "This would help *Ed* and *Dean* build a better forecast, right?"

Frame the Customer Within Three UATTRA Dimensions

Good knowledge concerning your team's customers enables the team to have a long "tail" on its "up and to the right arrow." This foundation prepares the team to address individual and team effectiveness on three behavioral dimensions that will define the "point" of the UATTRA. These three dimensions are interrelated and lead team members to look inward and outward and to consider the present as well as the future.

Why three dimensions? Simplicity and "actionability." For any model intended to improve team interaction to become popular, it needs to be memorable and usable. These three dimensions define a minimal yet sufficient set of team behaviors that will guide teams of knowledge workers toward effective results. Additions to this model are welcome; individuals and teams have unique needs that require customization of any model for organizational development. However, often "less is more" when trying to change human behavior. Excessive additions to the model may lessen the model's effectiveness, depending on the work team.

Table 29.2 summarizes the three dimensions. A more detailed explanation of each follows.

Table 29.2. UATTRA Dimensions, Goals, and Key Elements

Dimension	Behavioral Goal	Strive to Be *Conscious* About
Self and Others Balance a sense of our own interests, needs, and capabilities with those of other team members.	Each member "chooses" to join in the team's effort and does so with knowledge of each participant's abilities and weaknesses (including his or her own) relative to the team's objective.	Self-honesty and consensus around: • Rules of the game (for team communication, problem solving, meeting management). • Roles and expected contributions. • Personal confidence to speak one's mind. • Gut check: "I *want* to be here and do this."
Objectives Versus Time Understand exactly what the group is expected to deliver or produce, in what timeframe.	All participants believe that the team's objective can be accomplished, in the required timeframe, through an understood and agreed-on process.	• Shared credibility that the team's objectives can be achieved. • Each participant understands and accepts the process whereby the team's work will lead to achievement of all objectives. • The team objectives are aligned with the business's objectives.
Motivation Ensure each team member is motivated to contribute to the team based on intrinsic (personal and private) drivers as well as external expectations for reward or outcome.	Each participant pledges commitment to the team's success after reflection on the reasons "why" each chooses to work on this effort.	• Personal understanding of and excitement around "What's in it for me?" (WIIFM) • Group understanding of how the team's efforts will be measured. • Shared understanding of how the team's deliverables serve its customers.

Self and Others

The first dimension, Self and Others, asks us to look inside and outside, taking stock of ourselves and others: "What do I bring to this group?" "What does each of us bring?"

Think back to how we formed play teams as children. Very often we began with a discussion of roles and abilities: "I'm really good at being the pitcher." "I run really fast." "Do we play keep-away?" "I'll be the race car." There were even more important discussions: "You got to be pitcher last time," "I don't know the rules," or "I don't want to play anymore; this isn't any fun." As children we openly spoke about what we were good or bad at (or at least *thought* we were good or bad at!) and made sure everyone knew the rules to the game. We only did stuff that met our standards for "fun" and "interest." We didn't hesitate to change the rules if circumstances required this, for example, a soccer field became defined by the space available. Three strikes? Maybe baby brother Joey was permitted five. Whatever our game, we talked about it with our playmates and developed "operating norms" on the playground.

Our adult work team behaviors don't have to be much different. Sure, we may not have the option of "not playing" simply because the game (of work) is not "fun," but we assemble as a team and get the abilities of each "player" and the rules out on the table. At the first meeting it is important to publicly clarify what everyone brings to the team and what members expect to contribute. It is also important to develop "team's rules" or norms and to have everyone pledge to behave in accordance with them. Be conscious or aware. Make it verbal. Be genuine and honest.

Activities such as these will enable each team member to decide whether to "opt in" to the team, or to "opt out." A personal "opt in" by each member is a first step toward goal achievement. We understand this lesson well enough: if we don't commit our energies and ourselves to the team, there will be a consequence at some point in the team's journey. Perhaps the impact will be minor, such as a tardy deliverable, or more significant, such as a contribution of poor quality. Either consequence impacts the team and the customer.

Kari moves to the whiteboard in the conference room and begins to list the names of those in the room. "Let's take a moment to discuss who's who in this zoo!" she lightheartedly announces. Next to her name, she writes, "project lead." "I'll start. As you know, I'm tagged with delivering the goods and coordinating the execution of the show. No, I've not produced an event like this before, but have coordinated a number of development projects in my position. I believe I bring the necessary organizational and project management skills to the group but have not worked with a project requiring this level of travel and scheduling intensity. Everything leads to a fixed week on the calendar where it all has to come together. I'm a little nervous about that and expect to learn a lot here as we work together.

But I think what you'll see is that I am pretty good at making sure that the resources we need to do our jobs are made available to us. I'm good at nagging and wheedling management." Kari goes on to talk about her expectations for team members and ends her remarks by asking for questions or comments.

After answering a few questions, Kari invites team members to share a little about themselves, their perception of their roles and their qualifications, and the expectations they have for themselves and others on the team. She encourages members to mention particular strengths that relate to the project and tactfully encourages members to identify any areas where their lack of experience or knowledge needs be thought about as a developmental need.

When it's Nancy's turn to share, Kari inwardly cringes and privately pre-judges her contribution: "I wonder if she's got any experience at all in travel coordination. We'll have big problems if such a critical function isn't professionally managed." Kari manages a smile despite her moody thoughts.

"Okay," begins Nancy. "I'm Nancy Hearn and I support Stew Smith, our group vice president of operations. I've been taking on more and more projects relating to logistics planning for our support groups and wanted to expand my involvement in travel coordination, so I volunteered to represent the travel agency in this kickoff planning. I've planned travel arrangements and meeting planning for small departmental groups before, but never for such a large gathering as this. I'm expecting to get a lot of help from our travel agency, of course, and definitely promise to do my best at this."

"So, let me make sure I understand this," pipes Todd, arms folded and voice stern. "I'm from finance, where we're already squeamish over the spending budget on this kickoff. Since travel and lodging expenses have historically accounted for over one-third of the total budget, you're telling me that you've no experience with negotiating and arranging group travel packages?" Kari picked up on the exasperation in Todd's tone.

"So I'm not the only one to have misgivings about Nancy's ability to deliver results," thinks Kari. She moves to intercede: "I share your concern, Todd. Without disrespect to Nancy and her abilities, I think we need some discussion about this role and what's expected from it. In addition, I want to comment that this is exactly the sort of discussion that we need to have at this time, sorting out our individual and collective strengths and weaknesses as we approach this assignment."

Discussion continues on the responsibilities of the travel coordination role as it relates to the needs of the team. With Nancy's concurrence (and enthusiastic support), agreement is reached for Kari and Nancy to explore how additional expertise can be added to the team to buttress Nancy's limited experience.

Others continue to share their roles, expectations, strengths, and weaknesses. Kari and others take notes as others speak, and team members commit to additional follow-up actions.

Kari clicks forward in her presentation to a simple slide titled "Rules of the Road." It contains only a few bullet points, but the ensuing discussion about individual responsibilities and team behaviors is spirited. Kari concludes the discussion of this slide by reminding the group that this slide will be revisited from time to time during the team's work and congratulates the group on its openness even at this early stage of team formation.

Rules of the Road

- We respect each other's voice
- Our discussions are open and honest
- We'll track action assignments and pledge ourselves to their followthru
- We're accountable for our results, both individually and as a group
- Other?

Kari, continuing her presentation, clicks to the last slide that has only four words: "How do I opt?" Larry takes the bait, "Opt? What do you mean, 'opt'?"

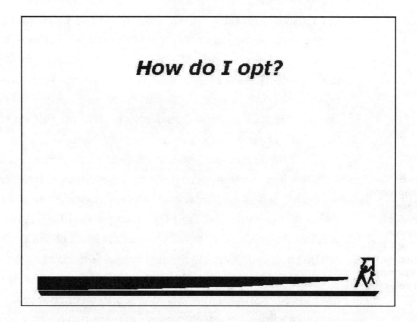

"Simply that we choose whether or not to be here and work on this kickoff event," replies Kari. "Look, we've got a ton of work to do to make this happen. And even though I'm tagged with being the coordinator of this year's event, that doesn't mean that I know all the tasks that we need to work through; that's why we're all here to help see it through. I'm here because it's part of my job, yes, but also because I 'opt' to be here. I'm excited—and a little anxious—to work on this; I want to be here."

"You know, this is going to be a lot of work. And a lot depends on our success. This isn't the best of times for the business. This economy has made it tough for us, and the people in the field are feeling the pain big time." She nods to Ken, from sales, who volunteers his perspective. "Pain? You better believe it. These people are wondering how they're going to eat next month if business doesn't pick up! So, yeah, I'm in. I opt in." Kari turns to the others: "What about you? Opt in or opt out?"

What if we "opt out?" Do we even have the option of choosing? Very often, especially in smaller companies or in firms where specialized expertise is concentrated in a select few, we are "assigned" to teams. It may seem unrealistic to offer participants the freedom to choose membership on a team. How can individuals "opt out" if their contributions are critical to the team's efforts? In fact, even if we are assigned to a team, we do choose whether or not to participate in the team's work. More precisely, we choose the *degree* to which we participate in the team's work. If we accept the team assignment reluctantly because we have too much else to do or genuinely don't want to contribute for one reason or another, we are likely to deliver "just enough." We might fulfill the minimal expectations of the team or, worse, deliver a contribution of poor quality that diminishes the team's deliverables as a whole.

Even if management assigns individuals to teams, the "opt-in" discussion is important and valuable.

Even if management assigns individuals to teams, the "opt-in" discussion is important and valuable, as it helps all members understand how team members are constrained by their other responsibilities and how they feel about the work of the team. However, will team members' statements about opting in or out be absolutely honest? Because a team's success heavily depends on the contributions of its members, it must create an environment where honest answers are offered. Team members may need to be encouraged by their teammates to speak candidly, because adjustments—in project scope, resources, or conflicting priorities—can be addressed if known in advance. Understanding the degree to which each individual will participate helps the team to plan how it will achieve its objectives in the allowed time. This is discussed in the section to follow, "Objective versus Time."

Ed is the first to speak. "I don't know about you, but I've got a job that's 24/7 already. Keeping the website up, with the new e-commerce initiative and the new intranet, is trouble enough for me. I don't know what this kickoff project will require, but I've got to tell you up-front that it's not going to be priority one for me." His resolute tone left no doubt about his position, although his voice betrayed some hesitation and perhaps some embarrassment in speaking with such honesty to strangers.

"That's fair," offered Kari. "The company still has to run while we plan this kickoff. Sales have to be made, operations have to be run; nobody's off the hook for their 'day' jobs. How much time can you commit? And would it make sense to bring on someone from your team to help us in this planning? Perhaps a junior member, working in tandem with you? I'm not trying to suggest a final solution at this point. We've only begun to sketch the task. Let's remain open to various ideas about how to obtain what is needed from you given your limited availability."

It is common to feel that we are already under too much pressure at work to deliver "extraordinary results," "operate efficiently," or "enhance productivity," as well. Corporate mandates like this often lead employees to feel that they are being asked to "do more with less." Once a team has discussed the issue of opting in, it must clarify its assignment and assess whether it can do what it has been asked to undertake. This is the focus of the next UATTRA dimension.

Objective Versus Time

This dimension seems clear enough. After all, we presume that we gather as a workgroup to accomplish something. But what, exactly? "Can I and everyone on the team clearly articulate what we're doing? And by when?" The time allotted to complete the objectives of the team will focus team thinking about what has to be done by whom and the issue of team resources. A team may need to weigh whether the accomplishment of the objectives is even possible. The scope of the objectives and the time given for their achievement are obviously connected. Our business world today has an insatiable appetite for faster and faster accomplishment of more and more things. Whatever it is, do more of it—faster.

As children, we quickly quit a game if it became apparent that no one could possibly win. We learned to change the rules (or even change the game) to make the play more "fair" or more interesting. Similarly, as work team members we must be able to state the "rules" of our teamwork, our route to the team's goals, and what these goals are. An arbitrary pronouncement by management that a team will achieve a particular objective or objectives by a particular date is never well-received. Often, we won't play the "team's game" well unless we're empowered, or we may not play at all if we feel we can't win. And a team that doesn't believe it can achieve its objectives may already have failed. The team must believe that it can achieve its objectives in the time allowed, with the members and resources that it has. Researchers argue that this collective belief by the team in the possibility of success is the single greatest factor in its ultimate success or failure (Kline, 1999; Yancey, 1998).

Belief by the team in the possibility of success is the single greatest factor in its ultimate success.

Once empowered, we ask: "Where are we going? And how are we going to get there? Are we there yet?" A five-year-old will ask these questions without hesitation from the back seat of the family car. A five-year-old may or may not have much to say about whether he or she goes along on the trip and we seldom ask more of our five-year-old passengers than to stay quiet. In contrast, we offer adults in UATTRA the opportunity to opt in or opt out and, if they opt in, we expect that they will be more than just a "passenger" in the team vehicle. However, we need to ask the similar questions asked by that five-year-old to ensure that we all understand our destination and can "buy in" to the path to reach it.

> "Kari, I have a question," began Todd, from finance. "You know, we've got a budget for this kickoff event that's about 10 percent less than last year's. And that's the budget we were given before this latest round of cutbacks; the budget may get trimmed before it's all through. I don't want to rain on anyone's parade here, but how are we supposed to give the sales folks a stronger kickoff message than last year if we can't even spend the budget allocated last year? Costs have undoubtedly gone up."
>
> Nancy adds her two cents: "Well, I expect that travel costs are going to be higher this year. Certainly we know that the hotel rooms are more expensive. I haven't made any calculations yet, but I doubt that we'll be able to offer the same travel and lodging arrangements as last year for any less money."
>
> Kari responds to both Todd and Nancy, and everyone else, for that matter: "Yes, it's true that we've got to work with less money overall. Don't blame only the economy, though; we would probably have trimmed the budget anyway. Finance wants us to manage spending better than last year. But no, I don't have the answers on how we'll do it for less. We probably should spend some time thinking about this."
>
> Todd shares his own perspective, but probably speaks for the group: "Well, I agree that we should spend some time working on the overall plan. Based on what I know now, I just don't know if we can *do* the kickoff in its current form with this budget. At least for me, it doesn't seem possible."

A team needs to devote considerable attention to the *objective versus time* dimension. Each team member must understand, agree to, and personally "buy in" to each part of the plan that leads to the accomplishment of team objectives. Participation from each team member is required as the objectives, action plan, and roles of team members are discussed and clarified. "Buy-in" cannot be tacit: every member must verbalize his or her willingness to work with team members on the implementation of a plan designed to achieve the team's goals. A team must eventually believe that its objective can be accomplished in the given timeframe.

Motivation

This UATTRA dimension influences the discussion by team members of the other two. Our motivation will determine how hard we will work, and the motivation demonstrated by team members may occur for different reasons. We will only "jump in" with our full commitment to a team effort and work hard on team tasks if our motivation is real and personal: "What do I as an individual hope to gain from participation with these people? What's in this for me?"

Motivation is reflected in the energy and enthusiasm we bring to and demonstrate in working on a task (Rossett, 1999; Zander & Zander, 2000). As children our energy and enthusiasm were easily discerned by others—when we were either excited or reluctant to "participate" in activities, such as practicing the piano, going to swimming class, or being the baby sitter for little brothers or sisters. If we *wanted* to put in the effort—practice our music lessons, for example—not only was the task accomplished, but a quality result was far more likely. If we were forced to practice, attend swim class, or baby sit our siblings, our attitude influenced our efforts and the quality of results we ultimately achieved.

What were the rewards that motivated us to exceptional performance when we were young? Were extrinsic, tangible rewards better motivators than intrinsic, intangible rewards? Did money given to us by our parents for doing chores bring out our best? Did praise for doing well from a private tutor encourage us to study harder? Did experiencing the thrill of competition or membership on a sports team push us toward athletic excellence?

As children, the best motivators were usually attainments that made us "feel good" in some way and that were important to us. If the reward was extrinsic or tangible, such as money from adults, we often used it to buy a toy, a book, tickets to a thrill park or a movie. When the reward was intrinsic or intangible—perhaps a "high five" from a teammate on our soccer team or praise for an artistic product from someone we admired—we took away a warm glow that made us a little bit bigger in our own minds. We thought a lot about our own well-being when growing up and centered our interests around making ourselves happy. Even as children, we had a "customer" that we cared about: ourselves.

Although we are adults now, we really don't behave much differently. When we work together in groups, we especially need to be genuinely motivated to "jump in" to the team's effort. We think twice about working with others to accomplish things; it really does take extra effort to collaborate with others, and we want others to work as hard as we will. Psychologists speak about children's judgment of what is worthy of enthusiasm and energy and note that "anything that is too hard to do alone" will be scored low (Gregerman, 2000). Things haven't changed just because we're older.

It's okay to want something for ourselves individually as a reward for our participation. It may be tangible and visible, such as a plaque or certificate, a promotion or bonus, or intangible, such as praise, learning something new, or the pride that accompanies an achievement. Whatever it is, go ahead and identify it. Be a little selfish; it's good for us *and* for the team. Be sure that *we* are one of our team's customers.

We also turn to our customer personas as a source of inspiration and motivation. As we noted, the team exists to serve a customer. A desire to serve a customer provides one reason for team participants to "jump in" together and invest their time and energy. Whether the motivation to contribute to the team comes from serving the customer or from some other source, each team member needs to identify what will influence his or her motivation.

Kari starts off: "We really do have to pull together as a group to make this kickoff happen. And yes, we're doing this in addition to everything else that's on our plates. It's not like we're all going to 'jump in with both feet' just because we got this memo inviting us—or assigning us—to this kickoff planning team. No, we've got to individually choose to join in this effort and, if we do, we've got to find the motivation within ourselves to commit a lot of time and energy over the next two months to planning the best kickoff we can. There's a huge amount at stake for the company, and no one can describe that better than Ken, who joins us to represent our customers, the Dean's, Joan's, and Ed's of sales. Our efforts here are very much able to contribute to the company's success and, if we are successful in this regard, we can come away from this experience with a very real sense of accomplishment.

"We also need to gain personally from being here. Believe me, we each need to get something out of this individually for each of us to give our all during these next eight weeks. We won't be at our best unless this is a 'win' for each of us as well as for the team.

"I'm pleased to share that the top managers are aware of the sacrifices that we'll likely have to make to bring this all together. Understanding the significance of this kickoff and recognizing the extra effort and work time that we'll be putting in during the next few weeks, they've already okayed a bonus week of vacation time for all of us. I, for one, am hugely appreciative."

Nods from some and excited murmuring from others signal enthusiasm for the unexpected vacation time. Ed, however, quickly pipes up: "Maybe time off is a good motivator for you, but what about me? I'm already three weeks behind in my vacation time. No way that I'll be able to take more time off, given the backlog of work that I've got to do. More time off only means that more work piles up for me."

Understanding, Kari nods: "Yes, that doesn't sound fair. Let's take this offline, Ed, and plan a meeting with your manager. Sounds like we need to think through a rebalance of workload and maybe some additional resources to help you. We should spend some time to figure out how to make this a 'win' for you, too!"

Putting It All Together: UATTRA

As discussed earlier, "up and to the right" is the desired direction for a chart showing business success. It's the picture we usually want to see when our business results are charted over time. Graphs of financial results that rise from the lower left-hand corner and burst through the upper right corner generally signal "success."

To plot our UATTRA, we pose a series of questions for each dimension of the UATTRA to derive numeric scores that, when charted, will graphically illustrate an arrow-like form. Assessment questions for each UATTRA dimension and a template on which scores can be placed are provided in Exhibit 29.1. The symmetry of the arrow and distance of each plot point from the UATTRA center provides a visual check of the team's strengths and weaknesses. The goal is for as large and symmetric an arrow as possible (review Figure 29.3, p. 517), demonstrating balance and depth across these interrelated dimensions. Our UATTRA will have as many "tails" in the lower-left quadrant as needed, each reflecting the degree to which we understand our particular customers.

Plot points very near the UATTRA origin indicate weakness in a dimension and suggest a priority for individual or team action. For example, the UATTRA assessment illustrated in Figure 29.4 indicates a rather short *Motivation* dimension, certainly far shorter than the plots of *the Self and Others* and *Objectives Versus Time* dimensions. This suggests that team members should consider how they might improve their individual or collective commitment to the team's cause.

Figure 29.4. UATTRA with Short Motivation Dimension

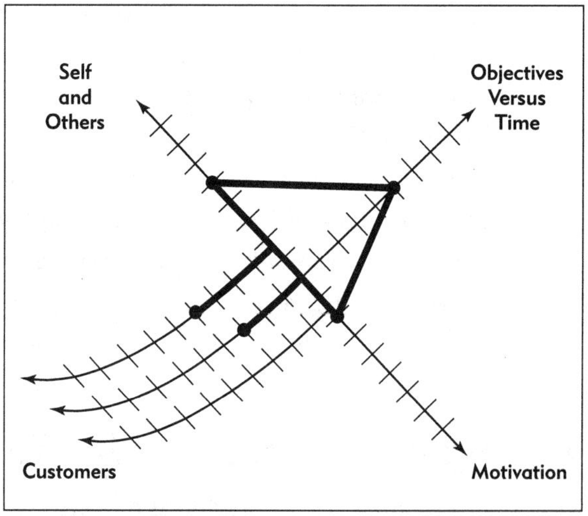

Following completion of the UATTRA a team should work first on the dimension that is the "weakest link."

Borrowing from popular television, following completion of the UATTRA, a team should work first on the dimension that is the "weakest link," the shortest or most out of sync.

The UATTRA assessment can be brought to teams when they form. If the entire team cannot or chooses not to carry out the assessment, individual team members can complete it on their own. Even one team member completing the UATTRA assessment can improve team effectiveness if he or she is determined to pursue actions that lead to more "strongly agrees" on the individual dimensions.

Concerning the UATTRA assessment questions and scoring template provided in Exhibit 29.1, each tic mark along the dimensions in the template represents a scored "point" from the assessment questionnaire. All assessment questions are equally important and count the same. The value of the assessment primarily is the individual reflection and team discussion it prompts. The "up and to the right" arrow reminds us to focus on team attributes and factors that will lead us most surely to business success!

> *"Coming together is a beginning,*
> *Keeping together is progress,*
> *Working together is success."*
> Henry Ford*

Epilogue

Teams are a vital component of today's workplace. Business success depends on people working together. But in business, time is money; work *teams* can spare little time before team*work* is expected. Business demands work team results quickly. The pressure is on us to fast form and fast norm into effective work teams as never before.

The challenge, of course, is how to do it.

The Customer. Self and Others. Objectives Versus Time. Motivation. The UATTRA dimensions form a framework that permits team members to reflect on and to discuss such important issues as the team's clients and their needs; the commitment of members to the team; team roles; team preparedness; team objectives; and the team's timeline, plan, and resources. The use of the UATTRA assessment can lead to outstanding results—results that we and our business desire and our customers expect.

Acknowledgments

The author is indebted to the insights and encouragement provided by Theresa Kline of the University of Calgary and author of *Remaking Teams*.

---

* Source: www.quoteworld.org.

Exhibit 29.1. UATTRA Assessment

Customer _____ Instructions: Complete for each customer of the team. Check and chart your understanding of how your team's deliverables will meet each customer's needs. Assess and separately chart each served persona.	Strongly Disagree	Disagree	Neither Disagree nor Agree	Agree	Strongly Agree
1. The team knows how this customer will benefit from our outputs.					
2. The team knows how specific goals of this customer will be aided by our team's outputs.					
3. The team has discussed the primary goals of this customer as they relate to our team's work.					
4. The team has prepared a specific persona for this customer.					
5. The team understands the persona for this customer.					
6. The team's understanding of this customer is based on direct, observational research.					
7. The team refers to the customer persona by name during our team interactions.					
8. The team has discussed scenarios in which this customer will leverage our team's outputs.					
9. The team's goals include measures of how our deliverables will benefit this customer.					
10. The team understands the consequences to this customer if our objectives are not achieved.					
Add the number of checks in each column:					
Multiply by this number:	-2	-1	0	1	2
Result:					
Add together the Result products of all columns (if less than 0, enter 0):					

Enter that value onto one of the "Customer" arms of the UATTRA chart:

After you've completed each of the four sections, the scores can be transferred to the large chart at the end of the assessment.

Exhibit 29.1. UATTRA Assessment, Cont'd

Self and Others Look inward and outward along the "Self and Others" dimension. Score your own and others' preparedness for team participation. Plot your perspective on the UATTRA Chart.	Strongly Disagree	Disagree	Neither Disagree nor Agree	Agree	Strongly Agree
11. I want to join this team.					
12. I know my role on this team.					
13. I know what deliverables are expected of me.					
14. I have all the skills and knowledge necessary to complete my contribution.					
15. I understand the role and expected contribution of each team member.					
16. Everyone on the team understands my role and expected contribution.					
17. As a group, the team discussed everyone's roles and expectations.					
18. Team members have agreed to follow norms or operating guidelines for group interactions.					
19. A role for a leader of the team is agreed on.					
20. I know who the customers are for this team.					
Add the number of checks in each column:					
Multiply by this number:	−2	−1	0	1	2
Result:					
Add together the Result products of all columns (if less than 0, enter 0):					
Enter that value onto the "Self and Others" arm of the UATTRA chart:					

Exhibit 29.1. UATTRA Assessment, Cont'd

Objectives Versus Time What do you think about the team's plan to achieve its objectives in the given timeframe? Score and chart your perspective on the team's "Objectives Versus Time" dimension.	Strongly Disagree	Disagree	Neither Disagree nor Agree	Agree	Strongly Agree
21. Everyone on the team understands the objectives.					
22. The team understands the steps and the process that will be followed to accomplish its goals.					
23. The team can achieve its objectives in the time allotted.					
24. The goals of the company are aligned with the team's objectives.					
25. The team's objectives address its customer(s) needs.					
26. The team has the correct action plan to accomplish its objectives in the planned timeframe.					
27. The time scheduled for the team's work is sufficient to accomplish its objectives.					
28. The team has agreed to the scope and timeframe for its deliverables.					
29. The team has a plan to regularly review its progress toward the objectives.					
30. I have the resources necessary to complete my contribution to the team.					
Add the number of checks in each column:					
Multiply by this number:	−2	−1	0	1	2
Result:					
Add together the Result products of all columns (if less than 0, enter 0):					
Enter that value onto the "Objectives Versus Time" arm of the UATTRA chart:					

Self and Others — Objectives Versus Time — Customers — Motivation

Exhibit 29.1. UATTRA Assessment, Cont'd

Motivation WIIFM? (What's in it for me?) Or for us? Are we ready to give "all we've got" to the team's effort? Evaluate and chart your position along the "Motivation" dimension to gauge your commitment.	Strongly Disagree	Disagree	Neither Disagree nor Agree	Agree	Strongly Agree
31. The results of our team's work are important to the company.					
32. The team will be rewarded for its accomplishments.					
33. Management has confirmed the importance of our team's contribution.					
34. I believe that I will be recognized for being on this team.					
35. I believe that my contribution to this team's effort is relevant to my own work.					
36. Our team has discussed our individual knowledge, skills, and abilities as relevant to our goals.					
37. I believe that being on this team is important for my career goals.					
38. Our team knows how its results will be evaluated.					
39. I will learn important skills or knowledge from contributing to this team.					
40. Our team has a plan to celebrate its accomplishments.					
Add the number of checks in each column:					
Multiply by this number:	–2	–1	0	1	2
Result:					
Add together the Result products of all columns (if less than 0, enter 0):					
Enter that value onto the "Motivation" arm of the UATTRA chart:					

Exhibit 29.1. UATTRA Assessment, Cont'd

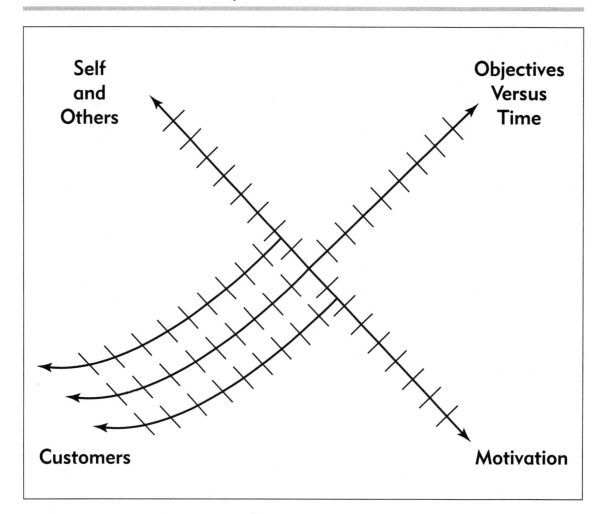

CHAPTER 30

Building and Using Virtual Learning Environments

Deborah Hurst and Scott Follows

MANY ORGANIZATIONS are introducing virtual teams to break the barriers of distance, time, and space (Boudreau, Loch, Robey, & Staub, 1998; Duarte & Snyder, 1999; Lipnack & Stamps, 1997). However, in addition to the typical challenges associated with teaming, in virtual teams there is the potential for miscommunication due to differences in geography, organization, time zone, language, culture, access to technology, and one's ability to use technology. These challenges can be overcome to some extent through training and team building done online. This chapter presents an example of virtual training as a method for increasing teams' ability to deal with those challenges—a virtual learning environment (VLE). The VLE consists of a simulation that mirrors complex organizational characteristics. Facilitated discussion can be used to aid learning during the VLE experience.

Many organizations are introducing virtual teams to break the barriers of distance, time, and space.

Virtual Learning Environments

The VLE is presented in two phases. The first phase is a CD-ROM-based virtual world that is designed to simulate real-world experiences. Analogous to a flight simulator for pilot training, the learner develops an understanding of content by engaging in team experiences through his or her interactions with simulated team members. The second phase of the VLE is an Internet chat site where a facilitator guides a small group of learners to work together as a virtual team. The module is thus interactive, technology-mediated, delivered at a distance, and deals with real team dynamics and communications issues in practice and content. The primary learning objectives of the team dynamics and communication module are (a) to understand how teams function, whatever the locale; (b) to learn how to build a successful and high-performing collaborative team; and (c) to allow individuals the opportunity to assess their personal strengths and weaknesses as team players.

Training is interactive, technology-mediated, and delivered at a distance.

In the sections that follow, experiences of the virtual learning environment for challenging value assumptions and building intellectual capital in skills and competencies needed for effective collaborative teaming are considered. The discussion begins with a description of the Canadian Professional Logistics Institute (2000) team training experience to provide a sense of what each professional learner encounters. We ask why the VLE is considered a powerful tool for this type of training, followed by a discussion of learners' actual experiences of the module. Of specific interest is how individuals build team-based skills and insight and how much impact technology-mediated learning has. In the final section of the chapter, learners' and facilitator's experiences are compared to initial questions regarding the VLE's ability to develop intellectual capital and provide the groundwork for cultural value change.

Virtual Teams

Teams are not the solution to every organization's current and future needs. Teams will not solve every problem, enhance every group's results, nor help every manager address every performance challenge. When misapplied, teams can be both wasteful and disruptive and interfere with collaboration. Nonetheless, teams can usually outperform other groups and individuals, and they represent one of the best ways to support the broad-based changes necessary for collaborative work in high-performing organizations (Katzenbach & Smith, 1999).

Teams are defined as a small number of people with complementary skills, committed to a common purpose, performing interdependent tasks for a common goal to which they hold themselves mutually accountable. Virtual teams take this one step further and move beyond co-location to span distance, time zones, and organizational boundaries (Lipnack & Stamps, 1997). (For additional information, see Chapter 7, Developing and Assessing a Climate for Creativity in Virtual Teams.)

It is assumed here that the implementation of any kind of team requires specific attention to cultural values that encourage listening constructively, responding to others' points of view, giving the benefit of the doubt, providing support, and recognizing the interests and achievements of others. Furthermore, teams are assumed limited in becoming effective collaborative work systems if they are introduced into a culture that does not support their functioning. Within the reality of introducing teams and hence the cultural changes to support them, there are obviously some important barriers to consider. The Canadian Professional Logistics Institute (2000) believes that most individuals approach teams cautiously, particularly the idea of putting one's fate into the hands of others. Mutual promises and accountability cannot be coerced any more than people can be made to trust one another. (See Chapter 8 on accountability as a leadership responsibility.) Moreover, people may have personalities and aspirations that are incompatible with a team approach. These individuals may have a propensity toward analysis, quick action, and a need for control and rely on considered opinions or formal process techniques rather than a discussion of values. Many people in organizations are trained to focus on decisions, outcomes, performance, measures, and actions. As a result, people become more adept at logical analysis and critical thinking than at developing and building relationships. Teams composed of such action-oriented people can fail unless they are challenging existing organizational and personal values regarding how teams form and the phases of development that teams go through.

Mutual promises and accountability cannot be coerced.

Cultural assumptions are laden with values about how we work and communicate and about how teams function. Cultural assumptions within traditional hierarchies that demand upward communication and accountability are contradictory and can limit team autonomy and functioning. Effective teaming requires organizations to nurture communications that flow downward, upward, across, and outside of the organization to build complex collaborative relationships and adapt different processes. With the emergence of strategic partnerships and global supply chains, inter-organizational collaboration demands now dominate business development. Effective team dynamics involves more than just members from the same department or several departments within the same organization; indeed, they may involve different agendas from constituencies that are culturally distinct and geographically dispersed. Virtual teams often do not meet in the same place at the same time; some communicate synchronously, others asynchronously. Whatever the challenge, real teams do not emerge unless individuals on them take risks involving conflict, trust, interdependence, and hard work.

Real teams do not emerge unless individuals on them take risks.

The Team Dynamics Module

In recognition of the complexities of teams in organizational life and learning, the Canadian Professional Logistics Institute created a program comprised of both virtual and traditional (face-to-face) modes of delivery. The team dynamics and communication module discussed here is part of a package of modules that includes integrated logistics networks and logistics process diagnosis delivered virtually, supply chain strategies, leading and managing change, ethics, and leadership delivered in a face-to-face format. The program works to mix soft and hard skill development as well as learning in different environments in an effort to build intellectual capital and promote supporting values for effective collaborative work within the logistics profession. The team dynamics and communications module facilitates practical skill development, understanding, and insight regarding team dynamics and virtual learning. Learners build on insights taken from Katzenbach and Smith (1999), among other thought leaders on teams, to develop key success indicators of teams.

The Team Dynamics Module is an interactive virtual learning environment that presents team experiences in two phases over a six-week period. In Phase One, learners engage in an extended case that simulates experiences that many individuals encounter as members of a new team. The learner interacts with virtual team members known as the simulated or "Sim-Team" on a time-sensitive, critical mission and experiences team and team-relevant issues as he or she progresses through various scenarios in an asynchronous learning environment. The setting for the VLE is a remote area where lightning has started a forest fire and also damaged a telecommunications tower. The learner is part of an emergency response crew that has been called together to repair the tower. The team must travel by canoe and arrive within a set period of time. If the team functions poorly and arrives late, telecommunications go down and firefighters will not be able to prevent the forest fire from approaching a small town. Each decision is shown to have immediate consequences within the virtual simulated world and collectively conveys the risk of failure.

Making mistakes creates teachable moments.

Although a poor decision or mistaken action taken by the learner may cause the team to lose time on the trip, making mistakes creates teachable moments. Failure is considered to be an opportunity to learn by determining "What went wrong?" A virtual coach provides just-in-time feedback (positive and negative) and content to the learner based on the learner's decisions. The learner is therefore able to learn from mistakes in a private and safe environment.

Instead of presenting information sequentially, the script is similar to a multiple path storybook, where the story depends on choices made by the learner. Learning becomes customized as learners spend greater amounts of time dealing with concepts and skills that are unfamiliar to them. The VLE also incorporates storytelling as a means of relating the content and experiences back to the workplace. As individuals learn and practice each new skill, they are thought to gain a deeper understanding of team dynamics and communications.

Woven into the module design are different aspects of team structure, process, culture, accountability, and politics occurring within the different stages of team development.

Learners are asked from time to time to make note of what they are thinking and feeling about the experiences so that they can use it later in online discussions. Self-evaluation tools are embedded within the module at strategic points to give learners an opportunity to focus on specific issues of interest and to more fully develop and reflect on the new skills and competencies under scrutiny. Examples of the self-evaluation tools include discovering communication preferences, leadership style, and handling conflict situations.

In Phase Two of the virtual learning environment, learners form another team, known as the Real-Team, with other learners who have also worked through the CD-ROM experience. They leave the asynchronous virtual world of the CD-ROM and enter an Internet-based synchronous chat environment within the Canadian Professional Logistics Institute's Learning Centre website.

During the initial chat room meeting, learners are arranged into smaller teams, introduce themselves, discuss their impressions of the CD-ROM experience, and then come up with a team name as part of their icebreaker activities.

The Real-Team is then assigned the task of creating a reverse logistics plan, assuming that the telecommunications tower is repaired. This task provides some continuity with the previous work within the CD-ROM and gives the team some further time to get to know one another. During this first exercise, team members become familiar with working in the chat environment, and it is often necessary for them to establish and re-establish how conversations will take place and what order members will speak in to ensure that all have their say and to create process rules to ensure that each member does participate fully. To launch the team to this task, they are advised that the fire is almost under control and that the crew will be finished repairing the communication tower in six hours. Their task is to get the used and remaindered supplies and members back to the point of origin. They are given three possible options to discuss, as well as many contingencies to consider, and are asked to come up with a detailed reverse logistics plan through consensus. During this initial exercise, the facilitator introduces additional information regarding transport routes, modes, environmental conditions, wildlife, handling disposing of dangerous/hazardous goods, and alternative options to challenge the team and bring out creative and different points of view. The goal of this exercise is to surface differences to allow team members the opportunity to experience and work through new ideas, skills, and competencies regarding team dynamics and communications during the learning.

The second task assigned to the team is the creation of a team charter template. The completed team charter template resembles a checklist and contains what the team believes to be the important issues to be addressed for creating and deploying an effective team as quickly and meaningfully as possible. (For more information on team charters, see Chapter 4.)

This forms the takeaway document for participants and covers topics such as how the team is formed and structured, purpose, processes, development of team culture, collaboration, accountability, measurement of success, and high performance functioning. The charter template is an important goal of this phase of the module, as this is where learning crystallizes and the team takes stock of what has been learned individually and collectively. Throughout this phase of the module, work is facilitated through weekly team meetings held synchronously, during which learners make decisions about how the work will be completed. Team members are encouraged to take control of their work. For example, if the team members decide to hold additional unmoderated meetings or assign tasks to subgroups of individuals to prepare for meetings, they are encouraged to do so. They are given a message board to post longer documents so that they can be shared and reviewed prior to meetings.

Phase Two activities intend to ground the learner's new skills and knowledge in additional collaborative experience. This phase also provides the opportunity to discuss views with other participants and a subject area facilitator. Collectively, the new team develops insight into team dynamics and communication processes and, as part of their collective work, designs a team charter template applicable to global teams in their field of expertise.

Overall, the VLE focuses on skills needed for effective team dynamics and virtual teaming: team process discussion, role assignment, leadership, conflict resolution, decision making, and planning for goal success. Many of the scenarios crafted were taken from real experiences highlighting the most salient issues of team development. Information on how different people store information and label organizational stories was used to construct the decision paths in each scene of the scenario. Cultural ideas around likely failures and interpretations of the failures were used to inform the scripting. The resulting scenarios were dramatic and encouraged participation. Other aspects of team member roles and competencies include the need to coordinate and collaborate autonomously. Organizational factors included networking, knowing the organizational landscape, and maintaining guidelines. The use of technology category was concerned with when to communicate, coordinate, and collaborate; how to communicate effectively; and communication etiquette. The personal management category includes the ability to prioritize work, set limits, create opportunities for learning and growth, collect and provide feedback, discuss strengths and weaknesses, manage boundaries, and understand different cultural perspectives and how differences can impact perception.

Why a Virtual Learning Environment?

Because this VLE is a virtual tool, it can be used in various contexts across or within organizations. This tool gets beyond significant challenges faced by traditional forms of corporate training and university teaching regarding how to provide experiential learning to employees or students given the impracticalities of cost, time frame, and risk.

Schank (1997) believes that real learning can only occur when people are thrown into scenarios, asked to make decisions, solve problems, make mistakes, and have access to an expert as required to answer questions and give advice. Because simulations are private, people are more willing to fail, and failure when attached to a goal is the most powerful stimulant for learning. Failure in organizations is perceived negatively, and this often stifles creativity.

 People can fail with dignity in a simulation rather than be publicly humiliated; the computer does not care or blame someone when a mistake is made. Failure, fun, and stories are all critical to real learning, as they can induce intense emotional feelings. Furthermore, the computer can store the learning that has occurred and retrieve it later if a similar pattern is observed later on. People need to practice skills, make mistakes, practice more, make further mistakes, and at some point hear what an expert has to say. Learning is most powerful when individuals learn to do something rather than being told about something, because knowledge gained through experience becomes tacit (Schank, 1997; Stewart, 2001a).

Learner and Facilitator Experiences

In this section of the chapter, comments are organized according to how the learners and the facilitator experienced the technical and content aspects of the module. To date, the team dynamics and communications module has been offered to participants of the Institute eleven times. The evaluation data referred to in this paper were taken from the first six offerings (2000–2001) of the module. As each round of the module provided new learning opportunities, improvements have been incorporated into the tool.

During the initial offerings of the module, some of the learners experienced technical challenges. The challenges were not only related to computer incompatibility issues but also to the degree of readiness displayed. For many in the module, there was an underlying hesitancy and fear associated with learning in a technologically mediated environment. Many thought that it "was fun, challenging . . . an overall good learning experience . . . although, my first experience in utilizing a chat line . . . it was quite different and a little scary in the beginning."

For some participants, technical problems and learner frustrations persisted throughout the module, signaling something else to the facilitator and developers. On further investigation, these people seemed worried that they would fail in a public way due to their unfamiliarity with the technique and as a result become embarrassed. This highlights one of the strengths of the VLE that Schank (1997) describes regarding the ability of learners to take risks and fail in private to prevent public embarrassment. The strength of the apprehension around failure prior to entry into the VLE was very interesting. As a result, facilitation was introduced before learners used the CD-ROM in order to encourage a comfort level among learners and minimize their stress.

VLE enables learners to take risks and fail in private to prevent public embarrassment.

Once the technical difficulties in Phase One of the program were dealt with, the learners began to comment on the positive aspects of their experience, for example: "I thought the interactive CD was very well put together and a neat way to learn. I know I now have a better understanding of team building, conflict resolution, and the importance of communication." The level of comfort in Phase Two increased after the first chat experience. One learner noted that, "I initially found it difficult to converse electronically with ten other people, although I see my children doing it all the time. Once I got the 'hang of it,' it became enjoyable." People commented increasingly on the content of the module throughout Phase Two, particularly as they became more comfortable with the technology and the use of it became tacit.

The facilitator reported that by entry into Phase Two, many of the learners appeared quite knowledgeable on the importance of virtual teams for organizations. The reflective exercises in the CD-ROM were provocative and useful to clarify ideas throughout the VLE, as well as to help learners prepare their thoughts for their individual contributions during the second part of the module. Once learners completed Phase One, they were directed to the website at a specified time as set by the facilitator so that they could participate in a synchronous discussion. Short introductions at the outset of Phase Two were intended to help the individuals get to know one another quickly and to build confidence and comfort with the new communications medium. Learners were then asked to name their team. In each case, the team brainstormed ideas in the chat room and, with the help of a facilitator, worked to develop and use a consensus decision-making process to settle on the final team name.

In the first offering of the module, the introductory session was considered "too short" by most learners. The facilitator noted that individuals appeared to take longer than expected to warm up to each other and develop trust within the team. Early communications seemed strained and factual, whereas later in the module, learners opened up to each other to the point of telling jokes.

After the introductory exercises, team members were asked to review a chat protocol provided by the Canadian Professional Logistics Institute so that all are aware of expectations at the outset. The chat protocol follows:

- Allow each learner to complete his or her thought before responding. This means do not interrupt or intrude with your thought while another is speaking.

- Be patient; not everyone has advanced keyboard skills.

- Avoid having side conversations; it's rude not to pay attention.

- Signal when you've finished a statement [some use a happy face to signal they have completed their input ☺]

- Signal when you don't understand something; use a question mark to get the facilitator's attention.

- Signal your "reactions" by using an exclamation mark (!) for surprise or a sad face for disagreement ☹ or some combination of symbols.

- Do not shout [CAPITALS MEAN THAT YOU ARE SHOUTING].

- Do not leave your computer during a scheduled session; it is impossible to get your attention if you leave the room.

- Officially sign on and off so that everyone knows when you are present.

- Keep statements brief and to the point; the chat box has a limit of 256 characters per statement; you can keep talking, but in spurts.

- Prepare notes and key ideas ahead of time so that you can engage in the discussion without trying to figure out how to word your statements.

Learners in each session underscored the importance of reviewing the chat protocol time and time again. One learner noted, "At times it was difficult to follow the conversation. In the time it took me to type my answer to someone's statement or question, two or three more players had answered and sometimes changed the subject; therefore my answer seemed to be inappropriate. Right from the beginning, there should be a clear understanding concerning the rules and the proper procedures of the chat system."

As learners became more comfortable and developed skill in the chat environment, they also contributed information for how to improve their communications on the team. One suggestion was to develop a speaker's order so that all would have a chance to contribute to the conversation in turn. This development improved the team's performance regarding their communication and collaboration in subsequent tasks. The team was then ready to do its main assigned work. The first major task that individuals were asked to complete was a reverse logistics plan. This exercise linked participants back to the Sim-Team experiences in Phase One of the module and provided an opportunity to discuss their experiences and reflections from that phase. To get the learners working on the reverse logistics planning and to relate their experiences of Phase One of the module, the following scenario was presented: "The fire is slowly being brought under control. The crew will finish repairing the communications tower in six hours. It is necessary to get used and remaindered supplies, as well as crew members, back to the point of origin."

Three options are presented to the learners at this point. They are asked to discuss the options and as a team develop and present a "reverse logistics plan" by selecting the most appropriate option to return to base camp. They are reminded by the facilitator that they must consider issues such as transport routes and modes, materials to be transported or disposed of, materials valuation, logistics valuation, handling and disposing of dangerous/hazardous goods, condition of personnel, alternative options, and potential costs such as using helicopters, environmental impacts, nature issues such as river currents, bears at the garbage dump, weather, and so on. Throughout the exercise, the facilitator adds other ideas for consideration and encourages the team to tease out all possible issues and hazards. The team then sets out to create its plan.

The facilitator noted, "It was interesting to hear what the learners chose to discuss." Many participants commented on the different Sim-Team characters from Phase One and how these encounters helped them to better understand themselves. For example, the strong character, Maureen, was often in discussions. This individual was extremely driven and analytical and was often stressed and pressed for time. One of the learners offered "to throw Maureen overboard." Another noted that he "misunderstood Maureen for most of the trip and realized why I was doing that in the end. I will take this experience and understanding to my daily work now." The learner was referring to his reaction to the communication style presented. As a result of his learning via the discussion and diagnostic tests, he gained a clearer understanding of his reaction in relation to others.

In the second major task of Phase Two, learners created a team charter template. The finished version of the team charter template most resembled a checklist containing the most important issues and questions raised when creating a new team. Learners were asked first to respond individually to the questions posed and then work in their teams to synthesize the information to create one common document. Individuals attended meetings in the chat room to discuss what should/should not be included in the document.

The team charter template most resembled a checklist containing the most important issues and questions.

The roles of leader, scribe, and timekeeper were rotated to give all participants a chance to develop additional skills. By the time learners were given this assignment, they were very comfortable with the virtual environment and appeared to "forget the lack of face-to-face cues."

In each offering of the module thus far, learners completing the task spend most of their time discussing team structure and process issues. As they discuss issues, teams often also experience the same issues. During a recent session, a discussion took place around conflict resolution. There was mild disagreement in how conflicts at an impasse should be resolved. Some members of the team thought that "troublemakers had the option to leave the team." Others noted that this was not an appropriate option; instead, they believed that "consensus must occur." The discussion heated up and circled for some time until the facilitator pointed out the similarities between the topic under discussion and the discussion itself. Since they had already discussed effective listening at length, they were then able to recognize the value of the discussion and develop a process that they could all live with, namely consensus. The learning opportunity was noted as one in which concepts were both discussed and experienced.

The final task of Phase Two asked learners to comment on what they found to be the most positive characteristics of the team experience and their team members. Interestingly, during the first pilot offering of the module, team members decided that they did not want to comment on each individual in the way requested because, they argued, they were a team. They met to discuss this and the team as a unit presented their revised version of the exercise to the facilitator. The facilitator was pleased with how "the team took on the issue and discussed it actively." She noted that "One individual, on behalf of the team, suggested that the team wanted to handle the task in a slightly different way and asked first if they could, as they had the full agreement of the team. I watched them come together with a force that night while they displayed excellent consensus decision making. I believe that the activity worked to catalyze the team and pushed them to a higher performance level in terms of their morale and functioning."

Once finished, team members expressed satisfaction with the result of the exercise and their experience and input into it. Overall, it appeared that the VLE provided opportunities as well as obstacles for learners. One noted positively that the "online experience was good in bringing people together from across the country and different areas of business. I found that people seem to be more open online than they are in a classroom setting." Another participant said, "The group dynamics were very realistic, the group came together by the final chat. . . . There was a natural flow to using e-mails. . . . We took the path of least resistance because it was effective for our group." Others remained a bit unsure of the technology and seemed reluctant to use it in the way intended. A lot of the resistance regarding the technology was overcome when the facilitator re-emphasized the expectations of working within the VLE and provided a detailed problem-solving document.

Resistance regarding the technology was overcome when the facilitator re-emphasized the expectations of working within the VLE.

Even though expectations were provided to learners at the beginning of the module, these had to be repeated again and again due to the initial discomforts with the technology. Because individuals were worried about their ability to perform in a VLE and were unsure or nervous about expectations in the virtual learning environment, they perhaps did not hear the messages and instructions provided. Each chat session lasted approximately two hours; however, earlier meetings during the module were somewhat longer (2.5 hours) and some of the teams asked for additional meeting time during the week. The first chat meeting was labor-intense as the learners struggled with expectations and interacting in the new environment. However, as they learned techniques, they took control of their learning, making the meetings much more efficient and creative.

Developing Intellectual Capital

Some interesting insights were gained as a result of testing and using the VLE thus far that lead us to believe that the VLE does have the capability to develop intellectual capital in terms of soft and hard skill development, as well as contribute to cultural values and assumptions. We know that intellectual capital encompasses a wide range of activities designed to get maximum value of knowledge continuously generated. We also know that organizations are largely social institutions that draw intellectual capital value from individuals within the firm. However, these same individuals also take value out of the firm by virtue of their interactions with colleagues.

Therefore, the organization needs to create structures and processes for employees, such as those collaborating on teams, that enable rather than constrain social activities and knowledge sharing (Birkinshaw, 2001). (See Chapter 21 on creating intellectual capital through communities of practice.)

While some very positive learning occurred, we must be cautious in interpretations. Many learners commented on the team's ability to come together: "The team jelled quite well and I think that the final document was something that could be used in a practical application." Another noted, "The exchanges were good and . . . everyone participated to the achievement of the team's objectives." However, some of the virtual teaming aspects presented a bit of a struggle for some, as they felt that a more social environment would have helped them. One learner noted, "A lot of the subtle aspects in forming a team did not come out in the [VLE] environment. . . . Examples of this include eye contact (used to convey trust or disbelief), body language (used to show enthusiasm or lack of interest), voice inflections (anger, skepticism, consoling, etc.)."

Technological tools for sharing and codifying knowledge were critical here and appeared to do well to capture explicit forms of knowledge, but they could not always capture the tacit knowledge that exists nor easily allow for knowledge or skill development. Still, the technology used worked to facilitate performance in the virtual team. The degree of social presence and information richness required for each task at hand needs to be examined further to allow for the most effective result (Duarte & Snyder, 1999). With the VLE implementation, social presence was more important to learners in the early phase, until they became comfortable with one another and began to trust. The early team development phase seemed somewhat ill-defined and frightening to learners, requiring them to spend a bit more time getting to know one another. Learners suggested that biographies be sent ahead of time, possibly photos as well, so that they could have a better idea who they were dealing with. It seemed that there was also a need for people to express emotion and personal views and/or frustrations. The issues surrounding social presence, however, were not altogether unlike those experienced in face-to-face teams during the early development stages.

As team members gained more comfort with one another and confidence in the virtual learning environment, their needs around information richness replaced the social aspects as most critical.

Team needs around information richness replaced the social aspects as most critical.

The amount and variety of information that learners were required to review increased with assigned tasks, making it important for them to post and review work completed asynchronously prior to synchronous chat meetings. Through practice and use of the technology, learners developed tacit knowledge around the most effective combined use of the message board and the synchronous chat used for team meetings.

Practical Applications

There were many valuable lessons gleaned from the VLE that were transferable to the everyday work world of the learners. The emergency response team was created as one form of virtual action team for the purpose of the VLE. The learning that occurred can be easily related to other forms of teaming such as management, service, production, project, or networked teams. The experience of teaming virtually that occurred in this module did seem to mirror the complexity that real virtual teams encounter due to time, distance, organizational, communication, and collaboration challenges. Virtual team members faced challenges of integrating their work methods and dealing with their different work habits, processes, goals, and cultures. The Real-Team within the VLE was receiving explicit knowledge about virtual teams while they were practicing as a virtual team. They were doing so using collaborative technology in a facilitated learning environment. As they worked their way through the module, each learner developed different leader and team member skills and competencies. There was also an indication that the VLE allowed for skills to develop among those typically less comfortable with contributing in a face-to-face environment.

The VLE allowed skills to develop among those less comfortable with a face-to-face environment.

"I felt that without seeing or hearing the other people there was no need to feel reserved in what we had to say, no body language to get in the way. I know that other team members felt the same way and, after a few sessions, the team jelled. For these reasons, I think that threaded discussion is an excellent medium for team brainstorming, a spawning ground for new ideas." Another noted something similar: "I found myself speaking out more in the chat room environment, probably more than I normally would have had I been in a normal classroom environment. The majority of my team was very enthusiastic about completing the assigned tasks. . . . I think for the majority, like for me, it was a first-time, unique experience working together on a project using the Internet."

Team members had ample opportunity to develop and practice soft skills, such as providing constructive feedback, listening actively, resolving conflict, building consensus and trust, and handling change. All occurred virtually. Team members also developed additional hard skills in logistics planning within their CD-ROM and web environment work. As a result of knowledge accumulated and skills developed, each learner began to develop explicit and implicit intellectual capital on what it takes to succeed in a virtual team. Of course, the module experience was just the beginning. A learner noted, "I think that the CD concept was very well-thought-out and did provide me with new insight on how teams should work. The second part of the course expanded on that knowledge. I normally find the experience of working with my peers always forces me to stretch my abilities and learn new ways of doing things. This group was no different than any other; some members contributed more than others. The important lesson here is that we proved that the team was able to accomplish more than we as individuals could have."

Intellectual capital with respect to the use of technology to mediate work on a team was gained as a result of the module in both explicit and tacit forms. Individuals gained knowledge of the hard skills by virtue of using the technology for meetings and sharing work as well as for how to make it work well for them as individuals.

Concluding Comments

As noted earlier, the VLE was developed assuming that adults learn best when there is an opportunity to directly experience what they are learning. In order for the learner to experience the development of collaborative work within teams, the VLE placed the learner in simulated and real-life situations that demanded practice of specific skills deemed important by theory and principles underlying the building and functioning of a successful team. The simulated experience was similar to what one would expect to face as a member of any new team. The learner interacted with virtual team members and solved a series of problems and/or made decisions in order to acquire knowledge and skills. The multi-path format employed allowed each learner to make decisions, safely experience failure, and learn from his or her mistakes by receiving just-in-time expert coaching from within the VLE. The learner then worked as part of a real virtual team in order to practice and reinforce the skills and knowledge.

Given our work, we found a few key insights regarding the development and use of virtual learning tools. First, the initial investment for the creation of the learning environment must be carefully considered. As stated, the adult learning or experiential learning approach works best for this type of material. Learners are provided with an opportunity to learn about specific topics intellectually while they also engage with the ideas experientially. Private trial and error experiences allow for a more receptive learner, subsequently developing deeper levels of learning and development of forms of tacit knowledge and perhaps new ways of thinking or new values regarding specific issues. However, development of such tools can be costly and can deter organizations from creating high quality VLE tools. There is an important caution here to consider when making the assessment of the costs and benefits of creating VLE tools. Adult learners prefer to be challenged with materials that they find useful and applicable. Just as in a classroom setting, virtual learners may become impatient or tune out if the tool presented is too elementary or non-engaging. Although the initial development investment may be substantial, there are important savings to consider during the delivery phases. VLE tools are immediately useful once developed. They can be used at multiple locations, in different time zones, with individuals remotely or groups of individuals within organizations simultaneously. Continuous improvements can be made to VLEs more quickly and less costly then redevelopment and delivery costs often associated with face-to-face development programs. High profile, leading facilitators can be recruited without the burden of busy schedules or reluctance to travel or extra travel and accommodation expense.

The second key insight found as a result of this research deals with the degree to which teams appear to need social cues with which to develop effective teaming and collaborative work relationships. We found social cues extremely important early in the team development process.

It seemed that participants were looking for social connections early, perhaps due to some of the technical problems experienced and their unfamiliarity with how to learn in a virtual environment. The social connections helped to alleviate the early stresses surrounding the uncertainties of the learning environment. To alleviate some of the early discomfort, we therefore built in more time for learners to become accustomed to one another and expectations with a VLE. We introduced additional time for discussions around impressions of the CD-ROM and asked what happened in the CD-ROM related to their everyday work experiences. As participants became more open with one another, we asked them to brainstorm ideas for team names. As comfort levels improved, participant needs became less socially oriented and more associated with information richness.

To answer participants' increasing need for information richness, we added diagnostic tools. The tools we used concentrated on communication (Robbins, 1992), leadership (Lloyd, 1996), team building (Quick, 1992), and conflict resolution (Kindler, 1996). Throughout the facilitated discussions, where different aspects of team formation and processes were highlighted, participants found the information taken from the diagnostics very useful. The tools provided insight to individuals privately as well as collectively through discussion. In each case, the insights gained experientially facilitated the team's learning and growth.

The final take-away from the module was the development of a team charter template or checklist, as it is referred to above. We developed the format for this exercise using ideas regarding the intricacies of team formation, processes, culture, politics, and accountability from the work of Aranda, Aranda, and Conlon (1998). In each offering of the course, participants have commented on the usefulness of the work completed during the module, with particular emphasis around the creation of the team charter template. In one participant's words, "The team charter planning tool is quite useful, I'm now using it with my team to revamp some of our work."

Finally, it is our view that the use of virtual learning environments can potentially allow organizations to bring about innovative developments, such as collaborative work systems and virtual teams, and bypass some of the institutionalized inertia of "organization" embedded in traditional cultural values, ideas, and assumptions that typically limit success of such innovations. The design and process of VLE use described in this chapter provide a roadmap for developing additional tools for educating team members online in competencies that can significantly enhance their performance.

CHAPTER 31

The Dynamics of Conflict Resolution

Jimmy A. Nelson

MOST OF US DO NOT HANDLE CONFLICT VERY WELL. Often, we were taught to handle conflict in one of two ways: stand and fight or run away. Fight or flight techniques can lead to instant escalation of the conflict, years of hidden bad feelings toward a co-worker, or a highly dangerous escalation of the conflict later. Often, especially in a work environment, unresolved conflict leads to losses in productivity, high absenteeism, loss of motivation, loss of job satisfaction, dissatisfaction with our surroundings, and finally, termination of employment (either voluntary or involuntary). Work conflicts can also negatively impact our lives outside of work. They can lead to stress at home, misdirected anger, or poor family relationships. Think about the last time you brought your complaints about work home with you.

Most of us do not handle conflict very well.

What we need to learn is a new way to handle this conflict. We need to learn how to focus not on "managing" conflict, but on *resolving* conflict, so we can keep conflict from negatively impacting our lives. In this chapter we will examine what conflict is, look at what causes conflict to occur, and discover the styles people use in conflict situations. We will then have a better understanding of the dynamics of conflict resolution and be ready to learn some very effective techniques that can be used daily to resolve conflict. In addition, we will look at why these techniques are so effective at resolving conflict for the people who know how to use them correctly. Our intent here is to offer information and tools that will enable you to prevent and work through conflict and enjoy a better work and home life. (See Chapter 19 for a discussion of the sources of conflict between organization groups and departments and their remedies.)

What Is Conflict?

Conflict is defined as the under-utilization or under-valuation of the thoughts, feelings, ideas, or strengths of one individual in a relationship, with relationship meaning "any interaction between two individuals." Consider the last time you observed (or were involved in) a conflict situation. What was occurring? One person was trying to explain (strongly) his or her point of view to another person, who in turn was trying to (strongly) get his or her point of view across to the other. Both were so wrapped up in trying to get the other person to understand a different point of view that neither heard what the other had to say. Both were frustrated because their thoughts, ideas, or opinions were not being utilized or valued by the other person. An underutilized or undervalued person always means conflict.

How Is Conflict Handled?

To really understand what conflict is, we must understand first that people handle conflict in many different ways. We will examine five of the most common ways.

The five basic styles we will focus on are the most often mentioned in the literature on conflict: smoothing, avoiding, competing, compromising, and integrating (see Figure 31.1).

Figure 31.1. Conflict Resolution Model

Adapted from K. Thomas, "Conflict and Conflict Management," in M.D. Dunnett (Ed.), *Handbook of Industrial and Organizational Psychology* (Santa Monica, CA: Goodyear Publishing Company, 1976).

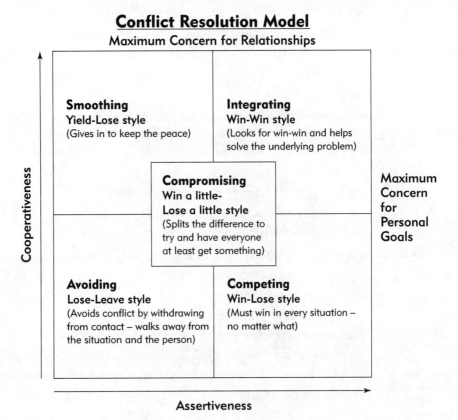

The conflict resolution model has two general dimensions: the amount of *assertiveness* a person demonstrates in a conflict situation and the amount of *cooperativeness* demonstrated. For example, if in conflicts you tend to be highly assertive yet low on the cooperation scale, you fall in the *competing* category. This means in most conflict situations you will "compete" with the others involved. This style is often called the win-lose style because you focus on winning and on the other person losing. On the other hand, if you have very high cooperativeness and very low assertiveness, you would fall in the *smoothing*

category. This means that in most conflict situations you will attempt to "smooth the conflict over." This style is often called the yield-lose style because you focus on smoothing over conflicts by yielding to other's feelings and desires. Conflicts never are resolved so the others lose.

While we can change our style to fit the situation or the person we are dealing with in a conflict situation, most of us utilize one of the five basic styles shown most of the time.

To illustrate in practical terms the five different styles shown in the model, let's pretend that we are co-workers working in the same area. We each must use the same box to get our work done, but the placement of the box is causing conflict. You want the box to be placed next to your station and I want the box to be placed next to my station. Let's examine what happens when each of the five styles is used to resolve the conflict.

Smoothing

If my basic style were smoothing, as soon as I experienced the conflict, I would simply give you what you wanted—the box on your side. But is the conflict resolved? It might seem to be resolved for you, but maybe it is just beginning for me. This time you want the box on your side, next you borrow my pen, then you take the cupcake I was saving, and so on. If I continue to "give in" to you over time, my resentment will build until one day I explode with no warning.

Smoothing or capitulation does not necessarily resolve conflict.

Smoothing or capitulation does not necessarily resolve conflict. Now, if the issue or concern had little or no meaning to me and does not cause great internal distress or discomfort, then smoothing the conflict may be appropriate. But don't fall into the trap of saying something is not important while internally negative feelings are building.

Avoiding

A second style is avoiding. Using the box dilemma again, if my basic style were avoiding, as soon as I felt the conflict, I would completely stop our discussion and, as before, probably just let you take the box (lose-leave style). I would turn my back on the situation and I would not care where the box was, just as long as I did not have to deal with it or with you. Once I felt that conflict, I would not look at you, I wouldn't talk to you, I wouldn't sit in the cafeteria where I could see you, and I would avoid walking down your office corridor. In short,

I would completely avoid contact. Even if you appeared later to try to resolve the issue, I would simply not want to talk about it. Does avoiding the conflict resolve it? Obviously not. The conflict and discomfort would still be within both of us, so it is not resolved.

Competing

Okay, how about competing? Returning to our box dilemma, if my basic style were competing I would simply grab the box from your hands, place it next to my workspace, and tell you that if you touched the box again I would cut your hands off! (I win-you lose style) Did that resolve the conflict? Would you feel okay about this solution? No. Most often this would just escalate the conflict toward a larger battle, especially if you also utilized the compete style. I am not saying that people who compete always escalate conflict, just that in a conflict situation competing will not resolve the conflict for both parties and often just makes it worse.

Compromising

By now you are saying, "Fine, let's not smooth, avoid, or compete; let's compromise. I have always heard that people get along much better if they would just learn to compromise." Unfortunately, as good as compromise sounds on the surface, it doesn't really resolve conflict. Let's return to our box situation and see how compromise would work. Since you want the box next to your machine, and I want the box next to my machine, the logical compromise is to put the box half-way between our stations, right? Okay, did that entirely resolve the conflict? You probably say yes, but no is the real answer. Now I have to walk half-way to get to the box and you have to walk half-way to get to the box. Neither one of us is especially pleased, and that is why I call this style lose-lose. Our solution didn't give either one of us what we wanted, did it? In fact, over time one of us might have a little compete in our system and decide to move the box closer to our station, creating a whole new conflict. The "box in the middle" is a solution, but not necessarily the best solution.

Here is another example of compromise. I have two teenage daughters who both want an orange. I only have one orange, so what do I do if I am compromising? Cut it in half, right? If I give half of anything to two teenage siblings, what automatically happens? They would make comments like, "Her half is bigger," or "Why does she always get the better side?" or "You like her better." Both would either feel that they did not get everything they wanted or that they received something less than the other. Am I correct? You know it is true. So I didn't necessarily resolve the conflict by sharing the orange.

A better approach that truly resolves conflict is integrating, or the win-win style.

Integrating

A better approach that truly resolves conflict is integrating, or the win-win style. Again using the box example, if my basic style were integrating, as soon as I experienced the conflict I would try to figure out what you wanted, tell you what I wanted, and then we would both brainstorm ways we could make both of our wants or needs reality. One simple solution would to get another box— you probably thought of that already. Sounds like a good solution, right? But when you are involved in a conflict, especially when emotions are high, the simple solutions often don't even come to mind. Because integration is the only way conflict will really be resolved, when you are involved in a conflict you must be able to control your emotions for the moment and focus on how to create a win-win situation—even if initially you don't want to.

So what if we couldn't get another box because it was made of gold and bolted to the floor or our supervisor told us no? Then we would need to work together creatively to integrate our needs, desires, thoughts, feelings, and ideas into a solution we were both truly happy with so that we would both win! Does this sound easy? It is not. In fact, this is the most difficult part of resolving conflict: being open-minded enough to consider solutions other than the one that first comes to mind and most of the time the one we are strongly attached to. If a second box could not be obtained, we would need to brainstorm some other possible solutions. What are some that come to mind? Could we move our desks or workstations closer together? Or could we eliminate the need for the box entirely by changing our process—for example, by installing a belting system? Or alter our shifts so we could each use the box? The major idea here is that both people involved in the conflict must work together to develop a solution that satisfies each of their needs.

At this point, you might be saying that you could have lived with a box located half-way between the two of you instead of wasting time with this brainstorming and the struggle to resolve this simple problem. If that is true for you, great. But you could use this simple conflict to develop skill in identifying win-win alternatives. When a person is sufficiently skilled in identifying win-win outcomes, he or she can enter conflicts involving larger problems and resolve them in ways that create very positive results. Just imagine how great it would be if you were able to eliminate conflicts and find positive, creative, innovate, helpful solutions to tough problems.

Working with a variety of organizations, I have seen some outstanding results when simmering conflicts have been resolved. For example, a vinyl processing plant went from seventy-hour to forty-hour workweeks for employees by simply having employees on two shifts sit down and, in this instance, integrate the "hot items report process" between shifts. This change also saved the company over $500,000. At another plant, resolving a conflict between the grinding and maintenance departments led to a dramatic reduction in plant shutdown time for maintenance—from an eight-hour total plant shutdown to a two-hour partial plant shutdown. In a third organization, the purchasing department eliminated $650,000 worth of "old" inventory and $400,000 worth of "improper receipts" by brainstorming a creative solution with the receiving department on bar coding issues.

The solution to conflict in each case involved individuals asking themselves, "How creative can we be in resolving this conflict?"

There are many more examples I could provide, but the solution to conflict in each case involved individuals asking themselves, "How creative can we be in resolving this conflict?"

Communication Techniques for Conflict Resolution

So is that all there is to resolving conflict, *understanding* conflict styles? The answer is, no. Certain communication techniques practiced by one or both parties in a conflict situation are also important. There are three communication techniques that are crucial in effectively handling conflict.

The first technique is *observation and the ability to objectively see what is happening in a relationship.* The key word here is objectively. In a conflict situation, those who are involved rarely can see anything except their own points of view. In fact, most don't even realize—don't see—how angry, mad, or upset they are. Their emotions make them lose their ability to objectively look at anything. It is surprising to see how emotionally involved people can become over small issues—who uses a copier first, for example. One person may want to go first because of time pressures, while the other may want to go first because he or she was at the copier first. Eventually they may let the conflict get to the point where they resort to throwing punches—over a stack of paper! If you are involved in conflict, try to think *objectively* and halt the conflict process before you or other individuals involved lose emotional control. Quickly bring the conflict back to the objective facts and realities of the situation, with both or all perspectives in clear view. This often means controlling your own emotions first when you are involved in a conflict, which permits you to be objective. Often a statement such as, "Wait a minute. Arguing about this is getting us nowhere; let's take a minute to see what would be best for both of us," will calm both participants down and create an opportunity to resolve the conflict.

The second communication technique is *listening or the ability to "hear and understand" what is being said and not said.* By listening we don't just mean paying attention to words.

By listening we don't just mean paying attention to words.

We have to pay attention to the tone, pitch, rate, verbal emphasis, and rhythm of remarks, as well as associated hand and arm gestures and facial expressions. How something is said can be more important to attend to than what is said. When I recently got a new puppy, I tried an experiment. I said in a low, mean tone, as if I were angry, "You beautiful puppy come over and eat this delicious food." The words were positive, but what was the impact? It took me three days of soft, quiet coaxing just to get him to return to the feeding dish. The puppy wasn't responding to what I said, but was responding instead to *how* I said it. Here is another example: Say, "I never said he stole my money," seven times, emphasizing a different word each time you say the statement. How many different meanings did you hear? Seven, right?

We have to be aware of how things are said and be aware that it is possible to misinterpret this information. For example, a negative tone may have more to do with someone's morning commute to work than with something you have said or done.

Returning to the issue of conflict, when you are in a conflict situation, be very sure as you listen to another that your understanding of him or her is correct.

The final communication technique is *questioning or the ability to get information or feedback from another.* After you have patiently observed and really listened to achieve understanding, your final step in handling the conflict comes in the form of focused questioning. You cannot start with questioning. Often, this will escalate the conflict. What kind of questions do you ask? You simply ask each member involved what it will take to resolve the underlying problem. Ask them what they need, in specific terms, to satisfy their concerns—their win. Sound easy? It's not. But it will open up the communication channels that will lead to eventual resolution of the conflict if used properly. To return to an earlier example, if John and I have a conflict over the use of the photocopy machine first, I can start by asking, "John, how long will it take you to finish your copying?" After he answers me, I have more information about his win, so I am in a better position to structure a win-win solution. Or perhaps I have come upon a similar situation involving John and Sally. I would simply ask, "John, how long will it take you to finish your copying and what is your time frame, and Sally, how long will it take to finish your copying and what is your time frame?" I could then help them prioritize who should go first or offer a creative solution: I could tell them the location of another copy machine or I could offer to perform the copying for both John and Sally, returning the finished products to them when complete. It is often easier to help others solve their conflict than to solve your own.

The Three R's

The conflict-handling techniques of observing, listening, and questioning can be used in a model of conflict resolution that is called the three R's. Each R suggests a particular action by an individual who is attempting to resolve a conflict. Here is how it looks:

> *Reflect* the other's feelings;
>
> *Restate* the underlying issue; and
>
> *Resolve* the conflict with a win/win solution.

Reflect

First, *reflect* how the other person is feeling. Simply state to him or her the emotion he or she seems to be showing: "You seem angry or mad or hurt." This is where listening skill and the ability to identify nonverbal signals become important. If you are paying attention to the speaker, you have a better chance of learning what he or she is feeling. Proper reflecting reduces the intensity of the emotions the other person is feeling and allows him or her to see this intensity through your eyes. The speaker also becomes aware that you understand how he or she feels, because you were able to reflect it back to him or her. One note of caution: Don't ever say, "I understand how you feel." First of all, you don't—you are not the other person—and, second, the other person doesn't think you do yet. Don't say you understand; just reflect the emotions you see the person feeling.

Restate

Next, *restate.* Many things are said in the heat of a conflict that are not very positive. In fact, most people take the opportunity of a conflict to practice what I call *alternative language* or *disrespectful speaking.* This is a place where good listening skills and utilizing your emotions in a positive way will benefit you in the long run. Allowing them to vent, even when they use this alternative language or disrespectful speaking, is a great second step, although this is not restating. Restating will be discussed shortly. Allowing individuals to vent is not easy, and many people have said that this step is really the most difficult to actually perform, but you must succeed in this step if you wish the conflict to be resolved. Also, during this venting, they are releasing pent-up anger, which moves them toward resolution.

As the listener, you should try to understand the underlying issue, the root of the conflict. This is also where questioning skills can come in handy. You should listen with the intent of discovering what is really causing the person to be concerned, upset, angry, or hurt. This is difficult, but by asking the right type of questions you can often get the other person to clarify the real problem and discover the root issue. You should also realize that you have two ears and one mouth and you should use them in that proportion.

Realize that you have two ears and one mouth and you should use them in that proportion.

For the moment, ignore the alternative language or disrespectful speaking, including put-downs and name calling, while you try to discern the real problem. Sometimes people ask me why they should let someone call them names or be disrespectful while trying to resolve conflict. I tell them that this is just step two and we will handle those issues in the next step! I also truly believe that underneath all conflicts there is a problem that must be solved to settle the conflict. Your job in handling conflict at this stage is to discover that problem or issue and nothing more. Just imagine where the conflict would end up if you reacted to what the other person was saying instead of listening for the underlying issue. That's right—more conflict and no solution.

What do you do once you think you know what the problem or issue is? This involves restating. You simply restate exactly what the person said the underlying issue is, without using any of the alternative language or disrespectful speaking and being very aware of your own nonverbal behavior. This means for the moment that you ignore the fact that the person called you a moron, or that he or she placed dispersions on your heritage, or that the person was screaming at you at the top of his or her lungs. You simply state what you believe the underlying issue is in a calm and straightforward manner.

Resolve

Next, and probably most important, is *resolving*. Conflicts should not be "managed"; they should be resolved. How many of us want to be managing the same conflicts six months from now? Not very many of us, I would guess. So we should focus on resolution. After you have reflected the person's feelings and restated the underlying issue, most people are ready for resolution. Why? Because they know that you both understand how they feel and what they have said. Resolution is finding the win/win solution to the underlying problem.

Resolution is finding the win/win solution to the underlying problem.

But what exactly does that mean? It means that each person should be given the chance to express what a win is for him or her (how each thinks the underlying problem should be solved from his or her perspective). The individuals involved must then agree to a solution that incorporates *both* wins. This takes imagination, creativity, ingenuity, and always a lot of communication, but it can be done. Remember this is not compromise; it is cooperation—two individuals working together to create a solution better than either one could have created by him- or herself. A very powerful question that facilitates this process is: "What can *we* do to solve this issue to *our* satisfaction?" Often this is where the two individuals will need help. It is hard to find a win/win solution when you are emotionally involved in the situation. But once the two people find it, it is like magic—conflict resolved!

The following list of ten communication skills summarizes much of what we have said above:

1. Don't take it personally (you must control your own emotions for a positive outcome);

2. Let the person in conflict vent his or her feelings (it is tough to listen to someone else's perspective, especially if it is disrespectful or a put-down);

3. Listen (we like to talk more than listen);

4. Maintain eye contact (it is hard to look someone who is angry in the eye);

5. Use the person's name (this defuses some emotion);

6. Take notes (even if only mentally);

7. Ask appropriate questions ("Are you stupid or something?" is *not* an appropriate question);

8. Understand the other person's perspective first (not a normal thing to do);

9. Offer your own perspective last (you always want to speak first); and

10. Do your best to help the person solve the problem (we may think, "Why help this person when *he or she* is the problem?).

Remember also that you cannot resolve conflict for anyone but yourself. Sounds like common sense, doesn't it, but if I had a nickel for every time someone said he tried to resolve conflict for someone else and failed, I would have pockets bulging with nickels. The individuals involved in the conflict must come to their own resolution. You can try to suggest solutions, but often your job is simply to guide them through the process we have just discussed. Take each one of the participants and help them reflect, restate, and resolve. Attempt to get them to agree to a solution largely of their own making. I often see managers use the old, "Okay you two, I want this conflict to end, so shake hands and say it's over" technique, but it rarely works. Using the three R's would be much more effective.

Conflict should be viewed as an opportunity to surface and resolve underlying problems.

To summarize, when conflicts occur it is critical that you view this as a sign or signal that something is being missed or overlooked. Conflict should be viewed as an opportunity to surface and resolve underlying problems and to improve relationships and performance. I keep a keen eye out for any type of conflict signal or sign—sighing, movement suggesting discomfort, folded arms, the absence of eye contact, tight lips, red face, a sudden outburst of swearing—especially when I am involved with a group and we are trying to make a decision or plan a course of action. These signs tell me that conflict is present and, as a consequence, the group is not going to structure the best decision or plan. I immediately begin using the communication skills covered in the chapter and transition into the three R's for resolving the conflicts. A successful outcome and greater success in our work together are usually my reward.

CHAPTER 32

Increasing Collaboration Success Through New Meeting Behavior

Gerald D. Klein

"NONE OF US IS AS SMART AS ALL OF US."** So goes a maxim about using small groups to solve business problems. The use of groups is increasingly necessary in organizations, as more decisions require all kinds of specialized knowledge that is seldom found within one person. At the heart of collaboration in organizations are meetings by small groups—meetings within departments and meetings of members of different departments.

In organizations meetings are held for different purposes. The focus of this chapter is on problem-solving meetings, meetings where individuals come together to identify, discuss, and resolve issues or problems.

Most human beings are capable of tremendous creativity in solving problems, and groups are especially good to use when problems are complex and creative and fresh approaches are desired. Group meetings are essential when both the understanding and acceptance of decisions are required. Decision acceptance is necessary if decisions are to be implemented.

At the heart of collaboration in organizations are meetings by small groups.

But the way individuals behave in meetings and how meetings are structured and led often cause individuals, groups, and collaboration to fall far short of their real potential. Group meetings should foster energetic and creative participation and result in feelings of solidarity and elation that come from successfully solving problems and improving the organization. Instead, participants in meetings often complain about boredom, irritation, impatience, hostility, and rivalry.

Meeting Problems

What are the key problems in meetings? A number of people who have studied problem-solving groups in organizations and in laboratory settings (see especially Bradford, 1976; Maier, 1967, 1970) have pinpointed the following:

- *People perceive a meeting as a competition between themselves and others.* Individual members attempt to "sell" a particular view or problem solution—to "win the argument," according to Maier (1967), rather than attempting to create a high-quality solution from the viewpoints of all.

- *Group members instinctively react to an idea's weaknesses rather than to its strengths,* thinking they are being entirely reasonable and sensible in doing so. This inbred reflex makes people hesitant to suggest new ideas.

- *A desire to be accepted and well-regarded by others causes individuals to repress both their ideas and their reactions to the ideas of group members.*

- *The individuals who dominate a meeting are not aware that they may not be the source of the best ideas in the group.*

- *Individuals at a meeting are not clear why they are there.*

- *Group members, each of whom often has a pressing need to discuss different problems, attempt to bring group discussion back to their own topics* if a meeting is not sufficiently organized. Meetings in which the focus continually shifts are not likely to be successful.

- *The group leader, often the head of an organizational unit, discourages—sometimes unwittingly—creativity, spontaneity, and thinking deeply about a problem.* For example, he or she may move through issues too quickly, not giving group members opportunities to express their thoughts.

- *The group leader, by virtue of his or her organizational role and group role, exerts too much influence* on both the content of the discussion and its flow.

Meetings can be much more productive and satisfying for members with a few minor changes in behavior on the part of group members and the group leader. The following sections describe these changes and provide other tips for having productive and good meetings. Implementing just some of these can significantly improve the climate of and outcomes from meetings. When the climate is right, group members actually look forward to meetings.

What Group Members Need to Do

- *Group members need to be aware that others may see problems from a different perspective.* These differences need to be valued and respected in order for a group to come up with innovative and complete problem solutions. They must treat differences in opinions as stimulating rather than as annoying and view participants who disagree, not as troublemakers, but as group *assets*—persons with potentially good ideas.

- *Group members must listen to others with the purpose of learning* and building on their ideas rather than with the purpose of refuting or criticizing.

- *It is desirable that they comment on that part of a group member's idea or suggestion that has the most merit,* rather than criticizing that part which represents the idea's weakest point.

- *They must give all ideas a fair hearing,* even those that are offered once the group's decision has started to jell. Research suggests that good ideas introduced after this point, particularly in leaderless groups, are often ignored and have little impact (Maier 1967, 1970).

- Rather than discarding an idea that is difficult to accept or implement as proposed, *group members should work to create variations or transformations of the idea.*

- *Group members should feel free to float before the group their ambivalence about or hesitancy to support a particular problem solution.* Typically, others are also sharing some of these feelings. The late psychologist, Carl Rogers, noted that often what is most personal is most general: what you are experiencing others are experiencing, too (Rogers, 1961). The group should use ambivalence expressed by members to strengthen a decision and make it more complete.

- To encourage widespread participation in discussions, *individual members should address their remarks to all,* not just to the leader or to a few members.

What Group Leaders Need to Do

- The group leader, instead of being the controller or director, should *become the servant of the group or servant to the participants.* In this role, his or her goals focus on ascertaining the issues that members want to discuss, bringing out the best ideas from each member and fully using the human resources assembled to solve problems.

- *Both the leader and the group should seek (1) high-quality group decisions, rich in detail and responsive to member concerns and (2) decisions that are widely understood and accepted.*

- *A leader should not call meetings just to announce decisions or to dispense information.* He or she should see groups as able to take preliminary decisions and *improve them* and as able to identify the ramifications and implications of information *that he or she cannot see.* Meetings called just to announce decisions or to transmit information will likely be seen as a waste of time, since there are other, more efficient ways of doing these things.

- *A leader should delay the group's rush to a decision.* Research suggests that groups will often and erroneously equate an acceptable decision with a high-quality one (Gouran, 1982; Maier, 1967, 1970). A leader should prudently prolong discussion until a high-quality decision is achieved. If a group decides on a course of action too quickly, he or she should have the group explore its positives and negatives or its requirements, costs, consequences, and alternatives.

- *A leader should try to hear from and use every member of the group or team.* He or she should encourage contributing through eye contact or by a verbal invitation to join in, for example: "John, I'd like to know your feelings on this issue."

- *A leader should help members to interact with each other and with the group, rather than just with him or her.* The leader can model this by scanning the group as he or she speaks. Also, the leader can make sure that group members direct their comments to the most appropriate recipients. A circular table rather than a rectangular table with a leader at its head also leads to greater member-to-member interaction (Brilhart, 1982; Hare & Bales, 1963).

- *A leader should think of the meeting process as having two separate and distinct steps, idea generation and idea evaluation.* Effective group work usually consists of these two major activities. Idea evaluation slows down the process of idea generation. At various points in a meeting, a leader should carry out a freewheeling idea-generation phase when no evaluation is permitted (brainstorming or having members write down their ideas before sharing them) *followed* by an idea-evaluation stage. Alternatively, group members should keep comments of evaluation brief so that the momentum of the group is not sapped.

The group leader— and other members— should periodically summarize the discussion.

- *The group leader—and other members—should periodically summarize the discussion as it unfolds,* rather than trying to control it. This moves the discussion away from issues that have been resolved and focuses the group's attention on those that require discussion.

- *The leader must seek out the views of others.* Effective meeting leaders don't push their views too much. Research shows that group leaders have influence just by virtue of their position, even when their ideas are not necessarily the best available in the group. A leader's contribution, whether he or she likes it or not, receives better treatment than that of other members of a group (Maier, 1967, 1970).

- *A leader must make sure no one is put on the defensive* or suffers blows to his or her self-esteem as a consequence of offering his or her views. The leader can model considerateness when disagreeing with a member, for example, by starting a statement of disagreement with, "With all due respect, . . ." or "I wish I could agree with you; however, . . ."(Gouran, 1982, p. 165). The leader can also suggest to a group that it establish ground rules that outlaw interruptions, sarcasm, and put-downs (Lippincott, 1999).

- *A leader should protect the person with the minority view* and give the person the opportunity to influence the majority position. The leader can do this by requesting that members listen carefully and respectfully to a member with a different view. There is little danger that a group will accept an inferior alternative, as research shows that a minority view influences a group only when facts favor it (Maier, 1967).

- *The leader should move the meeting along to prevent boredom* (see "Other Tips," below) *and to reduce the possibility of fatigue-type solutions, yet move the meeting along without closing off full discussion.* Fatigue-type solutions occur when members agree merely to get out of a meeting.

Group leaders who practice this style of running meetings will permit group members to have a say and to have significant influence; and being able to influence things is extremely important to group members.

Other Tips for Having Good Meetings

In problem solving, there is a natural and logical sequence of steps, which, if followed, invariably leads to successful results:

1. Group discussion begins with problem identification or listing.

2. Problems are then precisely described or defined.

3. Problems are ordered in terms of their importance or urgency.

4. Select the most important and urgent problem and identify its causes.

5. Generate solutions that address each cause.

6. Evaluate each of the solutions, identifying its pros and cons or strengths and weaknesses.

7. Based on this analysis, create an action plan for addressing the problem.

8. Information needs to be gathered to learn if the action plan was effective in solving the problem it was meant to address. Develop a plan for information gathering.

9. Implement the action plan and gather information.

10. Carefully analyze this information to determine whether or not the problem has been solved.

Among the challenges for a group and its leader are preventing too little discussion of a step and discussion of a step out of turn, such as discussing solutions before the problem is clear.

In addition to making sure a group tackles problems in this systematic way, the following are also important guidelines:

- *Always work from an established agenda.*

- *Permit group members to influence the agenda prior to the meeting.* Opening the agenda to group input assures that the agenda reflects the interests of all members. Although this may lead to the scheduling of additional meetings as items are added, it is usually for the better. Whatever needs to be addressed and discussed will be.

- *Work on the important items on the agenda first,* and consider member availability and guests. Both influence the final order of the discussion topics. For the convenience of guests, topics involving guests are usually addressed first.

- *Discuss an item and achieve closure on it before moving on to the next item.* Closure is achieved when the group either reaches a decision or decides that it can't decide at this time. When a group decides that it can't or shouldn't reach a decision on an item, additional discussion on the item is scheduled for (or postponed until) another time.

Avoid bogging down on an agenda item and resist jumping among the various items on the agenda ("frogging").

- *Avoid bogging down on an agenda item* and resist jumping among the various items on the agenda ("frogging").

- *Write down decisions and their rationales.* This prevents the rehashing of issues and permits decisions to be communicated to others not included in the meeting.

There is much more that can be learned about having productive and successful meetings. The reader is encouraged to consult the many good resources that are available in this area, including Jay (1976), Lippincott (1999), and Yukl (1998).

CHAPTER 33

A Tool Approach to Forgotten Team Competencies

Michael M. Beyerlein

COLLABORATIVE SUCCESS DEPENDS ON A LOT OF FACTORS—
world-class performance on any stage does. Perhaps the most commonly addressed factor is training. It ought to be viewed as a subset of learning, just as teams ought to be viewed as a subset of collaborative practice. This chapter in the Fieldbook suggests shifting the perspective on how to think about training of team competencies as tools and adding some new areas to the training to enable teams and members to develop mastery of some key performance areas. The following types of tool sets should be included in the learning system: mind, conversation, decision making, technical, support systems alignment, project management, and business. Types under each tool set are identified that are rarely covered in team training, with rationales about why development of those particular competencies would be valuable.

Shifting the Perspective on Training

Training has evolved as a formal approach to creating learning opportunities. Cutting-edge practices in training are quite effective, although they are not practiced as widely as they should be. For example, using multimedia presentations to enable trainees with different learning styles to master the material is fairly widely practiced, but training sessions using interactive exercises based on adult learning principles remain surprisingly rare.

Formal training is not enough.

Formal training is not enough; it must be heavily supplemented by informal methods such as mentoring, coaching, and modeling. A broader view of learning may improve the perspective decision makers use. For example, Duffy (1995) defines learning as (1) a "body" of knowledge, (b) a change process, (c) application and involvement in the real world, and (d) ethical activity. These all rely on sensemaking, which is often based on collaborative activity. You can't use knowledge that you can't make sense of.

The goal of the training is change in performance—that means change in behavior (mental or physical). Performance depends on knowing a lot: knowing what, knowing how, knowing why, and caring why (Quinn & Anderson, 1996). The last two components of learning are not always addressed in training. The biggest challenge is that new learning fits on a continuum from explicit to tacit. Tacit knowledge includes the rules of the road, the tricks of the trade, building an instinct for handling certain situations, and other competencies of experienced employees that cannot be easily communicated in formal training. Experiential approaches to training do help some, but informal methods play critical roles in passing tacit knowledge from one employee to another.

Learning is typically thought of as an individual activity. After all, working solo is strongly enforced in elementary and secondary schools. However, learning can be a collaborative activity when it is a shared experience or the experienced help the inexperienced learn. In Figure 33.1, ten steps have been identified that tie learning into effective action. The process can be interrupted or sidetracked at any of the linking points identified by arrows. In addition, the subprocesses within a single step may be inadequate for laying a foundation for the next step.

Figure 33.1. The Collaborative Knowledge Generation Process

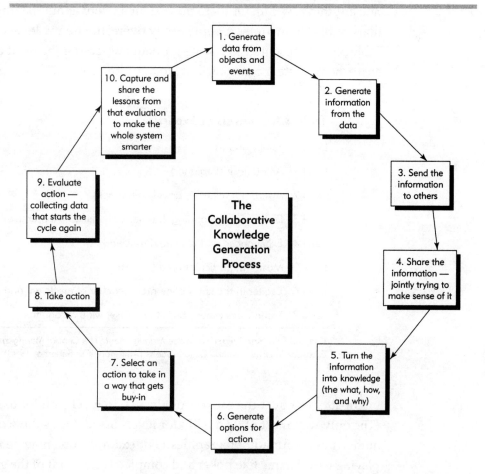

The level of performance on any issue depends on the quality of teamwork in each of the ten steps and in each of the transition arrow processes. Analysis of the processes should reveal the flaws and provide opportunities for improvement. Inherent in the cycle is opportunity for learning at individual, team, and organizational levels.

The step that is missing in this rather standard model is becoming open to learning. The culture of the learning organization (Watkins & Marsick, 1993) is recommended as a context to support such openness, but it is also an individual choice. There may be a hubris about what one knows that interferes with letting anything new in. Or there may be an anxiety about making one's limitations public. Sometimes, people easily overestimate the level of expertise, so Table 33.1 is presented as a scale for better assessing the need to learn in any area where mastery can contribute to performance.

Table 33.1. Levels of Expertise

Level 0: Totally unaware

Level 1: Amateurish (Beginner)

Level 2: Aware but relatively unskilled (Novice)

Level 3: Deeper understanding, but narrowly skilled (Apprentice)

Level 4: Experienced and reliable (Proficient)

Level 5: Master of particular area (Expert)

Level 6: Leader in the knowledge area, teacher of proficient and expert

Level 7: World-class expert, broad expertise, wide recognition

Adapted from Karl Wiig, *Knowledge Management: The Central Management Focus for Intelligent-Acting Organizations* (Arlington, TX: Schema, 1993).

Most of us cover the range from level 0 to level 5 on thousands of topics. (The only way most of us qualify for levels 6 and 7 is as the world's foremost authorities on our autobiographies.) For example, one may be fairly expert at playing a card game like poker and completely ignorant of the game of bridge, have a high level of expertise about quality management and a low level about team-based organizing, or understand testing procedures for metals under stress and not know how to fill out a travel voucher. The problem lies in not having an accurate assessment of what level applies to what topic area and so failing to recognize how much learning is required before informed judgments can be made and thus intelligent action begun.

Recognize how much learning is required for informed judgments. Below are some competency areas where proficiency or expertise would make a difference in performance. These areas are usually not assessed in planning of training content; they are ignored or taken for granted, so no developmental efforts are made. As a result, team members at all levels of the organization tend to remain at the novice and beginner levels of expertise.

Tool Sets

Seven categories of tools for effective collaborative practice are identified here: *mind, conversation, decision making, technical, support systems alignment, project management,* and *business.* Training is usually organized to cover only a subset of these categories. When the budget is lean, technical training tends to be retained and the "softer" (but more difficult) training dropped. As collaboration and social networking increase in importance within the shift to knowledge-based and service-based economies, weaknesses in soft skills will diminish the ability of an organization to compete.

Mind as Tool

The mind of the individual is usually considered to be the source of knowledge. Training is often aimed at pumping more information into that mind. Information has value, but information processing competencies, including learning how to learn and seeing the big picture, are more important.

An important aspect of "mind as tool" is attention. As most performance requires sustained attention, performance suffers when concentration is below par. Most performance requires sustained attention. Focused attention is reduced by distraction, ambiguity, anxiety, frustration, distance from the goal, indifference, and hurdles in the environment. Sustaining focus depends on fitness of the system—ability, vitality, and appropriateness. Ability to concentrate includes some natural ability and some learned skill, but mostly it requires interest. Part of what is learned is what to attend to. The facets of mind that can be enhanced through training are listed in Table 33.2. Having each member of the team rate himself or herself will produce a profile for each member.

Each of the eight facets represents a mental strength or cognitive asset. We all have some of each of these assets; however, in any group, members will be strong and weak on differing ones. That is part of why working in a group can offset individual weaknesses. Here are simple definitions for each of the eight scales: The ability to (1) focus attention, (2) analyze and plan, (3) learn complex and subtle material, (4) let in new ideas and methods, (5) recall clearly and completely what has happened in the past, (6) generate new and innovative ways of seeing a problem or approaches to it, (7) value the resources in the people in the group and environment around them, and (8) take calculated risks.

Table 33.2. Cognitive Assets

Cognitive Assets	Scale: 1 = low; 5 = extraordinary				
Attentive mind	1	2	3	4	5
Thinking mind	1	2	3	4	5
Learning mind	1	2	3	4	5
Open mind	1	2	3	4	5
Remembering mind	1	2	3	4	5
Creating mind	1	2	3	4	5
Appreciating mind	1	2	3	4	5
Entrepreneurial mind	1	2	3	4	5

Each member of the organization is characterized by a profile that indicates how strong or weak each facet is. Scaling these on a 1 to 5 measure might result in a profile like this: 4, 3, 2, 1, 5, 3, 2, 2. Such a profile suggests that reliance on memory and resistance to new learning result in mediocre levels of creativity and low levels of entrepreneurial behavior. All of the decisions and insights of this person are constrained by the low ratings on these facets. Hence, performance levels are limited. Training in focusing of attention, analytical and synthesizing thinking skills, openness to new learning, and so forth can enhance that performance level. Each of these competency areas is important to team performance. When change in one team member's profile is difficult, balance it with the strengths of another member, so the whole team has a complete array of strengths.

Complexity challenges teams' mental tools.

As the complexity of the challenges teams face increases, the set of mental tools they have available needs to improve.

A good start in choosing competencies to focus on comes from the book *Common Fire: Leading Lives of Commitment in a Complex World* (Daloz, Keen, Keen, Parks, & Parks, 1997). The authors argue that three thinking skills are essential:

1. Critical and systemic thinking that allows for the complex exploration of issues and the surfacing of underlying assumptions;

2. Ability to engage in perspective taking and withholding judgment; and

3. Searching for common values while honoring diversity of perspective and committing to creating a safe, civil, and inclusive work space.

These three complex skills represent valuable ways of working together, but they also represent the level of quality needed in thinking about competencies for the 21st Century. In comparison, much training and development in the past has been overly simplistic.

Conversation as Tool

Conversation is about building meaning and building alliances. However, both these goals are often unreachable. Conversations may be ritualized, gaming, deceiving, indirect, or obfuscating because of lack of skill or openness. But it remains the most important tool in effective collaboration and effective operation. Mohrman (Mohrman & Tenkasi, 1997) stated that the work of the knowledge worker takes place through conversation. A single conversation can have an enormous impact on subsequent conversations by the way it is conducted (even more than by its subject matter or its outcome). Yet there is a tendency to take conversation for granted; neither the skill nor the infrastructure receive the developmental attention they deserve.

Conversation as tool includes a sequence from the simplest to the most sophisticated and valuable levels: (a) data transmitted, (b) information given, (c) information received, (d) information exchanged, (e) knowledge shared, (f) sense-making, (g) dialogue and development of shared mental models, and (h) creation of a synergistic understanding.

This list of eight levels is hierarchical. Higher levels depend on lower levels, but lower levels usually add less value. The people who are good at higher levels tend to be creative decision makers. Level one can include observational data, such as nonverbal behavior, as well as symbolic data like numbers, words, graphs, and schematics. Level 8 represents those times when the group works so well together that the outcome is clearly a leap above what any individual in the group could have created alone. The most valuable outcomes from these processes on communication are meaning making and creative synergies. However, flaws in the early steps undermine those parts.

There is a website that makes the point that translation erodes meaning, that is, the need to convey information from one person or group to another may result in that information being altered as a result of the conversion from one language to another, for example, when an electrical engineer talks with a production supervisor or when a team member in the warehouse talks with a salesperson in the field. At www.tashian.com/multibabel, a simple phrase can be typed in and run through translation to another language, such as English to

German, and back. Repeating the translation cycle several times results in amusingly distorted results. For example, "I'm a little tea pot, short and stout" from the children's song becomes "They are a small potentiometer, short circuits and a beer of malzes of the tea." The first sentence of this paragraph translated into French and back to English becomes, "There is a website which makes the remark that the translation erodes the significance." Such erosion of meaning is a common experience across disciplines. "Dilbert" cartoons illustrate the problem frequently. The worst problem is not that erosion of meaning occurs, but that it is ignored.

There are many common problems with communications in addition to the translation problem. A challenging one involves making a complex statement that is also clear. There is a tendency to oversimplify a complex issue in describing it to someone who is new to it. The complexity of the problem-solving system must match the complexity of the problem, so oversimplification of explanations will not erode the ability to respond to a situation. The development of complex and clear understanding evolves through discussion. Here are the conditions for what Gregg Walker calls "collaborative argument": (a) valuing disagreement, (b) desire to learn, (c) willingness to risk, (d) open-mindedness, (e) distinguish between arguers and arguments, (f) positive regard for the other, and (g) ethical responsibility.

Establishing these conditions depends on both training and setting of norms. It raises the standard of conversation to a new level. Training members of the organization to recognize the value of conversation as a tool for building shared meaning and coordinated action and in the skills of that process of exchange, especially active listening, will help when the team tackles complex issues.

Decision-Making Continuum as Tool

As work teams become more empowered and accountable, the nature of their problem solving shifts from the routine to the nonroutine, the familiar to the novel. The latter type takes significantly more capability for effective problem solving. Novel, ambiguous problems require consensus problem definition as well as consensus decision making. Such problems have been referred to as soft (Robards & Gillespie, 2000), wicked (Rittel & Webber, 1984), creative (Mumford, 2000), ill-structured (Ambrose, 1996), macroproblems (Ambrose, 1996), and fuzzy (Liedtka, 2000). Wicked problems must be dealt with when complex tradeoffs occur, such as choosing layoffs or risking new enterprise, when strate-

Wicked problems involve complex tradeoffs.

gic planning is required, and when multiple perspectives conflict, such as union and management views or front-line workers and engineers.

Table 33.3 illustrates the differences between tame and wicked problems on a decision-making continuum. At the left end of the continuum, problems are simple enough to define and solve that routine responses, formulae, recipes, and algorithms can do the job. On the right end of the continuum, problems are ambiguous, complex, and viewed through multiple perspectives, so agreement on the problem is as difficult as determining how to proceed with a solution. Design of new products, service configurations, and organizations are ill-defined or wicked. Treating them as well-defined oversimplifies and so leads to failure to achieve objectives.

Table 33.3. Decision-Making Continuum of Problem Types

Tame	Ill-Defined	Wicked
Clear problem definition	Defining the problem *is* the problem	Goals are unclear
Limited set of options		May have to invent the means to achieving the goals
Algorithmic solutions	Iterative solutions are needed	Conflicting views of problem
Right and wrong, true or false solutions	Heuristic solutions	Better or worse, good or bad solutions, not right or wrong
	More reliance on insight	
Objective measure of success	Goals may be clear	No objective measure of success is adequate
Focus on tasks more than problems	Open-ended; problem is ongoing	
Clear goals	Defining and solving processes go back and forth as both develop	Trial-and-error method
		Iterative process—successive approximation—every trial counts
		Solution is a unique creation; can't be reused in a new situation
		Moral, political, or professional issues with failure; have no right to be wrong
		Every wicked problem is a symptom of another problem, and they are interdependent
		Insight and creativity become most essential

Routine, established responses to well-defined problems create efficiencies. Routine responses to ill-defined and wicked problems create errors, rather like a knee-jerk reaction to a complex problem. Differentiating the types of problems and shifting the approach to match the degree of ambiguity and complexity requires awareness, disciplined thinking, and willingness to avoid premature selection of solutions. It becomes a process of the joint creation of meaning that leads up to consensus decision making (Mutch, 1999). Collaborative processes involving customers enable the problem and the solution to be iteratively defined—a jointly managed process of successive approximation as understanding grows and tradeoffs become more clear.

Technology as Tool

Tools are devices that extend our reach—physical, social, or mental. Tools may be tangible or intangible. Technology develops and maintains tools. However, we have developed the habit of using the term "technology" to represent a specific type of tools, namely hardware. Software is often included as technology, but not liveware (people). The technology of organizing, interacting, teaming, and collaborating has been evolving rapidly over the past century, yet many questions remain, particularly those involving efficient and effective use of such tools. The first training agenda item here is that of building awareness about the social technology that is available for improving work flow, including such things as dedication to the success of peers and focusing on the quality of relationships within the internal supply chain, taking care of one's immediate customers and suppliers. That awareness is a first step toward integrating the use of hard and soft technologies.

A great deal has been written about the failure of technology investments to achieve expected return-on-investment. The common problem identified by those writers has been the tendency to omit people from the planning and implementation of technology changes. Hardware and software have limited value, unless the users understand and appreciate them. That attitude is created through involving users in planning and implementation, rather than imposing new hardware and software on them. Training of IT personnel in effective relating and consulting with end users becomes a leverage point for increasing the value of hardware and the performance of employees.

Support System Alignment as Tool

In her work with eleven high-tech companies, Mohrman discovered that "Ninety percent of the teams failed because of context factors" (Mohrman & Tenkasi, 1997). The problems were not within the teams, but outside them in their environments. Support systems were not delivering relevant support. Work at the Center for the Study of Work Teams has generated the following list of critical support systems: (a) organization and team design, (b) leadership, (c) performance management, (d) integration of teams and systems, (e) financial, (f) learning, (g) physical workspace, (h) change/renewal, and (i) creativity and innovation. (For more information on these critical factors, see Chapters 1 and 11.)

Research by Mohrman and her colleagues and others (Hall, 1998; Mohrman, Cohen, & Mohrman, 1995; Moran, 1996; and Wageman, 1997) has identified critical support systems. Perhaps the most important is the executive leadership support for the teaming initiative, but organization and team design is also critical. These writers address the alignment of support systems with team needs. They do not specifically address the issue that training of support system members as service providers to line teams is critical or that training of team members to assertively seek support is critical. Although alignment of support systems is the responsibility of top management in the strategic design role and of the leaders of each support system, team members need to learn ways to communicate upward their needs and frustrations around support. That feedback, assertively and articulately delivered, will provide a valuable corrective action.

Project Management as Tool

Project management provides rigorous guidelines for people in oversight positions. Some of those tools should be pushed down to the bottom level of the organization. One of the ways that teams have created value is through generating project ideas and executing them. Projects may represent improvements in process, product, or service. (Chapter 5 describes a method of capturing the value of process improvements.) Knowledge of some project management tools, such as planning and assessment, can create more successes for those teams.

The critical success factors (CSFs) for project management can be taught to all teams, not just new product development. The CSFs should include (a) managing scope; (b) establishing sponsorship from a higher level; (c) setting and meeting milestones; (d) tracking costs, benefits, and risks; (e) pilot testing; and (f) presenting the business case for the change. A half day of training with some added just-in-time support is likely to produce significant gains.

Business Tools

There is a story of an employee in a factory who had worked there for thirty years. On his last day of work before retirement, the employee was given a tour of the plant. At the end of the tour, he said, "Oh, now I know what I was building." Lack of knowledge of the business as a whole, including financial knowledge, reduces the number of ways an employee can contribute. Open book management (Case & Carney, 1996) is based on openly sharing information about the financial side of the business and teaching employees to understand it.

Training and communication can help employees answer questions such as (a) What is the bottom line? (b) How can I contribute to the bottom line? (c) What payoff is there for me in contributing to the business? and (d) What business outcomes are of value besides the quarterly profit statement? Training employees to think about the business as a whole increases not only their understanding, but also their caring, and their ability to play a better partnership role in making the business thrive.

Conclusion

Training is often viewed in narrow and traditional terms. When that happens, there is limited value added for the investment. The return-on-investment from training may also be underestimated when there is a failure to recognize the value of developing more sophisticated competencies in team members. The suggestions here about broadening the scope of training aim at enabling the members of the organization to become fully functioning partners in the organization and at enhancing their ability to contribute. The focus on mind tools builds intellectual capital; the focus on conversation tools builds intellectual and social capital; and the focus on decision-making tools builds process and innovation capital. The focus on social technology builds human and organizational capital. The work on support systems alignment builds organizational and structural capital. The focus on project management competencies builds process capital. And the focus on business knowledge builds financial and customer capital. All of these build competitive advantage and organizational excellence. They require an investment, but that will pay back a range of tangible and intangible benefits over the ensuing years.

CHAPTER 34

Balancing Skills for Collaboration with Individual Development

Gayle Porter

COLLABORATION HAS A LOT TO OFFER in today's information intensive companies, but it doesn't always work. Insight on the reasons for this difficulty can be pieced together, starting with some basic observations about human nature:

Observation #1: Weak Links Won't Make a Strong Chain. Few managers would argue with this logic. However, the quality of the individual contributor is typically considered only in the selection process, not as an ongoing development responsibility. Effective collaboration requires developing individuals who are capable of both contributing to and benefiting from interdependency.

Observation #2: People Have a Stronger Willingness to Work for Something That Feels Like a Part of Themselves. When the work is viewed as an extension of what they're all about, individuals begin to think of their time and effort as a personal investment, rather than a transaction in which the goal is to get the best exchange for the least given. This idea is a basic premise of workplace empowerment, but the term empowerment is often distorted to cover any passing on of responsibility, whether personally meaningful or not.

Observation #3: People Have a Tendency to Seek Out Those Things They Feel They Are Lacking. They may consciously understand that something is missing or experience only a vague, unclear feeling. But in either case, they will somehow move toward filling the void. Unfortunately, and partly because this process often occurs at an unconscious level, they frequently fill that void with whatever is most conveniently available and offers some immediate resolution.

In summary, these three observations emphasize the need to develop individuals who embrace the work as a part of their identity and who understand that identity in a broad context. A useful perspective for accomplishing this objective is to focus on balance and compatibility. By this we mean the balance of organizational objectives with compatible individual interests; balance of individual development with compatible skills specific to collaboration; and balance of the workplace as one development context within and compatible with broader life experience.

Any reference to balance implies consideration of multiple inputs or perspectives. Overall, the following discussion addresses the need for individual development in order to improve collaboration success (Observation #1). The first two sections offer an explanation of psychological ownership, which increases individual investment in the work (Observation #2), and indicates as well how this element of personal development contributes to collaboration potential. The narrative here addresses the importance of considering development important to the individual, along with the development of skills in collaboration.

The third section compares the roots of ownership to typical team-building efforts. Next is discussion of the potential negative behaviors that may result if efforts toward collaboration happen in the absence of development needed for psychological ownership—the disjoint that occurs when team building and personal development are not in balance. This disjoint creates a gap the person may attempt to fill through the most readily available source (Observation #3).

If that source restricts the inputs for individual development, it will likely result in a dysfunctional variation of ownership.

The final sections of this chapter offer suggestions for organizational action to promote more balanced development, and managers are reminded that creating and supporting balanced development is important in the accomplishment of organizational goals.

The Proactive Investment of Ownership

Notice the follow-through when people in a meeting put forward a suggestion. It's usually apparent whether that idea is their own or one they are relaying on behalf of their boss or another. For their own ideas, people will work much harder to promote acceptance or, at least, to gain a fair hearing. For a suggestion they have not adopted as their own, even the most conscientious effort lacks that sense of personal investment. The difference is *ownership*.

One recent article (Pierce, Kostova, & Dirks, 2001) elaborates on the idea of *psychological ownership* as an element of employees' relationship to their work and the workplace. Psychological ownership is explained as a feeling of being tied to an object to the extent that the object becomes an important part of the individual's identity. When the object is an organization, actions that benefit the organization also simultaneously reinforce the identity of the individual. The organization is then an extension of self, so a variety of rights and responsibilities begins to seem appropriate. For example, the individual is more likely to seek out needed information for job performance (a "right" to acquire what is needed) and, formally or informally, to help others perform (a "responsibility" to the overall effort or the community of the workplace).

Psychological ownership has three roots or elements. The first is a sense of efficacy.

Psychological ownership has three roots or elements (Pierce, Kostova, & Dirks, 2001). The first is a sense of efficacy—the belief in one's ability to complete a task. This belief develops as the individual experiences a connection between controlling effort expended and achieving desired outcomes of that effort. For example, making a change in work process that leads to greater efficiency provides the person who made the change with evidence of cause and effect (effort to performance) and, therefore, a sense of ownership in the improvement.

The second factor in building ownership is self-identity. Work is an expression of identity, a way of defining individuality to others.

The third factor is that of having a place—establishing a territory or home space. As the workplace provides for these psychological needs (efficacy, expression of identity, and an identifiable territory), the bond between work and self strengthens into a feeling of ownership.

The one downside to feelings of organizational ownership is the potential for dysfunctional behaviors. As with many things, there is a variation that seems to reverse the outcomes. Rather than the positive behaviors that support organizational goals, distortions can turn ownership into negative outcomes for the organization. Rather than developing a healthy sense of efficacy, a person may cling to control by refusing to share information or to delegate authority to others. Identity and territory are still very important factors, along with performance. The performance outcomes, however, are achieved through extreme control rather than comfort with ability to affect desired results. In this variation, the person may demonstrate strong individual achievement but be working against organizational objectives in the larger realm of collaborative effort. Information is carefully guarded, assistance withheld, and interaction takes the form of competition rather than mutual endeavor. The difference between positive and negative ownership attitudes is particularly important when work groups are attempting high levels of collaboration.

Individual Development and Collaboration

Companies have experienced mixed results from their efforts to promote collaboration at work.

Companies have experienced mixed results from their efforts to promote collaboration at work. Decades of studying group dynamics have provided a wealth of knowledge, yet we continue to struggle with successful implementation of coordinated, collective effort. To help uncover the source of difficulty, we can look at the traditional training offered during a shift to a team-based organization. We do not mean to suggest that the training content is inappropriate, but we wish to examine whether it might be inadequate. For some workers, the attention to team skills lights a path for collaborative and focused effort toward organizational goals. For others, the same skills become surface-level techniques, at best. Trainees learn the buzzwords, but the work does not improve. Something more is needed.

Training for collaboration typically consists of teaching people about effective communication, the importance of trust, step-by-step decision-making processes, goal setting, and conflict resolution. Each of these topics deals with the interaction among members. However, as pointed out long ago in *The Paradox of Group Life* (Smith & Berg, 1987), the strongest teams are made up of strong individuals. Perhaps one problem with teaching people how to collaborate is that the guidance offered does not also include efforts toward strengthening what each brings to the team as a unique individual.

There are a number of theories about personal development over an individual's lifetime. Some theories emphasize tendencies that stabilize into personality types well before the time in life that people would be entering a business organization. The Myers-Briggs profiles fit into this category and have been used by many companies to help clarify and communicate the value of diverse talents among employees. The use of this tool can offer increased understanding among individuals, but is that enough? Beyond general understanding, identifying types is a tool that limits the organization's options to selection and placement of personnel in hopes of matching the optimal type to open positions. When the labor market tightens—as it has in recent years for many skilled positions—it becomes increasingly necessary to adopt a more comprehensive strategy.

A second class of development theory specifies stages or tasks people complete on the way to realizing their potential. Work by Arthur Chickering is an example of this approach. His work specifically delineates developmental tasks encountered by college students (see Exhibit 34.1). His concern is with the development of young adults rather than the development of children. These are tasks to surmount during the time of life that people are realizing substantial transition in the way they view themselves and others in the adult world. In the recent versions (Chickering & Reisser, 1993), the authors acknowledge the differing ages and life experiences of people now attending college. (It is reasonable here to also acknowledge that not all people go to college.)

Exhibit 34.1. Seven Developmental Tasks of College-Age Students

The seven tasks are summarized as follows:

Achieving a sense of competence—developing intellectual and social abilities as well as physical and manual skills and believing in those abilities; the capacity to cope with what comes along and complete targeted goals.

Moving through autonomy toward interdependence—the balance of inner direction and recognizing of the importance (benefits and contributions) of others in a social system.

Managing emotions—finding new and more useful patterns of expression and control by recognizing that personal feelings provide relevant information on decisions about behavior.

Establishing identity—comfort and consistency through understanding self, as well as sustaining congruent roles and behavior.

Freeing interpersonal relationships—developing tolerance for a wide range of persons; being willing to express trust, independence, and individuality in relationships.

Clarifying purposes—formulating plans and priorities that integrate a full range of life activity.

Developing integrity—adopting a set of personal beliefs that have consistency and provide a guide for behavior.

Paraphrased from Chickering & Reisser, 1993.

Further, going to college is no guarantee that an individual will succeed in working through these developmental tasks. For purposes of this discussion, keep in mind that the workplace contains people at all stages of personal development, college graduates or not. Therefore, information on development during transition into adulthood is useful for considering the connections from developmental tasks to individual work habits and job performance.

The developmental tasks do not occur in the same sequence for everyone; nor is there necessarily a clear completion of one before focus shifts to another. Through experiences that allow for growth, various task-related events are likely to dovetail, reinforcing one another in an ongoing development process. One event may stand out in memory as a notable change, but others may quietly build in a more gradual development evolution.

All development occurs in some context or setting, and that context can be managed. This means there is opportunity to influence the process by making room for, and even encouraging, personal growth. Managers may, at first, consider this to be outside the realm of their concern. Personal development that doesn't seem directly job-related might be construed as crossing a boundary that is potentially inappropriate and probably uncomfortable. In spite of that discomfort, it's important to recognize that the outcome of whether or not this development occurs is certainly of concern to the organization. Providing a suitable context is, therefore, a consideration for good management.

Team Building, With or Without Ownership

The traditions of organizational life have long emphasized individual achievement and control through extensive policies and procedures, rather than open interactions based on trust. With increased competitive pressure in the marketplace, organizations now find it necessary to move quickly and have greater flexibility. Many have responded to this requirement by training people in the skills for collaboration, often under the umbrella term of team building. To work collaboratively, people must be able to communicate effectively, offer and receive some trust from members of the work group, learn to set shared goals, make collective decisions, and find some way to transform potentially divisive differences of opinion into innovative solutions. Training packages are plentiful for developing these collaborative skills.

For some this training is new skill acquisition; for others it is a message that personal skills, previously possessed but set aside while at work, are now valued on the job. Referring back to Chickering's developmental tasks, the topics covered in classic team-building processes would relate strongly to the tasks described as interpersonal relations and managing emotions.

Figure 34.1 offers an overview of personal development. It shows that, while classic team-building topics relate to the developmental tasks that involve interpersonal relations and managing emotions, other developmental tasks strongly parallel the roots of psychological ownership previously discussed. The fully developed person will have experienced achievement in two areas: how to collaborate with others and how to comfortably face the more individually focused issues of competence, identity, and moving from autonomy to interdependence.

Figure 34.1. An Overview of Personal Development

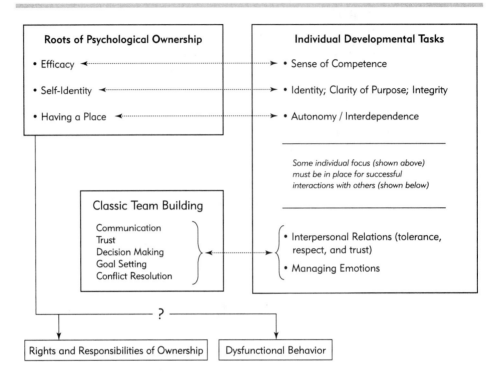

Many companies that are seeking to increase and improve collaborative activity have, traditionally, only rewarded outstanding independent effort. There is certainly a need for development activities that fall in the category of classic team building. If nothing else, this training shows a level of seriousness about the need to recapture skills that employees previously may have been discouraged from using. The faulty assumption, however, is that this skill set can simply be plugged in, as if everyone has arrived on the job with high-level development on the more individually focused tasks. In some cases the assumption that individual development is already there holds true. These are the people for whom the team building is most effective.

What does team building do for the others? It may actually stimulate their feeling a need to fill in around those collaboration skills, to seek out more definitive feelings of competence, identity, and one's appropriate place in an interdependent system. Okay, this sounds good so far. If individuals begin to sense a need for more, it is likely to spur further development. Unfortunately, people tend to latch onto messages of their environment in the places and forms they are most readily available. In other words, they will take easily accessible information unless some conscious effort guides them to a broader context.

Avoiding Dysfunctional Potentials

Ideally, a person's sense of competence derives from broad-based life skills as well as from the ability to make a living at a specific job task. A worker prepared for the jobs today may or may not be prepared for what they will face in tomorrow's scramble for individual competitive advantage. People benefit from a sense that they will be able to meet new demands that are not yet defined. Similarly, identity and purpose are best realized in as large a context as possible. The recognition of interdependence is as important to family functioning as to work teams, and learning to balance the give-and-take between the two is increasingly important in today's two-earner households. These factors should not be defined exclusively within the context of the job.

Generally speaking, employee development that takes into consideration the whole person is more likely to allow for feelings of ownership and behavior that supports organizational objectives, including collaboration. If identity is determined only in relation to the job, problems may arise. For example, changes in work assignment, definition of rank, and every potential symbol of status might take on exaggerated importance.

Employee development that takes into consideration the whole person is more likely to allow for feelings of ownership and behavior that supports organizational objectives.

Consider the evidence of layoff victims who seriously question their self-worth rather than seeing themselves as competent employees caught in an unfortunate but temporary situation. If the job environment is the only situation in which people have a clear-cut sense of their place in the world, they are at risk whenever that context shifts in unpredictable ways. Attention to personal development in a broader context does not diminish the potential to connect with and realize organizational objectives. Rather, it leads to the voluntary behaviors that will give *long-term support* to the desired outcomes.

Figure 34.2 summarizes the process described above. Efforts in team building and collaboration cause people to attempt to draw from related, more individually focused development. If that foundation exists, the collaboration skills easily integrate with a balanced perspective of competence, identity, and comfort with interdependence. If the foundation does not exist, the individuals may supplement from the most readily available information and over-emphasize the workplace as the sole context for individual reinforcement. This leads to dysfunctional behaviors as a quick means to avoid or offset any sense of lacking.

Figure 34.2. Paths from Team Building to Constructive or Dysfunctional Behavior

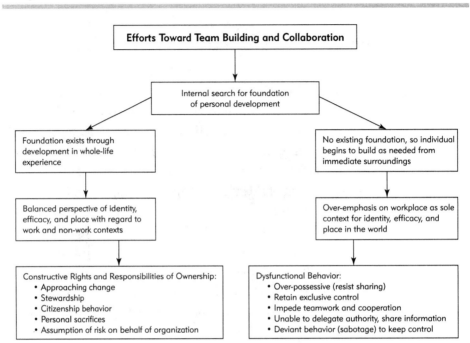

Those who have no broader perspective are likely to be over-controlling. They cannot share information for fear their importance in the system will decrease. They cannot risk cooperative effort or delegate authority. In many ways, these people will passively block the potential for collaboration. If the threat persists, they will even actively sabotage a team's effort in order to retain control of the situation. This pathological behavior has also been described in terms of workaholism or addiction to work (Porter, 1996). When control of the job becomes people's only source of feeling good about themselves, they will do almost anything to protect that source.

Some Specific Action Suggestions

By this point, skeptics might be rolling their eyes and sighing as they envision every extreme "touchy-feely" style workshop that has hit the headlines in the past decade. Erase that image and focus on something a little more mundane but possibly neglected in what your organization currently offers. Consider the following examples.

Offering Career Planning and Development

Most companies have backed away from any involvement in individual career planning efforts. Because the organization no longer promises predictable advancement or long-term employment, career concerns are increasingly defined as the individual's responsibility. However, a good career-planning workshop would contain personal goal setting that would involve defining one's values and charting a path to live those values.

A good career-planning workshop would contain personal goal setting that would involve defining one's values and charting a path to live those values.

This is a foundation for solidifying identity and recognizing opportunities to build compatible competencies. There seems to be a fear that providing a forum for career planning might highlight the fact that the current job and company are not always the best long-term investment for the employee. Yes, that's possible but not always such a bad thing.

Many people are better able to apply themselves to a job that is not 100 percent fulfilling when they have identified that it is something they are doing now because it fills a specific need, for example, while finishing school, until the spouse becomes established in his or her career, or to put the kids through college. Before the people in these situations consciously identify the need that's keeping them there—in the context of their full life involvement—they may be chronically unenthusiastic or frustrated over details that don't deserve the focus they receive. Strengthening their sense of self and place in the world can free them to take ownership of the job, for whatever time they remain, in a way that was previously blocked.

There is even the potential that activities focusing on the individual's career ambitions might strengthen their link to the current organization. They might realize more importance in what they currently do, find creative in-house paths to match their interests, or become *intra*preneurial in pursuit of personal opportunity. Companies that are encouraging collaboration in the form of topical communities of practice are allowing personal interests to provide a foundation for interaction that can gradually evolve into profitable pursuits for the organization. This format is more successful when the individual employees have identified which interests motivate them to take more initiative.

Reinstating career planning activities within the company is one way to help build the roots of ownership. The few people who choose to leave as a result of such planning may be causing less damage through that action than they would by staying on the job without building any sense of ownership in the organization.

Supporting Broad-Based Development

The emphasis today is on doing more with less. Those who remain after all the restructuring and downsizing must cover as much or more work. The job must be done, even when the company cannot locate or recruit all the people with specialized skills that are needed. Under these intense demands, time for training and development is limited to necessary, job-related skills and information. Even those companies that cover formal education through tuition reimbursement programs often restrict payment to narrowly defined courses and degree programs. Although economically defensible, these practices can also create a pattern of defining personal growth only in terms of job-relevant activities.

Can, or should, more personally enriching interests be pursued only on personal time? This luxury is increasingly difficult in two-earner households, where each person is working fifty to sixty plus hours per week, commuting more hours per day than at any time in history, rushing home in hopes of saying hello to the kids before bedtime, and sacrificing sleep to keep up with household responsibilities. Loosening the grips a little on what is considered valuable development—recognizing the worth of a more well-rounded life—is a way to remind employees of the broader context.

Allowing people to develop in a general sense and then discover how that feeds into their professional lives is, again, a potential path to creating feelings of organizational ownership.

Requiring Work/Life Balance

Organizations frequently make one (or both) of two mistakes in their programs designed to support work/life balance. First, they may focus on providing services and benefits that make it easier for people to spend more time on the job. Concierge services, on-site childcare, and so forth are wonderful ways to alleviate stress of competing demands, but only among those people who want smoother integration of their work and home responsibilities. Some people really would rather keep those activities segregated. These individuals may feel their lives already are overrun with job-related demands. Now, with these new "benefits," they have even fewer acceptable options for drawing a distinct line between home and work.

The second mistake organizations make is being satisfied that they have provided a benefit by simply offering balance opportunities—believing that available options will be utilized by people who want or need better work/life balance. Yet the subtle messages that go out to employees often contradict those offerings. Having a policy that allows personal time off doesn't eliminate the potential that actually using it might interfere with a future promotion. One person disappears periodically for events involving the children, while another candidate for the same promotion is consistently at the office ten hours a day. History has demonstrated that the person who puts the job first will move up, regardless of new family-friendly policies being in place.

It is important that companies explore a range of work/life balance options, giving consideration to both the people who want easier integration and those who prefer segregation—who want to maintain clearly separate job and home activities. In addition, there should be *serious* organizational support for use of options for life balance:

- Require employees to use their vacation time and discourage contact while they are gone;

- Make sure high-ranking executives model balanced behavior and publicly applaud those who take time off for family and personal lives;

- Develop performance indicators that do not solely rely on face time or whose car is in the parking lot the most hours; and

- Question what is wrong when any employees' lives seem consumed by their work.

Returning to Collaboration

The above are just a few suggestions. Each organization is different, and defining the correct action depends on the existing situation. Return briefly to Figures 34.1 and 34.2, as a reminder of where these potential actions fit into the focus on better collaboration. Strong individuals make better collaborators. Employees who have developed their identity, feelings of competence, and sense of having a place have the roots for organizational ownership and can thrive in interdependent work relationships when skills in collaboration are added. If these features of personal development become totally vested in the job-related activities, people are more susceptible to dysfunctional behavior that can sabotage collaboration.

Is it management's responsibility to provide personal development? Perhaps not. In an ideal world, this development would happen through life experience, and people would arrive on the job as well-balanced, fully defined beings. That ideal isn't reality. The question then becomes: Can any organization afford to ignore the importance of ongoing personal development?

Can any organization afford to ignore the importance of ongoing personal development?

Consider the dollars wasted in training people to collaborate if the needed, compatible personal skills are not in place or also being addressed. Consider the impact on profitability when individuals are working against collaborative effort because their sense of competence and identity relies on total control. It is management's responsibility to recognize when things aren't working as well as they could be and to consider feasible remedies. If your company's efforts in collaboration are not succeeding as well as you would like, consider the possibility that individual employee development might also be needed.

Reflecting on the Lessons Learned

THIS FIELDBOOK CONTAINS THIRTY-FOUR CHAPTERS arranged under six sections that represent the areas that demand attention when building a collaborative organization. A rich array of ideas, tools, and examples was presented. In reviewing the offerings, the editing team has captured some of the key lessons the sections contained. They are arranged below by section. Most lessons apply to all three levels of collaborative work systems: teams, team-based organizations, and the collaborative organization.

As explained in the introduction to this book, for an organization to leverage the benefits of collaboration to its fullest, the organization must align six key components:

- Strategy and goal setting;
- Leadership and culture;
- Structure and overall design;
- Work processes and communications;

- Human resource processes; and
- Individual, interpersonal, and team competencies and skills.

Strategy and Goal Setting

High-performing organizations require leaders to align the collaboration strategy of team-based organizations with the higher-level business strategy. Practitioners and consultants have developed a variety of tools and approaches for creating this alignment. These approaches include highly participative events such as Search Conferences and other large group events. In addition to participation, goal setting is an important vehicle for creating alignment. High-performing organizations establish goals for the implementation of teams and other collaborative mechanisms. These goals relate directly to activities that promote team performance and collaboration. Related to the goal-setting process is the measurement of the outcomes associated with high involvement. Innovative organizations create return-on-investment models that measure the bottom-line, financial impact of involvement and teams. These provide strong justification for support and funding of involvement strategies.

Leadership and Organizational Culture

Organizations do not magically transform into team-based systems. Successful team-based organizations anticipate and make plans for re-engineering the internal systems that guide individual behavior. A system of control based on fear and reward gives way and a new leader emerges in the team-based system—a leader who empowers, respects, and encourages the contributors he or she jointly works with to fulfill company objectives. In addition, for team-based organizations, members' identities have changed. The values and belief systems that worked for traditional, hierarchical organizations are counterproductive for teaming and collaboration. An organizational culture that supports participation, innovation and creativity, teamwork, and rapid learning is needed. People need a safe environment for passion and responsibility to spring forth in collaborative work systems. Those who lead, manage, and steer change initiatives to team-based systems need to assess organizational readiness; develop a vision for change; create an effective design and guide the implementation of that design; actively communicate with those involved in the change; and model collaboration and teaming themselves. Understanding and dealing with resistance to change is also crucial.

Structure and Overall Design

Successful team-based organizations require fundamental changes in the structure of the organization, including the chain of command, departmentalization, definition of roles and responsibilities, and integrating mechanisms. These areas represent the business answer to the question "how to organize work and distribute power." Effectiveness depends on a sharing of power through participation and involvement. Influence must flow upward as well as downward, and communication and problem solving must flow laterally, across the functional and project boundaries.

Work Processes and Communication Systems

Team-based organizations require more sophisticated work and social interaction processes. In some cases these interactions are face-to-face, but are increasingly virtual (separated by space, time, or organizational boundaries). There are different approaches for designing and fostering these interactions. Some of these approaches are analytical, while others are more intuitive. These work flows and social interactions have become broader and more complex. In addition to exchanging information between departments, team-based organizations are also turning their focus to designing knowledge-creating systems with other companies and across geographic/cultural/organizational boundaries.

Human Resource Processes

Team-based organizing requires a different approach to all the processes underlying human resources, since the primary unit of focus shifts from the individual to the team. This does *not* mean that there is no consideration of the individual. It simply means that the emphasis shifts to the team—its construction, motivation, performance, and improvement. Individual selection, motivation, performance, and improvement all remain important, but as a general rule of thumb, they can no longer be pursued in ways that would be to the detriment of the overall team. As a result, the team-based human resource systems that are beginning to emerge reflect a dual system that must be carefully balanced between a system for teams and a system for individuals. The HR field has not yet reached the maturity level that reflects this state in a systemic way. However, the practices provided in this section collectively lead the way in demonstrating how such HR systems could be constructed.

Individual, Interpersonal, and Team Competencies and Skills

Effective change depends on learning (and unlearning). The development of a team-based organization or collaborative work system requires development of new competencies by all members of the organization. Individual learning at the lowest level of the hierarchy cannot be optimized without support from the top. If collaborative activity is not valued and modeled by top management, it will not be valued and practiced at lower levels. Strong norms support the effort and risk to learn new ways of working together. The most difficult part of that is learning to take initiative, express curiosity, and practice collegiality. The culture of the collaborative organization makes that development possible.

The Change Process

The Fieldbook represents an extensive compilation of work organized around six major categories that represent key criteria for organizational excellence. The thirty-four chapters cover tools, methods, perspectives, and examples for creating effective collaborative work systems. Examining the content of those chapters shows an emphasis on values, ways of organizing, business goals, and change processes and tools. Change is the core of the book, because most organizations have a long journey of transformation before reaching excellence in collaborative systems and practices. The need for excellence in collaboration shows up at all levels: teams fail, companies fail, mergers fail, and so on, on a daily basis. Building collaborative capacity can enable those teams and organizations to function more intelligently and respond more smoothly to environmental changes.

Several chapters present pictures of the change process. Chapter 9, Sustaining Leadership Teams at the Top: The Promise and the Pitfalls by Mindy Gewirtz

and Peter Gumpert, provides a detailed example of the stages of change starting at the top of the organization, including the following steps:

Early Intervention

- A stable framework of meetings for the executive team;
- Emphasis in this stage is on creating safety, creating a containing or hold-
ing environment in which difficult issues could surface and be discussed;
- Emphasis placed on creating interpersonal trust by creating a structure
and process for re-framing volatile issues;
- Major accomplishment of this stage is executives able to engage in dia-
logue regarding hot conflicts; and
- Major learning for consultants in this stage—speak the truth.

Middle Stage

- Emphasis on building a track record for success for resolving conflicts,
solving difficult problems and difficult decisions; more training in iterative dialogue with executives;
- Executives learn to use dialogue rather than sheer power or manipulation; and
- Consultants learn (1) resistance never stops; (2) there is a looped learning between working on interpersonal and business issues.

Termination Stage

- Emphasis on holding up a mirror to team members and to individual
coaching;
- Executives learn participative leadership is not just "icing on the cake";
and
- What consultants learned: honor, ride, and manage resistance.

Chapter 3, The Transformation Grid: A Framework for TBO Conversions by
Tom Devane, presented the Transformation Grid as a framework for planning
the change process. It included five phases: Initiation, Direction Setting, Design,
Implementation, Operating and Continuous Improvement. Devane used the

grid process to aid the organization in developing capability in five areas: leadership development, participative planning, process awareness, high participation, structuring, and support systems.

Both of these examples for change process phases demonstrate the long-term investment and complexity involved in transforming an organization to a team-based organization. It is a daunting task with major payoffs. However, some organizations are not ready to commit to such an endeavor and yet have a need to build collaborative practices and capabilities. That can be done with either a formal emphasis or an informal emphasis. The formal emphasis includes a focus on teams, such as training and selection interventions. Part 6, Individual, Interpersonal, and Team Competencies and Skills, contains five chapters focusing on competency development for teams. But other chapters also address team interventions, such as Chapter 23, Team Member Selection: "Tell Us About a Time When. . ." by Carole Townsley and Susan Larkin, and Chapter 27, Keeping Teams Afloat: Critical Coaching Competencies by Sarah Bodner and Lori Bradley.

The informal focus looks at culture and social networks for developing collaborative capability. Chapter 21, Making Space for Communities of Practice: Creating Intellectual Capital Through Communicative Action by David O'Donnell and Gayle Porter, examines dialogue, community, and knowledge absorption within a culture designed for the creation of new knowledge. Although researchers debate whether communities of practice can be actively managed or not, there is little question about their ability to build intellectual capital for the organization. In Chapter 30, Building and Using Virtual Learning Environments, Deborah Hurst and Scott Follows also focus on the relationship of culture and intellectual capital—for virtual team effectiveness. Theodore Wohlfarth and Michael Stevens also include culture as a critical variable in Chapter 26, Creating and Measuring Ways to Win Together.

Whether the goal is incremental improvement in collaborative practice at the team level, cultural change, transformation to team-based organizing, or inter-organizational partnerships, effective practices depend on attention to culture, values, change process, and structural goals, as well as to business outcomes. Chapter 5, Return on Teaming Initiative (ROTI): Measuring Teaming Outcomes to Optimize Their Performance by Frances Kennedy, and Chapter 6, ROI and Strategy for Teams and Collaborative Work Systems by Alec Levenson, both help tie the teaming and change work back to business results. That continues to be the focus of effective change processes and of the Fieldbook. An organization that does not produce a positive balance sheet does not survive long enough to produce anything else. Effective collaborative practices and structures contribute to that balance sheet, directly and indirectly.

Conclusion

This Fieldbook provides ideas, frameworks, tools, and examples to support the processes and practices of building effective team-based organizations and enhancing collaborative work systems. The lessons learned by three dozen authors over a combined half millennium of experience help develop a roadmap for new and renewed efforts in organizations. As efforts continue by leaders and teams to incorporate these lessons into their daily activities, we hope a sharing of new lessons learned will emerge from the experience. The Center for the Study of Work Teams and Jossey-Bass/Pfeiffer have websites to support that sharing. Only the accumulation of wisdom about effective collaboration will enable us all to capitalize on it in making our organizations better contributors to their members and to the world. As we conclude this book, we would like to summarize some of our thoughts in each of these areas.

What the fieldbook demonstrates is the remarkable breadth and depth of the tools and techniques that have sprung up to support the movement toward collaborative work systems. Moreover, the contents of this book are just the tip of the iceberg. The collection and assembly of the material in this book was a collaborative effort on the part of the editors and authors. We hope it will stimulate even more sharing of methods in this arena. As the practitioners in this field already understand, there is no underestimating the challenges inherent in moving toward a truly collaborative organization. However, we anticipate that this volume enhances the likelihood of sustained progress. It also represents our humble attempt to practice what we preach.

While we believe that the fieldbook has met its stated intent, we also feel it is important to at least mention what it does not address. It does not deal with organizational ethics and the purposes to which teamwork and collaboration are put. Any organizational approach can be used for benefit or detriment. History is replete with examples of teamwork used to benefit the few at the expense of the many. As we write this book, the Enron case is unfolding. While the root causes await others in our field to identify and analyze, it is already apparent that the company could not have pursued its course if it had not been for a remarkable degree of collaboration. Collaboration was extensive both within the company and with many other institutions—its partnerships and subsidiaries, auditors and auditing community, investment banks, management consulting firms, and governmental entities, including regulatory agencies, Congress, and the executive branch. Indeed, this case may emerge as a classic on the dark side of collaboration. So despite our enthusiasm for the need for collaboration, we would be remiss in not bringing up this issue.

If anything, the Enron case appears to demonstrate the extraordinary efficacy of collaboration. It is entirely plausible that if Enron had simply curbed the excessive degree of its practices, it would still be considered one of the most highly valued companies, despite the true facts. From a purely technical standpoint, there are no doubt useful collaborative tools that can be extracted from this case. More importantly, however, is the need to learn when and why collaboration is inappropriate. Collaboration can only be broadly beneficial when it is counter-balanced with adequate oversight, arms-length relationships, and regulation. Another way to cast this issue is to ask, "When does collaboration become collusion?"

So we have come full circle to our primary premise, which is that teamwork and collaboration are not ends in themselves, but means to an end. In today's complex, interdependent world, we anticipate that this approach will clearly emerge as the major competitive strategy on the social side of organizations.

REFERENCES

Ackoff, R.L., & Emery, F.E. (1972). *On purposeful systems*. London: Tavistock.

Ambrose, D. (1996). Panoramic scanning: Essential element of higher-order thought. *Roeper Review, 18*(4), 280–285.

Ansari, S., Bell, J., Klammer, T., & Lawrence, C. (1999). *Activity-based management*. [Management accounting: A strategic focus. A modular series.] New York: McGraw-Hill/Irwin.

Appelbaum, E., & Batt, R. (1994). *The new American workplace: Transforming work systems in the United States*. Ithaca, NY: Cornell University Press.

Aranda, E.K., Aranda, L., & Conlon, K. (1998). *Teams: Structure, process, culture and politics*. Upper Saddle River, NJ: Prentice Hall.

Asch, S. (1952). *Social psychology*. Upper Saddle River, NJ: Prentice Hall.

Axelrod, R.H. (2000). *Terms of engagement: Changing the way we change organizations*. San Francisco, CA: Berrett-Koehler.

Baldrige National Quality Program. (2000). *Education criteria for performance excellence* [On-line]. Available: www.quality.nist.gov/Education_Criteria.2000.htm

Baskin, K. (2001, May 23–25). *What your body would tell you if it could talk.* Keynote presentation, Collaborative Work Systems Symposium, University of North Texas, Denton, Texas.

Beckhard, R., & Harris, R. (1977). *Organization transitions.* Reading, MA: Addison-Wesley.

Bedeian, A.G., & Zammuto, R.F. (1991). *Organizations: Theory and design.* Hinsdale, IL: The Dryden Press.

Beer, M., & Nohria, N. (2000). *Breaking the code of change.* Cambridge, MA: Harvard Business School Press.

Bell, A.H. (2001). How to use behavior-based structured interviewing. *Workforce* [On-line]. Available: www.workforce.com [last accessed August 27, 2001]

Bernhut, S. (2001). Measuring the value of intellectual capital. *Business Quarterly, 65*(4), 16–20.

Beyerlein, M. (1997a). Why do teams fail? Let me count the ways: The macro level. *Center for the Study of Work Teams Newsletter, 7*(2).

Beyerlein, M. (1997b). Why do teams fail? Let me count the ways: The micro level. *Center for the Study of Work Teams Newsletter, 7*(2).

Beyerlein, M. (1998). *Team effectiveness model.* Unpublished paper.

Beyerlein, M.M., Freedman, S., McGee, C., & Moran, L. (2002). *Beyond teams: Building the collaborative organization.* San Francisco: Jossey-Bass/Pfeiffer.

Beyerlein, M., Hall, C., Harris, C., & Beyerlein, S. (1997, September). The failure of transformation to teams. *Proceedings of the 1997 International Conference on Work Teams.* Dallas, TX: University of North Texas.

Beyerlein, M.M., & Harris, C.L. (2001). *Team-based organizing: Crafting the conditions for collaborating.* Pre-conference workshop at the 12th Annual International Conference on Work Teams, Dallas, Texas.

Beyerlein, S.T., Beyerlein, M., & Richardson, S. (1993). *Summary survey feedback report: Technical professional employees in teams.* Denton, TX: Center for the Study of Work Teams.

Bion, W.R. (1961). *Experiences in groups.* London: Tavistock.

Birkinshaw, J. (2001). Making sense of knowledge. *Ivey Business Journal, London, 65*(4), 32–36.

Bloom, A., Giroux, A., & Jarvis, K. (2000). *Case study: Wind driven generator project* (A U.S./Dutch engineering design project). An unpublished report.

Boudreau, M.C., Loch, K.D., Robey, D., & Straub, D.W. (1998). Going global: Using information technology to advance the competitiveness of the virtual transnational organization. *The Academy of Management Executive, 12*(4), 120–128.

Bradford, L.P. (1976). *Making meetings work.* San Francisco: Jossey-Bass/Pfeiffer.

Brandenberger, A.M., & Nalebuff, B.J. (1996). *Co-opetition.* New York: Doubleday.

Brassard, M., & Ritter, D. (1994). *The memory jogger II.* Boston, MA: Goal/QPC.

Brilhart, J.K. (1982). *Effective group discussion* (4th ed.). Dubuque, IA: William C. Brown.

Brown, J.S., & Duguid, P. (1991). Organizational learning and communities of practice: Toward a unified view of working, learning, and innovation. *Organization Science, 2*(1), 40–57.

Brown, M.C., Hitchcock, D.E., & Willard, M.L. (1994). *Why TQM fails & what to do about it.* Chicago, IL: Irwin.

Buckingham, M., & Coffman, C. (1999). *First, break all rules.* New York: Simon & Schuster.

Bunker, B., & Alban, B. (1996). *Large group interventions.* San Francisco: Jossey-Bass.

Cabana, S. (1995, November/December). Can people restructure their own work? *Target, 11*(6).

Cabana, S., & Fiero, J. (1995, July/August). Motorola, strategic planning and the search conference. *Journal for Quality and Participation,* pp. 22–31.

Canadian Professional Logistics Institute. (2000). *Team dynamics and communications courseware.* Toronto, Ontario, Canada: Author.

Cascio, W. (1998). *Applied psychology in human resource management* (5th ed.). Upper Saddle River, NJ: Prentice Hall.

Case, J., & Carney, K. (1996, February). Fun ways to learn about the P & L. *HR Magazine.* Also available: www.shrm.org/hrmagazine/article/default.asp?page=0296open.html [last accessed August 6, 2002]

CASE: Counsel and advice to senior executives. Retrieved from www.case-jc.demon.co.uk/iip.htm.

Chickering, A.W., & Reisser, L. (1993). *Education and identity.* San Francisco: Jossey-Bass.

Coleman, H.J., Jr. (1999). What enables self-organizing behavior in businesses. *Emergence, 1*(1), 33–49.

Collins, J.C., & Porras, J.I. (1994). *Built to last: Successful habits of visionary companies.* New York: HarperBusiness.

Cooper, A. (1999). *The inmates are running the asylum.* Indianapolis, IN: SAMS (division of Macmillan Publishing).

Cooperrider, D.L., & Whitney, D. (1999). *Collaborating for change: Appreciative inquiry.* San Francisco: Berrett-Koehler.

Cordery, J.L. (2000). Work teams in Australia. In M. Beyerlein (Ed.), *Work teams: Past, present, and future* (pp. 183–192). Boston, MA: Kluwer Academic Press.

Corporate Leadership Council. (1999). *The compelling offer: A quantitative analysis of career preferences and decisions of high value employees* (p. 51). Washington, DC: Author.

Cote, S. (1999). Affect and performance in organizational settings. *Current Directions in Psychological Science, 8*(2), 65–68.

Cramton, C. (1999). *The mutual knowledge problem and its consequences in geographically disperse teams.* Fairfax, VA: George Mason University.

Cramton, C., & Orvis, K. (2001, April 3–4). *Facilitating effective information processing in virtual teams.* Paper presented at the University of Southern California's Center for Effective Organizations, Creating Conditions for Effective Virtual Teams: A Meeting of Minds and Sharing of Practice, Los Angeles, California.

Daft, R.L., & Lengel, R.H. (1984). Information richness: A new approach to managerial behavior and organization design. In B.M. Staw & L.L. Cummings (Eds.), *Research in organizational behavior, volume 6* (pp. 191–233). Greenwich, CT: JAI Press.

Daloz, L.A., Keen, C.H., Keen, J.P., Parks, S., & Parks, S.D. (1997). *Common fire: Leading lives of commitment in a complex world.* Boston, MA: Beacon Press.

Dalton, M. (1959). *Men who manage.* New York: John Wiley & Sons.

Dannemiller, K., James, S., & Tolchinsky, P. D. (2000). *Collaborating for change: Whole scale change.* San Francisco: Berrett-Koehler.

David, K. (1996). *Constructing cultural distance: BDDP's attempted takeover of BMP.* Munich, Germany: Society for Intercultural Education, Training, and Research.

David, K., & Lloyd, J.R. (2001). *Engineering across borders: Improving the effectiveness of globally distributed engineering design teams with transcultural incident reporting.* American Society of Mechanical Engineers–International Mechanical Engineering Congress and Exposition, New York.

David, K., & Terpstra, V. (1991). *The cultural environment of international business.* Cincinnati, OH: South-Western.

Deming, W.E. (1982). *Out of the crisis.* Cambridge, MA: Massachusetts Institute of Technology.

Deutsch, M. (1973). *The resolution of conflict: Constructive and destructive processes.* New Haven, CT: Yale University Press.

Deutsch, M. (1985). *Distributive justice: A social-psychological perspective.* New Haven, CT: Yale University Press.

Devane, T., & Holman, P. (1999). *The change handbook: Group methods for shaping the future.* San Francisco: Berrett-Koehler.

Devine, D., & Clayton, L., (1999). Teams in organizations. *Small Group Research, 30*(6).

Dixon, N. (2000). *Common knowledge: How companies thrive by sharing what they know.* Boston, MA: Harvard Business School Press.

Doherty, E., Nord, W., & McAdams, J. (1989). Gainsharing and organizational development: A productive synergy. *Journal of Applied Behavioral Science, 25*(3), 371–399.

Duarte, D., & Snyder, N. (1999). *Mastering virtual teams: Strategies, tools, and techniques that succeed.* San Francisco: Jossey-Bass.

Duffy, M. (1995). Sensemaking: A collaborative inquiry approach to "doing" learning. *The Qualitative Report, 2*(2). Also available: www.nova.edu/ssss/QR/QR2–2/duffy.html

Dumaine, B. (1990, May 7). Who needs a boss. *Fortune.*

Dumaine, B. (1994, September 7). The trouble with teams. *Fortune.*

Ekvall, G. (1983). *Climate, structure, and innovativeness of organizations.* (Technical Report 1). Stockholm: Swedish Council for Management and Organizational Behavior.

Ellison, S. (1999). *Classic blunders in team implementation lessons learned from the 90s.* Denton, TX: Center for the Study of Work Teams. Also available: www.workteams.unt.edu/orderfrm.htm

Emery, E. (1999). Searching: The theory and practice of making cultural change. *Dialogues on work and innovation* (Vol. 4). Amsterdam/Philadelphia: John Benjamin.

Emery, E., & Purser, R. (1998). *The search conference: A powerful method for planning organizational change and community action.* San Francisco: Jossey-Bass.

Emery, F., & Emery, M. (1993). Participative design: Work and community life. In M. Emery (Ed.), *Participative design for participative democracy.* Canberra: Australian National University.

Emery, F.E. (1959). *Characteristics of socio-technical systems: The emergence of a new paradigm of work.* Canberra: Australian National University.

Emery, F.E. (1967). The democratization of the workplace. *Manpower and Applied Psychology, 1*(2), 118–130.

Emery, F.E., & Emery, M. (1976). *A choice of futures: To enlighten or inform.* Leiden: Martinus Nijhoff.

Emery, F.E., & Thorsrud, E. (Eds.). (1976). *Democracy at work.* Leiden: Martinus Nijhoff.

Emery, F.E., & Trist, E. (1978). Analytical model for sociotechnical systems. In W. Pasmore & J. Sherwood (Eds.), *Sociotechnical systems: A sourcebook.* New York: John Wiley & Sons.

Emery, M. (Ed.). (1993). *Participative design for participative democracy* (rev. ed.) Canberra: Australian National University.

Emery, M., & Devane, T. (2000). *Collaborating for change: Participative design workshop.* San Francisco: Berrett-Koehler.

Emery, M., & Purser, R. (1996). *The search conference: A powerful method for planning organizational change and community action.* San Francisco: Jossey-Bass.

Fisher, K. (1993). *Leading self-directed teams.* New York: McGraw-Hill.

Fisher, K. (2000). *Leading self-directed work teams* (rev. ed.). New York: McGraw-Hill

Fisher, K., & Fisher, M. (2001). *The distance manager: A hands-on guide to managing off-site employees and virtual teams.* New York: McGraw-Hill.

Fogg, C.D. (1994). *Team-based strategic planning: A complete guide to structuring, facilitating, and implementing the process.* New York: AMACOM.

Fox, W.M. (1988). Getting the most from behavior modeling training. *National Productivity Review, 17,* 238–245.

Friedlob, G.T., & Plewa, F.J., Jr. (1996). *Understanding return on investment.* New York: John Wiley & Sons.

Gergen, K.J. (1999). *An invitation to social construction.* Thousand Oaks, CA: Sage.

Godard, J. (2001). High performance and the transformation of work? The implications of alternative work practices for the experience and outcomes of work. *Industrial & Labor Relations Review, 54,* 776–796.

Goleman, D. (1995). *Emotional intelligence.* New York: Bantam.

Goodman, H. (1999, March 14). Everybody's hero: Commissioner John Timoney is shaking up the Philadelphia police force. *Philadelphia Inquirer Magazine.*

Gouran, D.S. (1982). *Making decisions in groups: Choices and consequences.* Glenview, IL: Scott, Foresman.

Graham-Moore, B., & Ross, T. (1990). *Gainsharing: Plans for improving performance.* Washington, DC: Bureau of National Affairs.

Green, P. (1998). *More than a gut feeling II. Benefits of behavior-based interviewing.* [Motion picture]. Des Moines, IA: American Media.

Greenhaus, J., Callanan, G., & Godshalk, V.M. (2000). *Career management.* Fort Worth, TX: The Dryden Press.

Gregerman, A. (2000). *Lessons from the sandbox.* Chicago, IL: Contemporary Books.

Habermas, J. (1984,1987). *The theory of communicative action* (Vols. 1 and 2) (T. McCarthy, Trans.). Boston, MA: Beacon. [*Theorie des kommunikativen Handelns,* 2 vols., Suhrkamp Verlag, Frankfurt am Main, 1981].

Hackman, J.R. (1977). Job design. In J.R. Hackman & J.L. Suttle (Eds.), *Improving life at work.* Santa Monica, CA: Goodyear.

Hackman, J.R., & Oldham, G.R. (1980). *Work redesign.* Reading, MA: Addison-Wesley.

Hall, C. (1998). *Organizational support systems for team-based organizations: Employee collaboration through organizational structures.* AAT 9841424. Denton, TX: University of North Texas.

Hannah, D. (September, 2001). *Second generation issues in high performance teams.* Workshop given at the 12th Annual International Conference on Work Teams: Leveraging Team Performance for Business Results, Dallas, Texas.

Hare, P.A., & Bales, R.F. (1963). Seating position and small group interaction. *Sociometry, 26,* 480–486.

Heifetz, R. (1994). *Leadership without easy answers.* Cambridge, MA: Belknap.

Hinrichs, G. (2001). *The enactment of HPWS in a brownfield site.* Unpublished dissertation. Ann Arbor, MI: University of Michigan.

Hitchcock, D., & Willard, M. (1995). *Why teams can fail and what to do about it: Essential tools for anyone implementing self-directed work teams.* Chicago, IL: Irwin.

Hodder, J.E., & Riggs, H.E. (1985, January-February). Pitfalls in evaluating risky projects. *Harvard Business Review.*

Hoerr, J., Polluck, M.A., & Whitestone, D.E. (1986, September 29). Management discovers the human side of automation. *Business Week.*

Hogan, R., Gordon, J.C., & Hogan, J. (1994). What we know about leadership effectiveness and personality. *American Psychologist, 49*(6), 493–504.

Holman, P., & Devane, T. (1999). *The change handbook: Group methods for shaping the future.* San Francisco: Berrett-Koehler.

Isar, Y.R. (1996). Keyote Speech at the International Congress of the Society for Intercultural Educationing, Training, and Research, Munich, Germany.

Jacka, J.M., & Keller, P.J. (2001). *Business process mapping: Improving customer satisfaction.* New York: John Wiley & Sons.

Jarvenpaa, S., & Leidner, D. (1998). Communication and trust in global virtual teams. *Journal of Computer Mediated Communication, 3*(4).

Jay, A. (1976, July/August). How to run a meeting. *Harvard Business Review,* pp. 43–57.

Johnson, D.W., & Johnson, R.T. (1989). *Cooperation and competition: Theory and research.* Edina, MN: Interaction Book Company.

Jones, S. (1999, September). *Developing team performance measures that capture the team strategy and align with business strategy.* Presentation at the 10th Annual International Conference on Work Teams, Dallas, Texas.

Katzenbach, J.R. (1998). *Teams at the top: Unleashing the potential of both teams and individual leaders.* Boston, MA: McKinsey.

Katzenbach, J.R., & Smith, D.K. (1993). *The wisdom of teams: Creating the high-performance organization.* Boston, MA: Harvard Business School Press.

Katzenbach, J.R., & Smith, D.K. (1999). *The wisdom of teams: Creating the high-performance organization* (rev. ed.). New York: HarperCollins.

Kayworth, T., & Leidner. D. (2000). The global virtual manager: A prescription for success. *European Management Journal, 18*(2), 183–193.

Kelleher, H. (1997). A culture of commitment. *Leader to leader* (Vol. 4) [On-line]. Available: www.pfdf.org/leaderbooks/L2L/spring97/kelleher.html

Kelley, H. (1973). The process of causal attribution. *American Psychologist, 28*(2), 107–128.

Kelly, R.E. (1998). *How to be a star at work: 9 breakthrough strategies you need to succeed.* New York: Times Books.

Kennedy, F.A. (2002). *Team performance: Using financial measures to evaluate the effect of support systems on team performance.* Unpublished doctoral dissertation. Denton, TX: University of North Texas.

Kepner, C.H., & Tregoe, B.B. (1981). *The new rational manager.* Princeton, NJ: Kepner-Tregoe.

Kerr, M.E., & Bowen, M. (1988). *Family evaluation: An approach based on Bowen theory.* New York: W.W. Norton.

Kerr, S. (1997). On the folly of rewarding A, while hoping for B. In R.P. Vecchio (Ed.), *Leadership: Understanding the dynamics of power and influence in organizations* (pp. 246–256). South Bend, IN: University of Notre Dame Press.

Kindler, H.S. (1996). *Managing disagreement constructively: Conflict management in organizations.* Menlo Park, CA: Crisp.

Klein, G.D. (1992, June). Assessing work behavior and performance. *Supervisory Management.*

Klein, J., & Barrett, B. (2000). One foot in a global team, one foot at the local site: Making sense out of living in two worlds simultaneously. In M. Beyerlein, D. Johnson, & S. Beyerlein (Eds.), *Advances in interdisciplinary studies of work teams (vol. 8): Virtual teams.* Greenwich, CT: JAI Press.

Klein, K.J., & Sorra, J.S. (1996). The challenge of innovation implementation. *Academy of Management Review, 21*(4), 1055–1071.

Kleingeld, P.A.M. (1994). *Performance management in a field service department: Design and transportation of a productivity measurement and enhancement system (ProMES).* Unpublished doctoral dissertation. Eindhoven, The Netherlands: Eindhoven University of Technology.

Kline, T. (1999). *Remaking teams.* San Francisco: Jossey-Bass/Pfeiffer.

Klinvex, K., O'Connell, M.S., & Klinvex, C.P. (1999). *Hiring great people.* A Briefcase book. New York: McGraw-Hill.

Kolb, D.A. (1984). *Experiential learning.* Upper Saddle River, NJ: Prentice Hall.

Kolb, D.A. (1985). *LSI learning style inventory: Self-scoring inventory and interpretation booklet.* Boston, MA: McBer.

Kostner, J. (1994). *Virtual leadership: Secrets from the round table for the multi-site manager.* New York: Warner Books.

Kotter, J.P. (1995, March/April). Leading change: Why transformation efforts fail. *Harvard Business Review,* pp. 59–66.

Kotter, J.P. (1996). *Leading change.* Boston, MA: Harvard Business School Press.

Kouzes, J., & Posner, B. (1999). *Encouraging the heart: A leader's guide to rewarding and recognizing others.* San Francisco: Jossey-Bass.

Kraut, A. (1976, Autumn). Developing managerial skills via modeling techniques: Some positive research findings. *Personnel Psychology,* pp. 325–361.

Labovitz, G., & Rosansky, V. (1997). *The power of alignment: How great companies stay centered and accomplish extraordinary things.* New York: John Wiley & Sons.

Larkin, S., Theismann, A., & Stephenson, J. (2000, August). *Basics of behavioral interviewing.* ISPI DFW Chapter Presentation, Fort Worth, Texas.

Lawler, E.E., III, (1992). *The ultimate advantage: Creating the high-involvement organization.* San Francisco: Jossey-Bass.

Lawler, E.E., III, Mohrman, S.A., & Benson, G. (2001). *Organizing for high performance: Employee involvement, TQM, reengineering, and knowledge management in the Fortune 1000 – The CEO report.* San Francisco: Jossey-Bass.

Ledford, G.E., Wendenhor, J.R., & Strahley, J.T. (1995, Winter). Realizing corporation philosophy. *Organization Dynamics*, pp. 5–18.

Lee, J., Sr. (2000). Knowledge management: The intellectual revolution. *IIE Solutions*, 32(10), 34–37.

Leibler, S.N., & Parkman, A.W. (1999). Human resources selection. In H.D. Stolovitch & E.J. Keeps (Eds.), *Handbook of human performance technology* (pp. 351–372). San Francisco: Jossey-Bass/Pfeiffer.

Leonard, D. (1998). *Wellsprings of knowledge: Building and sustaining the sources of innovation.* Boston, MA: Harvard Business School Press.

Levitt, B., & March, J.G. (1988). Organizational learning. *Annual Review of Sociology*, 14, 319–340.

Lewin, K., Lippitt, R., & White, R.K. (1939). Patterns of aggressive behavior in experimentally created social climates. *Journal of Social Psychology, 10*, 271–299.

Liedtka, J. (2000). In defense of strategy as design. *California Management Review*, 42(3), 8–31.

Likert, R. (1961). *New patterns of management.* New York: McGraw-Hill.

Likert, R. (1967). *The human organization.* New York: McGraw-Hill.

Lipnack, J., & Stamps, J. (1997). *Virtual teams: Reaching across space, time and organizations with technology.* New York: John Wiley & Sons.

Lippincott, S.M. (1999). *Meetings: Do's, don'ts and donuts: The complete handbook for successful meetings* (2nd ed.). Pittsburgh, PA: Lighthouse Point Press.

Lipshitz, R., & Bar-Ilan, O. (1996). How problems are solved: Reconsidering the phase theorem. *Organizational Behavior and Human Decision Processes, 65*(1), 48–60.

Litterer, J.A. (1966). Conflict in organizations: A re-examination. *Academy of Management Journal, 9*, 178–186.

Lloyd, S.R. (1996). *Leading teams: The skills for success.* West Des Moines, IA: American Media.

Lowe, J. (1998). *Jack Welch speaks: Wisdom from the world's greatest business leader.* New York: John Wiley & Sons.

Luehrman, T.A. (1998, July-August). Investment opportunities as real options: Getting started on the numbers. *Harvard Business Review*, pp. 51–67.

Lytle, W.O. (1993). *Starting an organization design effort: A planning and preparation guide.* Plainfield, NJ: Block Petrella Weisbord.

Lytle, W.O. (1998). *Designing a high-performance organization: A guide to the whole-systems approach.* Plainfield, NJ: Block Petrella Weisbord.

Mabey, C., Salaman, G., & Storey, J. (1988). *Strategic human resource management: A reader.* London: Sage.

Macy, B., & Hiroaki, I. Organizational change, design, and work innovation: A meta-analysis of 131 North American field studies—1961–1991. In R. Woodman & W. Pasmore, (Eds.), *Research in organizational change and development.* Greenwich, CT: JAI Press.

Maier, N.R.F. (1967). Assets and liabilities in group problem solving: The need for an integrative function. *Psychological Review, 4,* 239–249.

Maier, N.R.F. (1970). Leadership principles for problem solving conferences. In N.R.F. Maier, *Problem solving and creativity.* Monterey, CA: Brooks/Cole.

Martin, P. (2002). *The new accountability* [On-line]. Available: www.martintraining.net/knowledge/accountability.html.

Maslow, A. (1998). *Maslow on management.* New York: John Wiley & Sons.

McLagan, P., & Nel, C. (1995). *The age of participation: New governance for the workplace and the world.* San Francisco: Berrett-Koehler.

Miles, R.H. (1980). *Macro organizational behavior.* Glenview, IL: Scott, Foresman.

Mohrman, S.A., Cohen, S.G., & Mohrman, A.M., Jr. (1995). *Designing team-based organizations: New forms for knowledge work.* San Francisco: Jossey-Bass.

Mohrman, S.A., & Tenkasi, R. (1997). *Patterns of cross-functional work: Behaviors and benefits.* Paper presented at the May 1997 University of North Texas Symposium on Work Teams, Denton, Texas.

Mohrman, S.A., Tenkasi, R.V., & Mohrman, A.M., Jr. (2000). Learning and knowledge management in team-based new product development organizations. In M.M. Beyerlein, D.A. Johnson, & S.T. Beyerlein (Eds.), *Product development teams.* Greenwich, CT: JAI Press.

Moran, L. (1996). *Keeping teams on track: What to do when the going gets rough.* New York: McGraw-Hill.

Morehead, A.M. (1959). *The official rules of card games* (51st ed.). Cincinnati, OH: US Playing Card Company.

Morgan-Gould, R. (1994). *Revolution at Oticon A/S (B): Acquiring change competence in a "spaghetti" organization.* (Case Number: 494–017–1). The European Case Clearing House, Cranfield University, Bedfordshire, England.

Mumford, M.D. (2000). Managing creative people: Strategies and tactics for innovation. *Human Resource Management Review, 10*(3), 313–352.

Mutch, A. (1999). Critical realism, managers, and information. *British Journal of Management, 10*(4), 323–334.

Nadler, D.A., & Tushman, M.L. (1989). A model for diagnosing organizational behavior: Applying a congruence perspective. In D.A. Nadler, M.L. Tushman, & C. O'Reilly (Eds.), *The management of organizations: Strategies, tactics, analyses* (pp. 91–106). New York: Harper and Row.

Nadler, D.A., & Tushman, M.L. (1997). *Competing by design: The power of organizational architecture.* New York: Oxford University Press.

Nemiro, J. (1998). *Creativity in virtual teams.* Unpublished doctoral dissertation. Claremont, CA: Claremont Graduate University.

Nemiro, J. (2000a). The climate for creativity in virtual teams. In M. Beyerlein, D. Johnson, & S. Beyerlein (Eds.), *Advances in interdisciplinary studies of work teams: Team development,* Vol. 7 (pp. 79–114). New York: Elsevier Science.

Nemiro, J. (2000b). The glue that binds creative virtual teams. In Y. Malhotra (Ed.), *Knowledge management and virtual organizations* (pp. 101–123). Hershey, PA: Idea Group.

Nerdrum, L., & Erikson, T. (2001). Intellectual capital: A human capital perspective. *Journal of Intellectual Capital, 2*(2).

Nordstrom, C.R., Wendland, D., & Williams, K.B. (1998) To err is human: An examination of the effectiveness of error management training. *Journal of Business and Psychology, 12*(3), 269–282.

O'Donnell, D., O'Regan, P., & Coates, B. (2000). Intellectual capital: A Habermasian introduction. *Journal of Intellectual Capital, 1*(2), 187–200.

O'Hara-Devereaux, M., & Johansen, R. (1994). *Global work: Bridging distance, culture, and time.* San Francisco: Jossey-Bass.

Orsburn, J.D., Moran, L., Musselwhite, E., & Zenger, J.H. (1990). *Self-directed work teams: The new American challenge.* New York: Irwin.

Osborne, A. (1963). *Applied imagination: Principles and procedures of creative thinking.* New York: Scribners.

Oticon. (2001). *Oticon* [On-line]. Available: www.oticon.com

Owen, H. (1992). *Open space technology: A user's guide.* Potomac, MD: Abbott.

Pacanowsky, M. (1995). Team tools for wicked problems. *Organizational Dynamics, 23*(3), 36–52.

Papero, D. (1990). *Bowen family systems theory.* Needham Heights, MA: Allyn & Bacon.

Pava, C. (1984). *Managing new office technology: An organizational strategy.* New York: The Free Press.

Pavelek, G. (1998). *QE520: Behavioral interviewing in teams workshop.* Austin, TX.

Peters, T. (1988). Restoring American competitiveness: Looking for new models of organizations. *The Academy of Management Executive, 11*(2), 103–109.

Peters. T. (1992). *Liberation management.* New York: A.A. Knopf.

Pettinger, T., Jr. (1997, March 7). How Lynn Mercer manages a factory that manages itself. *Wall Street Journal,* p. B1.

Pfeffer, J. (1994). *Competitive advantage through people: Unleashing the power of the workforce.* Boston, MA: Harvard Business School Press.

Pfeffer, J. (1998). *The human equation: Building profits by putting people first.* Boston, MA: Harvard Business School Press.

Pierce, J.L., Kostova, T., & Dirks, K.T. (2001). Toward a theory of psychological ownership in organizations. *Academy of Management Review, 29*(2), 298–310.

Pondy, L.R. (1964, April). Budgeting and intergroup conflict in organizations. *Pittsburgh Business Review.*

Porter, G. (1996). Organizational impact of workalcoholism: Suggestions for researching the negative outcomes of excessive work. *Journal of Occupational Health Psychology, 1*(1), 70–84.

Pritchard, R.D. (1990). *Measuring and improving organizational productivity: A practical guide.* New York: Praeger.

Pritchard, R.D. (Ed.). (1995). *Productivity measurement and improvement: Organizational case studies.* New York: Praeger.

Purser, R.E., & Cabana, S. (1998). *The self-managing organization: How leading companies are transforming the work of teams for real impact.* New York: The Free Press.

Quick, T.L. (1992). *Successful team building.* New York: AMACOM.

Quinn, J.B., & Anderson, P. (1996). Leveraging intellect. *Academy of Management Executive, 10*(1), 7–28.

Rachlin, R., & Sweeny, A. (1996). *Accounting and financial fundamentals for nonfinancial executives.* New York: AMACOM.

Rath & Strong, Inc. (2000, October). *Rath & Strong's Six Sigma pocket guide.* Lexington, MA: Author.

Rehm, R. (1999). *People in charge.* Stroud, Gloucestershire, UK: Hawthorn Press.

Reina, D.S., & Reina, M.L. (1999). *Trust & betrayal in the workplace: Building effective relationships in your organization.* San Francisco: Berrett-Koehler.

Rittel, H., & Webber, M.M. (1984). Planning problems are wicked problems. In N. Cross (Ed.), *Developments in design methodology* (pp. 135–144). New York: John Wiley & Sons.

Robards, K.J., & Gillespie, D.E. (2000). Revolutionizing the social work curriculum: Adding modeling to the systems paradigm. *Journal of Social Work Education, 36*(3), 561–572.

Robbins, H.A. (1992). *How to speak and listen effectively.* New York: AMACOM.

Robbins, H.A., & Finley, M. (2000). *The new why teams don't work: What goes wrong and how to make it right.* San Francisco: Berrett-Koehler.

Robinson, D.G., & Robinson, J.C. (1989). *Training for impact: How to link training to business needs & measure the results.* San Francisco: Jossey-Bass.

Rogers, C.R. (1961). *On becoming a person.* New York: Houghton-Mifflin.

Romig, D.A. (1996). *Breakthrough teamwork: Outstanding results using structured teamwork®.* Austin, TX: Performance Research Press.

Romig, D.A. (2001). *Side by side leadership: Achieving outstanding results together.* Austin, TX: Bard Books.

Rossett, A. (1999). *First things fast.* San Francisco: Jossey-Bass/Pfeiffer.

Ruttenbur, B.W., Spickler, G.C., & Lurie, S.S. (2000). *Elearning: The engine of the knowledge economy.* New York: Morgan Keegan.

Samuel, M. (1999). Success through accountability participant workbook: An employee orientation module for achieving high performance and personal satisfaction. *Impaq* [On-line]. Available: www.ist.berkeley.edu/LeaderTeam/accountability2.html

Schank, R. (1997). *Virtual learning: A revolutionary approach to building a highly skilled workforce.* New York: McGraw-Hill.

Schein, E. (1996). Three cultures of management: The key to organizational learning. *MIT Sloan Management Review, 38*(1), 9–20.

Schine, E. (1996, April 22). Liftoff: How Mike Armstrong reinvented Hughes Electronics. *Business Week.*

Schwarz, R. (1994). *The skilled facilitator: Practical wisdom for developing effective groups.* San Francisco: Jossey-Bass.

Semler, S.W. (1997). Systematic agreement: A theory of organizational alignment. *Human Resource Development Quarterly, 8*(1), 23–40.

Senge, P. (1990). *The fifth discipline: The art and practice of the learning organization.* New York: Currency/Doubleday.

Senge, P., Kleiner, A., Roberts, C., Ross, R., & Smith, B. (1994). *The fifth discipline fieldbook: Strategies and tools for building a learning organization.* New York: Currency/Doubleday.

Sherif, M., & Sherif, C. (1953). *Groups in harmony and tension.* New York: Harper & Row.

Sloan, A.P. (1963). My years with General Motors. In J. McDonald & C. Stevens (Eds.), *A ghost's memoir.* Garden City, NJ: Doubleday.

Smith, K.K., & Berg, D.N. (1987). *Paradoxes of group life.* San Francisco: Jossey-Bass.

Spencer, L. (1989). *Winning through participation.* Dubuque, IA: Kendall/Hunt.

Steele, F.I. (1979). *Physical settings and organizational development.* Reading, MA: Addison-Wesley.

Stevens, T. (1999, July 19). Lights, camera, innovation! *Industry Week, 248*(14), 32–36.

Stewart, G., & Manz, C. (1990). *Leadership for the self-managing work teams: A typology and integrative model.* New York: Delta Consulting Group.

Stewart, G., & Manz, C. (1997). Understanding and overcoming supervisor resistance during the transition employee empowerment. In W. Pasmore & R. Woodman (Eds.), *Research in organizational change and development, vol. 10* (pp. 169–196). Greenwich, CT: JAI Press.

Stewart, T.A. (2001a). *The wealth of knowledge: Intellectual capital and the twenty-first century organization.* New York: Doubleday/Currency.

Stewart, T.A. (2001b, April 16). Accounting gets radical. *Fortune, 143*(8), 184–194.

Strauss, G. (1962). Tactics of lateral relationship: The purchasing agent. *Administrative Science Quarterly, 7,* 161–186.

Sundstrom, E., DeMuse, K.P., & Futrell, D. (1990). Work teams: Applications and effectiveness. *American Psychologist, 45,* 120–133.

Sundstrom, E.D. (1999). *Supporting work team effectiveness: Best management practices for fostering high performance.* San Francisco: Jossey-Bass.

Sussland, W.A. (2001). Creating business value through intangibles. *Journal of Business Strategy, 22*(6), 6–10.

Sveiby, K.E. (1997). *The new organizational wealth.* San Francisco: Berrett-Koehler.

Tenkasi, R.V. (1997). The socio-cognitive dynamics of knowledge creation in scientific knowledge work environments. In M. Beyerlein, D. Johnson, & S. Beyerlein (Eds.), *Knowledge work in teams* (pp. 163–204). Greenwich, CT: JAI Press.

Tornow, W., & London, M. (1998). *Maximizing the value of 360-degree feedback.* San Francisco: Jossey-Bass.

Townsend, A., DeMarie, S., & Hendrickson, A. (1996, September). Are you ready for virtual teams? *HR Magazine,* pp. 123–126.

Trist, E., & Emery, F. (1960). *Report on the Barford conference for Bristol/Siddeley Aero-Engine Corporation* (Document no. 598). London: Tavistock Institute.

Tuckman, B. (1965). Developmental sequence in small groups. *Psychological Bulletin, 63,* 384–399.

Tudor, T.R., & Trumble, R.R. (1996). Work-teams: Why do they often fail? *S.A.M. Advanced Mangement Journal, 61*(4), 31–41.

Urdan, T.A., & Weggen, C.C. (2000). *Corporate e-learning: Exploring a new frontier.* New York: WR Hambrecht.

Van Tuijl, H.F.J.M., Kleingeld, A., Schmidt, K., Kleinbeck, U., Pritchard, R.D., & Algera, J.A. (1997). Measuring and enhancing organizational productivity by means of ProMES: Three practical implications. *European Journal of Work and Organizational Psychology, 6*(3), 279–301.

Van Vijfeijken, H.T.G.A., Kleingeld, P.A.M., Van Tuijl, H.F.J.M., & Algera J.A. (2001, May 16–18). *Designing effective combinations of goal-setting & feedback and rewards: The role of task, goal, and reward interdependence.* Paper presented at the Third International Workshop on Human Resources Management, Seville, Spain.

Wageman, R. (1997). Critical success factors for creating superb self-managing teams. *Organizational Dynamics, 26*(1), 49–62.

Wageman, R., & Baker, G. (1997). Incentives and cooperation: The joint effects of task and reward interdependence on group performance. *Journal of Organizational Behavior, 18,* 139–158.

Walker, G. (2000). *Communicating well in conflict: Competence skills and collaboration.* Department of Speech Communication, Oregon State University. [On-line.] Available: www.orst.edu/instruct/comm440–540/comptent.htm

Walton, R.E. (1972, November/December). How to counter alienation in the plant. *Harvard Business Review,* pp. 70–81.

Walton, R.E. (1977). Work innovations at Topeka: After six years. *The Journal of Applied Behavioral Science, 13,* 422–433.

Walton, R.E., & Dutton, J.M. (1969). The management of interdepartmental conflict: A model and review. *Administrative Science Quarterly, 14,* 73–84.

Waterman, R. (1994). *What America does right: Learning from companies that put people first.* New York: W.W. Norton.

Watkins, K.E., & Marsick, V.J. (1993). *Sculpting the learning organization: Lessons in the art and science of systemic change.* San Francisco: Jossey-Bass.

Webber, A.M. (1999). Learning for a change. *Fast Company, 24,* 178–188.

Weick, K. (1979). *The social psychology of organizing* (2nd ed.). New York: McGraw-Hill.

Weick, K. (1999). Sensemaking as an organizational dimension of global change. In D. Cooperrider & J. Dutton (Eds.), *Organizational dimensions of global change: No limits to cooperation* (pp. 39–56). Thousand Oaks, CA: Sage.

Weisbord, M.R. (1992). *Discovering common ground: How future search conferences bring people together to achieve breakthrough innovation, empowerment, shared vision, and collaborative action.* San Francisco: Berrett-Koehler.

Weisbord, M., & Janoff, J. (2000). *Future search.* San Francisco: Berrett-Koehler.

Wenger, E.C., & Snyder, W.M. (2000, January/February). Communities of practice: The organizational frontier. *Harvard Business Review,* pp. 139–145.

Werther, W.B., & Davis, K.I. (1996). *Human resources and personnel management* (5th ed.). New York: McGraw-Hill.

Whitely, R. (1991). *The customer-driven company: Moving from talk to action.* Reading, MA: Addison-Wesley.

Wiig, K.M. (1993). *Knowledge management: The central management focus for intelligent-acting organizations.* Arlington, TX: Schema.

Wilson, J., George, J., & Wellins, R. (1994). *Leadership trapeze: Strategies for leadership in team-based organizations.* San Francisco: Jossey-Bass.

Wohlfarth, T.A. (2001). *Learning to win together.* St. Louis, MO: EnTeam Institute.

Yancey, M. (1998). *Work teams: Three models of effectiveness* [On-line]. Available: www.workteams.unt.edu/reports/Yancey.html

Yukl, G. (1998). Leading meetings. In G. Yukl, *Leadership in organizations* (4th ed.) (pp. 380–404). Upper Saddle River, NJ: Prentice Hall.

Zander, R.S., & Zander, B. (2000). *The art of possibility.* Boston, MA: Harvard Business School Press.

MICHAEL M. BEYERLEIN, PH.D., is director of the Center for the Study of Work Teams (www.workteams.unt.edu) and professor of industrial/organizational psychology at the University of North Texas. His research interests include all aspects of collaborative work systems, organization transformation, work stress, creativity/innovation, knowledge management and the learning organization, and complex adaptive systems. He has published in a number of research journals and has been a member of the editorial boards for *TEAM Magazine, Team Performance Management Journal,* and *Quality Management Journal.* Currently, he is senior editor of the JAI Press/Elsevier annual series of books, *Advances in Interdisciplinary Studies of Work Teams,* as well as this new series of books on collaborative work systems. In addition, he has been co-editor with Steve Jones on two ASTD case books about teams and edited a book on the global history of teams, *Work Teams: Past, Present and Future.* He has been involved in change projects at the Center for the Study of Work Teams with such companies as Boeing, Shell, NCH, Advanced Micro Devices, Westinghouse, and Xerox and with government agencies such as the Bureau of Veterans' Affairs, Defense

Contract Management Agency, the Environmental Protection Agency, and the City of Denton, Texas.

JAMES R. BARKER, PH.D., is director of research and professor of organizational theory and strategy in the Department of Management at the U.S. Air Force Academy. His research interests focus on the development and analysis of collaborative control practices in technological and knowledge-based organizations. His research projects include collaborations with scientists at the Los Alamos and Sandia National Laboratories and with scholars at the University of Melbourne and the University of Western Australia. Dr. Barker's work has appeared in a number of professional journals, including *Administrative Science Quarterly, Journal of Organizational and Occupational Psychology,* and *Communication Monographs.* His new book, *The Discipline of Teamwork,* is now available from Sage Publications. He won the 1993 Outstanding Publication in Organizational Behavior award from the Academy of Management and the 1999 *Administrative Science Quarterly* Scholarly Contribution Award for his research on self-managing teams. He has lectured on teamwork in organizations at many universities and organizations, including the Sloan School of Management at the Massachusetts Institute of Technology and the University of Western Australia. He served as associate editor of the *Western Journal of Communication* and on the editorial boards of *Administrative Science Quarterly, Journal of Organizational Change Management,* and *Management Communication Quarterly.*

SUSAN TULL BEYERLEIN, PH.D., holds a B.A. in English from the University of Oregon, an M.S. in general psychology from Fort Hays State University, and a Ph.D. in organization theory and policy with a minor in education research from the University of North Texas, Denton. Since 1988, she has taught a variety of management courses as an adjunct faculty member at several universities in the Dallas metroplex, with a particular focus on strategic management at both the undergraduate and MBA levels. Dr. Beyerlein has served as a research scientist/project manager with the Center for the Study of Work Teams at the University of North Texas and has been a recipient of research grant awards from the Association for Quality and Participation, the National Science Foundation, and corporate donors. Since 1995, she has co-edited the Elsevier/JAI Imprint annual book series, entitled *Advances in Interdisciplinary Studies of Work Teams,* and during the same period has served as an *ad hoc* reviewer for *The Academy of Management Review*. She has published book reviews on contemporary business offerings in *Business and the Contemporary World*, and her work has also appeared in *Structural Equation Modeling: A Multidisciplinary Journal, Teams: The Magazine for High Performance Organizations* (UK), *Journal of Management Education, Empirical Studies of the Arts*, and *Multiple Linear Regression Viewpoints*. She is a member of the Academy of Management, Beta Gamma Sigma—the honor society for collegiate schools of business—and Phi Kappa Phi National Honor Society.

MICHAEL M. BEYERLEIN, PH.D., is director of the Center for the Study of Work Teams (www.workteams.unt.edu) and professor of industrial/organizational psychology at the University of North Texas. His research interests include all aspects of collaborative work systems, organization transformation, work stress, creativity/innovation, knowledge management and the learning organization, and complex adaptive systems. He has published in a number of research journals and has been a member of the editorial boards for *TEAM Magazine* and *Quality Management Journal.* Currently, he is senior editor of the JAI Press/Elsevier annual series of books *Advances in Interdisciplinary Study of Work Teams.* He is also organizing the launch of a new series of books for Jossey-Bass/Pfeiffer on collaborative work systems. The flagship book in that series is *Beyond Teams: Building the Collaborative Organization,* written with Sue Freedman, Craig McGee, and Linda Moran. In addition, he has been co-editor with Steve Jones on two ASTD case books about teams and edited a book on the global history of teams, *Work Teams: Past, Present and Future.*

Dr. Beyerlein has been involved in change projects at the Center for the Study of Work Teams with such companies as Boeing, Shell, NCH, AMD, Westinghouse, and Xerox and with government agencies such as the Bureau of Veterans Affairs, DCMAO, EPA, and the City of Denton, Texas. Dr. Beyerlein may be reached at beyerlei@unt.edu.

CRAIG MCGEE, PH.D., has over twenty years of experience in change management, with an extensive background in organization development, organization design, process improvement management/ executive development, new company/plant startups and technology implementation. He has served in external consulting, corporate staff, and line management roles, and has the ability to blend a strong technical background with pragmatic, sound business judgment.

Dr. McGee worked as an internal consultant, line manager, and executive in manufacturing for ten years. He helped start up new plants and subsidiaries for Anheuser-Busch, developing a startup model to accelerate profitability. He assisted in the integration of newly acquired companies. Since 1989, Dr. McGee has served as an external consultant. He brings experience in a wide range of change methodologies (including large group, rapid change) and works with the client group to craft and execute a change process that best suits their needs. Dr. McGee can be contacted at cmcgee@aol.com.

GERALD D. KLEIN, PH.D., is associate professor of organizational behavior and management in the College of Business Administration at Rider University, Lawrenceville, New Jersey. As a member of the Department of Management and Human Resources, he teaches in both the undergraduate and MBA programs.

His teaching responsibilities reflect his scholarly and professional interests: interpersonal, management, and team skills; career management and career management systems in organizations; and organization leadership and design. He has a longstanding interest in collaboration in organizations and in teams, particularly self-directed work teams. He has taught about self-directed teams virtually since their inception in this country in the early 1970s, and has researched and written about these and other forms of employee empowerment. Dr. Klein has been an invited presenter at the International Conference on Self-Managed Work Teams and has organized and chaired panels at this conference on the supervisor's role under team self-management and self-directed teams in services.

His work experience includes project management for the Behavioral Science Center, a consulting and training firm in Boston and Washington, D.C. Dr. Klein was also special consultant to the assistant secretary for planning and evaluation, Department of Health and Human Services in Washington, D.C. He has been a consultant to Squibb Corporation, Alcoa Aluminum, the U.S. Department of Commerce, Procter & Gamble, The New Jersey Agricultural Society, and other organizations.

He is a graduate of Drexel University and received an MBA from Harvard University. His doctoral degree in organizational behavior is from Case Western Reserve University in Cleveland, Ohio.

Dr. Klein is the author of many published papers that have appeared in such periodicals as the *California Management Review, National Productivity Review, Supervisory Management, Compensation and Benefits Review, Personnel,* and the *Journal of Management Education.* He is a former chair of his department, a past and present chair or member of standing and ad hoc campus committees, and a recipient of the College of Business Innovative Teaching Award. At Rider University in 1995 he received the University's Award for Distinguished Teaching. Dr. Klein can be contacted at kleinger@rider.edu.

JILL E. NEMIRO, PH.D., is an assistant professor in the Behavioral Sciences Department at California State Polytechnic University, Pomona, and an adjunct professor in the Human Resources Design Masters' Program at Claremont Graduate University. Her research interests are in the area of organizational and team creativity and the virtual workplace. She has published numerous articles on the topics of creativity and virtual teams. Most recent articles can be found in *Creativity Research Journal* and the *Journal of Creative Behavior.* Her recent book chapters can be found in *Advances in the Interdisciplinary Study of Work Teams, The Encyclopedia of Creativity,* and *Knowledge Management and Virtual Organizations.* She has also presented papers at the Academy of Management Conference, International Conference for Advances in Management, Institute for Behavioral and Applied Management, Western Psychological Association Conference, and the University of North Texas' Symposiums on Individual, Team, and Organizational Effectiveness and Collaborative Work Systems, and the International Conference on Work Teams.

Professionally, Dr. Nemiro has worked for twenty years in the entertainment industry as a film and videotape editor, specializing in management training and corporate videos, children's television programs, and documentaries. She has also worked as a research associate for the Museum of Creativity Project at the Milken Foundation, for the Institute for the Academic Advancement of Youth with Johns Hopkins University, and for WestED.

Dr. Nemiro received her Ph.D. in organizational psychology from Claremont Graduate University. She received a master's degree from California State University, Los Angeles, and a bachelor's degree from the University of California, Los Angeles. Dr. Nemiro can be contacted at jnemiro@csupomona.edu.

LAURIE BROEDLING, PH.D., is the vice chair of the California Team Excellence Award Council. She is also president of LB Organizational Consulting. Her firm provides services in strategic human resource management, collaborative work systems, quality improvement, change management, and aligning organizational systems to support organizational goals. Dr. Broedling has held executive positions in human resources and quality, including as senior vice president of human resources and quality for McDonnell Douglas Corporation, vice president of employee involvement and people systems for Boeing, Deputy Under Secretary of Defense, and associate administrator of NASA. She can be contacted at lbroedling@earthlink.net.

SARAH L. BODNER is a consultant who works with companies going through various stages and forms of organizational redesign, including team-based organization. She is in the process of completing the coursework for a Ph.D. in industrial/organizational psychology at the University of North Texas. Her consulting experience began at the Center for the Study of Work Teams, specializing in teams, and has broadened from there. Her interests include teaming in organizations, organizational assessment, change management, leadership development, and empowerment.

LORI BRADLEY is in her last year of doctoral coursework in industrial/organizational psychology at the University of North Texas. She is an associate of the Center for the Study of Work Teams and a member of the International Association of Facilitators.

Ms. Bradley's experience in working with team-based organizations and with organizations that are in the midst of a move to a team-based structure has been concentrated in the alignment of support systems and work teams and in the development of team coaches. She has facilitated numerous strategic focus groups in the banking, real estate, and information services industries and has ten years' experience in designing and facilitating educational programs and working with cross-functional teams in the aviation industry.

She recently participated in the administration of a train-the-trainer course for facilitators in a team-based organization and is currently leading a project to design a facilitator training program for an international banking company. She is currently involved in research on virtual teams and virtual facilitation.

CATHERINE BRADSHAW draws on twelve years of experience as an organization effectiveness consultant to help organizations become high-performance, collaborative workplaces. She has worked in a variety of arenas, including the garment, paper products, and insurance industries, as well as education, health care, and human services. She is trained and practiced in the use of the Search Conference and participative design workshop, as well as a variety of other participative methodologies. Ms. Bradshaw holds a master of arts in whole systems design and organization systems renewal from Antioch University in Seattle.

SYLVIA CHEUY has more than ten years' experience as a consultant whose strong analytical and facilitation skills have assisted individuals and groups to advocate for, clarify, and implement transformational change in their lives, their organizations, and their communities. Her bias is one of collaboration and high participation, and the methods she uses reflect this. She has training and experience in the use of the Search Conference and the participative design workshop, which she has used in both corporate and community settings.

KENNETH DAVID, PH.D., received his doctorate from the University of Chicago and MBA in international business from Michigan State University. He is a professor of anthropology at Michigan State University with a specialty in organizational studies and project studies. He has done organizational research in Europe, Asia, and the United States. This research focuses on inter-organizational relationships (acquisitions, joint ventures, long-term consulting relationships, and strategic alliances). He has published a variety of articles on these topics and co-authored the widely adopted *Cultural Environment of International Business.*

He and co-author Dr. John Lloyd are co-PIs on an NSF-sponsored grant studying geographically dispersed and culturally disparate teams of engineers doing design work in China, Mexico, The Netherlands, Russia, Spain, and the United States.

DONALD DE GUERRE, PH.D., was appointed to an assistant professorship in the Department of Applied Human Sciences, Concordia University, in 1999, where he teaches in the graduate program in human systems intervention. He was appointed manager, organization effectiveness, Syncrude Canada Ltd. in 1989, where he led a total organization redesign process. Prior to Syncrude, Dr. De Guerre worked internationally on the development of TBOs in various industries and economic sectors. His ongoing research interests have to do with participative planning and policymaking and the development of new forms of work organization. He holds a Ph.D. in human and organization systems (1999) from The Fielding Institute.

TOM DEVANE is an internationally recognized consultant, author, and workshop leader who helps clients integrate business strategy, processes, and human factors in large-scale change efforts. Coaching assistance includes team-based strategic planning, business process redesign, metrics development, and implementation of team-based organizational structures.

Prior to founding Premier Integration in 1988, Mr. Devane held management positions at two Big Five consulting firms and an energy company. He was co-author of *The Change Handbook: Group Methods for Shaping the Future,* a contributor to *The Organization Development and Training Sourcebook* series, *The Consultant's Toolkit,* and *Executive Excellence Magazine* on the topics of performance improvement and large-scale change. He holds bachelor's and master's degrees in finance from the University of Illinois.

KEVIN DOWLING is presently finishing his master's degree in the industrial/organizational program at the University of North Texas. He has been an associate of the Center for the Study of Work Teams for two years, with clients including Xerox, Toyota, Wellmark Industries, Tadiran Microwave Networks, and Boeing. His work at Boeing has included working closely with managers and functional managers and a cross-functional steering team in the strategic planning for and implementation of a team-based endeavor. He has a master's degree in psychology from the University of West Georgia.

SCOTT FOLLOWS, PH.D., is an associate professor in the School of Business Administration and director of the Acadia Centre for Virtual Learning Environments at Acadia University, Canada. Considered by Acadia University to be a "champion" of technology-enhanced learning, Dr. Follows founded the Acadia Centre for Virtual Learning Environments (ACVLE). The ACVLE has produced a number of virtual learning environments for the university and corporate training markets. His work focuses on the evaluation of technology tools in education.

MINDY L. GEWIRTZ, PH.D., principal of GLS Consulting, Inc., is a trusted advisor and strategic thought partner for senior leadership in the public and private sectors. Dr. Gewirtz has over twenty years of experience in management, creating systemic business culture change, leadership development, and executive coaching. She is currently presidential advisor to American Type Culture Collection (ATCC), a global bio-resource center. Prior to GLS, she was adjunct faculty at Boston University; president, Strategic Business Solutions; and founder of the North American Network of Jewish Information Services and Eldercare Connection of Greater Boston Jewish Family Services. She maintains a clinical practice and appears in *Who's Who of American Women.*

Dr. Gewirtz received her Ph.D. in organizational sociology from Boston University and post-graduate certification in HR and organization development from the Boston Institute for Psychotherapy. A Diplomate in clinical social work, she earned her MSW from State University of New York.

PETER GUMPERT is a principal and co-founder of GLS Consulting, Inc. He has more than twenty-five years of experience working in the private and public sectors. At GLS Consulting, Dr. Gumpert provides strategic consultation specializing in leadership development, executive coaching, organizational design, systemic business culture change, and cross-functional team development.

Prior to joining GLS, Dr. Gumpert was a professor of psychology at Columbia University and Boston University. He continues to teach at the Boston Institute for Psychotherapy, where he founded the organization development and human resource consultation program for the post-graduate training of consultants. He has received several research grants from the National Science Foundation and National Institute of Mental Health, is a member of the American Association for the Advancement of Science, the American Group Psychotherapy Association, and the Massachusetts Psychology Association. He earned a Ph.D. in psychology from Columbia University.

CHERYL L. HARRIS, is a consultant and researcher affiliated with the Center for the Study of Work Teams (CSWT) at the University of North Texas. She recently completed a year of research at the Center for Creative Leadership in Colorado Springs, where she led projects on the topic of team-based organizations (TBOs). Previously, she spent four years at CSWT while completing coursework for a Ph.D. in industrial/organizational psychology at the University of North Texas. While at CSWT, she led research on teams, consulted with an organization on redesign into a TBO, assisted several graduate level classes, and presented at numerous conferences. Her interests include TBOs, support systems for teams, organizational change, organizational design, and learning in organizations.

GINA HINRICHS, PH.D., worked at John Deere for twenty-three years in various positions. She began in industrial engineering, moved to manufacturing engineering, reengineering, and finally the total quality manager for Worldwide Combine, John Deere Harvester Works. Dr. Hinrichs is currently working as a consultant for process improvement and organizational development.

She has a B.A. in history, a B.S. in industrial engineering, an M.M. from Northwestern's Kellogg Business School, a master's in organizational behavior from Benedictine University, and her Ph.D. in organizational development from Benedictine University.

DEBORAH HURST, PH.D., is associate professor with the Centre for Innovative Management, Athabasca University, Alberta, Canada. Her area of specialization is located within the study of cultural organization change, with an interest in knowledge work and development of intellectual capital through ongoing competency development and virtual learning. Her current research program is concerned with the experiences of contingent knowledge workers, the development, retention, and valuation of intellectual capital, the use of virtual learning environments to enhance intellectual capital, transmission and alignment of cultural values, and the de-institutionalization of the psychological employment contract. For more information regarding

Dr. Hurst's work or background, check the Athabasca University Centre for Innovative Management website at www.mba.athabascau.ca.

FRANCES KENNEDY, PH.D., is an assistant professor at Clemson University in the Department for Accountancy and Legal Studies. She has five years' experience in public accounting with a regional CPA firm and eight years of managerial accounting experience with a Fortune 500 company. Her industrial accounting experience includes the pilot start-up of a team-based system in a manufacturing facility, as well as participation on a product development team as a core team financial analyst.

AD KLEINGELD, PH.D., currently holds a research position at the faculty of technology management, at Eindhoven University of Technology, The Netherlands. His Ph.D. is in industrial engineering and management science. His current research focuses on tools for supporting problem solving and task strategy development of individuals and groups and on the design of reward systems which fit with existing task and goal interdependencies.

SUSAN LARKIN is an independent performance consultant with over twenty years' experience in the travel and transportation industry. Her experience includes team hiring, orientation development, competency modeling, and instructional design. She is a skilled facilitator and is proficient in moderating groups through process improvement, team hiring projects, and change management initiatives. She is currently working toward a certificate in human performance improvement through ASTD. Ms. Larkin is a member of both the international and local Dallas/Fort Worth International Society of Performance Improvement chapters, in addition to the national chapter of ASTD.

ALEC R. LEVENSON, PH.D., is a research scientist at the Center for Effective Organizations, University of Southern California. His research focuses on personnel and the economics of human resources. Topics include the return on investment for virtual teams and HR systems; the bottom-line rationale for implementing workplace-based basic education programs; and factors impacting attraction, retention, and motivation of frontline employees. Dr. Levenson received his M.A. and Ph.D. in economics from Princeton University and B.A. in economics and Chinese language from the University of Wisconsin, Madison.

JOHN R. LLOYD received his Ph.D. at the University of Minnesota. He is a university distinguished professor of mechanical engineering at Michigan State University. He is a Fellow of the American Society of Mechanical Engineers, and he has received the Melville Medal and the Heat Transfer Memorial Award from ASME. He was awarded the degree Doctor of Technical Science Honorus Causa by the Russian Academy of Sciences. He also currently serves as senior vice president-engineering of that society. He is an editor of several international technical journals.

WILLIAM O. LYTLE is the head of William O. Lytle & Associates of Lincoln, Massachusetts. Using both traditional and accelerated approaches, he helps organizations design and implement high-performance work systems. He brings more than twenty-five years of experience to his organization development practice.

Working at all organization levels, Mr. Lytle has consulted on issues of change with a variety of manufacturing, research, financial, government, and non-profit groups. His clients have included Monsanto, Georgia-Pacific, Esso Chemical Canada, First Union, Rohm & Haas, Scott Paper, A.E. Staley, and the Canada Department of National Defense. He has helped both management and union representatives find common ground through new high-participation/ high-performance work designs.

In addition, Mr. Lytle is a frequent presenter at public workshops and conferences. He is also a respected developer of organization simulations and books to guide those involved in change efforts.

BIJAN MASUMIAN has a Ph.D. in instructional design and technology from the University of Texas at Austin. His professional experience includes working as curriculum design specialist for Northland Pioneer College in Arizona and as instructional designer for the State of Texas. From 1995 through 2000, Dr. Masumian worked as the lead computer-based training and web-based training developer for the Austin, Texas, site of Advanced Micro Devices. He has also developed websites and electronic performance support systems, such as the Managers.Compass. He currently heads the e-learning operation at the Austin site of AMD.

GARRY MCDANIEL, PH.D., is responsible for corporate leadership and succession planning at Advanced Micro Devices. In this role, he coordinates the development of emerging leaders and executives on a global basis. Dr. McDaniel has over twenty years of experience in the field of training, education, and organization development. He is a frequent national and international speaker, has authored numerous articles and book chapters, and is author of the book *Managing the Business.* He is a board member for ACC Center and Community Based and Non-Profit Organizations and serves on the curriculum committee for Leadership Austin. He received his doctorate from The University of Texas at Austin and his master's degree from Southwest Texas State University in San Marcos, Texas.

JIMMY A. NELSON, PH.D., is a professional speaker and trainer who holds a doctorate in organizational psychology. He is also an adjunct instructor for Davenport University and a "retired" Dale Carnegie® instructor. He is internationally published in *TEAMS* magazine and is an expert in areas such as team development, behavior change training, conflict management, facilitation/meeting management skills, and leadership/coaching skills. He has worked with teams, leadership, and coaching since 1980 when he was trained as a Deming quality facilitator. He is the founder and owner of Nelson Training & Development.

DAVID O'DONNELL is a knowledge consultant and researcher on the intangible nature of value, or intellectual capital; consultant courseware designer for the e-Business Certification Institute (EBCI); senior consultant on IC and KM issues with The Eglinton HR Group; and CKO and founding member of The Intellectual Capital Research Institute of Ireland, a loosely coupled virtual international research network. He has been published in the *Journal of Intellectual Capital, International Journal of Manpower Studies, Journal of European Industrial Training, Southern African Business Review,* and *Industrial & Commercial Training* and has contributed to numerous books on business strategy and intellectual capital, plus various international conference proceedings.

GAYLE PORTER, PH.D., is a member of the management faculty at Rutgers University School of Business in Camden, New Jersey. Her industry experience includes technical work in the oil and gas industry, finance and accounting with a Fortune 500 company, and consulting on training programs and employee development. She received her Ph.D. in management from The Ohio State University. At Rutgers she teaches courses in organizational change, leadership, training and development, organizational behavior, and social responsibility.

Dr. Porter's research explores various organizational supports for realization of employees' full potential. Her publications highlight leader/member relations, learning orientation, team diversity and interpersonal trust, and workaholism.

KEVIN RICKE joined Deere & Company in May of 1977 as an inspector at the John Deere Harvester Works. He is a member of UAW Local 865 and has served as a representative in the following positions: welder, assembler, machinist, shop floor steward, alternate steward, Election Committee member, United Way campaign chairperson, and continuous improvement pay plan facilitator. He has been in his current assignment as a CI process coordinator for the past two years. He is currently involved in CI process implementation at John Deere Harvester Works.

JOAN ROBERTS is a professional consultant specializing in organizational development and strategic planning. After a varied career in human services and municipal government, she has recently completed her M.A. in human systems intervention from Concordia University. She led a Search Conference for her thesis/intervention and has joined with the other authors in a Toronto-based consulting practice, Open System Design Associates, specializing in the open system tools of Search Conference and participative design.

DENNIS ROMIG, PH.D., is the president of Performance Resources, Inc., of Austin, Texas, a management consulting firm that has provided leadership and teamwork training around the world with Texas Instruments, Dell Computer, and others. He has been facilitating the development of collaborative work systems since his widely recognized work with Motorola's Participative Management Program in the 1980s. His book, *Breakthrough Teamwork,* presented control group research and case studies with high-tech, energy, and manufacturing companies that documented the business case for team-based organizations. Dr. Romig's book, *Side-by-Side Leadership,* presents the 20 to 40 percent improvement in business results when leaders combine mutual leadership, visionary goals, creativity, and structure with empowered teams.

KELLY RUPP'S leadership experience spans twenty years of high-tech marketing, sales, and business management responsibilities. As managing director of Lead To Results, he helps build the strategic and tactical bridge between businesses and their target customers. He emphasizes thorough understanding of customers as well as corporate work teams in his work, successfully transforming work processes as well as marketing programs towards accelerated business growth. Prior to founding Lead To Results, his vita includes executive roles at WebCriteria (website analysis), Mentor Graphics, and Synopsys (electronic design automation), Tektronix (electronics test equipment), and Intel (semiconductors). He is an accomplished author and public speaker. He holds bachelor's and master's degrees in computer science and psychology from Southern Illinois University.

MICHAEL J. STEVENS, PH.D., is a management professor at the University of Missouri-St. Louis and consults widely with organizations in the business and not-for-profit sectors. His primary areas of expertise include improving organizational performance through empowerment and teamwork; individual assessment and selection (especially for teams); executive coaching and leadership development; and interpersonal effectiveness in the workplace. He received his Ph.D. from the Krannert School of Management at Purdue University and won the Ralph G. Alexander Best Dissertation Award from the National Academy of Management. He has published book chapters and research articles in highly respected management journals and regularly gives presentations at professional conferences and meetings. He is also the principal co-author of The Teamwork-KSA Test, an employment test widely used in industry to measure an individual's aptitude for working successfully in a self-directed team environment. He is currently active in several professional societies and has held management and board positions in industry, government, consulting, and nonprofit organizations.

CAROLE TOWNSLEY works as an organizational effectiveness consultant at Sabre, Inc. Her current projects include developing performance measures for virtual teams and redesigning organizational structures and systems to better support work teams. Prior to joining Sabre, she worked as an associate at UNT's Center for the Study of Work Teams, where she gained experience in benchmarking virtual teams and co-authored several publications. Ms. Townsley recently completed her master of science degree in industrial/organizational psychology at the University of North Texas.

HARRIE VAN TUIJL, PH.D., earned a doctorate in experimental psychology from Nijmegen University. He is presently associate professor in personnel management at Eindhoven University of Technology,

The Netherlands. During the past decade, he has been involved in a number of applied research projects, both in profit and in not-for-profit organizations, on the design and implementation of feedback and goal setting systems, based on the ProMES-method (Productivity Measurement and Enhancement System). His main research interests are cooperative work, productivity enhancement, organizational learning, group problem solving, self-management, and consistency between control systems. He has published several journal articles and book chapters on these topics.

THEODORE A. WOHLFARTH is a researcher who founded the St. Louis-based EnTeam Institute in 1995 to develop team-building programs by combining the principles of game theory and experiential learning with a dose of fun. By using unique versions of volleyball, baseball, and other sports, as well as games like chess, he developed the EnTeam method for measuring the ability to collaborate. The EnTeam Institute's projects work well in business and youth programs. Mr. Wohlfarth has a bachelor's degree in economics from Stetson University; his master's degree and doctoral work are in the areas of human resources and economics at Florida State University. He held both academic and corporate research positions prior to founding EnTeam.